Communicology

BY THE AUTHOR

The Psychology of Speech and Language: An Introduction to Psycholinguistics
Communication: Concepts and Processes (revised and enlarged edition)
General Semantics: Nine Lectures
General Semantics: Guide and Workbook (revised edition)
Language: Concepts and Processes
Psycholinguistics
Articulation and Voice: Effective Communication
The Interpersonal Communication Book

JOSEPH A. DEVITO

Queens College,
City University of New York

Communicology: An Introduction to the Study of Communication

Harper & Row, Publishers
New York/Hagerstown/San Francisco/London

Sponsoring Editor: James B. Smith
Special Projects Editor: Marlene Ellin
Project Editor: Karla B. Philip
Designer: Emily Harste
Production Supervisor: Marion Palen
Compositor: American Book–Stratford Press, Inc.
Printer and Binder: The Murray Printing Company
Art Studio: Danmark & Michaels Inc.

Photograph Credits

Below are listed the pages on which photographs appear.
Page 8, Franken, Stock, Boston; 23, Motlow, Jeroboam; 38, Optic
Nerve, Jeroboam; 50, Preuss, Jeroboam; 64, Payne, Jeroboam;
77, Johnson, Stock, Boston; 95, Vilms, Jeroboam; 121, Running,
Stock, Boston; 144, Weldon, De Wys; 158, Weldon, De Wys; 170,
Rogers, Monkmeyer; 186, Joel Gordon; 197, Wide World; 209,
Rosenthal, De Wys; 220, Joel Gordon; 229, Franken, Stock,
Boston; 241, Merrim, Monkmeyer; 262, Eckert, Jeroboam; 280,
Smolan, Stock, Boston; 289, De Wys; 304, Franken, Stock,
Boston; 316, Herwig, Stock, Boston; 335, Southwick, Stock,
Boston; 358, Weldon, De Wys; 371, Payne, Jeroboam; 385,
Albertson, Stock, Boston; 395, Cynara, DPI; 420, Franken, Stock,
Boston; 442, Englebert, De Wys; 455 Lejeune, Stock, Boston;
466, Kaplan, DPI; 477, Franken, Stock, Boston; 492, United
Nations; and, 508, Forsyth, Monkmeyer.

**Communicology:
An Introduction
to the Study
of Communication**

Copyright © 1978 by Joseph A. DeVito

Library of Congress Cataloging in Publication Data

DeVito, Joseph A   Date–
    Communicology.

    Includes index.
    1. Interpersonal communication.   I.   Title.
BF637.C45D485   301.14   77–17495
ISBN 0–06–041655–6

THE TITLE

Communicology is the study of the science of communication, particularly that subsection concerned with communication by and among humans. *Communicologist* refers to the communication student-researcher-theorist or, more succinctly, the communication scientist. Franklin H. Knower, founder of the International Communication Association, and Wendell Johnson, another major figure in the field of semantics, speech, and learning sciences, have long advocated the use of these terms.

The study of communication is still young, and still embroiled in the laborious process of defining itself. Until now, the term *communication* has been used as a catch-all to refer to three different areas of study: 1) the process or act of communicating, 2) the actual message or messages communicated, and 3) the study of the process of communicating. Communicology is a far more specific and accurate way to describe the focus of this book. It is not a piece of meaningless jargon; rather it represents an attempt to refine the language which relates to the field as a whole in order to pinpoint and clarify the broad areas of study within it.

Joseph A. DeVito

CONTENTS

CONTENTS IN DETAIL

PREFACE

I wrote this book to enable students to learn the essentials of communication. More specifically, I wrote it so that they would be able to understand, control, and analyze communication behaviors and events. I proceeded on the assumption that the student-communicator has at least a three-part responsibility—as a communication source, a communication receiver, and a communication analyst. I devote considerable attention to all three of these functions.

Communicology is a unique text. The book is divided into 34 short units rather than into long chapters. The unit approach makes the book easier and more pleasant to read, and since each unit is a self-contained whole they can be studied in any pattern that best suits the needs of a particular course or group of students. The major advantage of this approach is that it will enable you to read the units at almost anytime—during a break between classes, before dinner, during lunch, on a bus or train, or anywhere else you get the chance to read. We learn best when we learn in small doses, and I recommend that students read no more than one unit at any one sitting. It is best to read one unit, spend a while thinking about the contents, and about how they relate to your own communication behavior.

Each unit begins with a set of Learning Goals. They will help you focus on the major concepts. After reading the unit, return to these goals to see if you are in fact able to do what the goals state. If you are not, reread the unit.

Communicology consists of thirty-four units divided into three major parts. Part One (7 units) is devoted to the nature of communication and the self. It provides a comprehensive introduction to the structure and function of communication; some of the essentials of the self, such as self-awareness, self-disclosure, credibility, and ethics are discussed. Part Two, containing 11 units, covers communication messages: message reception, such as perception, attraction, and listening; verbal messages; nonverbal messages; and message effects. The 15 units in Part Three focus on communication contexts. Three units are devoted to each of the five major communication contexts: interpersonal communication; small group communication; public speaking; mass communication; and cross-cultural communication.

At the end of each unit is a list of sources which include both the references I used in preparing the text and the references I would suggest for further reading. I realize that most students do not do "further reading," especially in an introductory course. These suggestions are included in the hope that both this text and this course will be different—they are about you and your communication behavior, and perhaps you will be more motivated to study yourself than you are to memorize mathematical formulae.

A major part of the text is devoted to Experiential Vehicles. These are exercises designed to enable you to *experience* the concepts and principles discussed in the units rather than to learn them on a purely intellectual level. In fact, some instructors will prefer to devote all class time to the Experiential Vehicles and have students do the reading independently. Other instructors will prefer to devote some time to the vehicles and some to an explanation or elaboration of textual material. In either case, the Experiential Vehicles will make the concepts more interesting and enjoyable to learn and the material learned more meaningful and personal.

The boxes sprinkled throughout the text are designed to provide what I consider useful and interesting sidelights on the concepts discussed in the units. The photographs and drawings were carefully chosen to illustrate these concepts as well.

Throughout the text I have built in a certain degree of redundancy. For example, the characteristics of effective communication are considered in different contexts from different points of view in a few places rather than in just one unit. Similarly, I have stressed the importance of ethical considerations repeatedly, not just in the unit on ethics. As you read the text you will find this redundancy helpful. It will help you to focus your attention on the central concepts and processes in communication, and ultimately to internalize and be guided by them.

At the end of the text is a glossary of significant terms used in the study of communication. These brief definitions should enable you to better understand the concepts and processes discussed in the book and should prove useful in review.

Some portions of this book have been taken from my *The Interpersonal Communication Book*. In many instances these were rewritten, rearranged, and updated. The units on public speaking, small group communication, mass communication, cross-cultural communication, and assertiveness were written especially for this book. Some of the Experiential Vehicles were taken from *The Interpersonal Communication Book* while many others were designed especially for this book.

Joseph A. DeVito

PART ONE
Communication and the Self

P art One presents some of the elementary principles and concepts of communication. One could not begin to understand statistics without an understanding of such concepts as mean, median, standard deviation, and so on. Similarly, we cannot understand communication without first understanding the elements and processes of the communication act, self-awareness, credibility, ethics, and the like.

The purpose of this first part, then, is to introduce the essentials of the communicator and the communication act. Seven units are devoted to accomplishing this general aim. Units 1, "Universals of Communication," and 2, "Models of Communication," focus on the elements and processes involved in the communication act. In these two units the relevant terminology of communication is introduced and the communication act as a whole is pictured from a number of different perspectives. By first viewing individually the several components of communication (Unit 1) and the various ways in which these components interact with each other, and then combining them into what we call a communication act (Unit 2), we should gain a first grasp of what communication is and how the communication components and processes operate.

One of the perspectives adopted here is that communication is transactional —every element and every process influence every other element and process. Communication elements or processes, therefore, cannot be studied apart from each other. A necessary corollary here is that communication, by definition, is an ongoing, ever-changing process. It is never static, never at rest. Communication can only be fully understood as an event-in-motion. For purposes of explanation we sometimes talk as if communication components are isolated entities or as if communication is static, but we need to keep reminding ourselves that communication is a transactional process. This view of communication is illustrated in the discussion of the five postulates of communication (Unit 3). These postulates are taken from the works of transactional psychologists concerned with explaining and analyzing human behavior in terms of the various communication patterns. These postulates will provide an exceptionally useful framework for analyzing all forms and functions of communication. These five characteristics or postulates provide another kind of communication model, in this case a purely verbal one.

Once the individual components and the general structure of communication are understood, we can focus on the communicator. Everything we know about individual and group behavior (learned from psychological, anthropological, sociological, and, especially, communication research) is relevant to an understanding of the communicator. The more we know about human behavior the more we know about human communication (and, of course, vice versa).

Given the wealth of material that might be considered, we will focus on four topics which seem to have the most relevance for communication. Self-awareness (Unit 4) is the most encompassing topic and, therefore, the most logical to introduce the section on the self. In this unit I emphasize that an individual is not a single self but many selves, and that the more we understand these several selves the more we will understand and control our own communication behaviors. One of the selves discussed under self-awareness is the hidden self—the self we know but prefer to keep hidden from others. It is that part of us containing our carefully kept secrets. When we do reveal this hidden self we are engaging in a type of communication called self-disclosure. Self-disclosure, because of its central importance to self-awareness and to person-to-person communication, is discussed at length in Unit 5, "Disclosing the Hidden Self." Self-awareness focuses on the individual's understanding of himself or herself; self-disclosure focuses on the individual interacting with others.

Unit 6, "Credibility," focuses on still another aspect of the self—the self as seen by others. Here we consider those elements that go into making an individual believable or credible. We are greatly influenced not only by what others think of us but also by what we *think* others think of us. If we think others see us as credible we will communicate very differently than if we think others see us as noncredible. This point of view underscores the discussion of credibility and should serve to reemphasize the transactional nature of communication.

The last unit in this section, Unit 7, deals with the self in a different and broader perspective—in relation to the ethical issues involved in communication. In many works on communicology the discussion of ethics is confined to public speaking and the issues discussed are, for example, the falsification of information, extreme emotionalism, specious reasoning, and the like. Ethical considerations are not and should not be limited to such narrow concerns. Rather, the question of ethics is involved in every communication exchange. I do not attempt to spell out what we know about ethics, as I did with self-disclosure or credibility, for example. Rather, questions are posed which I feel are signicant and which every communicator should confront. The answers to these questions are individual; each person will answer the questions differently and so no individual answers are offered. Nor did I attempt an exhaustive listing of those situations in which ethical considerations are paramount. Rather, I selected four topics which I felt were especially significant and discussed these in depth. By considering the issues raised in Unit 7, you should be in a better position to formulate your own tentative theory of ethics—a set of principles that will guide your various communication interactions.

These first seven units will provide you with considerable insight into the nature of communication, how communication works, the dynamics of self-awareness and self-disclosure, and the role of credibility and ethical considerations in communication. These insights will then serve as a foundation for the exploration of communication messages, the substance of Part Two.

UNIT 1
Universals
of Communication

LEARNING GOALS

After completing this unit, you should be able to:

1. discuss the nature of the universals of communication
2. define the following terms: *communication context, sources and receivers, messages, competence and performance, encoding and decoding, noise, feedback, field of experience, communication effect, ethics,* and *process.*
3. explain the transactional nature of communication
4. diagram the model of communication presented in this unit, labeling all its parts
5. diagram and explain the relationship between competence and performance
6. construct an original model of communication that incorporates the following: context, source, receiver, message, encoding, decoding, noise, feedback, and field of experience

EXPERIENTIAL VEHICLE

1.1 PRELIMINARIES TO COMMUNICOLOGY

The purpose of this experiential vehicle is to enable you to explore some of the elements and processes involved in the act of communicating before beginning any reading or any formal training in communicology.

Examine the following diagram of the communication process and respond to the questions with reference to this diagram.

The Communication Process Diagrammed

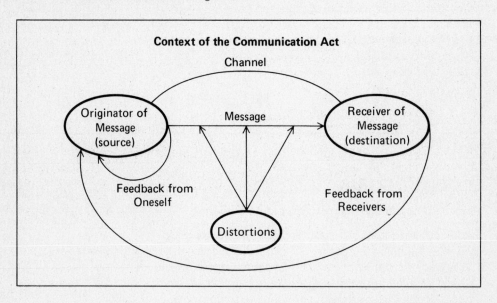

1. Who or what might be designated as a *source* of communication? Identify as many different types of communication sources as you can.
2. Who or what might be designated by the term *destination*? Identify as many different types of communication destinations as you can.
3. What forms might *distortions* take? That is, what types of distortions might enter or interfere with a communication system? From what sources might distortions originate?
4. How can distortions be reduced? Might a communication system ever be distortion free? Explain.

5. What kinds of information can be fed back from the destination to the source?
6. Of what value to the source is information fed back from the destination?
7. What kinds of information might the source receive from his or her own communications?
8. Of what value is information fed back that the source receives from his or her own communications?
9. What forms can a message take? That is, what signals can be used to communicate information?
10. Over what channels might a message be communicated? That is, what senses can be utilized by the source and by the receiver in sending and receiving information? What advantages and limitations do each of the senses have in terms of communication?
11. What are the dimensions or significant aspects of the context of the communication act? That is, in analyzing the context of communication, what factors would have to be investigated?
12. How might *interpersonal communication, small group communication, public communication,* and *mass communication* be defined and distinguished from one another on the basis of the elements noted in the preceding diagram?

This book is about communication and a definition seems a good place to begin. *Communication* refers to the act, by one or more persons, of sending and receiving messages distorted by noise, within a context, with some effect and with some opportunity for feedback. The communication act, then, would include the following components: *context, source(s), receiver(s), messages, channels, noise, sending* or *encoding processes, receiving* or *decoding processes, feedback,* and *effect.* These elements seem the most essential in any consideration of the communication act. They are what we might call the *universals of communication;*—the elements that are present in every communication act, regardless of whether it is *intrapersonal, interpersonal, small group, public speaking, mass communication,* or *intercultural* communication. We cannot proceed without first defining and explaining these several universals.

Universals may be treated as existing on a number of different levels. At the most general level, the universals of communication would include, for example, source, receiver, message, context, noise, effect, and ethics. We might also discuss universals of communication at more specific levels; we might consider those universals included in each of the general universals. For example, the universals included in the *general* universal of source would include self-awareness, self-disclosure, credibility, attitudes, and so on. The general universals of communication are illustrated in Figure 1.1.

Communication is a process; it is ongoing, and it is forever in motion. For

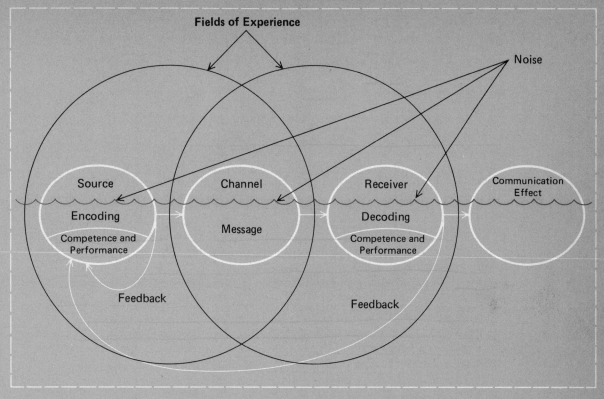

Figure 1.1
A Model of the Universals of Communication

the sake of convenience we may talk about communication elements such as source, context, and message as if they were static and discrete elements existing apart from their role in the total act of communication. But this is simply a technique for explaining and illustrating the various elements. In actual fact, these elements exist in transaction with the other elements. Thus, we should keep in mind the process nature of each of these elements even though the discussion may make them seem static.

Communication is best viewed as transactional. Sources and receivers are in constant transaction with each other and within the context—in fact, they are in constant transaction with each element in the total communication act. The source influences the receiver; at the same time, the receiver influences the source and the context influences both source and receiver. In turn, the context is influenced by both the source and the receiver and their interactions.

Simply, each element in the communication act influences and is influenced by each other element.

COMMUNICATION CONTEXT

Communication always takes place within a *context*. At times this context is not obvious or intrusive; it seems to be so natural that it is ignored, like background music. At other times, the context stands out boldly, and the ways in which it restricts or stimulates our communications are obvious. Compare, for example, the differences in communicating in a funeral home, a football stadium, a quiet restaurant, and a rock concert.

The context of communication has at least four dimensions: physical, social, psychological, and temporal. The room or hallway or park—that is, the tangible or concrete environment—in which communication takes place is the *physical context*. This physical context, whatever it is, exerts some influence on the content as well as the form of our messages. The *social dimension* of context includes, for example, the status relationships among the participants, the roles and the games that people play, and the norms and cultural mores of the society in which they are communicating. The *psychological context* consists of such aspects as the friendliness or unfriendliness of the situation, the formality or informality, and the seriousness or humorousness of the situation. Communications are permitted at a graduation party that would not be permitted at a funeral or in a hospital. The *temporal dimension* includes the time of day as well as the time in history in which the communication act takes place. For many people the morning is not a time for communication; for others, the morning is ideal. Some communication behaviors, for example, sexual interactions seem to many to be more appropriate at night than in the morning or afternoon. Time in history would be particularly important for the communication researcher since messages—their appropriateness, their importance, their impact, their insightfulness—depend in great part on the times in which they were uttered. Consider how difficult it would be to evaluate messages on racial, sexual, or religious attitudes and values if we did not know the time in which these messages were communicated.

These four dimensions of context interact with each other; each influences and is influenced by the others. If, for example, the temperature in a room becomes extremely hot (a physical change), it would probably lead to changes in the social and psychological dimensions as well. General discomfort seems to make people friendlier, as many have witnessed when a train or bus gets stuck. Change in the context, then, may be brought about in any of three general ways: 1) from outside influences, for example, a train failure; 2) from a change in one of the basic dimensions, for example, time or temperature change; or, 3) from the interaction among the dimensions, for example, friendliness increasing as a result of a train breakdown. The context in the communication model (Fig. 1.1) is depicted by a broken line to illustrate that the context is changing rather than static.

SOURCES AND RECEIVERS

In the model, communication is illustrated as taking place between two persons, a *source* and a *receiver*. If we wanted the diagram to illustrate *intra*personal communication, we would view the two "participants" as two roles or functions of the same person.

But regardless of whether there is one person (as in intrapersonal communication), two persons (as in interpersonal communication), or a mass of people (as in mass communication), communication, by definition, demands that someone send signals and someone receive them. One person, of course, might send and receive his or her own signals, as in talking to yourself.

Who people are, what they know, what they believe in, what they value, what they want, what they are told, how intelligent they are, what their attitudes are, and so on all influence what they say and how they say it, what messages they receive and how they receive them. A rich, pampered, well-educated child and a poor, neglected, uneducated child do not talk about the same things or in the same way. Nor, of course, will they receive messages of the same content in the same way or in the same form or style.

MESSAGES AND CHANNELS

The *messages* that are sent and received in communication may be of any form, that is, may be sent and received through any one or combination of sensory organs. Although we customarily think of communication messages as being verbal (oral or written), these are not the only kinds of messages that communicate. We also communicate nonverbally. For example, the clothes we wear communicate something to other people and, in fact, probably communicate to us as well. The way we walk communicates as does the way we shake hands or the way we cock our heads or the way we comb our hair or the way we sit or the way we smile or frown. In fact, everything about us communicates. All of this information constitutes our communication messages.

NOISE

Noise may enter into any communication system. *Noise* is anything that distorts or interferes with the message. Put differently, noise is present in a communication system to the extent that the message sent differs from the message received. The screeching of passing cars, the hum of an air conditioner, the lisp of the speaker, the sunglasses a person wears, may all be regarded as noise since they interfere with the effective and efficient transmission of messages from sender to receiver. Noise is also present in written communication. Such noise would include blurred type, the print that shows through from the back page, creases in the paper, poor grammar, and anything that prevents a reader from getting the message sent by the writer.

The concept of noise might also refer to psychological interference and would include biases and prejudices in senders and receivers which lead to distortions in processing information. Closed-mindedness is perhaps the classic example of noise preventing information from being received.

ENCODING AND DECODING

In communication theory the processes of speaking or writing and understanding or comprehending are referred to as *encoding* and *decoding*. The

---

Box 1
COMMUNICATION AMONG BEES

The language of the bees is perhaps one of the most intensively studied of all animal communication systems. We probably know more about bee communication than we do about the communication systems of any other nonhuman.

The beehive is an amazingly well-ordered society and some researchers have suggested that in order to study bees properly the hive must be studied much like the whole body of a human, and each individual bee must be looked at as would a cell of the human body. The hive consists basically of three types of bees: the queen, who lays the eggs, the workers (all females), who tend to the care and maintenance of the hive, and the drones (all males) whose principal task is to mate with the queen, after which they are driven from the hive to die.

The forager bees' (workers) task is to scout for food supplies. When a food supply is spotted the forager bee returns to the hive and does an intricate dance. By the type of dance she does, whether rounded or wagging, she indicates the general distance the food supply is from the hive. The frequency with which the bee turns, while dancing, indicates the distance in more precise terms. The vigor with which she dances indicates the richness of the food supply, which in turn dictates how many members of the hive should be sent out to collect the food and how many other scouts should be sent to look for additional supplies.

Perhaps most amazing is the manner in which the bees indicate the direction of the food from the hive. They do this by using sunlight for orientation. The bee dances so that the horizontal line connecting the two halves of her dance hits the rays of the sun at precisely the same angle that the rays of the sun hit the line connecting the hive with the food supply. In this way the bees know exactly at what angle to fly to get the nectar. If there is an obstruction between the hive and the food, say a large mountain, the bees will communicate this by giving the directional signals as if the bees were to fly through the mountain (that is,

act of producing messages, for example speaking or writing, is termed encoding. By putting our ideas into sound waves we are putting these ideas into
a code, hence *en*coding. By translating sound waves into ideas we are taking
them out of the code they are in, hence *de*coding. Thus we may refer to speakers or writers as encoders and to listeners or readers as decoders.

If further discrimination among the various communicative components is
necessary, the idea-generating aspect (that is, the brain) and the message-
producing aspect (such as the vocal mechanism) may be distinguished. The
idea-generating component would be referred to as the source, while the
signal- or message-producing aspect would be referred to as the encoder.
Or, if one were talking on a telephone, the source would be the speaker and
the vocal mechanism (and the telephone mouthpiece) would be the encoder.
Conversely, in listening the brain would be the receiver while the auditory

the "bee line") but the distance signals as if the bees were to fly around the
mountain.

One interesting parallel with human language is that bees appear to have
dialects. Austrian bees, for example, will perform a circle dance for close distances
and a wagging dance for far distances. But the Italian bee will, in addition to these
two dances, perform a sickle dance for intermediate distances. Also, the time
schedule for the two types of bees is slightly different. Interestingly enough,
these bees can live together and interbreed but when they attempt to communicate
about food supplies they run into problems. The Austrian bee taking directions
from the Italian bee will look for food too far away because of the differences
in the time schedules of the dances.

These dances, it should be noted, are innate. Bees, taken away from the hive
at birth, seem to have no problem in understanding the dances when returned
to the hive later on. Further, offspring bearing the markings of the Italian bee will
perform the Italian bee dance and offspring bearing the markings of the Austrian
bee will perform the Austrian bee dance.

Bees, of course, communicate about a great deal other than food. For example,
when a new home must be found scouts will go out and search for appropriate
places to house the new colony. When a possible homesite is found the scout returns to the swarm and does a dance, apparently debating the merits of the
home she has found. Other scouts will tell of their findings. Among the factors
the bees consider is the size of the home, the protection it affords from wind
and rain, the available food supply in the area and the distance from other hives,
lest competition among the hives result in some bees starving. There must be
unanimous agreement among the bees on the new home. Since there is only one
queen and since each hive must have a queen, they cannot split up with some
going to one home and others to another home. So the debates are very important to the future of the colony. One such debate was reported in which 21
scouts returned to the hive each reporting on a different possible homesite. Each
was attended to carefully and only after all reports were received was any decision
made.

mechanism would be the decoder. The listener in a telephone conversation would be the receiver while the auditory mechanism (and the earpiece of the telephone) would be the decoder.

COMPETENCE AND PERFORMANCE

Essential to an understanding of encoding and decoding are the concepts of *competence* and *performance*. Consider the "simple" act of speaking. Verbal messages are formed with no real problems; we open our mouths and will certain things to be said. Without any difficulty, they are said. At times we make an error and perhaps say what we did not want to say; but for the most part the vocal mechanism seems a most obedient servant. Similarly, when we listen to the words of others we have no difficulty understanding them, at least most of the time.

We are able to perform these linguistic feats without any problems because we have, among other things, what is called *linguistic competence*. We know the rules of the language (competence) and therefore can formulate and understand sentences (performance) (Figure 1.2). We are able to produce and understand sentences because we have a set of linguistic rules which in effect tell us that these sounds, structured together in this way, mean something specific. This set of linguistic rules—which we know but cannot necessarily verbalize—is our language competence. When we recognize an error in grammar, for example, we do this by matching up what was said with a rule that is part of our competence. Our competence, then, is a somewhat abstract set of grammatical rules that pairs or matches sound with meaning. Our actual speaking and comprehending are performance aspects of language.

Competence and performance differ in an important way. Competence is knowledge of language, which is uninfluenced by any psychological or physical processes. Performance, on the other hand, is influenced not only by competence but also by such factors as fatigue, anxiety, boredom, attention span, and interest. When we fail to understand what someone says, it may be due to our competence. More likely, however, it is due to our failing to attend to what was said or perhaps to our lack of interest—that is, to performance.

FEEDBACK

Another type of message is that of *feedback*. When we send a message, say in speaking to another person, we also hear ourselves. We get feedback from our own messages—we hear what we say, we feel the way we move, we see what we write, and so on. On the basis of this information we may correct ourselves, rephrase something, or perhaps smile at the clever turn of phrase. Even more important than this self-feedback is the feedback we get from others. In speaking with another individual, not only are we constantly sending

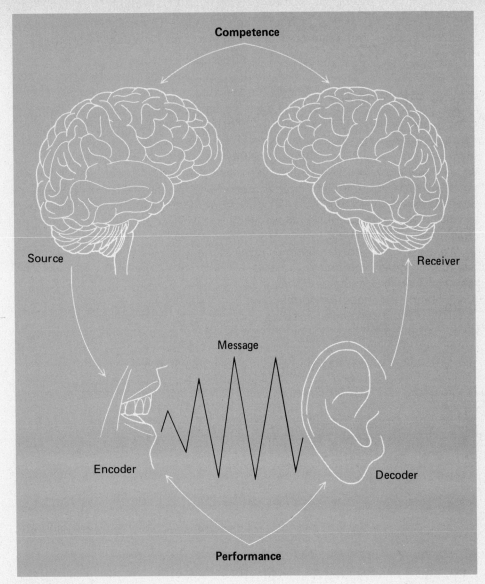

Figure 1.2
Competence and Performance

messages, but we are also constantly receiving messages. Both parties are sending and receiving messages at the same time. The receiver's messages (sent in response to the source's messages) are termed *feedback.* This feed-back, like other messages, can be in many forms: auditory, tactile, visual, gustatory, or olfactory. A frown or a smile, a yea or a nay, a pat on the back, or a shot in the mouth are all feedback.

Feedback may be positive or negative. Positive feedback tells the source that everything is fine and that one should continue as one has been going. Negative feedback tells the source that all is not well and that a reassessment of one's communication behavior is necessary. Negative feedback serves a corrective function by informing the communicator that something needs changing, something needs adjustment. Effectiveness in communication seems largely due to the ability of the communicator to respond appropriately to feedback. Teaching effectiveness may also be seen in the same way. Effective teachers seem to be those who can decode the responses of their students accurately and adjust their messages accordingly. Ineffective teachers seem oblivious to how students are responding and just continue to communicate as always.

FIELD OF EXPERIENCE

The overlapping circles in Figure 1.1 refer to what is called a *field of experience*. The assumption here is that communication can only take place to the extent that the participants share the same experiences. Communication is ineffective or impossible to the extent that the participants have not shared the same experiences. Parents have difficulty communicating with their children, in this view, because the children cannot share the parental experience and because the parents have forgotten what it is like to be a child or do not know what it is like to be a child today. When management forgets what it is like to be labor and when labor does not share any of management's experiences, communication becomes extremely difficult, if not impossible. Differences among people serve to make communication more and more difficult; the larger the differences the more difficult communication becomes. Although many differences cannot be eliminated, communication is still not hopeless. While we cannot, for example, share the actual experiences of our parents, we can perhaps attempt to role-play what it is like being a parent and perhaps in that way better extend the field of experience.

COMMUNICATION EFFECT

Communication *always* has some effect on one or more persons. For every communication act there is some consequence. The effect may be on the source or on the receiver or on both. When communication affects the environment or context, this is done through people. The effects of communication are, then, first on people; they are always personal. Even when we cannot observe an effect (which is perhaps most of the time), we assume that for every communication act there is an effect. As students of communication, part of our task is to determine what these effects are. But that, as we shall see, is a most difficult, though extremely important, undertaking.

A NOTE ON ETHICS

To the degree that communication has an effect, it also has an *ethical dimension*. Because communication has consequences, there is a rightness-wrongness aspect to any communication act. Unlike principles of effective communication, principles of ethical communication are difficult if not impossible to formulate. Often we can observe the effect of communication and on the basis of the observations formulate principles of effective communication. But we cannot observe the rightness or wrongness of a communication act. The ethical dimension of communication is further complicated by the fact that it is so interwoven with one's personal philosophy of life that it is difficult to propose universal guidelines.

Given these difficulties, we nevertheless include ethical considerations as being integral to any communication act. The decisions that we make concerning communication must be guided by considerations of ethics as well as effectiveness.

SOURCES

Communication concepts are considered in most of the available texts in communication. My reader, *Communication: Concepts and Processes,* revised and enlarged ed. (Englewood Cliffs, N.J.: Prentice-Hall, 1976), or that by Jean Civikly, *Messages: A Reader in Human Communication* 2d ed. (New York: Random House, 1977) would be good starting places. Brief introductions to the entire area are provided by Gerald Miller, *An Introduction to Speech Communication,* 2d ed. (Indianapolis: Bobbs-Merrill, 1973) and David L. Swanson and Jesse G. Delia, *The Nature of Human Communication* (Palo Alto, Cal.: SRA, 1976). An excellent introduction to communication terminology is provided by Wilbur Schramm in his *Men, Messages, and Media: A Look at Human Communication* (New York: Harper & Row, 1973). James C. McCroskey and Lawrence R. Wheeless' *Introduction to Human Communication* (Boston: Allyn & Bacon, 1976) provides an excellent introduction to the various elements and processes of communication. For a more thorough discussion of competence and performance, see Helen S. Cairns and Charles E. Cairns, *Psycholinguistics: A Cognitive View of Language* (New York: Holt, Rinehart & Winston, 1976).

EXPERIENTIAL VEHICLES

1.2 ME AS A COMMUNICATOR

Following are two sets of semantic differential scales. The first set is entitled "Me as a Communicator." After reading the instructions for completing semantic differential scales, complete the scale for yourself as a communicator. The second set of scales is entitled "The Ideal Communicator." Complete the scale as you see the ideal communicator.

After completing both sets of scales, compare them. On which dimensions do you match up to the ideal? On which do you fall short? How might you go about improving your own communication abilities? What suggestions might you make, on the basis of these ratings, for establishing the goals of this course?

A number of the exercises in this text make use of semantic differential scales such as these. The instructions given here should be followed whenever semantic differential scales are used.

Instructions for Completing Semantic Differential Scales

Taking the kind-cruel scale as an example, the seven positions should be interpreted as follows. If you feel that the concept being rated is *extremely* kind or *extremely* cruel mark the end positions as follows:

kind **X** : ___ : ___ : ___ : ___ : ___ : ___ cruel

or

kind ___ : ___ : ___ : ___ : ___ : ___ : **X** cruel

If you feel that the concept is *quite* kind or *quite* cruel mark the scale as follows:

kind ___ : **X** : ___ : ___ : ___ : ___ : ___ cruel

or

kind ___ : ___ : ___ : ___ : ___ : **X** : ___ cruel

If you feel that the concept is *slightly* kind or *slightly* cruel mark the scale as follows:

kind ____:____: **X** :____:____:____:____ cruel

or

kind ____:____:____:____: **X** :____:____ cruel

If you feel that the concept is neutral in regard to kind-cruel mark the scale in the middle position, that is,

kind ____:____:____: **X** :____:____:____ cruel

Note: Mark each scale in order; do not omit any scales. Mark each scale only once. Mark each scale on one of the seven scale positions; do not put a mark between positions.

ME AS A COMMUNICATOR

positive	____:____:____:____:____:____:____	negative
sad	____:____:____:____:____:____:____	happy
honest	____:____:____:____:____:____:____	dishonest
introverted	____:____:____:____:____:____:____	extroverted
fluent	____:____:____:____:____:____:____	disfluent
friendly	____:____:____:____:____:____:____	unfriendly
open	____:____:____:____:____:____:____	closed
stupid	____:____:____:____:____:____:____	intelligent
tense	____:____:____:____:____:____:____	relaxed
intellectual	____:____:____:____:____:____:____	nonintellectual
hot	____:____:____:____:____:____:____	cold
static	____:____:____:____:____:____:____	changeable
active	____:____:____:____:____:____:____	passive
calm	____:____:____:____:____:____:____	excitable
sympathetic	____:____:____:____:____:____:____	unsympathetic
rugged	____:____:____:____:____:____:____	delicate
conservative	____:____:____:____:____:____:____	liberal
hard	____:____:____:____:____:____:____	soft
fast	____:____:____:____:____:____:____	slow
humorous	____:____:____:____:____:____:____	serious
soft	____:____:____:____:____:____:____	loud
shallow	____:____:____:____:____:____:____	deep
strong	____:____:____:____:____:____:____	weak
optimistic	____:____:____:____:____:____:____	pessimistic
ferocious	____:____:____:____:____:____:____	peaceful

THE IDEAL COMMUNICATOR

positive	__ :	__ :	__ :	__ :	__ :	__ :	__ negative
sad	__ :	__ :	__ :	__ :	__ :	__ :	__ happy
honest	__ :	__ :	__ :	__ :	__ :	__ :	__ dishonest
introverted	__ :	__ :	__ :	__ :	__ :	__ :	__ extroverted
fluent	__ :	__ :	__ :	__ :	__ :	__ :	__ disfluent
friendly	__ :	__ :	__ :	__ :	__ :	__ :	__ unfriendly
open	__ :	__ :	__ :	__ :	__ :	__ :	__ closed
stupid	__ :	__ :	__ :	__ :	__ :	__ :	__ intelligent
tense	__ :	__ :	__ :	__ :	__ :	__ :	__ relaxed
intellectual	__ :	__ :	__ :	__ :	__ :	__ :	__ nonintellectual
hot	__ :	__ :	__ :	__ :	__ :	__ :	__ cold
static	__ :	__ :	__ :	__ :	__ :	__ :	__ changeable
active	__ :	__ :	__ :	__ :	__ :	__ :	__ passive
calm	__ :	__ :	__ :	__ :	__ :	__ :	__ excitable
sympathetic	__ :	__ :	__ :	__ :	__ :	__ :	__ unsympathetic
rugged	__ :	__ :	__ :	__ :	__ :	__ :	__ delicate
conservative	__ :	__ :	__ :	__ :	__ :	__ :	__ liberal
hard	__ :	__ :	__ :	__ :	__ :	__ :	__ soft
fast	__ :	__ :	__ :	__ :	__ :	__ :	__ slow
humorous	__ :	__ :	__ :	__ :	__ :	__ :	__ serious
soft	__ :	__ :	__ :	__ :	__ :	__ :	__ loud
shallow	__ :	__ :	__ :	__ :	__ :	__ :	__ deep
strong	__ :	__ :	__ :	__ :	__ :	__ :	__ weak
optimistic	__ :	__ :	__ :	__ :	__ :	__ :	__ pessimistic
ferocious	__ :	__ :	__ :	__ :	__ :	__ :	__ peaceful

1.3 INITIATING COMMUNICATION

For this exercise each member of the class should talk with a stranger for at least ten minutes and report back to the class on what transpired. Here are a number of guidlines that should be followed.

1. Play it safe. It is probably unwise to go up to a stranger on a dark street or in a deserted area and attempt to communicate. When in doubt select another person.
2. Do this exercise alone. Do not do it with a group. The other person should not feel that he or she is being studied.
3. Do not tell the person that this is an exercise for a communication course. You may tell the person after the conversation but do not tell him or her before.
4. Do not interview the person. "Just" communicate.
5. Select a stranger with whom you would not normally communicate. The

person should be different from you on at least one significant variable, for example, age, race, educational background, or social status.

Discussion should center on at least the following:

1. Describe:

   a. the person with whom you communicated
   b. the communication context (physical, social, psychological, temporal)
   c. the types of feedback received
   d. the kinds of noise that interfered with communication
   e. the respective fields of experience
   f. the possible effects (on you, on the stranger)

2. How did you open the conversation? Describe the stranger's initial responses.
3. Who did most of the talking? Explain.
4. What did you talk about? Why was this topic used?
5. Was the conversation at all worthwhile? Explain why.

UNIT 2
Models
of Communication

Functions of Models of Communication
A Sampling of Models of Communication
Some Summary Propositions

2.1 General Models of Communication
2.2 Specific Models of Communication

LEARNING GOALS

After completing this unit, you should be able to:

1. identify and explain the four functions of models
2. reproduce and explain at least three of the communication models developed by Aristotle, Lasswell, Gerbner, Berlo, Dance, Shannon and Weaver, Barnlund, Johnson, and Westley and MacLean
3. identify at least six summary propositions derived from the various communication models
4. construct a model of communication that visually represents one or more of the definitions of communication presented and one or more communication situation (see Experiential Vehicles)

Communication is an extremely complex process. Because of the tremendous complexity and the fact that in communication everything is constantly changing, we need to simplify and generalize the essential elements and processes so that we may better explain and understand the structure and function of communication. Communication models are perhaps the best way to accomplish this simplification.

The model presented in Figure 2.1 for example, was designed to illustrate some of the essential concepts or universals of communication as developed in this text. A few of the more popular models are presented here so that the broad spectrum of communication might be observed. First, however, some of the major purposes of such models should be noted.

FUNCTIONS OF MODELS OF COMMUNICATION

Communication models are visualizations of the communication process. In one sense they are basic theories concerning the elements of communication and how these elements operate and interact. More specifically, models of communication may serve any or all of four general functions. We here follow Karl Deutsch's general outline.

First, models serve to *organize* the various elements and processes of the communication act. Of course, no model can organize all the data pertaining

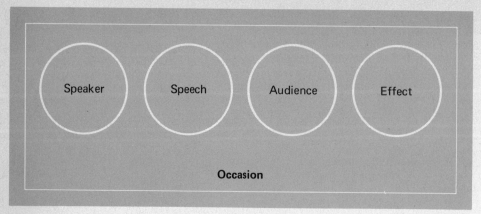

Figure 2.1
Aristotle's Model of Communication

to communication, but we can expect a reasonably good model to organize at least some of the data in a meaningful and interesting way.

Second, models aid in the *discovery* of new facts about communication; that is, they serve a heuristic function. The model should generate questions concerning communication that can be researched and hopefully answered, even if only in part.

Third, models enable us to *make predictions* concerning communication. They should help us to predict what will happen under certain conditions.

Fourth, models might provide a means of *measuring the elements and processes involved in communication*. For example, such a model might contain explicit statements concerning the relative importance of different communication channels and the means by which the information each transmits can be measured. This function is a particularly sophisticated one, and most models of communication do not even attempt to serve it.

The models presented here attempt to organize the elements and processes, to propose some questions, and to offer certain predictions about communication processes and elements.

A SAMPLING OF MODELS OF COMMUNICATION

Nine models of communication will be presented and discussed briefly. The models span a period of some 2300 years, beginning with Aristotle and moving to those constructed in the 1960s and 1970s by contemporary communication theorists. The purpose here is not to provide a complete account of each model, outlining their individual strengths and weaknesses, but rather to provide a general idea as to how various people, each approaching communication from a somewhat different perspective, conceptualized the essential con-

Table 2.1
Lasswell's Model of Communication

Communication component	Research area
Who	Control analysis
Says what	Content analysis
In what channel	Media analysis
To whom	Audience analysis
With what effect	Effect analysis

Source: Harold D. Lasswell, "The Structure and Function of Communication in Society," in Lyman Bryson, ed., *The Communication of Ideas* (New York: Harper & Row, 1948), p. 37.

cepts and processes involved in the communication act. Taken together they provide perhaps the best answer to the question, What is communication?

Probably the earliest systematic model of communication was presented by Aristotle, the Greek philosopher, in his *Rhetoric,* completed some 2300 years ago. The model is extremely simple, as can be seen in Figure 2.1. Aristotle included five essential elements of communication; the speaker, the speech or message, the audience, the occasion, and the effect. In his *Rhetoric,* Aristotle advises the speaker on constructing a speech for different audiences on different occasions for different effects. This model, as can be appreciated, is most applicable to public speaking.

The models devised by both Harold Lasswell and George Gerbner, presented in Tables 2.1 and 2.2, attempt to explain the essential elements in communication and the areas of study concerned with them. The Gerbner model expands on the five general components originally defined by Lasswell. Notice

Table 2.2
Gerbner's Model of Communication

Communication component	Research area
Someone	Communicator/audience research
Perceives an event	Perception research and theory
And Reacts	Effectiveness measurement
In a situation	Physical/social setting research
Through some means	Media investigation
To make available materials	Administration; distribution
In some form	Structure; organization; style
And context	Communicative setting
Conveying content	Content analysis; study of meaning
Of some consequence	Overall changes study

Source: George Gerbner, "Toward a General Model of Communication," *Audio-Visual Communication Review,* 4 (1956): 173.

Table 2.3
Berlo's Model of Communication

Source	Message	Channel	Receiver
Communication skills	Elements	Seeing	Communication skills
Attitudes	Structure	Hearing	Attitudes
Knowledge	Content	Touching	Knowledge
Social system	Treatment	Smelling	Social system
Culture	Code	Tasting	Culture

Source: David Berlo, *The Process of Communication* (New York: Holt, Rinehart & Winston, 1960), p. 72.

that the Lasswell model is not very different from that proposed by Aristotle some 2300 years ago.

David Berlo's model of communication attempts to explain the various components in the communication process (Table 2.3). The four basic components are source, message, channel, and receiver. For each of these four components there are five elements that need to be considered. The source and receiver are treated in essentially the same way. To study either we need to consider their communication skills (speaking and writing for the source, and listening and reading for the receiver), their attitudes, their knowledge, the social system of which they are a part, and the culture in which they operate. The message consists of both elements and structure, each of which may be

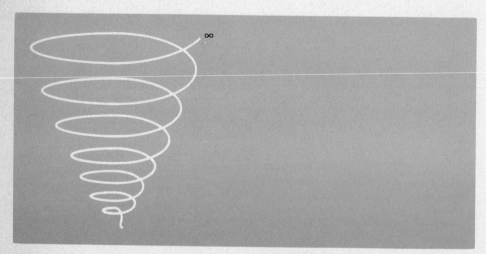

Figure 2.2
Dance's Helical Spiral (*Source:* Frank E. X. Dance, "Toward a Theory of Human Communication," in *Human Communication Theory: Original Essays,* F. E. X. Dance, ed. [New York: Holt, Rinehart & Winston, 1957], p. 296.)

broken down into content, treatment, and code. For the channel, Berlo lists the five senses, emphasizing that messages may be sent and received through any and all of the senses.

A model that appears relatively simple (compared with the other models reviewed) and yet says a great deal that is not obvious about the process of communication is the helical spiral proposed by Frank Dance. This model, presented in Figure 2.2, emphasizes that communication has no clear observable beginning and no clear observable end; the spiral continues indefinitely. No communication transaction may be said to have fixed boundaries. Each transaction is, in part, a function of previous communications and each transaction in turn influences future communications.

Perhaps the most famous of all the models of communication is that proposed by Claude Shannon and Warren Weaver, termed the Mathematical Theory of Communication (Figure 2.3). Communication, according to this model, follows a simple left to right process. The information source, let's say a speaker, selects a desired message from all the possible messages. The message is sent through a transmitter, for example, a microphone, and is changed into signals. In telephone communication these signals would be electrical impulses and the communication channel a wire. The signals are received by a receiver, for example, an earphone of some kind, changed back into a message and given over to the destination, a listener. In the process of transmission certain distortions are added to the signal which were not part of the message sent by the source, and these we call noise.

A model of communication that most clearly emphasizes the transactional

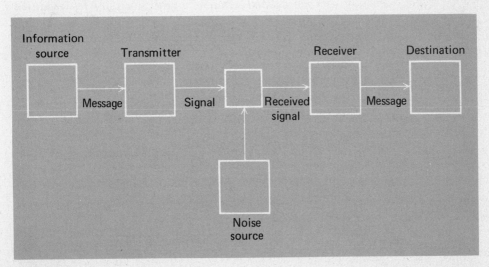

Figure 2.3
Shannon and Weaver's Model of Communication (*Source:* Claude E. Shannon and Warren Weaver, *The Mathematical Theory of Communication* [Urbana, Ill.: University of Illinois Press, 1949], p. 5.)

nature of communication has been proposed by Dean Barnlund. Barnlund's model is based on six communication postulates—six assumptions made about the process of communication. These are reviewed here briefly not only because they enable us to better understand the model but because they provide significant insight into communication in general.

1. *Communication is dynamic.* Communication is an ongoing event and not a static entity. moving + CHANGIng

2. *Communication is continuous.* Communication has no beginning and no end. It is "a continuing condition of life." Although we may, for convenience, stop the process and talk about when a particular communication act began, in reality the process can never be stopped and a beginning never clearly distinguished.

3. *Communication is circular.* When we consider communication as the passing of messages from speaker to listener we imply that the process begins with the speaker and ends with the listener. But communication is a circular process with each person serving each function, with each person influencing and being influenced by every other person.

4. *Communication is unrepeatable.* No action and no reaction is exactly repeatable. No person ever does the same thing in exactly the same way. All communications, to paraphrase the linguists, are novel communications.

5. *Communication is irreversible.* The processes of only some systems can be reversed. For example, water may be turned into ice and the ice may be turned back into water again. This is a reversible process. Other systems, however, are irreversible; the process can only go in one direction. Communication is an irreversible process. We can never undo what has already been done. What has been communicated remains communicated, however we may attempt to qualify it or negate it.

6. *Communication is complex.* The numerous types of communication, the numerous purposes communication serves, the numerous contexts in which communication may take place, and the numerous forms communication messages may take make a vast array of communication acts possible. There seems little question that communication is complex.

Barnlund's transactional model of communication is presented in Figure 2.4. Before explaining the process of communication we should explain the essential components. First, there is P_1 and P_2. These are the two persons involved in the communication act. The D and E stand for decoding and encoding, receiving and sending. Note that no distinction is made here between speaker and hearer; both parties send and both parties receive messages at the same time. C_{PU} stands for cues—public. These are cues derived from the environment available to all potential communicators and are created prior to the communication act. In this way these cues are distinguished from the communication messages which are naturally created during the communication act. Public cues may also be classified into natural cues, those created by nature, and artificial cues, those created by people. Cues—private (C_{PR}) are

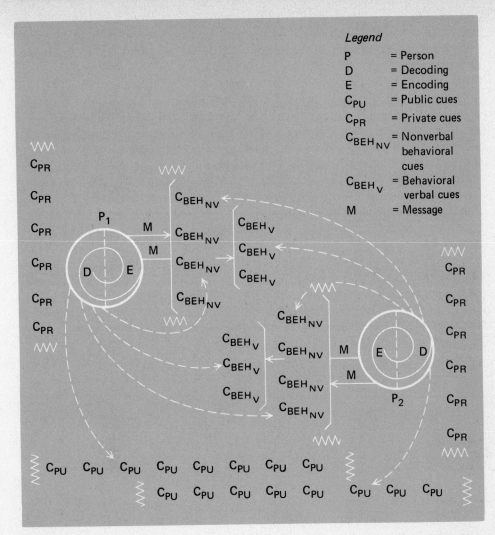

Figure 2.4
Barnlund's Transactional Model of Communication (*Source:* Dean C. Barnlund, "A Transactional Model of Communication," *Language Behavior: A Book of Readings in Communication,* J. Akin, A. Goldberg, G. Myers, and J. Stewart, comps. [The Hague: Mouton, 1970], p. 59.)

cues not available to other people; they are only available to one person. These cues would include, for example, a taste, a pain, or an itch that only one person perceives. Cues perceived with a microscope or an earphone to which others do not have access would also be considered private cues. C_{BEH_V} denotes verbal behavioral cues and $C_{BEH_{NV}}$ denotes nonverbal behavioral cues. The nonverbal cues are considered to include both deliberate nonverbal acts (combing one's hair) as well as unconscious nonverbal acts, such as biting one's lip or squinting. But the term *message, M,* according to Barnlund, is restricted to meaning that set of cues that are purposely controlled by one person in order to communicate with another.

Barnlund's model depicts communication between two people, but with minor modifications it can be altered to include small group communication, public speaking, or mass communication as well as communication with the self. Focus first on the arrows emerging from P_1. The dotted arrows represent the perceptions of P_1. These perceptions are actually of two types: private (C_{PR}) and public (C_{PU}). Notice that the dotted arrows go not only to the public cues but also to the verbal and nonverbal messages of P_2, as well as to the nonverbal messages of P_1 (and the verbal messages of P_1, it seems, should have been included here as well). The process is identical from the point of view of P_2.

One of the most insightful models and most clearly a model of interpersonal communication is that proposed by Wendell Johnson (Figure 2.5). Although it may seem complex, the model is actually rather simple when compared to the truly complex process of communication. The surrounding rectangle indicates that communication takes place in a context which is external to both speaker

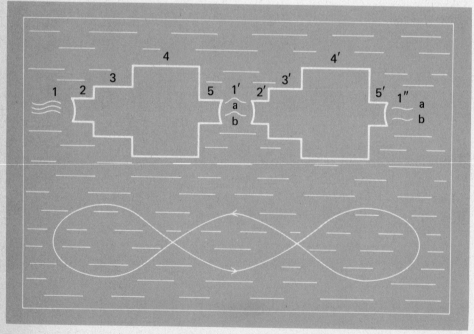

Figure 2.5
Johnson's Model of Communication (*Source:* Wendell Johnson, "The Spoken Word and the Great Unsaid," *Quarterly Journal of Speech* 37 [1951]:421.)

and listener and to the communication process as well. The curved loop indicates that the various stages of communication are actually interrelated and interdependent.

The actual communication process begins at 1 which represents the occurrence of an event, anything that can be perceived. This event is the stimulus. Although not all communication occurs with reference to such external stimuli, communication makes sense, Johnson argues, only when it does in some way relate to the external world. At stage 2 the observer is stimulated through one or more sensory channels. The opening at 2 is purposely illustrated as relatively small to emphasize that out of all the possible stimuli in the world, only a small part of these actually stimulate the observer. At stage 3 organismic evaluations occur. Here nerve impulses travel from the sense organs to the brain which effect certain bodily changes in, for example, muscular tension. At 4 the feelings aroused at 3 are beginning to be translated into words, a process that takes place in accordance with the individual's unique language habits. At stages 5, from all the possible linguistic symbols, certain ones are selected and arranged into some pattern.

At 1′ the words that the speaker utters, by means of sound waves, or the words that are written, by means of light waves, serve as stimulation for the hearer, much as the outside event at 1 served as stimulation for the speaker. At 2′ the hearer is stimulated, at 3′ there are organismic evaluations, at 4′ feelings are beginning to be translated into words, at 5′ certain of these symbols are selected and arranged, and at 1″ these symbols, in the form of sound and/ or light waves, are emitted and serve as stimulation for another hearer. The process is a continuous one.

Westley and MacLean have proposed a model of communication which is

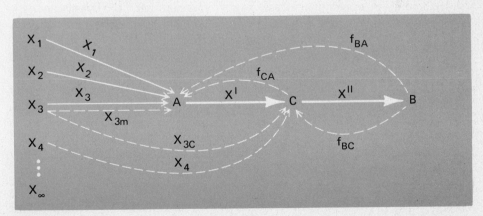

Figure 2.6
Westley and MacLean's Model of Communication (*Source:* Bruce H. Westley and Malcolm S. MacLean, Jr., "A Conceptual Model for Communication Research," *Journalism Quarterly* 34 [1957].)

particularly appropriate to describe the essential elements and processes involved in mass communication. The model is presented in Figure 2.6.

In this model there are three essential persons, represented by *A*, *B*, and *C*. *A* refers to the communicator, the person who selects and transmits messages purposively. *B* refers to the receiver or "the public." *C* designates an agent that selects and transmits messages received from *A* or from his or her own environment to *B*. The *X*'s refer to the objects in the sensory field of the individual to whom they are connected by arrows. X^I refers to the messages that *A* transmits to *C* about the *X*'s in his or her sensory field. X^{II} designates the messages transmitted by *C* to *B* about the *X*'s in his or her sensory field. The dotted lines going from right to left and designated f_{CA}, f_{BA}, and f_{BC} refer to the feedback messages which enable *A* and *C* to discover how *B* has reacted to their messages.

These models are certainly not complete explanations of the communication process. Rather, they are attempts to picture *some* of the most essential elements and processes and *some* of the relevant relationships which make up the communication act. These models should clarify some of the components and interactions that exist in communication. At the same time, they provide a kind of framework into which the more specific details of communication, to be discussed throughout the remainder of the text, may be fit. Finally, these models should serve to introduce a basic vocabulary of communication.

SOME SUMMARY PROPOSITIONS

As a kind of summary we might note a number of assumptions about communication that the models presented imply.

1. As all of the models point out, communication consists of several different elements in constant interaction with one another. The elements most frequently mentioned are source, receiver, encoder, decoder, feedback, message, noise, context, effect, and channel.
2. Each element, as both Lasswell and Gerbner note, may be associated with a specific area of research or methodology.
3. Each element in communication may be further broken down into more specific elements or components as Berlo notes in his source-message-channel-receiver (SMCR) model.
4. Communication has no clear observable beginning or end; communication transactions do not have fixed boundaries. This is illustrated most clearly in the models of Dance and Barnlund.
5. Each communication act influences future transactions and is influenced by past transactions. This assumption is made by most models but is visualized most clearly in Dance's helical spiral.
6. Noise is inevitable in any communication transaction—a point made most vividly by Shannon and Weaver but recognized by most other models as well.

7. As both Barnlund and Johnson note, communication is dynamic; communication is not a static event but rather one in constant process.

8. Communication is transactional; each element influences every other element. The transactional nature of communication seems most clearly recognized by Dance and Barnlund.

9. Communication is complex. This is a point made explicit by Barnlund but illustrated by all of the other models.

10. Encoders and decoders are interchangeable. Each party continually encodes and decodes. This characteristic is inherent in any transactional conception of communication but is made explicit by Barnlund and Johnson.

11. Feedback messages come from the source as well as from the receiver and provide the source with information as to the relative effectiveness of various messages. Westley and MacLean made the role of feedback an essential part of their model but it is implicit in the models of various others, most notably Dance and Barnlund.

12. Communication, as Johnson notes, makes sense only to the extent that the message relates to the external world.

13. Our communications, as both Barlund and Johnson note, make use of and reference to only a small part of our perceptions.

14. As Westley and MacLean note, it is useful to define an intermediary in communication—one that transmits the message from a source to a receiver, especially when one is dealing with mass communications or communication in which messages are passed from person to person.

15. Communication messages may be verbal as well as nonverbal. Communication takes place when we squint as well as when we speak. Berlo, Barnlund, and Johnson make this explicit.

16. Communication takes place in a context. This point is made by most theorists but is visualized most effectively in the models of Aristotle and Johnson.

17. Communication is inevitable. All behavior communicates. This proposition, although not stated explicitly in any model, is clearly deducible from most of them.

18. Each communication event is unique. No two communication acts are ever identical or repetitive. Both Barnlund and Johnson are clearest on this property.

19. Communication takes place through the continual encoding and decoding of signals—a process whereby signals transmitted in one code are received and translated into another code. Shannon and Weaver's model visualizes this most clearly.

20. All models are abstractions and are incomplete representations of the actual communication act.

SOURCES

For communication models see the summaries by Joseph A. DeVito, *The Psychology of Speech and Language: An Introduction to Psycholinguistics* (New York: Random House, 1970), from which much of the previous discussion was drawn; David Mortensen, *Communication: The Study of Human Interaction* (New York: McGraw-Hill, 1972); Ron Smith's article "Theories and Models of Communication Processes" in Larry L. Barker and Robert J. Kibler, eds., *Speech Communication Behavior: Perspectives and Principles* (Englewood Cliffs, N.J.: Prentice-Hall, 1971); Sara A. Barnhart, *Introduction to Interpersonal Communication* (New York: Crowell, 1976); or Robert Hopper, *Human Message Systems* (New York: Harper & Row, 1976). References to specific models may be found in any of these sources. For a more extended treatment of the functions of models see Karl Deutsch, "On Communication Models in the Social Sciences," *Public Opinion Quarterly,* 16 (1952). More sophisticated treatments of the theory and model of communication are presented by Leonard C. Hawes in "Elements of a Model for Communication Processes," *Quarterly Journal of Speech,* 59 (1973) and *Pragmatics of Analoguing: Theory and Model Construction in Communication* (Reading, Mass.: Addison-Wesley, 1975).

EXPERIENTIAL VEHICLES

2.1 GENERAL MODELS OF COMMUNICATION

Below are presented several definitions of communication. Each of these definitions presents a somewhat different view of the nature and function of communication. After reading each definition select the one that seems most meaningful to you and construct a model of communcation based on that definition—that is, construct a visual representation of communication as viewed by the definition selected.

After completing this model the class should separate into groups based on the definition chosen. Each group should then discuss the several visual representations and attempt to formulate a composite model that incorporates the best of the individual models.

These composite models should then be presented to the class as a whole in order to emphasize the many different ways in which communication may be viewed and in order to introduce some of the essential concepts and processes of communicology.

Definitions

1. "A word that describes the process of transferring meaning from one individual to another." (Robert S. Cathcart, *Post Communication: Criticism and Evaluation* [Indianapolis: Bobbs-Merrill, 1966], p. 1.)
2. "A process involving the selection, production, and transmission of signs in such a way as to help a receiver perceive a meaning similar to that in the mind of the communicator." (Wallace C. Fotheringham. *Perspectives on Persuasion* [Boston: Allyn & Bacon, 1966], p. 254.)
3. "Communication means that information is passed from one place to another." (George A. Miller, *Language and Communication* [New York: Mc-Graw-Hill, 1951], p. 6.)
4. "The discriminatory response of an organism to a stimulus." (S. S. Stevens, "Introduction: A Definition of Communication," *Journal of the Acoustical Society of America,* 22 [1950]: 689.)
5. "All behavior in an interactional situation has message value, i.e., is communication. . . ." (P. Watzlawick, J. H. Beavin, and D. D. Jackson, *Pragmatics of Human Communication* [New York: Norton, 1967], p. 48.)
6. "A process whereby a source elicits a response in a receiver through the transmission of a message, be it sign or symbol, verbal or nonverbal." (Andrea L. Rich, *Interracial Communication* [New York: Harper & Row, 1974], p. 4.)

7. "Communication occurs whenever persons attribute significance to message-related behavior." (C. David Mortensen, *Communication: The Study of Human Interaction* [New York: McGraw-Hill, 1972], p. 14.)

2.2 SPECIFIC MODELS OF COMMUNICATION

In groups of five or six construct a diagrammatic model of the essential elements and processes involved in one of the following communication situations. This model's primary function should be to describe what elements are involved and what processes are operative in the specific situation chosen. (It may be useful to define the situation chosen in more detail before constructing the model.)

1. Sitting silently on a bus
2. Thinking
3. Asking for a date on the phone
4. Conversing with a very close friend
5. Talking with three or four acquaintances
6. Delivering a lecture to a class
7. Watching television
8. Participating in a formal group discussion
9. Writing a speech for a political candidate
10. Reading a newspaper
11. Performing in a movie
12. Acting a role in a play
13. Arguing with your instructor
14. Selling insurance door-to-door
15. Persuading an angry crowd to disband

Each group should share their models with the rest of the class. Discussion might center on the following:

1. How adequately do the models explain the processes which they are supposed to represent? Do they incorporate all the essential elements and processes? Are the relationships among the elements and processes clear?
2. What insight into the actual processes of communication do these models provide? What new ideas or information may be found in these models?
3. What elements and processes included here might also be included in the general models of communcation discussed in the unit?
4. What functions do these models serve? Explain. (Respond to this question with specific reference to the functions of models presented by Deutsch.)

UNIT 3
Postulates
of Communication

The Impossibility of Not Communicating
Content and Relationship Aspects of Communication
Punctuation of Communication Sequences
Digital and Analogic Systems of Communication
Symmetrical and Complementary Interactions

LEARNING GOALS

After completing this unit, you should be able to:

1. explain the importance of the statement "we cannot *not* communicate"
2. identify the alternatives available when one does not wish to communicate but another person does
3. distinguish between the content and the relationship dimension of communication
4. distinguish among *confirmation*, *rejection*, and *disconfirmation* in communication
5. explain the concept of punctuation in communication
6. distinguish between *digital* and *analogic communication*
7. distinguish between *symmetrical* and *complementary interactions*

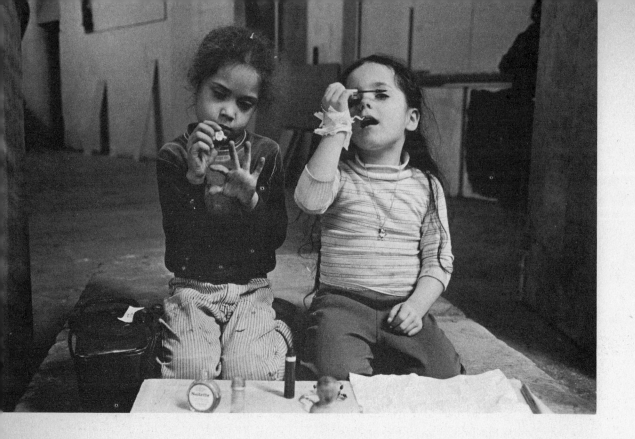

In *Pragmatics of Human Communication: A Study of Interactional Patterns, Pathologies, and Paradoxes,* Paul Watzlawick, Janet Beavin, and Don Jackson present an analysis of the behavioral effects of communication derived from the study of behavior disorders. Perhaps the most essential part of their analysis of human communication is the five postulates, or axioms, of communication—propositions that are essential to an understanding of communication in all its forms and functions. These postulates are universals of communication; they are descriptive of communication in all its forms and functions.

THE IMPOSSIBILITY OF NOT COMMUNICATING

Often we think of communication as being intentional, purposeful, and consciously motivated. In many instances it is. But in other instances we are communicating even though we might not think we are or might not even want to communicate. Take, for example, the student sitting in the back of the room with an expressionless face, perhaps staring at the front of the room, perhaps staring out the window. Although the student might say that he or she is not communicating with the teacher or with the other students, that sudent is obviously communicating a great deal—perhaps disinterest, perhaps boredom, perhaps a concern for something else, perhaps a desire for the class to be over with as soon as possible. In any event, the student is communicating whether he or she wishes to or not. We cannot not communicate.

Further, when we are in an interactional situation with this person we must respond in some way. Even if we do not actively or overtly respond, that lack of response is itself a response and communicates. Like the student's silence, our silence in response also communicates.

Watzlawick, Beavin, and Jackson give the example of two strangers on a plane; one wishes to communicate while the other does not. When we do not wish to communicate we have four general alternatives that may be employed.

1. We may simply and explicitly state the desire not to communicate. We may do this nonverbally which is perhaps the less socially offensive way or we may do this verbally. The expression of not wishing to communicate, whether verbal or nonverbal, obviously does not follow communication etiquette. Despite the fact that the person next to us is a complete bore and that we might just want to daydream, we are under social pressure not to ignore anyone. Yet the option to say we do not wish to communicate is still open to us.

2. We may simply give in and communicate. This, it seems, is the alternative that many people take, and it seems to be the road of least effort. In fact, it may take more psychic energy to tell this person that you do not wish to communicate than to communicate. And we can still hope that the person will soon tire and go away.

3. We may disqualify our communications in various ways. For example, we may contradict ourselves, speak in incomplete sentences, or change the subject without any apparent motivation. In all of these cases the intent is to get the other person bored or confused so that he or she will stop communicating. Of course it often happens that the person becomes all the more interested in figuring us out and consequently seems to stay with us for what seems like forever.

4. Perhaps the most ingenious way is to pretend to want to talk but to also pretend that something is preventing us from doing so. For example, we might say that we would like to talk but we are just so sleepy that we cannot keep our eyes open and then doze off. Or perhaps we feign a toothache which makes speaking difficult. Or we might pretend to be drunk or sick or deaf. At times, of course, the other person is aware that we are pretending. Yet this is a more socially acceptable manner of getting out of talking than honestly stating that we do not want to communicate.

Notice that regardless of what we do or do not do we are still communicating. All behavior is communication; all behavior has message value.

CONTENT AND RELATIONSHIP ASPECT OF COMMUNICATION

Communications, to a certain extent at least, refer to the real world or to something external to both speaker and hearer. At the same time, however, communications also refer to the relationships between the parties. For example, a teacher may say to a student, "See me after class." This simple message has a *content aspect,* which refers to the behavioral responses expected—namely that the student see the teacher after class—and a *relationship aspect,* which tells us how the communication is to be dealt with. Even the use of the simple command states that there is a status difference between the two parties such that the teacher can command the student. This is perhaps seen most clearly when we visualize this command being made by the student to the teacher. It appears awkward and out of place simply because it violates the normal relationship between teacher and student.

In any communication the content dimension may be the same but the relationship aspect different or the relationship aspect may be the same with the content different. For example, the teacher could say to the student, "You had better see me after class," or he or she could say, "May I please see you after class?" In each case the content is essentially the same; that is, the message being communicated about the behavioral responses expected is about the same in both cases. But the relationship dimension is very different. In the first it signifies a very definite superior-inferior relationship and even a put-down of the student, but in the second a more equal relationship is signaled and a respect for the student is shown. Similarly, at times the content may be different but the relationship essentially the same. For example, a child might say to his or her parents, "May I go away this weekend?" and "May I use the car tonight?" The content is clearly very different in each case and yet the relationship dimension is essentially the same. It is clearly a superior-inferior relationship where permission to do certain things must be secured.

Thus on the relationship level we communicate, not about the outside world of content, but about the relationship between the communicators. In such communications we offer a definition of ourselves. When we offer this definition of self the other person may make any of three general responses, according to Watzlawick, Beavin, and Jackson. In *confirmation* the other person verifies the individual's self-definition. The student who responds to the teacher's, "You had better see me after class" with "Yes, Professor Perrotta" confirms the teacher's definition of himself or herself. In *rejection* the other person rejects the individual's self-view. Such rejection may be constuctive as when a therapist rejects a patient's self-definition. The student who responds to the teacher's, "You had better see me after class," with "No, I don't feel like it," is rejecting the teacher's definition of self. Lastly, in *disconfirmation* the other person ignores or denies the right of the individual to even define himself or herself. The student who ignores the teacher's command is disconfirming the teacher's definition of self.

Many problems between people are caused by the failure to recognize the distinction between the content and the relationship levels of communication. For example, consider the engaged couple arguing over the fact that the woman made plans to study during the weekend with her friends without first asking her boyfriend if that would be all right. Probably both would have agreed that to study over the weekend was the right choice to make; thus the argument is not at all related to the content level. The argument centers on the relationship level; the man expected to be consulted about plans for the weekend whereas the woman, in not doing this, rejected this definition or relationship. Similar situations exist among married couples when one person will buy something or make dinner plans or invite a guest to dinner, as in an example given by Watzlawick, Beavin, and Jackson, without asking the other person first. Even though the other person would have agreed with the decision made, they argue over it because of the message communicated on the relationship level.

This is not to say that the relationship level is often discussed or even that it should be explicitly discussed by both parties. In fact, Watzlawick, Beavin, and Jackson argue the contrary: "It seems that the more spontaneous and 'healthy' a relationship, the more the relationship aspect of communication recedes into the background. Conversely, 'sick' relationships are characterized by a constant struggle about the nature of the relationship, with the content aspect of communication becoming less and less important."

We might also note that arguments over the content dimension are relatively easy to resolve. Generally, we may look something up in a book or ask someone what actually took place or perhaps see the movie again. It is relatively easy to verify facts that are disputed. Arguments on the relationship level, however, are much more difficult to resolve, in part because we seldom recognize that the argument is in fact a relationship one.

PUNCTUATION OF COMMUNICATION SEQUENCES

Communication events are continuous transactions. They are broken up into short sequences only for purposes of convenience. What is stimulus and what is response is not very easy to determine when we, as analysts of communication, enter after the communication transaction is underway. Consider, for example, the following incident. A couple is at a party. The wife is flirting with the other men and the husband is drinking; both are scowling at each other and are obviously in a deep nonverbal argument with each other. In explaining the situation the wife might recall the events by observing that the husband drank and so she flirted with the sober men. The more he drank the more she flirted. The only reason for her behavior was her anger over his drinking. Notice that she sees her behavior as the response to his behavior; his behavior came first and was the cause of her behavior.

In recalling the "same" incident the husband might say that he drank when she started flirting. The more she flirted, the more he drank. He had no intention of drinking until she started flirting. To him, her behavior was the stimulus and his was the response; she caused his behavior. Thus she sees the behavior as going from drinking to flirting, and he sees it as going from flirting to drinking.

This tendency to divide up the various communication transactions into sequences of stimuli and responses is referred to by Watzlawick, Beavin, and Jackson as the punctuation of the sequences of events. They do not argue that punctuation is wrong; obviously, it is a very useful technique in providing some organization for thinking about and talking about communication transactions. At the same time, because we each see things differently, we each punctuate events differently. To the extent that these differences are significant, the possibility for a communication breakdown exists.

DIGITAL AND ANALOGIC SYSTEMS OF COMMUNICATION

In human communication we make use of both *digital* and *analogic* information and utilize both digital and analogic communication systems. These two kinds of systems are actually quite simple to distinguish, although when we attempt to translate messages from one system to another we run into problems.

Digital systems are those that deal with discrete rather than continuous elements; they are systems that work on the all-or-none principle. For example, a light switch is a digital system; the light is either on or off. A calculator is a digital system; it gives answers in discrete numbers.

Analogic systems are those that are continuous rather than discrete; they are systems that work on the more-or-less principle. For example, a rheostat or dimmer is an analogic system; the light's intensity can be varied to different degrees of brightness. A slide rule is an analogic system; unlike the calculator the slide rule gives us an approximate rather than a discrete and exact answer.

Human communication makes use of both digital and analogic systems. Our verbal communication system, consisting of words and sentences, is digital; our words and sentences are discrete entities. On the other hand, most of our nonverbal system, for example, the loudness of our voice or the degree of our smile, is analogic and is more like the rheostat than the on-off light switch.

Watzlawick, Beavin, and Jackson note that the digital system is more likely to communicate the content message and that the analogic system is more likely to communicate the relationship message. We will verbalize about the outside world but our relationship to another person will more likely be communicated through nonverbal means; eye contact, touching behavior, the way we stand, and so on.

Watzlawick, Beavin, and Jackson also note that digital messages may be more complex and more abstract than analogic messages. It would be difficult, for example, to communicate highly complex and abstract notions nonverbally (or analogically) but we can easily talk about them in words and sentences (or digitally). Analogic messages are subject to greater ambiguity than are digital messages. Although digital messages may be ambiguous, there seems to be greater ambiguity or room for misinterpretation with analogic messages. As Watzlawick, Beavin, and Jackson point out we can cry and shed tears of both joy and sorrow; we can smile to convey both sympathy and contempt; we can appear reticent to convey both tact and indifference.

In translating analogic messages into digital messages we often run into problems. Consider, for example, how many times in attempting to write a message expressing deep emotions and thought one has wished to be able to say the message instead. In speaking we would have the use of the analogic communication system as well, but in the written message we have only the digital system. Similarly, as Watzlawick, Beavin, and Jackson point out, giving a gift is an analogic message. But when the receiver attempts to translate it into a digital message, he or she may consider it a sign of affection, a conscience present, or perhaps a bribe.

We also run into problems when we attempt to show people that we really understand how they feel and attempt to put their nonverbal or analogic messages into verbal or digital messages. At times we can do it with satisfaction but most often, it seems, we cannot. We fail, not necessarily because we are not insightful or cannot accurately read the nonverbal cues, but rather because one system does not translate into another system very easily. There are no one-to-one equivalencies between analogic and digital messages.

SYMMETRICAL AND COMPLEMENTARY INTERACTIONS

Symmetrical and complementary relationships are not good or bad in themselves. Both are usually present in normal, healthy relationships.

In a *symmetrical relationship* the two individuals mirror each other's behavior. The behavior of one party is reflected in the behavior of the other party. If one member nags, the other member responds in kind. If one member expresses jealousy, the other member expresses jealousy. If one member is passive, the other member is passive. The relationship is one of equality with the emphasis on minimizing the differences between the two individuals.

In a *complementary relationship* the two individuals engage in different behaviors, with the behavior of one serving as the stimulus for the complementary behavior in the other. In complementary relationships the differences between the parties are maximized. It is necessary in a complementary relationship for both parties to occupy different positions, one being the superior and one being the inferior, one being passive and one being active, one being strong and one being weak. At times such relationships are established by the culture as, for example, the complementary relationship existing between teacher and student or between employer and employee. Perhaps the classic complementary relationship would be between the sadist and the masochist, where the sadistic behavior of the sadist serves to stimulate the masochistic behavior of the masochist and vice versa.

Problems may arise in both symmetrical and complementary relationships. In the symmetrical relationship it is easy to appreciate that two individuals who mirror each other's jealousy will find very little security. The jealous behavior is likely to escalate to the point where one or both parties will quit from exhaustion. As Watzlawick, Beavin, and Jackson put it, "In marital con-

"Let's face it, Sarah, over-analyzing the basis of our
relationship is the foundation of our relationship."
(Cartoon by Gordon Shoemaker.)

flict, for instance, it is easy to observe how the spouses go through an escala-
tion pattern of frustration until they eventually stop from sheer physical or
emotional exhaustion and maintain an uneasy truce until they have recovered
enough for the next round."

Perhaps the classic example of problems created in complementary relationships, familiar to many college students, is that of rigid complementarity.
Whereas the complementary relationship between mother and child was at
one time vital and essential to the life of the child, that same relationship
when the child is older "becomes a severe handicap for his further development, if adequate change is not allowed to take palce in the relationship."

In review, the five postulates of communication are:

1. In an interactional situation it is impossible not to communicate
2. All communications have a content and a relationship dimension
3. The meaning of a communication transaction depends, in part, on its
   punctuation
4. Communication is both digital and analogic
5. Communication transactions may be symmetrical or complementary

These five postulates, as set forth by Watzlawick, Beavin, and Jackson,
seem essential to any introductory or advanced analysis of communication.
They provide us with insight into the nature and function of human com-

munication as well as into the intricacies of human relationships and interactions.

SOURCES

For this unit I relied on Paul Watzlawick, Janet Helmick Beavin, and Don D.
Jackson, *Pragmatics of Human Communication: A Study of Interactional Patterns, Pathologies, and Paradoxes* (New York: Norton, 1967). Another useful
work in this area is Jurgen Ruesch and Gregory Bateson, *Communication:
The Social Matrix of Psychiatry* (New York: Norton, 1951). Many of the ideas
set forth in *Pragmatics* may be found in the work of Bateson. For a useful
collection of Bateson's writings, see *Steps to an Ecology of Mind* (New York:
Ballatine, 1972). An alternative way of looking at communication is provided
by Gerald R. Miller and Henry E. Nicholson, *Communication Inquiry: A Perspective on a Process* (Reading, Mass.: Addison-Wesley, 1976). This book
is for the advanced or the ambitious beginning student of communication.

EXPERIENTIAL VEHICLE

3.1 ANALYZING AN INTERACTION

The five postulates of human communication proposed by Watzlawick, Beavin, and Jackson and discussed in this unit should prove useful in analyzing any communication interaction. To better understand these postulates and to obtain some practice in applying them to an actual interaction, a summary of Tennessee Williams' *Cat on a Hot Tin Roof* is presented. Ideally, all students would read the entire play or see the movie and then apply the five postulates to the interactions that take place. The brief summary is presented, then, more in the nature of a "mental refresher." (Note that the original play, as it has been published, differs from the film, particularly in the last act. The film version of the play is somewhat more positive. The summary presented here is from the original stage play, the version Williams prefers.)

Big Daddy and Big Mama Pollitt, owners of a huge estate, have two sons: Brick (married to Maggie, the cat), an ex-football player who has now turned to drink; and Gooper (married to Mae), a lawyer and father of five children with one on the way. All are gathered together to celebrate Big Daddy's sixty-fifth birthday. The occasion is marred by news that Big Daddy may have cancer for which there is no hope of a cure. A false report is given to Big Mama and Big Daddy stating that the test proved negative and that all that is wrong is a spastic colon—a sometimes painful but not fatal illness. It appears, to Maggie and perhaps to others as well, that Gooper and Mae are really here to claim their share of the inheritance.

The desire to assume control of Big Daddy's fortune (estimated at some $10 million and 28,000 acres "of the richest land this side of the valley Nile") has created considerable conflict between Gooper and Mae on the one hand and Maggie on the other. Brick, it appears, does not care about his possible inheritance.

Throughout the play there is conflict between Brick and Maggie. Brick refuses to go to bed with Maggie although Maggie desperately wants him. This fact is known by everyone since Mae and Gooper have the adjoining room and hear everything that goes on between Brick and Maggie. The cause of this conflict between Brick and Maggie goes back to Brick's relations with Skipper, his best friend. Brick and Skipper were football players on the same team and did just about everything together. So close were they that rumors about their love for each other began to spread. While Brick is in the hospital with a football injury Maggie confronts Skipper and begs that he either stop loving Brick or tell him of his love. In an attempt to prove Maggie wrong Skipper goes to bed with her but fails and as a result takes to drinking and drugs. Maggie repeatedly at-

46

tempts to thrash this out with Brick but he refuses to talk about it or even to listen to Maggie. All he wants to do is drink—waiting for the little click in his head that tells him he can stop.

In a confrontation with Big Daddy, Brick talks of his disgust with lying and his using liquor to forget all the lies around him. Under pressure from Big Daddy, Brick admits that Skipper called to make a drunken confession after his attempted relationship with Maggie but that Brick hung up and refused to listen. It was then that Skipper committed suicide. And this, it appears, is what Brick uses alcohol to forget. In his anger Brick tells Big Daddy that is dying of cancer.

Gooper and Mae confront Big Mama with the news that Big Daddy has cancer and attempt to get Big Mama to sign some papers concerning the disposition of the property now that Big Daddy has not much longer to live. Perhaps Gooper and Mae's major argument is that they are responsible (as shown by their five children), while Brick and Maggie are not responsible (as shown by Brick's drinking and by his refusal to sleep with Maggie and have a child, something Big Daddy wants very much). At this point Maggie announces that she is pregnant. Big Mama is overjoyed and seems to be the only one who believes her. This, Big Mama reasons, will solve all problems, even the problem of Brick's drinking. Brick of course knows that Maggie is lying but says nothing to betray her.

In the final scene Maggie locks up all the liquor and pressures Brick into going to bed with her in order to make her lie about her pregnancy become truth. Afterwards she promises to unlock the liquor so that they may both get drunk. She sobs that she really loves Brick while Brick thinks if only that were true.*

After reading the play or viewing the film, identify instances of and explain the importance of:

1. the impossibility of not communicating

   a. What alternatives does Brick use in attempting to avoid communicating with Maggie?
   b. What alternatives does Brick use in attempting to avoid communicating with Big Daddy?

2. the content and relationship aspects of communication

   a. How does Brick deal with the self-definitions of Maggie and Big Daddy?
   b. How does Big Daddy deal with Big Mama's definition of herself?
   c. Are any problems caused by the failure to recognize the distinction between the content and the relationship levels of communication?

* An interesting discussion of *Cat on a Hot Tin Roof* in terms of communication problems is provided by Philip C. Kolin, "Obstacles to Communication in *Cat on a Hot Tin Roof,*" *Western Speech Communication* 39 (Spring 1975): 74–80. For alternative views of Maggie, Kolin recommends the following articles, both of which should prove useful in analyzing the role of Maggie and in understanding the communication dimension of the play as a whole: James Ray Blackwelder, "The Human Extremities of Emotion in *Cat on a Hot Tin Roof,*" *Research Studies* 38 (1970): 13–21 and Paul J. Hurley, "Tennessee Williams: The Playwright as Social Critic," *Theatre Annual* 21 (1964): 40–56.

3. the punctuation of communication sequences

   a. How do Maggie and Brick differ in their punctuation of the events?
   b. Why do they punctuate the sequences differently?

4. the digital and analogic systems of communication

   a. Are any problems caused by attempting to translate analogic into digital messages? (Look specifically at Maggie's interpretation of Brick's communications and Brick's interpretation of Maggie's communications and of Big Daddy's communications. Also look at Big Mama's interpretation of Big Daddy's messages toward her.)
   b. From what can be constructed of Skipper's communications, how were they interpreted in digital versus analogic terms?

5. the symmertical and complementary interactions

   a. What type of relationship existed between Brick and Maggie, Gooper and Mae, Big Daddy and Big Mama, Big Daddy and Brick, Big Daddy and Gooper, Maggie and Mae?

UNIT 4
Self-Awareness

LEARNING GOALS

After completing this unit, you should be able to:

1. explain the structure and general function of the Johari window
2. define the open, blind, hidden, and unknown selves
3. provide examples of information that might be contained in each of the four selves

49

If we had to list some of the qualities we wanted to possess, that of self-awareness would surely rank high. We all wish to know ourselves better. The reason is that we are in control of our thoughts and our behaviors only to the extent that we understand ourselves, only to the extent that we are aware of ourselves.

This concept of self-awareness is basic to all forms and functions of communication and is best explained by the Johari Window, presented in Figure 4.1. The window is broken up into four basic areas or quadrants, each of which contains a somewhat different self.

THE OPEN SELF

The *open self,* the first quadrant, represents all the information, behaviors, attitudes, feelings, desires, motivations, ideas, and so on that are known to the self and also known to others. The type of information included here might vary from one's name, skin color, and sex to one's age, political and religious affiliation, and batting average. Each individual's open self will vary in size depending upon the time and upon the individuals he or she is dealing with. At some times we are more likely to open ourselves up than at other times. If, for example, we opened ourselves and got hurt because of it, we might then close up a bit more than usual. Similarly, some people make us feel

Open Self known to self known to others	**Blind Self** not known to self known to others
Hidden Self known to self not known to others	**Unknown Self** not known to self not known to others

Figure 4.1
The Johari Window (*Source:* Joseph Luft, *Group Processes: An Introduction to Group Dynamics* [Palo Alto, Cal.: National Press Books, 1970], p. 11.)

comfortable and support us; to them, we open ourselves wide, but to others we prefer to leave most of ourselves closed.

In some instances the size of the open self seems directly related to the degree of closeness with the individual: We might reveal most to those we are closest to and least to those we are least close to. It seems that some of our most important desires or motivations often concern the people we are closest to, thus we might not want them to learn such information. Should our need to open ourselves become too strong we might disclose our feelings to a stranger or relative stranger or at least to someone not closely involved with our daily life, for example, a religious conselor or a therapist of some sort. Sometimes a student will select a teacher or an athletic coach to confide in. Despite this variation each person has a "modal area," a kind of average which defines how open one will generally be.

The size of the open self also varies greatly from one individual to another (Figure 4.2). Some people are prone to reveal their innermost desires and feelings while others prefer to remain silent about both the significant and the insignificant things in their lives. Most of us, however, open ourselves to some people about some things at some times.

"The smaller the first quadrant," says Luft, "the poorer the communication."

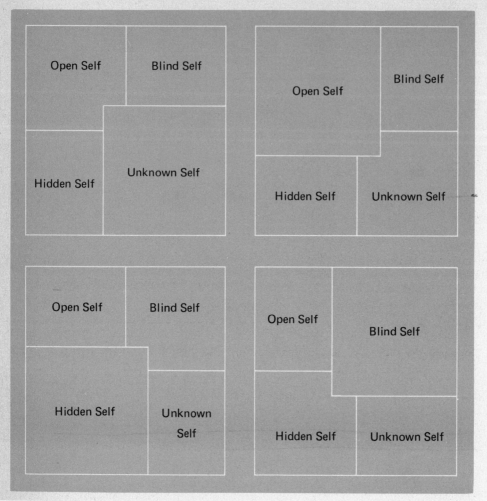

Figure 4.2
Johari Windows of Varied Structure

Communication is dependent upon the degree to which we open ourselves to others and to ourselves. If we do not allow others to know us (that is, if we keep the open self small), communication between them and us becomes extremely difficult if not impossible. We can communicate meaningfully only to the extent that we know each other and to the extent that we know ourselves. To improve communication, we have to work first on enlarging the open self.

We should also note that a change in the open area—in any of the quadrants—will bring about a change in the other quadrants. We might visualize the window as a whole as being of constant size but with each pane of glass as being variable, sometimes small, sometimes large. As one pane becomes smaller, one or more of the others must become larger. Similarly, as one pane becomes larger, one or more of the others must become smaller. For example, if we enlarge the open self this will shrink the hidden self. Further, this revelation or disclosure in turn will function to lead others to decrease the size of the blind self by revealing to us what they know and we do not know. Thus these several selves are not separate and distinct selves but interacting selves, each one dependent upon the other.

THE BLIND SELF

The *blind self* represents all those things about ourselves which others know but of which we are ignorant. This may vary from the relatively insignificant habit of saying "you know" or of rubbing your nose when you get angry or of a peculiar body odor, to something as significant as defense mechanisms or fight strategies or repressed past experiences.

Some people have a very large blind self and seem to be totally oblivious to their own faults and sometimes (though not as often) their own virtues. Others seem overly concerned with having a small blind self. They seek therapy at every turn and join every encounter group. Some are even convinced that they know everything there is to know about themselves, that they have reduced the blind self to zero. Still others only pretend to want to reduce the size of the blind self. Verbally they profess a total willingness to hear all about themselves. But when confronted with the first negative feature the defenses and denials go up with amazing speed. In between these extremes lie most of us.

Communication depends in great part on both parties sharing the same basic information about each other. To the extent that blind areas exist communication will be made difficult. Yet blind areas will always exist for each of us. Although we may be able to shrink our blind areas we can never totally eliminate them. If, however, we recognize that we do in fact have blind areas, that we can never know everything that others know about us, this recognition will help greatly in dealing with this most difficult and elusive self and with our other selves as well.

The only way to decrease the size of the blind self is to seek out information which others have and which we do not have. In everyday interactions, we influence how much of the blind area will be made open by others. This need not be done directly although at times it is, as when we ask someone's honest opinion about our appearance or our speech or our home. Most often, however, it is done indirectly; in fact, it is a consequence of everything we do. In any interaction with another person we invariably reveal how much of ourselves we want to know about, how much we prefer not to know, which aspects we want to know about, and which aspects we prefer to leave hidden. We also reveal in these interactions how we will react to such revelations. In some contexts we would react defensively, in other contexts openly. Through-out our interactions we give cues as to how we will react in future situations, and we in effect enable others to accurately predict our future behaviors. Generally, if we are open about ourselves and reveal our inner selves to others, others in turn will reveal what is contained in the blind area more readily than they would if we did not engage in any self-disclosure.

Although communication and interpersonal relations are generally enhanced as the blind area becomes smaller, it should not be assumed that people should, therefore, be forced to see themselves as we see them or to find out everything we know about them. Forcing people to see what we see may cause serious trauma. Such a revelation might cause a breakdown in defenses; it might force people to see their own masochism or jealousy or prejudice when they are not psychologically ready to deal with such information. It is important to recognize that such revelations, since they may cause problems, might best be dealt with in the company of trained personnel.

THE HIDDEN SELF

The *hidden self* contains all that you know of yourself and of others but which you keep to yourself. This area includes all your successfully kept secrets about yourself and others. In any interaction this area includes what is relevant or irrelevant to the conversation but which you do not want to reveal.

At the extremes we have the overdisclosers and the underdisclosers. The overdisclosers tell all. They keep nothing hidden about themselves or others. They will tell you their family history, their sexual problems, their marital difficulties, their children's problems, their financial status, their strategies for rising to the top, their goals, their failures and successes, and just about everything else. For them this area is very small and had they sufficient time and others sufficient patience it would be reduced to near zero. The problem with these overdisclosers is that they do not discriminate. They do not distinguish between those to whom such information should be disclosed and those to whom it should not be disclosed. Nor do they distinguish among the various types of information which should be disclosed and which should not be disclosed. To discuss one's wife's or husband's sexual relationships with coworkers might not be the wisest thing to do, and yet they do it.

The underdisclosers tell nothing. You get the feeling that they know a great deal about themselves but simply refuse to say anything. They will talk about you but not about themselves. Depending upon one's relationship with these underdisclosers we might feel that they are afraid to tell anyone anything for fear of being laughed at or rejected. Or we may feel somewhat rejected for their refusal to trust us. To never reveal anything about yourself comments on what you think of the people with whom you are interacting. On one level, at least, it is saying, "I don't trust you enough to reveal myself to you."

The vast majority of us are somewhere between these two extremes. We keep certain things hidden and we disclose certain things. We disclose to some people and we do not disclose to others. We are, in effect, selective disclosers.

At other times, however, it seems that we must carefully weigh the pros and cons because the consequences are so great. Consider, for example, the sociology professor. She is married with three school-age children. She recently received her Ph.D., had her first book published, and is now teaching a course in criminology. In discussing drugs and present laws, part of her wants to disclose that as a graduate student she was busted on drug charges and served two years in jail. But the other part of her, the practical part, wants to remain silent for fear of losing her job and therefore causing problems for her family. This is not at all a rare situation. In fact, such a decision-making process seems to occur with amazing frequency. All of us, it seems, hide something. But this takes energy—a fact that we probably do not appreciate as fully as we should. We are forced to expend great amounts of energy to keep parts of ourselves hidden. Hiding some aspects of ourselves is not a passive but an active process at which we must constantly work if we are to succeed. This principle seems to have been recently recognized by many homosexuals who have found that keeping their homosexuality hidden cost them a great deal in psychic energy and that once they moved this information from the hidden to the open area they have felt freer and less burdened.

Although it is comforting to tell ourselves that the information we disclose to others will be treated confidentially, we cannot always be sure that it will. The teacher who confidentially tells her class about her criminal record may have a very sympathetic audience that day. But after a rough mid-term she may lose some of her "friends" who may no longer wish to be "burdened" by this "secret."

As potential disclosers we should also recognize that we impose a burden upon the person to whom we disclose. In disclosing anything significant we are in effect saying, "I know you will be supportive and not reveal this to anyone else." But at times people cannot be supportive and at times people cannot or simply do not remember that this bit of information is to be classified as secret.

When dealing with our feelings, especially our present feelings, self-disclosure is especially useful, helpful, and conducive to meaningful dialogue. Last year, for example, on the first day of an interpersonal communication course I was teaching I became extremely nervous. I was not sure of the reason, but I was nervous. At that point I had three basic options open to me. One was to withdraw from the situation, for example, by saying I was not feeling well or that I had forgotten something and just walk out. Second, I could have attempted to hide the nervousness, hoping that it would subside as the class progressed. The third option and the one I chose (although I did not go through these options consciously at the time) was simply to tell the class that I was nervous and did not understand why. The class was most supportive, telling me I had nothing to be nervous about and that I should not worry. They revealed that they were the ones who felt anxious; for many, this was their first college class. I, in turn, assured them that they should not be nervous. After this very simple exchange, all of which happened without any conscious planning or strategy, as an expression of what our feelings were at the time, we worked together closely and warmly for the rest of the semester. This incident was not in itself responsible for the success of the course, yet it helped greatly to set the tone for an open and supportive atmosphere.

THE UNKNOWN SELF

The *unknown self* represents all that exists but which we nor others know about. One could legitimately argue that if neither we nor any one else knows what is in this area, we cannot know that it exists at all. Actually, we do not *know* that it exists but rather we *infer* that it exists.

We infer its existence from a number of different sources. Sometimes this area is revealed to us through temporary changes brought about by drug experiences or through special experimental conditions such as hypnosis or sensory deprivation. Sometimes this area is revealed by various projective tests or dreams. There seem to be sufficient instances of such revelations to justify our including this unknown area as part of the self.

Although we cannot easily manipulate this area we should recognize that it does exist and that there are things about ourselves and about others that we simply do not and will not know.

SOURCES

The Johari model is most thoroughly discussed in the works of Joseph Luft, particularly *Group Processes: An Introduction to Group Dynamics,* 2d ed. (Palo Alto, Cal.: Mayfield Publishing Company, 1970) and *Of Human Interaction* (Palo Alto, Cal.: Mayfield Publishing Company, 1969). Ronald B. Levy's books cover this area but in a more elementary fashion: *Self Revelation Through Relationships* (Englewood Cliffs, N.J.: Prentice-Hall, 1972) and *I Can Only Touch You Now* (Englewood Cliffs, N.J.: Prentice-Hall, 1973). John Powell's *Why Am I Afraid to Tell You Who I Am?* (Niles, Ill.: Argus Communications, 1969) and *Why Am I Afraid to Love?* (Niles, Ill.: Argus Communications, 1972) and *The Secret of Staying in Love* (Niles, Ill.: Argus Communications, 1974) are three of the most interesting and perceptive works in this area. They are deceptively simple so do not dismiss them if they appear too elementary. Nathaniel Branden's *The Psychology of Self-Esteem* (New York: Bantam, 1969) and *The Disowned Self* (New York: Bantam, 1971) and Henry Clay Lindgren's *How to Live With Yourself and Like It* (Greenwich,

Conn.: Fawcett, 1953) are useful for understanding ourselves. Patricia Niles Middlebrook, in her *Social Psychology and Modern Life* (New York: Knopf, 1974), provides a thorough overview of the social-psychological dimensions of the self. For a relatively detailed discussion of the self in communication, see Kenneth L. Villard and Leland J. Whipple, *Beginnings in Relational Communication* (New York: Wiley, 1976).

EXPERIENTIAL VEHICLES

4.1 YOUR JOHARI WINDOWS

This experiential vehicle is designed to enable you to become more familiar with the concept of the Johari window and to apply this concept to your own interactions with significant others.

The procedure is simple. Draw a Johari window—varying the sizes of the different selves as seems appropriate—for yourself as you interact with the following persons:

1. your mother
2. your father
3. your best same-sex friend
4. your best opposite-sex friend
5. your communication teacher
6. yourself

In small groups of five or six, discuss some of the implications of your windows on your interactions with these individuals. Look at this in at least two ways. First, how does the size of the different windows (selves) influence your interactions with these individuals? Second, how do your interactions with these individuals influence the structure of your windows? Try to be as concrete as possible, citing as many specific instances as you can.

4.2 SELF-AWARENESS

A model of the Johari window is presented in Figure 4.1. With specific reference to the four selves represented by the model, discuss in a small group of five or six 1) the selves of someone you most admire and 2) the selves of someone you least admire.

What do the most admired persons seem to have in common? What do the least admired persons seem to have in common? What insights can you derive from the discussion that might be pertinent to your own model of awareness? What general principles might you derive that are pertinent to communication?

4.3 I'D PREFER TO BE

This exercise should enable members of the class to get to know each other better and at the same time get to know themselves better. The questions asked here should encourage each individual to think about and increase awareness of some facet(s) of his or her thoughts or behaviors.

Rules of the Game

The "I'd Prefer To Be" game is played in a group of four to six people, using the following category listing. General procedure is as follows:

1. Each member individually rank orders each of the twenty groups using 1 for the most-preferred and 3 for the least-preferred choice.
2. The group then considers each of the twenty categories in turn, with each member giving his or her rank order.
3. Members may refuse to reveal their rankings for any category by saying, "I pass." The group is not permitted to question the reasons for any member's passing.
4. When a member has revealed his or her rankings for a category, the group members may ask questions relevant to that category. These questions may be asked after any individual member's account or may be reserved until all members have given their rankings for a particular category.
5. In addition to these general procedures, the group may establish any additional rules it wishes, for example, appointing a leader, establishing time limits, and so forth.

"I'D PREFER TO BE"

1. _____ intelligent
   _____ wealthy
   _____ physically attractive

2. _____ movie star
   _____ senator
   _____ successful businessperson

3. _____ blind
   _____ deaf
   _____ mute

4. _____ on a date
   _____ reading a good book
   _____ watching television

5. _____ loved
   _____ feared
   _____ respected

6. _____ alone
   _____ in a crowd
   _____ with one person

7. _____ brave
   _____ reliable
   _____ insightful

8. _____ adventurous
   _____ scholarly
   _____ creative

9. _____ hard
   _____ soft
   _____ medium

10. _____ traitor to a friend
    _____ traitor to one's country
    _____ traitor to oneself

11. _____ a lion
    _____ an eagle
    _____ a dolphin

12. _____ bisexual
    _____ heterosexual
    _____ homosexual

13. _____ angry
    _____ guilty
    _____ fearful

14. _____ traveling in uncharted areas
    _____ traveling in Europe
    _____ traveling in the United States

15. _____ the loved
    _____ the lover
    _____ the good friend

16. _____ introvert
    _____ extrovert
    _____ ambivert

17. _____ a tree
    _____ a rock
    _____ a flower

18. _____ the sun
    _____ the wind
    _____ the waters

19. _____ a leader
    _____ a follower
    _____ a loner

20. _____ married
    _____ single
    _____ living with someone but unmarried

Areas for Discussion

Some of the areas for discussion which might prove of value are:

1. What are the reasons for the individual choices? Note that the reasons for the least-preferred choice may often be as important or even more important than the reasons for the most-preferred choice.
2. What do the choices reveal about the individual? Can persons be differentiated on the basis of their choices to these and similar alternatives?
3. What is the homogeneity/heterogeneity of the group as a whole? Do the members evidence relatively similar choices or wide differences? What does this mean in terms of the members' ability to communicate with each other?
4. Do the members accept/reject the choices of other members? Are some members disturbed by the choices other members make? If so, why? Are some apathetic? Why? Did hearing the choices of one or more members make you want to get to know them better?
5. Did any of the choices make you aware of preferences you were not aware of before?
6. Are members reluctant to share their preferences with the group? Why?

4.4 SOME LAST WORDS

Each student should respond individually to the following questions:

1. If you knew that in five minutes you were going to die what would you say in these last five minutes and to whom?
2. What would you like your epitaph to read?
3. In *Edward Kennedy and the Camelot Legacy,* James MacGregor Burns writes that "the biographer looks in vain for indications of potential greatness. When pressed for a memorable remark, the headmaster of his London school could remember only that Teddy said he would 'pass up' a serving of cauliflower because 'I always bring that up.' " What memorable remark(s) might your biographer find?

These comments may be discussed in small groups of five or six or may be used as the basis for a general class discussion. Another alternative is to collect the papers (without names, of course) and read some of the responses aloud.

4.5 GOALS OF SELF AND OTHERS

1. Working in dyads, on Form 1 rank these twelve goals in order of their importance to you at this time in your life. Use 1 for the most important, 2 for the most important, and so on, using 12 for the least important.
2. On Form 2 rank these goals in order of their importance to your partner. That is, attempt to predict how your partner will rank these goals.
3. Exchange Form 2 with your partner so that both of you now have your own rankings and the rankings your partner gave you. Compute an error score by subtracting your own rankings from the rankings your partner gave you, disregarding sign (whether + or −). For example, if you ranked emotional security 4 and your partner gave you a ranking of 7 then there would be 3 error points. Note that since signs are disregarded there would also be 3 error points if your partner had given you a rank of 1 for emotional security. Do this for all 12 items.
4. Discuss with your partner the predictions each of you made. Consider, for example, the following:

   a. the basis for the predictions; that is, what cues were used for making the various predictions?
   b. the certainty or uncertainty you felt in making them
   c. the implications of your predictions for communication between the two of you
   d. the social constraints influencing your predictions
   e. the possible reasons for the accurate/inaccurate predictions
   f. whatever else may seen relevant to your communication behavior

Note: It may be useful to use those items for which there was a large error score as take-off points for discussion.

FORM 1 (SELF)

_____ Emotional security
_____ Sexual love
_____ Independence
_____ Knowledge
_____ Family love
_____ Financial security
_____ Friendship
_____ Self-regard
_____ Work
_____ Excitement
_____ Beauty
_____ Creative self-expression

FORM 2 (OTHER)

_____ Emotional security
_____ Sexual love
_____ Independence
_____ Knowledge
_____ Family love
_____ Financial security
_____ Friendship
_____ Self-regard
_____ Work
_____ Excitement
_____ Beauty
_____ Creative self-expression

UNIT 5
Disclosing
the Hidden Self

The Rewards of Self-Disclosure
Sources of Resistance to Self-Disclosure
Contexts for Self-Disclosure

LEARNING GOALS

After completing this unit, you should be able to:

1. define *self-disclosure*
2. distinguish between *history* and *story*
3. explain at least three rewards of self-disclosure
4. explain at least three sources of resistance to self-disclosure
5. explain the contexts of self-disclosure
6. explain the differences in self-disclosure in terms of topic, sex, and age

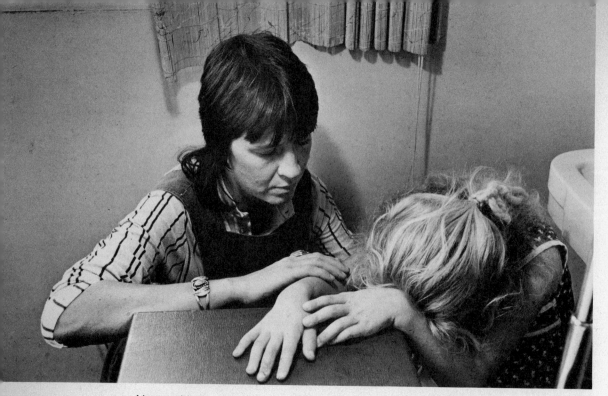

Along with the recent interest in encounter groups, integrity groups, and intra- and interpersonal communication generally, has come great interest in the concept of *self-disclosure.* In terms of the Johari wnidow discussed in the previous unit, self-disclosure consists of revealing information about yourself that is in the hidden area—that is, it is a process of moving information from the hidden area to the open area. More formally, we may define self-disclosure as a type of communication in which information about the self is communicated to another person. Special note should be taken of several aspects of this elementary definition.

Self-disclosure is a type of communication. Thus overt statements pertaining to the self as well as slips of the tongue, unconscious nonverbal movements, and public confessions would all be classified as self-disclosing communications.

Self-disclosure is information, in the information theory sense, meaning something previously unknown by the receiver. Information is new knowledge. To tell someone something he or she already knew would not be self-disclosure; in order to be self-disclosure some new knowledge would have to be communicated.

Self-disclosure involves at least one other individual. In order to self-disclose, the communication act must involve at least two persons; it cannot be an *intra*personal communication act. Nor can we, as some people attempt, "disclose" in a manner that makes it impossible for another person to understand. This is not a disclosure at all. Nor can we write in diaries that no one reads and call this self-disclosure. To be self-disclosure the information must be received and understood by another individual.

Gerard Egan, in *Encounter,* makes another distinction that may prove useful. He distinguishes between "history" which he calls "the mode of non-involvement" and "story" which he calls "the mode of involvement." *History* is a manner of revealing the self that is only pseudoself-disclosure. It is an approach that details some facts of the individual's life but does not really invite involvement from listeners. From a person's history we may learn what the individual did or what happened to him or her throughout that person's life, but somehow we really do not get to know the person.

Story, on the other hand, is authentic self-disclosure. In story individuals communicate their inner selves to others and look for some human response rather than just simple feedback. The speaker takes a risk, puts himself or herself on the line, and reveals something significant about who he or she is and not merely what he or she has done.

THE REWARDS OF SELF-DISCLOSURE

The obvious question when the topic of self-disclosure arises is, *Why?* Why should anyone self-disclose to anyone else? What is it about this type of communication that merits its being singled out and discussed at length? There is no clear-cut answer to these very legitimate questions. There is no great body of statistical research findings that attests to the usefulness or importance of self-disclosure. Yet there is evidence in the form of testimony, observational reports, and the like that has led a number of researchers and theorists to argue that self-disclosure is perhaps the most important form of communication in which anyone could engage.

One argument is that we cannot know ourselves as fully as possible if we do not self-disclose to at least one other individual. It is assumed that by self-disclosing to another we gain a new perspective on ourselves, a deeper understanding of our own behavior. In therapy, for example, very often the insight does not come directly from the therapist; while the individual is self-disclosing, he or she realizes some facet of behavior or some relationship that had not been known, before. Through self-disclosure, then, we may come to understand ourselves more thoroughly. Sidney M. Jourard in his *The Transparent Self* notes that self-disclosure is an important factor in counseling and psychotherapy and argues that people may need such help because they have not disclosed significantly to other people.

Closely related is the argument that we will be better able to deal with our problems, especially our guilt, through self-disclosure. One of the great fears that many people have is that they will not be accepted because of some deep dark secret, because of something they have done, or because of some feeling or attitude they might have. Because we feel these things are a basis for rejection, we develop guilt. If, for example, you do not love—or perhaps you hate—one of your parents, you might fear being rejected if you were to self-disclose such a feeling; thus a sense of guilt develops over this. By self-disclosing such a feeling, and by being supported rather than rejected, we are better prepared to deal with the guilt and perhaps reduce or even eliminate it. Even self-acceptance is difficult without self-disclosure. We accept ourselves largely through the eyes of others. If we feel that others would reject us, we are apt to reject ourselves as well. Through self-disclosure and subsequent support we are in a better position to see the positive responses to us and are more likely to respond by developing a positive self-concept.

Keeping our various secrets to ourselves and not revealing who we are to others takes a great deal of energy and leaves us with that much less energy for other things. We must be constantly on guard, for example, lest someone see in our behavior what we consider to be a deviant orientation, or attitude, or behavior pattern. We might avoid certain people for fear that they will be able to tell this awful thing about us, or avoid situations or places because if we are seen there others will know how terrible we really are. By self-disclosing we rid ourselves of the false masks that otherwise must be worn. Jourard puts this most clearly:

> Every maladjusted person is a person who has not made himself known to another human being and in consequence does not know himself. Nor can he be himself. More than that, he struggles actively to avoid becoming known by another human being. He works at it ceaselessly, twenty-four hours daily, and it is work! In the effort to avoid becoming known, a person provides for himself a cancerous kind of stress which is subtle and unrecognized, but none the less effective in producing not only the assorted patterns of unhealthy personality which psychiatry talks about, but also the wide array of physical ills that have come to be recognized as the province of psychosomatic medicine.

Self-disclosure is also helpful in improving communication efficiency. It seems reasonable to assume that we understand the messages of others largely to the extent that we understand the other individuals—that is, we can understand what an individual says better if we know the individual well. We can tell what certain nuances mean, when the person is serious and when joking, when the person is being sarcastic out of fear and when out of resentment, and so on. Self-disclosure is an essential condition for getting to know another individual. You might study a person's behavior or even live together for years, but if that person never self-discloses, you are far from understanding that individual as a complete person.

Perhaps the main reason why self-disclosure is important is that it is necessary if a meaningful relationship is to be established between two people. Without self-disclosure meaningful relationships seem impossible to develop. There are, it is true, relationships that have lasted for ten, twenty, thirty, and forty years without self-disclosure. Many married couples would fall into this category as would colleagues working in the same office or factory or people living in the same neighborhood or apartment house. Without self-disclosure, however, these relationships are probably not terribly meaningful or at least they are not as meaningful as they might be. By self-disclosing we are in effect saying to other individuals that we trust them, that we respect them, that we care enough about them and about our relationship to reveal ourselves to them. This leads the other individual to self-disclosure in return. This is at least the start of a meaningful relationship, a relationship that is honest and open and one that goes beyond the surface trivialities.

SOURCES OF RESISTANCE TO SELF-DISCLOSURE

For all its advantages and importance, self-disclosure is a form of communication that is often fiercely resisted. Some of the possible reasons for its resistance should be examined so that we may better understand our own reluctance to enter into this type of communication experience.

Perhaps the most obvious reason—and some would argue the only reason—for our reluctance to self-disclose, according to Gerard Egan, is that there is a societal bias against it, and we have internalized this bias. We have been conditioned against self-disclosure by the society in which we live. The hero in American folklore is strong but also silent; he bears responsibilities, burdens, and problems without letting others even be aware of them. He is self-reliant and does not need the assistance of anyone. Males have internalized this folk hero, it seems, at least to some extent. Women are a bit more fortunate than men. They are allowed the luxury of self-disclosure; they are allowed to tell their troubles to someone, to pour out their feelings, to talk about themselves. Men are more restricted. Women are allowed greater freedom in expressing emotions, to verbalize love and affection; men are somehow conditioned to avoid such expressions. These, men have been taught, are signs of weakness rather than strength.

Although it is difficult to admit, many people resist self-disclosing because of a fear of punishment, generally, rejection. We may vividly picture other people laughing at us or whispering about us or condemning us if we self-disclose. These mental pictures help to convince us that self-disclosure is not the most expedient course of action. We rationalize and say it is not necessary to tell anyone anything about ourselves. We are fine as we are, or so we tell ourselves.

We may also fear punishment in the form of tangible or concrete manifestations, such as the loss of a job, the loss of some office, or of some "friends." At times this does happen. The ex-convict who self-discloses his or her past record may find himself or herself without a job or out of political office. Generally, however, these fears are overblown. These fears are often in the nature of excuses which allow us to rest content without self-disclosing.

Gerard Egan, in *Encounter,* points out that this fear of rejection operates like a reverse halo effect. A *halo effect* refers to the generalizing of virtue from one area to another. For example, your communication teacher may know a great deal about communication and may be perceived as highly credible in that field. The halo effect operates to generalize that perceived credibility to other fields as well, and so when he or she talks about politics or economics or psychology we are more apt to see him or her as credible and knowledgeable in these areas too. The *reverse halo effect* operates in a similar manner. We wrongly assume that if we tell others something negative about ourselves their negative responses will generalize to other aspects of our behavior and they will see us as generally negative, much as we may see the teacher of one field as competent in other fields.

Another possible reason why we resist self-disclosure is what Egan calls *fear of self-knowledge.* We may have built up a beautiful, rationalized picture of ourselves—emphasizing the positive and eliminating or minimizing the negative aspects. Self-disclosure often allows us to see through the rationalizations. We see those positive aspects for what they are, and we see the negative aspects that were previously hidden.

CONTEXTS FOR SELF-DISCLOSURE

As a particular form of communication, self-disclosure occurs more readily under certain circumstances than under others. Generally, self-disclosure is reciprocal. In any interaction self-disclosure by A is more likely to take place if B engages in self-disclosure than if B does not. This seems quite obvious and predictable. Yet its consequences are interesting. It implies that a kind of spiral effect operates here, with each person's self-disclosure serving as the stimulus for additional self-disclosure by the other person which in turn serves as the stimulus for self-disclosure by the other person and on and on.

Self-disclosure, perhaps because of the numerous fears we have about revealing ourselves, is more likely to occur in small groups than in large groups. Dyads are perhaps the most frequent situations in which self-disclosure seems to take place. This seems true for any number of reasons. A dyad seems more suitable because it is easier for the self-discloser to deal with one person's reactions and responses than with the reactions of a group of three or four or five. The self-discloser can attend to the responses quite carefully and on the basis of the support or lack of support monitor the disclosures, continuing if the situation is supportive and stopping if it is not supportive. With more than one listener such monitoring is impossible since the responses are sure to vary among the listeners. Another possible reason is that when the group is larger than two the self-disclosure takes on aspects of exhibitionism and public exposure. It is no longer a confidential matter; now it is one about which many people know. From a more practical point of view it is often difficult to assemble in one place at one time only those people to whom we would want to self-disclose.

Research has not been able to identify fully the kind of person with whom self-disclosure is likely to take place. There seems a great deal of individual variation here. Some studies have found that we disclose more often to those people who are close to us, for example, our spouses, our family, our close friends. Other studies claim that we disclose to persons we like and not disclose to persons we dislike regardless of how close they are to us. Thus an individual may disclose to a well-liked teacher even though they are not particularly close and yet not disclose to a brother or sister with whom he or she is close but who is not liked very much. Other studies claim that a lasting relationship between people increases the likelihood of self-disclosure while still others claim that self-disclosure is more likely to occur in temporary relationships, for example, between prostitute and client or even between strangers on a train.

In their excellent review of research McCroskey and Wheeless discuss a number of correlates of self-disclosure. Among the major correlates noted are reciprocal self-disclosure, competence, trustworthiness, personality, anxiety, and liking-loving.

We tend to self-disclose when the person we are with also self-discloses. This probably leads us to feel more secure and, in fact, reinforces our own self-disclosing behavior. Competent people, it has been found, will engage in self-disclosure moreso than will people judged less competent. "It may very well be," note McCroskey and Wheeless, "that people who are more competent also perceive themselves to be more competent, and thus have the self-confidence necessary to take more chances with self-disclosure. Or, even more likely, competent people may simply have more positive things about themselves to disclose than less competent people."

Mutual trust seems to be a prerequisite to self-disclosing behaviors. Generally, the more we trust a person the more likely it is that we will self-disclose to him or her. Trust, however, is not a sufficient condition for self-disclosure; we do not self-disclose to everyone we trust. People who are highly sociable and extroverted generally self-disclose more than those who are less sociable and introverted.

Self-disclosure is strangely related to anxiety. Anxiety in general, or anxiety about some particular situation, seems to have the effect of increasing self-disclosure significantly or reducing it to a minimum. Perhaps the relationship between self-disclosure and liking and loving is the easiest to appreciate intuitively. Usually, the more we like or love someone the more likely we will self-disclose to that person. Although this is not always the case, it seems more true than false.

According to Jourard there are topic, sex, and age differences in self-disclosure communications. Certain areas are more likely to be self-disclosed than others. For example, we would be more likely to self-disclose information about our jobs or hobbies than about our sex lives or about our financial situation. Male college students are more likely to disclose to a close friend than to either of their parents, but college females will disclose about equally to their mothers and to their best friends but will not disclose very much to their fathers or to their boy friends. There are even differences in the amount of self-disclosure in different age groups. Self-discloure to a spouse or to an opposite sex friend increases from the age of about seventeen to about fifty and then drops off. As might be expected, husbands and wives self-disclose to each other more than they do to any other person or group of persons. ''This confirms the view,'' says Jourard in *The Transparent Self,* ''that marriage is the 'closest' relationship one can enter, and it may help us the better to understand why some people avoid it like the plague. Anyone who is reluctant to be known by another person and to know another person—sexually and cognitively—will find the prospective intimacy of marriage somewhat terrifying.''

''A penny for your thoughts.''
(Cartoon by Joseph Farris, from *Saturday Review,* October 16, 1971.)

SOURCES

On self-disclosure see Sidney M. Jourard's *Disclosing Man to Himself* (New York: Heinhold, 1968) and *The Transparent Self,* rev. ed. (New York: Reinhold, 1971). In writing this unit I relied heavily on the insights of Gerard Egan. See especially his *Encounter: Group Process for Interpersonal Growth* (Belmont, Cal.: Brooks/Cole, 1970) or, if you prefer a shorter version, *Face to Face: The Small-Group Experience and Interpersonal Growth* (Belmont, Cal.: Brooks/Cole, 1973). An overview of self-disclosure in communication is provided by W. Barnett Pearce and Stewart M. Sharp, "Self-Disclosing Communication," *Journal of Communication* 23 (December 1973): 409–425. This article also provides an excellent review of the research on self-disclosure and communication. Sam Keen and Anne Valley Fox's *Telling Your Story: A Guide to Who You Are and Who You Can Be* (New York: New American Library, 1973) provides some interesting insights on self-disclosure. James C. McCroskey and Lawrence R. Wheeless, *Introduction to Human Communication* (Boston: Allyn & Bacon, 1976) provide an excellent review of relevant research findings from which I drew freely. For a different point of view see Barrie Hopson and Charlotte Hopson, *Intimate Feedback: A Lovers' Guide to Getting in Touch with Each Other* (New York: New American Library, 1976). An overview of the self in relation to communication is provided by Stewart L. Tubbs and John W. Baird, *The Open Person . . . Self-Disclosure and Personal Growth* (Columbus, Ohio: Charles Merrill, 1976). Valerian J. Derlega and Alan L. Chaikin, *Sharing Intimacy: What We Reveal to Others and Why* (Englewood Cliffs, N.J.: Prentice-Hall, 1975) provide an excellent overview of self-disclosure. Especially interesting are the discussions of intimacy in friendship and in marriage.

EXPERIENTIAL
VEHICLES

5.1 SELF-DISCLOSURE QUESTIONNAIRE

Complete the accompanying questionnaire by indicating in the appropriate spaces your willingness-unwillingness to self-disclose these matters to members of a group of students chosen at random from this class.

In a group of five or six persons discuss the questionnaires, self-disclosing what you wish to self-disclose and not disclosing what you do not wish to disclose. Consider at least the following:

1. Are there any discrepancies between what you indicated you would self-disclose and what you were actually willing to self-disclose?
2. What areas were people most unwilling to self-disclose? Why? Discuss these reasons in terms of conditioning.
3. After the group got going and a number of people self-disclosed, did you feel more willing to self-disclose? Explain your feelings.
4. Were negative qualities (or perceived negative qualities) more likely to remain undisclosed? Why?
5. How would the results of your questionnaire have differed if this information was to be disclosed to your parents, a stranger you would never see again, a counselor, and a best friend? Would the results differ depending on the sex of the individual to whom the disclosures were to be made? Explain the reasons why.

SELF-DISCLOSURE QUESTIONNAIRE

	Would definitely self-disclose	Would probably self-disclose	Don't know	Would probably not self-disclose	Would definitely not self-disclose
1. My religious beliefs					
2. My attitudes toward other religions					
3. My attitudes toward different nationalities and races					
4. My political beliefs					
5. My economic status					
6. My views on abortion					
7. My views on pornography					
8. My views on premarital relations					
9. My major pastime					
10. My parents' attitudes toward other religions					
11. My parents' attitudes toward different nationalities and races					
12. My parents' political beliefs					
13. My parents' economic status					
14. My relationship with my parents					
15. My sexual fantasies					
16. My past sexual experiences					
17. My perceived sexual attractiveness					
18. My desired physical attractiveness					
19. My most negative physical attribute					
20. My physical condition or health					
21. My ideal mate					
22. My drinking behavior					
23. My drug behavior					
24. My gambling behavior					
25. My personal goals					
26. My most embarrassing moment					
27. My unfulfilled desires					
28. My major weaknesses					
29. My major worry					
30. My major strengths					
31. My present happiness-unhappiness					
32. My major mistakes					
33. My general attractiveness					
34. My general self-concept					
35. My general adequacy					

5.2 SELF-DISCLOSURE

General Discussion of Model

Refer to the Johair Window model. How might the information in the hidden self area, if not disclosed, prevent meaningful communication? How might this information, if disclosed, foster meaningful interaction? How might nondisclosure and disclosure work in reverse? What positive effects might self-disclosure have on the individual? Negative effects? What positive and/or negative effects might self-disclosure have on interpersonal interaction? In any decision pertaining to self-disclosure, what audience factors should the individual take into consideration? That is, what variables of the audience might influence an individual's decision to disclose or not disclose?

Open Self	**Blind Self**
Hidden Self	**Unknown Self**

The Johari Window

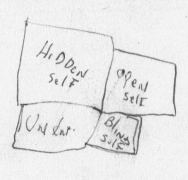

On an index card write a statement of information that is currently in the hidden self. Do not put your names on these cards; the statements are to be dealt with anonymously. These cards will be collected and read aloud to the entire group.[1]

Discussion of Statements and Model

1. Classify the statements into categories, for example, sexual problems, attitudes toward family, self-doubts, and so forth.

[1] The general idea for this exercise comes from Gerard Egan, *Encounter* (Belmont, Cal.: Brooks/Cole, 1970).

2. Why do you suppose this type of information is kept to the hidden self? What advantages might hiding this information have? What disadvantages?
3. How would you react to people who disclosed such statements to you? For example, what difference, if any, would it make in your relationship?
4. What type of person is likely to have a large hidden self and a small open self? A large open self and a small hidden self?
5. In relation to the other group members would your open self be larger? Smaller? The same size? Would your hidden self be larger? Smaller? The same size?

5.3 I WAS, I AM, I WILL BE

Each student should complete each of the following nine statements with the first things that come to mind. Do not try to write what might be regarded as socially acceptable or as "the right thing to do."

1. I was _____
2. I was _____
3. I was _____
4. I am _____
5. I am _____
6. I am _____
7. I will be _____
8. I will be _____
9. I will be _____

After all statements have been completed, discuss them in groups of five or six with particular reference to the concepts of self-awareness and self-disclosure. Groups may wish to consider some or all of the following questions.

1. Describe the differences between past, present, and future statements. Are we more apt to self-disclose negative things about the past than about the present? Why?
2. Which time period contains the most evaluatively positive statements? Is this the same for all members? Why is this so?
3. How close or how distant were the future statements to the present? That is, were they short-range or long-range characteristics? What difference does this make in terms of self-awareness and self-disclosure?
4. How realistic are the future statements? Does this matter?
5. Describe the interaction among the time periods, that is, how has the past influenced the present? How has the present influenced the perceived future? How does the perceived future influence our way of looking at the past and the present?

UNIT 6
Credibility

LEARNING GOALS

After completing this unit, you should be able to:

1. define *credibility*
2. define the three major types of credibility
3. define the dimensions of credibility and explain at least one way in which each may be established or communicated to a receiver
4. explain some of the ways in which the perception of credibility may vary
5. define *intrapersonal credibility*
6. recognize and identify credibility references in selected messages

EXPERIENTIAL VEHICLE

6.1 POETRY EVALUATION

Following are three poems. Please read each poem carefully.

1. Write a brief evaluation of each poem. Use any criteria you wish in evaluating these poems, that is, meaningfulness, universality, depth of insight, communicativeness, relevance, and so on.
2. In the upper right hand corner of the poem rank the poem in order of merit: 1 = the best of the three; 2 = the second best; and, 3 = the worst of the three.
3. Please do NOT talk while doing these evaluations.

Rank: _____

At the round earth's imagined corners blow
Forty years back, when much had place
Your trumpets, angels, and arise, arise
That since has perished out of mind.
Of souls, and to your scattered bodies go;
He spoke as one afoot will wind
All whom the flood did, and fire shall o'erthrow,
A morning horn ere men awake;
All whom war, death, age, agues, tyrannies,
His note was trenchant, turning kind.

Solemn and gray, the immense clouds of even
Despair, law, chance hath slain, and you, whose eyes
Pass on their towering unperturbed way
Shall behold God, and never taste death's woe.
Through the vast whiteness of the rain-swept heaven,
But let them sleep, Lord, and me mourn a space;
The moving pageants of the waning day;
The counterfeits that Time will break,
Brooding with sullen and Titanic crests
Teach me how to repent, for that's as good.
   —John Donne, *Prelude to God, VII*

Rank: _____

The forests were old and black,
   the clouds are heavy and brown.
But the world is red and gold,
   and its people pink and blue.

The heavens are pale and timid,
   the skies are still and cold.
But the water is pure and clear,
   and its people pink and blue.

The dogs are lonely and sad,
   the cats are crying and still.
But the streets are joyful and gay,
    and its people pink and blue.
      —Alexander Pope, *Elegy for Pink and Blue*

How doth the little crocodile   Rank: _____
   Improve his shining tail,
And pour the waters of the Nile
   On every shining scale!

How cheerfully he seems to grin,
   How neatly spreads his claws,
And welcomes little fishes in
   With gently smiling jaws.
      —Grace Whitherspoon, *The Crocodile*

After all three poems are evaluated and ranked, your instructor will provide you with some background material on these poems. Keep this material in mind and refer back to your evaluations as you read the unit. What conclusions are you willing to come to as a result of this experience?

We have all had the experience of speaking or listening to someone and as a result of who the person was or what the person said or how it was said, believing that person. Similarly, we must have also had the experience of disbelieving someone after speaking or listening to him or her. When teachers or researchers, for example, present their conclusions on a topic, some people believe us and some people do not believe us.

The question we should now consider is what leads us to believe some people and to disbelieve others? What is there about a person that makes him or her believable? This question, generally called *speaker credibility*, has been discussed and investigated for at least 2500 years and perhaps longer. Some 2300 years ago Aristotle, in his *Rhetoric,* said:

> Persuasion is achieved by the speaker's personal character when the speech is so spoken as to make us think him credible. We believe good men more fully and more readily than others; this is true generally whatever the question is, and absolutely true where exact certainty is impossible and opinions are divided.

> There are three things which inspire confidence in the orator's own character—the three, namely, that induce us to believe a thing apart from any proof of it: good sense, good moral character, and good will.

Although Aristotle was talking about the formal speech delivered in a court of law, a political meeting, or at some formal ceremony, the characteristics noted as contributing to persuasion—namely, good sense, good moral character, and good will—are essentially the same qualities stressed by modern theorists as being applicable to all forms of communication, whether they be formal public-speaking type situations or informal, interpersonal situations.

Hadley Cantril, in his study *The Invasion from Mars,* for example, concluded:

> It is a well known fact to the social psychologist, the advertiser, and the propagandist that an idea or a product has a better chance of being accepted if it can be endorsed by, or if it emanates from, some well known person whose character, ability, or status is highly valued.

Basically, there are two ways to examine credibility. One way is to examine effective versus ineffective individuals and explore the differences between them, specifically asking what makes one person effective and another person ineffective. Why is one person believed when the other person is disbelieved? The second way is to conduct controlled experiments. The typical design involves setting up two different but similar groups, say two sections of a college course in communication. One group is presented with a speaker, introduced as a person who runs a barber shop, whose topic is foreign policy. The other group hears the same speaker and the same speech but this time the person is introduced as a political science professor. The students are then tested on the extent to which they agreed or disagreed with the speaker. Invariably, the group that heard the speaker introduced as a political science professor evidences more agreement than the group hearing the speaker introduced as a barber. In other instances speakers may deliver essentially the same speech, but in one there might be references to noted and respected philosophers and in the other there would be no such references. Again, the references to philosophers give the speaker a much higher credibility rating. Elaborating on these basic procedures, researchers have discovered a great deal about this important dimension of communication.

TYPES OF CREDIBILITY

For our purposes, we should distinguish three general types of credibility: *initial, derived,* and *terminal.*

Initial Credibility

Initial or extrinsic credibility is that which the communicator is seen to have before the actual communication begins. Regardless of who we talk to or who we read, the source is seen as possessing or lacking some degree of credibility. Often this initial credibility is a function of the individual's title or position. Thus on the first day of class, the person who walks in the room to teach begins with some initial credibility by virtue of the position of teacher. If there is a "Dr." or "Professor" in front of his or her name, then that person's credibility is probably higher than if no such title appeared.

Derived Credibility

During any communication we naturally talk about ourselves, whether explicitly or implicitly. The topics we talk about, the vocal emphasis we give them, our facial expression as we talk about them, the degree of conviction we express, and so on all say something about ourselves. *Derived credibility* is the credibility that a listener perceives based on what takes place during the communication encounter. All communication is self-reflexive; all communication says something about the speaker or source. Consequently, all communications relate, directly or indirectly, to the speaker's credibility. Inevitably, in our communications we convey impressions of our intelligence, our morals, or our good will toward others.

Note, for example, how our impressions change when a person mispronounces a word we think he or she should know or when some kind of grammatical or factual mistake is made. When this happens we tend to think less of the individual's intelligence or competence and perhaps would be less likely to believe what the person is saying. Conversely, if a person is able to cite obscure facts or quote famous philosophers or do complicated mathematical operations, the credibility that person is seen to possess is likely to increase.

In many instances specific and direct attempts are made to exchange the perceived credibility of a particular individual. For example, when politicians are confronted with some wrong they have done or unpopular decision they have made, they quickly attempt to rebuild their credibility by stressing that they did this based on facts and figures not available to the general public (knowledge), that they are good people and would never do anything immoral (high moral character), or that they would only do what is right for the rest of the state or country and that the people's interests were really paramount (good will).

Teachers will often intersperse their lectures or discussions with credibility-building references. They may, for example, "casually" note that their new book will be out soon or that an article they have written will clarify important questions, or they may note how thorough their own education was. In all of these instances the teacher (knowingly or not) is building credibility or at least making an attempt to do so.

More specifically, we should ask what factors influence the perception of credibility in listeners. That is, what does a communicator do that enhances or detracts from his or her credibility? A great deal of research has been directed at discovering the various means of achieving high derived credibility.

The way in which the message is presented and constructed influences credibility a great deal. If a person communicates haltingly, with poor grammar, with numerous hesitations, and with an uneasiness, we would probably perceive that person to be of low credibility and not readily believe him or her. Conversely, the speaker who speaks with assurance, who speaks in accordance with the rules of grammar, and who appears self-confident seems to have a much better chance of being perceived as credible. Thus the words we choose in speaking, the way in which we arrange those words, the way in which we organize our arguments, questions, or responses influence our credibility.

The fairness with which one presents oneself seems also to influence the perception of credibility. If we feel that people have some kind of ulterior motive then we would be less likely to believe them. On the other hand, speakers who present themselves honestly seem to be believed more readily.

Generally, we perceive as believable people who are like ourselves. The more similar people are to our own backgrounds, attitudes and beliefs, goals and ambitions, the more likely it is that they will be perceived as credible. Closely related to this is the issue of "common ground." When people align themselves with what we align ourselves, they establish common ground with us and are generally perceived as more believable than people who do not establish this common ground. In the movie *Gypsy*, Rose carries around with her a collection of pins and buttons for various societies. If she meets an Elk she puts on the Elk pin; if she meets a Moose she dons the Moose pin. In this way she establishes common ground and stands a better chance of being believed. I guess we do not like to think that people who are like us would be anything but knowledgeable, of good character, and of good will.

Terminal Credibility

Terminal credibility is that which the communicator is seen to possess after the communication interaction is completed. This terminal credibility is a product of the interaction of initial and derived credibility. Based on the initial credibility and the derived credibility, a terminal credibility image is formed. At times this is higher than the initial credibility, and at times it is lower. But it is always a product of the interaction of the before, or initial, and the during, or derived, credibility. After the job interview, after the teacher and students finish the last discussion of the course, after the lovers kiss goodnight, there is some terminal credibility picture that is formed in the mind of each person about the other person.

DIMENSIONS OF CREDIBILITY

Lovers, entertainers, educators, salespersons, and in fact everyone who wishes to influence attitudes, opinions, beliefs, and behaviors is concerned with the components or dimensions of credibility. They are concerned with what goes

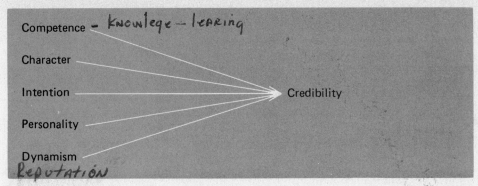

Figure 6.1
The Dimensions of Credibility

into making a person appear believable or credible. Although various writers put their emphases in different places, most agree with McCroskey who defines five major dimensions: *competence, character, intention, personality,* and *dynamism* (see Figure 6.1).

Dynamism - quality + Forcefulness [handwritten]

Competence

The more intelligent and knowledgeable a person is thought to be, the more that person will be perceived as credible, and the more likely it is that he or she will be believed. The teacher, for example, is believed to the extent that he or she is thought knowledgeable about the subject. Similarly, the textbook writer is thought credible to the extent that he or she is thought competent.

Competence is logically subject-specific. A person may be competent in one subject and totally incompetent in another subject. However, people often do not make the distinction between areas of competence. Thus a person who is thought competent in politics will often be thought competent in general and will thus be perceived as credible when talking on health or physical education.

Character *- morals* [handwritten]

We will perceive someone as credible if we perceive that person as having what Aristotle referred to as a high moral character. Here we would be concorned with the individual's honesty and basic nature. We would want to know if we could trust that person. A person who can be trusted is apt to be believed; a person who cannot be trusted is apt not to be believed.

Intention

An individual's motives or intentions are particularly important in determining credibility. The salesperson who says all the right things about a product is often doubted because his or her intentions are perceived as selfish; credibility is therefore low. The salesperson is less believable than a consumer advocate who evaluates a product with no motives of personal gain. Of course it is extremely difficult to judge when individuals are concerned with our good or with theirs. But when we can make the distinction, it greatly influences our perception of credibility.

Personality – *How you Act or Relate*

Generally, we perceive as credible or believable people we like rather than people we do not like. And, it seems, we like people who have what we commonly refer to as a "pleasing personality." We believe people who are friendly and pleasant rather than people who are unfriendly and unpleasant. Positive and forward-looking people are seen as more credible than negative and backward-looking people. Perhaps we reason that they have gotten themselves together and so are in a better position to know what is right and what is wrong. We would be leery of accepting marital advice from an unhappily married couple, perhaps for a similar reason. If they cannot solve their own problems, we reasonably doubt their ability to help us.

Dynamism

The shy, introverted, soft-spoken individual is generally perceived as less credible than the aggressive, extroverted, and forceful individual. The great leaders in history have generally been dynamic people. They were aggressive and empathic. Of course, we may still have the stereotype of the shy, withdrawn college professor who, though not very dynamic, is nevertheless credible. Generally, however, the more dynamic, the more credible the person is perceived to be. Perhaps it is because we feel that the dynamic person is open and honest in presenting himself or herself whereas the shy, introverted individual may be seen as hiding something.

In short, the person who is seen as competent, of good character, of legitimate intention, of pleasant personality and dynamic, will be perceived as credible. That person's credibility will decrease as any one of these five qualities decreases; his or her credibility will increase as any one of these five qualities increases.

VARIATIONS IN CREDIBILITY PERCEPTION

The answers about credibility are somewhat more complex when we attempt to examine the relative importance of these qualities. One of the reasons for the complexity is that the perception of credibility varies with the individual doing the evaluating and with the subject matter. To some people the most credible person is the most competent person, and issues such as personality and dynamism are relatively unimportant. To other people, a good character is the most important attribute; a person is thought credible if he or she is thought to be of good character. Similarly, the perception of credibility depends on the subject under consideration. When evaluating surgeons or physicians we would probably be most concerned with their competence. If they are perceived as competent they will be thought credible and believed. It would be an added bonus if they were of high character, pleasant, forceful, and so on but these would clearly be of minor importance. In thinking about a husband or wife, character may be more important than competence and personality more important than dynamism.

There are also differences among people in evaluating each of the five qualities. For example, one individual may be perceived by some people as pleasant but by others as unpleasant. Some teachers are perceived as friendly by some students and as unfriendly by others. Similarly, some people may like aggressiveness, whereas others may dislike it. Ministers may be perceived as highly credible by their congregations but as not credible by atheists or agnostics, for example. A colleague of mine sees fortune tellers and astrologers as highly credible whereas many others find these people to be of low credibility.

We might all agree that a person with a Ph.D. in nuclear physics from Harvard knows something about nuclear physics and is therefore credible in this area. Similarly, we might agree that the average high school freshman does not know much about nuclear physics and is therefore not credible. With these extremes there is seldom any difficulty in securing agreement as to the degree of credibility to be attributed. But in the middle there are many difficulties. Consequently, we cannot point to an individual and say that that person is credible and that this other one is not credible. Credibility is not intrinsic; it is in our perceptions. My friend sees Madame Xenovia, the fortune teller, as highly credible. Madame Xenovia herself is neither credible nor not credible. Whatever credibility she has is in the perceptions of others.

A NOTE ON INTRAPERSONAL CREDIBILITY

As viewed in this unit, and by most other writers, credibility is considered an interpersonal communication component; that is, credibility is seen as being perceived by one person about another person. But there is also an *intra*-personal credibility which should be explored. We all have images of ourselves. We all see ourselves as being competent or incompetent to some degree. We all see ourselves as having particular character traits. This view of ourselves leads us to react in certain ways and not in others, much as our view of others leads us to react in particular ways.

For example, consider the student who in taking an examination puts down one answer, sees that another student has put down a different answer, and changes his or her answer to conform with that of the other student. The students who change their answers are, in doing so, saying something about their perception of their own credibility, as well as about the credibility of the other students. The relative faith we have in our own decisions is largely a matter of the degree of credibility we perceive ourselves to have. People who view themselves as being of low credibility (and we all know such people) will constantly seek the advice of others who are of higher credibility before making any move at all.

The way in which we react to others, based on our perception of their credibility, seems very similar to the way in which we react to ourselves, based on our perception of our own credibility. We see ourselves much as we see other people. We evaluate their competence, character, and so on and we evaluate our own competence, character, and so on. On the basis of this credibility rating we believe or disbelieve others and believe or disbelieve ourselves. For example, given a task to accomplish, based on our credibility, we may believe or disbelieve that we could accomplish it.

It should be apparent that the degree to which we appear credible to others is greatly dependent upon the degree to which we appear credible to ourselves. People who do not believe in themselves are rarely going to find others who believe in them. If we think ourselves incompetent we can be fairly certain that others will agree with us. The comforting aspect of this is that it also works in reverse.

SOURCES

A summary of the experimental research on credibility through the 1960s is provided in Kenneth Andersen and Theodore Clevenger Jr., "A Summary of Experimental Research in *Ethos*," *Speech Monographs* 30 (1963):59–78. More up-to-date treatments may be found in Kenneth Andersen, *Persuasion: Theory and Practice* (Boston: Allyn & Bacon, 1971); James C. McCroskey, *An Introduction to Rhetorical Communication,* 2d ed. (Englewood Cliffs, N.J.: Prentice-Hall, 1972); Stephen W. King, *Communication and Social Influence* (Reading, Mass.: Addison-Wesley, 1975); and Thomas M. Steinfatt, *Human Communication: An Interpersonal Introduction* (Indianapolis: Bobbs-Merrill, 1977).

A study which presents somewhat different dimensions of credibility is Christoper J. S. Tuppen, "Dimensions of Credibility: An Oblique Solution," *Speech Monographs* 41 (1974):253–260. An interesting study pertinent to this class is James C. McCroskey, William E. Holdridge, and J. Keven Toomb, "An Instrument for Measuring the Source Credibility of Basic Speech Communication Instructors," *Speech Teacher* 23 (1974):26–33.

EXPERIENTIAL VEHICLES

6.2 CREDIBILITY ASSESSMENT

Below are a series of semantic differential scales designed to measure credibility. These particular scales, designed by Berlo, Lemert, and Mertz, measure three dimensions or aspects of credibility, namely trustworthiness, expertness, and personal dynamism.

Instruction

1. On Form A rate yourself as you feel you really are. (If necessary, reread the instructions in Unit 1 for completing the scales.)
2. On Form B rate yourself as you feel others see you.
3. On Form C have someone who knows you fairly well rate you.

FORM A

kind	___ :	___ :	___ :	___ :	___ :	___ :	___ cruel
friendly	___ :	___ :	___ :	___ :	___ :	___ :	___ unfriendly
honest	___ :	___ :	___ :	___ :	___ :	___ :	___ dishonest
experienced	___ :	___ :	___ :	___ :	___ :	___ :	___ inexperienced
informed	___ :	___ :	___ :	___ :	___ :	___ :	___ uninformed
skilled	___ :	___ :	___ :	___ :	___ :	___ :	___ unskilled
aggressive	___ :	___ :	___ :	___ :	___ :	___ :	___ meek
emphatic	___ :	___ :	___ :	___ :	___ :	___ :	___ hesitant
bold	___ :	___ :	___ :	___ :	___ :	___ :	___ timid
active	___ :	___ :	___ :	___ :	___ :	___ :	___ passive

FORM B

kind	____ : ____ : ____ : ____ : ____ : ____ : ____	cruel
friendly	____ : ____ : ____ : ____ : ____ : ____ : ____	unfriendly
honest	____ : ____ : ____ : ____ : ____ : ____ : ____	dishonest
experienced	____ : ____ : ____ : ____ : ____ : ____ : ____	inexperienced
informed	____ : ____ : ____ : ____ : ____ : ____ : ____	uninformed
skilled	____ : ____ : ____ : ____ : ____ : ____ : ____	unskilled
aggressive	____ : ____ : ____ : ____ : ____ : ____ : ____	meek
emphatic	____ : ____ : ____ : ____ : ____ : ____ : ____	hesitant
bold	____ : ____ : ____ : ____ : ____ : ____ : ____	timid
active	____ : ____ : ____ : ____ : ____ : ____ : ____	passive

FORM C

kind	____ : ____ : ____ : ____ : ____ : ____ : ____	cruel
friendly	____ : ____ : ____ : ____ : ____ : ____ : ____	unfriendly
honest	____ : ____ : ____ : ____ : ____ : ____ : ____	dishonest
experienced	____ : ____ : ____ : ____ : ____ : ____ : ____	inexperienced
informed	____ : ____ : ____ : ____ : ____ : ____ : ____	uninformed
skilled	____ : ____ : ____ : ____ : ____ : ____ : ____	unskilled
aggressive	____ : ____ : ____ : ____ : ____ : ____ : ____	meek
emphatic	____ : ____ : ____ : ____ : ____ : ____ : ____	hesitant
bold	____ : ____ : ____ : ____ : ____ : ____ : ____	timid
active	____ : ____ : ____ : ____ : ____ : ____ : ____	passive

Credibility Analysis

Scoring

1. Number the top scale positions 1 to 7, from left to right, for example,

```
            1     2     3     4     5     6     7
trustworthy ____ : ____ : ____ : ____ : ____ : ____ : ____ untrustworthy
```

2. Determine your scores and enter them on the Credibility Analysis Form.
3. Total the scores for each of the three forms. Enter these totals at the bottom of the analysis form.
4. Enter the average for each scale in the appropriate place, that is, the average for kind-cruel, for friendly-unfriendly, and so forth.

CREDIBILITY ANALYSIS FORM

Scale	Form A	Form B	Form C	Average
Kind-cruel				
Friendly-unfriendly				
Honest-dishonest				
Experienced-inexperienced				
Informed-uninformed				
Skilled-unskilled				
Aggressive-meak				
Emphatic-hesitant				
Bold-timid				
Active-passive				
Total				

Discussion

In dyads or small groups consider the following:

1. What does a low score on a form mean? A high score? An average score?
2. On which form is your score highest? Does this come as a surprise? Explain.
3. What do these scores tell you about the way you see yourself? About the way you think others see you? About the way others see you?
4. What do low difference scores among Forms A, B, and C mean? High difference scores?
5. What do you think accounts for the differences between the first two sets of scales (between Forms A and B)? (Try to think in terms of overt behaviors.)
6. What do you think accounts for the differences between Forms B and C? (Try to think in terms of overt behaviors.)
7. For which scales were there the largest differences? How might you account for this?
8. Do you think the ratings on Form C are typical of the ratings you would get from other people? Explain.

6.3 COMMUNICATOR CREDIBILITY

Each of the following excerpts are examples of attempts by communicators to establish their credibility. Examine each with special reference to the dimensions of credibility discussed in this unit and record the specific means used by each of the speakers to establish their credibility. The time span of some 100 years illustrates, I think, that the techniques for establishing credibility have not changed very much.

1. I am certain that my fellow Americans expect that on my induction into the Presidency I will address them with a candor and a decision which the present situation of our Nation impels. This is preeminently the time to speak the truth, the whole truth, frankly and boldly. Nor need we shrink from honestly facing conditions in our country today. This great Nation will endure as it has endured, will revive and will prosper. So, first of all, let me assert my firm belief that the only thing we have to fear is fear itself—nameless, unreasoning, unjustified terror which paralyzes needed efforts to convert retreat into advance. In every dark hour of our national life a leadership of frankness and vigor has met with that understanding and support of the people themselves which is essential to victory. I am convinced that you will again give that support to leadership in these critical days.

    —Franklin Delano Roosevelt, First Inaugural Address

2. Mr. Chairman and Gentlemen of the Convention: I would be presumptuous, indeed, to present myself against the distinguished gentlemen to whom you have listened if this were a mere measuring of abilities; but this is not a contest between persons. The humblest citizen in all the land, when clad in the armor of a righteous cause, is stronger than all the hosts of error. I come to speak to you in defense of a cause as holy as the cause of liberty—the cause of humanity.

    —Wililam Jennings Bryan, The Cross of Gold

3. Those of us—and they are most of us—who are more Americans than we are Democrats or Republicans, count some things more important than the winning or losing of elections.

    There is a peace still to be won, an economy which needs some attention, some freedoms to be secured, an atom to be controlled—all through the delicate, sensitive and indispensable processes of democracy—processes which demand, at the least, that people's vision be clear, that they be told the truth, and that they respect one another.

    —Adlai Stevenson, Address to the Southeastern Democratic Conference

4. The people of this state, the state which sent John Quincy Adams and Daniel Webster and Charles Sumner and Henry Cabot Lodge and John Kennedy to the United States Senate, are entitled to representation in that body by men who inspire their utmost confidence.

    For this reason, I would understand full well why some might think it right for me to resign. For me this will be a difficult decision to make.

    It has been seven years since my first election to the Senate. You and I share many memories—some of them have been glorious, some have been very sad. The opportunity to work with you and serve Massachusetts has made my life worthwhile.

    And so I ask you tonight, People of Massachusetts, to think this through with me. In facing this decision, I seek your advice and opinion. In making it, I seek your prayers. For this is a decision that I will have finally to make on my own.

—Edward M. Kennedy, Speech on Chappiquiddick

5. Then, in 1942, I went into the service. Let me say that my service record was not a particularly unusual one. I went to the South Pacific. I guess I'm entitled to a couple of battle stars. I got a couple of letters of commendation.

But I was just there when the bombs were falling. And then I returned to the United States, and in 1946 I ran for the Congress.

When we came out of the war, Pat and I—Pat during the war had worked as a stenographer, and in a bank, and as an economist for a government agency and when we came out, the total of our savings, from both my law practice, her teaching, and all the time that I was in the war, the total for that entire period was just a little less than $10,000—every cent of that, incidentally, was in government bonds—well, that's where we start, when I go into politics.

—Richard Nixon, Checkers Speech

6.4 QUINTILIAN COLLEGE

The purpose of this exercise is to explore the perception of credibility of others on the basis of their background and previous experiences.

Each student should read the directions and profiles and then rank the candidates in order of merit, using 1 for the first choice, 2 for the second choice, and so on. After these rankings are completed, groups of five or six students should be formed. The task of each group is to agree on a group ranking of the candidates, again using 1 for the group's first choice, 2 for the group's second choice, and so on.

After these rankings are completed, the groups should share their rankings with each other. Attention should be directed to at least the following:

1. the reasons for the rankings
2. the dimensions of credibility each group perceived in each candidate
3. the variations in the perception of credibility and the reasons for these (the variations among the individual students and the variations among the several groups)

The College and the Job

Quintilian College is a private midwestern coeducational institution with a student body of approximately 15,000. It is a four-year liberal arts college that wishes to be known for its progressiveness and responsiveness to the needs of the surrounding communities.

For the most part the students come from the surrounding towns and cities, although some come from other states and even from other countries. The student body is approximately 70 percent white, 20 percent black, and 10 percent Spanish and Mexican. Most of these students are from middle-class families. The tuition is approximately $1500 per semester.

Quintilian has been undergoing a number of problems, the major one being financial. The school has an annual deficit of over $1 million. Because of these financial problems it has cut back on a number of its academic programs and is now in danger of losing accreditation. The college is not, however, in serious danger of bankruptcy since it does own large areas of land. It has been reluctant to sell this land for the needed funds because the value of the land is increasing at approximately 20 percent per year.

The current president is retiring at the end of this year. A committee has been appointed to search for a new president and has submitted the names of the following candidates along with some information they think might be pertinent to the final selection. All candidates have indicated an eagerness to serve as president.

Profiles of the Candidates

HENRY BENSON, white, male, forty-five years old, married with two children, both college students. Currently, Professor of Classics. Author of numerous articles and books on Greek and Latin and currently working on a monograph on the phonological structure of irregular verbs of early Latin. Benson is a Danish citizen but has indicated that he would become a citizen of the United States if offered the presidency.

MARTHA WALLACE, white, female, forty-three years old, single. Currently, Professor of Economics. President of state chapter of Women's Liberation and author of articles and books on economics and women's liberation. Adviser to and a charter member of local group, Lesbian Liberation, and frequent speaker at gay liberation meetings.

JOHN RUSSELL, black, male, thirty-five years old, married, no children. Currently, Professor of Biological Sciences. Author of several monographs on the biological bases of language and cognitive processes. Academic adviser to several conservative black organizations.

ANDREW WILCOX, white, male, forty-six years old. Single. Currently, vice president of a large electronics corporation and former Professor of Linguistics. Author of numerous articles and books on computer languages and computational linguistics. An avowed supporter of black militancy and a frequent contributor to militant/radical papers and magazines.

MICHEL ANGUS, white, female, forty years old, divorced three times and now married with no children. Recently retired from a large investment firm which she founded and where she served as president. Received a B.B.A. degree from a correspondence school some ten years ago. She has been extremely successful in business (largely through her own investments) and is now a multi-millionaire.

MARTIN TORES, white, male, sixty years old, Catholic priest. Currently, president of St. Thomas University and former Professor of Philosophy. Author of several widely used philosophy texts and editor of a leading philosophy journal. A leading spokesman for the Spanish and Mexican-American causes. He has been jailed twice for his involvement in demonstrations against discrimination in employment and housing and school segregation.

UNIT 7
Ethical Considerations in Communication

Censorship
Ghostwriting
Conditioning—As Persuasion, As Therapy
The Prevention of Interaction

LEARNING GOALS

After completing this unit, you should be able to:

1. state some of the arguments relating to censorship, ghostwriting, conditioning, and the prevention of interaction
2. define *conditioning, positive reinforcement, negative reinforcement,* and *punishment*
3. identify examples from your own experience that illustrate the operation of conditioning principles
4. explain the prevention of interaction as a question of ethics
5. make predictions as to the state of censorship, ghostwriting, conditioning, and the prevention of interaction in the next 50 to 60 years.
6. take a tentative stand on issues relating to censorship, ghostwriting, conditioning, and the prevention of interaction

All communicators, regardless of their specific purposes and regardless of the specific form of communication utilized, need to take into consideration questions of ethics. Every communication act has consequences, whether for one person or for an entire culture, and, therefore, has an ethical dimension, a rightness and a wrongness dimension. Only a few of the areas where questions of ethics are particularly apparent are considered here, namely censorship, ghostwriting, conditioning, and the prevention of interaction.

CENSORSHIP

In 1973, in *Miller* v. *California,* the Supreme Court ruled in favor of a most rigid censorship law. Essentially, this ruling holds that the individual communities and local governments have the right to determine when an article, book, film, play, or other public communication appeals to "prurient interests" and should therefore be censored.

This decision has raised a number of important issues relative to free speech and more generally, to the human right to information. Shortly after the decision was made, numerous movies were banned by local communities —not only the X-rated films, such as *Deep Throat* or *The Devil in Miss Jones,* but also films such as *Carnal Knowledge* and *Paper Moon.* The reasons given for banning such movies have generally centered on the claim that these films offend community standards of morality.

Some people would agree that the community as a whole should have the right to determine what comes into the community, specifically what movies are shown in the local theatres, what programs appear on television, what books are made available at the local libraries or assigned in schools, and what magazines are sold. Still more people would agree to grant these rights to the community if that community was unanimous in its decisions. If every citizen in the community did not wish to have a picture shown in the local movie house then a strong argument could be made for it not being shown, that is, for it being banned. But what about decisions made by fewer than all of the people? Clearly these would include all the decisions or at least 99 percent of the decisions normally made on such issues. We might extend the argument and ask what if only one person wanted to read a particular book? Should the library make the book available? What if 10 percent of the people wanted to read it? Twenty percent? Forty-nine percent?

One of the many paradoxes that censorship laws have created concerns "the public will." It is argued that the local community should set the standards for what is pornographic and what is not pornographic and that the local community has the right to censor that which it considers pornographic. Given this situation we are compelled to wonder how theatres that show films considered to be pornographic by the "community"—and therefore subject to censorship—can manage to make a profit. Any theatre owner interested in making a profit would be a fool to schedule films that the members of the community are not going to see. But, of course, the theatre owner does make a profit; members of the community clearly do want to see such films. Yet throughout the country films are being ruled pornographic and banned on the basis of the argument that the community does not want to see them.

In early 1977 Larry Flynt, the publisher of *Hustler* magazine, was arrested, bond refused, and sentenced to 7 to 25 years in prison and fined $11,000. The charge was that Flynt published an obscene magazine and engaged in organized crime. "Engaging in organized crime," according to Ohio law, consists of five or more persons conspiring to commit a crime; Flynt was charged with working with his staff (of more than five persons) to publish *Hustler* magazine which was defined as obscene and hence a crime to publish. One of the many issues which this case raises is that this charge of "organized crime" can be used against any publisher. Hence we may ask, to what extent any publisher is (or should be) free from government interference? Further, if *Hustler* magazine is read by 3 million people—as it claims—then we must recognize that such a situation not only deprives the publisher from publishing the magazine but it also deprives 3 million people of reading the magazine. And would it matter if only 10 people read it or if 50 million people read it?

It is relatively easy to go back into history and find numerous works of literature that were at one time banned as pornographic. Where once people could not read *Lady Chatterly's Lover,* today many students are required to read it as part of some college course in English. Should we wonder if *Deep Throat* will become required viewing in film courses 10 or 20 years from now? Will the writings of Linda Lovelace or Xaveria Hollander become required reading in sex education courses? Such a situation probably seems absurd. But then so did the idea that the works of D. H. Lawrence might one day be required reading seem absurd not so many years ago.

We must recognize that morality and definitions of pornography are time bound as well as culture bound (at least according to most systems of ethics). What is considered pornographic in one culture and at one time may not be considered pornographic in another culture or at another time. However, the changing definitions that we have witnessed over time do not seem to be governed by any logic; they appear totally unpredictable.

Still another issue in regard to pornography and its regulation is that it is taken as an axiom that it is the obligation of those who would attempt to depict sexual activities to prove that such depictions are worthy of redeeming social significance. Underlying this notion seems to be the assumption that somehow sex is evil and is therefore to be hidden from public view. Most persons do not object to depictions of theft, murder, and war, and yet they do object to depictions of sexual activity.

It somehow seems to be assumed, though the line of reasoning seems a bit tenuous, that sexually oriented communications have undersirable effects on the persons viewing them. Although there seems little evidence to support this, it is nevertheless an empirical question and one which should be answered by evidence. Yet it is paradoxical that in the absence of such evidence the filmmaker, photographer, and writer must prove their innocence—contrary to the normal system where innocence is assumed and guilt must be proven.

Another assumption underlying these provisions seems to be that the effects of such communications can be predicted with a fair degree of accuracy. But this hardly seems the case. When *West Side Story* was shown on television some years ago, it apparently helped to reactivate gangs and gang wars in New York City and perhaps elsewhere as well. Should *West Side Story* have been banned?

There are other issues—which get at the interpersonal dimension more directly—that we need to consider under the heading of censorship. As citizens we all have the right to make our voices heard. The Constitution grants us that right. Each of us has the right (some would say the obligation) to voice our opinions and our beliefs when they do not endanger the lives or safety of others. Clearly we do not have the right to ruin someone's reputation with lies or yell "fire" in a theatre since this might endanger the lives of others. Yet, we do have the right to speak out for or against a particular way of life or political philosophy or economic policy. But as average citizens how can we do this? To speak and to have our voices heard today is an extremely expensive undertaking. The communications systems throughout the country and the world are too expensive for us to engage for even a single minute. If we wished, for example, to advertise in favor of one of our political views or in support of something we wish to defend, rather like the large corporations do, and we chose to run this ad in *Playboy* it would cost us at least a few years'

Box 2
THE FIRST AND FIFTH AMENDMENTS

The First Amendment to the Constitution of the United States

Congress should make no law respecting an establishment of religion, or prohibiting the free exercise thereof; or abridging the freedom of speech, or of the press; or the right of the people peaceably to assemble, and to petition the Government for a redress of grievances.

The Fifth Amendment to the Constitution of the United States

No person shall be held to answer for a capital, or otherwise infamous crime, unless on a presentment or indictment of a Grand Jury, except in cases arising in the land or naval forces, or in the Militia, when in actual service in time of War, or public danger; nor shall any person be subject for the same offence to be twice put in jeopardy of life or limb; nor shall be compelled in any criminal case to be a witness against himself, nor be deprived of life, liberty, or property, without due process of law; nor shall private property be taken for public use, without just compensation.

---

salary. It is interesting (yet frightening), for example, to reflect on the fact that Bell Telephone can use our money to advertise to millions of people how hard they are working to bring us the best service at the least possible cost but we, who use the phones everyday, cannot advertise to tell these same people of the difficulties we encounter in dealing with them. Of course, this problem is not limited to Bell Telephone, nor was it created by them. Could we purchase one minute of the "Tonight Show" to air our views? Clearly we could not, and yet this is exactly what we would have to do if we were to have an effective voice in influencing public opinion. The days of individuals in their basements with an old printing press, cranking out handbills to distribute in front of the local church, are gone forever. Such a procedure today would be ludicrous and ineffective.

Are we not effectively censored from communicating our views because we are not millionaires and only have access to interpersonal communication channels? Although there have been some efforts made to require television stations to allot a certain amount of time to the presentation of opposing views, it seems clear that the size of one's voice and hence influence are largely determined by the size of one's bank account.

This problem of expense has been discussed perhaps most often in connection with political campaigning. Without a substantial financial backing it seems impossible to get elected to any high public office. A potential candidate without any money would not be able to advertise, would not be able to buy air time, would not be able to travel to deliver speeches, would not be able to have posters printed and circulated, and so on. And so (if one is at all serious about running for political office) one must obtain this financial backing. And we are well aware that one does not obtain substantial financial backing without giving something in return. And this "something in return" is often given at the expense of the very people who will eventually elect this candidate.

At the same time that we may see dangers in censorship it seems equally clear that some restrictions may be helpful and useful. Most would probably agree that people with access to military information should not be allowed to reveal certain facts which might prove damaging to national security. We might also agree that restrictions on the basis of age might be legitimate. Perhaps certain information, on subjects such as alcohol and cigarettes, should be restricted to "adults," however we might define that term. And so while we might agree that certain lines may be useful to draw, we seem far from agreeing on exactly where the lines should be.

GHOSTWRITING

One of the perennial topics raised in any discussion of communication is that of ghostwriting. Ghostwriting, broadly conceived, refers to the practice of em-

"You're working entirely too hard, congressman . . .
maybe you should try to get off the ethics committee."

ploying professional writers to prepare one's speeches or articles and then presenting them as if they were one's own.

The most familiar example of this practice is among politicians who invariably employ a staff of writers to prepare their speeches. But the practice is much more widespread and certainly is not limited to politics and politicians. Broadly viewed, ghostwriting would include, for example, 1) the student who turns in a term paper or delivers a speech obtained from the fraternity file, from *Reader's Digest,* or from some agency that specializes in preparing such compositions for college students; 2) the student who pays to have his or her thesis or dissertation written by a professional writer; 3) the college teacher who "demands" or "accepts" coauthorship for an article or book actually written and researched by a graduate student; 4) the news reporter who reads the news copy prepared by another individual; and, of course 5) the politician who presents a speech written by a speech staff. Clearly there are differences among these several examples of ghostwriting; yet each of them raises significant questions.

We might sympathize with the politician on any number of bases. There is not enough time for the politician to prepare all the speeches, especially when campaigning throughout the country. The speeches, if they are to be at all effective, must be individualized for perhaps hundreds of different audiences and must resemble interpersonal communications as much as possible. No one person could possibly have the time necessary for such a monumental undertaking. Certainly the president does not have the time to prepare relatively polished speeches to present over television or at various conferences and conventions. We might further argue that since everyone knows that the politicians are not writing their own speeches, no one is really deceived by the practice. Should one politician attempt to write his or her own speeches, such speeches would surely not be as effective as those of the opponent. Thus by not employing such writers one is, in effect, practically giving up all chances for election.

We might also note that numerous politicians—Franklin D. Roosevelt and Adlai Stevenson are perhaps the clearest examples—guide the speechwriting process of their ghostwriters very carefully. On this basis we might argue, as many have done, that these were really their speeches and not those of their staff.

These are at least some of the familiar arguments used to show that ghostwriting—at least among politicians—should be accepted. But are we or should we be willing to accept this practice? Does practical necessity make a practice acceptable?

When we are attempting to make up our minds regarding the qualifications of several opposing political candidates, is it fair that none of the candidates is actually delivering campaign speeches which he or she has written? Is it fair that politicians would have us listen to a humorous and enlightening speech on, for example, educational reform, when they in fact know nothing

---

Box 3
ETHICS AND GHOSTWRITING

David D. Draves

A Prevalence of Ghosts

What follows is not a defense of ghost-written and plagiarized student papers but a partial explanation of why students feel at ease in using ghostwriters to help them to earn college credits:

1. When I prepare for what my civics teacher tells me is my highest political responsibility as a commonplace citizen, voting intelligently in a public election, I must base my decisions on candidate speeches which have been created by a stable of ghostwriters.

2. When I read a professor's research article, I am never sure whether the writer did all the background grubbing or used the labors of ghost graduate students.

3. When my term paper or examination paper is evaluated for a large college lecture course, it generally is read by a ghost graduate student.

4. When I enroll in an introductory college English course, or French course, or mathematics course, very likely I will be instructed by a gost graduate student— a Miss Zagano—who is teaching me so that the famous person whose reputation helped to bring me to that campus can do more important things.

5. When I enjoy Audrey Hepburn in yet another TV rerun of "My Fair Lady," I hear a ghost's voice sing the songs of Eliza Doolittle.

6. When I end the day half-listening to Johnny Carson, I hear not the wit of Carson but that of a coterie of ghostwriters.

7. When I relax with an autobiography of a contemporary athlete or movie star, more likely than not I am reading the words of an "as-told-to" or "with" ghost.

Ghosts are all around me, accepted, and, when not graduate students, highly paid. Why should not I employ a ghostwriter to help me accomplish one task for a course which represents less than 3 percent of my college work?

Source: The New York Times Magazine, July 6, 1975. Reprinted by permission of *The New York Times* and David D. Draves.

---

about educational reform and are themselves totally humorless? Does the fact that a practice is universal mean we should accept it? Does the fact that everyone is doing it make it right and justified?

Consider the case of the student handing in a term paper or delivering a speech as his or her own when in fact it was obtained from someone else— perhaps a friend, a magazine, or a professional agency. If the student gets caught there is little that can save the student from failing the course or at least the assignment. Most instructors would state without reservation that the student's behavior is unethical.

Yet consider the case of the college instructor who is pressured to publish scholarly articles. A bright graduate student comes along and produces a term paper worthy of publication. This much the instructor knows. So a few suggestions for improvement are made along with some stylistic suggestions, and the instructor offers to have it published with the student as coauthor. The assumption when two names appear on an article or a book is that both persons shared in producing the work, but it seems that this instructor did little—certainly not half. And yet the professor's name appears on the article as coauthor. If this instructor gets enough good graduate students he or she may become widely known on the basis of a number of articles with which he or she actually had little to do. Students may even enroll in this instructor's classes or attend the school at which the instructor is teaching because of this reputation. Yet, in fact, this instructor may know very little and may not have had anything significant to do with the publications responsible for this wide reputation. (This situation, I should add, is actually not at all exaggerated. There are many instructors in all disciplines who make this type of thing a common practice.)

We might argue that the instructor has provided the stimulation necessary for this kind of work and that the value of this stimulation is surely half the work. Further, the student would not have known enough about procedures to get the article published alone. Also, the instructor did make some changes in the paper and who can say that these changes were not the very thing that led to the paper's acceptance for publication? Are these arguments sufficient to justify this widespread practice?

Take the case in which the graduate student, pleased with the guidance received from the instructor, asks the instructor to coauthor the paper. Is the instructor justified in accepting this? Has the instructor a right to pose to the academic world as an expert on a topic he or she may know very little about? And again, is the widespread nature of this practice sufficient to justify it, to make it acceptable? Like the busy politician who must prepare and present several speeches a week, the college instructor must publish—otherwise the instructor does not get promoted and is not granted tenure. But is need enough to justify practice?

This system is similar to that of news reporters who do not prepare their own news reports. A staff of reporters assemble the facts, professional writers write up the copy, and "news reporters" simply present it to the public. Their qualifications may be nothing more than a pleasant voice and a handsome face. Surely we would rather look at a handsome face than an ugly one and would want to hear a pleasant voice rather than a harsh and rasping one. Who would turn on the news to listen to an unpleasant individual? The ratings would drop to near zero and advertisers would cancel. And so the practice is justified for purely economic reasons. The problem with this is that, like instructors who gain reputations for being experts in fields they know nothing about, these attractive people with pleasant voices get reputations for being authorities on world events when in fact they may know nothing and care less about the politics of the world. The character of Ted Baxter on *The Mary Tyler Moore Show* is perhaps the classic example. But it seems there are "Ted Baxters" all over the channels.

Because these several practices are so widespread there is an increasing need not for passive acceptance but for active and thorough evaluation. We need to ask if we are doing ourselves an injustice and if we are actually fostering deception by accepting such practices.

CONDITIONING—AS PERSUASION, AS THERAPY

In one of the most widely read, condemned, praised, and generally discussed books of this century, *Beyond Freedom and Dignity*, B. F. Skinner sets forth the case for conditioning—a psychological technique for controlling behavior.

According to Skinner, all learned behavior is learned through a process of conditioning, a process governed by rewards and punishments. Put generally, the "theory" of conditioning states that we will learn and repeat those behaviors that have been rewarded in the past, and we will not learn or not repeat those behaviors that have been unrewarded or punished. Behavior may be rewarded through either of two basic means. *Positive reinforcement* involves the presentation of some kind of reward after some bit of behavior has been emitted. The result is that this type of behavior is strengthened in frequency and will be more likely to occur in the future under similar circumstances. *Negative reinforcement,* on the other hand, involves the removal of an aversive or painful stimulus (for example, an unpleasant sound) after some bit of behavior has been emitted. This, too, results in the behavior being strengthened and in its being more likely to occur under similar circumstances in the future. Behavior that is not reinforced, or that is punished, will not be learned—or, if already learned, will be extinguished or weakened.

According to Skinner all learned human behavior can be explained in essentially this way although there are rather complex types of conditioning schedules to account for the learning of different types of behaviors. But the essence of conditioning is that we learn according to the principles or laws of reinforcement.

Skinner's argument in *Beyond Freedom and Dignity* did not receive so much attention from all segments of the population because it presented a new psychological theory; actually Skinner had presented the same theory decades ago and it can be found in practically every basic psychology textbook. The reason this particular book received so much attention was simply that here Skinner applied the results of laboratory studies to society and denied the existence of what we normally call freedom of choice. We act and behave, according to Skinner, not because we are free to choose, but because of the way in which we have been conditioned. In this work, as well as in his novel *Walden Two,* Skinner portrayed and advocated a society organized on the basis of the principles of conditioning.

This thesis proved particularly disturbing to many people. Skinner's critics argued that society should not be based on such principles and that we would be morally unjustified in establishing a society where certain people were granted the right to reward and punish and thus control the behaviors of its people. Skinner's argument, however, is that we do not have a choice in whether or not we wish to be controlled by conditioning. According to Skinner, we *are* so controlled; that is simply in the nature of being human. And the question then becomes, Do we want to organize this process or do we want to leave it to the inconsistent applications, such as we now have?

Admittedly, this is a rather disturbing notion. We all want to be free, to think we are free, and to act as if we are free. Yet, Skinner's arguments and evidence are not easy to dismiss. If we accept Skinner's basic assumptions about conditioning, then we are left with two basic choices. Either we accept the present system in which our behaviors are controlled by rewards and punishments, although in a very inconsistent and often illogical manner, or we establish a society in which these rewards and punishments are organized so that the behaviors of the individuals within the society are controlled for the good of the whole. Naturally, there are intermediate positions; but according to Skinner, we do not have the choice of whether or not we want to be controlled by conditioning. We are human and because of that we learn and we behave according to the principles of reinforcement.

It now seems clear that we are influenced greatly (perhaps even "controlled") by conditioning. The questions we should ask concern the use to which such conditioning principles should be put. We are all, according to Skinner, both objects of conditioning and agents of conditioning. Our behavior is controlled by the reinforcements of others and we, in turn, control the behaviors of others by the reinforcements we apply.

In Anthony Burgess' *A Clockwork Orange* we see the protagonist conditioned to the point where he becomes extremely ill when presented with scenes of violence—scenes in which he would have eagerly participated before this conditioning. So thorough is his conditioning that he is powerless to defend himself when attacked. This is perhaps conditioning in its extreme, but we need to examine similar situations and attempt to ferret out the significant issues they raise.

In mental institutions, conditioning is widely applied as a means of behavior control. For example, disruptive and self-destructive behavior may be severely punished in order to reduce it or perhaps eliminate it fully. Small children are at times so self-destructive that they will literally chew huge hunks of flesh out of their arms and legs. Presented with such extreme cases we may be willing to accept the application of conditioning principles to control such behavior. But would we be willing to accept its application in other situations?

One crime that is currently on the books in most states, if not all, is suicide. If an individual attempts to commit suicide he or she is generally judged insane. Such an individual could be conditioned to prevent another suicide attempt. Currently, we grant society this right; that is, we have granted society the right to judge a potential suicide victim insane and to apply whatever treatment it deems effective. But should an individual have the right to take his or her own life? And does society have the right to prevent someone and in effect force someone to learn, through conditioning, contrary behavior patterns?

One type of conditioning receiving a great deal of attention is *aversive conditioning.* In this procedure the individual goes through the particular behaviors the therapist wishes to eliminate and is administered some aversive stimulus (for example, an electric shock) while engaging in these behaviors. In relatively short order such behaviors are weakened or eliminated. In one widely publicized case a small child would not keep food in his system. Whatever he was fed, he would throw up. In this case conditioning was used. The infant was wired in such a way so that he would receive a severe electric shock whenever any muscular movements were made in the direction of throwing up after he was fed. Within a matter of days the child stopped throwing up his food and apparently is a healthy young boy today. This same general procedure is used on those who exhibit behavior that society has chosen to con-

---

Box 4
THE PROBLEM OF RESPONSIBILITY IN COMMUNICATIONS

Margaret Mead

It therefore seems that it is important to arrive at a phrasing of responsibility which will meet this fear of misused power and develop an ethic of communications within a democracy such as ours. Once a climate of opinion expressing such an ethic begins to develop, appropriate institutional forms may be expected to emerge, either slowly or under intensive cultivation.

Such an ethic might take the form of an insistence that the audience be seen as composed of *whole* individuals, not artificial cut outs from crowd scenes, such as are represented on the dust jacket of a recent book on radio. It might take the form of insisting that the audience be seen as composed of individuals who could not be manipulated but could only be appealed to in terms of their systematic cultural strengths. It might include a taboo on seeing any individual as the puppet of the propagandist, and focussing instead on the purposeful cultivation of directions of change. It would then be regarded as ethical to try to persuade the American people to drink orange juice, as a pleasant and nutritional drink, by establishing a style of breakfast, a visual preference for oranges, and a moral investment in good nutrition, but not by frightening individual mothers into serving orange juice for fear that they would lose their children's love, or their standing in the community.

Source: Margaret Mead, "Some Cultural Approaches to Communication Problems," in *The Communication of Ideas,* ed. L. Bryson (NY: Harper, 1948), p. 24.

demn (such as homosexuals). At times these individuals will put themselves under the care of such a conditioning therapist and with this we would probably not wish to quarrel. Clearly they have a right to attempt to change their behavior should they wish to. But at times no choice is given. In mental hospitals or prisons, people are sometimes forced to submit to such conditioning. And it does not really matter to the issues involved here whether they are conditioned by a trained psychologist or by an ignorant prison guard. Both are probably effective in altering the behavior. But the question is whether they should be in the position of administering such conditioning without the consent of the individual.

We might argue that such rights are granted to society for its own well-being and, in fact, preservation. This license to alter behavior is then granted for the good of the general population. This argument or reasoning may sound convincing until we recall that in the not so distant past this same argument was used for sterilization of "undesirables" and for the elimination of millions. True, the conditions and times are different now. But are they sufficiently different to risk allocating such great power to a relatively small group?

THE PREVENTION OF INTERACTION

There are laws in our society—sometimes ignored by the courts and sometimes applied to the letter—that prevent various interactions among adult citizens.

Among the most obvious of these are the laws prohibiting interracial marriage and the laws prohibiting homosexual relations. These laws literally prohibit certain groups of persons from interacting in the manner in which they wish. If an interracial couple wishes to get married, the state in which such a marriage is performed must be chosen carefully. But perhaps more important than the actual laws are the societal codes, which are unwritten but which are prohibitive in a much more insidious way. Interracial couples will run into difficulty in finding housing, employment, and, most significantly, acceptance into a community. Likewise, homosexuals will have difficulty in much the same way, and consequently, many of them are forced to live "straight" lives—at least on the surface.

If you run a business, for example, should you have the right to refuse a job to a person because that person is married to an individual of another race or because that person prefers to interact sexually with persons of the same sex? And if you do have the right to choose your employees on the basis of such preferences, do you still retain the rights to protection of the law which the society as a whole has granted to everyone?

Homosexuals are currently prevented from holding jobs as teachers, policemen, firemen, and so forth, in most states. These discriminatory laws are not terribly effective. But this not the issue. The relative ineffectiveness of such prohibitions should not blind us to the social realities that these laws incorporate. What should be considered is that the homosexual teacher, for example, cannot teach as a homosexual but only as a heterosexual. The teacher is permitted to teach only if he or she—at least on the surface—denies the fact of his or her homosexuality and behaves as a heterosexual. We do not ask that a black teacher act white—although society once did demand this in often subtle ways. We do not ask a Jew to act like a Christian or a Christian to act like a Jew if he or she wants a job—although, again, some persons do. Yet, we do ask homosexuals that they not reveal their true identity. These persons are only accepted if they act like the majority. But are we being fair when we ask for such concealment of identity?

Take a somewhat different example. A mother of a student recently found birth control pills in her daughter's dresser. The mother was incensed and said, "You don't use these." The young woman confessed that she did, in fact, use them. "No, you don't use them," said the mother, "and I don't ever want to hear about them again." And out of the room she stomped. This act—in somewhat different form—is a frequentlly occurring one. The mother, because she could not approve of her daughter's behavior, attempted to prevent her sexual interaction.

There are, of course, many different issues which such prohibitions of interactions raise. But I think the central issue they raise is whether any one group—however large and however sanctioned by state or church—has the right to set down rules of behavior for others and to literally prevent them from their own self-actualization. It is no wonder that so many interracial marriages end in divorce, that so many homosexuals are unhappy, and that suicide is one of the major causes of death among college students. In fact, in January 1975 an Associated Press article noted that teenage suicides are now at 30 per day and that more than 50 percent of the patients in psychiatric hospitals are under twenty-one years of age. Is society fostering marital discontent, homosexual unhappiness, and student despair by preventing people from being themselves, from interacting as they wish, from presenting themselves to others as they feel they really are? Lest we all ease our consciences too easily, let us recognize that it is we who constitute this "society," and it is we who give it the power it has—the very power we may deplore as we sit comfortably in the camp of the sanctioned majority.

SOURCES

On communication and ethics see Thomas R. Nilsen, *Ethics of Speech Communication,* 2d ed. (Indianapolis: Bobbs-Merrill, 1974), Richard L. Johannesen, *Ethics in Human Communication* (Columbus, Ohio: Charles E. Merrill, 1975), and R. Johannesen, ed., *Ethics and Persuasion: Selected Readings* (New York: Random, 1967). For ghostwriting, see especially Ernest G. Bormann, "Ethics of Ghostwritten Speeches," *Quarterly Journal of Speech* 47 (1961):

262–267. The discussion in this unit owes much to this Bormann article. Franklyn S. Haiman's "Democratic Ethics and the Hidden Persuaders," *Quarterly Journal of Speech* 44 (1958):385–393 is particularly relevant to this unit. An interesting and relevant discussion of academic freedom is presented in David Rubin's *The Rights of Teachers* (New York: Avon, 1972). For a discussion of ethics as related to efficiency see Robert T. Oliver, "Ethics and Efficiency in Persuasion," *Southern Speech Journal* 26 (1960):10–15. Ethical considerations and how they relate to language is covered in Jane Blankenship, *A Sense of Style* (Belmont, Cal.: Dickenson, 1968). Also see Franklyn S. Haiman's "The Rhetoric of the Streets: Some Legal and Ethical Considerations," *Quarterly Journal of Speech* 53 (1967):99–114. Patricia Niles Middlebrook (*Social Psychology and Modern Life* [New York: Knopf, 1974]), in her discussion of the emotional approach to changing attitudes and her thorough treatment of intensive indoctrination, provides a clear analysis of the effectiveness of these techniques. You may wish to read these two discussions with the issues of ethics we raised here in mind.

EXPERIENTIAL VEHICLES

7.1 ETHICAL PRINCIPLES

Complete the following statements as you would have them read for an ideal society.

1. Censorship should be instituted under the following conditions: . . . . .
2. Ghostwriting should be considered justified when . . .
3. Conditioning should be utilized by social institutions because . . .
4. Parents and society generally should prevent interactions between or among . . . , under the following circumstances: . . . .

After each student has completed these four statements a number of different procedures may be followed. One procedure is to divide up into small groups of five or six and discuss the various completions. The groups might then attempt to construct a compromise statement for each of the four areas in a manner not unlike that which would be followed by government committees. Another procedure is simply to discuss the statements with the class as a whole, again attempting to formulate some general statements that everyone can live with. A third procedure is to collect the various statements (without names on them) and read them aloud to the entire class. The problems and/or advantages of each statement or each type of statement may then be considered.

7.2 SOME QUESTIONS OF ETHICS

This exercise is designed to raise only a few of the many questions that could be raised concerning the ethics of communication, and to encourage you to think in concrete terms about some of the relevant issues. The purpose is not to persuade you to a particular point of view but rather to encourage you to formulate your own point of view.

The exercises consist of a series of cases, each raising somewhat different ethical questions. These exercises will probably work best if you respond to each of the cases individually and then discuss your decisions and the implications in groups of five or six. In these small groups simply discuss those cases that you found most interesting. The most interesting cases for small group discussion will probably be those that were the most difficult for you to respond to, that is, those that involved the most internal conflict. A general discussion in which the various groups share their decisions and insights may conclude the session.

As an experience in self-disclosure and perception the group members may attempt to guess what each individual would do in each of these specific situations. Reasons for their choices or guesses would then be considered; for example, what led the group to guess that Person X would act one way rather than another way? Reasons for the accurate and/or inaccurate guesses might then be discussed.

Guidelines

1. Carefully read each of the following cases and write down your responses. By writing your decisions many issues that may be unclear will come to the surface and may then be used as a basis for discussion.
2. Your responses will not be made public, these papers will not be collected, and your decisions will be revealed only if you wish to reveal them. If individuals wish not to reveal their decisions, do not attempt to apply any social pressure to get them to make these decisions public.
3. Do not attempt to avoid the issues presented in the various cases by saying, for example, "I'd try other means." For purposes of these exercises "other means" are ruled out.
4. In the small group discussions focus some attention on the origin of the various values implicit in your decisions. You might, as a starting point, consider how your parents would respond to these cases. Would their decisions be similar or different from yours? Do not settle for "conditioning" as an answer. If you wish to discuss the development of these values in terms of conditioning, focus on specific reinforcement contingencies, the rewards and punishments received which may have led to the development of these various values.
5. Devote some attention to the concept of change. Would you have responded in similar fashion five years ago? If not, what has led to the change? Would you predict similar responses five or ten years from now? Why? Why not? This concept of change is also significant in another respect. Focus attention on the changes or possible changes that might occur as a result of your acting in accordance with any of the decisions. That is, is the student who sells drugs the same indivdual he or she was before doing this? Can this student ever be the same individual again? How is the student different? If we accept the notion, even in part, that how we act or behave influences what we are, how does this relate to the decisions we make on these issues?
6. Consider the concept of acceptance. How willing is each group member to accept the decisions of others? Are you accepting of your own decisions? Why? Why not? Would you be pleased if your children would respond in the same way you did?
7. Note that there are two questions posed after each case: What *should* you do? and What *would* you do? The distinction between the two questions is crucial and is particularly significant when your answers for the two ques-

tions are different. When answers for the *should* and the *would* questions differ, try to analyze the intrapersonal dynamics. How do you account for the difference? Is there intrapersonal conflict? Are these differences the result of changes you are going through? How pleased/displeased are you with the differences in answers?

GHOSTING

You are a capable and proficient writer and speaker and have, for the past three years, worked full time for a large political organization as a ghostwriter. During these three years you have prepared papers for publication and speeches to be delivered by the various officers of the organization. Throughout this time you have been firmly committed to the aims and methods of the organization. Consequently, no problem arose. You were serving your political party by making their appeals and policies more persuasive, in addition to earning an extremely high salary as a ghostwriter. Recently, however, the party has decided to endorse a bill which you feel would not be in the public interest. On this issue your attitudes are diametrically opposed to those of the party. As ghostwriter for the organization you are asked to speak in favor of this bill. These informal talks are to be held throughout the state. You realize that if you do not comply you will lose your job. At the time, however, you wonder if you can ethically give persuasive force to a proposal which you feel should not be supported. Not being effective in these interpersonal encounters will not work since you would be fired after one such interaction.

1. What should you do?
2. What would you do?

BUYING A PAPER

You are presently taking an elective course in anthropology. You need an "A" in this course in order to maintain the average you think you will need to get into graduate school. Although you have done the required work you are running only a "B—" at best. The instructor has told you that he will give you an "A" if you write an extra paper and get an "A" on it. You want to write this paper but are too pressed for time; you need to put what time you do have available into your major courses. You hear about one of the "paper mills" which, for approximately $50, will provide you with a paper that should get you an "A" in the course. You can easily afford the $50 fee.

1. What should you do?
2. What would you do?

THE CHILDREN'S HOSPITAL

You have been put in charge of raising money for your town's new children's hospital—a hospital that is badly needed. There are a number of crippled children who are presently wearing heavy braces and who must walk with crutches.

These children, you reason, would be very effective in influencing people to give to the hospital fund. As a conclusion to a program of speeches by local officials and entertainment you consider having these children walk through the audience and tell the people how desperately they need this hospital. An appeal by these children, you feel, would encourage many of the people to make donations which they would not make if a more reasoned and logical appeal was presented. You know from past experience that other available means of persuasion will not be effective.

1. What should you do?
2. What would you do?

BECOMING A STAR

You are being tested for the lead role in an important new movie. You very much want this part since you know that it will make you a major star, something you have worked extremely hard to achieve. The old stories you have heard about "couch casting" now become a reality. The producer has indicated that the part is yours should you agree to become sexually familiar. The contracts would not be drawn up for at least a week or two. During this time you would be expected to move in with the producer. After the contracts are signed both you and the producer know that you become a free agent. This is presented to you as a business arrangement; no long-term emotional commitments or attachments are expected or desired by the producer. If you do not agree to the producer's terms the part will go to someone else.

1. What should you do (if the producer were a person of the preferred sex)?
2. What should you do (if the producer were a person of the unpreferred sex)?
3. What would you do (if the producer were a person of the preferred sex)?
4. What would you do (if the producer were a person of the unpreferred sex)?

SCHOLARSHIP COMPETITION

You are competing with a fellow student for a full scholarship to law school. Both of you need the scholarship and both of you seem to deserve it equally— your grades, service to the school and community, law board scores, and so on are about the same. Unfortunately, there is only one scholarship to be awarded. The committee charged with selecting the winner is a most conservative group and would vote against candidates should they find out anything about their personal lives of which they would disapprove. You have recently learned that your competitor is an ex-convict. You could easily leak this information to the committee in which case you would surely get the scholarship. No one (not even the members of the committee) would know that you were the source of this information.

1. What should you do?
2. What would you do?

7.3 A TENTATIVE THEORY OF COMMUNICATION ETHICS

Formulate here what might be called, "My Tentative Theory of the Ethics of Communication." Formulate a theory that you feel is reasonable, justified, internally consistent, and consonant with your own system of values. Construct your theory so that it incorporates at least all of the situations presented in the previous exercise. That is, given this statement of ethical principles another individual should be able to accurately predict how you would behave in each of the situations presented in the cases in Experiential Vehicle 7.2.

PART TWO
Communication Messages

art Two focuses on verbal and nonverbal messages, their nature, their reception, and their effects. The first two units deal with the ways in which we respond to people and their messages, that is, to communicators and to communications. Our responses to people are discussed in Unit 8, "Perception in Communication" and our responses to messages are discussed in Unit 9, "Listening in Communication." As will be apparent throughout these two units, it is a great deal easier to separate these two processes verbally than in reality; in reality one could never hope to separate the communicator from the communication. *Perception* and *listening* are discussed first because it will be particularly helpful to understand our general response tendencies and the ways in which these responses can be made more effective before we consider specific types of messages. The processes of perception and listening should be kept clearly in mind throughout our consideration of messages (Units 10–15).

Communication takes place through the exchange of both verbal and nonverbal symbols. When we talk we also gesture; when we compliment someone we also smile; and when we verbalize fear our eyes and our entire body echo our words. For convenience, however, we will separate verbal and nonverbal messages. In Unit 10, "Verbal Interaction: Nine Principles," some general properties of *verbal messages* are discussed. These nine principles detail significant characteristics of verbal messages that will guide you in understanding the structure and the functions of all verbal messages. Unit 11, "Verbal Interaction: Six Barriers," focuses on some of the potential barriers to mutual understanding and how they might be eliminated or at least reduced. Together these two units provide both the theoretical insights for understanding and the practical guidelines for improving our verbal communications.

From verbal messages we proceed naturally to *nonverbal messages*. In Unit 12, "Characteristics of Nonverbal Messages," we focus on five general properties of nonverbal messages (communicative, contextual, believable, packaged, and metacommunicational). These properties should provide a framework for considering the major forms of nonverbal messages: *kinesics* or body communication (Unit 13), *proxemics* or spatial communication (Unit 14), and *paralanguage* (Unit 15). Along with these major forms we also explain other carriers of nonverbal messages, such as body type and touch.

Communication would not exist without the desire to alter attitudes and behaviors. That is, a message is communicated for one or more purposes. Unit 16, "Attitudes in Communication," and Unit 17, "Attitude and Behavior Change" deal with matters prefatory to the consideration of these specific purposes, namely the general issues of attitudes and their relationship to behavior and how attitudes and behaviors are changed. (The more specific purposes are considered in Part Three.) The issue of change is approached from two different points of view: one is purely behavioral, the other cognitive. By juxtaposing these alternative explanations of the ways attitudes and behaviors are changed, I hope to make clear that both approaches are useful for understanding communication.

The following ten units, then, should provide you with insight into three related areas concerned with messages: (1) the way in which a message is received (perception and listening); (2) the actual verbal and nonverbal message; and (3) the effect a message can have on attitudes and behaviors.

With this as a background we will be able to focus on the major contexts of communication—the substance of Part Three.

UNIT 8
Perception
in Communication

Stages in the Perception Process
Perceptual Judgments
Perceptual Processes

8.1 Perceiving My Selves
8.2 Perceiving Others
8.3 Perceiving a Stranger

LEARNING GOALS

After completing this unit, you should be able to:

1. define *perception*
2. explain the three stages in the perception process
3. distinguish between *static* and *dynamic judgments*
4. define and supply at least one example of each of the three principles of perception
5. define and supply at least one example of each of the three bases for judgment
6. explain the influence of the following variables on accuracy in perception: age, sex, intelligence, cognitive complexity, popularity, personality characteristics, effects of training
7. recognize the bases for our own judgments of people
8. define *primacy* and *recency*
9. explain the influence of primacy-recency on perception
10. define the *self-fulfilling prophecy*
11. explain the influence of the self-fulfilling prophecy on perception
12. define *perceptual accentuation*
13. explain the influence of perceptual accentuation on perception
14. define an *implicit personality theory*
15. state at least three propositions that are part of your own implicit personality theory
16. explain the influence of an implicit personality theory on perception
17. define *consistency*

18. explain the influence of consistency on perception
19. define *stereotype*
20. explain the influence of stereotyping on perception
21. recognize the different ways in which you perceive and are perceived by others

Perception is the process by which we become aware of objects and events in the external world through our various senses: sight, smell, taste, touch, and hearing. Perception is an active rather than a passive process. Our perceptions are only in part a function of the outside world; in large measure they are a function of our own past experiences, our desires, our needs and wants, our loves and hatreds. Hans Toch and Malcolm MacLean express the essence of this transactional view of perception most clearly. "Each percept [that which is perceived]," note Toch and MacLean, "from the simplest to the most complex, is the product of a creative act. . . . We can never encounter a stimulus before some meaning has been assigned to it by some perceiver. . . . Therefore, each perception is the beneficiary of all previous perceptions; in turn, each new perception leaves its mark on the common pool. A percept is thus a link between the past which gives it its meaning and the future which it helps to interpret."

In communication we are particularly concerned with that area of perception that focuses on people, often called people perception or interpersonal perception, and the judgments we make about them.

STAGES IN THE PERCEPTION PROCESS

Before we explain person perception, some understanding of the general nature of the process of perception seems essential. For convenience, we might consider the process of perception as occurring in three stages or steps. These stages are not discrete and separate as the discussion might imply; in reality they are continuous and blend into one another.

Sensory Stimulation Occurs

At this first stage the sense organs are stimulated—we hear Donna Summer's "Try Me," we see someone we have not seen for years, we smell perfume on the person next to us, we taste a juicy steak, we feel a sweaty palm as we shake hands.

We all have different abilities to hear, see, smell, taste, and feel. Some people can hear very high-pitched sounds whereas others cannot. Similarly, some can see great distances whereas others have trouble seeing ten feet away.

Even when we have the sensory ability to perceive stimuli we do not always do so. For example, when you are daydreaming in class you do not hear what the teacher is saying until your own name is called. Then you wake up. You know your name was called but you do not know why. This is a clear and perhaps too frequent example of our perceiving what is meaningful to us and not perceiving what is not meaningful (or at least what we now judge to be not meaningful).

Perhaps the most obvious implication to be drawn from this stage of the perceptual process is that what we do perceive is only a very small portion of what could be perceived. Much as we have limits on how far we can see, we also have limits on the quantity of stimulation that we can take in at any given time. When we walk down a street we see a great number of things but we fail to see even more. Similarly, we hear the teacher calling our name but fail to hear the birds sing, the student next to us chew gum, the folding of papers, the tapping of the foot, the whispers of the student behind us, the sound of the chalk on the board (unless it squeaks), and so on. One of the goals of education, or so it would seem, is to train us to perceive more of what exists whether it be art, politics, music, communication, social problems, or any other conceivable source of sensory stimulation.

Sensory Stimulation Is Organized

At the second stage the sensory stimulations are organized in some way and according to some principles. Exactly how our sensory stimulations are organized and what principles such organization follow is not always agreed upon. But the principles of perceptual organization put forth by the Gestalt psychologists seem to offer perhaps the best beginning. Generally, four principles are considered.

Proximity and Resemblance

Stimuli that occur close to each other or that resemble each other are generally grouped together and are considered a whole. Those stimuli that are more physically separated are considered as being apart, as different, and as belonging to some other grouping.

Good Form

According to the Gestalt psychologists the perception of good form is evidenced by continuation and symmetry. Visualize two series of dots. In the first, the dots occur in a row or in a column. Here our eye would perceive the dots as having continuation—one dot is perceived as following another and so on. We perceive some system, some order to the arrangement. In the second, the dots occur randomly. Here we would find no continuation and hence no "good form." Perhaps the clearest example of symmetry is a figure that is identical on all sides, for example, a circle or a square. Asymmetrical or irregular figures, on the other hand, are not considered good form.   *balance*

Closure

This is perhaps the most well known of all the Gestalt principles of organization and refers to the tendency to perceive as closed or complete a figure that is in reality unclosed or incomplete. For example, a broken circle will be perceived as a circle even though part of it is missing. Even a series of dots or dashes arranged in a circular pattern will be perceived as a circle. In language we see the same principle operate when we fill in sentences containing missing words or when we listen to speech and unconsciously fill in a word that may have been omitted by the speaker or drowned out by some outside noise.

Common Fate

Figures possessing common fate appear to us to be moving in the same direction, for example, two lines moving left to right or two or more series of dots going from top to bottom.

Sensory Stimulation Is Interpreted-Evaluated

The third step in the perceptual process is interpretation-evaluation, a term which we hyphenate and consider together to emphasize that in reality they cannot be separated. This third step is inevitably a subjective process involving evaluations on the part of the perceiver. Our interpretations-evaluations, then, are not based solely on the external stimulus but rather are greatly influenced by past experiences, our needs, our wants, our value systems, our beliefs about the way things are or should be, our physical or emotional states at the time, our expectations, and so on. It should be clear from even this very incomplete list of influences that there is here great room for disagreements between and among people. Although we may all be exposed to the same external stimulus, the way it is interpreted-evaluated will differ with each person and from one time to another for the same person. We may both hear Donna Summer but one person may say it is terrible and the other say it is great. The sight of someone we have not seen for years may bring joy to one person and anxiety to another. The smell of perfume may be pleasant to one person and repulsive to another. The taste of a juicy steak may make one person feel great and the other person choke. A sweaty palm may be perceived by one person to indicate nervousness and by another to indicate excitement.

PERCEPTUAL JUDGMENTS

Types of Judgments

Static judgments refer to those characteristics of another person that are relatively unchanging. Judgments of such characteristics as race, occupation, age, or nationality would be examples of static judgments, since these characteristics are relatively enduring. We often also make judgments about an individual's habitual response to specific situations. For example, such statements as "He's a soft touch when anyone needs help," or, "She drives carefully," or, "He eats well," represent static judgments. Similarly, we make judgments concerning an individual's general behavior without regard to specific situations. Examples include the statement that an individual is quick tempered, that he or she is extroverted, or that he or she is mercenary. We also make numerous general *sociometric judgments.* These are judgments concerning relations among people, for example, "He loves her," "She hates her brother," or "The children are afraid of their father." All of these are static judgments since they refer to lasting or habitual characteristics.

Dynamic judgments, on the other hand, refer to the characteristics of other people that change more rapidly. One type of dynamic judgment would concern the specific response of an individual, for example, "He wants to leave the party," "She is having a good time," or "He is tired." These are judgments concerning a specific situation at a specific time. Judgments of affect would also be of the dynamic type. We can, for example, judge the moods of different people ("He is afraid," "She is happy," "He is in love"). A final type is what Mark Cook calls *regulation judgments.* These judgments refer to the behavior of people in social situations. For example, when we are in a group we do not talk when someone else is talking (at least not usually). When that person has finished we may make a regulation judgment that it is proper for us to talk now. We also make regulation judgments about the type of social situation we are in. Consequently, we regulate the topics and the language that might be appropriate or inappropriate. At a family dinner we would probably not talk about the same things or speak in the same way as we would in a locker room. These social-type judgments allow us to regulate appropriate behavior.

Three Principles of Perception

Psychologists once thought that if one wanted to understand perception all one had to do was study the stimuli being perceived. If these stimuli were analyzed fully and accurately enough, perception would be explained. The role of the perceiver in the process of perception was ignored.

Few psychological processes are that simple, and perception is no exception. In order to understand perception we need to understand some of the principles or "rules" that perceptual processes seem to follow. The three noted here seem among the most important for communication: *subjectivity, stability* and *meaningfulness.*

Subjectivity

Perception is an active rather than a passive process. We do not perceive the world unfiltered and in pure form; rather, we actively interact with the world as we perceive it. To a great extent we actually create the perceptions we have. Consequently, we will often perceive what we expect to perceive or what we want to perceive.

In perceiving people we do not simply perceive their individual bits of behaviors; we perceive some structured whole. In interpersonal or people perception, then, our expectations and our wants or needs will be particularly important. We may, for example, have been told that Jack is honest and warm and that Bill is dishonest and cold. If we then observe the exact same behaviors of these two individuals we would probably perceive them in very different ways depending upon our previous conceptions of what these people are like.

"Beauty is in the eye of the beholder," the old saying goes, and in terms of perception theory it clearly is. That is why the same individual can be perceived as ugly by one person and as beautiful by another, why the same person can be perceived as humorous by one and as "sick" by the other, why the same person can be perceived as "encouraging students to use their full potential" by one and as "unrealistic in his or her demands" by another.

Stability

In order to better understand the concept of *stability* (or invariance), focus on an object at least twenty feet away, say a picture or a book or a person. Now walk toward that object until you are a foot or less away. Physically, of course, the object did not change in size; it also did not change in size psychologically, despite the fact that the size of the image on the retina changed drastically as you approached it. Psychologically, we adjust our perceptions because we ''know'' from past experiences that things do not change in size as we get closer. We know how to adjust our perceptions of size on the basis of the retinal image, distance, and object size.

In people perception we function in a very similar way. We perceive various behaviors of a friend as that friend is talking with a group of people. Naturally, this friend has never acted in this exact way before; no behaviors are ever repeated exactly. We do not focus our attention on the specific bits of behaviors but on those aspects which are more or less unchanging, for example, his or her purposes, motivations, values. Consequently, our perception of these behaviors is relatively stable; we see the behavior of our friend as being consistent with our previous conceptions.

Assume, for a moment that you know several people who seem constantly to be praising themselves. At every turn they tell you how great they are. You might then label them as ''egomaniacs'' or ''egocentrics.'' Now notice what effect that label will have on your perception of the future behaviors of these individuals. Upon seeing them again, the easiest way to structure your perception and make sense of it is to categorize it as egomaniacal. In doing this you are assuming that there is a certain stability to people's behavior and that there is a certain degree of invariance.

Meaningfulness

One of the best ways of appreciating the principle of meaningfulness is to view a film of a dream sequence that is—at least at the time of viewing— without any meaning. Things seem to happen without cause and without expected effect. We sit there and wonder what we are seeing. We have difficulty perceiving this kind of presentation because the assumed meaningfulness of people is absent.

Generally, we assume that people are sensible and that their behaviors stem from some logical antecedent. We assume, in other words, a certain degree of predictability in other people's behavior. We assume that they will be consistent from one occasion to another, or at least relatively so.

If you are sitting in a classroom and a student raises his or her hand you perceive him or her to have a question. Logically, of course, there could be any number of reasons for a student's hand being up. If that same behavior were evidenced at a football game or while swimming or while cooking you would perceive the raised hand as having a different meaning. Thus we attribute to the behavior a meaning that is sensible in the context in which it occurs.

In any people perception experience these three principles of subjectivity, stability, and meaningfulness will operate with varying degrees of influence.

And people differ in the extent to which they are subjective or the extent to which they seek stability or meaningfulness. These principles, although always present, influence the people perception process in different ways and to different extents depending upon the perceiver and the perceived.

Bases for Judgments

The judgments that we make about other people are based on behaviors (or appearance) of the individual and some rule or rules that link that behavior with some type of judgment. For example, we see a person with thick glasses and conclude that he or she is studious. To make that judgment ("studious"), however, we must have, somewhere in our perceptual system, a rule that goes something like this: "Persons who wear thick glasses are studious."

The question we need to ask now is how we acquire the rules we have, that is, how did the rules develop. Generally such rules are derived from experience, analogy, and/or authority (Figure 8.1).

Experience

Perhaps the most obvious ways to formulate rules about people and their characteristics is from experience. This experience may be derived from our own personal interactions or it may be from the interactions of others that we observe either in reality or in fiction (radio, television, movies, novels).

Analogy

Another way of formulating rules is on the basis of analogy. We assume that person X will respond in a particular way because person Y, who is similar to person X, has responded in this way. Such analogies are perhaps most often formed on the basis of one's own behavior but are also formed on the basis of the behavior of one's friends, one's family, and one's heroes.

Thus, for example, if I as a teacher were to assume the role of mediator with

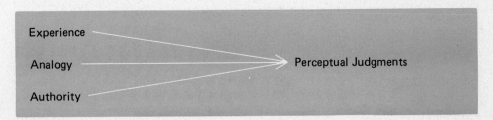

Figure 8.1
The Bases for Judgments

a group of arguing students I might then infer that another teacher would also assume the role of mediator given a similar situation. My implicit rule might be something like: "Teachers, when with a group of arguing students, will assume mediator roles." Very often when we are trying to predict how another individual will react we attempt to reason by analogy and ask, "What would I do in this situation?" The assumption here is that other people act as we do.

Authority

When we were growing up we learned a great many rules from our parents about other people and about the ways in which they behave. Depending upon the orientation of the family, these rules might have been in the form of traditional stereotypes about various racial, religious, and national groups or perhaps in the form of suggested modes of behavior. For example, we might have learned that "all foreigners are untrustworthy," "all Americans are materialistic," "all Italians are religious," and so on. Or we might have learned such rules as, "people who study hard will achieve success," or, "honest people will come out ahead in the long run," and so on.

In many instances (and probably in most), our judgments are made on the basis of some complex system of rules derived from all three sources rather than from just one. Thus, for example, you may see a person from your home town and make some kind of judgment. That judgment would be based on rules derived from your experience with home town people, from an analogy with your own behavior or general response tendency, or from something you learned when you were young or something you read or heard from an authoritative source.

It is not possible to examine a judgment and discover the specific basis for the rules that were used to formulate that judgment. But by being aware of the ways in which such rules are formed, we are in a better position to examine the judgments we make, and to evaluate and perhaps revise them.

Accuracy in Perception

Children can tell what a person is really like, even though adults might have
    difficulty.
Women are just naturally better judges of people than men.
He or she is so popular with everyone; he or she must be an excellent judge
    of people.
After going on an encounter weekend we should be able to judge people
    more accurately.

These and perhaps various other types of statements reflect our concern with accuracy in people perception. Some of these statements seem logical on the basis of our experience. Some seem logical because of some rule of analogy—we went on an encounter weekend, improved our accuracy, and therefore conclude that encounter improves perception accuracy for people in general. Some seem logical because some authority told us so.

Actually much experimental research, clearly synthesized by Mark Cook, has been directed at testing these and similar statements to determine the characteristics of persons who are particularly accurate in people perception. Some of the more prominent factors or variables are noted here.

Age

Contrary to the popular notion that children can tell what a person is really thinking or really like, accuracy in people perception increases with age rather than decreases. For example, it has been found that judgments of emotion from facial and vocal cues, as well as sociometric judgments, increase in accuracy with age.

Sex

The popular notion that women are more accurate interpersonal perceivers than men has some—but not overwhelming—support. Differences on the basis of sex have not been found in most sudies. In the few studies that have found differences, women have performed at a slightly better level than men.

Intelligence

Generally, the more intelligent the person the better he or she is at accurately judging other people. This variable of intelligence is probably closely related to that of cognitive complexity.

Cognitive Complexity

Individuals who are "cognitively complex" are those who have a great number of concepts for describing people and are generally better at judging others than are those of less cognitive complexity. These cognitively complex individuals differentiate more finely and will not group people together as much as will those with less cognitive complexity.

Popularity

It is generally assumed that people who are popular and socially favored have achieved their standing because they are accurate judges of people. A number of studies have sought to investigate this but no definite conclusions seem warranted. At times, of course, accurate perception may prove a hindrance to popularity if this skill enables the individual to see all the faults in others. On the other hand, if it gives an individual better insight into other people, then it probably functions to improve social relationships.

Personality Characteristics

A great deal of research has focused on the personality characteristics of accurate perceivers. Are accurate perceivers more sociable or less sociable, more empirically oriented or less empirically oriented, more independent or more dependent? Here there is much confusion. Generally the personality characteristics of accurate judges include sociability, toughmindedness, empiricism, nonconformity, independence, strong will, and dominance. When the sex of the judge is controlled, however, a somewhat different picture emerges. "The picture of the good male judge that emerges," says Cook, "is rather unexpected. The good male judge of males is described as a rather insensitive, aggressive person while the good male judge of females is described as very ineffectual. The good female judges are described slightly more favorably."

Effects of Training

It is generally assumed that training will increase one's ability at almost anything. We seem to have an undying faith in the ability of individuals to be educated to the point where they can do just about anything. With people perception, however, training has not been found to be effective, at least not generally. People perception has been improved when judges were given immediate knowledge of results, but T-groups and clinical training, for example, have not resulted in improved perception. It should be noted that such training does provide people with a host of new labels and terms, and this makes it appear that their accuracy has improved. Actually, however, it has not. Or so say the experimental studies.

PERCEPTUAL PROCESSES

People, or interpersonal, perception is an extremely complex affair. Perhaps the best way to explain some of these complexities is to examine at least some of the psychological processes involved in people perception (Figure 8.2).

Primacy–Recency

Assume for a moment that you were enrolled in a course in which half the classes were extremely dull and half the classes were extremely exciting. At the end of the semester you are to evaluate the course and the instructor. Would the evaluation be more favorable if the dull classes constituted the first

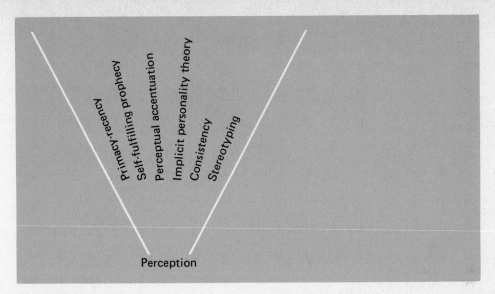

Figure 8.2
Perceptual Processes

half of the semester and the exciting classes constituted the second half of the semester or if the order were reversed? If what comes first exerts the most influence, we have what is called a *primacy effect.* If what comes last (or is the most recent) exerts the most influence, we have a *recency effect.*

In an early study on the effects of primacy-recency in people perception Solomon Asch read a list of adjectives describing a person to a group of subjects and found that the effects of order were significant. A person described as "intelligent, industrious, impulsive, critical, stubborn, and envious" was evaluated as more positive than a person described as "envious, stubborn, critical, impulsive, industrious, and intelligent." The implication here is that we utilize early information to provide us with a general idea as to what a person is like, and we utilize the later information to make this general idea or impression more specific. Numerous other studies have provided evidence for the effect of first impressions. For example, in one study subjects observed a student (actually a confederate of the experimenter) taking a test. The task of the subject was to estimate the number of questions the student got right and to predict how well the student would do on a second trial. The confederate followed two different orders. In one order, the descending order, the correct answers were all in the beginning. In the ascending order, the correct answers were toward the end. In each case, of course, there were the same number correct and incorrect. Subjects judged the descending order to contain more correct responses. They also estimated that students in the descending order would do better on a second trial and judged them to be more intelligent.

Self-Fulfilling Prophecy

Perhaps the most widely known example of the self-fulfilling prophecy is the *pygmalian effect,* now widely popularized. Basically, teachers were told that certain pupils were expected to do exceptionally well—that they were late bloomers. However, the names of these students were selected at random by the experimenters. The results were not random. Those students whose names were given to the teachers actually did perform at a higher level than did the other students. In fact, these students even improved in I.Q. scores more than did the other students.

Eric Berne in *Games People Play* and Thomas Harris in *I'm O.K., You're O.K.* both point out the same type of effect but in a somewhat different context. These transactional psychologists argue that we live by scripts which are given to us by our parents and that we essentially act in the way in which we are told to act. Much like the children who were expected to do well, we all, according to transactional psychology, live by the scripts given to us as children.

Consider, for example, people who enter a group situation convinced that the other members will dislike them. Almost invariably they are proven right; the other members do dislike them. What they may be doing is acting in such a way as to encourage people to respond negatively. Or similarly, when we enter a classroom and prophesize that it will be a dull class, it turns out, more often than not, to be a dull class. Now it might be that it was in fact a dull class. But it might also be that we defined it as dull and hence made it dull; we made a prophecy and then fulfilled it.

Perceptual Accentuation

"Any port in a storm" is a common enough phrase that, in its variants, appears throughout our communications. To many, even an ugly date is better than no date at all. Spinach may taste horrible but when you are starving, it can taste like filet mignon. And so it goes.

In what may be the classic study on need influencing perception, poor and rich children were shown pictures of coins and later asked to estimate their size. The poor children estimated the size as much greater than did the rich children. Similarly, hungry people perceive food objects and food terms at lower recognition thresholds (needing fewer physical cues) than people who are not hungry.

In terms of people perception, this process, called *perceptual accentuation,* leads us to see what we expect to see and what we want to see. We see people we like as being better looking than people we do not like; we see people we like as being smarter than people we do not like. The obvious counter-argument to this is that we actually prefer good-looking and smart people—not that people whom we like are seen as being handsome and smart. But perhaps that is not the entire story.

As Zick Rubin describes it, male undergraduates, for example, participated in what they thought were two separate and unrelated studies; it was actually two parts of a single experiment. In the first part each subject read a passage; half the subjects were given an arousing sexual seduction scene to read, and half were given a passage about seagulls and herring gulls. In the second part of the experiment, subjects were asked to rate a female student on the basis of her photograph and a self-description. As might be expected, the subjects who read the arousing scene rated the woman as significantly more attractive than did the other group. Further, the subjects who expected to go on a blind date with this woman rated her more sexually receptive than did the subjects who were told that they had been assigned to date someone else. How can we account for such findings?

Although this experiment was a particularly dramatic demonstration of perceptual accentuation, this same general process occurs every day. We magnify or accentuate that which will satisfy our needs and wants. The thirsty person sees a mirage of water, the sexually deprived person sees a mirage of sexual satisfaction, and only very rarely do they get mixed up.

Implicit Personality Theory

We each have a theory of personality. Although we may not be able to verbalize it, we nevertheless have the rules or systems that constitute a theory of personality. More specifically, we have a system of rules that tells us which characteristics of an individual go with which other characteristics. Consider, for example, the following brief statements. Note the characteristic in parentheses that best seems to complete the sentence:

John is energetic, eager, and (intelligent, stupid).
Joe is bright, lively, and (thin, fat).
Jim is handsome, tall, and (flabby, muscular).
Jane is attractive, intelligent, and (likeable, unlikeable).
Mary is bold, defiant, and (extroverted, introverted).
Susan is cheerful, positive, and (attractive, unattractive).

It is not important which words you selected. And certainly there are no right or wrong answers. What should be observed, however, is that certain of the words "seemed right" and others "seemed wrong." What made some seem right was our implicit personality theory, the system of rules that tells us which characteristics go with which other characteristics. The theory tells us that a person who is energetic and eager is also intelligent, not stupid, although there is no logical reason why a stupid person could not be energetic and eager.

Consistency

There is a rather strong tendency to maintain balance or consistency among our perceptions. As so many of the current theories of attitude change demonstrate, we strive to maintain balance among our attitudes; we expect certain things to go together and other things not to go together. On a purely intuitive basis, for example, respond to the following sentences by noting the expected response.

1. I expect a person I like to (like, dislike) me.
2. I expect a person I dislike to (like, dislike) me.
3. I expect my friend to (like, dislike) my friend.
4. I expect my friend to (like, dislike) my enemy.
5. I expect my enemy to (like, dislike) my friend.
6. I expect my enemy to (like, dislike) my enemy.

According to most consistency theories, our expectations would be as follows: We would expect a person we liked to like us (1) and a person we disliked to dislike us (2). We would expect a friend to like a friend (3) and to dislike an enemy (4). We would expect our enemy to dislike our friend (5) and to like our other enemy (6). All of these—with the possible exception of the last one—should be intuitively satisfying. With some reflection even the last (6) should seem logical.

Further, we would expect someone we liked to possess those characteristics that we liked or admired. And we would expect our enemies not to possess those characteristics that we liked or admired. Conversely, we would expect persons we liked to lack unpleasant characteristics and persons we disliked to possess unpleasant characteristics.

In terms of people perception this tendency for balance and consistency may influence the way in which we see each other. It is easy to see our friends as being possessed of fine qualities and our enemies as being possessed of unpleasant qualities. Donating money to the poor, for example, can be perceived as an act of charity (if from a friend) or as an act of pomposity (if from an enemy). We would probably laugh harder at a joke told by a well-liked comedian than at that very same joke if told by a disliked comedian.

Stereotyping

One of the most frequently used shortcuts in people perception is that of *stereotyping*. Originally, "stereotype" was a printing term that referred to the plate that printed the same image over and over again. A sociological or psychological stereotype, then, is a fixed impression of a group of people. We all have stereotypes whether they be of national groups, religious groups, or racial groups, or perhaps of criminals, prostitutes, teachers, plumbers, or artists.

When we have these fixed impressions we will often, upon meeting someone of a particular group, see that person primarily as a member of that group. Then all the characteristics we have in our minds for members of that group are applied to this individual. If we meet someone who is a prostitute, for example, we have a host of characteristics for prostitutes which we are ready to apply to this one person. To further complicate matters, we will often see in this person's behavior the manifestation of various characteristics which we would not see if we did not know that this person was a prostitute. Stereotypes distort our ability to accurately perceive other people. They prevent us from seeing an individual as an individual; instead the individual is seen only as a member of a group.

SOURCES

An excellent introduction to perception and communication is provided by Hans Toch and Malcolm S. MacLean, Jr., '''Perception and Communication: A Transactional View,'' *Audio Visual Communication Review* 10(1967): 55–77. Also see Thomas M. Steinfatt, *Human Communication: An Interpersonal Introduction* (Indianapolis: Bobbs-Merrill, 1977) for a general overview. A thorough summary of this area is contained in Mark Cook's *Interpersonal Perception* (Baltimore: Penguin, 1971) on which I relied heavily for the entire unit. A more thorough and scholarly presentation of this area is by Renato Tagiuri, "Person Perception," in *The Handbook of Social Psychology,* edited by G. Lindzey and E. Aronson, 2d ed. (Reading, Mass.: Addison-Wesley, 1969) 3:395–449. Standard reference works in this area include Michael Argyle, *Social Interaction* (London: Methuen, 1969) and Renato Tagiuri and Luigi Petrullo, eds., *Person Perception and Interpersonal Behavior* (Stanford, Cal.: Stanford University Press, 1958). A brief but insightful account of people perception is provided by Albert Hastorf, David Schneider, and Judith Polefka in *Person Perception* (Reading, Mass.: Addison-Wesley, 1970). I also found Zick Rubin's *Liking and Loving: An Invitation to Social Psychology* (New York: Holt, 1973) a most useful source. Much of the discussion of the perceptual processes is based on the insights provided by Rubin. The cited study by Solomon Asch is "Forming Impressions of Personality," *Journal of Abnormal and Social Psychology* 41(1946):258–290. The cited study on forming impressions of exam-taking students was conducted by Edward E. Jones, Leslie Rock, Kelley G. Shaver, and Lawrence M. Ward: "Pattern of Performance and Ability Atribution: An Unexpected Primacy Effect," *Journal of Personality and Social Psychology* 10(1968):317–340. Both of these studies are discussed by Rubin.

EXPERIENTIAL VEHICLES

8.1 PERCEIVING MY SELVES

The purposes of this experiential vehicle are to get us to better understand how we perceive ourselves, how others perceive us, and how we would like to perceive ourselves. In some instances and for some people these three perceptions will be the same; in most cases and for most people, however, they will be different.

Following this brief introduction are eleven lists of items (animals, birds, colors, communications media, dogs, drinks, fish, food, music, sports, and transportation). Read over each list carefully attempting to look past the purely physical existence of the objects to their "personality" or "psychological meaning."

1. First, for each of the eleven lists indicate the one item that best represents how you perceive yourself—not your physical self but your psychological-philosophical self. Mark these items *MM* (Myself to Me).

2. Second, for each of the eleven lists select the one item that best represents how you feel others see you. By "others" is meant acquaintances—neither passing strangers nor close friends but people you meet and talk with for some time, for example, people in this class. Mark these items *MO* (Myself to Others).

3. Third, for each of the eleven lists select the one item that best represents how you would like to be. Put differently, what items would your ideal self select? Mark these items *MI* (Myself as Ideal).

After all eleven lists are marked three times, discuss your choices in groups of five or six persons in any way you feel is meaningful. Your objective is to get a better perspective on how your self-perception compares with your perception by others and your ideal perception. In discussions you should try to state as clearly as possible why you selected the items you did and specifically what each selected item means to you at this time. You should also welcome any suggestions from the group members as to why they think you selected the items you did. You might also wish to integrate consideration of some or all of the following questions into your discussion.

1. How different are the items marked *MM* from *MO*? Why do you suppose this is so? Which is the more positive? Why?
2. How different are the items marked *MM* from *MI*? Why do you suppose this is so?

3. What does the amount of or the number of differences between the items marked *MM* and the items marked *MI* mean for personal happiness?
4. How accurate were you in the items you marked *MO*? Ask members of the group which items they would have selected for you.
5. Which of the three perceptions (*MM*, *MO*, *MI*) is easiest to respond to? Which are you surest of?
6. Would you show these forms to your best same sex friend? Your best opposite sex friend? Your parents? Your children? Explain.

ANIMALS

_____bear
_____cobra
_____deer
_____elephant
_____fox
_____horse
_____hyena
_____leopard
_____lion
_____monkey
_____rabbit
_____squirrel
_____tiger
_____turtle

BIRDS

_____albatross
_____canary
_____chicken
_____eagle
_____flamingo
_____hawk
_____hummingbird
_____ostrich
_____owl
_____parrot
_____pelican
_____penguin
_____pigeon
_____seagull

_____sparrow
_____swan
_____turkey
_____vulture

COLORS

_____black
_____blue
_____brown
_____green
_____grey
_____orange
_____pink
_____purple
_____red
_____violet
_____white
_____yellow

COMMUNICATIONS MEDIA

_____body language
_____book
_____face-to-face
_____film
_____fourth-class mail
_____gossip
_____magazine article
_____radio
_____records
_____smoke signals
_____sky writing
_____special delivery letter
_____tapes
_____telegraph
_____telephone
_____television

DOGS

_____afghan
_____boxer
_____chihuahua
_____cocker spaniel
_____collie
_____dalmatian
_____doberman pinscher
_____German shepherd
_____greyhound
_____husky
_____Irish wolfhound
_____mutt
_____poodle
_____St. Bernard

DRINKS

_____beer
_____champagne
_____club soda
_____coffee
_____coke
_____milk
_____orange juice
_____prune juice
_____red wine
_____scotch
_____7-up
_____sherry
_____water
_____white wine

WATER CREATURES

_____angelfish
_____blowfish
_____dolphin
_____eel
_____goldfish
_____mermaid
_____piranha
_____salmon
_____shark
_____starfish
_____tuna
_____whale

FOOD

_____apple pie
_____Big Mac
_____caviar
_____filet mignon
_____french fries
_____gum drops
_____ice cream sundae
_____jello
_____noodle soup
_____peanut butter
_____tossed salad
_____white bread

MUSIC

_____broadway/film
_____country western
_____disco
_____folk
_____hymns
_____jazz
_____opera
_____popular
_____rock
_____symphony
_____synthesized
(computerized)

SPORTS

_____auto racing
_____baseball
_____boxing
_____bridge
_____bullfighting
_____chess
_____fishing
_____ice skating
_____mountaineering
_____polo
_____skydiving
_____tennis
_____weight lifting
_____wrestling
_____yachting

TRANSPORTATION

_____bicycle
_____bus
_____Edsel
_____jet plane
_____horse and wagon
_____kiddy car
_____motorcycle
_____Rolls Royce
_____Porsche
_____skateboard
_____train
_____van
_____Volkswagen

8.2 PERCEIVING OTHERS

List the name of the person in this class who you would most like to:

1. have a date with
2. go into business with
3. have dinner with
4. have meet your family
5. discuss your inner feelings with
6. work on a class project with
7. have at a party
8. have as a group leader

9. borrow money from
10. room with
11. drive cross-country with
12. be happy with
13. be sad with
14. be locked in a jail cell with
15. go camping with

Class members should discuss their results as a whole. Specifically, consider the following:

1. What cues did the people give you that led you to feel as you did about them?
2. What quality of the person named led you to select him or her for that purpose?
3. Think of (but do not verbalize) the persons with whom you would least like to do the fifteen things listed. Why? That is, what cues did these people give that led you to feel as you did about them?
4. What quality of the person thought of led you to reject him or her for that purpose?
5. For which purposes do you think other people would select you? What qualities do people see in you that would lead them to select you for one or more of these fifteen items?

8.3 PERCEIVING A STRANGER

The purpose of this exercise is to explore the bases you use in perceiving and judging people you see for the first time.[1] Since we all make judgments of people upon seeing them, we need to investigate the ways and means we use in making these judgments.

A stranger (someone you have not seen before) will be brought into class. Look the stranger over and answer the questions that follow. For this phase of the exercise no interaction between you and the stranger should take place. Use the number "1" to indicate your answers.

After this you will be able to interact with the stranger for five or ten minutes. Ask him or her any questions you wish though none can be directly related to the exercise questions. The stranger should answer any questions posed as fully as he or she thinks necessary. The stranger should not, however, answer any questions that relate directly to the questions posed in the exercise. After this interaction, again answer the questions, this time using "2" to mark your answers.

After the answers have been recorded the stranger or the instructor will go

[1] This exercise, though in a somewhat different form, was suggested by James C. McCroskey, Carl E. Larsen, and Mark L. Knapp in their *Teacher's Manual* for *An Introduction to Interpersonal Communication* (Englewood Cliffs, N.J. Prentice-Hall, 1971).

over each of the questions, specifying which answers the stranger thinks are most appropriate.

Discussion should focus on at least the following:

1. Which judgments were static judgments? Which were dynamic judgments?
2. Explain how rules from experience, analogy, and/or authority influenced your perceptions of the stranger.
3. Explain how the principles of subjectivity, stability, and meaningfulness operated in your perceptions of the stranger.

Instructions

Before interaction with the stranger answer the questions by placing the number "1" in the appropriate space. After interaction answer the questions by placing the number "2" in the appropriate space.

The stranger would most likely:

1. read

   _____ *The Best of Mad*
   _____ *War and Peace*
   _____ *The Sensuous Man/Woman*
   _____ *Knots*
   _____ *Slaughterhouse Five*

2. see

   _____ a romantic movie
   _____ a western
   _____ a comedy
   _____ an erotic movie
   _____ a foreign film
   _____ a detective film
   _____ a musical

3. participate in

   _____ football
   _____ tennis
   _____ golf
   _____ skiing
   _____ none of these

4. listen to

   _____ classical music
   _____ rock music
   _____ country western music
   _____ popular music

5. watch on television

_____ a situation comedy
_____ the news
_____ an educational show
_____ a detective show
_____ a sports show
_____ a soap opera

6. prefer to be

_____ alone
_____ in a crowd with friends and acquaintances
_____ with one person
_____ with family

7. go to

_____ a rock concert
_____ an art museum
_____ a sports event
_____ an opera
_____ a play
_____ a movie

8. look for in a mate

_____ intelligence
_____ looks
_____ personality
_____ money

9. study

_____ sciences
_____ languages
_____ music/art/drama
_____ business
_____ communications
_____ social sciences

10. subscribe to

_____ *Playboy/Playgirl*
_____ *National Geographic*
_____ *Time/Newsweek*
_____ *Popular Mechanics*
_____ *Good Housekeeping*

11. behave

_____ as an extrovert
_____ as an introvert
_____ as an ambivert

12. act

_____ very aggressively
_____ very unaggressively
_____ fairly aggressively
_____ fairly nonaggressively

13. be

_____ very energetic
_____ very lazy
_____ fairly energetic
_____ fairly lazy

14. behave in most situations

_____ very emotionally
_____ very rationally
_____ fairly emotionally
_____ fairly rationally

15. be generally

_____ very happy
_____ very unhappy
_____ fairly happy
_____ fairly unhappy

16. Also, what is the stranger's:

Age _____
Occupation _____
Educational level reached _____
Marital status _____
Financial status _____

17. Describe the stranger's personality in two, three, or four adjectives.

18. How does the stranger feel now? Explain.

UNIT 9
Listening
in Communication

The Nature and Importance of Listening
Listening and Feedback
Obstacles to Effective Listening
Guides to Effective Listening

9.1 Sequential Communication
9.2 Feedback in Communication

LEARNING GOALS

After completing this unit, you should be able to:

1. define *listening*
2. explain the importance of feedback to listening
3. explain the five characteristics of effective feedback
4. explain the role of feedback in communication accuracy
5. list and explain the five obstacles to effective listening
6. list and explain the five guides to effective listening
7. identify and explain the three basic processes in sequential communication

There can be little doubt that we listen a great deal. Upon awakening we listen to the radio. On the way to school we listen to friends, to people around us, and perhaps to screeching cars, singing birds, or falling rain. In school our listening day starts in earnest and we sit in class after class listening to the teacher, to comments by other students, and sometimes even to ourselves. We listen to friends at lunch and return to class to listen to more teachers. We arrive home and again listen to our family and friends. Perhaps we then listen to records, radio, or television. All in all we listen for a good part of our waking day.

THE NATURE AND IMPORTANCE OF LISTENING

Numerous studies have been conducted to determine the percentage of our communication time devoted to listening as compared with speaking, reading, and writing. In one study, for example, it was found that adults in a variety of occupations spent approximately 70 percent of their day in one of the four communication activities. Of that time, approximately 42 percent was spent in listening, 32 percent in talking, 15 percent in reading, and 11 percent in writing. Listening percentages for students are even higher.

That we listen a great deal of the time, then, can hardly be denied. Whether we listen effectively or efficiently, however, is another matter. Although we might occasionally complain about having to study writing in elementary school, in high school, and again in college we would probably not deny its usefulness. Despite occasional problems in such courses, most people would admit that improvement in writing is both necessary and possible. With listening, however, our attitudes are different. For some reason we do not feel that it is necessary to improve our listening or that it is even possible. If you search through your college catalog you will find numerous courses designed to improve writing skills. And, of course, you will even find courses designed to improve your tennis, golf, and fencing abilities. Yet you will probably not find a single course in listening, despite its importance and its pervasiveness. The one exception to this general rule is found in music departments, where courses in listening to music will be offered. If it is useful to teach "music listening," would not a similar concern for language and speech be logical? It seems to be assumed that because we listen without a great deal of effort, we open our ears something like we open a drain. But this view, as we shall see, is far from accurate.

In actual practice most of us are relatively poor listeners, and our listening behavior could be made more effective and more efficient. Given the amount of time we engage in listening, the improvement of that skill would seem well worth the required effort. And it does take effort. Listening is not an easy matter; it takes time and energy to listen effectively.

By listening we mean *an active process of receiving aural stimuli.* Contrary to popular conception, listening is an *active* rather than a passive process. Listening does not just happen; we must make it happen. Listening takes energy and a commitment to engage in often difficult labor.

Listening involves *receiving* stimuli and is thus distinguished from hearing as a physiological process. The word "receiving" is used here to imply that stimuli are taken in by the organism and are in some way processed or utilized. For at least some amount of time, the signals received are retained.

Listening involves *aural* stimuli, that is, signals (sound waves) received by the ear. Listening therefore is not limtied to verbal signals but encompasses all signals sent by means of fluctuations in air—noises as well as words, music as well as prose.

Make special note of the fact that there is nothing in this definition that implies that listening as a skill is limited to formal speaking situations, such as when a public speaker addresses a large audience. Listening is a skill that is of crucial importance in interpersonal and in small group communication, as well as in public speaking and mass communication.

Jesse S. Nirenberg, in his *Getting Through to People,* distinguishes three levels of listening. First, there is the level of *nonhearing.* Here the individual does not listen at all; rather, he or she looks at the speaker and may even utter remarks that seem to imply attention such as "O.K.," "yes," and "mm" but there is really no listening. Nothing is getting through. The second level is the level of *hearing*. Here the person hears what is being said and even remembers it but does not allow any of the ideas to penetrate beyond the level of memory. Third is the level of *thinking* where the listener not only hears what the speaker is saying but also thinks about it. The listener here evaluates and analyzes what is being said. It is this third level, the level of *listening-thinking,* that we are defining as listening.

LISTENING AND FEEDBACK

The concept of *feedback* is crucial to an understanding of listening as an active process. Feedback refers to those messages sent from listeners and received by speakers which enable speakers to gauge their effects on their receivers. If speakers are to learn the effects of their messages and if they are to adapt their messages more effectively, then listeners must be trained to send these messages of feedback to speakers. Here are some guides for effective use of the feedback mechanism in communication. Effective feedback is immediate, honest, appropriate, clear, and informative.

Immediate Feedback

The most effective feedback is that which is most immediate. Ideally, feedback is sent immediately after the message is received. Feedback, like reinforcement, loses its effectiveness with time; the longer we wait to praise or punish, for example, the less effect it will have. To say to children that they will get punished when Daddy comes home probably does little to eliminate the undesirable behavior simply because the punishment or feedback comes so long after the behavior.

Honest Feedback

Feedback should be honest. To say this is not to provide license for overt hostility or cruelty. It is to say, however, that feedback should not merely be a series of messages that the speaker wants to hear and which will build up his or her ego. Feedback should be an honest reaction to a communication.

Feedback concerning one's understanding of the message as well as one's agreement with the message should be honest. We should not be ashamed or afraid to admit that we did not understand a message, nor should we hesitate to assert our disagreement.

We can, of course, consistently give speakers the feedback they want. You can shake your head, indicating understanding, as the teacher pours forth some incomprehensible dribble and nod agreement with his or her equally incomprehensible theories. This may make the teacher feel that you are intelligent and clever. But note the effect that this kind of behavior has: It reinforces the behavior of the teacher. It will lead that teacher to continue addressing classes with this same incomprehensible dribble. In effect, you have told the teacher that he or she is doing a good job by your positive feedback. The same is true with any speaker in any type of communication situation.

The quality of teaching and in fact of all the communicative arts are in large part a reflection of the listeners; we are the ones who keep the levels of communication where they are.

Appropriate Feedback

Feedback should be appropriate to the general communication situation. For the most part we have learned what is appropriate and what is not appropriate from observing others as we grew up. And so there is no need for spelling out what is and what is not appropriate. We should recognize, however, that appropriateness is a learned concept; consequently, what is appropriate for our culture is not necessarily apropriate for another culture. Thus for students to stamp their feet when a teacher walks in might signal approval or respect in one culture but might signal hostility in another.

We should also note that feedback to the message should be kept distinct from feedback to the speaker. We need to make clear, in disagreeing with speakers, for example, that we are disagreeing with what they are saying and not necessarily rejecting them as people. We may dislike what a person says but like the person saying it. When students say that a class session is boring, they are not saying that they dislike the teacher personally, but merely that they disliked the class session.

Clear Feedback

Feedback should be clear on at least two counts. It should be clear enough so that speakers can perceive that it is feedback to the message and not just a reflection of something you ate that did not agree with you. Second, the feedback should be clear in meaning; if it is to signal understanding then it should be clear to the speaker that that is what you are signaling. If you are disagreeing then that, too, should be clear.

Informative Feedback

The feedback you send to speakers should convey some information; it should tell them something they did not already know.

In any classroom there are always some students who sit with the same expression on their faces regardless of what is going on. You could lecture on the physics of sound or you could show a stag film and their expression would remain unchanged—or at least relatively so. These people communicate no information and serve only to confuse the speaker.

Similarly, to always respond in the same way conveys no information. To communicate information responses must be, in part at least, unpredictable. If speakers are able to completely predict how you will respond to something they say then your response conveys no information and does not serve any useful feedback function.

The importance of listening can hardly be denied. We spend most of our communication time in listening, and we probably learn more from listening than from any other means. In any form of communication, listening and feedback are so closely related that we cannot be said to listen effectively if immediate, honest, appropriate, clear, and informative feedback is not given.

OBSTACLES TO EFFECTIVE LISTENING

Listening is at best a difficult matter. Yet it may be made easier, more pleasant, and more efficient if some of the obstacles or barriers to effective listening were eliminated. Although there are many that could be identified, five general classes of obstacles are considered here.

Prejudging the Communication

Whether in a lecture auditorium or in a small group of people there is a strong tendency to prejudge the communications of others as uninteresting or irrelevant to our own needs or to the task at hand. Often we compare these communications with something we might say or with something that we might be doing instead of "just listening." Generally, listening to others comes in a poor second.

By prejudging a communication as uninteresting we are in effect lifting the burden of listening from our shoulders. If we have already determined that the communication is uninteresting, for example, then there is no reason to listen. So we just tune out the speaker and let our minds recapture last Saturday night.

All communications are, at least potentially, interesting and relevant. If we prejudge them and tune them out we will never be proven wrong. At the same time, however, we close ourselves off from potentially useful information. Most important, perhaps, is that we do not give the other person a fair hearing.

Rehearsing a Response

For the most part we are, as Wendell Johnson put it, our own most enchanted listeners. No one speaks as well or on such interesting topics as we do. If we could listen just to ourselves, listening would be no problem.

Particularly in small group situations but also in larger settings the speaker may say something with which we disagree; for the remainder of that speaker's time we rehearse our response or rebuttal or question. We then imagine his or her reply to our response and then our response to his or her response and so on and on. Meanwhile, we have missed whatever else the speaker had to say—perhaps even the part that would make our question unnecessary or irrelevant or which might raise other and more significant questions.

If the situation is a public speaking one, and the speech is a relatively long one, then perhaps it is best to jot down the point at issue and go back to listening. If the situation is a small group one then it is best to simply make mental note of what you want to say and perhaps keep this in mind by relating it to the remainder of what the individual is saying. In either event the important point is to get back to listening.

Filtering Out Messages

I once had a teacher who claimed that whatever he could not immediately understand was not worth reading or listening to; if it had to be worked at it was not worth the effort. I often wonder how he managed to learn, how he was intellectually stimulated if indeed he was. Depending on our own intellectual equipment, many of the messages that we confront will need careful consideration and in-depth scrutiny. Listening will be difficult but the alternative—to miss out on what is said—seems even less pleasant than stretching and straining our minds a bit.

Perhaps more serious than filtering out difficult messages is filtering out unpleasant ones. None of us want to be told that something we believe in is untrue, that people we care for are unpleasant, or that ideals we hold are self-destructive. And yet, these are the very messages we need to listen to with great care. These are the very messages that will lead us to examine and reexamine our implicit and unconscious assumptions. If we filter out this kind of information we will be left with a host of unstated and unexamined assumptions and premises that will influence us without our influencing them. That prospect is not a very pleasant one.

Inefficiently Using the Thought–Speech Time Differential

It should be obvious that we can think much more quickly than a speaker can speak. Consequently, in listening to someone our minds can process the information much more quickly than the speaker can give it out. At conventions it was especially interesting to listen to Ralph Nichols, a nationally known expert on listening. Unlike most speakers, Nichols would speak very rapidly. At first, his speech sounded peculiar because it was so rapid. Yet it was extremely easy to understand; our minds did not wander as often as they did when listening to someone who spoke at a normal speed. I would not recommend that we all speak more rapidly since there are various side-effects that are difficult to control. But it is important to realize that in listening there is a great deal of time left over; only a portion of our time is used in listening to the information in the messages.

Given this state of affairs, we are left with a number of possibilities—from letting our mind wander back to that great Saturday night to utilizing the time for understanding and learning the message. Obviously, the latter would be the more efficient course of action. With this extra time, then, we might review concepts already made by the speaker, search for additional meanings, attempt to predict what the speaker will say next, and so on. The important point is that we stay on the topic with the speaker and not let our thoughts wander to distant places from whence they will not return.

Focusing Attention on Language or Delivery

For many people in communication, having studied language and style for so long, it is difficult not to concentrate on the stylistic peculiarities of an individual. In hearing a clever phrase or sentence, for example, it is difficult to resist the temptation to dwell on it and analyze it. Similarly, it is difficult for many to ignore various gestures or particular aspects of voice. Focusing on these dimensions of communication only diverts time and energy away from the message itself. This is not to say that such behaviors are not important, but only that we can fall into the trap of devoting too much attention to the way the message is packaged and not enough to the message itself.

GUIDES TO EFFECTIVE LISTENING

Listening ability—like speaking, reading, and writing abilities—can be improved. As in the case of these other abilities, there are no easy rules or simple formulas. There are, however, some guidelines which should be of considerable value if followed.

Listen Actively

Perhaps the first step to listening improvement is the recognition that it is not a passive activity; it is not a process that will happen if we simply do nothing to stop it. We may hear without effort but we cannot listen without effort.

Listening is a difficult process; in many ways it is more demanding than speaking. In speaking we are in control of the situation; we can talk about what we like in the way we like. In listening, however, we are forced to follow the pace, the content, and the language set by the speaker.

Perhaps the best preparation for active listening is to act like an active listener. This may seem trivial and redundant. In practice, however, this may be the most often abused rule of effective listening. Students often, for example, come into class, put their feet up on a nearby desk, nod their head to the side, and expect to listen effectively. It just does not happen that way. Re-call, for example, how your body almost automatically reacts to important news. Almost immediately you assume an upright posture, cock your head to the speaker, and remain relatively still and quiet. We do this almost reflexively because this is how we listen most effectively. This is not to say that we should be tense and uncomfortable but only that our bodies should reflect our active minds.

Listen for Total Meaning

In listening to another individual we need to learn to listen for total meaning. The total meaning of any communication act is extremely complex, and we can be sure that we will never get it all. However, the total meaning is not only in the words used. The meaning is also in the nonverbal behavior of the speaker. Sweating hands and shaking knees communicate just as surely as do word and phrases.

Along with the verbal and nonverbal behaviors we should also recognize that the meaning of a communicaiton act lies also in what is omitted. The speaker who talks about racism solely in the abstract, for example, and who never once mentions a specific group is communicating something quite different from the speaker who talks in specifics.

Listen with Empathy

It is relatively easy to learn to listen for understanding or for comprehension. But this is only a part of communication. We also need to *feel* what the speaker feels; we need to empathize with the speaker.

To empathize with others is to feel with them, to see the world as they see it, to feel what they feel. Only when we achieve this will we be able to fully understand another's meaning.

There is no fast method for achieving empathy with another individual. But it is something we should work toward. It is important that we see the teacher's point of view, not from that of our own, but from that of the teacher. And equally it is important for the teacher to see the student's point of view from that of the student. If students turn in late papers, teachers should attempt to put themselves in the role of the students to begin to understand the possible rea-sons for the lateness. Similarly, if teachers fail papers because they are late, students should attempt to put themselves in the role of teachers and attempt to understand the reason for the failure.

So often we witness the behavior of others which seems, to us at least, foolish and ridiculous. We see, for example, a child cry because he or she lost money. From our point of view the amount lost is insignificant and it therefore seems foolish to cry over it. What we need to do, however, is to see the situation from the point of view of the child—to realize that the amount of money is not insignificant to the child and that perhaps the consequences of losing the money are extremely serious. Popular college students might intellectually understand the reasons for the depression of the unpopular student but that will not enable them to emotionally understand the feelings of depression. What popular students need to do is to put themselves in the position of the unpopular student, to role play a bit, and begin to feel his or her feelings and think his or her thoughts. Then these students will be in a somewhat better position to "really understand," to emphathize.

William V. Pietsch, in his imaginative *Human BE-ing,* makes the point that most of our education has been concerned with objective facts to the almost total neglect of subjective feelings. We need to recognize that understanding and problem solving cannot be achieved solely with reference to the intellect; the emotions as well need to be examined. "Real listening," says Pietsch, "means 'tuning in' to what the other person is *feeling* so that we *listen to emotions,* not simply to 'ideas'."

Listen with an Open Mind

Listening with an open mind is an extremely difficult thing to do. It is not easy for us, for example, to listen to arguments against some cherished belief. It is not easy to listen to statements condemning what we so fervently believe. It is not easy to listen to criticisms of what we think is just great.

In counseling students one of the most difficult tasks is to make them realize that even though they may dislike a particular teacher they can still learn something from him or her. For some reason many people will attempt to punish the people they dislike by not listening to them. Of course, if the situation is that of teacher and student, then it is only the student who suffers by losing out on significant material.

We also need to learn to continue listening fairly even though some signal has gone up in the form of an out-of-place expression or a hostile remark. Listening often stops when such a remark is made. Admittedly, to continue listening with an open mind is a difficult matter yet here it is particularly important that listening does continue.

Listen Critically

Although we need to emphasize that we should listen with an open mind and with empathy it should not be assumed that we should listen uncritically. Quite the contrary. We need to listen fairly but critically if meaningful communication is to take place. As intelligent and educated citizens, it is our responsibility to critically evaluate what we hear. This is especially true in the college environment. While it is very easy to simply listen to a teacher and take down what is said, it is extremely important that what is said is evaluated and critically analyzed. Teachers have biases too; at times consciously and at times unconsciously these biases creep into scholarly discussions. They need to be identified and brought to the surface by the critical listener. Contrary to what most students will argue, the vast majority of teachers will appreciate the responses of critical listeners. It demonstrates that someone is listening.

SOURCES

On the nature of listening and for numerous studies see C. William Colburn and Sanford B. Weinberg, *An Orientation to Listening and Audience Analysis* (Palo Alto, Cal.: SRA, 1976); Larry L. Barker, *Listening Behavior* (Englewood Cliffs, N.J.: Prentice-Hall, 1971); and Carl Weaver, *Human Listening: Processes and Behavior* (Indianapolis: Bobbs-Merrill, 1972). Perhaps the classic in the area is Ralph Nichols and Leonard Stevens, *Are You Listening*? (New York: McGraw-Hill, 1957). On listening and feedback the chapter by Kathy J. Wahlers in Barker's *Listening Behavior* was most helpful. Listening from the point of view of auditory attention is covered in Neville Moray's *Listening and Attention* (Baltimore, Penguin, 1969). Ella Erway's *Listening: A Programmed Approach* (New York: McGraw-Hill, 1969) covers the nature of listening, its importance, and the ways in which it can be improved.

The obstacles to effective listening covered here are also covered in a number of books on listening such as those listed above. Similarly, the guides to effective listening presented here are also considered in other texts in different ways. A useful overview is Ralph Nichols' "Do We Know How to Listen? Practical Helps in a Modern Age," *Speech Teacher* 10(1961):118–124. This article contains ten suggestions for improving listening. Most of the suggestions for improving listening, such as those presented here as well as those presented in other texts, owe their formulation to the work of Ralph Nichols. Another useful and informative source is Wendell Johnson's *Verbal Man* (New York: Colliers, 1969). For serial (or sequential) communication read William V. Haney, "Serial Communication of Information in Organizations," *Communication: Concepts and Processes,* Joseph A. DeVito, ed., revised and enlarged edition (Englewood Cliffs, N.J.: Prentice-Hall, 1976) and Haney's *Communication and Organizational Behavior: Text and Cases,* 3rd ed. (Homewood, Ill.: Irwin, 1973). Barrie Hopson and Charlotte Hopson's *Intimate Feedback: A Lovers' Guide to Getting in Touch with Each Other* (New York: New American Library, 1976) contains much that is relevant to effective listening.

EXPERIENTIAL VEHICLES

9.1 SEQUENTIAL COMMUNICATION

This exercise is designed to illustrate some of the processes involved in what might be called "sequential communication," that is, communication that is passed on from one individual to another.

This exercise consists of both a nonverbal (visual) and a verbal part; both are performed in essentially the same manner. Taking the visual communication experience first, six subjects are selected to participate. Five of these leave the room while the first subject is shown the visual communication. He or she is told to try to remember as much as possible as he or she will be asked to reproduce it in as much detail as possible. After studying the diagram the first subject reproduces it on the board. The second subject then enters the room and studies the diagram. The first diagram is then erased and the second subject draws his or her version. The process is continued until all subjects have drawn the diagram. The last reproduction and the original drawing are then compared on the basis of the processes listed below.

The verbal portion is performed in basically the same way. Here the first subject is read the statement once or twice or even three times; the subject should feel comfortable that he or she has grasped it fully. The second subject then enters the room and listens carefully to the first subject's restatement of the communication. The second subject then attempts to repeat it to the third subject and so on until all subjects have restated the communication. Again, the last restatement and the original are compared on the basis of the processes listed below.

Members of the class not serving as subjects should be provided with copies of both the visual and the verbal communications and should record the changes made in the various reproductions and restatements.

Special attention should be given to the following basic processes in sequential communication.

1. *Omissions.* What kinds of information are omitted? At what point in the chain of communication are such omissions introduced? Do the omissions follow any pattern?
2. *Additions.* What kinds of information are added? When? Can patterns be discerned here or are the additions totally random?
3. *Distortions.* What kinds of information are distorted? When? Are there any patterns? Can the types of distortions be classified in any way? Are the dis-

tortions in the directions of increased simplicity? Increased complexity? Can the sources or reasons for the distortions be identified?

Nonverbal (Visual) Communication

Verbal Communication

Millie is a particularly bright and energetic chimp. She lives at the Queen's Zoo, one of the country's most famous attractions. Frequently, Millie has been discovered throwing bananas at passers-by when she thinks no one is looking. The keeper has punished her by taking away her food but she persists. And in fact she has been found teaching her two babies to do the same thing. If this continues the authorities may have to get rid of her or confine her to the indoors.

9.2 FEEDBACK IN COMMUNICATION

The purpose of this exercise is to illustrate the importance of feedback in communication. The procedure is to have a listener at the blackboard and a speaker prepared to communicate under various different conditions.

The object of the interactions is for the speaker to communicate to the listener instructions for reproducing a diagram. The different conditions under which this task is attempted should enable you to investigate the importance of feedback in communication.

First Condition

The speaker is given a diagram which is neither too complex nor too simple. With his or her back to the listener, the speaker must communicate instructions for reproducing the diagram. The listener is not allowed to speak.

Second Condition

The speaker is given another diagram and must tell the listener how to reproduce it. This time the speaker may observe what the listener is doing and may comment on it. The listener is not allowed to speak.

Third Condition

The speaker is given a third diagram and must tell the listener how to reproduce it. The speaker may again observe what the listener is doing and may comment on it. This time, however, the listener may ask any questions he or she wishes of the speaker. Members of the class should see the diagrams.

Discussion should center on the accuracy of the drawings and the confidence the listeners had in their attempts at reproducing the diagrams. Which is the most accurate? Which is the least accurate? To what extent did the feedback, first visual and then both visual and auditory, help the listener reproduce the diagram?

In the following conditions, how would the lack of feedback influence the communication interactions:

1. A trial lawyer addressing a jury
2. A teacher lecturing to a class of students
3. A used car salesperson trying to sell a car
4. An amorous lover with the loved one
5. A typist typing a letter

UNIT 10
Verbal Interaction: Nine Principles

Immanent Reference
Determinism
Recurrence
Contrast and the Working Principle of Reasonable Alternatives
Relativity of Signal and Noise
Reinforcement/Packaging
Adjustment
The Priority of Interaction
The Forest and the Trees

10.1 The Case of *Waldon v. Martin and Company*

LEARNING GOALS

After completing this unit, you should be able to:

1. distinguish between *immanent reference* and *displacement*
2. define and explain the principle of determinism
3. define *recurrence* in verbal interaction
4. explain the principle of contrast and the working principle of reasonable alternatives
5. explain the relativity of signal and noise
6. explain reinforcement/packaging
7. explain the way the principle of adjustment operates in communication
8. explain the principle of the forest and the trees as it applies to the analysis of communication interactions
9. identify the operation of the universals of verbal interaction in the verbal interactions of others
10. identify at least three or four instances of your own behavior in which these universals were operative

Perhaps the most common and the most sophisticated means of communication is that of verbal interaction: talking and listening. The best way to approach this area is to focus on those characteristics or features that are present in all verbal interactions regardless of their specific purpose, their particular context, or their unique participants. There are nine principles of verbal interaction. Rather than being limited to specific kinds or types of verbal interactions, these principles are universal. They are, in effect, generalizations applicable to any and all verbal interactions.

Universals such as these are significant for at least two major reasons. First, they provide a rather convenient summary of essential principles of verbal interaction. In effect, they define what constitutes a verbal interaction: what is its nature, and what are its essential aspects. Second, these universals provide us with a set of principles for analyzing verbal interactions. These principles should prove useful for analyzing any interaction which is primarily or even partially linguistic. These universals provide us with a set of questions to ask about any verbal interaction.

The nine principles, or universals, are taken from one of the most interesting research studies in the entire area of language. Three researchers (Robert Pittenger, Charles Hockett, and John Danehy) pooled their talents to analyze in depth the first five minutes of a psychiatric interview. Each word, phrase, and sentence; each intonation, pause, and cough were subjected to an incredibly detailed analysis. At the conclusion of this research the authors proposed nine "findings" (principles) which they felt would be of value to future students and researchers attempting to understand and analyze verbal interactions.

IMMANENT REFERENCE

It is true that human beings have the ability to use what Leonard Bloomfield called "displaced speech" and what Charles Hockett labels "displacement": Human language may make reference to the past as well as to the future; humans can talk about what is not here and what is not now. Nevertheless, all verbalization makes some reference to the present, to the specific context, to the speaker, and to the listener. All verbal interactions, in other words, contain *immanent references.*

In attempting to understand verbal interaction, then, it is always legitimate to ask such questions as, "To what extent does this communication refer to this particular situation?" "To what extent does this communication refer to the speaker?" "In what ways is the speaker commenting on the listener?"

The answers to such questions may not be obvious. In many instances, in fact, the answers may never be found. Yet these questions are potentially answerable and thus always worth asking.

DETERMINISM

All verbalizations are to some extent determined; all verbalizations are to some extent purposeful. Whenever something is said, there is a reason. Similarly, when nothing is said in an interactional situation there is a reason. Words, of course, communicate and there are reasons why the words used are used. But silence also communicates and there are reasons why silence is used. Watzlawick, Jackson, and Beavin, in their *Pragmatics of Human Communication,* put it this way: one cannot *not* communicate. Whenever we are in an interactional situation, regardless of what we do or say or don't do or say, we communicate. Words and silence alike have message value; they communicate something to other people who in turn cannot *not* respond and are, therefore, also communicating.

Consequently, it is always legitimate in analyzing interactions to ask the reasons for the words as well as the reasons for the silence. Each communicates and each is governed by some reason or reasons; all messages are determined.

RECURRENCE

In our interactions individuals will tell us—not once but many times and not in one way but in many ways—about themselves—who they are, how they

Box 5
THE FUNCTIONS OF SPEECH

Speech may serve any number of different functions. Different researchers have offered different schemes for describing the various functions. The one offered here is based on the six essential elements in communication: source, channel, message, code, receiver, and referent. Each of these components has a specific function of speech associated with or oriented to it.

1. *Emotive* speech, closely associated with the source or speaker, serves a psychological function and is seen most readily in speech used to express the feelings, attitudes, or emotions of the speaker. The clearest example of speech serving a psychological function is probably seen in catharsis, a process whereby the speaker frees his mind of certain pressing problems.

2. *Phatic* speech creates social relationships and may be considered identical to what Bronislaw Malinowksi referred to as phatic communion. Phatic speech cannot be interpreted literally; rather, its meaning rests in great part on the immediate and specific communication situation. The greeting *How are you?* is in most situations phatic speech. The speaker does not expect or want the listener to tell him how he actually feels but rather is merely saying *Hello*. Another way of looking at this function is as speech whose purpose is to keep the channels of communication open and in good working order. Logically, this function is oriented to the channel.

3. *Cognitive* speech makes reference to the real world and is frequently referred to as referential, denotative, or informative. It is most closely associated with the referent.

perceive themselves, what they like, what they dislike, what they want, what they avoid, and so on.

Whatever is perceived as important or significant to an indivdual will recur in that person's verbal interactions; he or she will tell us in many different ways and on many different occasions what these things are. Of course, they will rarely be communicated in an obvious manner. People who find themselves in need of approval do not directly ask others for approval. Rather, they go about obtaining approval responses in more subtle ways, perhaps asking how others like their new outfit, perhaps talking about their grades on an examination, perhaps talking about how they never betray a confidence, and so on.

CONTRAST AND THE WORKING PRINCIPLE
OF REASONABLE ALTERNATIVES

For any signal to communicate information, two prerequisites are necessary. First, receivers must not know with certainty which signal will be communicated. Second, receivers must be able to recognize the signal they do receive.

If to every question I asked you said yes, and I knew that to every future question I would ask you would also say yes, your responses would not com-

4. *Rhetorical* speech, also referred to as directive or conative, is probably the most complex of all the functions. Rhetorical speech seeks to direct or influence thought and behavior. It is the language of the clergy, of the politician, and of the salesman. It is the speech of persuasion and associated most directly with the receiver.

5. *Metalingual* speech is used to talk not about the objects and events in the real world but about speech itself. It is a higher order or more abstract speech and is oriented to the code of communication.

6. *Poetic* speech serves to structure the message, to which it has its primary orientation, so that it may be more appealing from an aesthetic point of view or more distinctive.

To this basic list other functions could be added. For example, one could consider speech which seeks to communicate aggression or speech which seeks to conceal facts. On closer inspection, however, it will be found that these functions can be viewed as subheadings under the six general functions discussed here, though it would be hazardous to claim that all conceivable functions could be included.

Any given utterance may serve any number of functions. This classification does not imply that only one purpose or function can exist at any one time. In fact, almost any speech sample will be found to serve a number of functions at the same time. One function, however, is likely to be more obvious or more dominant than others.

Source: From *The Psychology of Speech and Language: An Introduction to Psycholinguistics,* by Joseph A. DeVito. Copyright © 1970 by Random House, Inc. Reprinted by permission of the publisher.

municate any information to me. And of course there would be no point in my continuing to ask you questions. I would already know your answer. Your answers, and in fact all your messages, communicate information only when they cannot be predicted with certainty.

The second requisite is more obvious. If I am to receive information from you I must be able to recognize the signals you are sending. If, for example, you send signals in a language I do not understand, then I cannot recognize them and they will communicate no information to me.

My recognition of a particular signal is dependent upon my ability to discern both what that signal is and what that signal is not. If I am to receive information from a signal I must know what that signal is as well as what that signal contrasts with. My understanding of the signal "cat" rests on my ability to recognize the /k/ sound as well as to recognize that the sound is not /r/ or /p/ or /m/.

In short, in understanding and in analyzing verbal interactions we need to ask not only what the signals were, but what were the reasonable alternatives that could have been used; why did the sender use the signals instead of the possible alternatives.

Box 6
THE POLLYANNA HYPOTHESIS

One of the most interesting hypotheses about language usage to be advanced is that of the Pollyanna Hypothesis. The Pollyanna Hypothesis states that "there is a universal human tendency to use evaluatively positive (E+) words more frequently, diversely and facilely than evaluatively negative (E—) words." Put differently, we all tend to say the positive rather than the negative thing more often, in more different situations, and with greater ease. Some examples of the kind of evidence used to formulate this hypothesis might make this clearer still. In one situation the experimenters gave 100 high-school boys in 13 different language communities a list of 100 culture-common nouns. The boys were instructed to write down the first qualifier that occurred to them for each of the 100 nouns. In 12 of the 13 language communities, more E+ words were supplied than E— words.

In the language of children this Pollyanna effect is also present. When the vocabularies of children are analyzed it is found that the frequency and diversity of the usage of E+ terms is much higher than that of E— terms. Although this difference gets smaller as the child grows older, E+ words are still more frequently and more diversely used in adult language.

Numerous studies have shown that E+ words are easier to learn than E— words. E+ words can be learned in less time and with fewer errors than can E— words. Also, it has been demonstrated repeatedly that E+ words can be recognized at lower recognition thresholds than can E— words. That is, the stimulus has to be more intense (brighter, louder) for E— words to be recognized than for E+ words.

Two major theories have been advanced to account for this effect. One position argues that the positive evaluation leads to the high frequency of usage. That is, the words are used more frequently because they are of positive evaluation. The other position argues that the high frequency leads to positive evaluation. That is, the words that are used most frequently become more positive in evaluation. This position is also known as the "mere exposure" hypothesis and although at first it may appear totally inaccurate and illogical, there is much experimental support in its favor. In terms of language usage, however, the first position seems the more accurate.*

* For more information see Jerry Boucher and Charles E. Osgood, "The Pollyanna Hypothesis," *Journal of Verbal Learning and Verbal Behavior* 8 (1969): 1–8.

RELATIVITY OF SIGNAL AND NOISE

What is a signal and what is noise in any given communication is relative rather than absolute. If we are interested in hearing a particular story and the speaker, in narrating it, breaks it up by coughing, we might become annoyed because the coughing (noise) is disturbing our reception of the story (signal). But suppose this individual seeks some form of medication and in his or her

---

Box 7
ALICE AND HUMPTY DUMPTY ON MEANING

After doing some calculations, Humpty Dumpty said to Alice:

". . . And that shows that there are three hundred and sixty-four days when you might get un-birthday presents."
"Certainly," said Alice.
"And only *one* for birthday presents, you know. There's glory for you!"
"I don't know what you mean by 'glory,' " Alice said.
Humpty Dumpty smiled contemptuously. "Of course you don't—till I tell you. I meant 'there's a nice knock-down argument for you'!"
"But 'glory' doesn't mean 'A nice knock-down argument,' " Alice objected.
"When *I* use a word," Humpty Dumpty said, in rather a scornful tone, "it means just what I choose it to mean—neither more nor less."
"The question is," said Alice, "whether you *can* make words mean so many different things."
"The question is," said Humpty Dumpty, "which is to be master—that's all."
Alice was too much puzzled to say anything; so after a minute Humpty Dumpty began again. "They've a temper, some of them—particularly verbs: they're the proudest—adjectives you can do anything with but not verbs—however, *I* can manage the whole lot of them! Impenetrability! That's what *I* say."
"Would you tell me please," said Alice, "what that means?"
"Now you talk like a reasonable child," said Humpty Dumpty, looking very much pleased. "I mean by 'impenetrability' that we've had enough of that subject, and it would be just as well if you'd mention what you mean to do next, as I suppose you don't mean to stop here all the rest of your life."
"That's a great deal to make one word mean," Alice said in a thoughtful tone.
"When I make a word do a lot of work like that," said Humpty Dumpty, "I always pay it extra."

---

interactions with the doctor coughs in a similar way. To the doctor this coughing might be the signal; the coughing might communicate an important message to the doctor. Similarly, when listening to a stutterer tell a story we may focus on the story, which would be the signal. The stuttering would be the noise interfering with our reception of the signal. But to the speech pathologist the stutters are the signals to which he or she attends and the story might be the noise.

The point is simply this: What is signal to one person and in one context might be noise to another person in another context.

REINFORCEMENT/PACKAGING

In most interactions messages are transmitted simultaneously through a number of different channels. We utter sounds with our vocal mechanism but we

Box 8
DENOTATION AND CONNOTATION

In order to best explain these two types of meaning let us take as an example the word *death*. To a doctor this word might simply mean, or denote, the time when the heart stops. Thus to the doctor this word may be an objective description of a particular event. On the other hand, to the dead person's mother (upon being informed of her son's death) the word means much more than the time when the heart stops. It recalls to her the son's youth, his ambitions, his family, his illness, and so on. To her it is a highly emotional word, a highly subjective word, a highly personal word. These emotional or subjective or personal reactions are the word's connotative meaning. The *denotation* of a word is its objective definition. The *connotation* of a word is its subjective or emotional meaning.

Some words are primarily and perhaps even completely denotative. Words like *the, of, a,* and the like are perhaps purely denotative; no one seems to have emotional reactions to such words. Other words are primarily denotative, such as *perpendicular, parallel, cosine, adjacent,* and the like. Of course, even these words might have strong connotative meanings for some people. Words such as *geometry, north* and *south, up* and *down,* and *east* and *west*—words which denote rather specific directions or areas—often produce strong emotional reactions from some people. For example, the student who failed geometry might have a very strong emotional reaction to the word even though to most people it seems a rather unemotional, objective kind of word. Other words, such as derogatory racial names and curse words, are primarily connotative and often have little denotative meaning. The very simple point that is trying to be made here is just that words may vary from highly denotative to highly connotative. A good way to determine the word's connotative meaning is to ask where it would fall on a good-bad scale. If "good" and "bad" do not seem to apply to the word then it has little, if any, connotative meaning for you. If, however, the term can be placed on

also utilize our body posture and our spatial relationships at the same time to reinforce our message. We say no and at the same time pound our fist on the table. One channel reinforces the other. The message is presented as a "package."

The extent to which simultaneous messages reinforce each other or contradict each other, then, is extremely important in understanding human communication. The same verbal message when accompanied by different nonverbal messages is not the same message and cannot be responded to in the same way.

ADJUSTMENT

Communication may take place only to the extent that the parties communicating share the same system of signals. This is obvious when dealing with speakers of two different languages; one will not be able to communicate with the other to the extent that their language systems differ.

the good-bad scale with some degree of conviction, then it has connotative meaning for you.

Another distinction between the two types of meaning has already been implied. The denotative meaning of a word is more general or universal, that is, most people agree with the denotative meanings of words and have similar definitions. Connotative meanings, however, are extremely personal and few people would agree on the precise connotative meaning of a word. If this does not seem correct, try to get a group of people to agree on the connotative meaning for words such as *religion, God, democracy, wealth,* and *freedom.* Chances are very good that it will be impossible to get agreement on such words.

The denotative meaning of a term can be learned from a good dictionary. When we consult a dictionary it is the denotative meaning for which we are looking. The dictionary would tell us, for example, that *south* means "a cardinal point of the compass directly opposite to the north, the direction in which this point lies" and so on. Connotative meaning, on the other hand, cannot be found in a dictionary. Instead it must be found in the person's reactions or associations to the word. To some people, for example, *south* might mean poverty, to others it might mean wealth and good land investment, to still others it might recall the Civil War or perhaps warmth and friendliness. Obviously, no dictionary could be compiled for connotative meanings simply because each person's meaning for a word is different.

Denotative meaning differs from connotative meaning in yet another way. Denotative meanings are relatively unchanging and static. Although definitions of all words change through time, denotative meanings generally change very slowly. The word *south,* for example, meant (denotatively) the same thing a thousand years ago that it does now. But the connotative meaning changes rapidly. A single favorable experience in the south, for example, might change completely one's connotative meaning for the word. With denotative meaning, of course, such changes would not occur.

This principle takes on particular relevance, however, when we realize that no two persons share identical signal systems. Parents and children, for example, not only have different vocabularies to a very great extent but even more importantly, have different denotative and especially different connotative meanings for the terms they have in common. Different cultures and subcultures, even when they share a common language, often have greatly differing nonverbal communication systems. To the extent that these systems differ, and unless a language adjustment is made, communication will not take place.

THE PRIORITY OF INTERACTION

This principle simply states that in understanding and in analyzing verbal interactions we must begin with the interaction itself, with the actual behavior. Only when we begin here can we effectively go on to deal with such questions as purpose, motivation, mental processes, and so forth.

This does not mean that questions of purpose and motivation are meaningless or even that they are of less importance than questions focusing on more objective areas. However, we need to first fully analyze the actual interaction behavior and only then can we legitimately deal with the various mental concepts.

THE FOREST AND THE TREES

This last principle is included as a warning, as a cautionary note. The previous principles have mostly focused attention on microscopic analysis, that is, on a detailed dissection of the verbal interaction. And certainly this is a valid way of approaching verbal language.

Yet it must not be forgotten that any interaction is *more* than the sum of its parts. It is a whole that cannot be fully understood from an analysis only of its parts, much like the forest is more than the individual trees. There is a possible danger, then, of missing the forest while concentrating solely on the trees—this principle calls this to our attention.

SOURCES

The nine universals of verbal interaction are taken from Robert E. Pittenger, Charles F. Hockett, and John J. Danehy's *The First Five Minutes: A Sample of Microscopic Interview Analysis* (Ithaca, N.Y.: Paul Martineau, 1960). Also in this area see Eric H. Lenneberg, "Review of *The First Five Minutes,*" *Language* 38(1962):69–73. For additional material on expressive language see Robert E. Pittenger and Henry Lee Smith, Jr., "A Basis for Some Contributions of Linguistics to Psychiatry," *Psychiatry* 20(1957):61–78 and Norman A. Mc-Quown, "Linguistic Transcription and Specification of Psychiatric Interview Material," *Psychiatry* 20(1957):79–86. On methods of analysis see Frederick Williams, "Analysis of Verbal Behavior," and Mervin D. Lynch, "Stylistic Analysis," in Philip Emmert and William D. Brooks, eds., *Methods of Research in Communication* (New York: Houghton Mifflin, 1970). Alternative approaches to the analysis of verbal interactions are discussed in Gerald R. Miller and Henry E. Nicholson, *Communication Inquiry: A Perspective on a Process* (Reading, Mass.: Addison-Wesley, 1976).

EXPERIENTIAL VEHICLE

10.1 THE CASE OF *WALDON* v. *MARTIN AND COMPANY*

The purpose of this experience is to enable you to better understand the universals of verbal interaction covered in this unit. All students should first carefully read the case presented.

Six people should be selected—hopefully from volunteers—to role play the six characters involved in this case. Each person should develop his or her role as he or she feels the person would probably act.

All others should pay close attention to the drama as it unfolds. After about five minutes or so try to jot down examples of the universals of verbal interaction. Write down the phrases or sentences used by the role players that illustrate the various univerals of verbal interaction.

Recently, a popular national magazine specializing in "the new and the different" ran an article which asked the reader's help in "conducting a scientific experiment on visual perception." Briefly, the article advised the readers to cut out "the specially treated card" inserted in the magazine, dissolve the card in menthanol (CH_3OH), drink the mixture, and focus on some bright object such as the sun or a powerful lamp. The readers were assured that if they did this they would have reactions "never experienced before," that they would be able "to see with amazing accuracy and clarity," and that they would "have insights into themselves and the world at large impossible to attain in any other way." The reader was then advised to write down any comments or reactions on a specially prepared form in the magazine and send it to the author, Professor I. C. Kleerly.

One week after the publication of this issue, Mr. and Mrs. William Waldon brought suit against Martin and Company, publishers of the magazine. Their son Robert, a high-school student of sixteen who was interested in chemistry, had tried the experiment and almost died. (Methanol, or wood alcohol, is a poisonous liquid formed in the distillation of wood and now generally made synthetically by the catalytic reaction of carbon monoxide and hydrogen under pressure. It is used chiefly as a solvent or antifreeze.) The Waldons seek to have the magazine banned and to recover damages.

The attorney for the Waldons argues that the publishers, in allowing this article to be published, clearly demonstrated a lack of a responsible and ethical editorial policy and thereby pose a threat to society. Although it is not now known, it is likely that other readers have attempted or will attempt the experiment with similar results. Any magazine that encourages its readers to take a poisonous substance without specifying that it is in fact poison should be prevented from publishing. Robert Waldon is now in the hospital with severely damaged intestines and throat burns which can never be healed completely. There is some question as to whether he will survive. For damages incurred as a result of this article the Waldons seek $1 million. They also seek to have the current issue of the magazine taken off the stands and the magazine forbidden to publish any longer.

The attorney for Martin and Company points out that the article was clearly presented in the nature of a satire on scientific experiments. The name of the author alone should have made this clear. No person, they assumed, would be naive enough to think that this was a valid scientific study. As of this time no one else has even written a letter of complaint. The magazine is clearly addressed to "adults only" (largely because of the nude pictures). No magazine, they argue, can attempt to prevent people who should not be reading the magazine in the first place from harming themselves. The publisher does not and in fact cannot pass judgment on the scientific accuracy of the articles appearing in its magazines. Furthermore, the magazine has already made commitments for publishing articles and advertisements for another year. If prevented from doing so, the result would be financial disaster not only for the publishing company and its stockholders but for its 200 employees as well. Lastly, the attorney argues that any such attempt to prevent publication of the magazine would be in violation of the company's right of free speech. The magazine is totally owned by Martin and Company which in turn is totally owned by Terrie Shore and Linda Blass, two sisters.

Both attorneys feel that this matter can be settled out of court and have invited the principals to meet for discussion. These include:

Ms. Margaret Waldon, mother of Robert
Mr. Raymond Waldon, father of Robert
Ms. Patricia Realyo, attorney for the Waldons
Ms. Terrie Shore, part owner of Martin and Company
Ms. Linda Blass, part owner of Martin and Company
Mr. James Basmanian, attorney for Martin and Company

After completing the drama, indicate examples of each of the nine principles of verbal interaction:

1. Immanent reference
2. Determinism
3. Recurrence
4. Contrast and the working principle of reasonable alternatives
5. Relativity of signal and noise
6. Reinforcement/packaging
7. Adjustment
8. The priority of interaction*
9. The forest and the trees*

* These two principles should be discussed as they apply to the discussion of the first seven principles. They are useful when we analyze communications by means of the first seven principles or in fact by means of any set of principles.

UNIT 11
Verbal Interaction: Six Barriers

Polarization
Intensional Orientation
Fact-Inference Confusion
Allness
Static Evaluation
Indiscrimination

11.1 E-Prime
11.2 Facts and Inferences
11.3 I, You, and He and She Talk

LEARNING GOALS

After completing this unit, you should be able to:

1. define *polarization*, *intensional orientation*, *fact-inference confusion*, *allness*, *static evaluation*, and *indiscrimination*
2. identify examples of these six misevaluations in the media
3. identify examples of these six misevaluations in your own communications

Although communication may break down at any point in the process from sender to receiver, perhaps the most obvious site of breakdown is in the actual message. Breakdown, of course, may occur in any form of communication and the breakdowns noted here are applicable to all forms of communication.

POLARIZATION

Polarization refers to the tendency to look at the world and to describe it in terms of extremes—good or bad, positive or negative, healthy or sick, intelligent or stupid, rich or poor, and so on. It is often referred to as the "fallacy of either-or" or "black and white." Although it is true that magnetic poles may be described as positive or negative and that certain people are extremely rich and others are extremely poor, the vast majority of cases are clearly in the middle, between these two extremes. Most pople exist somewhere between the extremes of good and bad, healthy or sick, intelligent or stupid, rich or poor. Yet there seems to be a strong tendency to view only the extremes and to categorize people, objects, and events in terms of these polar opposites.

This tendency may be easily illustrated by attempting to fill in the polar opposites for such words as the following:

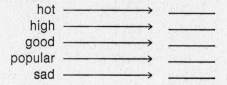

Filling in these opposites should have been relatively easy and quick. The words should also have been fairly short. Further, if a number of people supplied opposites we would find a high degree of agreement among them.

Now, however, attempt to fill in the middle positions with words meaning, for example, "midway between high and low," "midway between hot and cold," and so on. These midway responses (compared to the opposites) were probably more difficult to think of and took more time. The words should also have been fairly long or phrases of two, three, four, or more words. Further, we would probably find rather low agreement among different people completing this same task.

It might be helpful to visualize the familiar bell-shaped curve. Few items exist at either of the two extremes, but as we move closer to the center, more and more items are included. This is true of any random sample. If we selected a hundred people at random we would find that their intelligence, height, weight, income, age, health, and so on would, if plotted, fall into a bell-shaped or "normal" distribution. Yet our tendency seems to be to concentrate on the extremes, on the ends of this curve, and ignore the middle which contains the vast majority of cases.

With certain statements it is legitimate to phrase them in terms of two absolutes. For example, this thing that you are holding is either a book or it is not. Clearly the classes of book and not book include all possibilities. And so there is no problem with this kind of statement. Similarly, we may say that the student will either pass this course or will not pass it, these two categories including all possibilities.

We create problems, however, when we use this basic form in situations in which it is inappropriate, for example, "the politician is either for us or against us." Note that these two possibilities do not include all possibilities; the politician may be for us in some things and against us in other things, or he or she may be neutral. During the Vietnam War there was a tendency to categorize people as either hawk or dove, but clearly there were many people who were neither and many who were probably both—hawks on certain issues and doves on others.

What we need to beware of is implying and believing that two extreme classes include all possible classes, that an individual must be a hawk or a dove and that there are no other alternatives. "Life is either a daring adventure or nothing," said Helen Keller. But for most people it is neither a daring adventure nor nothing but rather something somewhere in between these two extremes.

INTENSIONAL ORIENTATION

Intensional orientation (the *s* in intensional is intentional) refers to the tendency to view people, objects, and events in terms of the way in which they are talked about or labeled rather than in terms of the way they actually exist and operate.

Extensional orientation, on the other hand, is the tendency to first look to the actual people, objects, and events and only after this, to their labels. It is the tendency to be guided by what we see happening rather than by the label used for what is happening.

Intensional orientation is seen when we act as if the words and labels are more important than the things they represent, when we act as if the map is more important than the territory. In its extreme form intensional orientation is seen in the person who, afraid of dogs, begins to sweat when shown a picture of a dog or when hearing people talk about dogs. Here the person is responding to the labels, to the maps, as if they were the actual thing or territory.

Intensional orientation may be seen clearly in the results of the numerous studies on prestige suggestion. Basically, these studies demonstrate that we are influenced more when we assume that the message comes from a prestigious personality than when it comes from an average individual. Such studies have shown that if given a painting, we will evaluate it highly if we think it was painted by a famous artist. But we will give it a low evaluation if we think it was produced by a little-known artist. Other studies have focused on our agreement with dogmatic statements, our judgments of literary merit, our perception of musical ability, and so on. In all of these studies the influencing factor is not the message itself—that is, the painting, the piece of literature, the music—but the name attached to it. Advertisers, of course, have long known the value of this type of appeal and have capitalized on it quite profitably.

One of the most ingenious examples of intensional orientation requires that you role play for a minute and picture yourselves seated with a packet of photographs before you. Each of the photographs is of a person you have never seen. You are asked to scratch out the eyes in each photograph. You are further told that this is simply an experiment and that the individuals whose pictures you have will not be aware of anything that has transpired here. As you are scratching out the eyes you come upon a photograph of your mother. What do you do? Are you able to scratch out the eyes as you have done with the pictures of the strangers or have you somehow lost your ability to scratch out eyes? If, as many others, you are unable to scratch out the eyes you are responding intensionally. You are, in effect, responding to the map (in this case the picture) as if it were the territory (your own mother).

In a study conducted not long ago Philip Goldberg claimed that women were

Box 9
THE NAME OF THE SITUATION AS AFFECTING BEHAVIOR

B. L. Whorf

In the course of my professional work for a fire insurance company, in which I undertook the task of analyzing many hundreds of reports of circumstances surrounding the start of fires . . . it became evident that not only a physical situation . . . but the meaning of that situation to people, was sometimes a factor, through the behavior of the people, in the start of the fire. . . .

Thus around a storage of what are called "gasoline drums," behavior will tend to a certain type, that is, great care will be exercised; while around a storage of what are called "empty gasoline drums" it will tend to be different—careless, with little repression of smoking or of tossing cigarette stubs about. Yet the "empty" drums are perhaps the more dangerous, since they contain explosive vapor. Physically the situation is hazardous, but the linguistic analysis according to regular analogy must employ the word "empty," which inevitably suggests lack of hazard. . . .

In a wood distillation plant the metal stills were insulated with a composition prepared from limestone and called at the plant "spun limestone." No attempt was made to protect this covering from excessive heat or the contact of flame. After a period of use the fire below one of the stills spread to the "limestone," which to everyone's great surprise burned vigorously. Exposure to acetic acid fumes from the stills had converted part of the limestone (calcium carbonate) to calcium acetate. This when heated in a fire decomposes, forming inflammable acetone. Behavior that tolerated fire close to the covering was induced by use of the name "limestone," which because it ends in "stone" implies noncombustibility. . . .

A tannery discharged waste water containing animal matter in an outdoor settling basin partly roofed with wood and partly open. This situation is one that ordinarily would be verbalized as "pool of water." A workman had occasion to light a blow-torch nearby, and threw his match into the water. But the decomposing waste matter was evolving gas under the wood cover, so that the setup was the reverse of "watery." An instant flare of flame ignited the woodwork, and the fire quickly spread into the adjoining building. . . .

Beside a coal-fired melting pot for lead reclaiming was dumped a pile of "scrap lead"—a misleading verbalization, for it consisted of the lead sheets of old radio condensers, which still had paraffin paper between them. Soon the paraffin blazed up and fired the roof, half of which was burned off.

Such examples, which could be greatly multiplied, will suffice to show how the cue to a certain line of behavior is often given by the analogies of the linguistic formula in which the situation is spoken of, and by which to some degree it is analyzed, classified, and allotted its place in that world which is "to a large extent unconsciously built up on the language habits of the group." And we always assume that the linguistic analysis made by our group reflects reality better than it does.

Source: From "The Relation of Habitual Thought and Behavior to Language," in *Language, Culture, and Personality, Essays in Memory of Edward Sapir,* edited by Leslie Spier, A. Irving Hallowell, Stanley S. Newman, pp. 75–77. Menasha, Wisconsin, Sapir Memorial Fund, 1941, University of Utah Press, reprint edition. Reprinted by permission.

prejudiced against women. Specifically, he found that women felt that articles written by men were more authoritative and more valuable than identical articles with feminine by-lines. This result was found for messages in "traditionally masculine fields," such as law and city planning, as well as in "traditionally feminine fields," such as elementary school teaching and dietetics. Again this is a clear example of intensional orientation, of our tendency to look at the label (in this case the by-line) and to evaluate the territory (in this case the actual article) only through the label.

In a letter addressed to Ann Landers a young lady wrote that she was distressed because her parents reacted so negatively to the idea of her fiance becoming a nurse. Ann Landers offered some comfort but added, "But I do feel that they ought to call male nurses something else." This is a rather classic example of intensional orientation.

An experiment conducted with stutterers should further illustrate this notion of intensional orientation. Early research has found that stutterers will stutter more when talking with persons in authority than with subordinates. Stutterers will stutter very little when talking with children or when addressing animals, for example, but when it comes to teachers or employers they stutter a great deal. Another finding on stuttering is that of adaptation. This refers to the fact that as a stutterer reads a particular passage he or she will stutter less and less on each successive reading. In this experiment the researcher obtained from the stutterers the names of the persons to whom they had most difficulty speaking. At a later date the researchers had each stutterer read a passage five times. As predicted the stuttering decreased on each reading to the point where it was almost entirely absent on the fifth reading. Before the sixth reading the experimenter placed in front of the stutterer a photograph of the person the stutterer had named as most difficult to speak to, and on the sixth reading the stuttering increased approximately to the level during the first reading of the passage. Again, the individual was responding to the photograph, the label, the map, as if it were something more, as if it were the actual thing.

Labels are certainly helpful guides but they are not the things, and they should not be confused with the things for which they are only symbols.

FACT-INFERENCE CONFUSION

We can make statements about the world that we observe, and we can make statements about what we have not observed. In form or structure these statements are similar and could not be distinguished from each other by any grammatical analysis. For example, we can say, "She is wearing a blue jacket," as well as "He is harboring an illogical hatred." If we diagrammed these sentences they would yield identical structures, and yet we know quite clearly that they are very different types of statements. In the first one we can observe the jacket and the blue color. But how do we observe "illogical hatred?'' Obviously, this is not a descriptive statement but an inferential statement. It is a statement that we make not only on the basis of what we observe but on the basis of what we observe plus our own conclusions.

There is no problem with making inferential statements; we must make them if we are to talk about much that is meaningful to us. The problem arises, then, not in making inferential statements but in acting as if those inferential statements are factual statements.

Consider, for example, the following anecdote: A woman went for a walk one day and met her friend, whom she had not seen, or heard from, or heard of, in 10 years. After an exchange of greetings, the woman said, ''Is this your little boy?'' and her friend replied, ''Yes, I got married about six years ago.'' The woman then asked the child, ''What is your name?'' and the little boy replied, ''Same as my father's.'' ''Oh,'' said the woman, ''then it must be Peter.''

The question, of course, is how did the woman know the boy's father's name if she had not seen or heard from or heard of her friend in the last ten years? The answer, of course, is obvious. But it is obvious only after we recognize that in reading this short passage we have made an inference which, although we are not aware of our having made an inference, is preventing us from answering a most simple question. Specifically, we have made the inference that the woman's friend is a woman. Actually, the friend is a man named Peter.

This is very similar to the example used to illustrate sexism in the language. One version goes something like this: A boy and his father are in an accident. The father is killed and the little boy is rushed to the hospital to be operated on. The surgeon is called in, looks at the boy, and says, ''I can't operate on this boy; he's my son.'' The question is, how could the boy be the surgeon's son if his father was killed in the accident? This question should not have caused any problems, but we were sensitized to making inferences on the basis of sex. Of course, the surgeon is the boy's mother. This is a particularly good example for illustrating our expectations in regard to male and female occupations. Because of our prior conditioning we almost feel compelled to qualify the term surgeon if the surgeon is female but not if the surgeon is male. Similarly, we speak of women lawyers and women doctors but of male nurses.

Perhaps the classic example of this type of fact-inference confusion concerns the case of the ''empty'' gun that unfortunately proves to be loaded. With amazing frequency we find in the newspapers examples of people being so sure that the guns are empty that they point them at another individual and fire. Many times, of course, they are empty. But, unfortunately, many times they are not. Here one makes an inference (that the gun is empty) but acts on the inference as if it is a fact and fires the gun.

Some of the essential differences between factual and inferential statements are summarized in Table 11.1.

Table 11.1
Differences Between Factual and Inferential Statements

Factual statements	Inferential statements
1. may be made only after observation	1. may be made at any time
2. are limited to what has been observed	2. go beyond what has been observed
3. may be made only by the observer	3. may be made by anyone
4. may only be about the past or the present	4. may be about any time—past, present, or future
5. approach certainty	5. involve varying degrees of probability
6. are subject to verifiable standards	6. are not subject to verifiable standards

Distinguishing between these two types of statements does not mean to imply that one type is better than another type. Neither is better than the other. We need both types of statements; both are useful, both are important.

The problem arises when we treat one type of statement as if it were another type. Specifically, the problem arises when we treat an inferential statement as if it were a factual statement.

Inferential statements need to be accompanied by tentativeness. We need to recognize that such statements may prove to be wrong, and we should be aware of that possibility. Inferential statements should leave open the possibility of other alternatives. If, for example, we treat the statement, "The United States should enforce the blockade," as if it were a factual statement, we eliminate the possibility of other alternatives. When making inferential statements we should be psychologically prepared to be proven wrong. This requires a great deal of effort but it is probably effort well spent. If we are psychologically prepared to be proven wrong we will be less hurt if and when we are shown to be incorrect.

ALLNESS

The world is infinitely complex and because of this we can never say all about anything—at least we cannot logically say all about anything. And this is particularly true in dealing with people. We may *think* we know all there is to know about individuals or about why they did what they did, yet clearly we do not know all. We can never know all the reasons we ourselves do something, and yet we often think that we know all the reasons why our parents or our friends or our enemies did something. And because we are so convinced that we know all the reasons, we are quick to judge and evaluate the actions of others with great confidence that what we are doing is justified.

We may, for example, be assigned a textbook to read and because previous texts have been dull and perhaps because the first chapter was dull we infer that all the rest will likewise be dull. Of course, it often turns out that the rest of the book is even worse than the beginning. Yet it could be that the rest of the book would have proved exciting had it been read with an open mind. The problem here is that we run the risk of defining the entire text (on the basis of previous texts and perhaps the first chapter) in such a way as to preclude any other possibilities. If we tell ourselves that the book is dull it probably will appear dull. If we say a course will be useless ("all required courses are useless") it will be extremely difficult for that instructor to make the course anything but what we have defined it to be. Only occasionally do we allow ourselves to be proven wrong; for the most part we resist rather fiercely.

The parable of the six blind men and the elephant is an excellent example of an allness orientation and its attendant problems. You may recall from elementary school that the poem by John Saxe concerns six blind men of Indostan who came to examine an elephant, an animal they had only heard about. The first blind man touched the elephant's side and concluded that the elephant was like a wall. The second felt the tusk and said the elephant must be like a spear. The third held the trunk and concluded that the elephant was much like a snake. The fourth touched the knee and knew the elephant was like a tree. The fifth felt the ear and said the elephant was like a fan. And the sixth grabbed the tail and concluded that the elephant was like a rope. Each of these learned men reached his own conclusion regarding what this marvelous beast, the elephant, was really like. Each argued that he was correct and that the others were wrong. Each, of course, was correct; but at the same time each was wrong. The point this poem illustrates is that we are all in the position of the six blind men. We never see all of something; we never experience anything fully. We see part of an object, an event, a person—and on that limited basis conclude what the whole is like. This procedure is a relatively universal one; we have to do this since it is impossible to observe everything. And yet we must recognize that when we make judgments of the whole based only on a part we are actually making inferences that can later be proven wrong. If we assume that we know all of anything we are into the pattern of misevaluation called *allness*.

Students who walk into a class convinced that they cannot learn anything will probably not learn anything. And while it may be that the teacher was not very effective, it may also be that the students have closed their minds to the possibility of learning anything. Disraeli once said that "to be conscious that you are ignorant is a great step toward knowledge." That observation is an excellent example of a nonallness attitude. If we recognize that there is more to learn, more to see, more to hear, we will leave ourselves open to this additional information and will be better prepared to assimilate it into our existing structures. An implicit or explicit *etc.* should end every sentence.

STATIC EVALUATION

In order to best understand the concept of static evaluation try to write down a statement or two that makes no reference to time—that is, we must not be able to tell whether the statement refers to the past, present, or future. Write this statement down before reading on. Next, attempt to date the following quotation. Approximately when was it written?

> Those states are likely to be well administered in which the middle class is large, and larger if possible than both the other classes or at any rate than either singly; for the addition of the middle class turns the scale and prevents either of the extremes from being dominant.

These two brief exercises should illustrate an interesting dimension of the English language. It was probably extremely difficult, if not impossible, to produce a sentence which made no reference to time whatsoever. Time, in English, is an obligatory category which means that all sentences must contain some reference to past, present, or future. Our verb system is constructed in such a way that it is impossible to produce a sentence without including a reference to time in the verb. This is not true in all languages. Second, in dating the quotation, most persons would find themselves missing the actual date by at least a few hundred years. The statement was actually written by Aristotle in his *Politics* approximately 2300 years ago.

Thus while it is impossible to make statements without reference to past, present, or future it is almost impossible to tell when statements were produced. These, of course, are obvious statements about language. Yet their consequences are not often so obvious.

Often when we form an abstraction of something or someone—when we formulate a verbal statement about an event or person—that abstraction, that statement, has a tendency to remain static and unchanging while the object or person to whom it originally referred may have changed enormously. Alfred Korzybski used an interesting illustration in this connection: In a tank we have a large fish and many small fish which are the natural food for the large fish. Given freedom in the tank the large fish will eat the small fish. After some time we partition the tank with the large fish on one side and the small fish on the other, divided only by a clear piece of glass. For a considerable time the large fish will attempt to eat the small fish but will fail each time; each time it will knock into the glass partition. After some time it will "learn" that attempting to eat the small fish means difficulty and will no longer go after them. Now, however, we remove the partition and the little fish swim all around the big fish. But the big fish does not eat them and in fact will die of starvation while its natural food swims all around. The large fish has learned a pattern of behavior and even though the actual territory has changed, the map remains static.

While we would probably all agree that everything is in a constant state of flux, the relevant question is whether we act as if we know this. Put differently, do we act in accordance with the notion of change, instead of just accepting it intellectually? Do we realize, for example, that because we have failed at something once we need not fail again? Do we realize that if someone does something to hurt us that they too are in a constant state of change? Our evaluations of ourselves and of others must keep pace with the rapidly changing real world; otherwise we will be left with attitudes about and beliefs in a world that no longer exists.

T. S. Eliot, in *The Cocktail Party,* said that "what we know of other people is only our memory of the moments during which we knew them. And they have changed since then . . . at every meeting we are meeting a stranger."

INDISCRIMINATION

Nature seems to abhor sameness at least as much as vacuums, for nowhere in the universe can we find two things that are identical. Everything is unique and unlike everything else.

Our language, however, provides us with common nouns, such as teacher, student, friend, enemy, war, politician, liberal, and the like which lead us to focus on similarities. Such nouns lead us to group all teachers together, all students together, all friends together and perhaps divert attention away from the uniqueness of each individual, each object, each event.

The misevaluation of *indiscrimination,* then, is one in which we focus on classes of individuals or objects or events and fail to see that each is unique, each is different, and each needs to be looked at individually.

This misevalaution is at the heart of the common practice of stereotyping national, racial, and religious groups. A stereotype is a relatively fixed mental picture of some group which is applied to each individual of the group without regard to his or her unique qualities. It is important to note that although stereotypes are usually thought of as negative they may also be positive. We can, for example, consider certain national groups as lazy or superstitious or mercenary or criminal but we can also consider them as intelligent, progressive, honest, hard working, and so on. Regardless of whether such stereotypes are positive or negative, however, the problem they create is the same. They provide us with short-cuts which are most often inappropriate. For example, when we meet a particular individual our first reaction may be to pigeonhole him or her into some category—perhaps a religious one, perhaps a national one, perhaps an academic one. Regardless of the type of category we attempt to fit him or her into we invariably fail to devote sufficient attention to the unique characteristics of the individual before us. As college students you may resent being stereotyped by other students. Each group seems to stereotype the other

Table 11.2
Barriers to Verbal Interaction

Be careful of:	Be conscious of:
1. Polarization; either-or thinking	1. Multivalued orientation; many-sided perspective
2. Intensional orientation	2. Extensional orientation; the word is not the thing
3. Fact-inference confusion	3. Facts are NOT inferences; inferences are NOT facts
4. Allness	4. Nonallness; the word is not ALL the thing; use the *etc.*
5. Static evaluation	5. Process Evaluation; date all statements
6. Indiscrimination	6. Nondiscrimination; index all nouns

quite readily while just as rapidly deploring the unfair stereotyping that goes on in a supposedly academic community.

It should be emphasized that there is nothing wrong with classifying. No one would argue that classifying is unhealthy or immoral. It is, on the contrary, an extremely useful method of dealing with any complex matter. Classifying helps us to deal with complexity; it puts order into our thinking. The problem arises not from classifying itself. It arises from our classifying, then applying some evaluative label to that class, and then utilizing that evaluative label as an "adequate" map for each individual in the group. Put differently, indiscrimination is a denial of another's uniqueness.

A summary of the "do's" and "don't's" of verbal interaction appears in Table 11.2.

SOURCES

The barriers to verbal interaction owe their formulation to the work of the General Semanticists. I would especially recommend the following for beginners: John C. Condon, Jr., *Semantics and Communication,* 2nd ed. (New York: Macmillan, 1975); William V. Haney, *Communication and Organizational Behavior: Text and Cases,* 3d ed. (Homewood, Ill.: Richard D. Irwin, 1973); S. I. Hayakawa, *Language in Thought and Action,* 3d ed. (New York: Harcourt Brace Jovanovich, 1972).

The nature of E-prime, explained in Experiential Vehicle 11.1, is discussed in detail in D. David Bourland, Jr., "A Linguistic Note: Writing in E-Prime," *General Semantics Bulletin,* nos. 32 and 33, 1965/1966.

Much that appears in this unit appears in more detail in my *General Semantics: Guide and Workbook,* rev. ed. (DeLand, Florida: Everett/Edwards, 1974). A number of the exercises are taken from this book as well. My cassette tape series *General Semantics: Nine Lectures* (DeLand, Florida: Everett/Edwards, 1971) also covers this material. For somewhat different points of view see Gerard Nierenberg and Henry Calero, *Meta-Talk: Guide to Hidden Meanings in Conversations* (New York: Simon and Schuster, 1973) and John C. Condon, Jr., *Interpersonal Communication* (New York: Macmillan, 1977).

EXPERIENTIAL VEHICLES

11.1 E-PRIME

E-prime is normal English minus the verb *to be*. The term E' refers to the mathematical equation, $E - e = E'$, where $E =$ the English language and $e =$ the verb *to be*. E', therefore, refers to normal English without the verb *to be*.

D. David Bourland, Jr. suggests that if we wrote and spoke without the verb *to be* we would more accurately describe the event. The verb *to be* often suggests that qualities are in the person or thing rather than in the observer making the statement. We often forget that these statements are evaluative rather than purely descriptive sentences. For example, we say "Johnny is a failure" and imply that failure is somehow *in* Johnny instead of in someone's evaluation of Johnny. This type of thinking is especially important in making statements about ourselves. We say, for example, "I can't learn mathematics," or "I'm unpopular," or "I'm lazy" and imply that these qualities (the inability to learn mathematics, the unpopularity, and the laziness) are *in* us. But these are simply evaluations which may be incorrect or, if at least partly accurate, may change. The verb *to be* implies a permanence which simply is not true of the world we live in.

To further appreciate the difference between statements that use the verb *to be* and those that do not, try to rewrite the following sentences without using the verb *to be* in any of its forms, that is, *is, are, am, was*, or any other variants.

1. I'm ugly.
2. He is unhappy.
3. What is love?
4. Is this helpful?
5. This exam was unfair.
6. Hate is a useless emotion.
7. Is life meaningful?
8. Was the book good?
9. This course is difficult.
10. This class is the best in the school.

11.2 FACTS AND INFERENCES

Carefully read the following report and the observations based on it.* Indicate whether you think the observations are true, false, or doubtful on the

* This experiential vehicle is taken from Joseph A. Devito, *General Semantics: Guide and Workbook*, rev. ed. (Deland, Florida: Everett/Edwards, Inc., 1974), p. 55.

basis of the information presented in the report. Circle T if the observation is definitely true, circle F if the observation is definitely false, and circle ? if the observation may be either true or false. Judge each observation in order. Do not re-read the observations after you have indicated your judgment and do not change any of your answers.

> A well-liked college teacher had just completed making up the final examinations and had turned off the lights in the office. Just then a tall, dark, broad figure appeared and demanded the examination. The professor opened the drawer. Everything in the drawer was picked up and the individual ran down the corridor. The Dean was notified immediately.

1. The thief was tall, dark, and broad.   T   F   ?
2. The professor turned off the lights.   T   F   ?
3. A tall figure demanded the examination.   T   F   ?
4. The examination was picked up by someone.   T   F   ?
5. The examination was picked up by the professor.   T   F   ?
6. A tall, dark figure appeared after the professor turned off the lights in the office.   T   F   ?
7. The man who opened the drawer was the professor.   T   F   ?
8. The professor ran down the corridor.   T   F   ?
9. The drawer was never actually opened.   T   F   ?
10. In this report three persons are referred to.   T   F   ?

11.3 I, YOU, AND HE AND SHE TALK

The way in which we phrase something will often influence the way in which something is perceived. This is especially true when we are dealing with and talking about people. We do not talk about ourselves as we do about the people we are with or about the people we know but are not with.

Recognizing this simple language habit, Bertrand Russell, the British philosopher and mathematician, proposed a conjugation of "irregular" verbs. One example he used was:

I am firm.
You are obstinate.
He is a pig-headed fool.

The *New Statesman* and *Nation* picked up on this and offered prizes for contributions in the style of these irregular verbs. One of the best ones was:

I am sparkling.
You are unusually talkative.
He is drunk.

> Ten sentences that are phrased in the first person follow. Using Russell's lead, conjugate these irregular verbs.

1. I speak my mind.
2. I believe in what I say.
3. I take an occasional drink.
4. I like to talk with people about people.
5. I smoke.
6. I study.
7. I like to eat a good meal.
8. I am a creative thinker.
9. I have been known to get upset at times.
10. I am open-minded.

UNIT 12
Characteristics of Nonverbal Communication

Communicative
Contextual
Believable
Packaged
Metacommunicational

12.1 Breaking Nonverbal Rules

LEARNING GOALS

After completing this unit, you should be able to:

1. explain the principle that holds that nonverbal communication occurs in a context
2. explain that reasons why nonverbal behaviors in an interactional situation always communicate
3. identify the reasons for assuming that nonverbal communication is highly believable
4. explain the *packaged* nature of nonverbal communication
5. define *metacommunication*
6. provide at least three examples of the ways in which nonverbal behavior is frequently metacommunicational
7. cite at least three examples of unwritten nonverbal rules of behavior

Today everyone seems interested in nonverbal communication, or what is more popularly called "body language." The gimmick used in selling the books or articles is the promise that we will learn to decipher what other people are thinking simply by observing their "body language." The cover of Julius Fast's *Body Language,* for example, shows the picture of a woman sitting in a chair with her arms folded and her legs crossed. Surrounding the woman are such questions as "Does her body say that she's a loose woman?" "Does your body say that you're hung up?" "Does his body say that he's a manipulator?" and so on. Who could resist learning this kind of information? It would be indispensable at parties and all sorts of social gatherings. Success in one's business and social life are almost assured should one just learn to read body language.

But, as anyone who has read such works knows, such significant insight is not so easy to attain. Perhaps the primary reason is simply that we do not know enough about nonverbal communication to enable the layman to make instant and accurate readings of the inner workings of the mind. And yet we have—especially in the last 10 years—learned a great deal about this nonverbal communication business.

Here we identify a few assumptions pertaining to nonverbal communication which seem valid and useful. These assumptions should provide a kind of framework through which we might better view the specifics of nonverbal communication. These assumptions may be stated briefly in preface. (1) All nonverbal behavior in an interactional situation is *communicative.* (2) Nonverbal

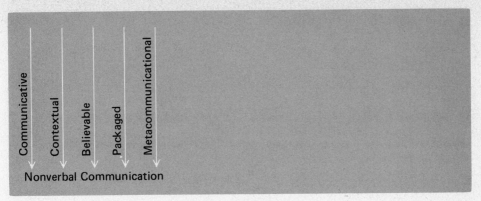

Figure 12.1
The Characteristics of Nonverbal Communication

communication is inevitably *contextually-bound.* (3) Nonverbal communication is highly *believable.* (4) Nonverbal communication occurs in *packaged* forms. (5) Nonverbal communication is frequently *metacommunicational* (see Figure 12.1).

The goal of such discussion is not to provide the means for personality diagnosis or for dating success or for determining when someone is bluffing in a poker game. The purposes are 1) to enable us to better understand ourselves, 2) to enable us to better understand others, and 3) to enable us to communicate more effectively.

COMMUNICATIVE

Nonverbal behavior in an interactional situation always communicates. This observation is true of all forms of communication, but it seems particularly important to stress it in regard to nonverbal communication. All behavior in an interactional situation is communicative. It is impossible not to behave, and consequently, it is impossible not to communicate. Regardless of what one does or does not do, one's nonverbal behavior communicates something to someone (assuming that there is an interactional setting).

Sitting silently in a corner and reading a book communicates to the other people in the room just as surely as would verbalization. Staring out the window during class communicates something to the teacher just as surely as would your saying, "I'm bored." Notice, however, an important difference between the nonverbal and the verbal statements. The student looking out the window, when confronted by the teacher's, "Why are you bored," can always claim to be just momentarily distracted by something outside. Saying, "I'm bored" however, prevents the student from backing off and giving a more socially acceptable meaning to the statement. The nonverbal communica-

Box 10
TEACHING CHIMPS TO TALK

The human urge to communicate is seen, perhaps in its most blatant form, in our effort to communicate with the lower animals, particularly the chimpanzees.

W. N. and Louise Kellogg were perhaps the first to record their efforts to teach Gua, a 7½-month-old chimp, a human language. The Kelloggs raised Gua along with their son Donald, two months Gua's senior. Gua was treated in almost every way like a human child and like the human child no special effort was made to teach her language. Although there was some success, for the most part the experiment ended in failure. Gua did learn to produce different sounds to mean different things but these were relatively few. She did manage to understand numerous different sentences (approximately 70 it was reported) and even surpassed Donald in her apparent comprehension of language. But the interesting thing was that even though Gua at one time surpassed Donald in comprehension she could not be made to respond appropriately to novel utterances, that is, to sentences she had not been explicitly taught.

Improving somewhat on the procedures used with Gua, Keith and Cathy Hayes began seeing their chimp almost immediately after birth and took her into their house when she was only six weeks of age. The Hayeses treated their chimp, Viki, like a retarded child and gave her specific instructions in language. According to the Hayeses, Viki learned to say three words, though not terribly distinctly, and responded to a number of different utterances. She is reported to have responded appropriately to novel utterances, but the extent of this ability does not seem clear.

Some researchers have reasoned that chimps have failed to learn human language not so much because they are incapable intellectually but rather that they are physiologically incapable of producing the sounds. Since the speech signals are not essential to language, recent attempts have focused on teaching chimps human language but through a means which is natural to their species. Allen and Beatrice Gardner of the University of Nevada attempted to teach Washoe sign

tion, however, is also more convenient from the point of view of the teacher. The teacher, if confronted with the student's "I'm bored," must act on that in some way. Some of the possibilities include saying, "See me after class," "I'm just as bored as you are," "Who cares?" "Why are you bored?" and so on. All of them, however, are confrontations of a kind. The teacher is in a sense forced to do something even though he or she might prefer to ignore it. The nonverbal staring out the window allows the teacher to ignore it. This does not mean that the teacher is not aware of it or that the staring is not communicating. Rather, nonverbal communication allows the "listener" an opportunity to feign a lack of awareness. And, of course, this is exactly what so many teachers do when confronted by a class of students looking out the window, reading the newspaper, talking among themselves, and so on.

There are, however, exceptions to this general rule. Consider, for example, language, the language of the deaf. Washoe learned a number of words and simple sentences but it was not always clear if she was also learning the rules for sentence construction. She was able to respond appropriately to many novel utterances and learned to use approximately 300 two-word sentences, but Washoe soon became too difficult to handle and the experiment had to be abandoned.

Sarah, under the direction of psychologist David Premack, is reported to have learned language with remarkable rapidity. Premack created a language for Sarah consisting of plastic pieces which adhere to a magnetic board. Each plastic piece corresponded to a word. In learning the language Sarah had to place the appropriate pieces on the magnetic board. Thus, if she was shown a banana and wanted it she had to first select the plastic piece that meant banana and place it on the board. In one report Sarah was said to have learned 8 names of people, 21 verbs, 6 colors, 21 food names, and 27 concepts, for example, key, table, shoe, dress, and so on. Sarah was also able to create and respond appropriately to sentences as complex as "Sarah, insert apple red dish, apple banana green dish." But perhaps the most remarkable feat Sarah is reported to have learned is the concept "name of." When teaching Sarah a new concept she is shown the object and the word (plastic piece) and the relationship term "name of" and apparently has been able in this way to quickly learn the terms for new concepts. The implications of this single accomplishment are vast. Conceivably—and apparently this is one of the main motives of the study—Sarah, after mastering the language fully, might well be able to teach it to her offspring who in turn might teach it to theirs and so on. The days of *Planet of the Apes* are perhaps far away but chimps and humans communicating might not be.

Another attempt at using sign language is being conducted by Herb Terrace in New York with a chimp named Nim. Elaborate socialization procedures have been instituted and Nim apparently lives her life much as would a human child. Nim seems to be functioning at quite a high level although the exact extent of her ability to use language seems unclear, at least at the time of this writing. It seems likely that we will be hearing more from Nim in the not-too-distant future.

if the student, instead of looking out the window, gave the teacher some unmistakable nonverbal signal such as the thumb pointing down gesture. This type of nonverbal communication is not so easy to feign ignorance of. Here the teacher must confront this comment just as surely as he or she would have to confront the comment, "I'm bored."

Even the less obvious and less easily observed behaviors also communicate. The smaller movements of the eyes, hands, facial muscles, and so on also communicate just as do the gross movements of gesturing, sitting in a corner, or staring out a window.

These small movements are extremely important in interpersonal relationships. We can often tell, for example, when two people genuinely like each other and when they are merely being polite. If we had to state how we know this we would probably have considerable difficulty. These inferences, many of which are correct, are based primarily on these small nonverbal behaviors of the participants, the muscles around the eyes, the degree of eye contact, the way in which the individuals face each other, and so on. All nonverbal behavior, however small or transitory, is significant—each has a meaning, each communicates.

CONTEXTUAL

Like verbal communication, nonverbal communication exists in a context and that context helps to determine to a large extent the meanings of any nonverbal behaviors. The same nonverbal behavior may have a totally different meaning when it occurs in another context. A wink of the eye to a beautiful person on a bus means something completely different from the wink of the eye that signifies a put-on or a lie. Similarly, the meaning of a given bit of nonverbal behavior will differ depending on the verbal behavior it accompanies or is close to in time. Pounding the fist on the table during a speech in support of a particular politician means something quite different from that same fist pounding in response to news about someone's death. When divorced from the context it is impossible to tell what any given bit of nonverbal behavior may mean. Of course, even if we know the context in detail we still might not be able to decipher the meaning of the nonverbal behavior. In attempting to understand and analyze nonverbal communication, however, it is essential that full recognition be taken of the context.

BELIEVABLE

For some reasons, not all of which are clear to researchers in nonverbal communication, we are quick to believe nonverbal behaviors even when these behaviors contradict the verbal behavior. Consider, for example, a conversation between a teacher and a student. The student is attempting to get a higher grade for the course and is in the process of telling the teacher how much hard work was put into and how much enjoyment was derived from the classes. Throughout the discussion, however, the student betrays his or her real intentions with various small muscle movements, inconsistent smiles, a lack of direct eye contact, and so on. Somehow, the teacher goes away with the feeling, based on the nonverbal behavior, that the student really hated the class. For the most part, research has shown that when the verbal and the nonverbal messages differ, we will believe the nonverbal. In fact, Albert Mehrabian argues that the total impact of a message is a function of the following formula: Total Impact = .07 verbal + .38 vocal + .55 facial. This formula leaves very little influence for verbal messages. Only one-third of the impact is vocal (that is, paralanguage, rate, pitch, rhythm), and over half of the message is communicated by the face.

Why we believe the nonverbal over the verbal message is not clear. It may be that we feel verbal messages are easier to fake. Consequently, when there is a conflict, we distrust the verbal and accept the nonverbal. Or it may be that the nonverbal messages are perceived without conscious awareness. We learned them without being aware of any such learning and we perceive them without conscious awareness. Thus when such a conflict arises we somehow get this "feeling" from the nonverbal. Since we cannot isolate its source, we assume that it is somehow correct. Of course, a belief in the nonverbal message may simply result from our being reinforced for conclusions consistent with nonverbal behavior; consequently, we tend to repeat that kind of judgment. Perhaps in the past we have been correct in basing judgments on nonverbals and so continue to rely on these cues rather than on verbal ones.

PACKAGED

Nonverbal behaviors, whether the hands, the eyes, or the muscle tone of the entire body, are normally accompanied by other nonverbal behaviors that reinforce or support each other. The nonverbals occur in packaged forms. We do not express fear in our eyes, for example, while the rest of our body relaxes as if sleeping. We do not express anger through our posture while our face smiles. Rather, the entire body expresses the emotion. For purposes of analysis we may wish to focus primarily on the eyes or the facial muscles or the hand movements but we need to recognize that these do not occur apart from other nonverbal behaviors. In fact, it is physically difficult to express an intense emotion with only one part of the body. Try to express an emotion with say your face while ignoring the rest of the body. You will probably find that the rest of the body takes on the qualities of that emotion as well. You will probably experience considerable difficulty if you attempt to restrict the expression of this emotion to only one part of the body.

It is even more difficult to express widely different or contradictory emotions with different parts of your body. For example, when you are afraid of something and your body tenses up, it becomes very difficult to relax your facial muscles and smile.

In any form of communication, whether interpersonal, small group, public speaking, or mass media, we generally do not pay much attention to the packaged nature of nonverbal communication. So expected is it that it goes unnoticed. But when there is an incongruity, when the weak handshake belies the smile, when the nervous posture belies the focused stare, when the constant preening belies the relaxed whistling or humming, we take notice. Invariably we are led to question the credibility, the sincerity, the honesty of the individual. And research tells us that our instincts serve us well in this type of situation. When nonverbal behaviors contradict each other, there seems good reason to question the believability of the communicator.

METACOMMUNICATIONAL

All behavior, verbal as well as nonverbal, can be metacommunicational. Any given bit of behavior can make reference to communication. We can say,

"This statement is false," or, "Do you understand what I am trying to communicate to you?" In each case these statements have made references to communication and are called *metacommunicational statements*.

Nonverbal behavior is very often metacommunicational. That is why this principle or assumption is noted here specifically. Nonverbal behaviors frequently function to make a statement about some verbal statement. The most obvious example of course is the crossing of the fingers behind one's back when telling a lie. We observe frequently someone making a statement and winking. The wink functions as a comment on the statement. These are obvious examples. Consider more subtle metacommunication. Take the first day of class as an example. The teacher walks in and says something to the effect that he or she is the instructor for the course and might then say how the course will be conducted, what will be required, what the goals of the course will be, and so on. But notice that much metacommunication is also going on. Notice that the clothes the teacher wears and how he or she wears them, the length and style of hair, the general physical appearance, the way he or she walks, the tone of voice and so on all communicate about the communication—as well as, of course, communicating in and of themselves. These nonverbal messages function to comment on the verbal messages the instructor is trying to communicate. On the basis of these cues, students will come to various conclusions. They might conclude that this teacher is going to be easy even though a long reading list was given or that the class is going to be enjoyable or boring or too advanced or irrelevant.

The metacommunicational function of nonverbal communication is not limited to its role as an adjunct to verbal communication; nonverbal communication may also comment on other nonverbal communication. This is actually a very common type of situation. For example, the individual who, when meeting a stranger, both smiles and presents a totally lifeless hand for shaking is a good example of how one nonverbal behavior may refer to another nonverbal behavior. Here the lifeless handshake belies the enthusiastic smile.

Most often, when nonverbal behavior is metacommunicational it functions to reinforce (rather than contradict) other verbal or nonverbal behavior. You may literally roll up your sleeves when talking about cleaning up this room, or smile when greeting someone, or run to meet someone you say you are anxious to see, or arrive early for a party you verbally express pleasure in attending. On the negative, though still consistent side, you may arrive late for a dental appointment (presumably with a less than pleasant facial expression) or grind your teeth while telling off your boss. The point is simply that much nonverbal communication is metacommunicational. This does not mean that nonverbal communication may not refer to people, events, things, relationships, and so on (that is, be *object* communication), nor does it mean that verbal communication may not be metacommunication. We merely stress here the role of nonverbal communication as metacommunication because of its frequent use in this role.

SOURCES

General introductions to nonverbal communication are plentiful. Mele Koneya and Alton Barbour, *Louder Than Words . . . Nonverbal Communication* (Columbus, Ohio: Charles Merrill, 1976) is a brief introduction to the various areas of nonverbal communication. Mark Knapp's *Nonverbal Communication in Human Interaction* (New York: Holt, 1972) surveys the same area but in greater detail and with more attention to the numerous experimental and descriptive studies. Similar coverage is provided by Dale G. Leathers, *Nonverbal Communication Systems* (Boston: Allyn & Bacon, 1976). A brief collection of readings has been edited by Haig A. Bosmajian, *The Rhetoric of Nonverbal Communication: Readings* (Glenview, Ill.: Scott, Foresman, 1971). Albert Mehrabian provides a brief but insightful overview in his "Communication Without Words," *Psychology Today* 2 (September 1968). A section by Mehrabian, "Nonverbal Communication," in C. David Mortensen and Kenneth K. Sereno, *Advances in Communication Research* (New York: Harper & Row, 1973) provides an excellent review of significant literature and presents four experimental studies on various aspects of nonverbal communication. Flora Davis's *Inside Intuition* (New York: Signet, 1973) provides an excellent popular review of nonverbal communication. A most interesting collection of articles and original essays on all aspects of nonverbal communication is provided by Lawrence Rosenfeld and Jean Civikly, *With Words Unspoken* (New York: Holt, Rinehart and Winston, 1976).

EXPERIENTIAL VEHICLE

12.1 BREAKING NONVERBAL RULES

The general objective of this exercise is to become better acquainted with some of the "rules" of nonverbal communication and to analyze some of the effects of breaking such rules.[1]

Much as we learn verbal language (that is, without explicit teaching) we also learn nonverbal language—the rules for interacting nonverbally. Among such rules we have learned might be some like the following:

1. Upon entering an elevator turn to the door and stare at it or at the numbers indicating where the elevator is until your floor is reached.
2. When sitting down in a cafeteria take a seat that is as far away from the next person as possible.
3. When sitting next to someone (or in the general area) do not invade their private space with your body or your belongings.
4. When sitting directly across from people do not stare at them (that is, directly at their eyes) for more than a second or two.
5. Members of the opposite sex should not stare at the various sexual parts of the other person's body while that person is watching you.
6. When strangers are talking, do not enter their group.
7. When talking with someone do not stand too close or too far away. You may move closer when talking about intimate topics. Never stand close enough so that you can smell the other person's body odor. This rule may be broken only under certain conditions, for example, when the individuals involved are physically attracted to each other or when one individual is consoling another or when engaged in some game where the rules require this close contact.
8. When talking in an otherwise occupied area, lower your voice so that other people are not disturbed by your conversation.
9. When talking with someone look at their eyes and facial area only occasionally. Do not stare at them nor avoid their glance completely.
10. When talking with someone do not touch them more than absolutely necessary. This is especially important when the parties do not know each other. Some touching is permitted when the parties are well acquainted. Touching is more permissible for women than it is for men—that is, it is more permissible for women to touch men than for men to

[1] This exercise was suggested to me by Pofessor Jean Civikly.

touch women and more permissible for women to touch women than for men to touch men.

Procedure

The procedures are relatively simple. Groups of two students are formed; one student is designated as rule breaker and one is designated as observer.

The task of the rule breaker is simply to enter some situation where one or more rules of nonverbal communication would normally be operative and break one or more rules. The task of the observer is to record mentally (or in writing if possible) what happens as a result of the rule breaking.

Each group should then return after a specified amount of time and report back to the entire class on what transpired.

UNIT 13
Kinesics

Areas of Kinesics
Types of Movements

    13.1 Instructing Nonverbally
    13.2 Control by Nonverbal Communication

LEARNING GOALS

After completing this unit, you should be able to:

1. define and distinguish between *prekinesics*, *microkinesics*, and *social kinesics*
2. provide two or three examples of nonverbal behaviors meaning different things in different cultures
3. define and provide at least two examples of *emblems*, *illustrators*, *affect displays*, *regulators*, and *adaptors*
4. identify instances of the five types of movements in the behaviors of others and in your own behaviors

AREAS OF KINESICS

The field of *kinesics* or body communication can, for convenience, be divided into three major areas; *prekinesics, microkinesics,* and *social kinesics.* Each of these areas is interrelated and interdependent with each other area.

Prekinesics is concerned with the physiological aspects of bodily movements. Prekinesics provides a method for the description of all bodily movements, although not all of the possible bodily movements have specific meaning. For example, not all of the hand or eye movements have individual and unique meanings. Some do and some do not. Each individually produced bodily motion is termed a *kine.*

Microkinesics is concerned with bodily motions that communicate different meanings. In microkinesics we are concerned with analyzing kines into classes. The range of movements that are functionally important or that communicate different meanings are termed *kinemes* and are analogous to *phonemes,* which define the range of speech sounds functionally important in the language or which communicate different meanings. For example, in the analysis of the English sound system an aspirated [kʰ] and an unaspirated [k=], as in "key" and "ski," respectively, are two sounds that belong to the same /k/ phoneme. These sounds do not communicate different meanings;

we could not in English find two words which differed solely on the basis of whether the [k] was aspirated or unaspirated, that is, on whether there is a puff of air expired (aspirated, as in "key") or not (unaspirated, as in "ski"). Similarly, in the analysis of bodily movements we would find that although we could distinguish eleven positions of the eyelid, not all of these function to communicate different meanings. In fact, only four positions of the eyelid have been found to communicate different meanings. Their specific meanings, however, seem to vary depending upon the context and their collocation with other linguistic features. For example, the most open position might signify anything from surprise to fear, while the almost closed position might mean anything from exhaustion to suspicion. The eleven discernible positions are kines whereas the four meaningful positions are kinemes.

The kineme, like the phoneme, is defined for a particular language community. Although, for example, aspirated [kʰ] and unaspirated [k=] belong to the same phoneme in English they are different phonemes in Hindi. In other cultures only two or perhaps as many as five or six positions of the eyelid might be meaningfully different.

Social kinesics, the third major area, is concerned with the role and meanings of different bodily movements. Whereas microkinesics seeks to explore the meaningful body movements, social kinesics seeks to explore the specific meanings that these movements communicate. Research in this area focuses on the general communicative function of the larger bodily gestures as well as on the relationship between the more minute movements and vocal-auditory communication.

One interesting example used by Ray Birdwhistell to illustrate the role of social kinesics is particularly appropriate here. In this study an analysis was made of leadership in group discussion. It was found that two leaders emerged in this particular discussion among nine boys. One leader spoke a great deal and had the highest percentage of initiated conversations. The other leader, however, only originated an average number of conversations but became a leader by virtue of his bodily movements, particularly those of the face and head. He literally directed and to an extent controlled the group by head and facial movements.

It is the cross-cultural studies, however, that probably provide the most provocative examples of the meaningfulness and meaning of different movements or kinemes. Weston La Barre, the cultural anthropologist, provides a number of fascinating examples. Spitting in most Western cultures is a sign of disgust and displeasure. However, for the Masai of Africa it is a sign of affection and for the American Indian it may be an act of kindness when, for example, the medicine man spits on the sick in order to cure them.

Sticking out the tongue to Westerners is an insult; to the Chinese of the Sung dynasty it served as a symbol to mock terror or to make fun of the anger of another individual; and to the modern South Chinese it serves to express embarrassment over some social mistake.

Mediterranean peoples have a number of hand gestures which communicate quite specific meanings. For example, kissing the fingers means approval, stroking the fingers on the chin signifies a lack of knowledge and concern over a particular event or statement, and forward movement of the hand with the palm downward means "don't worry," "take it slow." For other peoples these gestures have no meanings. Since there is no real relationship between the gestures and the meanings they signify, the meanings cannot be deduced simply by observing the individual kinemes.

TYPES OF MOVEMENTS

In dealing with nonverbal movements of the body, a classification offered by Paul Ekman and Wallace V. Friesen seems the most useful. These researchers distinguish five classes of nonverbal movements based on the origins, functions, and coding of the behavior: emblems, illustrators, affect displays, regulators, and adaptors (Figure 13.1).

Emblems

Emblems are nonverbal behaviors that rather directly translate words or phrases. Emblems include, for example, the O.K. sign, the peace sign, the come here sign, the hitchhiker's sign, the "up yours" sign, and so. Emblems

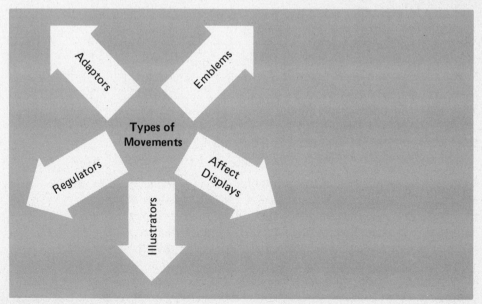

Figure 13.1
Types of Movements

are nonverbal substitutes for specific verbal words or phrases and are probably learned in essentially the same way as are specific words and phrases—without conscious awareness or explicit teaching and largely through a process of imitation.

Although emblems seem rather natural to us and almost inherently meaningful, they are as arbitrary as any word in any language. Consequently, our present culture's emblems are not necessarily the same as the emblems of 300 years ago or the same as the emblems of other cultures.

Emblems are often used to supplement the verbal message or as a kind of reinforcement. At times they are used in place of verbalization, for example, when there is a considerable distance between the individuals and shouting would be inappropriate or when we wish to "say" something behind someone's back.

Illustrators

Illustrators are nonverbal behaviors that accompany and literally "illustrate" the verbal messages. In saying, "Let's go up," for example, there will be movements of the head and perhaps hands going in an upward direction. In describing a circle or a square you are more than likely to make circular or square movements with your hands. You shake your head up and down to indicate yes and from side to side when indicating no. So well learned are these movements that it is physically difficult to reverse them or to employ inappropriate ones. Try, for example, saying "yes" while shaking your head from side to side. After a few seconds you will probably notice that your head will begin to move up and down.

In using illustrators we are aware of them only part of the time; at times they may have to be brought to our attention and our awareness.

Illustrators seem more natural and less arbitrary than emblems. They are partly a function of learning and partly innate. Illustrators are more universal; they are more common throughout the world and throughout time than are emblems. Consequently, it is likely that there is some innate component to illustrators, contrary to what many researchers might argue.

Eight types of illustrators are distinguished by Ekman and Friesen:

batons: movements that accent or emphasize a particular word or phrase
ideographs: movements that sketch the path or direction of thought
deictic movements: movements that point to an object, place or event
spatial movements: movements that depict a spatial relationship
rhythmic movements: movements that depict the rhythmic or pacing of an event
kinetographs: movements that depict a bodily action, or some nonhuman physical action
pictographs: movements that draw a picture in the air of the shape of the referent

emblematic movements: emblems used to illustrate a verbal statement, either repeating or substituting for a word or phrase

Affect Displays

Affect displays are more independent of verbal messages than are illustrators and are less under conscious control than are emblems or illustrators.

Affect displays are the movements of the facial area that convey emotional meaning; these are the facial expressions that show anger and fear, happiness and surprise, eagerness and fatigue. They are the facial expressions that "give us away" when we attempt to present a false image and that lead people to say, "You look angry today, what's wrong?" We can, however, also consciously control affect displays, as actors do whenever they play a role.

Affect displays may be unintentional—as when they give us away—but they may also be intentional. We may want to show anger or love or hate or surprise and, for the most part, we do a creditable job. Actors are often rated by the public for their ability to accurately portray affect by movements of their facial muscles. And we are all familiar with the awkward attempt of the would-be lover to seem seductive only to appear ludicrous—a kind of Woody Allen attempting to seduce Sophia Loren.

Regulators

Regulators are nonverbal behaviors that "regulate," monitor, maintain, or control the speaking of another individual. When we are listening to another we are not passive; rather, we nod our heads, purse our lips, adjust our eye focus, and make various paralinguistic sounds such as "mm-mm" or "tsk." Regulators are clearly culture bound and are not universal.

Regulators in effect tell speakers what we expect or want them to do as they are talking—"Keep going," "What else happened?" "I don't believe that," "Speed up," "Slow down," and any number of other speech directions. Speakers in turn receive these nonverbal behaviors without being consciously aware of them. Depending on their degree of sensitivity, they modify their speaking behavior in line with the directions supplied by the regulators.

Regulators would also include such gross movements as turning one's head, leaning forward in one's chair, and even walking away.

Adaptors

Adaptors are nonverbal behaviors that when emitted in private—or in public but without being seen—serve some kind of need and occur in their entirety. For example, when you are alone you might scratch your head until the itch is put to rest. Or you might pick your nose until satisfied. In public, when people are watching us, we perform these adaptors, but only partially. And so you

---

Box 11
BODY TYPE

We can probably describe some of the major characteristics of physique in males and to a lesser extent in females, under three general headings: 1) endomorphy, the fatty dimension; 2) mesomorphy, the muscular dimension; and 3) ectomorphy, the skinny dimension. We might then attempt to classify any given body in terms of the degree to which it possessed each of these three dimensions. Each body would be described by a three digit number. The first number would describe the endomorphic dimension, the second the mesomorphic dimension, and the third the ectomorphic dimension. An extremely fat individual, for example, the fat man or woman of the circus, would be described as 7-1-1 indicating that he or she is high on endomorphy but low on the other two dimensions. Mr. America, Hercules, and Atlas would be described as 1-7-1—all muscle. The thin man or woman of the circus would be 1-1-7—just skin and bones. Of course few persons are at these extremes. We might attempt to illustrate this by estimating the body types of persons who most of us have seen. Johnny Carson, for example, might be described as 2-5-4 whereas Merv Griffin might be described as 3-4-2. Joe Namath might be described as 3-6-1 whereas Mick Jagger might be 1-3-6. These, of course, are simply estimates that illustrate the concept; they are not accurate measurements. These three-digit numbers, then, represent one's *somatype*, or the degree to which a person is fat, muscular, and skinny. Male examples are used here because these body types were formulated on the basis of studies of the male body.

Try to picture the following individuals as they are described; try to see their physical characteristics or, better still, attempt to draw them.

Person 1. This man is dominant, confident, impetuous, domineering, enterprising, adventurous, competitive, determined, and hot-tempered.

Person 2. This man is dependent, contented, sluggish, placid, affable, tolerant, forgiving, sociable, generous, soft-hearted.

Person 3. This man is tense, anxious, withdrawn, cautious, serious, introspective, suspicious, cool, precise.

---

might put your fingers to your head and move them around a bit but you probably would not scratch enough to totally eliminate the itch. Similarly, you might touch your nose but probably you would not pursue this simple act to completion.

In observing this kind of nonverbal behavior it is difficult to tell what the partial behavior was intending to accomplish. For example, in observing someone's finger near the nose we cannot be certain that this behavior was intended to pick the nose, scratch it, or whatever. These reduced adaptors are emitted without conscious awareness.

Three types of adaptors are generally distinguished. *Self-adaptors* are not intended to communicate information to others but rather serve some personal need, for example, grooming, cleaning, excretory, and autoerotic activity

Object adaptors are nonverbal behaviors that make use of some kind of

If your responses were consistent with those of others to whom similar tests were given, you probably pictured Person 1 as high on mesomorphy, as having a rather muscular build. Person 2 was probably pictured as high in endomorphy, as rather short and fat. Person 3 was probably pictured as high in ectomorphy, as relatively tall and thin.

There is considerable debate over the relationship between personality characteristics, such as those listed above, and somatype. Much research does seem to indicate a rather strong relationship between body build and personality. The further question and the inevitable one is to what this relationship can be ascribed. Is it genetic? Are persons born with tall skinny bodies also born with certain personality traits, such as tenseness, withdrawnness, and so on. Is the relationship cultural? Are persons who are fat expected to be affable, sluggish, tolerant, forgiving, and so on, and do they therefore take on these characteristics which everyone seems to think they possess anyway? This question has not been settled. What is clear is that people have certain reactions to different body types; the body types communicate something to us. We expect the fat person to be sociable, generous, and affable. We expect the muscular individual to be dominant, confident, impetuous, and hot-tempered. We expect the skinny person to be tense, precise, cool, and suspicious. At least in general we seem to have these expectations. Whether or not our judgments are well founded, we do seem to make inferences about people's personality from merely looking at their body build. And just as we have expectations of others based on their body build, they will have expectations of us based on our body build. Further, if these stereotypes are strong enough— and in many cases they seem to be—we will have expectations about ourselves based on our body build. The fact that these characteristics, these stereotypes, are so common across large sections of the population attests to the importance of body build in nonverbal communication.

It should also be noted that because of these different perceptions we will also have different perceptions of the same actions when they are performed by persons of different body build. For example, if a man at a dance sits in the corner with his head down and his arms clasped in front of him we would probably read different things into it if he were fat, or muscular, or skinny.

prop—a pencil, a tie, a cigarette or pipe—but in which the prop does not serve any instrumental function. Object adaptors would not include writing with a pencil or tying a tie or smoking a cigarette; rather, they include banging the desk with the pencil or chewing on it or playing with one's tie or chewing on a pipe.

Alter adaptors include the movements learned in the manipulation of material things—in fixing a car, in changing a tire, in sewing a dress, in licking an envelop.

In many of the more popularized versions of nonverbal behavior it is to adaptors that most attention is given. Here the authors talk about people crossing their legs a certain way—which is supposed to indicate sexual invitation— or crossed in another way—which indicates introversion—or crossed still

---

Box 12
PAY OF FAT EXECUTIVES IS FOUND LEANER THAN CHECKS OF OTHERS

Detroit, Jan. 1 (UPI)—A survey of 15,000 executives by an employment agency showed today that fat executives received less pay than lean ones did.

"By exploiting the overweight, too many American companies are literally living off the fat of the land," said Robert Half, president of a New York-based company that finds jobs for financial and computer executives.

"Some fat people pay a penalty of $1,000 a pound," he said.

The survey, he said, also showed that overweight persons are less likely to advance as quickly or as high as lean persons.

Mr. Half conducted the survey by asking the branch offices of his company, Robert Half Personnel Agencies, to pick 1,000 of the company's clients at random in 15 cities and check their executives' height, weight and salaries. The results were released by his branch here.

The results were checked against insurance industry charts. Persons who weighed 10 per cent more than the chart figures were considered overweight.

Of 1,500 executives who earned between $25,000 and $45,000, the survey found, only 9 percent were more than 10 pounds overweight.

But of 13,500 executives paid between $10,000 and $20,000, nearly 40 per cent were more than 10 per cent overweight.

Mr. Half said that his company had received thousands of requests from employers for "thin" men and women but only one request in 25 years for a "plump" executive.

"And that request came from a company that makes clothing for overweight men," he said.

He said that his company refused to supply information about the weight of prospective executives on the ground that such action constituted discrimination.

"The overweight," he said, "have become America's largest, least protected minority group."

Source: The New York Times, January 2, 1974. Reprinted by permission of *The New York Times.*

---

another way—to indicate agressiveness—and so on. The attempt here is to identify nonverbal behaviors that are performed without conscious awareness and that reveal some kind of inner desires or tendencies.

SOURCES

Perhaps the most authoritative source for body communication is Ray L. Birdwhistell's *Kinesics and Context: Essays on Body Motion Communication* (New York: Ballantine Books, 1970). This paperback contains 28 articles by Birdwhistell on body communication plus a most complete bibliography of research and theory in this area. Another interesting source is *Approaches to Semiotics,* edited by Thomas A. Sebeok, Alfred S. Hayes, and Mary Catherine

Bateson (The Hague: Mouton, 1964). This volume also contains an excellent study by Weston LaBarre, "Paralinguistics, Kinesics, and Cultural Anthropology" and articles by Alfred S. Hayes and Margaret Mead which are particularly useful for the study of kinesics. The discussion and classification of "types of body movements" is from P. Ekman and W. V. Friesen, "The Repertoire of Nonverbal Behavior: Categories, Origins, Usage, and Coding," *Semiotica* 1 (1969):49–98. Two works by Albert E. Scheflen will be found both interesting and informative: *Body Language and the Social Order* (Englewood Cliffs, N.J.: Prentice-Hall, 1972) and *How Behavior Means* (Garden City, N.Y.: Anchor Press, 1974). Portions of the discussion of the areas of kinesics were taken from my "Kinesics—Other Codes, Other Channels," *Today's Speech* 16(April 1968): 29–32. Good general introductions include Flora Davis, *Inside Intuition* (New American Library, 1973) and Gerald Nierenberg and Henry Calero, *How To Read a Person Like a Book* (New York: Pocket Books, 1971).

EXPERIENTIAL VEHICLES

13.1 INSTRUCTING NONVERBALLY

The purpose of this exercise is to heighten your awareness of nonverbal communicátion, particularly communication with one's body.[1]

In this exercise the class is broken up into groups of five or six. One member from each group leaves the room for approximately a minute. When these "subjects" are out of the room each group is given an instruction which they must communicate to the subject, and the nonverbal cue or cues to which they are restricted. All groups, of course, should be given the same instruction and be limited to the same nonverbal cue or cues so that the task will be equally difficult for all groups.

The first group to get the subject to comply with their instruction wins the round and gets 10 points. After the instruction is complied with the process is repeated, this time with another subject chosen from the group, another instruction, and another nonverbal cue or cues. The exercise is completed when one group wins 50 points, when time is up, or when some other point is reached.

Some sample instructions and types of nonverbal cues follow. Instructors may wish to compile their own list of instructions to insure that they have not been seen by any member of the class.

Sample Instructions

leave the room
give the teacher a pat on the back
shake hands with each member of the group
open (close) all the windows
open (close) the door
bring into the class someone who is not a member of the class
write the time on the board
find a red pen
raise your hand
clap hands
sit on the floor
put your shoes on the wrong feet

[1] This exercise was adapated from one developed by my students in interpersonal communication.

get a drink of water
hold up a notebook with the name of the school on it
comb your hair

Nonverbal Cues

vocal (but nonverbal) cues
hand and arm movements
eye movements (but not head movements)
head movements
the entire body
tactile cues
manipulation of the objects in the room
leg movements (including feet movements)

13.2 CONTROL BY NONVERBAL COMMUNICATION[2]

Write the letters of a phrase or statement on pieces of typing paper or cardboard, one letter on each piece. Shuffle them randomly, and distribute one to each student. (Select a phrase or statement that contains as many letters as there are students.)

Tell the students to form a phrase or statement without talking or writing anything. The students should attempt to arrange themselves so that the letters they are carrying spell out the phrase or statement.

After the phrase or statement is formed, consider the following:

1. Did anyone emerge as leader?
2. What nonverbal behaviors were used by the leader to direct or control the behavior of the group members?
3. Did others attempt to take charge? When? In what way? With what non-verbal behaviors did they indicate a desire to take charge?
4. Were some members turned off? How did they signal this nonverbally?
5. How did you feel being directed by other people without any talking?

[2] This exercise is adapted from one developed by my students in Small Group Communication.

UNIT 14
Proxemics

Proxemic Dimensions
Proxemic Distances

14.1 Spatial Relationships I and II

LEARNING GOALS

After completing this unit, you should be able to:

1. define *proxemics*
2. define the following: *postural-sex identifiers, sociofugal-sociopetal orientation, kinesthetic factors, touch, vision, thermal factors, smell,* and *loudness*
3. identify and explain the four proxemic distances
4. give examples of the kinds of communications that would take place in each of the four proxemic distances
5. explain at least five messages communicated by different seating arrangements

Edward T. Hall, in the study he calls "Proxemics," has provided much new and significant insight into nonverbal communication by demonstrating how messages from different channels may be analyzed by relating them to the spatial dimensions of communication. More formally, in "A System for the Notation of Proxemic Behavior," Hall has defined *proxemics* as the "study of how man unconsciously structures microspace—the distance between men in the conduct of their daily transactions, the organization of space in his houses and buildings, and ultimately the layout of his towns."

Like verbal behavior, proxemic behavior communicates; space speaks just as surely and just as loudly as do words. Speakers who stand close to their listener, with their hands on the listener's shoulders and their eyes focused directly on those of the listener, clearly communicate something very different from the speaker who sits crouched in a corner with arms folded and eyes to the floor.

Like verbal and kinesic behavior, proxemic behavior is learned without any conscious or direct teaching by the adult community. Children are merely exposed to certain spatial relations which they internalize unconsciously, much as children seem to acquire the particular codes of speech or body motion.

PROXEMIC DIMENSIONS

The best way to explain proxemics is to briefly present the eight general classes of proxemic behaviors and their more specific categories as systematized by Hall.

Postural-sex identifiers refer to the posture and sex of the communication source and receiver. Hall has divided this class into six possible categories: man prone, woman prone, man sitting or squatting, woman sitting or squatting, man standing, woman standing.

Sociofugal-sociopetal orientation, referring to the physical directness of the communication, specifies the relationship of one person's shoulders to the other person's shoulders. These positions are categorized on a nine-point scale, ranging from face-to-face communication in which the shoulders of both parties are parallel, through the situation in which the shoulders of the two parties form a straight line, to the situation in which there is back-to-back communication and the shoulders are again parallel. The nine positions are: parallel face-to-face, 45° angle, 90°, 135°, 180°, 225°, 270°, 315°, and parallel back-to-back communication.

Kinesthetic factors refer to the closeness of the two persons involved in communication and the potential that exists for the holding, grasping, or touching of each other. The four major categories are: within body contact distance, within touching distance with the forearm extended, within touching distance with the arm extended, and within touching distance by reaching. More specific degrees of closeness which lie between any two of these four major classes—for example, just outside body contact distance—might also be recorded.

Touch, referring to the amount and type of physical contact between the two parties, is quantified along a seven-point scale: caressing and holding, caressing and feeling, extended holding, holding, spot touching, brushing or accidental touching, and no contact.

Vision, the extent of visual contact between the two persons, is divided into four categories: sharp, focused looking at the other person's eyes; clear, focused looking at the person's face or head; peripheral, looking at the person in general but not focused on the head; and no visual contact.

Thermal factors, the amount of body heat of one person perceived by the other, are categorized into four types: detection of conducted heat, detection of radiant heat, probable detection of some kind of heat, and no detection of heat.

Loudness, or vocal volume, is described on a seven-point scale: silent, very soft, soft, normal, somewhat above normal, loud, and very loud.

Smell is categorized into five types: detection of differentiated body odor, detection of undifferentiated odor, detection of breath odor, probable detection of some odor, and no detection.

These categories may appear at first to be somewhat rigid or too finely delineated. In analyzing proxemic behavior, however, adjacent categories can be combined to form more general ones or, if additional distinctions are needed, the categories may be further divided. Hall has presented this system as a *tentative* strategy for analyzing proxemic behaviors.

PROXEMIC DISTANCES

One of the earliest references to space as communication occurs in the Gospel of Luke (14:1–11):

When thou are invited to a wedding feast, do not recline in the first place, lest perhaps one more distinguished than thou have been invited by him. And he who invited thee and him, come and say to thee, "Make room for this man"; and then thou begin with shame to take the last place. But when thou art invited, go and recline in the last place; that when he who invited thee comes in, he may say to thee, "Friend, go up higher!" Then thou wilt be honored in the presence of all who are at table with thee. For everyone who exalts himself shall be humbled, and he who humbles himself shall be exalted.

This brief passage illustrates one of the concepts or meanings that space communicates, namely status. We know, for example, that in a large organization status is the basis for determining how large an office one receives, whether that office has a window or not, how high up the office is (that is, on what floor of the building), and how close one's office is to that of the president or chairperson.

In interpersonal communication space is especially important, although we

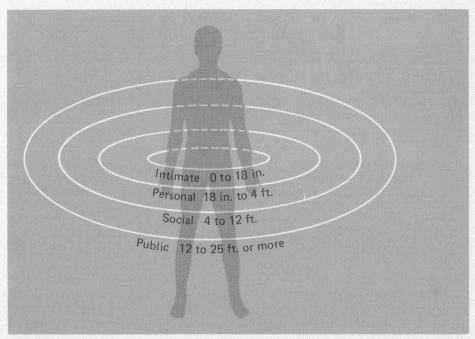

Figure 14.1
Proxemic Distances

seldom think about it or even consider the possibility that it might serve a communicative function. Edward Hall, for example, distinguishes four distances which he claims define the type of relationship permitted. Each of these four distances has a close phase and a far phase, giving us a total of eight clearly identifiable distances (Figure 14.1).

In *intimate distance,* ranging from the close phase of actual touching to the far phase of 6 to 18 inches, the presence of the other individual is unmistakable. Each individual experiences the sound, smell, and feel of the other's breath.

The *close phase* is used for lovemaking and wrestling, for comforting and protecting. In the close phase the muscles and the skin communicate while actual verbalizations play a minor role. In this close phase whispering, says

---

Box 13
TOUCH

Touch is perhaps the most primitive form of communication. In terms of sense development, it is probably the first to be utilized; even in the womb the child is stimulated by touch. Soon after birth the child is fondled, caressed, patted, and stroked by the parents and by any other relative who happens to be around. The whole world wants to touch the new infant. Touch becomes for the child a pleasant pasttime and so he or she begins to touch. Everything is picked up, thoroughly fingered, and put into the mouth in an attempt to touch it as closely as possible. The child's favorite toys seem to be tactile ones—cuddly teddy bears, teething rings, and even pieces of blankets. Much in the same way as children touch objects in the environment, they also touch themselves; children play with toes and fingers, nose and lips, and ears and genitals. At some point, children are stopped from picking their noses and playing with their genitals. No reason is given other than the admonition, "Don't do that," or a gentle slap on the hands. As children mature and become sociable, they begin to explore others through touch, though again there are certain parts that are forbidden to touch or have touched by others.

Touching as a form of communication can serve any number of functions. In fact, one would be hard pressed to name a general function of communication which could not be served by tactile communication. Special note, however, should be made of two major functions normally served by tactile communications.

Perhaps the most obvious is a sexual one. Touch seems to be the primary form of sexual interaction. From fondling one's genitals as a child, to kissing, to fondling another individual, to sexual intercourse, touch plays a primary role. Men shave or grow beards, women shave their legs and underarms, and both use body oils and creams to keep their skin smooth in conscious or subconscious awareness of the powerful role of touch as a form of communication.

Touch also serves a primary role in consoling another individual. For example, we put our arms around people, hold their heads in our hands, hold their hands, or hug them in an attempt to empathize with them more fully. It seems like an attempt to feel what other people are feeling by becoming one with them—perhaps

Hall, has the effect of increasing the psychological distance between the two individuals.

The *far phase* allows us to touch each other by extending our hands. The distance is so close that it is not considered proper in public and because of the feeling of inappropriateness and discomfort (at least for Americans) the eyes seldom meet but remain fixed on some remote object.

Each of us, says Hall, carries around with us a protective bubble defining our *personal distance,* which allows us to stay protected and untouched by others.

In the close phase of personal distance (from 1.5 to 2.5 feet) we can still hold or grasp each other but only by extending our arms. We can then take into our protective bubble certain individuals—for example, loved ones. In the

---

the ideal in empathic understanding. Try to console someone, even in role playing, when you are not allowed to touch, and you will see how unnatural it seems and how difficult it is to say the appropriate words.

In almost all group encounter sessions touch is used as a supportive gesture. Generally, we do not touch people we dislike (except in fighting with them). Otherwise, we only touch people we like and so the very act of touching says, "I like you," "I care about you," "I want to be close to you," and so on.

Touching implies a commitment to the other individual; where and how we touch seems to determine the extent of that commitment. To shake someone's hand, for example, involves a very minor commitment. Our culture has, in effect, defined hand shaking as a minor social affair. But to caress someone's neck or to kiss someone's mouth implies a commitment of much greater magnitude.

The location, amount, and intensity of tactile communication is also culturally determined, at least in part. For example, southern Europeans will touch each other a great deal more than will northern Europeans or Americans. Women seem to be allowed to touch more and to be touched more than men. For example, it has been shown that females are touched more often than are males by same sex friends, different sex friends, mothers, and fathers. This seems true even for infants; girls between 14 and 24 months, for example, are touched more than boys of the same age. Similarly, mothers touch both male and female children more than do fathers who, in fact, hardly touch more than the hands of their children.

Touching ourselves, of course, also communicates. Lily Tomlin in her role as Ernestine the telephone operator touches herself a great deal in an attempt to communicate a certain egocentric personality which, together with the power of the telephone company, can even call on the president and make trouble. In real life we are all familiar with the individual who is constantly fixing his or her hair—to the point where we feel like screaming and perhaps sometimes do.

Although we have learned somewhere that certain ways of touching oneself are forbidden, at least in public, there are still people who pick their nose, scratch their head, stick their fingers in their ears, or scratch their genitals or anus without the least concern for those around who might not care to witness this exercise in self-gratification.

far phase (from 2.5 to 4 feet) two people can only touch each other if they both extend their arms. One person can touch the other by extending his or her arms fully to the point where the two people can touch only if both extend their arms. This far phase is the extent to which we can physically get our hands on things and hence it defines, in one sense, the limits of our physical control over others.

Even at this distance we can see many of the fine details of an individual— the gray hairs, teeth stains, clothing lint, and so on. However, we can no longer detect body heat. At times we may detect breath odor but generally at this distance etiquette demands that we direct our breath to some neutral corner so as not to offend (as the television commercials warn us we might do).

This distance is particularly interesting from the point of view of the body odor and the colognes designed to hide it. At this distance we cannot perceive normal cologne or perfume. Thus it has been proposed that the cologne has two functions: First, it serves to disguise the body odor or hide it; and second, it serves to make clear the limits of the protective bubble around the individual. The bubble, defined by the perfume, simply says you may not enter to the point where you can smell me.

At the *social distance* we lose the visual detail we had in the personal distance. The close phase (from 4 to 7 feet) is the distance at which we conduct impersonal business, the distance at which we interact at a social gathering. The far phase (from 7 to 12 feet) is the distance we stand at when someone says, "Stand away so I can look at you." At this level business transactions have a more formal tone than when conducted in the close phase. In offices of high officials the desks are positioned so that the individual is assured of at least this distance when dealing with clients. Unlike the intimate distance, where eye contact is awkward, the far phase of the social distance makes eye contact essential—otherwise communication is lost. The voice is generally louder than normal at this level but shouting or raising the voice has the effect of reducing the social distance to a personal distance. It is at this distance that we can work with people and yet both not constantly interact with them and not appear rude. At certain distances, of course, one cannot ignore the presence of another individual. At other distances, however, we can ignore the other individual and keep to our own business.

This social distance requires that a certain amount of space be available. In many instances, however, such distances are not available; yet it is necessary to keep a social distance, at least psychologically if not physically. For this we attempt different arrangements with the furniture. In small offices in colleges for example, professors sharing an office might have their desks facing in different directions so that each may keep separate from the other. Or they may position their desks against a wall so that each will feel psychologically alone in the office and thus be able to effectively maintain a social rather than a personal distance.

In the close phase of *public distance* (from 12 to 15 feet) an individual seems protected by space. At this distance one is able to take defensive action should one be threatened. On a public bus or train, for example, we might keep at least this distance from a drunkard so that should anything come up (literally or figuratively) we could get away in time. Although at this distance we lose any fine details of the face and eyes we are still close enough to see what is happening should we need to take defensive action.

At the far phase (more than 25 feet) we see individuals not as separate individuals but as part of the whole setting. We automatically set approximately 30 feet around public figures who are of considerable importance, and we seem to do this whether or not there are guards preventing us from entering this distance. This far phase is of course the distance from which actors perform on stage; consequently, their actions and voice will have to be somewhat exaggerated.

These four distances, according to Hall, correspond quite closely to the four major types of relationships: intimate, personal, social, and public.

SOURCES

For spatial communication the work of Edward T. Hall is perhaps the most well known and the most insightful. The discussion of proxemic dimensions comes from his "A System for the Notation of Proxemic Behavior," *American Anthropologist* 65(1963):1003–1026. The discussion of proxemic distances comes from his *The Hidden Dimension* (New York: Doubleday, 1966). Hall's first popular work on spatial communication and perhaps still one of the most famous is *The Silent Language* (New York: Doubleday, 1959). Robert Sommer also deals with spatial communication, but from a somewhat different point of view. Particularly interesting are his *Personal Space: The Behavioral Basis of Design* (Englewood Cliffs, N.J.: Prentice-Hall, 1969); *Design Awareness* (San Francisco: Rinehart Press, 1972); and, *Tight Spaces: Hard Architecture and How to Humanize It* (Englewood Cliffs, N.J.: Prentice-Hall, 1974). The Experiential Vehicles on seating positions (14.1 and 14.2) are based on the work of Sommer summarized in *Personal Space*.

EXPERIENTIAL VEHICLES

14.1 SPATIAL RELATIONSHIPS—PART I

Below are presented diagrams of tables and chairs. Imagine that the situation is the school cafeteria and that each is the only table not occupied. For each of the eight diagrams place an X where you and a friend of the same sex would seat yourselves for each of the four conditions noted.

1. Conversing, to talk for a few minutes before class

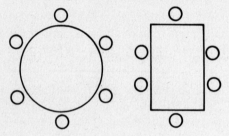

2. Cooperating to study together for the same exam or to work out a math problem

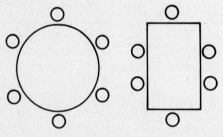

3. Co-acting to study for different exams

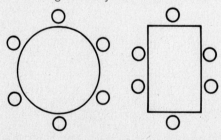

[1] This exercise is based on studies conducted by Robert Sommer and reported in *Personal Space: The Behavioral Basis of Design* (Englewood Cliffs, N.J.: Prentice-Hall, 1969).

4. Competing against each other in order to see who would be the first to solve a series of puzzles

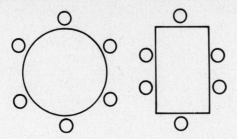

For Discussion

1. Why did you select the positions you did?
2. Explain the differences in the opportunity for nonverbal interaction which the different positions chosen allow.
3. How do these different positions relate to verbal communication?
4. Would you have chosen the same positions if the other person were of the opposite sex? Explain.
5. Compare your responses with the responses of others. How do you account for the differences in seating preferences?
6. Are there significant differences in choices between the round and the rectangular tables? Explain.

14.2 SPATIAL RELATIONSHIPS—PART II

Below are presented diagrams of tables and chairs. Imagine that the situation is the school cafeteria and that this is the only table not occupied. In the space marked X is seated the person described above the diagram. Indicate by placing an X in the appropriate circle where you would sit.

1. A young man/woman to whom you are physically attracted and whom you would like to date but to whom you have never spoken

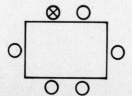

2. A person whom you find physically unattractive and to whom you have never spoken

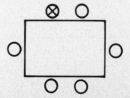

3. A person you dated once and had a miserable time with and whom you would never date again

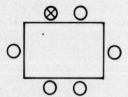

4. A person you have dated a few times and would like to date again

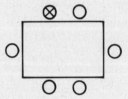

5. An instructor who gave you an "F" in a course last semester which you did not deserve and whom you dislike intensely

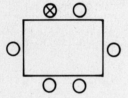

6. Your favorite instructor who you would like to get to know better

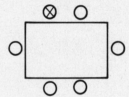

For Discussion

1. Why did you select the positions you did? For example, how does the position you selected enable you to better achieve your purpose?

2. Assume that you were already seated in the position marked X. Do you think that the person described would sit where you indicated you would (assuming the feelings and motives are generally the same)? Why? Are there significant sex differences? Significant status differences? Explain.

3. What does the position you selected communicate to the person already seated? In what ways might this nonverbal message be misinterpreted? How would your subsequent nonverbal (and perhaps verbal) behavior reinforce your intended message? That is, what would you do to insure that the message you intend to communicate is in fact the message communicated and received?

UNIT 15
Paralanguage

The Structure of Paralanguage
Judgments Based on Paralanguage

15.1 Paralanguage Communication

LEARNING GOALS

After completing this unit, you should be able to:

1. define *paralanguage*
2. identify three or four major classes of paralinguistic phenomena
3. explain at least three messages that variations in paralinguistic phenomena might communicate

An old exercise to increase the student's ability to express different emotions, feelings, and attitudes was to have the student say the following sentences while accenting or stressing different words: "Is this the face that launched a thousand ships?" Significant differences in meaning are easily communicated depending on where the stress is placed. Consider, for example, the following variations:

1. IS this the face that launched a thousand ships?
2. Is THIS the face that launched a thousand ships?
3. Is this the FACE that launched a thousand ships?
4. Is this the face that LAUNCHED a thousand ships?
5. Is this the face that launched a THOUSAND SHIPS?

Each of these five sentences communicates something different. Each, in fact, asks a totally different question even though the words used are identical. All that distinguishes the sentences is stress, one of the aspects of what is called *paralanguage*. Paralanguage may be defined as the vocal (but nonverbal) dimension of speech. Paralanguage refers to the manner in which something is said rather than to what is said.

THE STRUCTURE OF PARALANGUAGE

An outline of a classification offered by George L. Trager is presented in Table 15.1. More important than the specifics of this table is that paralanguage en-

Table 15.1
Paralanguage: A Classification

I. Voice Qualities
  A. Pitch Range
    1. Spread
      a. Upward
      b. Downward
    2. Narrowed
      a. From above
      b. From below
  B. Vocal Lip Control
    1. Rasp
    2. Openness
  C. Glottis Control
    1. Sharp transitions
    2. Smooth transitions
  D. Pitch Control
  E. Articulation Control
    1. Forceful (precise)
    2. Relaxed (slurred)
  F. Rhythm Control
    1. Smooth
    2. Jerky
  G. Resonance
    1. Resonant
    2. Thin
  H. Tempo
    1. Increased from norm
    2. Decreased from norm

II. Vocalizations
  A. Vocal Characterizers
    1. Laughing/crying
    2. Yelling/whispering
    3. Moaning/groaning
    4. Whining/breaking
    5. Belching/yawning
  B. Vocal Qualifiers
    1. Intensity
      a. Overloud
        1. somewhat
        2. considerably
        3. very much
      b. Oversoft
        1. somewhat
        2. considerably
        3. very much
    2. Pitch Height
      a. Overhigh
        1. slightly
        2. appreciably
        3. greatly
      b. Overflow
        1. slightly
        2. appreciably
        3. greatly
    3. Extent
      a. Drawl
        1. slight
        2. noticeable
        3. extreme
      b. Clipping
        1. slight
        2. noticeable
        3. extreme
  C. Vocal Segregates
    1. Uh-uh
    2. Uh-huh
    3. Sh
    4. (Pause)

Source: George L. Trager, "Paralanguage: A First Approximation," *Studies in Linguistics* 13(1958):1–12; George L. Trager, "The Typology of Paralanguage," *Anthropological Linguistics* 3(1961):17–21; and Robert E. Pittenger and Henry Smith, Jr., "A Basis for Some Contributions of Linguistics to Psychiatry," *Psychiatry* 20(1957):61–78.

Box 14
JABBERWOCKY

Lewis Carroll

'Twas brillig, and the slithy toves
    Did gyre and gimble in the wabe:
All mimsy were the borogoves,
    And the mome raths outgrabe.

'Beware the Jabberwock, my son!
    The jaws that bite, the claws that catch!
Beware the Jubjub bird, and shun
    The frumious Bandersnatch!'

He took his vorpal sword in hand:
    Long time the manxome foe he sought—
So rested he by the Tumtum tree,
    And stood awhile in thought.

And, as in uffish thought he stood,
    The Jabberwock, with eyes of flame,
Came whiffling through the tulgey wood,
    And burbled as it came!

One, two! One, two! And through and through
    The vorpal blade went snicker-snack!
He left it dead, and with its head
    He went galumphing back.

'And hast thou slain the Jabberwock?
    Come to my arms, my beamish boy!
O frabjous day! Callooh! Callay!
    He chortled in his joy.

'Twas brillig, and the slithy toves
    Did gyre and gimble in the wabe:
All mimsy were the borogoves,
    And the mome raths outgrabe.

compasses a great deal of vocal expression and can be classified and analyzed rather precisely for various different purposes.

Although in outline form the breakdown of paralinguistic phenomena is as shown, the four major classes are: *voice qualities, vocal characterizers, vocal qualifiers,* and *vocal segregates.*

The sounds used in vocal segregates are not the same as those sounds when used in words—that is, the *sh* which means "silence!" is not the same sound as in *shed.*

The "pause" noted as a vocal segregate is classified in a somewhat different area by many contemporary researchers. This area, generally referred to as "hesitation phenomena," is concerned with all forms of hesitations, pause being only one of these.

Some of the classifications are actually continuous scales. Vocal lip control may be analyzed as ranging from rasp through openness rather than simply as either rasp or open.

If we assume the validity of the proposition that nothing never happens, that all behavior serves a communicative function, then we must further assume that each of these paralinguistic features also communicates meaning. Thus the speaker who speaks quickly communicates something different from the one who speaks slowly. Even though the words might be the same, if the speed differs the meaning we receive will also differ. And we may derive different meanings from "fast talk" depending on the speaker. Perhaps in one person we might perceive fear, feeling that he or she is hurrying to get the statement over with. In another we might perceive annoyance or lack of concern, inferring that he or she speaks rapidly so that not too much time is wasted. In still another we might perceive extreme interest, feeling that the person is speaking quickly so that he or she can get to the punch line and hear our reaction.

JUDGMENTS BASED ON PARALANGUAGE

With all of the features of paralanguage we will perceive different things depending on the specifics of the situation and on the other nonverbal and verbal cues we perceive.

We are a diagnostically oriented people, quick to make judgments about another's personality based on various paralinguistic cues. At times our judgments turn out to be correct, at other times incorrect. But the number of times correct and incorrect does not seem to influence the frequency with which we make such judgments. We may, for example, conclude that speakers who speak so softly that we can hardly hear them seem to have some kind of problem. Perhaps they feel inferior—they "know" that no one really wants to listen, "know" that nothing they say is significant, and so speak softly. Other speakers will speak at an extremely loud volume, perhaps because of an overinflated ego and the belief that everyone in the world wants to hear them, that what they have to say is so valuable that they cannot risk our not hearing every word. Speakers who speak with no variation, in a complete monotone, seem uninterested in what they are saying and seem to encourage a similar disinterest from the listeners—if any are still around. We might perceive such people as having a lack of interest in life in general, as being rather bland individuals. All of these conclusions are, at best, based on little evidence. Yet this does not stop us from making such conclusions.

It is important for us to inquire into the relationship between paralanguage and impression formation. It does seem that certain voices are symptomatic of certain personality types, of certain problems, and specifically that the personality orientation leads to the vocal qualities. When listening to people speak —regardless of what they are saying—we form impressions based on their paralanguage as to what kind of people they are. Our impressions seem to consist of physical impressions (about body type perhaps and certainly about sex and age), personality impressions (they seem outgoing, they sound shy, they appear aggressive), and evaluative impressions (they sound like good people, they sound evil and menacing, they sound lovable, they have vicious laughs).

Much research has been directed to the question of the accuracy of these judgments—that is, how accurately may we judge a person on the basis of voice alone. One of the earliest studies on this question was conducted by T. H. Pear. Pear used nine speakers and had over 4000 listeners make guesses about these nine speakers. The sex and age of the speaker appeared to be guessed with considerable accuracy. However, the listeners were only able to accurately guess the occupations of the clergymen and the actor.

Other studies, perhaps taking their cue from that of Pear, pursued the investigation of the relationship between vocal characteristics and personal characteristics. Most studies suggest, in agreement with Pear, that sex and age can be guessed accurately on the basis of the voice alone. This is not to say that complete accuracy is possible with age but it does seem able to be guessed within relatively small ranges.

Some studies report that listeners can guess the occupation of the speaker whereas other studies report that they cannot. In some studies listeners have been able to match voices to photographs and to the people themselves, although other evidence suggests that this is not always possible.

One of the most interesting findings on voice and personal characteristics is that which shows that listeners can accurately judge the status (whether high, middle, or low) of speakers from hearing a 60-second voice sample. In fact, many listeners reported that they made their judgments in less than 15 seconds. It has also been found that the speakers judged to be of high status were rated as being of higher credibility than those speakers rated middle and low in status.

There is much greater agreement in the literature when we consider the question of identifying the emotional states of listeners from their vocal expression. Generally, in these studies the content of the speech is nonexistent or is held constant. Thus in a content-free situation the speaker would attempt to communicate anxiety, for example, by saying the alphabet or perhaps by reciting numbers. In the situation where the content is held constant the speakers say the same sentences (generally rather unemotional ones) for all the emotions they are to communicate.

It has been found that speakers can communicate or encode emotions through content-free speech or through content that is unrelated to the emotions, and listeners are able to decode these emotions.

A typical study would involve speakers using numbers to communicate different emotions. Listeners would have to select the emotions being communicated from a list of 10 emotions that they were given. In situations like this listeners are generally effective in guessing the emotions.

Listeners vary in their ability to decode the emotions, speakers vary in their ability to encode the emotions, and the accuracy with which emotions are guessed depends on the emotions themselves. For example, while it may be easy to distinguish between hate and sympathy, it may not be so easy to distinguish between fear and anxiety. This type of study is used as the basis for the exercise at the end of this unit.

SOURCES

For a classification and introduction to paralinguistic phenomena see George L. Trager's "Paralanguage: A First Approximation," *Studies in Linguistics* 13(1958):1–12 and "The Typology of Paralanguage," *Anthropological Linguistics* 3(1961):17–21. Mark Knapp's *Nonverbal Behavior in Human Interaction* (New York: Holt, 1972) provides an excellent summary of research findings as does Dale Leathers' *Nonverbal Communication Systems* (Boston: Allyn & Bacon, 1976). George F. Mahl and Gene Schulze likewise provide a thorough summary of the research and theory in this area. See their "Psychological Research in the Extralinguistic Area," in T. A. Seboek, A. S. Hayes, and M. C. Bateson, eds., *Approaches to Semiotics* (The Hague: Mouton, 1964). For a collection of research studies on paralanguage see Joel R. Davitz, ed., *The Communication of Emotional Meaning* (New York: McGraw-Hill, 1964). For the study by T. H. Pear see his *Voice and Personality* (London: Chapman and Hall, 1931). For a thorough review of paralanguage see (in addition to the Mahl and Schulze and Knapp) Ernest Kramer, "Judgment of Personal Characteristics and Emotions from Nonverbal Properties," *Psychological Bulletin* 60(1963) and Albert Mehrabian, *Silent Messages* (Belmont, Cal.: Wadsworth, 1971).

EXPERIENTIAL VEHICLE

15.1 PARALANGUAGE COMMUNICATION[1]

In this exercise a subject recites the alphabet attempting to communicate each of the following emotions:

anger
fear
happiness
jealousy
love
nervousness
pride
sadness
satisfaction
sympathy

The subject may begin the alphabet at any point and may omit and repeat sounds, but the subject may use only the names of the letters of the alphabet to communicate these feelings.

The subject should first number the emotions in random order so that he or she will have a set order to follow which is not known to the audience, whose task it will be to guess the emotions expressed.

As a variation, have the subject go through the entire list of emotions: once facing the audience and employing any nonverbal signals desired and once with his or her back to the audience without employing any additional signals. Are there differences in the number of correct guesses depending on which method is used?

For Discussion and Response

1. What are some of the differences between encoding-decoding "emotional meaning" and "logical meaning"?
2. Davitz and Davitz found the number of correct identifications for these emotions to be as follows: anger (156), nervousness (130), sadness (118), happiness (104), sympathy (93), satisfaction (75), love (60), fear (60), jealousy (69), and pride (50). Do these figures correspond to those obtained in class?

[1] This exercise is based on J. R. Davitz and L. J. Davitz, "The Communication of Feelings by Content-Free Speech," *Journal of Communication* 9(1959):6–13.

What conclusions would you draw relevant to the relative ease-difficulty of expressing the several emotions?

3. Do you think there is a positive relationship between encoding and decoding abilities in situations such as this? Is the person adept at encoding the emotions also adept at decoding them? Explain.

4. What variables might influence encoding ability? Decoding ability?

5. What personality factors seem relevant to the encoding and decoding of emotions?

UNIT 16

Attitudes
in Communication

Atttiude and Related Concepts
Functions of Attitudes

LEARNING GOALS

After completing this unit, you should be able to:

1. define *attitude*
2. distinguish among *attitude, belief, faith, opinion,* and *value*
3. identify and define the four major functions of attitudes

Central to the study of any form of communication, especially communication that seeks to influence people, is the concept of *attitude*—a tendency to respond in one way rather than in another. Unlike communication messages or noise, attitudes cannot be observed directly. We cannot see attitudes or touch them or hear them. What we do see or touch or hear are behaviors which we ascribe to the influence of attitude. So, for example, if a person constantly compliments us, asks us to go out, invites us to all sorts of activities, is always with us, and so on, we might conclude from these behaviors that this person has a favorable attitude toward us. We do not see the favorable attitude but rather we infer it exists from the behaviors that we can observe. Attitude is thus a hypothetical construct. It is a useful concept which we create to simplify our descriptions and explanations of behavior.

Take the case of a young man we observed engaging in the following behaviors: 1) criticized the police for whatever they do; 2) fought with his sister because she dated a policeman; 3) refused to talk with a cousin who became a policeman; and 4) referred to policemen with the least favorable expressions he could think of. We might then attempt to explain these behaviors by postulating stimuli for each of these responses. The individual might then be seen as depicted in Figure 16.1.

In attempting to predict the possible causes for these various behaviors, we

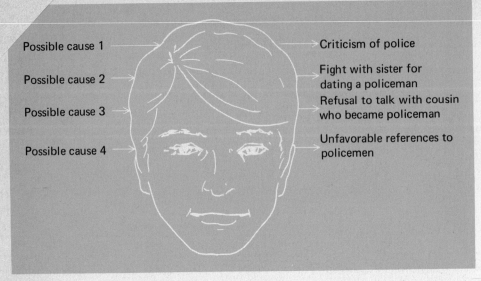

Possible cause 1 → Criticism of police

Possible cause 2 → Fight with sister for dating a policeman

Possible cause 3 → Refusal to talk with cousin who became policeman

Possible cause 4 → Unfavorable references to policemen

Figure 16.1
Stimuli and Responses

must be careful to also include the behaviors feeding back and becoming causes of themselves and of other behaviors. That is, calling policemen vulgar names may now become a stimulus for other behavior, say throwing things. This circular kind of process must also be explained. This type of analysis can get extremely complicated.

ATTITUDE AND RELATED CONCEPTS

Enter the concept of attitude. Because of the tremendous complexity of behavior we need a kind of summary statement that will enable us to describe and explain (at least on one level) the behaviors we observe as well as those we cannot or have not yet observed. *Attitude* serves these functions well. By postulating a negative attitude toward policemen we can describe and to some degree explain the individual's behavior. Also, the concept of attitude will help us to predict what this individual might do on other occasions. If, for example, the individual has an unfavorable attitude toward policemen, we may then be in a better position to predict what he will do if his brother wishes to become a policeman or if a policeman performs some kind of service for him.

We may define attitude as *a predisposition to respond for or against an object.* An attitude is a *predisposition* or a kind of *readiness to respond.* The attitude is not the behavior but only a mental or internal state of readiness that we postulate. Attitudes are predispositions to respond *for or against* something. Attitudes, by definition, are evaluative; they are predispositions to respond favorably or unfavorably and, obviously, anywhere between these two extremes. Theoretically, at least, we can have neutral attitudes, fairly favorable, quite unfavorable, and extremely favorable attitudes, and, in fact, attitudes covering any possible gradation from extremely unfavorable to extremely favorable. Attitudes are predispositions to respond for or against *an object.* The word "object" is used here in its broadest sense to include things, people, situations, events, ideas, and so on. Attitudes, then, are not merely abstract evaluations but have connections to referents.

The term *attitude* is often used interchangeably with a number of other terms and at times it is confused with them. Some of the more closely related terms are noted here so that the concept of attitude may be clarified still further. We here follow the insights provided by Joseph Cooper and James McGaugh.

Belief

We have an attitude *toward* something but we have a belief *in* or *about* an object or person or event or idea. According to Martin Fishbein, *beliefs* may be viewed as the cognitive dimension of attitude rather than the affective or emotional dimension. Whereas attitudes vary from favorable to unfavorable, beliefs vary from true to false, probable to improbable, existent to nonexistent, likely to unlikely. Thus when we have an attitude toward something we are favorable or unfavorable to it, but when we have a belief in something we believe it to be true or false, probable or improbable, and so on. Beliefs are in some ways the bases or foundations of attitudes. If we believe x, y, and z about someone, then we may develop an attitude toward him or her on the basis of these beliefs. Thus if we believe that this person steals, cheats, and beats children, then we would develop an unfavorable attitude toward this person. However, note that the process goes in the other direction as well. If we have an unfavorable attitude toward someone then we are more likely to believe negative things about this person and less likely to believe positive things. Similarly, if we have a favorable attitude toward someone we are more likely to believe positive things and less likely to believe negative things.

Given this relationship between attitudes and beliefs we can easily imagine two general ways to change attitudes and beliefs. Attempts at change may be directed at the affective component or at the cognitive component. We might attempt to develop or change an existing favorable or unfavorable attitude toward an object by appeals to the emotional dimension; on the other hand, we might attempt to change individuals beliefs about an object which in turn will lead them to change their attitudes. For example, we might change our negative attitudes toward the person mentioned earlier if we were first made to change our beliefs about him or her. So if we were made to believe that this person did not steal, did not cheat, and did not beat children, then we would have no reason for an unfavorable attitude toward him or her and might even develop a favorable attitude.

Beliefs are often used to make predictions about the future or even guesses about the past that is unknown. If we believe that Jane is the brighest kid in the world then we might predict that she will do well on her examinations and that she will get into the college of her choice and so on. Or if we believe that Jane is a drunk we might guess—information to the contrary—that when she came home late last night it was because she first stopped at a local bar. Although not all predictions are made on the basis of beliefs, the majority of our guesses seem related in some way to our system of beliefs.

Faith

Faith is a type of attitude that is primarily emotional in meaning. To have faith in someone or something, for example, is to have an emotional attachment of some sort. Faith is a kind of belief; to have faith in someone is to believe in him or her. Like belief, we also often use faith to predict the unknown. If we did not know what happened to our favorite team in some game we might predict their behavior on the basis of our faith in them. Faith is also a kind of ideology in that it is often used to explain some phenomenon. Faith, for example, may enable us to explain the cycle of life and death, the achievements and failures of people and nations, the goodness and the cruelty of humankind.

Opinion

Of all the terms considered here, *opinion* is perhaps the most frequently used; we express our opinions, we listen to the opinions of others, we read the results of opinion polls, we gauge public opinion. Opinions are perhaps best viewed as tentative conclusions regarding some object, person, or event. Opinions are tentative and thus change rather quickly. Attitudes on the other hand are relatively enduring. In fact, many writers make this enduring quality an essential part of the definition of attitude.

When opinion is used in the phrase "public opinion," we are speaking of a general or collective mind with a given opinion or more concretely, the opinion of the majority or at least a large portion of the people.

Value

Value refers objectively to the worth of an object or subjectively to the perceived worth of an object. Some would argue that value is inherent in an object and hold, for example, that a Rembrandt painting is inherently valuable and would be so even if there were no people to evaluate it. Others, however, would argue that value is in the observer's evaluation rather than in the object and that the Rembrandt is valuable because millions of people perceive it to be of value.

In one sense, a value is an organized system of attitudes. If, for example, we have a cluster of favorable attitudes pertaining to various issues relating to freedom of speech, for example, then we might say that one of our values is that of free speech.

In another sense, a value is an organizing system for attitudes. If we have a particular value, say financial success, then this will give us guidelines for developing and forming attitudes. Thus we will have favorable attitudes toward high-paying jobs, marrying into a wealthy family, and inheriting money because of the value we place on financial success. Values also provide us with guidelines for behavior; in effect, they direct our behavior so that it is consistent with the achievement of the values of goals we have.

FUNCTIONS OF ATTITUDES

Daniel Katz has distinguished four functions of attitudes which are important to consider in any attempt to understand how attitudes operate and why they operate as they do: utilitarian, ego defensive, value expressive, and knowledge.

Utilitarian

Some attitudes are directed at objects that will enable us to reach our goals (in which case they are favorable) or to avoid undesirable goals (in which case they are unfavorable). *Utilitarian* attitudes, as the term implies, are formed on the basis of the perceived usefulness-uselessness of the object to the individual.

Typical utilitarian attitudes of college students might be, for example, favorable attitudes toward high grades, scholarships, admission to graduate school, athletic prowess, and popularity with peers. Unfavorable attitudes might be directed toward low grades, unpopularity, conservatism, and meaningless courses. These attitudes are utilitarian in that they are directed at objects which can help or hinder the individual in his or her attainment of goals.

Utilitarian attitudes are generally formed on the basis of associations. For example, if the mother satisfies the child's hunger need, the child will develop favorable attitudes toward the mother, toward the food, and perhaps toward the general situation in which this need is satisfied. We have a favorable attitude toward high grades because high grades have been associated in the past (and we predict will be associated in the future) with social reinforcement, entrance into the school of our choice, and so on.

Utilitarian attitudes are formed on the basis of the rewards and the punishments that we receive. For example, if upon studying we are positively reinforced, for example, by a social reward, then studying will become positive for us—that is, we will develop favorable attitudes toward studying. If, on the other hand, studying was punished, say by peer criticism as it often is in high school, then we might develop unfavorable attitudes toward studying.

Ego Defensive

Many of our attitudes are developed to protect our rather sensitive egos. At times such attitudes might protect us from the real or imagined dangers which we face in the outside world and at other times they may protect us from discovering something about ourselves which might be ego deflating. If we are unpopular with our peer group we might develop attitudes that will protect our egos from this kind of realization; we might, for instance, develop unfavorable attitudes toward these members, considering them generally inferior, stupid, immoral, dull, or whatever. By putting this group down we elevate ourselves (in our own minds at least) and in this way protect our egos.

Thus *ego-defensive attitudes* are not created in response to an object in the outside world and its relationship to our goals, as is the case with utilitarian attitudes. They are created in response to some inner need or conflict. Consequently, such ego-defensive attitudes may be destructive rather than constructive. For example, if we develop negative attitudes toward this peer group with whom we are unpopular, then we do not confront the issue of our own unpopularity with other people but rather take refuge in the idea that these people are dull, or whatever other designation is handy and ego protecting.

Value Expressive

Some attitudes are *value expressive,* that is, they express the values we hold and thus help us to articulate to ourselves and to others the kind of person we are or wish ourselves to be. For example, I see myself as a progressive instructor. Consequently, I have a number of attitudes which are appropriate expressions of this "progressive teacher" value. For example, I have favorable attitudes toward maintaining office hours for students, preparing thoroughly for classes, grading papers as soon as they are turned in, keeping on top of the new developments in the field, and so on. These attitudes reflect to some extent my own self-image.

We all see ourselves differently. But regardless of how we see ourselves we maintain attitudes that are expressions of the values we believe in. If we value freedom of expression, then we would have unfavorable attitudes toward censorship and laws limiting free expression and favorable attitudes toward whatever is positively related to this freedom of expression value.

Knowledge

Many of our attitudes help us to give meaning to the world by providing us with standards against which various objects and actions may be measured. For example, if we have a negative attitude toward a particular form of education then this attitude will be useful by providing us with a frame of reference, *knowledge,* into which we may fit new information about this type of education.

Similarly, we may have a favorable attitude toward a certain philosophy. This may provide us with the standard against which we can evaluate or judge new courses of action or evaluate decisions which have to be made.

Attitudes may serve any or all of these functions, singly or in combination; a single attitude may serve one function or all four at the same time.

The importance of appreciating these different functions is two-fold. First, by recognizing these four functions we will be in a better position to understand our own attitudes—how they are developed, how they are maintained, and, to some extent, the usefulness-uselessness of them to our own self-image and our own goals. Some attitudes are unproductive and in fact destructive and these need to be examined and altered. Perhaps a prerequisite is the understanding of the functions our attitudes now serve.

Second, attitudes serving different functions will not be susceptible to the same forces of change. Should we, for example, attempt to change someone's attitude, the way it will change, the appeals it will be responsive to, the resistance we will run into, and the chance for success will in large measure depend on the function that the attitude is now serving. An attitude serving important ego-defensive needs, for example, will be highly resistant to change and will obviously not respond to the same kinds of appeals as would an attitude that serves primarily a knowledge function.

SOURCES

Attitudes are covered in most social psychology texts in considerable detail. On the dimensions and functions of attitudes see "The Functional Approach to the Study of Attitudes" by Daniel Katz, *Public Opinion Quarterly* 24(1960):163–204. I relied heavily on this article for the discussion of the dimensions and the functions of attitudes presented here. Perhaps the most comprehensive work on attitudes is that of William J. McGuire, "The Nature of Attitudes and Attitude Change" *The Handbook of Social Psychology,* 2d ed., edited by Gardner Lindzey and Elliot Aronson, vol. 3 (Reading, Mass.: Addison-Wesley, 1969), pp. 136–314.

Excellent collections of articles on attitude are *Readings in Attitude Theory and Measurement,* edited by Martin Fishbein (New York: Wiley, 1967) and *Attitudes,* edited by Marie Johoda and Neil Warren (Baltimore: Penguin, 1966). Joseph B. Cooper and James L. McGaugh's "Attitudes and Related Concepts," used here extensively, is reprinted in Jahoda and Warren's *Attitudes.*

Herbert W. Simons, *Persuasion: Understanding, Practice, and Analysis* (Reading, Mass.: Addison-Wesley, 1976) surveys the area of attitudes and attitude theories most clearly.

EXPERIENTIAL VEHICLES

16.1 THE ATTITUDE GAME

This game is played in groups of approximately six people. The procedure is as follows: One member is selected through some random means to be the first subject. If the group members do not know each other, the subject should introduce himself or herself with a brief talk (no more than one or two miuntes). After this introduction the group members, one at a time, attempt to guess the objects toward which the subject has a favorable attitude. Proceeding clockwise, the group members each guess a favorable attitude of the subject until one member guesses incorrectly. Naturally, the subject should respond honestly to the various guesses of the group. When an incorrect guess is made, the guessing stops. The group then focuses on the reasons for their success or failure to guess accurately. The individual who is the subject should lead this discussion and should attempt to discover what cues he or she gives off which led the group members to guess as they did. At any point the subject may conclude the discussion and ask that the group go onto another person. The subject's wishes should be respected and another member should be chosen, again in some impartial manner.

The same general procedure may be repeated to deal with unfavorable attitudes, positive values, and negative values. Ten or fifteen minutes should be reserved so that the group as a whole might discuss and evaluate the game. DO NOT READ ANY FURTHER UNTIL THE GAME HAS BEEN PLAYED.

After completing the game the group members should focus on at least some of the following questions:

1. How brave were the group members in guessing meaningful and significant attitudes and values?
2. How honest was each player in telling the group members whether they were right or wrong?
3. To what extent did the group members make the subject feel that they were really interested in his or her attitudes and values? How did they indicate this interest or disinterest?
4. To what extent are the members of this group homophilous? Heterophilous? Are their specific areas of similarity and difference?
5. Do you feel you know anyone better as a result of this exercise? Explain.

16.2 THE ATTITUDES AND VALUES GAME

The purpose of this exercise is to explore the nature of attitudes and values in more specific and more personal terms than is possible in any reading.

Groups of six or seven persons should be formed; members may or may not be familiar with each other. It is best to have all members either familiar with each other or all members unfamiliar with each other rather than to have groups composed of some members who know each other and other members who do not know anyone. The exercise also may be effectively played with the entire class as one group.

Each member of the group should complete the accompanying Attitudes and Values Form as honestly as possible. Each member should respond to the questions with those attitudes and values most important to him or her.

ATTITUDES AND VALUES FORM

1. Among those objects toward which I have favorable attitudes, some of the most important are:

    a.
    b.
    c.

2. Among those objects toward which I have unfavorable attitudes, some of the most important are:

    a.
    b.
    c.

3. Among those objects for which I have high positive value, some of the most important are:

    a.
    b.
    c.

4. Among those objects for which I have high negative value, some of the most important are:

    a.
    b.
    c.

The papers should be collected, shuffled randomly, and read aloud to the group by one member. The first objective is for members to attempt to guess the person whose form was read. After all forms are read, discussion should focus on some or all of the following areas:

1. To what extent do these attitudes and values reveal something of the individual? To what extent do they enable one to predict other attitudes and values? Test this by actually making some predictions.
2. What functions do these attitudes and values serve (using a system such as that described in this unit, that is, utilitarian, ego defensive, value expressive, knowledge)?
3. To what extent are these attitudes and values resistant to change?—that is, how difficult would it be to change these attitudes and values? What types of appeals would be most effective in trying to change these attitudes and values? Why?
4. Do any of these attitudes and values create psychological discomfort? How is this dealt with?
5. Can the origin of these attitudes and values be determined?—that is, how did the individual come to hold these attitudes and values?
6. How do the attitudes and values differ from those that would be expressed by the parents of the group members? Test this by asking some parents.
7. Was it easier to guess the forms of some people rather than others? Why?
8. Do you feel you know anyone better as a result of this exercise? Explain.

UNIT 17
Attitude and Behavior Change

17.1 Everybody's Talking

Conditioning and Attitude and Behavior Change
Cognitive Balance and Attitude and Behavior Change

17.2 The Related Attitudes Game

LEARNING GOALS

After completing this unit, you should be able to:

1. define *conditioning, positive reinforcement, negative reinforcement,* and *punishment*
2. explain how conditioning principles may account for the development, maintenance, and change of attitudes
3. specify the five principles of behavior control
4. define the concept of *balance* as it applies to attitude
5. state the conditions under which attitudes are balanced and unbalanced
6. define *cognitive dissonance*
7. state the conditions necessary for dissonance to develop
8. state the possibilities for dissonance reduction—that is, the ways in which dissonance may be reduced
9. explain how dissonance operates in forced compliance, decision making, exposure to information, and social support

EXPERIENTIAL VEHICLE

17.1 EVERYBODY'S TALKING

This exercise should be completed individually. Before reading this unit respond to the following questions with the first statements that come to your mind. Do not try to say the "right thing"; be honest—no one will see what you have written. As you read the unit, especially the section on cognitive balance, refer back to your statements to determine to what extent this theory was able to predict your responses.

1. If you could overhear what your two best friends are saying about you, what three things would you predict they are saying?

   a.
   b.
   c.

2. If you could overhear what your two worst enemies are saying about you, what three things would you predict they are saying?

   a.
   b.
   c.

3. If you were talking about your two best friends, what three things would you be most likely to say? (Specify the type of audience you are addressing.)

   a.
   b.
   c.

4. If you were talking about your two worst enemies, what three things would you be most likely to say? (Specify the type of audience you are addressing.)

   a.
   b.
   c.

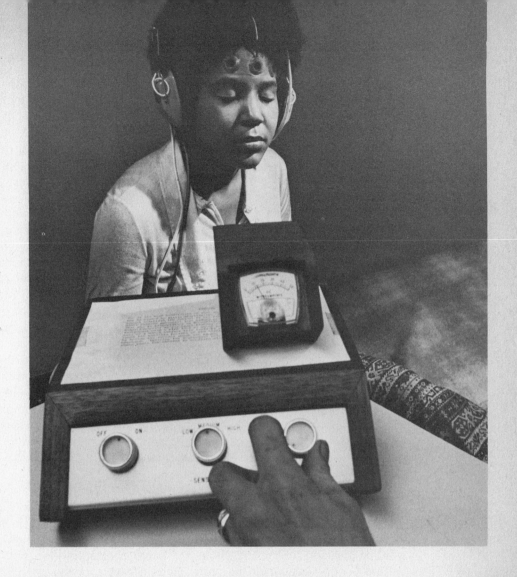

CONDITIONING AND ATTITUDE AND BEHAVIOR CHANGE

Perhaps the branch of psychology most often in the popular news is that of behaviorism. The techniques of conditioning and reinforcement as applied to learning, behavior problems, and social planning are by now familiar to most. For our purposes, however, some of the basics of conditioning need to be considered before its relationship to attitude and attitude change may be discussed.

The Operation of Conditioning

Operant behavior—that form of behavior that is peculiarly human, unlike reflexive behavior—is behavior that is dependent upon its consequences. If the behavior is rewarded its strength, frequency, and/or likelihood of occurrence will increase. If the behavior is punished or ignored then its strength and frequency will decrease and the behavior may be extinguished or eliminated.

Behavior may be rewarded in two general ways. First, and perhaps the method most familiar, is by positive reinforcement, which is what we normally think of when we talk about reward. Positive reinforcement is simply the presentation of a positive or rewarding stimulus. For example, if after pressing a lever we present the rat with food, we are positively reinforcing the lever-pressing behavior. We can also reward through negative reinforcement. If, for example, a person is equipped with earphones through which a painful sound is passed, and if upon his or her performing the desired behavior we shut the sound off for 10 seconds, we are engaged in negative reinforcement. Notice that shutting off the sound—more formally, the removal of an aversive stimulus—is rewarding for the individual in a way similar though not identical to that of positive reinforcement. Punishment is simply the presentation of an aversive or unpleasant stimulus or the removal of a pleasant stimulus. Thus, for example, we may punish a child by spanking or by taking away candy.

According to behaviorists, most of our behaviors are learned through this system of reinforcement. We learn to respond to other people in the way we do because we have in the past been reinforced for some behaviors and punished for other behaviors. Similarly, we learned to smoke, for example, through reinforcement (probably social) when we were younger. Alternatively, we unlearn behaviors through the same basic means. Smoking behavior, for example, may be unlearned by making punishment contingent upon it and reward contingent upon nonsmoking behavior.

The theories of operant conditioning may be utilized to explain how attitudes are developed and how they are maintained. Take a simple issue, such as eating popcorn. Eating popcorn was accompanied by hunger satisfaction which is rewarding or positively reinforcing and so the popcorn comes to have a positive meaning for the individual. On future occasions—for example, when we are hungry—we would be more likely to reach for the popcorn because this has in the past been associated with reward. On the other hand, if the popcorn made us violently ill, that is, if it were punishing, then our tendency to reach for the popcorn would be lessened or perhaps extinguished entirely. On the basis of the consequences of the behavior we develop favorable or unfavorable attitudes—favorable attitudes if the consequences were positive or rewarding and unfavorable attitudes if the consequences were negative or punishing. Thus we would have a predisposition to reach for or not reach for the popcorn because of its previous consequences and this predisposition we choose to call *attitude.*

It is often said that children are not born with prejudices but must learn them from their parents. A prejudice may be viewed as a negative attitude toward a class of people which is unrealistic and not based on any concrete evidence. It is an irrational attitude. Consider how this type of attitude or prejudice might develop in a child. The child comes home from nursery school and tells the parents about this new child whose skin was a different color and whose eyes did not look like everyone else's. Immediately the child is told how bad these other children are and how they should not be associated with. Notice that this relatively simple kind of expression of prejudice in effect tells the child that negative consequences will follow or that rewards will be withdrawn if this child is played with. Because of this kind of teaching the child now has a predisposition to respond against another child of a different skin color and this predisposition we simply call an unfavorable attitude.

Perhaps the most difficult type of attitude to account for in operant terms is that which we normally term moral behavior. Take the situation of a student who is caught with a term paper he or she did not write. The instructor discovers that another student wrote the paper and attempts to get the name of the paper writer from this student. Even when faced with all sorts of unpleasant consequences the student refuses to tell on his or her friend. Even if the instructor were to offer a reward for telling (say, letting the student off with no penalty), he or she opts to take the punishment and remain silent. On the surface it would seem that this type of behavior defies what has already been said about behavior being governed by its consequences. With somewhat more analysis, however, we can see that this type of behavior is similar to that of the popcorn or even to the rat pressing the lever. Even in this situation there are rewards and punishments but here they are internalized. By not telling on his or her friend the student gets rewarded through the social reinforcement of his or her peers and also avoids the punishment that would be received if he or she had told. To the student the peer group reinforcement is the more powerful. In a similar manner we may engage in behavior that has immediate unpleasant consequences—for example, studying on a warm Saturday night when everyone else is on a date—in order to get a positive reinforcement at a later time—perhaps in the form of a good grade and possible social reinforcement as well. The ability to delay our rewards is dependent in great part on maturity. Children have great difficulty in delaying rewards: they are not satisfied to be told they can have ice cream tomorrow or even in an hour. They want it when they want it and that is that.

Principles of Behavior Control

We also want to know how behavior is controlled through this system of rewards and punishments. Perhaps the best way to explain the operation of behavior conditioning principles is to specify the steps necessary to alter the behavior of an individual. Let us assume, then, that we wish to stop a particular behavior, say smoking. There are five basic steps to be followed.

Specify the Behavior to Be Learned or Unlearned

This principle may seem unnecessary except that it emphasizes *behavior*. In applying the principles of conditioning we are dealing with behavior, not with internal emotions. We do not attempt to extinguish anxiety; we do attempt to extinguish nail biting or foot stamping. The behavior in our example is smoking behavior; that is what we are attacking, not any symptoms or causes of the behavior but the behavior itself—the puffing and inhaling to be exact.

Establish and Apply the Reinforcers

To control behavior we manipulate the consequences of the behavior. To learn a particular bit of behavior we use reinforcement; to unlearn behavior we use punishment. Now the questions that naturally arises is what is reinforcing. David Premack has suggested a relatively simple but ingenious method for determining what is a reinforcer. The theory, called variously the *Premack principle* or the *differential probability hypothesis,* states that high frequency behaviors may be used to reinforce low frequency behaviors. If, for example, telephoning behavior is extremely frequent, then that behavior may be used to reinforce other behavior which is normally less frequent, for example, studying behavior. The application of the principle requires that telephoning behavior be allowed only as a reward for engaging in the less rewarding (or less immediately rewarding) studying behavior. The specific application of the re-

"Nope; no chess problems until you've finished your quadratic equations!"

ward will depend on the individual case. For example, if you cannot seem to study for more than one hour at a time then it is the short period of time that needs to be increased. Thus in the beginning you may allow yourself one telephone call for each hour of studying. After this period is no longer such a strain, increase it to one hour and a quarter and only after that time allow yourself the phone call. In this way you will be able to increase the time you engage in normally "undesirable" behaviors.

With punishment we generally know what works and what will not work. At times the punishment needs to be extreme whereas at other times it may be relatively mild. For example, you may make a "contract" with yourself which goes something like this: for every cigarette I smoke I will send $5 to the American Cancer Society. Assuming you stick to this contract you will stop smoking or go broke in very short order. I smoked almost three packs of cigarettes a day for 15 years. When I decided to stop I chose a somewhat more drastic punishment which I applied three times: For every cigarette I smoked I would stick my fingers down my throat until I threw up. I must confess that this was not the most pleasant experience and yet it did get me to stop smoking, at least for a time. At that time I stopped for six months and then went back to smoking. The reason for the failure of this application was that I allowed myself to cheat. It is very easy to cheat ourselves; we are such easy marks. At any rate, I cheated by concluding that cigars were not in the original contract I made with myself and so I smoked cigars. As many cigarette smokers who attempt cigars know, they are relatively unsatisfying if you do not inhale. And so for about a month I inhaled about 20 cigars a day. The house smelled so bad that guests would refuse to enter. Of course, it was not difficult for me to cheat myself one step further and conclude that the evil of cigarettes was far less than that of cigars. With cigars not only was I going to lose my health but my friends as well. And so I went back to cigarettes and smoked for four years until the second and last conditioning. In some cases it is possible to be your own contingency manager and to monitor the contract you make with yourself. At other times it is not so easy, as I learned. The only real change I made in the procedure was to have someone else monitor the no smoking agreement and to apply the punishment. In this case it was electric shock administered as I held a cigarette in my mouth. After approximately five hours of this treatment (spread over five days) and discussion pertaining to my reasons and rationalizations for smoking I was "cured." I still consider myself a smoker—rather like the alcoholic who has ceased drinking—but one who does not smoke. At the time of this writing it has been approximately five years since I had a cigarette.

Utilize the Stimulus Properties of the Situation

If a rat is repeatedly shocked in a maze it will attempt to avoid the maze. This is not a particularly profound discovery on the part of the rat but it is a useful one. The maze takes on stimulus properties of the original stimulus, the shock. Because of this we need to structure our learning situations so that the stimulus properties of the situation will work for rather than against us. Consider, for example, instructors who use the classroom as a place for discussion of personal problems and then expect the students to work when told to do so. The classroom, in this situation, has become the stimulus for reading the newspaper, playing tic-tac-toe, or just daydreaming. Instructors who think they can turn the situation around at whim are fools and should be told so. Notice how effective instructors do utilize the stimulus properties of the situation to advantage. Many students have difficulty studying because of the failure to properly utilize the stimulus properties of the situation. The student who wants the situation to stimulate studying behavior needs to study and only study in the same place. If this is a desk then one should do nothing else at that desk but study. When one wishes to read a magazine or make a phone call one should sit somewhere else. In this way studying behavior will be stimulated by sitting at the desk. Similarly, many people have difficulty sleeping because they do things other than sleep in bed.

Smoking behavior is often situational: Our smoking behavior is often triggered by various situations. For example, having coffee after eating stimulates smoking behavior in most smokers as does having a drink at a bar; important phone conversations also stimulate smoking behavior. Situations that stimulate the behavior that we wish eliminated should be avoided, especially at the beginning of the period when we are modifying behavior.

This issue is closely related to the perceived rewarding value of the actual smoking behavior. For example, smokers will say that smoking relaxes them, but we know that physiologically smoking does not relax the body; it tenses it. Actually, the smoking is closely related to relaxing but in itself has nothing to do with it. The smokers among the readers should imitate the act of taking a drag on a cigarette. Notice how deep we breathe when we smoke. It is this deep breathing that is relaxing and because it is associated with the smoking we perceive the smoking to be relaxing.

Reinforce Immediately

Reinforcers lose their effectiveness over time. Teachers who return examinations or papers after weeks of time should be made to realize that the effects of their reinforcement or punishment are much less than they would be if the papers were returned after only a short time. The mother who says to the child that he or she will be punished when father gets home does nothing to extinguish the undesirable behavior because the time between the actual behavior and the reinforcement is too long. If we wish the reinforcer to have its maximum effect it must be applied immediately. It should in fact be the next thing in time after the behavior itself.

One instructor attempting to teach students about teaching and especially about teacher-student communication equipped the student teachers with a receiving set so that as they gave their sample lectures he was able to reinforce immediately.

At times, of course, the desired behavior does not manifest itself, and we simply do not have the time to wait for it. What we do in this case is to reinforce successive approximations of the desired behavior. This procedure is called *shaping behavior*. If we are teaching a pigeon to make the classic S-shape design, we reinforce any movement in the desired direction until the complete S is formed.

With smoking behavior the punishment must come immediately after the cigarette is taken or even while the cigarette is being held. If we wait until a whole pack is smoked, for example, then the effectiveness of the punishment is going to be minimal.

Introduce Uncertainty

One of the more interesting aspects of conditioning is that constant reinforcement does not work as effectively as intermittent reinforcement. For example, if the pigeon is reinforced every time it presses the lever the frequency of its lever-pressing behavior will be less than if it is reinforced only intermittently. Ideally, the time of the reinforcement and the form of the reinforcement should be somewhat unknown to the individual whose behavior we are trying to shape or mold.

If, for example, we are shocked for every fifth puff on a cigarette, this will be less effective in curbing smoking behavior than if we were shocked on a quasi-random schedule, even if this averages one shock for every five puffs. The reason is simple enough: If we know that we will be shocked on every fifth puff we will be able to enjoy the first four and so the association between the behavior and the punishment is not established. But if we do not know when the shock will come then we will be apprehensive on each puff and the association between the smoking and the shock will be more firmly established. When we are our own contingency manager we cannot apply this principle but it is most useful when we are attempting to control another's behavior.

COGNITIVE BALANCE AND ATTITUDE AND BEHAVIOR CHANGE

Instead of concentrating solely on the behavior, the *consistency* or *balance theory* "goes into the mind" and attempts to explain some of the cognitive dynamics involved in the process of attitude change. The fundamental assumption of all balance theories—and there are a number of different variations—is that there is a universal tendency to maintain homeostasis, psychological balance, or consistency. *Balance* might best be defined as a state of psychological comfort in which all the attitude objects in our minds are related as we would want them to be or as we would psychologically expect them to be. Imbalance or inconsistency, then, is a state of psychological discomfort in which the attitude objects in our minds are not related as we would want or expect them to be.

The Nature of Cognitive Balance

Let us say that we positively evaluate Peter and Patricia and that we negatively evaluate Neil and Nancy. Our minds would be balanced under the following conditions:

1. if Peter liked Patricia/if Patricia liked Peter
2. if Neil liked Nancy/if Nancy liked Neil
3. if Peter and Patricia liked us
4. if Neil and Nancy disliked us
5. if Neil and Nancy disliked Peter and Patricia/if Peter and Patricia disliked Neil and Nancy

We expect people we like to like us (3) and expect people we dislike to dislike us (4). Similarly, we expect people we like to like each other (1) and expect people we dislike to like each other (2). Further, we expect people we like to dislike people we dislike (5). With a little reflection these should be intuitively satisfying.

From these examples we can deduce the states of imbalance:

6. if Peter disliked Patricia/if Patricia disliked Peter
7. if Neil disliked Nancy/if Nancy disliked Neil
8. if Peter and Patricia disliked us
9. if Neil and Nancy liked us
10. if Neil and Nancy liked Peter and Patricia/if Peter and Patricia liked Neil and Nancy

The assumption in all balance theories is that when our attitudes are in a state of balance we are psychologically comfortable and are not motivated to change our attitudes or our behaviors. On the other hand, when we are in a state of imbalance or inconsistency, we are psychologically uncomfortable and are motivated to change our attitudes and our behaviors. (It should be noted that some theories argue that given a state of imbalance, attitude change is automatic. Other theories claim that given a state of imbalance, we must be motivated to change our attitudes; it is not automatic.)

Let us take one of the imbalanced examples and attempt to predict the type of changes that would bring this imbalanced condition into a state of balance: "If Peter disliked Patricia." Visualizing our minds as containing a positive side for favorable attitude objects and a negative side for unfavorable attitude objects, we might diagram this as in Figure 17.1 (the line connecting the two attitude objects is the expressed relationship which in this case is negative, Peter *dislikes* Patricia):

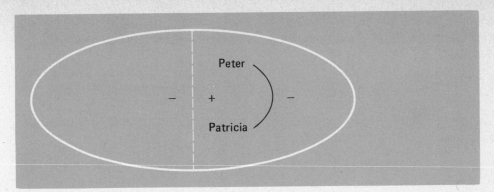

Figure 17.1
Attitudes in an Unbalanced State

We should now consider what kinds of changes would bring this model into balance. Obviously, if Peter changed his attitude toward Patricia and liked her, it would bring the model into balance. But this is an alternative over which we do not always have control, although we sometimes do convince ourselves that one person likes or dislikes another simply to suit our own needs. Generally, however, the choices open to us are 1) to change our attitude toward Peter or 2) to change our attitude toward Patricia. If one of them (but not both of them) were evaluated negatively, we would be in a state of psychological comfort and balance. This change may seem very mechanical and unrealistic when viewed in terms of the diagram and the clear-cut divisions between positive and negative. But the general procedure or process by which attitudes are changed does not seem much different from the situation as depicted here. We might change our attitude toward Peter and explain it in any number of ways, for example, if Peter does not like Patricia then he is the one who has problems. Or we might change our attitude toward Patricia and reason that if Peter does not like her there must be something wrong with her.

This process is perhaps seen most clearly when we are confronted with a neutral attitude object, that is, an object about which we do not feel very positive or very negative. However, when a positive or a negative bond is created between this neutral object and an object toward which we do have a definite attitude then we change our attitude from neutral to either positive or negative depending upon which would produce a balanced state. For example, if Bill No. 75, about which we feel neutral, is introduced and supported by a politician toward whom we feel positive then we would soon feel positive toward the bill, perhaps reasoning that if this politician supports it it must have merit. In this case then, we have a positive bond between two positively evaluated objects. This is similar to situation (1), Peter liking Patricia. On the other hand, if the politician was someone toward whom we had a negative attitude then we would develop a negative attitude toward the bill, reasoning that this incompetent politician could not possibly support anything worthwhile. Here we are creating a positive bond between two negatively evaluated objects, similar to situation (2), Neil liking Nancy.

In order to explain this consistency approach more clearly we shall explain one of the balance theories in greater depth. The theory to be considered here is that of *cognitive dissonance* which is perhaps the most interesting of all the theories in social psychology today. It is also the most general and the most applicable to communication.

Cognitive Dissonance

The theory of *cognitive dissonance* was formulated by Leon Festinger and originally presented in his *A Theory of Cognitive Dissonance.* Since then there have been thousands of studies conducted to test the implications and the predictions of cognitive dissonance.

Dissonance and *consonance* refer to relationships between elements, cognitions, or "knowledges" about oneself, about other people, or about the world. Elements or cognitions may be beliefs, attitudes, feelings, behaviors, desires, and so on. In our examples the elements were, for example, "Peter likes Patricia" or "Neil and Nancy dislike us."

Dissonance (similar to imbalance) and consonance (similar to balance) exist when there is a relation between two elements. The relation is dissonant when *the obverse of one element follows from the other element.* Two elements, A and B, are dissonant if, given A, non-B would be expected to follow. For example, A might be "I like Peter" and B might be "Peter does not like me." Given that I like Peter (A) it would follow that Peter likes me (which is the obverse of B). Hence this relation would be dissonant. Or take an example alluded to earlier. As a smoker I had the following cognitions: (A) smoking is unhealthy and (B) I am a heavy smoker. Given A, it would be more logical if non-B followed. That is, given the fact that I know smoking is unhealthy my being a heavy smoker would not follow. Hence this relationship was dissonant.

On the other hand consider the following relations: (A) I like Peter, and (B) Peter likes me. Given A, B would logically follow; hence this relationship is consonant. Similarly, consider these two relationships: (A) Smoking is unhealthy and (B) I no longer smoke. Given A, B would be logical to follow and hence this is a state of balance or consonance. Consonance, then, exists when, given one element, the other would be psychologically or logically expected.

When we are in a dissonant state there is pressure to reduce the dissonance and restore consonance; there are a number of alternatives to accomplish this. Obviously, if there is a great deal of dissonance there will be much pressure to reduce it; if there is little dissonance there will be little pressure to reduce it.

Explaining the alternative modes of dissonance reduction will be simplified if we worked through an example. Suppose that I am a skydiver and that I very much enjoy this experience. But I know that it is dangerous and so the two elements (I skydive, skydiving is dangerous) are dissonant. Now, what are my alternatives to reduce the dissonance?

First, I could change the behavior, that is, I could stop skydiving and that would eliminate the dissonance. Similarly, the person who smokes and yet knows that smoking is unhealthy can reduce the dissonance by stopping the behavior. But, as any smoker knows, this is not always easy. The typical unrequited love story presents a dissonant relationship to the person who loves but is not loved in return. To change the behavior and get himself or herself to not love may not be possible, and so he or she may have to eliminate changing behavior as one alternative to reducing dissonance.

A second method to reduce dissonance is to change the environmental element. This is often the most difficult of all alternatives. In the case of my skydiving it would involve making skydiving safe or at least less dangerous. Similarly, for the smoker it would involve making smoking healthy or at least not unhealthy. For the lover it would involve getting the other person to love in return. At best these are extremely difficult to accomplish. Of course, there are situations when changing the environment is not out of the question, as it is in the examples given. We might for example be riding in a car with bad brakes. Our two elements are (A) I ride in this car and (B) this car has bad brakes and is therefore dangerous. Here it is quite possible to change the environment and get the brakes fixed, reducing the danger, and eliminating the dissonance.

A third alternative to reduce dissonance is to acquire new elements. As a skydiver I might read about the numerous precautions being taken to make skydiving safe and perhaps read about how dangerous automobile travel is or about how people are dying every day and have never had the thrill of skydiving. As a smoker the person might read about the biased nature of the research linking smoking to cancer or perhaps rationalize that smoking has enabled him or her to accomplish a great deal of work by relieving tension. The lover might attempt to find faults with the loved one. These new elements would reduce the dissonance perhaps to the point where it would no longer be uncomfortable.

In order to see the relevance of cognitive dissonance to communication we should examine the four situations Festinger notes as applicable to the theory: forced compliance, decision making, exposure to information, and social support.

Forced Compliance

Dissonance is created when our public behavior contradicts our private attitudes. Such a situation might be brought about by the individual being promised a reward for compliance or by being threatened for noncompliance. But the amount of dissonance created will vary with the nature of the reward or threat. Consider, for example, a situation used in one of the many experiments designed to test dissonance. Subjects participated in an extremely boring experiment. After they participated in this boring experience they were asked to lie to subjects who were waiting to participate in the same experiment and to tell them that the experiment was interesting. Some subjects received $20 for this lying whereas other subjects received only $1. In which group would more dissonance be created? The measure of the amount of dissonance was taken to be the amount of attitude change that took place after the lying; thus after completing the experiment the subjects rated the experiment in terms of how interesting it was, then they lied to the other subjects, and then they again rated the experiment. The results of the experiment showed that the group that was paid $20 changed their attitudes very little and thus were judged to have experienced little dissonance. The subjects who were paid only $1, however, changed their attitudes a great deal (now feeling that the experiment was not so boring) and were judged to have experienced much dissonance. This seems quite logical after some reflection. The subjects who were paid $20 were able to justify their lying; they had received a significant reward for a relatively minor lie. But the subjects who were paid only $1 could not justify their behavior because the reward was too small.

In another study students were offered rewards for writing essays advocating shorter summer vacations, a position with which they did not agree. The group receiving the greatest reward showed the least attitude change in the direction of shorter summer vacations whereas the group receiving the smallest reward showed the most attitude change and hence the greatest dissonance. Again, their reward was not sufficient to justify taking a position contrary to that which they really believed.

This procedure of forced compliance with the resulting attitude change is obviously something many hucksters and charlatans have long known. One of the most obvious techniques of persuaders is to get you to verbally agree with them or to try their product even if it means it will be at an initial loss to them. The product is generally offered for a minimal amount or at times given free. The object here is to get you to use the product and by the mere fact that you have used it you will develop a more positive attitude toward it and hence will be more likely to use it in the future.

Decision Making

Dissonance is created after making any decision, according to the theory. The reasoning is that any decision involves the acceptance of one alternative, and the rejection of one or more other possible alternatives. In accepting A, for example, we also accept all the negative features of A and of course we reject all the positive features of B, C, D, and so on. For example, suppose you are going to buy a stereo and are deciding between a Pioneer and a Marantz. In selecting the Pioneer you are also accepting its negative features and rejecting (by not buying) the positive features of the Marantz. Because of this, dissonance is created after making decisions. The closer the items and the harder the decision, the more dissonance will be created. If, for example we are offered two prizes but may select only one to keep, we would experience much dissonance if the prizes were about equal in value; we would experience little dissonance if one item was valuable and the other worthless.

In one experiment new car buyers were investigated and were found to read more advertisements of the car they had finally bought and less advertisements of the car they had considered but not bought. The reasoning here is that the advertisements for the car they had bought would provide support for their decision and would reduce the dissonance. If they had read advertisements for the car they were going to buy but did not buy, they would in effect be told that they had made the wrong decision. Hence their dissonance would be increased rather than decreased.

Exposure to Information

When we experience dissonance we may attempt to reduce it by seeking new information. We expose ourselves to information which will decrease our dissonance as in reading the advertisements for the car that we purchased and avoiding ads for the car we did not buy.

The way in which we expose ourselves to information is particularly important in our interpersonal relationships. Take for example people who ask us how they look. They want to be told they look great. Similarly, a new pair of pants or a new jacket brings on a kind of "tell me what you think" attitude. But in doing this they are really attempting to expose themselves to dissonance-reducing information. They are expecting us to to tell them that they look great, that the pants or jacket look fine, and so on. In fact, we often expose ourselves to those people who are normally complimentary so that our dissonance may be reduced.

As a smoker I used to avoid the commercials by the American Cancer Society or the Heart Association. I did not want to be reminded that smoking was dangerous and uncomfortable for others. And at the same time I would actively dwell on advertisements depicting the pleasures of cigarette smoking. Now, however, my behavior is reversed. I actively seek out the commercials against smoking as a kind of reinforcement and avoid the ads for cigarettes. Even my decision to stop smoking created dissonance. By not smoking I have given up the pleasures of smoking; consequently, I experience dissonance. My behavior with the different kinds of advertisements is clearly directed at reducing the dissonance. Even in reading this unit and especially these examples of smoking, the reader who smokes will experience a great deal of dissonance, the reader who stopped smoking will derive reinforcement, and the reader who has never smoked will wonder why there's all the fuss about smoking.

Social Support

The social group is a powerful influence on both the creation of cognitive dissonance and on its reduction. If a group disagrees with us, finds us unpleasant, or ignores us this will create dissonance in us. On the other hand, if the group supports us dissonance will be reduced.

Not all groups or group members produce dissonance equally. The credibility of the group members is significant in the amount of dissonance produced. If members are of high credibility then they are able to produce a great deal of dissonance by disagreeing with us. On the other hand, if they are of low credibility, their disagreeing with us would produce only slight dissonance. Another factor is the number of members who disagree with us. The greater the number of members who disagree with us, the greater the amount of dissonance that will be created. The cohesiveness of the group is also significant. If the group is very cohesive then it will have much more influence in producing or in reducing dissonance than if the group was not a very cohesive one. In fact, one of the important functions that peer groups serve is the reduction of dissonance for its members. When parents do not understand their son or daughter he or she can always go to the peer group who will give the social support necessary to reduce the dissonance created by parental disagreements.

When there is dissonance resulting from disagreement with a social group there are three major ways of reducing it. One way is to change one's attitude so that it is in agreement with that of the group. This is the route taken by many young people who are afraid to be loners or who are afraid that the group might withdraw its support from them because of disagreements. A second way is to change the opinions of those who disagree. When confronted by the disagreement of the group we might at first attempt to change their opinions so that they will be consistent with ours and so that dissonance will be reduced. This method is rather like changing the environment discussed earlier. Third, we might attempt to make the group members somehow different from us so that they now have little effect in producing dissonance. We might attribute to the group some undesirable trait; we might say, for example, that they disagree with us because they are prejudiced or because they are mercenary or immature. When these undesirable traits are attributed to them, their attitudes and opinions are given less importance.

Cognitive dissonance is only one of the many balance theories of attitude change. It was selected for discussion because it seems to be the most widely applicable. It should not be thought that there are no problems with the theory of cognitive dissonance. All theories have problems. Yet the theory seems to provide an amazing degree of insight into the processes of communication.

SOURCES

For conditioning, the works of B. F. Skinner are essential. Particularly valuable are the recent *Beyond Freedom and Dignity* (New York: Knopf, 1971) and *About Behaviorism* (New York: Knopf, 1974). Arthur W. Staats' *Complex Human Behavior* (New York: Holt, Rinehart and Winston, 1963) and *Learning, Language, and Cognition* (New York: Holt, Rinehart and Winston, 1968) clarify much of the research and theory relating to conditioning. The five principles of behavior control are taken from my "The Teacher as Behavioral Engineer," *Today's Speech* 16(February 1968):2–5. For Premack's principle see David Premack, "Toward Empirical Behavior Laws: I. Positive Reinforcement," *Psychological Review* 66(1959).

A summary of the theories of consistency in attitude change are presented in my *The Psychology of Speech and Language: An Introduction to Psycholinguistics* (New York: Random House, 1970). The original work on cognitive dissonance is Leon Festinger's *A Theory of Cognitive Dissonance* (Stanford, Cal.: Stanford University Press, 1957). Extensions of the theory and additional experimental evidence are provided by J. W. Brehm and A. R. Cohen in their *Explorations in Cognitive Dissonance* (New York: Wiley, 1962).

An assessment of consistency theories of attitude change is provided by William J. McGuire, "The Current State of Consistency Theories" and "Cognitive Consistency and Attitude Change," both in Martin Fishbein, ed., *Readings in Attitude Theory and Measurement* (New York: Wiley, 1967). A recent and excellent overview and analysis is provided by Patricia Middlebrook, *Social Psychology and Modern Life* (New York: Knopf, 1974).

Perhaps the best introduction to this general area is Philip Zimbardo, Ebbe Ebbesen, and Christina Maslach's *Influencing Attitudes and Changing Behavior,* 2d ed. (Reading, Mass.: Addison-Wesley, 1977).

EXPERIENTIAL VEHICLE

17.2 THE RELATED ATTITUDES GAME

Attitudes toward or against an object are seldom unrelated to other attitudes. An individual probably does not hate dogs and love all other animals. Rather, he or she probably has a generally favorable or unfavorable attitude toward animals and then more specific attitudes toward various classes of animals. Similarly, the person who has a favorable attitude toward animals is probably unfavorable toward hunting wild animals and toward wearing wild animal fur. This same person may then have a favorable attitude toward efforts of ecologists to preserve the natural environment and an unfavorable attitude toward pollution, littering, and so on. Thus one attitude is often related to another attitude which in turn is then related to another attitude and so on.

The object of this game is to explore the degree to which attitudes are related, and it is played like "twenty questions." Groups of approximately six persons are formed. One person is selected to be the first subject, and the subject thinks of one of his or her attitudes. It is generally best that the subject write the attitude down without showing it to the group. In this way there will be no arguments later on. The subject then identifies the area which the attitude is in. That is, rather than animal-vegetable-mineral, the general area is identified—for example, political, social, religious, economic, educational, psychological. The group members may then ask a maximum of 20 questions which may be answered by the subject with only "yes" or "no." The object is to guess the attitude the subject has written down.

The game should continue until all members have had a chance to be subjects or until the members feel that they have understood the concepts sufficiently. Discussion and response should then focus on some of the following questions:

1. We may predict that the attitudes that were the most difficult to guess were also the ones that somehow did not seem to fit into the general orientation of the individual subject. Was this true?
2. Why would dissonance-producing attitudes be more difficult to guess than consonance-producing attitudes? Why would dissonance-producing attitudes be less likely to be selected by the subjects for guessing? Were any dissonant attitudes used?
3. A pool of inconsistent attitudes should be collected by each group and then shared with the entire class. Why are these attitudes inconsistent with other attitudes? What would the parents of these members say about these attitudes? (Do *not* settle for an easy answer to these questions.)

PART THREE
Communication Contexts

In this section we focus on five major forms or types of communication, namely interpersonal communication, small group communication, public communication, mass communication, and intercultural communication. Each of these five forms is discussed in three, or in the case of interpersonal communication five, units each.

These five forms are the major contexts in which communication occurs and taken together provide a thorough survey of the broad area of human communication. These are the forms through which relationships as well as hostilities are established, brilliant and productive as well as ignorant and destructive decisions are reached, large groups are informed and moved to action for the betterment of all as well as incited to riot and wage war, people are entertained and informed as well as lulled into inactivity and false security, and mutual understanding and respect as well as mutual distrust and hatred among different groups are achieved. In short, those activities that are most human (as well as most inhuman) occur within these five communication contexts.

Our major purpose in each of these discussions is to provide you with insight into the nature of these forms, how they operate, and how they might be analyzed. Ultimately, we are concerned with how these five contexts might be better controlled or mastered by the student of communication.

The organizational structure followed here is standard. Our discussion begins with the smallest communication unit, interpersonal communication, and continues through small group, public communication, and mass communication. The fifth form, intercultural communication, overlaps with the previous four and focuses on communication between or among individuals who are members of different social or cultural groups.

More specifically, Unit 18, "Preliminaries to Interpersonal Communication," Unit 19, "Attraction in Interpersonal Communication," Unit 20, "Conflict in Interpersonal Communication," Unit 21, "Assertiveness in Interpersonal Communication," and Unit 22, "Transactional Analysis in Interpersonal Communication," deal with the purposes and elements accounting for interpersonal communication effectiveness, the ingredients of attractiveness, the nature of conflict and the methods of conflict resolution, the role of assertiveness in communication, and how the insights of transactional analysis might be used to understand and ultimately improve our own interpersonal communications.

The purposes and characteristics of effective interpersonal communication are covered in the first of these units and in considerable detail because they best answer the question, What is interpersonal communication? and explain how this form of communication differs from those forms considered in succeeding units. One significant variable, attractiveness, is then singled out for extended treatment so that we may see in depth the complexity of communicating interpersonally. Attractiveness is also a logical choice here because it plays such an important role in both the initiation and in the maintenance of interpersonal relationships. When attraction breaks down, one possible alternative is conflict and this important area is the substance of Unit 20 where we cover the nature of conflict, the relationship between communication and conflict, and the ways in which conflict may be resolved. Assertiveness is included here because I find that interpersonal relationships are, especially among the young, hindered and sometimes destroyed because of a lack of assertiveness. Lastly, I devote considerable attention to transactional analysis because of all the methods available for analyzing messages, transactional analysis seems to provide the greatest insight into the problems of interpersonal communication as well as the most efficient means for facilitating interpersonal communication.

Units 23, "The Nature of Small Group Communication," 24, "Members and Leaders in Small Group Communication," and 25, "Small Group Analysis and Evaluation," explain the nature and the various types of small groups, the roles of both members and leaders in small group communication, and some of the various ways in which small group interaction may be analyzed.

As with the consideration of interpersonal communication, the first unit here attempts to illustrate what small group communication is and how it differs from the other forms considered. The discussion of members and leaders approach small group communication from the point of view of the participants of the small group and attempts to provide both theoretical and practical insight into the dynamics operating when people interact in a small group. The final unit in this section approaches small group communication from the point of view of the critic-observer and provides not only ways in which small group communications may be studied or described, but also the criteria by which small group interactions may be evaluated.

Units 26, "Preliminaries to Public Communication," 27, "The Speech in Public Communication," and 28, "The Speaker and Receiver in Public Communication," explain the nature of public communication, its purposes and methods, the ways in which public communications are structured, supported, and worded, and the role of audience analysis and delivery in the presentation of the public communication. Because many communication courses include a substantial section on public communication, often with the student preparing and delivering public communications, these three units are longer than other units in the text and also have a more extensive practical as well as a theoretical orientation. Units 26, 27, and 28 might be considered a handbook of public communication. There is included here that information that will provide the student with an understanding of the principles and techniques needed to prepare and deliver a wide variety of public communications as well as those principles and techniques needed to function as a critical consumer of public communications.

Units 29, "The Nature of Mass Communication," 30, "The Functions of Mass Communication," and 31, "The Flow of Mass Communication," concentrate on the nature and forms of mass communications and its audiences, the functions or purposes that mass communication fulfills in our society, and how messages, particularly messages of influence, pass from media to people and from people to media.

The early units on interpersonal, small group, and public communication attempt to provide—in addition to the theoretical insights into these communication forms—practical insights for improving your own communication behaviors. The units on mass communication do not attempt to provide the skills needed to master the intricacies of mass communication. Few of us will actually become mass communicators but all of us will spend a great deal of time as consumers of the media. Consequently, our focus will be on understanding how the mass media function, on our roles as consumers of the mass media, and on the ways in which the media may be made more responsive to society.

Units 32, "Culture, Subculture, and Communication," 33, "Language Relativity and Universal Language," and 34, "Some Intercultural Communication Conflicts," attempt to explore the nature of culture, subculture, and communication; the role of language within a cultural context; and lastly, some of the possible conflicts that might arise in attempting to communicate across different subcultures, for example, communication between males and females, gays and straights, whites and blacks, and teachers and students.

The first of these units, Unit 32, sets the role of communication in a cultural-subcultural context; it is against this background that we may look at the specifics of any given communication act. Because language is so central to culture and to crosscultural communication particularly, Unit 33 is entirely devoted to it. Here the two sides of the proverbial coin are considered: 1) the differences among languages and 2) the attempts to bridge these differences with a universal language. Unit 34 is an attempt to confront the very practical issues of communicating with people who belong to different social or subcultural groups. Although we cannot resolve or eliminate the differences between gays and straights and whites and blacks, for example, we can become sensitive to some of the potential obstacles to effective communication and can perhaps, with this increased sensitivity, begin to find ways to lessen the differences.

Taken as a whole these 17 units should provide you with insights into the various forms or contexts of communication, whether interpersonal, small group, public, mass, or intercultural communication.

UNIT 18
Preliminaries to Interpersonal Communication

The Purposes of Interpersonal Communication
Effectiveness in Interpersonal Communication

18.1 Interpersonal Communication Concepts
18.2 Me and You: Communicating Interpersonally
18.3 Effective Interpersonal Interaction

LEARNING GOALS

After completing this unit, you should be able to:

1. cite examples of interpersonal communication from your own experiences and observations
2. define *interpersonal communication*
3. explain at least three purposes of interpersonal communication
4. define *openness* and identify the three aspects of interpersonal communication to which it refers
5. define *empathy* and distinguish it from *sympathy*
6. define *supportiveness*
7. define *positiveness* and explain the three aspects of interpersonal communication to which it refers
8. define *equality* as it relates to interpersonal communication
9. identify the presence of openness, empathy, supportiveness, positiveness, and equality in interpersonal interactions

You enter your sociology class and spot a person you would like to date. You get the person's phone number from a mutual friend and call that evening. A previous engagement prevents this person from saying yes, and you decide to call next week. At the same time, you wonder if this "previous engagement" was merely another way of saying no.

You are sitting on a bus reading a book when a person who smells of cigar smoke sits next to you. The odor is so strong that you change your seat.

You are on a basketball team and are discussing strategy for the next quarter with the other members. The captain wants to do certain things while other members want to do something else. The members argue and fight.

You are having dinner with your family and the conversation covers a variety of topics—what each person did during the day, the accident that happened down the street, the plans for tomorrow, and so on.

These and thousands of similar examples are interpersonal communication situations. More formally, we might define *interpersonal communication* as the sending of messages by one person and the receiving of messages by another person, or small groups of persons, with some effect and with some opportunity for immediate feedback. The nature and scope of interpersonal communication will be further clarified through a consideration of the major purposes and characteristics of effective interpersonal interaction.

THE PURPOSES OF INTERPERSONAL COMMUNICATION

All behavior, as already noted, is determined; all behavior has one or more purposes and although these purposes may not always be obvious, we can be certain that they do exist. More specifically, what are the purposes of interpersonal communication?

Four general purposes which seem among the most significant may be noted here. Put differently, interpersonal communications are determined by one or more of the following four purposes (at least generally): personal discovery, discovery of the external world, establishing meaningful relationships, and changing attitudes and behaviors (see Figure 18.1). It should be noted that the purposes of the communication need not be conscious at the time of the interpersonal encounter nor is it essential that individuals agree that they are in fact communicating for these purposes. Purpose is a most peculiar concept; it may be subconscious as well as conscious, unrecognizable as well as recognizable.

Since interpersonal communication involves at least one other person, all four of these purposes affect both the self and other(s). These purposes are

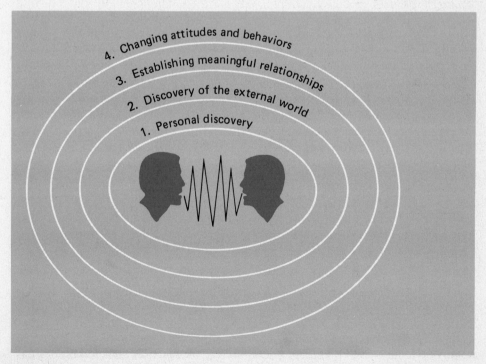

Figure 18.1
The Purposes of Interpersonal Communication

motivating factors to varying degrees. They are not all-or-none issues; rather, they motivate participation in varying degrees depending upon the individuals involved, their needs, wants, and histories, the context of the communication, and the numerous other factors we have already noted as being essential to any communication act.

Personal Discovery

One of the major purposes of interpersonal communication which is not shared by public speaking or mass communication is that of personal discovery. When we engage in an interpersonal encounter with another person we learn a great deal about ourselves as well as about the other person. In fact, our self-perceptions are in large part a result of what we have learned about ourselves from others during interpersonal encounters.

Interpersonal communication provides an almost unique opportunity for us to talk about our favorite subject—ourselves. Nothing seems as interesting or exciting or as worthy of discussion as our own feelings, our own thoughts, our own behaviors. By talking about ourselves with another individual we are provided with an excellent source of feedback on our feelings, thoughts, and behaviors. From this type of encounter we learn, for example, that our feelings about ourselves, others, and the world are not so different from someone else's feelings. And the same is true about our behaviors, our fears, our hopes, our desires. This positive reinforcement helps to make us feel "normal."

We also learn how we appear to others, what our strengths and weaknesses are, who likes us and who dislikes us and why. Usually, we choose our interpersonal partners carefully so that most of what we hear is positive or at least more supportive than not. And this helps to build a stronger self-image.

Discovery of the External World

Much as interpersonal communication enables us to better understand ourselves and the other person with whom we are communicating, it also enables us to better understand the external world—the world of objects, events, and other people. Much of the information we now have comes from interpersonal interactions. In fact, our beliefs, attitudes, and values have probably been influenced more by interpersonal encounters than by the mass media. While it is true that a great deal of information comes to us from the media, it is often discussed and ultimately "learned" or internalized through interpersonal interactions.

Recall the meaningful educational experiences that you have had up to this point. Very likely interpersonal encounters with teachers or parents would rank high, certainly higher than would any individual lecture.

Establishing Meaningful Relationships

One of the greatest desires (some would say "needs") people have is that of establishing and maintaining close relationships with other people. We want to feel loved and liked and in turn we want to love and like others. Much of the time we spend in interpersonal communication is devoted to establishing and maintaining social relationships with others. Recall the times you spotted a friend on campus and felt good about it; you were not concerned with the topic that would be discussed but rather simply with the idea that a relationship would be established. Or, even better, recall your wanting to date someone. It was the relationship between you and this other person that was the important point. The importance of this is probably best seen in our lack of concern for the subject matter of discussion when we are with someone we care for a great deal. It does not matter whether we talk about a movie, about philosophy, about cars, or about people. What does matter is that we are together and that we are relating to each other.

This seems an appropriate place to also note that much of our interpersonal communication time is spent in giving and in receiving strokes, that is, in giving and in getting proverbial pats on the back. We actively seek reinforcement for our thoughts, our behaviors, and our feelings; most often we seek this reinforcement in our numerous interpersonal encounters.

Changing Attitudes and Behaviors

Many times we attempt to change the attitudes and behaviors of others in our interpersonal encounters. We may wish them to vote a particular way, try a new diet, buy a particular item, listen to a record, see a movie, read a book, enter a particular field, take a specific course, think in a particular way, believe that something is true or false, value some idea, and so on. The list is endless. We spend a good deal of our time engaged in interpersonal persuasion.

It is interesting to note that the studies that have been done on the effectiveness of the mass media versus interpersonal situations in changing attitudes and behaviors seem to find that we are more often persuaded through interpersonal communication than through mass media communication.

Two major qualifications should be noted here. First, no list of communication purposes can be exhaustive. Obviously there are other purposes for interpersonal communication. The four considered here seem the major ones and, hence, were singled out for discussion. Second, no communication interaction is motivated by one factor. Single causes do not seem to exist in the real world and so any interpersonal communication interaction is probably motivated by a combination of factors rather than only one factor.

EFFECTIVENESS IN INTERPERSONAL COMMUNICATION

Interpersonal communication, like any form of behavior, can vary from being extremely effective to extremely ineffective. Probably no interpersonal encounter is a total success or a total failure; it could have been better, but it could have been worse. Here we attempt to characterize effective interpersonal communication, recognizing that each communicative act is different and that principles or rules must be applied judiciously with a full recognition of the uniqueness of communication events.

Effective interpersonal communication seems to be characterized by at least the following five qualities: openness, empathy, supportiveness, positiveness, and equality (Figure 18.2).

Openness

The quality of *openness* refers to at least three aspects of interpersonal communication. First, and perhaps most obvious, is that effective interpersonal communicators must be willing to open up to the other people with whom they are interacting. This does not mean that we should immediately pour forth our entire life history. Interesting as that may be, it is not usually very helpful to the communication or interesting to the other individuals. Openness simply means a willingness to self-disclose, to reveal information about oneself that

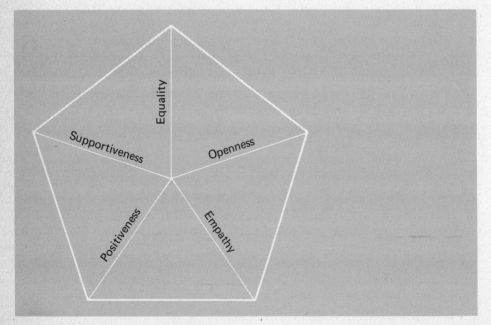

Figure 18.2
Effective Interpersonal Communication

might normally be kept hidden but which is relevant to the interpersonal encounter.

The second aspect of openness refers to the willingness of a communicator to react honestly to incoming stimuli. Silent, uncritical, and immovable psychiatrists may be of some help in a clinical situation, but they are generally boring conversationalists. We want (and have a right to expect) people to react openly to what we say. Nothing seems worse than indifference; even disagreement seems more welcome. Of course there are extremes here too.

The third aspect of openness I take from Arthur Bochner and Clifford Kelly's concept of owning feelings and thoughts. To be open in this sense is to acknowledge that the feelings and thoughts we express are ours and that we bear the responsibility for them. We do not attempt to shift the responsibility for our feelings to others. Bochner and Kelly put it this way: "the person who owns his feelings or ideas makes it clear that he takes responsibility for his own feelings and actions. Owning shows a willingness to accept responsibility for oneself and commitment to others. It is the antithesis of blaming others for the way one feels." Bochner and Kelly advise us not to say, "Isn't this group supposed to listen to people?" but rather, "I feel ignored. I don't think people in this group listen to me."

This difference is interesting from another point of view as well. When we own our feelings and thoughts we say in effect "This is how *I* feel," "This is how *I* see the situation," "This is what *I* think," with the *I* always paramount. And so instead of saying "This discussion is useless" we would say something like "*I* think this discussion is useless" or "*I*'m bored by this discussion" or "*I* want to talk more about myself" or any other such statement that includes reference to the fact that *I* am making an evaluation and not describing objective reality. By including in such statements what the general semanticists call "to me-ness," we make explicit the fact that our feelings are the result of the interaction between the outside reality and our own preconceptions, attitudes, prejudices, and the like.

Empathy

Perhaps the most difficult of all the communication qualities to achieve is the ability to *empathize* with another individual. By empathizing is meant a feeling with the individual; to empathize with someone is to feel as that person does. To sympathize, on the other hand, is to feel for the individual, to be sorry for the person, for example. To empathize is to feel as the individual feels, to be in the same shoes, to feel the same feelings in the same way. If we are able to empathize with people, we are then in a position to understand where they are coming from, where they are now, and where they are going. Also, we are less likely to judge their behaviors or attitudes as being right or wrong.

Supportiveness

An effective interpersonal relationship is one that is *supportive.* Open and empathetic interpersonal communication cannot survive in a threatening atmosphere. If participants feel that what they say will be criticized or attacked, for example, they may be reluctant to open up or to reveal themselves in any meaningful way.

In a supportive environment silence does not take on a negative value. Rather, silence is seen as a positive aspect of communication; an opportunity for relating nonverbally.

Positiveness

Positiveness in interpersonal communication refers to at least three different aspects or elements. First, interpersonal communication is fostered if there is a certain positive regard for the self. The persons who feel negative about themselves will invariably communicate these feelings to others, who in turn will probably develop similar negative feelings. On the other hand, people who feel positive about themselves will convey this feeling for themselves to others, who in turn are likely to return the positive regard.

Second, interpersonal communication will be fostered if a positive feeling for the other person is communicated. This obviously will make the other person feel better and will encourage more active participation on a more meaningful level. One will, for example, be more likely to self-disclose.

Third, a positive feeling for the general communication situation is important for effective interaction. Nothing is more unpleasant than communicating with someone who does not enjoy the exchange or does not respond favorably to the situation or context. A negative response to the situation makes one feel almost as if one is intruding and communication seems sure to quickly break down.

Equality

Equality is a peculiar characteristic. In any situation there is probably going to be some inequality. One person will be smarter, richer, better looking, or a better athlete. Never are two people absolutely equal in all respects. Even identical twins would be unequal in some ways. Despite this inequality, interpersonal communication is generally more effective when the atmosphere is one of equality. This does not mean that unequals cannot communicate. Certainly they can. Yet their communication, if it is to be effective, should recognize the equality of personalities. By this is meant that there should be a tacit recognition that both parties are valuable and worthwhile human beings and that each has something important to contribute.

Equality should also characterize interpersonal communication in terms of speaking versus listening. If one participant speaks all the time while the other listens all the time, effective interpersonal communication becomes difficult if not impossible. There should be an attempt at achieving an equality of sending versus receiving. Depending on the situation, one person will normally speak more than the other person, but this should be a function of the situation and not of the fact that one person is a "talker" and another person is a "listener."

People in varied occupations often develop a certain snobbishness about communication. The professor may not feel it worthwhile to communicate with a salesperson in an atmosphere of equality. The college graduate may feel it worthless to communicate equally with high-school dropouts. The truck driver may feel it useless to communicate with a scientist as an equal. All in their way are interpersonal communication snobs. All assume that they have nothing to gain from such interactions and that time is better spent talking to "equals." This is a particularly harmful attitude since it prevents each from learning what the other person has to offer. But perhaps we have to experience the rewards from such communications before we can believe that they are in fact enjoyable, profitable, and generally rewarding.

A Note on Homophily-Heterophily

These five characteristics of effective interpersonal communication are qualities that can be learned, and so it seems important that they be singled out for discussion. We should, however, make note here of the concepts of homophily and heterophily. *Homophily* refers to the degree of similarity between the parties engaged in interpersonal communication and *heterophily* refers to the degree of difference between the parties. The similarity and difference may refer to just about any characteristic—age, religion, political leaning, financial status, educational level, and so forth.

Generally, research has shown that interpersonal communication is more effective when the parties are homophilous. James McCroskey, Carl Larson, and Mark Knapp, for example, state: "More effective communication occurs when source and receiver are homophilous. The more nearly alike the people in a communication transaction, the more likely they will share meanings." We will, according to this principle, communicate best with people who are most like ourselves. Butchers will communicate best with butchers, Texans will communicate best with Texans, and college students will communicate best with college students.

Because of the contribution that homophily-heterophily makes to the study of interpersonal communication it needs to be discussed in relation to the five characteristics of effective interpersonal communication. The more homophilous individuals are, the more open they will be with each other. This seems to follow since we seem to be most comfortable with those who are like us. Consequently, we are more apt to reveal ourselves and to self-disclose to people like ourselves. We feel perhaps that they would reveal themselves and disclose to us. And so by being open we do not risk as much as we would in a heterophilous situation.

Empathy is greatest when people are homophilous and least when people are heterophilous. We can more easily feel as other people do (which is the essence of empathy) when we are like them to begin with. There is little distance to travel in order to empathize when we are similar to the individuals but much distance when they are not like us. Consider the difficulty a poor person would have empathizing with the disappointment of a rich one because he or she must give up the second car, or the difficulty a rich person would have in empathizing with a poor person's hunger.

It seems that we all want to support people who are like us more than people who are very different from us. By supporting homophilous people we are in effect supporting ourselves. People like us, we may feel, will be supportive to us and so we respond in kind and support them. We can be silent with people who are like us and not be uncomfortable. We do not feel we have to impress them with our knowledge or intelligence.

When we are with people who are homophilous we feel more positive toward ourselves because we are not made to feel inferior as we might be made to feel if we were with heterophilous people. We generally enjoy the act of communicating in a homophilous situation more than we would in a heterophilous one. Of course, we generally like people who are like us more than we like people who are unlike us. In a sense, being with homophilous individuals provides a kind of confirmation of self.

Perhaps the most obvious relationship that exists with homophilous people is that of equality. By definition, homophilous people are equal to us, neither inferior nor superior. Hence there is more likely to be an atmosphere of equality, a free give and take of ideas, and an awareness that both participants have something to contribute.

Although communication is most effective when the individuals are homophilous, we should note that change is often brought about when the parties involved are "optimally heterophilous" in regard to the subject under discussion. According to McCroskey, Larson, and Knapp, if the two people are homophilous in regard to the subject matter then neither will be competent enough to change the attitudes, beliefs, or behaviors of the other. Also, when the individuals are too far apart in their competence on a subject, the more competent one will obviously not be changed by the less competent one, and the less competent one will probably have difficulty in understanding the other. Consequently, no change will take place here either. But when one party is optimally heterophilous, optimally more competent than the other, he or she will be better able to effect change in the other.

A Note on Rhetorical Sensitivity

One of the most interesting formulations of effectiveness is that by Roderick Hart and Don Burks—they call it *rhetorical sensitivity*.

Hart and Burks first distinguish between the expressive and the instrumental aspects of communication. In the *expressive* aspect we communicate to express our own feelings and thoughts, to get things off our chest. In the *instrumental* aspect we communicate to influence others; communication is a means to the end of persuasion. It is the instrumental function of communication to which Hart and Burks address their five characteristics of the rhetorically sensitive individual.

First, the rhetorically sensitive individual attempts to accept role-taking as a necessary part of the human condition. This characteristic focuses on the fact that we are actually many different selves and not a single self. We are different selves to different people; we are different selves at different times; and we are different selves with different contexts (objects, events, situations, and so on). The assumption Hart and Burks make here is that we inevitably take on different roles depending upon the context, person, or time and that we need to recognize this. Most importantly we need to be trained to effectively select among the roles available to us. Training in communication, according to Hart and Burks, would involve enabling the student "(1) to widen this repertoire of selves or roles in order to deal more effectively with his interpersonal environment and (2) to discover those roles he enjoys taking."

Second, the rhetorically sensitive person attempts to avoid stylized verbal behavior. By this is meant that one leaves behind any preference for consistency for the sake of consistency. This person recognizes that the various roles he or she takes on may be very different from each other and, in fact, often contradictory. One should select the role on the basis of the specifics of the situation and not on the basis of consistency with previous behavior. "Rhetorical consistency," note Hart and Burks, "if it does occur, should result from situational decisions; a passion for regularity should not guide or sustain rhetorical behavior."

Third, the rhetorically sensitive person is willing to adapt on the basis of the communication interaction. A willingness to adapt is a willingness to change—to change our thoughts, our beliefs, our attitudes, and even our behaviors. We should enter a communicative situation with the willingness to change, to adapt. Hart and Burks put it this way: "Rhetorical sensitivity encourages one to (1) consider making adaptations *before* breaking off an interaction and (2) not engage in a self-fulfilling prophecy whereby one predicts, without sufficient data, that even making adaptations one is capable of making would have no social effect."

Fourth, the rhetorically sensitive person attempts to distinguish between all available information on the one hand and that information that is acceptable for communication on the other. At certain times and in certain situations, the rhetorically sensitive thing to do is to say nothing. Further, some ideas should not be stated, regardless of how they are phrased. Put differently, the rhetorically sensitive person first determines what it is possible to say, that is, the information that seems relevant, and then determines how much of it should be said, given the particular situation and the particular people with whom he or she is interacting. Hart and Burks believe that total candor—when we say whatever is on our minds—can often be destructive. "It is a rare human association indeed," note Hart and Burks, "that can thrive without judicious consideration being given to its rhetorical character and to the ideas to be given utterance in the context of that relationship."

Fifth, and last, the rhetorically sensitive person recognizes that ideas can be expressed in different (multiform) ways. That is, once we know what ought to be communicated, we have to consider how that information or feeling is to be expressed. The consideration, or lack of it, that we give to the ways in which we express our feelings and thoughts often distinguishes between the expressive and the instrumental forms of communication. In the expressive form we are simply concerned with venting our emotions but in the instrumental form we are concerned with influencing behavior and hence must be concerned with how our ideas or feelings are expressed. The need to consider alternative ways of expression is perhaps most significant when emotions run high. There are many ways, for example, to express our anger or our frustration; some ways can be productive but other ways can be destructive. The rhetorically sensitive person recognizes this and demonstrates this in his or her communications.

SOURCES

The nature of interpersonal communication is surveyed in a number of excellent sources. See, for example, Gerald Miller and Mark Steinberg, *Between People* (Chicago: Science Research Associates, 1975); Kenneth Sereno and Edward Bodaken. *Trans-Per: Understanding Human Communication* (Boston: Houghton Mifflin, 1975); and, Dennis R. Smith and L. Keith Williamson, *Interpersonal Communication: Roles, Rules, Strategies, and Games* (Dubuque, Iowa: Brown, 1977). Two brief but excellent introductions are John C. Condon, *Interpersonal Communication* (New York: Macmillan, 1977) and Catherine Konsky and David Larsen, *Interpersonal Communication* (Dubuque, Iowa: Kendall/Hunt, 1975).

For the discussion of effectiveness I relied (sometimes consciously and at other times subconsciously) on the work of Jack Gibb, particularly his most insightful "Defensive Communication," *Journal of Communication* 11 (1961): 141–148. This article has been reprinted in a number of different places, for example, in the readers by DeVito and Civikly, cited in Unit 1. For an overview of homophily and heterophily see James C. McCroskey, Carl E. Larson, and Mark L. Knapp, *An Introduction to Interpersonal Communication* (Englewood Cliffs, N.J.: Prentice-Hall, 1971). For a more extensive treatment see E. M. Rogers and F. F. Shoemaker, *Communication of Innovations* (New York: Free Press, 1971). See Mark I. Alpert and W. Thomas Anderson, Jr., "Optimal Heterophily and Communication Effectiveness: Some Empirical Findings," *Journal of Communication* 23(September 1973):328–343 for a recent review of relevant findings and an example of an experimental study on this question. A book which provides an excellent transition between the characteristics of effective interpersonal communication and the self is Edmond G. Addeo and Robert E. Burger, *Egospeak: Why No One Listens To You* (New York: Bantam, 1973). See Murray S. Davis, *Intimate Relations* (New York: Free Press, 1973) for a look at interpersonal communication from the point of view of the sociologist and Kurt Danziger, *Interpersonal Communication* (New York: Pergamon, 1976) for the point of view of the psychologist. These two works are excellent complements to the work by communicologists emphasized here. The concept of owning feelings and thoughts comes from Arthur P. Bochner and Clifford W. Kelly, "Interpersonal Competence: Rationale, Philosophy, and Implementation of a Conceptual Framework," *Speech Teacher* 23 (November 1974):279–301. The discussion of rhetorical sensitivity is based on Roderick P. Hart and Don M. Burks, "Rhetorical Sensitivity and Social Interaction," *Speech Monographs* 39 (June 1972):75–91.

EXPERIENTIAL VEHICLES

18.1 INTERPERSONAL COMMUNICATION CONCEPTS

The following concepts are generally considered essential ingredients in even the most basic model of interpersonal communication. Read over the terms and their definitions (in Unit 1 or in the Glossary) and construct an original visual representation of the process of *interpersonal* communication which includes (as a minimum) the concepts noted below.

source
encoder
message
decoder
receiver
channel
context
noise
feedback
effect
field of experience

When each student has completed the model, groups of five or six should be formed so that members may pool their insights in order to construct one improved model of communication. After this is completed all models should be shared with the entire class.

18.2 ME AND YOU: COMMUNICATING INTERPERSONALLY

The purpose of this experience is to enable you to participate in an interpersonal communication encounter in which: 1) there will be relatively immediate feedback, 2) you will be able to explore some of your own feelings about yourself, 3) you will have the opportunity to self-disclose as much or as little as you like, and 4) you will be able to explore some of the ways others form impressions of you and you form impressions of others.

Instructions

Dyads are formed with persons who do not know each other well. In the first phase one person (A) reads the following list of words to the other person (B) one at a time. B responds aloud to each of the words with a sentence or two in which he or she attempts to relate the word or concept to himself or herself. The process is continued for all ten words. In the second phase, the process is repeated with person B reading the words to person A who likewise responds to each of the words.

After each person has responded to all ten words, write a short paragraph about your impressions of the other person. Ideally, these paragraphs should be based solely on the interactions that just took place. Inevitably, however, they will be influenced by previous interactions. The paragraphs are to be written from the point of view of how this person appears to you, not from the point of view of "what this person really is" (assuming that that question could ever be answered). After the paragraphs are completed, exchange and discuss them in any way that seems meaningful to you.

Stimulus Words *

love
death
your family
occupation
yourself
the future
school
war
God
sex

18.3 EFFECTIVE INTERPERSONAL INTERACTION

In order to see the characteristics of effective interpersonal communication in actual operation, the following role-playing situations have been designed. The procedure is as follows:

1. Participants should be selected (hopefully from volunteers) to role play the characters in the situations described below.
2. Participants should act out the parts, developing their roles and the interactions as seems logical at the time.
3. In these role-playing situations the participants will either closely follow the characteristics of effective interpersonal communication or clearly violate the characteristics as they are instructed by the group leader or instructor.
4. The remainder of the class should monitor the role playing, observing how closely the participants are following or violating the characteristics of ef-

---

* Other stimulus words may, of course, be used. However, the same words should be used for both participants.

fective interpersonal communication. Two general procedures have been found useful for this monitoring:

a. The observers may stop the role-playing session as soon as any member fails to follow his or her instructions. The person who stops the role playing should naturally explain why he or she felt that the participants were not following instructions. After essential discussion the role playing should resume to be stopped again when any role player fails to follow instructions. *Note:* If this procedure is used, it is best not to stop the role playing during the first three minutes. This will allow the members an opportunity to begin to feel the characters they are playing.

b. The observers may take notes during the role playing, reserving all discussion of the characteristics of effective interpersonal communication until the role-playing session is completed. If this procedure is followed, it is generally useful to first ask the role players how closely they felt they were following the instructions.

Role-Playing Situations

Any or all of the following situations may be used to illustrate 1) following the characteristics of effective interpersonal communication or 2) violating the characteristics. It is recommended that at least one of the situations be used to illustrate following and one violating the characteristics so that the differences between the two interactions may be more easily noted.

1. *Participants:*

   Joan Davis (college sophomore)
   Homer Davis (Joan's father)
   Ann Davis (Joan's mother)

   Situation:

   Joan wants to go away for the weekend with her boyfriend and use the family car. Homer and Ann are totally against this. First, they thoroughly detest Joan's boyfriend. Second, they disapprove of unmarried couples spending weekends together. Third, they want to use the car themselves.

2. *Participants:*

   Chris Martin (Diane's husband)
   Diane Martin (Chris' wife)
   Marlene Jason (Diane's mother)

   Situation:

   Diane and her mother have just gone to purchase new furniture for the Martins' home. They have picked out extremely expensive furniture which Chris and Diane cannot afford. Upon hearing of this Chris becomes angry and demands that different furniture (which they can afford) be selected.

Marlene says that she will pay for the furniture since she wants her daughter to have the best. Chris argues that what comes into the house should be bought by Diane and himself and that they should not accept such gifts since there will inevitably be strings attached as there have been in the past.

3. *Participants:*

   James and Thelma (married couple)
   Frank and Carol (married couple)

   Situation:

   James and Frank want to go bowling alone. Thelma and Carol want to go to dinner and the movies with their husbands. The husbands feel that this is their one day out a week and that their desire to spend it bowling does not seem unreasonable. The wives argue that this, too, is their only chance to go out and that they have a right to this outing.

4. *Participants:*

   Dr. Mary James (professor)
   Michell Russo (student)
   Daniel Miller (student)
   Ronald Kennedy (student)

   Situation:

   Michell, Daniel, and Ronald have just received their grades for their Introduction to Communication course and have gone to complain to Dr. Mary James. Michell received a C+, Daniel received an *F*, and Ronald received a *D.* All three students feel that they deserved better grades. Dr. James feels that the grades the students received—based on their class performance and their examination scores—were fair.

5. *Participants:*

   Dr. Michael Craeman (professor)
   Joan Mitchell (student)
   Danny Santos (student)
   Molly McCoy (student)
   Dr. Joseph Bartlett (professor)

   Situation:

   Joan, Danny, and Molly have written a letter of complaint against Dr. Michael Craeman and submitted it to Dr. Bartlett, chairperson of the Sociology Department. The students claim that Dr. Craeman's classes are dull, that he is often late to class, that his tests are impossible to pass, and that they are not learning anything.

UNIT 19
Attraction in Interpersonal Communication

LEARNING GOALS

After completing this unit, you should be able to:

1. define *interpersonal attraction*
2. define *attractiveness* and explain its influence in interpersonal attraction
3. explain the relativity of physical and personal attractiveness
4. define *proximity* and explain the ways in which it influences interpersonal attraction
5. explain the "mere exposure" hypothesis
6. define *reinforcement* and explain how it enters into interpersonal attraction
7. define *similarity* and explain how it operates in interpersonal attraction
8. define *complementarity* and explain the ways it influences interpersonal attraction

EXPERIENTIAL VEHICLE

19.1 THE QUALITIES OF INTERPERSONAL ATTRACTION: PART I

In order to test the principles and findings discussed in this unit, complete the following questionnaire before reading any further.

CHARACTERISTICS OF A PERSON
YOU WOULD BE MOST ATTRACTED TO:

Age	_____
Sex	_____
Height	_____
Weight	_____
General physical attractiveness	_____
Race	_____
Religion	_____
Nationality	_____
Intelligence	_____
Years of formal education	_____
Profession or professional goal	_____
At least three major personality characteristics	_____
	_____

List the names of five people to whom you are very attracted (do not list relatives):

1.
2.
3.
4.
5.

List the names of five people to whom you are not attracted (do not list relatives):

1.
2.
3.
4.
5.

We are all attracted to some people and not attracted to others. In a similar way, some people are attracted to us and some people are not. This seems to be the universal human condition. If we were to examine the people we are attracted to and the people we are not attracted to we would probably be able to see patterns in the decisions or judgments we make. Even though many of these decisions seem subconsciously motivated, we can nevertheless discern patterns in the interpersonal choices we make.

We are all probably attracted to "a type" of person or to "types" of people. This ideal type (which differs for each person) can probably be found, in varying degrees, in each of the people we are attracted to and its opposite, in varying degrees, in each of the people to whom we are not attracted. It has been found that most people are interpersonally attracted to others on the basis of five major variables: *attractiveness, proximity, reinforcement, similarity,* and *complementarity* (Figure 19.1).

ATTRACTIVENESS

Attractiveness comes in at least two forms. When we say, "I find that person attractive," we probably mean either 1) that we find the person physically attractive or 2) that we find that person's personality or ways of behaving attractive. For the most part we tend to like physically attractive people rather than physically ugly people, and we tend to like people who possess a pleasant personality rather than an unpleasant personality. Few would find fault with

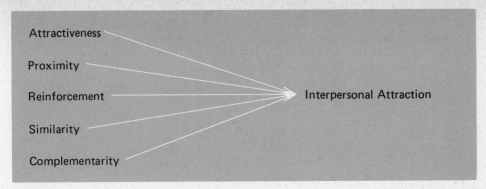

Figure 19.1
The Qualities of Interpersonal Attraction

these two generalizations. The difficulty arises when we try to define "attractive." Perhaps the best way to illustrate this difficulty is to look at some old movies, newspapers, or magazines and compare the conceptions of beauty portrayed there with those popular now. Or even better, examine the conceptions of beauty in different cultures. At some times and in some cultures people who are fat (by our standards) would be considered attractive but in other cultures they would be unattractive. Where at one time fashion models were supposed to be extremely thin (remember Twiggy?) they are now allowed to have some flesh on their bones. The same difficulty besets us when we attempt to define "pleasant personality." To some people this would mean an aggressive, competitive, forceful individual whereas to others it might mean an unassuming, shy, and bashful individual.

Similarly, we would probably look for different physical and personality characteristics depending on the situation in which we were going to interact. In a classroom it might be most important to sit next to someone who knows all the answers. So regardless of this person's physical appearance, this "answer machine" is perceived as attractive. To go on a swimming date, however, we might select someone with a good body and not be too concerned with his or her intellectual abilities. When inviting someone to join a football team we might choose someone heavy and strong.

Although attractiveness (both physical and personality) is difficult to define universally (impossible is perhaps closer to the truth), it is possible to define it for any one individual for specific situations. Thus if Person A were interested in dating someone, he or she might choose someone who possessed x, y, and z characteristics. For Person A, in this situation, these are the characteristics that are considered "attractive." And in all probability, given this same person in another similar situation, he or she would again look for someone who possessed these same characteristics. That is, we seem relatively consistent in the characteristics we find "attractive."

We also tend to attribute positive characteristics to people we find attractive and negative characteristics to people we find unattractive. If people were asked to predict which qualities a given individual possessed they would probably predict the possession of positive qualities if they thought the person attractive and negative characteristics if they thought the person unattractive.

PROXIMITY

If we look around at the people we find attractive we would probably find that they are the people who live or work close to us. This is perhaps the one finding that emerges most frequently from the research on interpersonal attraction. In one of the most famous studies Festinger, Schachter, and Black studied friendships in a student housing development. They found that the development of friendships was greatly influenced by the distance between the units in which the people lived and by the direction in which the units faced. The closer the students' rooms were to each other the better the chances were that they would become friends. It was also found that the students living in units that faced the courtyard had more friends than the students who lived in units facing the street: The people who became friends were the people who had the greater opportunity to interact with each other. We might add that the vast majority of marriages are between people who have lived very close to each other physically.

As might be predicted, physical distance is most important in the early stages of interaction. For example, during the first days of school, proximity (in class or in dormitories) is especially important. It decreases (but always remains significant) as the opportunity to interact with more distant others increases.

The importance of physical distance also varies with the type of situation one is in. For example, in anxiety-producing situations we seem to have more need for company and hence are more easily attracted to others than when we are in situations with low or no anxiety. It is also comforting to be with people who have gone through or who will go through the same experiences. We seem especially attracted to these people in times of stress. We would also be more susceptive to being attracted to someone else if we had previously been deprived of such interaction. If, for example, we were in a hospital or prison without any contact from other people we would probably be attracted to just about anyone. Anyone seems a great deal better than no one. We are also most attracted to people when we are feeling down or when self-esteem is particularly low. If, for example, we have been put down by a teacher, friend, or parent, then we seem to have a greater need to interact with others and are more easily attracted to someone. Perhaps we assume that this person will pull us out of the state we are in.

When we attempt to discover the reasons for the influence that physical closeness has on interpersonal attraction we can think of many. We seem to have positive expectations of people and consequently fulfill these by liking or being attracted to others. If we go to a party, for example, it is a lot easier to go with the idea that the people we will meet will be pleasant ones. Since we have this expectation, we fulfill the prophecy ourselves.

Another reason is that proximity allows us the opportunity to get to know the other person, to gain some information about him or her. We come to like people we know, because we can better predict their behavior and perhaps because of this they seem less frightening to us than complete strangers.

Still another approach argues that mere exposure to others leads us to develop positive feelings for them. Just two examples of the many that could be cited to illustrate the influence of "mere exposure" should be sufficient to make the point. In one study women were supposedly participating in a taste experiment and throughout the course of the experiment were exposed to other people. The subjects were exposed to some people ten times, to others five times, to others two times, to others one time, and to others not at all. The subjects did not talk with these other people and had never seen them before this experiment. The subjects were then asked to rate the other people in terms of how much they liked them. The results showed that they rated highest those persons they saw ten times, next highest those they saw five times, and so on down the line. How can we account for these results except by "mere exposure." Consider another study. Three groups of rats were selected at random. One group listened to recordings of Mozart for 12 hours for 52 days. Another group listened to recordings of Schoenberg for 12 hours for 52 days. A third group listened to no music at all. After these 52 days each rat was placed in a specially designed cage so that it could select the music it wished to listen to. The music selected by the rats was written by the same composer as the music that they had been exposed to for the 52-day period. Thus the rats raised on Mozart selected Mozart; the rats raised on Schoenberg selected Schoenberg. Mozart was also preferred by the rats raised without music. To make this experiment more unbelievable we should emphasize that the music that the rats heard during the 52-day period was not the same as that selected by the rats in their specially designed cages; it was only written by the same composer. Again, can we account for these findings in any way other than mere exposure?

Connected to this "mere exposure" concept is the finding that the greater the contact between people, the less they are prejudiced against each other. For example, whites and blacks living in housing developments became less prejudiced against each other as a result of living and interacting together. It is interesting to speculate on the influence that architects could have on interpersonal interaction, attraction, prejudice, and the like.

The most obvious reason for the effects of proximity (which is not considered in any work on interpersonal attraction) is simply that people are basically attractive. By interacting or being exposed to them, we find this out and are thus attracted to them. Put differently, perhaps we are attracted to people because they are attractive.

REINFORCEMENT

Perhaps the most obvious statement anyone could make about interpersonal attraction and the reasons we like or dislike people is that we like those who like us and dislike those who dislike us. Naturally there are exceptions; there are some who love people who do not love them and there are those who hate those who love them. For most of us, for most of the time, however, we like those who like us. Put in more behavioral terms, we tend to like those who reward or reinforce us. The reward or reinforcement may be social, as in the form of compliments or praise of one sort or another, or it may be material, as in the case of the suitor whose gifts eventually win the hand of the beloved.

Like most things, reinforcement too can backfire. When overdone, rewards lose their effectiveness and may even lead to negative responses. The people who try to reward us constantly soon become too sweet to take and we come, in short order, to discount whatever they say.

Also, if the reinforcement is to work it must be perceived as genuine and not motivated by selfish concern. The salesperson who compliments your taste in clothes, your eyes, your build, and just about everything else is not going to have the effect that someone without ulterior motives would have. In all probability the salesperson is acting out of selfish concerns; he or she wants to make the sale. Hence this person's "reinforcements" would not lead us to be attracted to him or her since they would not be perceived as genuine.

SIMILARITY

If people could construct their mates they would look, act, and think very much like themselves. By being attracted to people like ourselves we are in effect validating ourselves, saying to ourselves that we are worthy of being liked, that we are attractive.

Generally, although there are exceptions, we like people who are similar to ourselves in color, race, ability, physical characteristics, intelligence, and so on. We are often attracted to mirror images of ourselves.

Similarity is especially important when it comes to attitudes. We are particularly attracted to people who have attitudes similar to our own, who like what we like, and who dislike what we dislike. This similarity is most important when dealing with salient or significant attitudes. For example, it would not make much difference if the attitudes of two people toward food or furniture differed (though even these can at times be significant), but it would be of great significance if their attitudes toward children or religion or politics were very disparate. Marriages between people with great and salient dissimilarities are more likely to end in divorce than are marriages between people who are a lot alike.

Generally, by liking people who are similar to us and who like what we like, we maintain balance with ourselves. It is psychologically uncomfortable to like people who do not like what we like or to dislike people who like what we like. And so our attraction for similarity enables us to achieve psychological balance or comfort.

Agreement with ourselves is always reinforcing. The person who likes what we like, in effect, tells us that we are right to like what we like. Even after an examination it is helpful to find people who wrote the same answers we did. It tells us we were right. Notice the next time you have an examination how reinforcing it is to hear that others have put down the same answers.

Another reason we are attracted to similarly minded people is that we can predict that since they think like us they will like us as well. And so we like them because we think they like us.

We have often heard people say that the pets of people come to look and act like their owners. This misses the point. Actually, the animals do not change. Rather, the owners select pets that look and act like them at the start. Look around and test this out on people who have dogs and cats.

COMPLEMENTARITY

Although many people would argue that "birds of a feather flock together," others would argue that "opposites attract." That opposites attract is the principle of complementarity.

Take, for example, the individual who is extremely dogmatic. Would he or she be attracted to others who are high in dogmatism or would he or she be attracted to those who are low in dogmatism? The similarity principle would predict that this person would be attracted to those who were like him or her (that is, high in dogmatism), while the complementarity principle would predict that this person would be attracted to those who were unlike him or her (that is, low in dogmatism). The sadist, we know, is not attracted to another sadist but is instead attracted to a masochist who in turn is attracted not to another masochist but to a sadist.

It may be found that people are attracted to others who are dissimilar only in certain situations. For example, the submissive student may get along especially well with an aggressive teacher rather than a submissive one, but may not get along with an aggressive fiance or spouse. The dominant wife may get along with a submissive husband but may not relate well to submissive neighbors or colleagues.

Theodore Reik, in his *A Psychologist Looks at Love,* argues that we fall in love with people who possess characteristics which we do not possess and which we actually envy. The introvert, for example, if he or she is displeased with his or her shyness might be attracted to an extrovert.

Conclusive evidence on the complementarity versus the similarity principle is not available. There seems some evidence to support each position. It seems that at times we are attracted to people who are similar and at other times to people who are dissimilar. Who would want complete predictability?

SOURCES

The area of interpersonal attraction is surveyed most thoroughly in Ellen Berscheid and Elaine Hatfield Walster's *Interpersonal Attraction* (Reading, Mass.: Addison-Wesley, 1969). I relied heavily on the review and the insights provided by Patricia Niles Middlebrook in her *Social Psychology and Modern Life* (New York: Random House, 1974). Zick Rubin's *Liking and Loving: An Invitation to Social Psychology* (New York: Holt, 1973) covers the area of interpersonal attraction in a most interesting and insightful manner. The experiments on "mere exposure" (the women in the taste experiment and the rats listening to music) are discussed by Rubin. The original references are Susan Saegert, Walter Swap, and Robert B. Zajonc, "Exposure, Context, and Interpersonal Attraction," *Journal of Personality and Social Psychology* 25(1973): 234–242 and Henry A. Cross, Charles G. Halcomb, and William W. Matter, "Imprinting or Exposure Learning in Rats Given Early Auditory Stimulation," *Psychonomic Science* 7(1967):233–234. The study on friendships in college housing was conducted by Leon Festinger, Stanley Schachter, and Kurt W. Back, *Social Pressures in Informal Groups: A Study of Human Factors in Housing* (New York: Harper & Row, 1950). The most authoritative source for the "mere exposure" hypothesis is Robert B. Zajonc, "Attitudinal Effects of Mere Exposure," *Journal of Personality and Social Psychology Monograph Supplement,* vol. 9, no. 2, part 2 (1968). For methods of measuring attraction see James C. McCroskey and Thomas A. McCain, "The Measurement of Interpersonal Attraction," *Speech Monographs* 41 (August 1974):261–266.

EXPERIENTIAL VEHICLE

19.2 THE QUALITIES OF INTERPERSONAL ATTRACTION: PART II

After reading the unit return to the questionnaire at the beginning of the unit and consider the following questions relevant to your responses.

1. Concerning the characteristics of a person you would be most attracted to:

   a. Would the person whose characteristics you described be considered physically attractive? Physically unattractive? Would this person have an attractive personality? An unattractive personality?
   b. What specific characteristics did you emphasize in terms of attractiveness (physical or personality)?
   c. How similar are the characteristics you see yourself as possessing?
   d. Were the attitudinal characteristics especially important?
   e. Could instances of complementarity be identified? That is, did you list characteristics that would complement your own?

2. Concerning the persons listed as being those you are attracted to:

   a. Are these persons attractive in terms of physical and personality characteristics?
   b. Do they live or work close to you?
   c. Do they reinforce you frequently? Socially? Materially?
   d. Are they similar to you in what they like and what they dislike? Are they similar to you in terms of physical and personality characteristics? Especially, are their attitudes toward significant issues similar to yours?
   e. Do they complement you in any way? How are they different from you? Are these differences complementary?

3. Concerning the persons you listed as being those you are not attracted to:

   a. Are they generally unattractive? Physically? In terms of personality? What specific behaviors do you find unattractive?
   b. How does proximity enter into your choices? Do any of the persons listed live or work very close to you?
   c. Do these people reinforce you? If so, how do they do this? Why does their "reinforcement" not have the effect generally predicted?
   d. How similar-dissimilar are the persons listed to you? Physically? Intellectually? Attitudinally?
   e. In what ways are you and they complementary? That is, do these persons have characteristics which would complement your own?

4. How valuable are the five variables discussed in this unit in explaining the bases for your own interpersonal attraction? What other variables seem significant to you?

UNIT 20
Conflict in Interpersonal Communication

The Nature of Conflict
Conflict and Communication
Conflict Resolution

20.1 Red and Blue Game
20.2 Sandy

LEARNING GOALS

After completing this unit, you should be able to:

1. define *conflict*
2. provide at least three examples of conflict situations
3. state at least three conditions under which conflict is likely to occur
4. explain some of the effects that conflict has on communication
5. explain some of the principles of communication that are relevant to conflict and its resolution
6. explain at least four pseudoconflict resolution methods
7. explain the four stages in conflict resolution

Relating to the matter under consideration

Some years ago, a group of 11-year-old boys at camp unknowingly became subjects in a most interesting study of conflict. There were three main stages in this simulated war, devised by Muzafer Sherif and his colleagues. In the first stage the boys were divided into two groups and each group was isolated from the other. The boys developed close interpersonal relations with members of their respective group and a feeling of group cohesiveness became strong. The groups called themselves the Eagles and the Rattlers.

The second stage involved the creation of friction between the two groups. The groups were placed in a number of competitive and mutually frustrating activities. A high level of intergroup hostility was thus developed.

The third stage focused on attempts to reduce the conflict. At first the experimenters brought the groups together for mutually satisfying activities such as seeing a movie, eating, and participating in a series of experiments. The effect of these activities was to produce outward displays of conflict and hostility, both verbal and nonverbal. The experimenters then set up a series of supraordinate goals, goals that required mutual cooperation between the groups. In one situation the researchers staged a water shortage. The cooperation of all the boys was needed if the water was to be turned on again. In another situation both groups had to contribute to pay to obtain a movie they all wanted to see but for which neither group had enough money by themselves. In the third situation the two groups were removed from the camp and had to perform a number of cooperative tasks such as using their combined efforts to start a stalled truck.

The outcome of these situations was that the hostility between the two groups was significantly reduced and was attributed by the experimenters to the interpersonal experiences of cooperation between the two groups. It seems universally agreed that if conflict is to be reduced it is to be reduced through interpersonal interaction. The corollary to this seems equally agreed upon: If conflict is to be generated and maintained, it is to be done through interpersonal interaction as well. Conflict, both its generation and its resolution, seems largely an interpersonal communication process.

In this unit we examine conflict from a number of different perspectives. First, we inquire into the nature of conflict, the ways in which it is manifested, and some of the problems, as well as some of the values, to be derived from conflict. Second, we inquire into the relationship between conflict and communication, considering the effect of conflict on communication and of communication on conflict. Third, we look at conflict resolution, both the pseudo methods of resolution and the stages which might go into a model of conflict resolution. In the final unit of the text (Unit 34) we will return to conflict and consider some specific conflicts that occur frequently in our culture. The insights provided here into the general nature of conflict and conflict resolution should provide a useful base for examining these more specific conflicts.

THE NATURE OF CONFLICT

In its most insidious form, conflict is war between individuals or nations. The object of the game is to bring the enemy to surrender. To accomplish this anything goes. In sports, boxing perhaps comes closest to real conflict. Although disguised as competition and supported as analogous to baseball or football, the object of boxing is to harm your opponent to the point where he will surrender or to the point where he is rendered incapacitated for 10 seconds. The greater the harm a fighter inflicts on his opponent the closer he is to winning the bout and being proclaimed a hero. Verbally abusing one another would be conflict as well. It is a kind of verbal version of the boxing ring, as, for example, in slander or libel.

In its less extreme form conflict may be seen as competition. Perhaps the most familiar example of competition is professional or amateur sports. Baseball, football, horse racing, chess, and in fact most activities in which someone wins and someone loses are clear examples of competition. Another unambiguous example of competition is the auction sale where two or more people are bidding for the same object; one will win and the others will lose. Competition is more relevant to interpersonal interactions when, for example, two or more people are vying for the affection of another or perhaps vying to marry a particular person. Here one will win and the others will lose. In a similar way siblings compete for the attention and rewards of their parents and relatives.

Conflict is likely to occur when both parties want or perhaps need the same thing—a particular river, grazing land, a protective mountain, a desirable job, an important promotion—and the only way to secure the desired object is to beat down any other person or group intent on taking it from you. Conflict is also likely to occur when one or more parties are threatened. Perhaps the classic version of this is in the fighting of young boys where one of the boys is threatened to the point where he cannot extricate himself in a socially acceptable manner without actually fighting and so delivers the first blow. In more mature versions the same basic pattern is followed, only the threats are more subtle and more sophisticated and the consequences more lethal. Even among nations the same general pattern is followed. First, the threats are verbal; then they are physical, but on a small scale, for example, blockading ships or shooting down a plane. When the threats can no longer be ignored—for physical, psychological, or social reasons—actual conflict results.

Naturally, conflict is more likely to occur among persons who dislike or hate each other, though there is also much conflict in marriage and among supposed lovers. And this suggests another condition under which conflict is likely to occur, namely, when one party has been hurt. When this happens, he or she is often likely to hurt back. If, for example, the husband hurts the wife by not responding favorably to her advances, she in turn may attempt to hurt him. As a result he in turn may attempt to hurt her. As a result she in return may attempt to retaliate and hurt him and he again may respond in kind. The process of conflict spirals with one response serving as the stimulus for another response and so on. Each attack becomes more and more deadly.

Although the usual view is that conflict is negative, as the examples above indicate, there are also a number of values or benefits to be derived from conflict, and explicit note should be made of these. Alan Filley in his *Interpersonal Conflict Resolution* considers four major values. (1) Many conflict situations have the effect of diffusing more serious conflicts. This is especially the case when the conflicts (perhaps more accurately described as competitive exchanges) are played out according to a system of rules. The disagreements that result often reduce the probability of more significant conflicts arising. (2) Conflict situations lead us to acquire new information, new ways of looking at things. They energize our creativity and force us to explore new ideas and new ways of behaving. (3) When the conflict is an intergroup one then conflict functions to increase group cohesiveness. One of the most powerful ways to encourage members of a group to interact cooperatively and efficiently is to put the group into conflict with another group. (4) Lastly, Filley notes that conflict provides an opportunity for individuals or groups to measure their power, strength, or ability since it is in conflict situations that such qualities are mobilized to their peak.

When there is conflict within an interpersonal relationship and when we attempt to resolve that conflict, we are saying in effect that the relationship is worth the effort. To confront such a conflict we must care, at least to some degree, about the relationship, otherwise we would walk away from it. Although there may be exceptions, as when we confront conflict to save face or to gratify some ego need, it seems generally true that confronting a conflict indicates a degree of concern, of commitment, of desire to preserve the relationship.

CONFLICT AND COMMUNICATION

As already noted, the generation as well as the resolution of conflict are essentially communication processes. Consequently, there are two general areas concerning conflict and communication that need to be explored. The first concerns the effects that conflict has on communications. The second concerns the principles of communication which may be relevant to conflict resolution or, put differently, the effects that communication has on conflict. Each of these areas will be explored in turn.

In considering the effects that conflict has on communication, review the characteristics of effective interpersonal communication discussed in Unit 18.

Conflict leads to increased negative regard for the opponent. At times this negative feeling is passed down from generation to generation as with warring families, tribes, or nations, for example. Generally, the more conflict, the deeper the negative regard. Again, there is a spiral effect here. The conflict leads to negative regard which leads to still more conflict and so on. Conflict leads to a tremendous waste of time and energy for both sides. War, for example, is seldom profitable for the winner or the loser. Most obviously, conflict can lead to serious damage or death, physical or psychological. Even in the most ritualized of all conflict situations, the boxing ring, men have died. But they also die in gang fights and in wars.

Conflict leads us to close ourselves off from the other individual—which seems a reasonable defensive strategy. It would not, for example, be to our advantage to reveal our weaknesses to our enemy who is attempting to harm us. Conflict is perhaps the opposite of supportiveness; conflict is destructiveness. We seek not to help but to destroy our opponent. In some cases conflict may lead people to develop an increased positiveness for themselves; perhaps the idea of glory due the conquering hero is still with us. But most reasonable people, it seems, would not take pride in killing. Conflict attempts to eliminate whatever equality may have been present at the start. If equality were to remain there would be a constant stalemate. By harming or thwarting or destroying the other we are in effect establishing superiority over them. Empathy, on the other hand, is perhaps increased in times of conflict. The only person who can empathize with the fighter who gets knocked cold in the first round seems to be another fighter who went through the same or similar experience. So perhaps the victim and the victor are not so far apart in their feelings.

Our goal in communicology should be to provide insight into how conflict might be resolved through the application of principles of effective communication. In an earlier unit five characteristics of effective interpersonal communication were considered: (1) openness, (2) empathy, (3) supportiveness, (4) positiveness, and (5) equality of both parties. These five principles might well be repeated here as guides to effective conflict management, but there are other principles that might be advanced which are perhaps more unique to conflict situations and their resolution.

Perhaps the most important point to recognize is that conflict is not necessarily bad. We have already elaborated on this point. Similarly, we should realize that conflict resolution is not synonymous with the elimination of differences. There will always be differences, even disagreements among people. These are as natural as they are inevitable. In conflict resolution we wish to lessen the destructive and unproductive fighting, not to eliminate difference and diversity.

In conflict situations, communication has to an extent broken down and consequently we need to quickly repair the damage done. One of the first tasks must be to reestablish mutual trust since it is likely that trust has been broken down.

A special attempt should be made in conflict situations to focus on the issues rather than on the personalities involved. Although we can never communicate objectively about the world without communicating about ourselves, we need to make a special effort in conflict to distinguish between these communications since there is such a strong tendency to blame someone for the conflict and to refocus the conflict onto this other person.

In any conflict there are areas and issues of agreement. In any discussion of conflict we need to capitalize on these agreements and perhaps use them as a basis to gradually approach disagreements and conflicts. Little is accomplished by emphasizing disagreement and minimizing agreement. In some instances we may have to journey far from the actual field of conflict to find such areas of agreement. In most cases, however, we will find them in the midst of the actual conflict.

We must also recognize that flexibility and a willingness to compromise are especially important in conflict situations. If we wish to resolve a conflict and approach it with the idea that things must be seen our way, then there will be little hope of agreement; instead there is a good chance that conflict will escalate. A willingness to change, to bend, to give seems essential in any attempt at conflict resolution.

Conflict cannot be resolved unless the communication channels are kept open. To walk out on conflict situations or to refuse to confront the issues creates more problems than it solves. This is not to say that we should constantly verbalize or that periodic moratoriums are not helpful. Rather, it is to emphasize that we need to be willing to communicate—to say what is on our minds and to *listen* to what the other party is saying.

CONFLICT RESOLUTION

There are a wide variety of ways to deal with conflict. Some of these are productive in the sense that they enable us to deal honestly and meaningfully with the conflict and to offer some promise of its ultimate resolution. Some of these ways (open communication, focusing on issues) were discussed under "Conflict and Communication." An alternative way of approaching conflict resolution is to focus on the various stages one would normally go through in resolving conflict. Before examining these stages, it will be beneficial to first look at those methods that, on the surface, appear to deal with conflict but which in reality do not. These methods are called pseudomethods of conflict resolution.

Pseudomethods of Resolution

Although many such pseudomethods might be identified, we concentrate here on the five that seem the most important. One of the values of going through some of these pseudomethods for resolving conflict is to enable us to better identify such strategies in the behaviors of others and ultimately in our own behaviors as well. This latter ability is not an easy one to develop; but its importance makes the effort worthwhile.

Avoidance or Redefinition

One of the most frequently employed methods of conflict "resolution" is to avoid the conflict. This may take the form of actual physical flight where the individual may leave the scene of the conflict or perhaps fall asleep and just mentally withdraw. Or it may take the form of emotional or intellectual avoidance where the individual leaves the conflict psychologically by not dealing with any of the arguments or problems raised.

A similar method is to redefine the conflict so that it becomes no conflict at all or so that it becomes irrelevant to the individuals and hence unnecessary to deal with.

Force

Perhaps the most common picture of a pseudomethod of conflict resolution is that involving physical force. When confronted with a conflict, many prefer not to deal with the issues but rather to simply force his or her decision, way of thinking or behaving on the other by physically overpowering the other individual, or at least by the threat of such physical force. At other times, the force used is more emotional than physical. In either case, however, the issues are avoided and the individual who "wins" is the individual who exerts the most force. This of course is the technique of warring nations and spouses.

Minimization

Sometimes we deal with conflict by making light of it, by saying and perhaps believing that the conflict, its causes, and its consequences are really not important. We might argue that if left alone time will resolve it. But time does absolutely nothing; over time *we* may do something but time itself never acts one way or the other.

Sometimes we minimize the conflict with humor and may literally laugh at the conflict. Sometimes it is obvious that our laughter is prompted by fear or embarrassment or personal inadequacy in dealing with the conflict situation. But in many instances the humor seems logical enough; it eases the tension and, at least for a time, makes for more effective interpersonal relations. The problem is that the laughter did nothing to get at the root of the problem and when the laughter dies the conflict is still very much alive.

Blame

Sometimes conflict is caused by the actions of one of the individuals; sometimes it is caused by clearly identifiable outside forces. Most of the time, however, it is caused by such a wide variety of factors that any attempt to single out one or two factors is doomed to failure. And yet, a frequently employed fight strategy is to avoid dealing with the conflict by blaming someone for it. In some instances we blame ourselves. This may be the result of a realistic appraisal of the situation or it may be an attempt to evoke sympathy or to gain pity from the other individual. More often, however, we blame the other person. If a couple has a conflict over a child's getting into trouble with the police, for example, the parents may—instead of dealing with the conflict itself—start blaming each other for the child's troubles. As can easily be appreciated (when we are not parties to the conflict), such blaming solves nothing other than temporarily relieving a degree of intrapersonal guilt.

Silencers

One of the most unfair but one of the most popular fight strategies is the use of silencers. By "silencers" I mean a wide variety of fighting techniques that literally silence the other individual. One frequently used silencer is crying. When confronted by a conflict and unable to deal with it or when winning seems unlikely, the individual cries and thus silences the other person. Another technique is to hurt the other individual to the extent that he or she is silenced. This might involve bringing up some embarrassing inadequacy or some physical or personality problem. "You should be put back in the mental hospital" or "How can you talk when you can't even get a job and support your family" may be totally irrelevant to the specific conflict but may go a long way toward silencing the other person.

Stages in Conflict Resolution

Any conflict situation may be approached as would a problem requiring a decision. The methods suggested for dealing with conflict are very similar to the

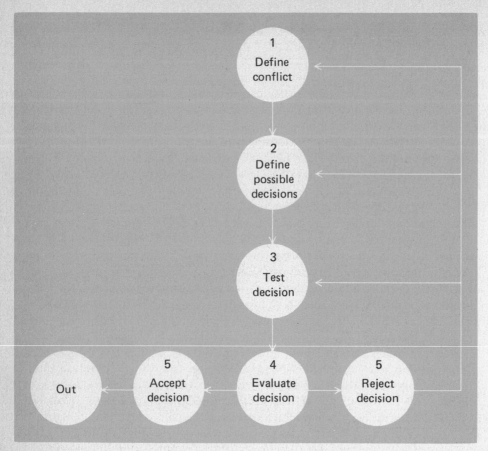

Figure 20.1
Stages in Conflict Resolution

methods of reflective thinking long taught as educational techniques and in small group communication classes. We here distinguish four principal stages in conflict resolution. A diagram of these essential stages is presented in Figure 20.1.

1. Define the Conflict

This step is perhaps the most essential and yet many attempts at conflict resolution omit this stage entirely. We need to ask ourselves what is the specific nature of the conflict and why does this conflict exist. It is at this stage that we should collect as much relevant data and opinions as we possibly can. Special care should be taken to insure that we collect data and opinions that may disagree with our position as well as the more supportive data and opinions.

In defining the conflict we should attempt to operationalize it as much as possible. Conflict defined in the abstract is difficult to deal with and resolve. Thus, for example, the husband who complains that his wife is "cold and unfeeling" is defining the problem in such abstract terms that it will be difficult to reach agreement as to the nature of the conflict let alone its resolution. There should be an attempt to deal with conflicts in behavioral terms if possible. Thus, it is one thing for a husband to say that his wife is "cold and unfeeling" and quite another to say she does not call him at the office or kiss him when he comes home or hold his hand when they are at a party. The latter behaviors can be dealt with whereas the abstract "cold and unfeeling" will be most difficult to handle. Further, it is useful to operationalize our conflicts because it forces us to be specific and to spell out exactly what we are fighting about. For a wife to say that her husband does not make her feel attractive but then fails to provide concrete examples of such behaviors is saying something quite different from the wife who says her husband does not make her feel attractive and who can easily rattle off 20 recent specific situations in which he, for example, criticized her appearance, laughed at her clothes, whistled at other women, and so on.

2. Define Possible Decisions

For any conflict there are a number of possible decisions that can be made. In some instances any one of three or four possible decisions would resolve the conflict; in other cases only one possible decision would work. But in all cases we need to first analyze all possible alternatives.

The word *decision* is used deliberately instead of the more common *solution*. To say that we will find a solution to a conflict assumes that we will eliminate the conflict. Very probably this is not what will happen—we actually strive to lessen the conflict. To imply that we will actually solve a conflict like we solve a mathematical equation is assuming too simplistic a view of human behavior and human interpersonal relationships. More likely we are attempting to make a decision so that future interactions may be undertaken in a somewhat more productive setting. For example, if a husband discovers that his wife is having an affair with a neighbor and they move to another city or neighborhood, they have not "solved" the problem, rather, they have made a decision so that future interactions may take place in a more productive atmosphere. In short, the word *decision* seems more descriptive of what actually goes on in conflict resolution.

In analyzing the possible decisions to the conflict we should attempt to predict the consequences of each of them. This is impossible to do with complete accuracy and yet some attempt should be made in this direction. We should guard against any tendency to dismiss possible decisions before we give them a fair hearing. Many excellent decisions are never put into operation because they at first seem strange, incorrect, or too difficult to implement.

3. Test Decision

The true test of any decision can only be made when the decision is put into operation. And so we play the odds—we select that decision that seems the most logical and try it out. Although each decision put into operation should be given a fair chance, we should recognize that if a particular decision does not work, another decision should be operationalized in its place. Putting a decision into operation with the idea that if this does not work that conflict resolution is impossible is self-destructive.

4. Evaluate the Decision

When the decision is in operation we need to evaluate it, examining the ways in which it helps to resolve (or aggravate) the conflict. Does it feel right? Does it make for improved interpersonal communication? Does it significantly lessen the conflict? If the decision works then we move to OUT on our diagram (Figure 20.1). If the decision does not prove satisfactory, then we can do one of three things. First, we might attempt to test another decision; perhaps the decision we ranked as number two will prove more satisfactory. And again we try it out. A second possibility is to redefine the various decisions and then test one of them. The third course of action is to go back and reanalyze and redefine the conflict itself. That is, we can reenter the conflict resolution process at any of the previous three stages. In any case, another decision must eventually be put into operation. Hopefully, it will work better than the previous one. And perhaps we will have learned something from the last decision-making process that will prove useful in subsequent conflict resolution attempts.

SOURCES

An excellent overview of conflict is provided by David Dressler, *Sociology: The Study of Human Interaction* (New York: Knopf, 1969). A more detailed overview is Alan C. Filley's *Interpersonal Conflict Resolution* (Glenview, Ill.: Scott, Foresman, 1975). Two works relating conflict and communication should be noted: Fred E. Jandt's *Conflict Resolution through Communication* (New York: Harper & Row, 1973) is a collection of 16 articles, many of which are helpful in conceptualizing the role of conflict in communication and the role of communication in conflict. *Perspectives on Communication in Social Conflict* (Englewood Cliffs, N.J.: Prentice-Hall, 1974), edited by Gerald R. Miller and Herbert W. Simons contains 8 thorough and perceptive articles on communication and conflict. This work also contains a bibliography of over 500 items.

George R. Bach and Peter Wyden's *The Intimate Enemy* (New York: Avon, 1968) is a popular, well-written, and insightful account of conflict and productive and unproductive ways of fighting.

The study of the boys at camp discussed in the beginning of the unit may be found in M. Sherif, O. J. Harvey, B. J. White, W. E. Hood, and C. W. Sherif, *Intergroup Conflict and Cooperation: The Robber's Cave Experiment* (Norman, Okla.: University of Oklahoma Book Exchange, 1961).

EXPERIENTIAL VEHICLES

20.1 RED AND BLUE GAME

For this exercise the class should be divided into dyads. One student is designated as Player 1 and the other student as Player 2. All players should inspect the accompanying matrix which contains the payoffs for each player, for each move. More specifically: Each player can play either RED or BLUE. (Follow this explanation while referring to the matrix.) The moves of Player 1 determine whether the payoffs come from the top two quadrants (if red is played) or the bottom two quadrants (if blue is played). The moves of Player 2 determine whether the payoffs come from the left two quadrants (if red is played) or the right two quadrants (if blue is played). Numbers before the slash are the payoffs for Player 1 and numbers after the slash are the payoffs for Player 2. If both players play BLUE, each player loses five points (−5). If both players play RED, each player wins five points (+5). If Player 1 plays RED and Player 2 plays BLUE, Player 1 loses ten points (−10) and Player 2 wins ten points (+10). If Player 1 plays BLUE and Player 2 plays RED, Player 1 wins ten points (+10) and Player 2 loses ten points (−10). The maximum amount of time allowed for each decision is one minute.

RED AND BLUE GAME

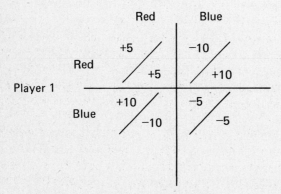

The game is played for 10 rounds and is scored on the score sheet like the one provided. Players reveal their decisions (that is, whether they choose BLUE or RED) only after they have entered them on the score sheet. Players must also record the amount won or lost and their balance in the spaces provided.

Discussion should center on at least the following:

1. How was cooperation evidenced?
2. How was conflict evidenced?
3. How would the amount won or lost have differed had greater cooperation or conflict been used?
4. How did your own history of conditioning influence your cooperation/ conflict behavior?
5. How does the "winner" feel?
6. How does the "loser" feel?
7. If you were playing for real stakes (for example, money, grades), how would your behavior have differed?

SCORE SHEET FOR RED AND BLUE GAME

Round	Decision	Amount Won or Lost	Balance
1			
2			
3			
4			
5			
6			
7			
8			
9			
10			

Total _____

20.2 SANDY

Sandy is a beautiful young woman, age 21, and a senior in college. Sandy is majoring in biology and is an honor student; she plans to work toward her master's degree in biology at night while teaching high school during the day.

At this particular high school, where Sandy has applied for a job, a committee of five members plus the school principal make all the hiring decisions. After reviewing Sandy's record—outstanding in every respect—the committee asks her in for a personal interview. This is a standard procedure with this high school. In this case, however, because Sandy's records and recommendations are so outstanding, the personal interview is regarded by the members of the committee and the principal as a formality. They are clearly eager to hire Sandy. Although there are other qualified applicants, none seems as outstanding as Sandy.

At the specified time Sandy appears to meet the committee. The members look at each other in shocked amazement; it seems obvious to them that Sandy is _____.* There is just no doubt that Sandy is, in fact, _____.

Thinking quickly, the principal, as committee chairperson, tells Sandy that the committee has fallen behind schedule and that they will see her in 15 minutes. Sandy leaves the room and sits outside waiting to be called back in. Sandy is well aware of their reactions and knows why they asked her to wait outside. She has seen those reactions before and is not surprised. She is _____ and as she sits waiting she ponders what the committee will do.

The committee, now alone for fifteen minutes, comes quickly to the point. The applicant is _____. "What should we do?" the principal asks.

Students should role play members of the committee and reach a decision as to what they should do in regard to Sandy. The members of the committee are:

Mrs. Markham, the school principal
Mr. Ventri, the biology department chairperson
Miss Colson, teacher of physical education
Mr. Garcia, teacher of chemistry
Ms. Goldstein, teacher of Romance languages
Mr. Jackson, teacher of art

Approximately 10 to 20 minutes should be allowed for the discussion. After this time, the class members should discuss the interactions that took place in the role playing session in terms of conflict and conflict resolution discussed in this unit. This discussion should have no rigid structure and may focus on any of the concepts considered under conflict and conflict resolution.

* Your instructor will fill this space.

UNIT 21
Assertiveness in Interpersonal Communication

Nonassertiveness, Aggressiveness, and Assertiveness
Principles for Increasing Assertiveness

LEARNING GOALS

After completing this unit, you should be able to:

1. define and give examples of *assertive behavior*.
2. distinguish among *assertiveness, nonassertiveness*, and *aggressiveness*
3. identify at least two types of situations in which one may choose not to be assertive
4. state and explain the five principles for increasing assertiveness
5. create a hierarchy for a specific desired assertive behavior
6. identify the cautions that should be observed in adopting new assertive behavior patterns

Recently there have been a number of best sellers devoted to what generally has been called assertiveness training. _Your Perfect Right: A Guide to Assertive Behavior; Stand Up, Speak Out, Talk Back: The Key to Self-Assertive Behavior; Don't Say Yes When You Want to Say No; Winning Through Intimidation; When I Say No, I Feel Guilty; The Assertive Woman_, and numerous others have done much to popularize the principles and techniques of assertiveness. The general assumption made by assertiveness theorists is that most of us are not assertive; most of us allow our rights to be trampled on; most of us are afraid to demand what is justly ours. As Fensterheim and Baer put it in their _Don't Say Yes When You Want to Say No_, "Parents, teachers, clergymen, and businessmen have unwittingly conspired to produce a nation of timid souls."

Thomas Moriarty has conducted a number of interesting experiments to illustrate just how passive we have learned to become. For example, in one experiment subjects were taking a psychological test and were placed near a confederate of the experimenter who played loud rock and roll music during the test. Of the 20 subjects, 16 made no comment at all. Even when the students were told that they would receive mild electric shocks for wrong answers, 16 of the 20 subjects still said nothing to the music player. Similar experiments were repeated in natural settings like the library and the movies, both with loud talking. Rarely did anyone object.

In perhaps the most clever variation, subjects approached people after they had left a phone booth saying that they had lost a ring and would the person mind emptying his or her pockets to see if he or she had perhaps picked up the ring. Of the 20 adult males who were approached 16 emptied their pockets. When the experiment was repeated using graduate students, 20 of the 24 men (83%) emptied their pockets. "I believe," concludes Moriarty, "that many of us have accepted the idea that few things are worth getting into a hassle about, especially with strangers. And I believe this is particularly true of younger people."

The aims of assertiveness training are to convince us that we should be more assertive and that we would be happier in doing so, and to show us how we might increase our own assertive behaviors.

Assertiveness is, as I see it, largely an interpersonal communication characteristic. It is mainly in interpersonal situations (though also in small groups and at times in large group situations) that the occasion and the need to assert ourselves arises. Our own assertiveness, or lack of it, will greatly influence our interpersonal interactions—a premise that will be demonstrated in this unit and in the experiential vehicles that follow.

It is also interesting to note that the qualities that assertiveness theorists consider characteristic of the assertive individual are also the qualities that communicologists consider characteristic of the effective interpersonal communicator. The relevance of assertiveness to interpersonal communication in particular and to communication in general will be even more apparent as we explain the distinctions among assertiveness, nonassertiveness, and aggressiveness and the characteristics of the assertive person and the principles for increasing assertiveness.

NONASSERTIVENESS, AGGRESSIVENESS, AND ASSERTIVENESS

There are two kinds of *nonassertiveness*. First, there is *situational nonassertiveness*. This is the nonassertiveness that is only displayed in certain situations, for example, situations that create a great deal of anxiety—perhaps because of the person one is interacting with or because of the topic being considered.

Generalized nonassertiveness is, as the term implies, behavior which is normally or typically nonassertive. These persons' behaviors are timid and reserved, and regardless of the specifics of the situation they are unable to assert their rights. These people do what others tell them to do, for example, parents, employers, and the like, without questioning and without concern for what is best for them. When these persons' rights are infringed upon they do nothing about it and even at times accuse themselves of being nonaccepting. Generalized nonassertive persons often ask permission from others to do what is their perfect right. Social situations create anxiety for these individuals and they more often than not find that their self-esteem is generally low. In the extreme, a generalized nonassertive person would be characterized as inhibited and emotionally unresponsive, one with feelings of personal inadequacy.

Aggressiveness may also be considered as being of two types: situational and generalized. *Situationally aggressive* people are aggressive only under certain conditions or in certain situations. For example, they may become aggressive after being taken advantage of over a long period of time or perhaps after being taken advantage of by someone for whom they have done a great deal. Or perhaps these people would be aggressive in dealing with teachers or fellow classmates or parents or older people. The important characteristic is that these people are usually not aggressive; only in certain situations do they behave aggressively.

Generally aggressive people, on the other hand, meet all or at least most situations with aggressive behavior. These persons seem in charge of almost all situations; regardless of what is going on they take over. These individuals appear to think little of the opinions, values, or beliefs of others and yet are extremely sensitive to others' criticisms of their own behavior. Consequently, they frequently get into arguments with others and find that they have few friends. They think little of others and others think little of them.

Assertive behavior is the desired alternative and has been characterized in various ways by various writers. Basically, assertive individuals are willing to assert their own rights but unlike their aggressive counterparts do not hurt others in the process. Assertive individuals speak their mind and welcome others doing likewise. Robert Alberti and Michael Emmons in *Your Perfect Right,* the first book on assertiveness training, note that "behavior which enables a person to act in his own best interest, to stand up for himself without undue anxiety, to express his honest feelings comfortably, or to exercise his own rights without denying the rights of others we call *assertive behavior.*" "The assertive individual," continue Alberti and Emmons, "is fully in charge of himself in interpersonal relationships, feels confident and capable without cockiness or hostility, is basically spontaneous in the expression of feelings and emotions, and is generally looked up to and admired by others." Surely this is the picture of a most effective individual.

According to Fensterheim and Baer there are four characteristics of the assertive individual. These four characteristics, although similar to those noted by Alberti and Emmons, should help to further clarify the nature of assertiveness.

First, the assertive individual freely reveals himself or herself to others. This person self-discloses without fear and says "Here I am. I think . . . , I do . . . , I want . . . ."

Second, the assertive person communicates openly, honestly, and fairly with all people whether they are intimate friends, family, or strangers. In short this individual communicates with those qualities that characterize effective interpersonal communication.

Third, the assertive person has an "active orientation to life." Rather than waiting for things to happen and passively accepting them, this person actively pursues his or her goals.

Fourth, the assertive individual respects himself or herself. This person recognizes his or her own weaknesses and failings but also honestly recognizes strengths and successes.

It should be emphasized that assertive people are assertive when they want to be but can be nonassertive if the situation seems to call for it. For example, we might wish to be nonassertive in a situation in which our assertiveness might emotionally hurt the other person. Let us say an older relative wishes us to do something for him or her. We might assert our rights and say no but in doing so we would probably hurt this person and so it might be easier to simply do as asked. But, of course, there are limits that should be observed. The individual should be careful, in doing what someone else asks to avoid hurting them, that he or she is not hurt instead. For example, the parents who wish the child to remain living at home until marriage may be hurt by the son's or daughter's assertive behavior. And yet the alternative is to hurt oneself and so here assertive behavior seems the better choice even though someone may be hurt in the process.

Also, it is generally not necessary to assert our rights after people have recognized them and have apologized. While waiting in line someone may step in front of us and then quickly realize what happened, step back, saying a simple "I'm sorry." Here of course it is unnecessary to be assertive. We often are tempted to do just that and to punish the other individual (with our assertive behavior) for "stepping on our toes."

PRINCIPLES FOR INCREASING ASSERTIVENESS

The general assumption made by most assertiveness trainers is that most people are situationally nonassertive. Most people can increase their assertive behavior with a resultant increase in general interpersonal effectiveness and in self-esteem.

Those who are generally nonassertive probably need extensive training with a trained assertiveness therapist. Those who are situationally nonassertive and who wish to understand assertiveness and perhaps behave a bit more assertively in certain situations should find the following principles of value. The rationale and the specific principles for increasing assertiveness derive from the behavior modification techniques of B. F. Skinner and the systematic desensitization techniques of Joseph Wolpe and others. In formulating these five principles, the techniques of these theorists, as well as the specific assertiveness training manuals noted in the introduction to this unit, were most helpful.

It should be said at the outset that assertiveness training deals with behavior and not with abstract or repressed needs and desires. The emphasis is on behavior and it is assumed that if one acts assertively he or she will in fact become more assertive. Further, it is assumed that these behaviors will reflect on the way in which we think of ourselves. If we act assertively we will soon think of ourselves as assertive individuals and more importantly our self-concept generally will be improved. The principles for increasing assertiveness follow.

1. Analyze the Assertive Behavior of Others

Perhaps the first step in increasing our own assertiveness is to understand the nature of assertiveness and how it differs from aggressiveness and nonassertiveness. This understanding on an intellectual level has hopefully already been achieved. What is necessary and even more important than intellectual understanding, however, is to understand actual assertive behavior. And the best way to start is to observe and analyze the behaviors of others, attempting to distinguish the differences between assertive, aggressive, and nonassertive behaviors. Consider what makes one behavior assertive and another behavior nonassertive or aggressive. Listen to what is said and to how it is said. Recall all the nonverbal behaviors we have already discussed and try to categorize nonverbal behaviors as assertive, aggressive, or nonassertive.

2. Analyze Your Own Behavior

It is generally easier to analyze the behaviors of others than your own. We find it difficult to be objective with ourselves. After we have acquired some skills in observing the behaviors of others we can turn our analysis to ourselves. We should be able to analyze those situations in which we are normally assertive, nonassertive, and aggressive. What characterizes these situations? What do the situations in which you are normally aggressive have in common? How do these situations differ from the situations in which you are normally nonassertive? What do the situations in which you are normally assertive have in common?

We should also be able to properly analyze our nonverbal behaviors. How do we stand when we are assertive? Aggressive? Nonassertive? What tone of voice do we use? What kind of eye contact do we maintain? What do we do with our hands? All our nonverbal behaviors are probably different for each of the three types of behaviors.

3. Record Your Behaviors

It is essential in any training program that you record your behaviors as accurately as possible. The advantages of this practice are many. The first advantage is that it will force you to pay special attention to all your behaviors and will force you to question whether they are assertive, aggressive, or nonassertive. Second, it will enable you to see if improvements have been made and, assuming they have been, this will provide reinforcement and will encourage you to continue your efforts. The third advantage is that this record will spotlight where improvement is particularly needed. This record will then serve as a guide for future behaviors.

A simple three-part form with space for recording assertive, aggressive, and nonaggressive behaviors will suffice. Be as specific as possible in recording your behaviors and give as many details of the actual situation as seem reasonable.

4. Rehearse Assertive Behaviors

A number of different systems have been proposed for effective rehearsal. One of the most popular is to select a situation in which you are normally nonassertive and build a hierarchy that begins with a relatively nonthreatening behavior and ends with the desired assertive behavior. For example, let us say that you have difficulty speaking in class and the desired behavior is to speak your mind in class. You might construct a hierarchy of situations that lead up to speaking in class. Such a hierarchy might begin with something like visualizing yourself sitting in class. You might then simply visualize yourself sitting in this class while you are in a state of relaxation. Once you have mastered this visualization you may proceed to the next step—visualizing the instructor asking a question. Once you are able to visualize this situation and remain relaxed throughout, visualize the instructor asking you the question. Visualize this situation until you can do so while relaxed. Then try visualizing yourself answering the question. Again, do this until you can do it while fully relaxed. Next you might rehearse visualizing your volunteering your opinion in class—the desired behavior. Do this until you can do it while totally relaxed.

This is the mental rehearsal. You might add an actual vocal dimension to this by actually answering the question you imagine the teacher asking you and vocalize your opinion. Again, do this until you have no difficulty. Next, try doing this in front of a supportive friend or group of friends. After this rehearsal you are probably ready for the next step.

5. Do It

This step is naturally the most difficult but obviously the most important. You can only become assertive when you *act* in an assertive manner; you cannot become assertive by acting nonassertively.

Again, do this in small steps. Staying with the previous example, attempt to answer a question that you are sure of before, say, volunteering an opinion or arguing with the position of the instructor. Once you have done this it is essential and most pleasant to reward yourself in some way. Give yourself something you want—an ice cream cone, a record, a new jacket. The assertive behavior will be more easily and permanently learned if you reward yourself immediately after engaging in the behavior. Try not to delay the reward too long; rewards are best when they are immediate.

After performing the behavior attempt to get some feedback from others. Start with people who are generally supportive. They should provide you with the social reinforcement so helpful in learning new behavior patterns.

In all behaviors but especially with new behaviors we should recognize that we may fail in what we are attempting to do. We might attempt to assert ourselves only to find that we have been unsuccessful. You might, for example, try to answer the teacher's question but find that not only do you have a wrong answer but that you did not understand the question either. Or you might raise your hand but find yourself lost for words when recognized. These incidents should not discourage us; we should recognize that in all attempts to change behaviors we will experience both failure and success. Naturally, we should try to develop these behaviors in situations that will result in success but any failures should not discourage us. They are only momentary setbacks but are not insurmountable problems.

A note of caution should be added to this discussion. It is easy to visualize a situation in which people are talking behind us in a movie and with our new-found enthusiasm for assertiveness, we assert ourselves and tell these people to be quiet. It is also easy to visualize our getting smashed in the teeth as a result. Equally easy to visualize is asserting ourselves with someone we care for only to find that as a result they burst into tears, totally unable to handle our new behaviors.

In applying these principles of assertiveness be careful that you do not assert yourself beyond that which you can handle—physically and emotionally. Do not assert yourself out of a job. It is best to be careful in changing any behavior but especially, it seems, in dealing with assertiveness.

SOURCES

I found the following works especially valuable in conceptualizing and in writing this unit. Robert E. Alberti and Michael L. Emmons' two books are perhaps the best starting places: *Your Perfect Right: A Guide to Assertive Behavior* (San Luis Obispo, Cal.: Impact, 1970) and *Stand Up, Speak Out, Talk Back: The Key to Self-Assertive Behavior* (New York: Pocket Books, 1970). Herbert Fensterheim and Jean Baer's, *Don't Say Yes When You Want to Say No* (New York: Dell, 1975) and Manuel J. Smith's, *When I Say No, I Feel Guilty* (New York: Bantam, 1975) are similar in many respects; both provide useful insight from assertiveness trainers. Robert J. Ringer's *Winning Through Intimidation* (Greenwich, Conn.: Fawcett, 1973) presents many ideas from the point of view of the real estate salesperson but they are applicable to everyone. S. Phelps and N. Austin's *The Assertive Woman* (San Luis Obispo, Cal.: Impact, 1975) addresses assertive behavior in relation to the particular problems women face. The experiments of Thomas Moriarty are reported in his "A Nation of Willing Victims,'' *Psychology Today* 8 (April 1975):43–50. Perhaps the most thorough discussion of assertiveness as communication is Ronald B. Adler's *Confidence in Communication: A Guide to Assertive and Social Skills* (New York: Holt, Rinehart and Winston, 1977). This book contains numerous exercises which may be used individually or in groups.

EXPERIENTIAL
VEHICLES

21.1 ASSERTIVENESS IN COMMUNICATION

Visualize the following communication situations and respond to each according to this five-point scale:

a. I have great difficulty with this situation
b. I have considerable difficulty with this situation
c. I have some difficulty with this situation
d. I have no difficulty with this situation
e. I enjoy this situation

_____ 1. You are called on in class when you know the answer.
_____ 2. You are in a group of friends and there is silence.
_____ 3. You are criticized by friends.
_____ 4. You are complimented by friends.
_____ 5. You are called on the phone for a date.
_____ 6. You are shown to be incorrect by friends.
_____ 7. You are approached by a stranger requesting information.
_____ 8. You are speaking before a large audience.
_____ 9. You are in a group and are ignored.
_____ 10. You are being interviewed for a job.
_____ 11. You are talking with someone who stands too close.
_____ 12. You are talking with someone who repeatedly touches you.
_____ 13. You are called on in class when you do not know the answer.
_____ 14. You burst out crying in front of friends.
_____ 15. You are told of unfavorable (but true) gossip about yourself.

1. Create a hierarchy (as explained in the fourth principle for increasing assertiveness) for one of the behaviors you responded to with an *a* (indicating "great difficulty") or *b* (indicating "considerable difficulty").
2. What characterizes those situations you have difficulty with? What characterizes those situations you have no difficulty with or those you enjoy? What are the essential differences?
3. Role play in your mind how you would act as the initiator of these various communications; for example, you criticize a friend, you compliment a friend, you call someone for a date, and so on. Does visualizing these situations contribute anything to your understanding of your own assertiveness in communication? Explain.

21.2 ASSERTIVENESS QUESTIONNAIRE

Indicate how you would respond to each of the 20 situations presented. Use the keys:

AS   Assertively
AG   Aggressively
NO   Nonassertively

Respond as you would instinctively rather than in the way you feel you should respond.

After each person has responded individually, discuss these situations and the responses in groups of five or six in any way you feel is meaningful.

_____ 1. A fellow student borrows a book and has not returned it in two weeks.

_____ 2. The people behind you in a movie are talking loudly.

_____ 3. Your neighbor is playing a stereo so loudly you have difficulty studying.

_____ 4. You are shortchanged by 25¢ at a supermarket.

_____ 5. Your meal in a restaurant arrives cold instead of hot.

_____ 6. A neighbor's dog repeatedly defecates in front of your house.

_____ 7. A neighbor's dog barks constantly during the day when the owner is out.

_____ 8. A friend borrows $5 but does not show any interest in returning it.

_____ 9. A neighbor repeatedly drops by for coffee without being invited.

_____ 10. A fellow student does no work on a group project for which each member will receive the same grade.

_____ 11. A teacher gives you a grade that you feel is unfair.

_____ 12. You are attracted to someone in class and want to ask the person on a date.

_____ 13. Your business partner does not do half of the work.

_____ 14. A friend is constantly late for appointments.

_____ 15. A group of fellow students is unfairly speaking against someone you know.

_____ 16. A persistent salesperson keeps showing you merchandise you do not want to buy.

_____ 17. Your friend wants to borrow your expensive watch and you are afraid it will be lost.

_____ 18. Your boss takes advantage by asking you to take on all sorts of responsibilities.

_____ 19. You are at a party where you know no one but the host.

_____ 20. Someone asks you on a date but you do not want to go.

21.3 ROLE PLAYING ASSERTIVENESS

In groups of five or six, each of the following four situations should be roll played so that each situation is played by an assertive, an aggressive, and a nonassertive behavior type. The roles should be rotated so that each person in the group gets an opportunity to demonstrate each of the three behavior patterns. The role of the initiator or stimulator should also be rotated.

Discussion should center on the following:

1. What nonverbal behaviors accompany each of the three behavior patterns?
2. What types of verbal statements are used to demonstrate the three behavior patterns?
3. Do some people have difficulty playing certain roles? Explain.
4. What kind of feelings accompany the playing of the various behavior types? Explain as concretely as possible.
5. Does assertiveness seem to come easier as the role playing progresses? Would this hold in the "real world?"
6. How might a hierarchy (as explained in the fourth principle for increasing assertiveness) be created for any one of the situations?

Situation One

You and another student turn in examination papers that are too similar for coincidence. The instructor accuses you of cheating by allowing the student behind you to copy your answers. You were not aware that anyone saw your paper.

Situation Two

You have just redecorated your apartment and have gone through considerable time and money in making it exactly as you want it. A good friend of yours brings you a house gift—the ugliest poster you have ever seen. Your friend insists that you hang it over your fireplace, the focal point of your room.

Situation Three

A friend borrows $10 and promises to pay you back tomorrow. But tomorrow passes as do 20 other tomorrows and yet there is no sign of the money. You know that the person has not forgotten about it and you also know that the person has more than enough money to pay you back.

Situation Four

A neighbor has been keeping a stereo at an extremely high volume late into the evening. This makes it difficult for you to sleep.

UNIT 22
Transactional Analysis in Interpersonal Communication

Ego States
Transactions
Life Positions

LEARNING GOALS

After completing this unit, you should be able to:

1. identify and define the three *ego states*
2. list the common verbal and nonverbal behaviors of each ego state
3. create dialogues that illustrate the way people in the different ego states would react in different situations
4. distinguish among and define *complementary*, *crossed*, and *ulterior transactions*
5. create dialogues that illustrate the three kinds of transactions and identify the type of transaction when given the dialogues
6. diagram the three types of transactions and identify the type of transaction when given the diagrams
7. explain the way people see themselves and others and the way they react in different situations when in the four life positions

One of the most insightful and certainly one of the most popular approaches to understanding interpersonal communication is that of *transactional analysis* (TA), a rather forbidding term for a relatively simple set of principles. Transactional analysis, popularized by Eric Berne in *Games People Play* and *What Do You Say After You Say Hello?*, and by Thomas Harris in *I'm O.K.—You're O.K.*, is an approach to or a means for analyzing and improving transactions between people.

The approach discussed here for understanding the self is not an alternative to the approaches considered earlier; rather, it is supplementary. Transactional analysis focuses on understanding the self through an analysis of interactions with others.

Some of the basic assumptions and principles of transactional analysis are presented here with two goals in mind: 1) to provide insight for better understanding ourselves and others, and 2) to provide a means for understanding and analyzing interpersonal encounters. To this end we consider the TA concepts of ego states, transactions, and life positions.

The *ego state* is a more or less stable pattern of feeling which corresponds to a pattern of behavior. In transactional analysis three such states are defined: Parent, Adult, and Child. *Transactions* refer to the patterns of interaction between two people. Complementary, crossed, and ulterior transactions are here distinguished. The *life positions* are the scripts or set of directions by which we live our lives. Four such scripts are considered here: I'm Not O.K., You're O.K.; I'm Not O.K., You're Not O.K.; I'm O.K., You're Not O.K.; and, I'm O.K., You're O.K.

EGO STATES

In transactional analysis distinctions are made among three ego states, which are defined as relatively consistent patterns of feelings that are or can be related to a corresponding consistent pattern of behavior. The three ego states are used in TA to describe the behaviors of people as they interact with each other. At any given time, individuals exhibit the behaviors characteristic of one of these ego states, although they may (and often do) shift from one ego state to another. The three ego states identified in TA are Parent, Adult, and Child. These ego states bear no relationship to the chronological age of the individual —a child may act as an Adult and an adult as a Child. (Note that the ego states are capitalized to distinguish them from actual parents, adults, and children.)

Parent

The ego state of *Parent* is one which is borrowed from one's real or substitute parents and may take the form of "mothering" or controlling. When in the ego state of Parent the individual acts and speaks like a real parent; verbally and nonverbally he or she assumes the role of the parent. The Parent makes frequent use of such expressions as "don't," "should," "shouldn't"—"Don't touch," "Be good," "Eat this," "I'll do it," "You'll get hurt," "Don't bother me now," "I'll get it," "Stop that," "Don't move from here," "Don't worry," "I'll fix everything," and so on. The Parent is especially evaluative and frequently uses such labels as good and bad, beautiful and ugly, healthy and sick, and similar terms to define an individual or group of individuals. Nonverbally, the Parent uses his or her body to supplement the words and makes frequent use of the accusing finger, the tapping foot (indicating impatience), the head shake (indicating "no"), the disapproving arms folded in front of the abdomen, the consoling arm on the shoulder, the approving cheek pinch, and so on.

Adult

In the ego state of *Adult* the individual is oriented to the world as it is, not as it is talked about. The Adult is logical rather than emotional, calm rather than excitable, inquiring rather than accusatory. The Adult is particularly oriented to accumulating and processing relevant information and to estimating the probabilities in any given situation. The Adult questions a great deal, asking How? What? Why? When? and Where? "What can we learn from this situation?" "What do the statistics say?" "What might we predict based on the probabilities?" (rather like the good reporter). Nonverbally, the Adult's body communicates interest and attention. This individual stands straight (but not rigid) and engages the attention of the other individuals by maintaining appropriate eye contact and physical distance and by moving close to the speaker to hear and see better.

Child

The ego state of *Child* may be either the Adapted Child State or the Natural Child State. In the Adapted Child State, individuals obey the directives of their parents, modify their behavior on the basis of the commands of the parents, do what the parents order or want, and perhaps even become what the parents want them to become when they get older. This Child may also adapt to the parents by withdrawing, crying, or having a temper tantrum. The Natural Child, on the other hand, is spontaneous, creative, intuitive, and rebellious. This Child does what he or she wants to do—and that is to have fun, play games, have sex, and otherwise please one's various appetites. This Child wants to explore new things and go to new places. The Child will frequently use such expressions as "can't," "don't want to"—"Is this O.K.?" "Let's play," "You don't love me," "Doesn't everybody love me?" "This is mine," "Don't hit me." Nonverbally, the Child cries and screams and maintains an uninhibited posture regardless of the social situation. The Child bites his or her nails and picks his or her nose whenever the urge presents itself.

Any individual in any interaction may be analyzed as operating in one of these three ego states. Transactional analysis provides a method for analyzing transactions in terms of these ego states. Whether the communication continues or is broken and what the outcome of the communication interaction will be is largely determined by the ego states of the individuals and by the type of transaction formed.

TRANSACTIONS

There are three basic types of transactions: *complementary*, *crossed*, and *ulterior*.

Complementary Transactions

Complementary transactions may be defined as those involving messages that are sent and received by the same ego state for each of the participants. That is, A's messages are sent by the same ego state that B is addressing, and B's messages are sent by the same ego state that A is addressing. Put differently and more simply, complementary transactions are those involving only two ego states.

In Type I complementary transaction we have the same ego states communicating with each other. This may be diagramed as follows:

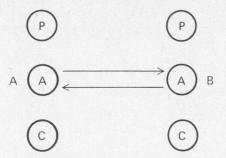

A dialogue representative of this kind of communication transaction might go something like this:

Spouse A: This is great furniture; too bad we can't afford it.
Spouse B: Yes, let's go downstairs; they're having a sale on floor samples and we might be able to get some good buys.

In Type II complementary transactions each person is in a different ego state but each addresses his or her messages to the other's current and therefore appropriate ego state. One such pattern is diagrammed as follows:

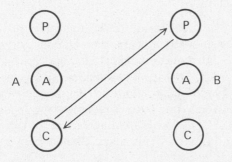

In this example, A's Child is addressing B's Parent, and B's Parent is addressing A's Child. This type of transaction might be identified from a dialogue such as:

Spouse A: Let's go on the town and get drunk.
Spouse B: Now, you know you get sick when you drink. There's more to life than just having fun.

Here A is in the Child state and wants to have fun, to play. B assumes the Parent state and restrains the Child.

In complementary transactions communication is productive and may con-

"Why do we have to have meaningful dialogues? . . . I'd
feel much better if we merely yell at each other!"
(*Grin and Bear It* by Lichty. Reproduced through courtesy
of Field Newspaper Syndicate.)

tinue indefinitely. In the Type I example, as long as the couple remain as two
Adults communication will continue with little chance of breaking down. In the
Type II example the same holds true. As long as A remains in the Child state
and B in the Parent state, no barriers will be established and communication
will continue.

Crossed Transactions

Trouble enters when one individual slips out of the ego state he or she is in
and into one that creates what is called a *crossed transaction*. Again there are
two general types. In Type I the communication—to use the most common
pattern—begins as Adult to Adult. That is, A as Adult says to B, also as Adult,
"This is great furniture; too bad we can't afford it." But in a crossed transaction B does not respond as Adult, nor does B address the message to A's
Adult. Rather, B responds as a Child to a Parent and says, for example, "Let's
buy it anyway. I want it. Buy it for me." This transaction might be diagramed as
follows:

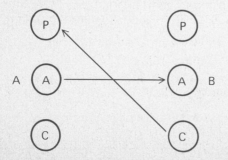

In Type II the transaction again begins with an Adult addressing an Adult, saying, to keep the same example, "This is great furniture; too bad we can't afford it." Here, however, B responds as a Parent to a Child saying, for example, "Now you know you can't afford it so why waste your time and mine looking at it." This dialogue, we might diagram as follows:

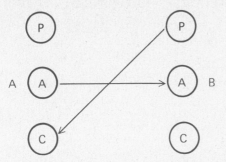

As you can see, it is with crossed transactions that problems in interpersonal communication arise. For example, in Type I-crossed, A (as Adult) may try to reason with B (as Child) but success will be almost impossible since A's arguments presuppose that B is in the Adult state, which B is not. Or A might switch to the Parent state and answer B as a parent would: "I told you we can't afford it and that finishes that." This may end the conversation but it does not clear up the communication breakdown. In Type II-crossed, A is again presented with a serious breakdown. A could attempt to reason with B and say something to the effect that A was just looking and did realize that there was not enough money and so on. But this kind of approach would only have an effect on someone in the Adult ego state.

We may generalize from these situations and note that communication broke down largely because messages were addressed to the inappropriate ego state.

Ulterior Transactions

A third class of transactions, somewhat more complex than the previous two, is that of *ulterior transactions.* In ulterior transactions more than two ego states are involved at the same time. Here there is an unspoken or hidden agenda, which is generally communicated nonverbally. Consider, for example, the following dialogue:

Student: (Handing the teacher a term paper while looking at the floor and speaking too softly) This is the best writing I could do on this extremely difficult topic you assigned me.

Teacher: (Accepting paper though with an expression of annoyance) Well, I'll read it and let you know.

On the surface the student's message is Adult to Adult, but the ulterior message is Child to Parent (I've been a bad student). The teacher responds on the surface as Adult but the ulterior and nonverbal message (the expression of annoyance) is from Parent to Child and punishes the student.

We might diagram this transaction as follows (dotted lines are generally used for ulterior transactions):

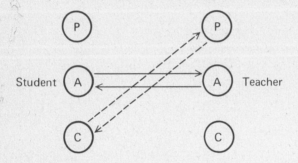

These ulterior transactions are the substance of game behavior. The problem with such games in terms of interpersonal relationships is that it is often difficult to tell when one is playing a game and when one is not playing. At times we may respond to someone as if that person was serious, only to find that a game was being played. And of course the reverse is just as much a problem, when we assume that someone is playing a game but later discover he or she was serious. The person who says, "My jacket is ugly," may mean it and may be simply stating an opinion. On the other hand, this person may be looking for reassurances that it is not ugly and that indeed it looks particularly attractive. When we know the individual involved we are in a better position to respond appropriately, but even here there is much room for error.

Some people play such games constantly; they are always "on." We are forever forced to look for hidden meanings in what they say and somehow feel that their real selves never come through. In the example of the student and teacher, the student is playing the game of "kick me," according to Berne's *Games People Play.* The student is, in effect, asking to be punished. In this example the teacher played too and "kicked" as the student asked.

Although individuals play games to win, the players are not winners in the usual sense. More often they are losers. "Games," note Muriel James and Dorothy Jongeward in *Born to Win,* "prevent honest, intimate, and open relationships between the players. Yet people play them because they fill up time, provoke attention, reinforce early opinions about self and others, and fulfill a sense of destiny."

LIFE POSITIONS

One of the basic tenets of transactional analysis is that we live our lives largely according to "scripts." These scripts are very similar to dramatic scripts, complete with a list of characters and roles, stage directions, dialogue, and plot.

Our culture provides us with one kind of script. This cultural script provides us with guides to proper dress; rules for sexual conduct; roles for men and women; a value system pertaining to marriage, children, money, and education; the concepts of success and failure; and so on. Families provide another kind of script. Family scripts contain more specific instructions for each of the family members—the boys should go into politics, the girls should get involved in social work, this family will always have its own business, "we may not earn much money but we will always have adequate insurance," the oldest son takes over the father's business, the oldest daughter gets married first, and so on.

From out of all our early experiences, particularly from the messages—both verbal and nonverbal—received from our parents, we develop a psychological script for ourselves and, for the most part, follow this throughout our lives.

Individual scripts are generally "written" by the age of three; they provide us with specific directions for functioning within the larger cultural script. Should we play the victim or the persecutor, the slave or the master, the clown or the intellectual?

Some children, for example, are told that they will be successes. Nonverbally, they are given love and affection; verbally, they are reinforced for numerous actions. Other children have been told they will never succeed. Statements such as, "No matter what you do, you'll be a success," as well as statements such as, "You'll never amount to anything," are extremely important in determining the script the child will assume in later life. Generally, people follow the scripts their parents have written for them. But such scripts can be broken. We do *not* have to follow the script written for us by our parents. One of the major purposes of transactional analysis is to break the negative and unproductive scripts and to substitute positive and productive scripts in their place. TA is used to prevent destructive messages from getting written into the script.

These scripts, which we all have, are the bases from which we develop what are called "life positions." In TA there are four basic life positions.

I'm Not O.K., You're O.K.

The person maintaining this life position sees others as being well-adjusted and generally effective (you're O.K.) but sees himself or herself as maladjusted and ineffective (I'm not O.K.). This is, according to Harris, the first position we develop as very young children. This is the position of the child who sees himself or herself as helpless and dirty and sees the adult as all-powerful and all-knowing. This person feels helpless and powerless in comparison to others and withdraws from confrontations rather than compete. This kind of life positions leads one to live off others, to make others pay for their being O.K. (and oneself being not O.K.). Such people are frequently depressed; at times they isolate themselves, lamenting, "If only . . ." or "I should have been . . ."

I'm Not O.K., You're Not OK.

People in this category think badly of themselves (I'm not O.K.) as well as of other people (you're not O.K.). They have no real acceptance of either themselves or others. They give themselves no support (because they are not O.K.) and they accept no support from others (because others are not O.K.). These people have given up. To them, nothing seems worthwhile and so they withdraw. Interpersonal communication is extremely difficult since they put down both themselves and others and intrapersonal communication does not seem particularly satisfying either. Attempts to give such people help are generally met with refusals since the would-be helpers are seen as "not O.K."

Such people seem to have lost interest in themselves, in others, and in the world generally. Living seems a drag. In the extreme they are the suicides and homicides, the autistics and pathologicals.

I'm O.K., You're Not O.K.

Persons in this position view themselves as generally effective (I'm O.K.) but see others as ineffective (you're not O.K.); "I am good, you are bad." These people have little or no respect for others and easily and frequently find fault with both friends and enemies. They are supportive of themselves but do not accept support from others. They are independent and seem to derive some satisfaction from *intra*personal communication but reject *inter*personal interaction and involvement. Literally and figuratively they need space, elbow room; they resent being crowded by those "not O.K." others. Criminals are drawn with disproportional frequency from this class, as are the paranoids who feel persecuted and who blame others for their problems.

I'm O.K., You're O.K.

This is the adult, normal, healthy position. This, says Berne in *What Do You Say After You Say Hello?*, is "the position of genuine heroes and princes, and heroines and princesses." These people approach and solve problems constructively. They have valid expectations about themselves and others and accept themselves and others as basically good, worthy, and significant human beings. These people feel free to develop and progress as individuals. They enter freely into meaningful relationships with other people and do not fear involvements. They feel neither inferior nor superior to others. Rather, they are worthy and others are worthy. This is the position of winners.

It is impossible to say how many people are in each class. Many pass through the "I'm not o.k., you're o.k." position. Few arrive at the "I'm o.k., you're o.k.'' position; few people are winners in this sense. Very probably the vast majority of people are in the "I'm not o.k., you're o.k." and "I'm o.k., you're not o.k." positions. It should be clear, of course, that these are general classes and that human beings resist each classification. Thus these four positions should be looked at as areas on a continuum, none of which have clear-cut boundaries and yet all of which are different.

Transactional analysis is perhaps the most effective means of understanding interactions among people and for making clear when and why interactions are effective and when and why interactions break down. It is an approach that enables us to look at our own communications and understand the ego state we are in; at the same time, it makes us aware of the effects our ego state has on others. Perhaps most important is that TA helps to bring to consciousness our own life positions so that we may change them to a more effective alternative.

It seems that these insights are prerequisite to understanding ourselves and our interpersonal communications—ultimately to make them more effective.

SOURCES

This unit is based on the theory of transactional analysis. New books on TA are constantly being written. Most of the popular works on TA cover essentially the same basics but apply them to different areas. In writing this unit I made most use of Thomas A. Harris, *I'm O.K., You're O.K.* (New York: Harper & Row, 1969) which I wholeheartedly recommend to any college student. Also useful are Muriel James and Dorothy Jongeward's *Born to Win: Transactional Analysis with Gestalt Experiments* (Reading, Mass.: Addison-Wesley, 1971) and Eric Berne's *Games People Play* (New York: Grove Press, 1964). Berne's book, I should mention, was a best seller for an extremely long time and apparently had considerable appeal; yet I found it dull, ponderous, and extremely difficult to stick with. A more simplified account of transactional analysis is *Success Through Transactional Analysis* by Jut Meininger (New York: New American Library, 1973). A useful collection of articles is contained in Gerald M. Goldhaber and Marylynn B. Goldhaber, eds., *Transactional Analysis: Principles and Applications* (Boston: Allyn & Bacon, 1976).

EXPERIENTIAL VEHICLES

22.1 PAC COMMUNICATIONS

These ten brief situations should be role played so that the differences among Parent (P), Adult (A), and Child (C) may be more easily seen. Three persons should be chosen for each situation, one to portray P, one to portray A, and one to portray C. After a neutral party or the instructor announces the general situation, for example, "A fellow employee enters the office crying," the three members interact in response to this situation according to the ego state each is to portray.

After this brief role playing members of the class should discuss the faithfulness of the roles to the ego state, offering other possible alternative ways of acting. Record what you feel are "ideal" responses for each ego state.

As a variation, three members may interact according to the situation without telling the class who is playing what role. Discussion may then center on the reasons for the ease or difficulty in identifying the roles.

Consider also how you would react in these situations without attempting to respond as would an Adult. Can you identify any influences that would lead you to respond as you would? Be as specific as possible.

1. A fellow employee enters the office crying.

   P
   A
   C

2. A student fails a course and tells friends.

   P
   A
   C

3. A relative has just died.

   P
   A
   C

4. A friend is to be married to a person of another race.

   P
   A
   C

5. A beggar asks for a dime.

    P
    A
    C

6. One's teenage child is arrested on drug charges.

    P
    A
    C

7. A local politician is found to have been taking graft.

    P
    A
    C

8. An auto accident occurs in the neighborhood.

    P
    A
    C

9. A favorite teacher on campus is fired.

    P
    A
    C

10. A close friend dies.

    P
    A
    C

22.2 MAPPING TRANSACTIONS

For this exercise dyads should be formed with a third person being the trans-actional analyst. The analyst selects a brief situation with some initial dialogue (one of the ten presented or one that does not appear here) and the two parties role play the situation in accordance with the initial dialogue they have been given. After this brief role playing, the analyst maps the transaction and all three members discuss the type of transaction it was and the effectiveness-ineffectiveness of the communications. "Map" the transaction by drawing arrows connecting the appropriate ego states expressed in the dialogue.

This exercise may also be done with two persons interacting and the rest of the class serving as analysts.

1. *Jim:* I wish you would stop drinking. You know this is not the place to get drunk.
   Sara: Have a drink with me. Come on, let's have some fun.

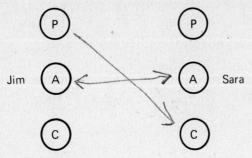

2. *Ronald:* I didn't finish my term paper. I just didn't know where to begin and couldn't seem to get it started.
   Dr. Hill: Now, don't worry. We'll talk about it and I'm sure you'll be able to do it once the directions are made clear.

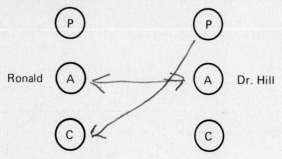

3. *Husband:* Why the hell aren't the kids in bed yet? I have to have some time to relax in quiet.
   Wife: (*Crying*) Stop yelling at me; can't you see I'm already upset.

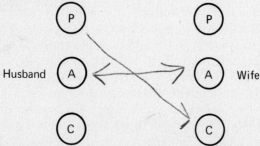

4. *Husband:* Can't you get a better job and make more money like everyone else?
Wife: If you weren't so ignorant of the economic conditions today you wouldn't ask such a stupid question.

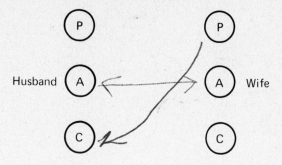

5. *Son:* I'm going to watch some television.
Mother: O.K.

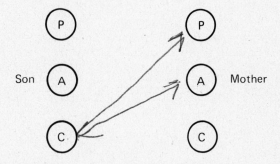

6. *Son:* I'm going to watch some television.
Mother: You're always watching television. Isn't there anything else you can do? You're going to grow up just like your father.

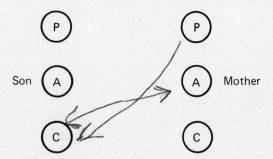

7. *Employer:* I'm sorry but we are going to have to lay you off for at least the next six months.
Employee: This company should fall apart.

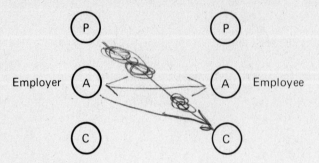

8. *Student:* Why is it that every teacher is so critical of everything I do. Don't I ever do anything right?
Teacher: I'm sure they don't criticize everything. I'm sure they are just trying to be helpful.

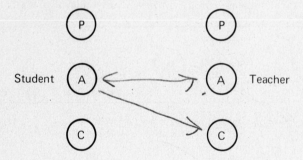

9. *Teenage boy:* How about going to a movie tonight?
Teenage girl: Aren't you ever going to grow up and ask me out to some sophisticated place? I'm almost seventeen!

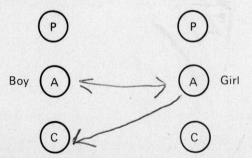

10. *Son:* Let's play in the sand.
    Father: O.K. Let's go.

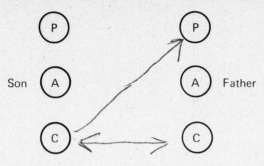

22.3 COMMUNICATIONS OF DIFFERENT LIFE POSITIONS

How would you respond to each of the following situations? Indicate what you think your initial response(s) would be.

1. Being offered a promotion to a position of responsibility
2. Being fired from a job held for the past five years
3. Being asked out on a date
4. Being robbed
5. Being designated leader in a small group situation
6. Being complimented for something you made
7. Being criticized for something you did
8. Being asked a favor that will take about an hour of your time
9. Being assigned an unpleasant job that will last about a month
10. Being given the opportunity to vote for or against the promotion of your in-personal communication instructor

After you have completed all ten, respond to the following ten situations, but this time determine how each of the four life positions would respond in the same situation.

1. Being offered a promotion to a position of responsibility

   a. I'm not O.K., You're O.K.
   b. I'm not O.K., You're not O.K.
   c. I'm O.K., You're not O.K.
   d. I'm O.K., You're O.K.

2. Being fired from a job held for the past five years

   a. I'm not O.K., You're O.K.
   b. I'm not O.K., You're not O.K.
   c. I'm O.K., You're not O.K.
   d. I'm O.K., You're O.K.

3. Being asked out on a date

   a. I'm not O.K., You're O.K.
   b. I'm not O.K., You're not O.K.
   c. I'm O.K., You're not O.K.
   d. I'm O.K., You're O.K.

4. Being robbed

   a. I'm not O.K., You're O.K.
   b. I'm not O.K., You're not O.K.
   c. I'm O.K., You're not O.K.
   d. I'm O.K., You're O.K.

5. Being designated the leader in a small group situation

   a. I'm not O.K., You're O.K.
   b. I'm not O.K., You're not O.K.
   c. I'm O.K., You're not O.K.
   d. I'm O.K., You're O.K.

6. Being complimented for something you made

   a. I'm not O.K., You're O.K.
   b. I'm not O.K., You're not O.K.
   c. I'm O.K., You're not O.K.
   d. I'm O.K., You're O.K.

7. Being criticized for something you did

   a. I'm not O.K., You're O.K.
   b. I'm not O.K., You're not O.K.
   c. I'm O.K., You're not O.K.
   d. I'm O.K., You're O.K.

8. Being asked a favor that will take about an hour of your time

   a. I'm not O.K., You're O.K.
   b. I'm not O.K., You're not O.K.
   c. I'm O.K., You're not O.K.
   d. I'm O.K., You're O.K.

9. Being assigned an unpleasant job that will last about a month

   a. I'm not O.K., You're O.K.
   b. I'm not O.K., You're not O.K.
   c. I'm O.K., You're not O.K.
   d. I'm O.K., You're O.K.

10. Being given the opportunity to vote for or against the promotion of your interpersonal communication instructor

    a. I'm not O.K., You're O.K.
    b. I'm not O.K., You're not O.K.
    c. I'm O.K., You're not O.K.
    d. I'm O.K., You're O.K.

Analyze your own responses in terms of the four life positions. Do you see any patterns in your responses? How would these responses influence your day-to-day experiences?

As an alternative, this exercise may be conducted by having the papers or forms on which each person indicates how he or she would respond collected (without names). The instructor or some member of the class would read the responses aloud and the class would attempt to classify these into the four life positions. More important than classification, however, would be a discussion of what these responses mean in terms of our views of ourselves and of others.

UNIT 23
The Nature of Small Group Communication

The Small Group
Types of Small Groups

LEARNING GOALS

After completing this unit, you should be able to:

1. define the nature of a *small group*
2. explain the four principles of brainstorming
3. identify the two ways in which therapeutic groups may be health producing
4. explain the distinction between the problem-solving group and the educational or learning group

We are all members of various small groups. The family is the most obvious example, but we also function as members of a team, a class, a collection of friends, and so on. Some of our most important and most personally satisfying communications take place within the small group context.

Before we can understand the nature of small group communication we need to inquire into the nature of the small group itself.

THE SMALL GROUP

For our purposes a *group* is best defined as a collection of individuals few enough in number so that all members may communicate with relative ease as both senders and receivers, and who are related to each other by some common purpose and with some degree of organization or structure among them. Each of these characteristics needs to be explained a bit.

A group is first of all a collection of individuals few enough so that all members may communicate with relative ease as both senders and receivers. This part of the definition touches on one of the most essential aspects of the small group—the number of individuals. Small groups are larger than two but not so large so that communication among the various individuals becomes impossible. Generally, a small group consists of approximately five to twelve people. The important point to keep in mind is that each member should be able to function as both source and receiver with relative ease. If the group gets much larger than twelve this becomes difficult if not impossible.

Box 15
SOLVING PROBLEMS IN GROUPS

Is it true that "two heads are better than one" or do "too many cooks spoil the stew"? There are arguments on both sides of the issue. It took thousands of scientists and technicians working harmoniously to conquer outer space, but Albert Einstein worked alone and announced the theory of relativity at age 26. Since the decision to work alone or with others has great practical implications, we can consider some of the factors that make group performance superior or that hamper group solutions.

The major advantage of working in groups is that you can pool your unique resources with those of others, and the different contributions of each group member can be combined into a new whole. The members of a group differ not only in intelligence but also in motivation. Some are more willing than others to do hard work, and some problems require time-consuming, painstaking chores. Working alone you may or may not be motivated to put forth the necessary effort. But with a group, the drudgery can be divided equally among the members. As the saying goes, "many hands make light work."

It is also easier for us to see other people's mistakes than to be aware of our own. Annoying as it may be, having our errors corrected by others is frequently helpful. Not only can the group filter out errors, but it may also stimulate ideas which would not have occurred to individuals working alone.

The most obvious disadvantage to group effort is the familiar impulse to let somebody else take the responsibility and slack off in our own effort. In addition, individuals come to the group bringing a variety of motives and these may interfere with the group enterprise. Some may want, consciously or unconsciously, to sabotage the group effort. Others may have self-oriented needs such as defeating rivals. impressing another group member, expressing pent-up feelings, or winning group approval. Members of a group may all want to solve the problem, yet have quite different ideas about how to go about it. If people are unwilling to compromise these different ideas can clash.

In addition, your status in a group also makes a difference in whether your ideas are incorporated in the group solution. Communication is important in group thinking, but it may be hampered by status differences. A group member may not want to criticize the ideas of high-ranking individuals, and low-ranking individuals may not want to speak out at all.

Many of these problems are negligible when groups use *brainstorming* to tackle their problems. The technique of brainstorming started with the assumption

The members of a group must be related to each other in some way. People in a movie house would not constitute a group since there is no relationship among the various individuals. With individuals constituting a small group the behavior of one member is significant for the other members whereas for individuals not constituting a small group the behavior of one member may not even be noticed by the other members.

There must be some common purpose among the members for them to

that creative ideas will be greatest when everyone feels free to communicate suggestions about a problem at hand. When a group is assembled to solve a problem, it is asked to follow some specific ground rules. During the initial phase of brainstorming (*green-light stage*), group members can put forth any idea they wish—no matter how impractical or ridiculous it may at first appear. No one is allowed to criticize anyone else's ideas. In this stage "killer thoughts" are forbidden: "We tried that before and it didn't work"; "You will never get people to cooperate"; "It's too expensive." All of the ideas are recorded until the flow of ideas dries up. Then in the next phase (*red-light stage*), all the suggestions are examined, evaluated, and criticized until a solution agreeable to the group is found. In many situations, brainstorming seems to work well. In others, it appears to be less effective than allowing individuals to work alone.

In an early study on brainstorming by Taylor, Berry, and Block (1958), subjects were assigned at random to work alone or in five-man groups. In both conditions five problems were posed, and 12 minutes were allowed to work on each one. The comparisons of individuals and groups in terms of the quantity and the originality of ideas produced showed that individuals working alone scored higher than the groups. (Individuals had an average of 68.1 ideas compared to 37.5 for groups.) Individuals also produced more creative ideas.

The fact remains that history records a preponderance of individual accomplishments and seldom reports spectacular group endeavors that have changed the course of mankind. Yet we know that groups have been incredibly successful. Perhaps the answer to whether groups or individuals are better problem solvers is: It depends—on the kind of problem undertaken and, of course, on the group.

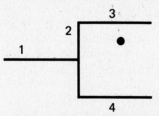

Can a group solve this puzzle faster than an individual? Set up a mini-test by giving the puzzle to several of your friends together, and then try to solve it on your own. The rules: Arrange four matchsticks as shown above and place a piece of "dirt" in the "shovel." By moving only two match sticks, get the dirt out of the shovel. No, you can't move the dirt! Solution appears in Box 15A, at the end of the unit.

Source: From Elton B. McNeil, *The Psychology of Being Human* (San Francisco: Canfield Press, 1974), p. 247.

constitute a group. This does not mean that all members must have exactly the same purpose in mind. Actually, this would be impossible. But generally there must be some similarity in the reasons for the individuals to interact.

The people must be connected by some organization or structure. Individuals not constituting a group have no such structure; the behaviors of the various individuals do not constitute any system; there is no pattern to their behaviors. In a small group there is pattern. At times the structure is a very rigid one as in groups operating under parliamentary procedure where each comment must follow prescribed rules. At other times, the structure is very loose as in a social gathering, dinner, or a card game. And yet in both groups there is some organization, some structure: two people do not speak at the same time, comments or questions by one member are responded to by others rather than ignored, and so on.

Another characteristic that is frequently included in other definitions of the small group is proximity. It is often held that the members must be face to face for them to constitute a small group. This is usually the case; however, with conference telephones becoming more and more popular we should recognize that the characteristic of proximity is only included because it is usually, but not always, present. Individuals on a conference call fulfill all the characteristics of a small group and should be recognized as such.

The area of small group communication, then, is concerned with the interaction process that occurs within small group settings. Alvin Goldberg and Carl Larson define the area more formally: "Group communication," says Goldberg and Larson, "is an area of study, research, and application that focuses not on group process in general, but on the communication behavior of individuals in small face-to-face discussion groups." If we eliminate the "face-to-face" characteristic, the definition seems a suitable one.

TYPES OF SMALL GROUPS

The number of the types of small groups is actually equal to the number of groups in existence because each group is unique and different from every other group. Yet, there are enough similarities among the groups to justify our considering some types as general classes. Here we distinguish six such general types.

The Problem-Solving Group

Perhaps the type of group most familiar to us when we think of small group communication is the problem-solving group. Here we have a group of individuals meeting to solve a particular problem or to at least reach a decision that may be a preface to the problem solving itself.

In one sense this is the most exacting kind of group to participate in since it requires not only a knowledge of small group communication techniques, but a thorough knowledge of the particular problem and usually a rather faithful adherence to a somewhat rigid set of procedural rules.

The Idea-Generation Group

Many small groups exist solely for the purpose of generating ideas, whether they are involved in advertising, politics, education, or, in fact, any field where ideas are needed and that would include all fields. Although members may get together and simply generate ideas, a formula is usually followed, particularly that formula called brainstorming.

Brainstorming is a technique for literally bombarding a problem and generating as many ideas as possible. In this system the group members meet in two periods, the first is the brainstorming period proper and the second is the evaluation period. The procedure is relatively simple. A problem is selected that is amenable to many possible solutions or ideas. Group members are informed of the problem to be brainstormed before the actual session so that some prior thinking on the topic is done. When the group meets each person contributes as many ideas as he or she can think of. During this idea generating session four general rules are followed.

No Negative Criticism Is Allowed

All ideas are treated in exactly the same way; they are written down by a secretary. They are not evaluated in this phase nor are they even discussed. Any negative criticism—whether verbal or nonverbal—is itself criticized by either the leader or the members.

Quantity Is Desired

The assumption made here is that the more ideas the better; somewhere in a large pile of ideas will be one or two good ones that may be used. The more ideas generated the more effective the brainstorming session.

Combinations and Extensions Are Desired

While we may not criticize a particular idea we may extend it or combine it in some way. The value of a particular idea, it should be noted, may well be in the way it stimulates another member to combine or extend it.

Freewheeling Is Wanted

By this is meant that the wilder the idea the better. Here the assumption is that it is easier and generally more profitable to tone an idea down rather than to spice it up. A wild idea can easily be tempered but it is not so easy to elaborate on a simple or conservative idea.

After all the ideas are generated, a period that takes no longer than 15 or 20 minutes, the entire list of ideas is evaluated and the ones that are unworkable are thrown out while the ones that show promise are retained and evaluated. Here, of course, negative criticism is allowed.

The Therapy Group

Therapy groups are designed to improve mental health in some way. Therapeutic groups may be effective or health producing in either of two general ways, as Charles Rossiter notes. First, they may be instrumentally therapeutic when they facilitate another health-producing activity. When a psychiatrist obtains information from a patient that will eventually be used to help the patient, the communication is said to be instrumentally therapeutic. Second, the group may be therapeutic in a consummatory manner when, for example, the group itself has a therapeutic effect as in the case of catharsis, where one speaks to rid himself or herself of pressing problems.

Another way of looking at these two general functions is to say that one is prefatory to therapeutic communication whereas the second is immediately therapeutic.

The Educational or Learning Group

In *educational* or *learning groups* the purpose is to acquire new information or skill and involves a mutual sharing of knowledge or insight. At times one person, say a teacher, will have the information and the group exists simply as a means for disseminating the information the teacher possesses. But this function is just as well, if not more effectively, served by a lecture. In most small group learning situations all members have something to teach and something to learn and the members pool their knowledge to the mutual benefit of all. Also included here would be the consciousness-raising groups currently enjoying considerable popularity. Perhaps the best examples of this are the numerous groups designed to raise the consciousness of women regarding sex roles, women's rights, and the like.

The Sensitivity Group

Currently, sensitivity groups are also enjoying considerable popularity. *Sensitivity groups* exist to deal with our psychological or sociological problems and provide us wtih greater insight into our own behaviors and the behaviors of others.

Sensitivity groups require considerable self-disclosure and a willingness to come to grips with one's vices as well as one's virtues.

The Social Group

Perhaps social groups are the most common of all small groups. *Social groups* exist for numerous reasons: They are fun—at least generally; they aleviate loneliness; they provide support for our ideas and thoughts by reinforcing all the nice things we want to know about ourselves.

"The topic for today is: What is reality?"
(Cartoon by Henry R. Martin, from *Saturday Review,* May 29, 1971.)

Social groups are found at parties, in restaurants, in school cafeterias and lounges, and wherever people come together for no obvious purpose other than to be with others.

The communications that take place in social groups may not be so important for the information they contain as for the relationships they imply. Thus, the fact that something is said may often be more important than what is said. Of course, this is not always the case but it is important to emphasize that certain messages are important because they serve to bind people together and make them feel a part of a larger group. That they also say something about the outside world may be of only secondary importance.

SOURCES

Introductions to the area of small group communication are plentiful and generally excellent. A particularly useful collection is that of Robert S. Cathcart and Larry A. Samovar, eds., *Small Group Communication: A Reader,* 2d ed. (Dubuque, Iowa: Brown, 1974). Other useful works include Dennis S. Gouran, *Discussion: The Process of Group Decision-Making* (New York: Harper & Row, 1974); B. Aubrey Fisher, *Small Group Decision Making: Communication and the Group Process* (New York: McGraw-Hill, 1974); and Alvin A. Goldberg and Carl E. Larson, *Group Communication: Discussion Processes and Applications* (Englewood Cliffs, N.J.: Prentice-Hall, 1975). In defining the therapeutic group I relied on Charles M. Rossiter, Jr., "Defining 'Therapeutic Communication'," *Journal of Communication* 25 (Summer 1975):127–130.

EXPERIENTIAL VEHICLES

23.1 INDIVIDUAL AND GROUP DECISIONS

The purpose of this experience is to explore the differences between individual and group decisions. The exercise is completed in two parts.

First, each individual should rank the 20 persons presented in the order in which they became president, using 1 for the person who was the earliest president, 2 for the person who was the next earliest, down to 20 for the person who was the most recent president. The 20 presidents listed are the 20 most recent.

Second, after each member has completed his or her ranking, groups of five or six should be formed. Each group should then construct its own ranking, again using 1 for the earliest president down to 20 for the most recent president.

After the group rankings are completed, the correct answers will be announced and each member should compute his or her own error score. In addition, the error score of the group should be computed. Error scores are computed as follows: Subtract the ranking you gave each president from the correct ranking without regard to + or − signs. For example, if you gave Harding a ranking of 13 and he was actually 16 then you would have 3 error points for this entry. Similarly, you would have 3 error points if you had ranked Harding 19 (19 from 16 is 3, disregarding the sign). Compute your individual error score by subtracting your rankings from the correct rankings for all 20 presidents and adding up the error points. This sum constitutes your error score. Compute the error score of the group in the same way. A low score is good (i.e., accurate) and a high score is bad (i.e., inaccurate).

Compare the error score of each individual member with the error score of the group. Did anyone achieve a better individual (i.e., lower) error score than the group? If so, why did this happen? For example, what did this person say when the group was constructing its ranking? Explain in detail.

This brief exercise should illustrate that, generally, group decisions, especially when dealing with questions of fact, are likely to be more accurate than individual decisions.

TWENTY UNITED STATES PRESIDENTS

_____ Jimmy Carter
_____ Harry S Truman
_____ Grover Cleveland
_____ Lyndon B. Johnson
_____ Calvin Coolidge
_____ Theodore Roosevelt
_____ James A. Garfield
_____ Warren G. Harding
_____ John F. Kennedy
_____ Rutherford B. Hayes
_____ Gerald R. Ford
_____ William McKinley
_____ Chester A. Arthur
_____ Benjamin Harrison
_____ Richard M. Nixon
_____ Dwight D. Eisenhower
_____ Franklin D. Roosevelt
_____ William H. Taft
_____ Herbert C. Hoover
_____ Woodrow Wilson

23.2 THE KIDNEY MACHINE*

At St. Francis Hospital in New York, the world famous kidney machine is a social curiosity—it saves lives in a most peculiar way. Some people suffer from a relatively rare kidney disease which 10 years ago was fatal. Today, a very expensive piece of equipment can keep people who have this disease alive but there are not enough opportunities to get at the machine to service everyone who needs it. People suffering from the disease must come once a week and remain hooked to the machine for 20 hours. That means only about 7 people can be served but there are many more people who seek the service.

At present, there are a number of foundations raising money to service more people suffering from the disease. One foundation, for example, has made it possible for any person who has access to the kidney machine to be treated without charge. Money is not an object in treatment. Another foundation is busily trying to raise funds to purchase another machine. They are getting close to their objective, but they are not there yet.

* This Kidney Machine problem has been around for a good number of years. It has been used repeatedly and has been printed in a number of books. Each instructor who uses this problem seems to make a few changes to suit his or her individual purposes and so the version printed here is actually the work of many hands. But the original problem and 95 percent of the writing and, hence, the credit for developing the problem is the work of Russel R. Windes of Queens College and it is used here with his permission.

Medical science can make a very accurate prognosis of who can profit from use of the machine. The medical decision, in fact, is quite easy to make, and once again, the doctors have a long list of people who could remain alive if they had access to the machine. The decision about who is serviced has to be made on *criteria other than medical.* St. Francis Hospital has solved this problem by appointing a volunteer citizens panel, ordinary people like you and me, to decide who should be served and who should not. They make their decisions on simple information. They are given a factual profile of medically eligible candidates and a psychologist's report which tells them something about the personality of potential subjects. The panel then meets, discusses the people, and makes a decision about who should be assigned as a patient to be served by the machine. The panel decides in its own way. They are not observed and they are not questioned. They meet, they talk, they decide, and they report their decision. They never meet the candidates; they do not see their pictures. In fact, the members of the panel are strangers to each other when they first come together, and they do not see each other except when they serve on the panel. They have the following basic criteria to consider:

1. People between the ages of 20 and 40 seem to have the best prognosis for a satisfactory life if served by the machine.
2. There is considerable potential for emotional disturbance in people who are served by the machine. Patients become dependent on the service, and they can become sullen and resentful. Some have been known to become very high handed and authoritarian with the doctors and nurses who supply the service. These people recognize the investment that the medical personnel have in successful treatment.
3. For those selected, money is no object.

Each person should carefully read the profiles of the ten candidates and select the one person to whom he or she would assign the kidney machine. In the event that the person dies before he or she is able to use the machine an alternate should also be selected.

After each person has selected the recipient of the kidney machine, groups of five or six should be formed and should act the part of a hospital board charged with the responsibility of making a final decision. Use any method of decision making that seems reasonable to you.

NORMAN D.

Age 31. Occupation: insurance underwriter. Wife: 30, employed as secretary in the office of the company for which her husband works. Son: 6, student in elementary school. Also caring for Mrs. D. (Norman's mother) who is ill. Holds B.B.A. degree from midwestern university. Family income: $15,000 per year, $9,000 from husband, $4500 from wife, and the remainder made up from social security payments to Mrs. D.

Personality Profile

Mr. D. expresses distress about his lot in life. He told the panel that he had hoped for a lot more when he graduated from college, and described in vivid detail what it is like to be a 9 to 5 man in the office of a large insurance company. He talked about his dreams of going to a warm place to write poetry and showed the panel some of the poetry he has written in his spare time. The panel agrees that the poetry is certainly expressive of his inner disturbance, but none was qualified to determine whether or not Mr. D. shows promise as a writer.

Mr. D. told the panel that he intends to write a daily journal of his feelings from "now until the end," in the hope that it can be published and the proceeds given as a legacy to his wife. He expressed considerable concern about the financial ability of his family, and told the panel several times that "there is no one else to help." He became very involved in a discussion of the plight of the middle-class American, with no one concerned about his welfare, and condemned the government for its activities on behalf of "people who really don't want to work and who just take jobs from people who want to get ahead."

Mr. D. is heavily involved in the activities of a political-religious Protestant church group, and also worked as a campaign worker for George Wallace. He told the panel that he turned to Wallace after the death of Senator Kennedy because "the country needs some kind of change in direction. Any kind of change may help us come to grips with the terrible problems that plague us." Mr. D. asserted that if he were permitted to live he would attempt to implement a cherished dream of entering politics and trying to make some important changes in the world.

CLARK B.

Age 24. Occupation: stevedore. Wife: 17, not employed. Daughter: 6 months. No education shown on record. Not literate. Family income: $8,000 per year.

Personality Profile

Mr. B. came to the area with his wife about six months ago, just before his baby was born. They had been working as migrant farm laborers. When his baby was born he sought and found permanent employment in the area. He hopes that he will be able to work "for a long time, til the child is grown," but he also expresses a dim view of his future since he is "not learned and not able to learn." The panel suggested commitment to a program of vocational training in the local junior college, and an attempt to acquire literacy through the general educational development program, but he did not appear to be interested in either.

Mr. B. spent a good deal of time before the committee inquiring about the availability of charitable services for his wife and child in the event of his death, and made it quite clear to the panel that he did not expect that "someone like me would be picked to stay alive."

CARTER P.

Age 30. Occupation: self-employed owner of public relations firm, freelance author. Wife: 20, employed as night club entertainer. No children. Holds B.S. degree in engineering from eastern university. Family income: Approximately $1 million per year (wife's share is about $55,000).

Personality Profile

Mr. P. is a hard-nosed, almost a stereotype, entrepreneur. He had little financial backing when he graduated from college. He started as a human relations consultant to industry and rapidly built his public relations consulting firm into one of the largest on the coast. He devotes a great deal of time to consultation on issues of community concern and is presently in charge of the governor's campaign against air and water pollution. He points with pride to his filmed commercials which are shown on most TV stations in the area.

He is proud of his wife. They have been married for less than a year. She is a singer in a local night club. He met her in Las Vegas, and he declares with pride that he married her within a week after he met her. They are presently planning the building of a home in a northern mountain area, which they characterize as their retreat. She also appears to support his community efforts and, in addition, she devotes herself to extensive work in fund raising for ghetto community action projects.

Colleagues of Mr. P. regard him as a man of high ethical principles, and they are unanimous in their praise of his skill at his chosen profession. He declares that if permitted to live, he knows he will "have the power to do something that matters in this society." He stipulates as a goal, "the total elimination of air and water pollution in this community to set a model for other communities all over the country to follow." He notified the panel that win, lose, or draw, he will contribute an amount of money equivalent to his care cost to one of the fund raising foundations and also indicated that he has devoted a segment of his firm to consulting in fund raising with the foundations at no cost to them.

JOHN W.

Age 39. Occupation: physician, instructor in medical school. Wife: 35, not employed. Son: 15, student in high school; son: 13, student in junior high school; daughter: 9, student in elementary school; son, 6, patient in school for the mentally retarded. Has B.A. and M.D. degrees. Family income: $54,000 per year contributed entirely by husband.

Personality Profile

John W. has been working with a medical team at the university hospital on a cancer research project. He seems to be very involved in this project and asserts that he is "on the verge of a major breakthrough in cancer detection." His colleagues regard him as a very competent, almost brilliant colleague, but somewhat impatient, volatile and a little difficult when working with groups.

Relations with his wife have not been good recently. Since the birth of their last son, there has been considerable talk of divorce, but both parties agreed that it would be wise to keep the family together in the interest of the children. There is no outward hostility in the home, but parents have little contact with each other. John W. is active in youth activities, particularly in Boy Scouts and Little League. He is a member of a suburban Rotary Club. Subject appears to have little contact with his daughter. Wife is active in various charitable groups and civic organizations and is an officer in the local chapter of the League of Women Voters. Some of John W.'s colleagues allege that he has been active in some John Birch society projects, particularly those opposing medical care programs operated by county welfare.

Mr. W. has received several honors for his medical research. Two years ago he was named by the American Medical Association as one of the ten best research physicians in the country. His advancement in the university has been rapid. He has published ten articles in medical journals, most of which have received a high evaluation.

He seems to be very anxious to be served by the machine. He impresses the panel as being very dedicated to his work, almost to the exclusion of other considerations, and the panel felt that he would be very productive, if permitted to continue.

WARREN G.

Age 36. Occupation: minister. Wife: 34, not employed. Daughter: 6, student in elementary school; son: 3. Has B.A. degree and D.D. from theological seminary. Family income: $35,000 ($20,000 from husband, $15,000 endowment income from wife's legacy).

Personality Profile

Warren G. has been heading his present congregation for six years. He came to it directly from military service (as a chaplain). It was a brand new congregation when he took it over, and he built it steadily from 5 families to its present 470 families. He will preside over the opening of his new church sometime next month.

His congregants regard him as an inspiring leader and point with pride to his skill as a community builder and fund raiser. The congregation has offered him a life contract. His wife is active in religious activities. She works with the congregation women's organization and also serves as a teacher in the afternoon school. She is Norwegian by birth and is raising her two children bilingually. She and the children have spent the last two summers in Norway while her husband enrolled for courses in the Division of American Studies at the local university.

Warren G. appears to be a self contained, almost austere man. He seems to take his illness as a matter of fact, and expressed to the panel a "what will be, will be" attitude. He asked questions about other possible candidates, expressing his willingness to lend his support to those "worth saving," but the committee, of course, keeps this information confidential. He discussed with the committee, at length, the possible merits of having people presently assigned to the kidney machine serve on the selection committee. "These people," he said, "would have greater insight into the kind of person that would profit most from being kept alive—the person who gives the most in return for the gift of life." The panel assured him that there were good reasons why current patients did not serve on the committee.

ARETHA N.

Age 22. Occupation: supervisor of neighborhood community center. Divorced, former husband now in prison. No children. L.A. graduate in social work. Income: $9,000 per year.

Personality Profile

Miss N. is a committed black activist. She functions under the name Selima X. and claims membership in the auxiliary organization to the Black Panthers. Her current program seeks to build psychological strength into black elementary school children. She also directs a program in literacy training for teenagers and young adults in her community center.

She talked at length with the panel about her goals for her people and seems quite selfless in her outlook. She conveys the strength and passion of a real leader of her people, and although she is frankly hostile to white people, she still seems to be in a frame of mind that would permit her to deal honestly with the white community. She explained to the panel that there were a few white people working with her community center that she trusted completely, and knew that they would be the bridge between the races. She sometimes talks of separatism, but most of the time seems to be realistic in her assessment of the future course of the black community.

She seems angry about her physical condition, almost paranoid, as though it was some kind of plot on the part of the community. She refused to meet with the panel twice on the grounds that there were no black psychologists on it. She finally appeared when we augmented our interview team with two of our black colleagues. Before speaking to the rest of us, she cross examined them about their attitudes on racial questions, and did not really submit to interview until she was satisfied with them.

MELVIN K.

Age 19. Student: Junior (philosophy) at local university. Father: age 44, owner of a men's clothing store; mother: deceased for 4 years; sister: 14, student in junior high school; sister: 10, student in elementary school. Scheduled to complete degree in about 18 months. No income.

Personality Profile

Melvin appears to be a sincere young activist. He has been involved in protest demonstrations, including spending one night in jail. He has and expresses deep convictions about the plight of man, particularly about the Vietnam War and about the state of life of inner-city dwellers. He expresses the hope that he might be able to work for an advanced degree in philosophy and work with young people. He also displays some ambiguity when he informs us that his father wants him to be a lawyer, and his mother encouraged him toward a career in medicine. He is currently engaged to a fellow student (age 18), and he informs us that her father is encouraging him to transfer into the school of business so that he can come into his plant after graduation.

Melvin has little contact with his family even though he attends college in his home town. His sisters inform us that he spends little time talking to them, and he seems either to treat them brusquely or not even recognize they are around. He is very intense as he talks about his political commitment, and shows little sense of humor. In commenting about his illness he said, "To die now might be better than to live, considering the direction the world is moving," but in almost the same breath he declared, "I'd hate to be denied my chance to do something about the world. I don't mean to seem arrogant, but maybe I'm the one who will have the idea that works. It would be so frustrating to die before finding out."

The panel feels that Melvin is fairly typical of our best university students. His grades are good, and his professors feel that he will have no trouble getting into graduate school or acquiring an advanced degree. They are prepared to help him because of his intellectual qualities, although they are unanimous in characterizing him as humorless and excessively serious.

PRESTON C.

Age 29. Occupation: garage mechanic. Wife: age 25, employed as legal secretary; son: 6, student in elementary school; son: 3. Withdrew from school in 8th grade and took training in night vocational-technical program (manpower training program). Family income: $14,000 ($8,000 from wife, $6,000 from husband).

Personality Profile

Mr. C. is deeply devoted to his family. He is currently attempting more courses in night school, hoping, he says, "to get enough skill to open my own garage." Although he lists his occupation as "garage mechanic," he does nothing more than lubricate automobiles. His employer is somewhat concerned about his capability to do anything more complicated.

His children are currently in the care of his wife's mother who lives with them. His wife is also working on an advancement program and is taking courses at business college. Mr. C. is involved in some community activities, particularly youth work. He participates in a recreation program at the local comm-center. He says, "I want no part of political activities, I just want to make a good living." He is also active in church work and his minister has no reservations about calling him "a good family man."

The panel is convinced that he is a good and honest man and an example to the people of his neighborhood. The panel is also convinced that he will not rise above the position he holds now, and that there is some potential of trouble between him and his wife as she continues to acquire professional skills.

He appears not to realize the severity of his illness. The panel is sure that he does not recognize this decision as crucial to his survival.

KATHARINE F.

Age 36. Occupation: Executive secretary to president of large corporation. Not married. Graduate of business college. Took special training in legal stenography and computer operation. Income: $17,000 per year.

Personality Profile

Miss F. is the pride of her office. Everyone who works with her talks of her indispensability, and her boss is the first to admit it. "Good women like her are hard to come by!" he declares. Miss F. has a reputation in her office of being a warm, earnest woman, yet she is efficient and keeps things moving. The panel regards her as being a genuine professional at her work.

During her interview with the panel, Miss F. indicated that she had never been very interested in marriage, and confessed to a brief and unsatisfying lesbian relationship while in her early twenties. She dated a bit in high school, but has had no social contact with men since her graduation. She is interested in musical activities, and sings lead with the local choral society. She is currently working on the Christmas production of Handel's "Messiah," which she is directing and singing lead in for the choral society. She has also been active in charitable work and is currently serving as a teacher on her weekends in a headstart program in one of the underprivileged neighborhoods.

She seems to be adjusted to her problem. She indicated to the panel that she has no qualms about dying provided that her body could make some contribution to medical research. She has willed the body to the medical school. At one point she volunteered to withdraw from consideration for a place on the machine in order to "simplify the judgment for the people who are confronted with that horrible task."

LAURA T.

Age 34. Occupation: housewife. Husband: 37, employed as bartender. Son: 16, student in high school; daughter: 15, student in high school; daughter: 13, student in junior high school; daughter: 12, student in junior high school; son: 10, student in elementary school; son: 8, student in elementary school; daughter: 6, student in elementary school; son: 3. Currently pregnant. Has high school diploma. Family income: $11,000 per year provided entirely by husband.

Personality Profile

Mrs. T. states that her goal is to be an "ideal mother." She seems inordinately devoted to her children, but is not terribly perceptive of her husband's problems in providing for a family that size. She appears to have no outside interests or activities outside of the family. She enrolled last year in a flower arranging course, but dropped out half way through because "it took too much time away from my children."

She is terribly distressed by her illness. She has already arranged for her mother-in-law to move in and take care of the children, and she has been spending a good deal of time in bed even though the testimony of the physicians seems to indicate that she need not do this.

She expressed to the panel serious fears about how her family would get on without her, and requested urgently that we take them into account more than her. Our attempts to get information from the children about relations with their mother were thwarted by Mrs. T.'s unwillingness to submit to an in-the-home interview. It is the feeling of the panel that there would be considerable hardship in the home if Mrs. T. were to die.

23.3 THE MILLIONAIRE

You and your fellow committee members, forming a group of five or six, are empowered to give one of the following persons one million dollars. You may not split up the money and may not keep any for yourself or, in fact, make any deals with the person selected. In order to help you make your decision brief profiles of the candidates follow. This is the only information you have or will have about these people. Select the person you would give the money to and also indicate your second choice.

Michael is a white college student majoring in biology with plans to become a doctor. Michael is not particularly bright but is a hard worker. He is extremely poor; his father is dead and his mother is a cleaning woman. Michael would like the money, he says, so that he might use it to help his mother and go to medical school.

Sharon is a white local prostitute with an elementary school education. For years she supported her mother and young son. But recently her mother died and the son was taken away from her by the courts. He now has a good home with a loving mother and father. Sharon would like to get out of her profession and perhaps go back to school. She is now 46 and this makes it difficult earning a living.

James is a black telephone repairman, 22 years old. James is now going to night school to earn his B.A. degree with hopes of becoming a teacher. James wants to use the money to set up a fund for needy students to go to college.

Linda is a white waitress, 37 years old, with no ambitions beyond this. She is married to an alcoholic but does not seem to mind very much; she buys him liquor and they both seem fairly contented. Linda has a daughter, 3, and a son, by a previous marriage.

George is a black Catholic priest who has taken a vow of poverty and so he would have to give the money away. He says that he will give it to the poor migrant workers in the southwest. George is 75 years old and has been a priest for 48 years.

Martha is a medical doctor working on cancer research. She said that she would use the money to further this research which she claims has great promise. Martha is wealthy in her own right having inherited a fortune from her parents some ten years ago. She has not yet used any of this money to further her research.

Ann is a white lesbian working for a fairly active lesbian organization without pay. Ann is 34 and has been with the same woman for the last 10 years. She would give the money to the organization for which she is now working.

Peter is a black young child of three years old. He does not know what a million dollars is but if awarded to him it would be put in a trust fund so that he would get it at 21. Peter's parents are dead and he is living with his grandmother.

Carl is a white businessman of 38 years of age. He has made a fortune in the stock market and says that he will turn this million dollars into 10 million within a year. His past experience seems to indicate that he will be able to do this. Carl is married with four children, ranging in age from 6 months to 17 years.

Frances is a white salesperson at the local variety store. Frances suffers from cerebral palsy and although this makes it difficult for her to work she insists on working rather than receiving some form of state or federal assistance. Frances is 40 years old and single.

23.4 SMALL GROUP COMMUNICATION PATTERNS

In this exercise we attempt to explore the efficiency and satisfaction of communication in different channel patterns.

Five groups of equal numbers are formed according to the following patterns:

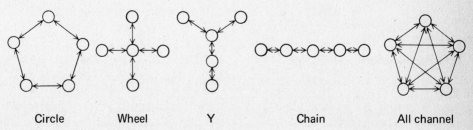

Circle   Wheel   Y   Chain   All channel

Arrows connecting two individuals indicate that communication may take place between them. Individuals not connected by arrows may not communicate directly but only indirectly through the individual(s) with whom they are connected.

The problem is the same for all groups. Each group is to reach *unanimous* agreement on how many square are contained in the following diagram:

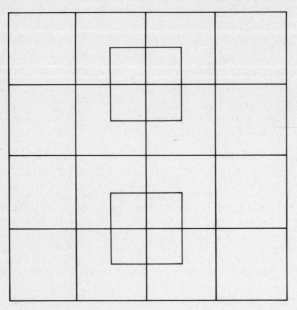

All messages are to be written on individual pieces of paper. Members may pass to other members only those messages that they themselves have written. Thus, if members receive a message they wish to pass on to another member, they must rewrite the message.

Efficiency and Satisfaction Indexes

The efficiency of the groups should be indexed in at least two ways. First, the time necessary for completion should be carefully noted. Second, the messages sent should be saved and counted. Efficiency will thus be indexed by the time it took to arrive at the correct answer and by the number of messages needed for communicating.

The satisfaction of the group members should be indexed by responses on the following scales.

Task Participation

Rate your participation in the task on the following scales:

interesting ____ : ____ : ____ : ____ : ____ : ____ : ____ boring
enjoyable ____ : ____ : ____ : ____ : ____ : ____ : ____ unenjoyable
dynamic ____ : ____ : ____ : ____ : ____ : ____ : ____ static
useful ____ : ____ : ____ : ____ : ____ : ____ : ____ useless
gocd ____ : ____ : ____ : ____ : ____ : ____ : ____ bad

Compute your mean score for these scales as follows: 1) number the scales from 7 to 1 from left to right; 2) total the scores from all five scales (this number should range from 5 to 35), and 3) divide by five to get your mean score.

Each group should then compute the group mean score by totaling the individual mean scores and dividing the sum by the number of participants.

Efficiency and Satisfaction Scores

| | Efficiency | | Satisfaction |
Channel Patterns	Time	Number of messages	Group mean scores
circle	_____	_____	_____
wheel	_____	_____	_____
"Y"	_____	_____	_____
chain	_____	_____	_____
all channel	_____	_____	_____

For Discussion

1. On what basis do you account for the differences in efficiency and satisfaction among the groups?
2. Are there realistic counterparts to these five communication structures? Do we find these communication structures and patterns in the "real world?" Where? What are some of the consequences of these various communication patterns?
3. How does structure influence function? Examine your own group situation and consider how the structure of the group (the positioning of the members for example) influenced the functions the members played. Does this have a realistic counterpart? In what ways do you function differently as a result of the structure in which you find yourself?
4. What implications would you be willing to draw from this experience for improved communication in the classroom?

Box 15A
SOLUTION TO MATCHSTICK PROBLEM

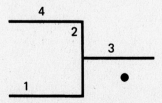

To solve the matchstick problem, *slide* match 2 up so that the end of it touches the end of match 1. Then, move match 4 so that it is above and parallel to match 1. Match 3 thus becomes the handle and the dirt is out of the shovel.

UNIT 24

Members and Leaders in Small Group Communication

24.1 Decision Making

Members' Roles in Small Group Communication
Leaders' Roles in Small Group Communication
Leadership Styles

24.2 Analyzing Leadership Styles

LEARNING GOALS

After completing this unit, you should be able to:

1. identify and define the three major types of member roles
2. provide at least two examples of each of the three major types of member roles
3. identify and explain at least four functions of leaders in small group communication
4. identify and define the three leadership styles
5. state at least one occasion under which each of the three leadership styles would be appropriate

EXPERIENTIAL VEHICLE

24.1 DECISION MAKING

Before beginning this unit, respond to the following cases and questions. Note the decision and one alternative by circling the appropriate number of the alternative.

Case A: The Interview

Mary is a graduating senior majoring in mass communication. Through some error she has scheduled two interviews for the same time; neither can be changed and neither can be made up at another time. She can only go to one interview.

One interview is with CBS for a job as assistant to the producer of an important TV series. The job pays $20,000 to start with promise of rapid advancement. The problem is that there are many applicants for this job and a recent college graduate with no experience stands only a fair chance of landing the job.

The second interview is with a local radio station as assistant to the producer of a mediocre radio show. The job pays $10,000 to start and goes up to $14,000 or $15,000. There are few applicants for this job; Mary's chances of landing this job are excellent.

What should Mary do?

1. Definitely go to the interview with CBS
2. Probably go to the interview with CBS
3. Probably go to the interview with the radio station
4. Definitely go to the interview with the radio station

Case B: The Investment

Frank has $5,000 to invest. This $5,000 is extra money; he does not need this for essentials. Frank is trying to decide between two businesses. Each business wants the $5,000 for a period of six months.

The first business is a new electronics store. The owner of the store thinks that she will be able to turn the $5,000 into $20,000 or $25,000 within the six-month period. However, since this is a new venture there is also the possibility that the money will be lost entirely if the business fails.

The second business is an established grocery store that wants to expand. The owner thinks that he will be able to pay Frank back $6,500 to $7,500 within the six-month period. Since the business is an already established one there is little possibility that the money would be lost.

What should Frank do?

1. Definitely invest in the electronics store
2. Probably invest in the electronics store
3. Probably invest in the grocery store
4. Definitely invest in the grocery store

Case C: The Grade

Carl is a student at Cicero College. He has a choice to take either of two teachers for cultural anthropology. Their grading procedures, however, are extremely different although their teaching is very similar.

Professor Jones gives only two grades. If you are in the top 50 percent you get an *A* but if you are in the bottom 50 percent you get an *F*.

Professor Smith follows the usual grading pattern where grades approximate a bell shaped curve with about 5 percent *A*'s, 15 percent *B*'s, 60 percent *C*'s, 15 percent *D*'s, and 5 percent *F*'s.

Which teacher should Carl take?

1. Definitely take Professor Jones
2. Probably take Professor Jones
3. Probably take Professor Smith
4. Definitely take Professor Smith

After each person has noted his or her alternatives the class should be divided into small groups of five or six persons. The groups should discuss each of the three cases in turn, devoting about five minutes to each case. After all cases are discussed, each person should individually reread the cases and again make decisions for each one. After these second decisions have been made, each person should read Box 17, "Risky Shift," in the following unit.

After reading the box on the risky-shift, record your decisions on the Decision Scores form. Write the number of your decisions (1–4) in the spaces provided.

Note that the lower the numbers of your choices, the greater the risk you were willing to have the individual take. According to the theory of the risky-shift, your decisions should have been more risky after your discussions, that is, the numbers for the second decision should be lower than the numbers for the first decision.

Next, respond to the following questions:

1. Did the risky-shift phenomenon manifest itself in these cases? If so, why? If not, why not?
2. Is your behavior in making individual decisions and in making decisions

after small group communication similar to that displayed in this exercise? Explain.

3. What factors do you feel account for the willingness to take the more risky position after the group discussion?

4. In Box 17 four major explanations for the risky-shift are discussed: (1) that risk is highly valued in certain roles, (2) that risk taking is a cultural value, (3) that the risky individual is the most influential in the group, and (4) that individual responsibility is diffused in the small group. Which of these explanations seems the best explanation for your individual behavior and for the behavior of the members of the group in which you participated?

DECISION SCORES

	First decision	Second decision
Case A		
Case B		
Case C		

In this unit, we consider the roles or functions of small group members and leaders. Each person may well serve all of these roles throughout his or her membership in various groups. More often, however, people fall into particular roles that they fulfill in every group in which they participate whether they wish to or not, whether the roles are productive or not. By gaining insight into the various roles of both members and leaders we will be in a better position to analyze our own small group behavior and to change it if we wish.

MEMBERS' ROLES IN SMALL GROUP COMMUNICATION

To function as a member (rather than as a leader) in a small group communication situation seems so natural that some considerations of the small group fail to devote any attention to members even though considerable time is spent on leaders and leadership. But obviously the members' roles are by far the more important. Furthermore, members and leaders are not so different from each other; members serve many of the functions normally considered to be in the province of leaders and leaders serve many of the functions normally considered the province of members.

Kenneth Benne and Paul Sheats (1948) proposed a classification of the roles of members in small group communication that seems to serve as the best overview of this important topic even though it is some 30 years old. Benne and Sheats classify member roles or functions into three general classes: group task roles, group building and maintenance roles, and individual roles. Each of these general functions may be served by different specific roles.

Group Task Roles

Twelve specific roles are distinguished as group task roles. The *initiator-contributor* presents new ideas or new perspectives on old ideas. He or she may suggest new goals, a new definition of the problem, or perhaps new procedures or organizational strategies. The *information* seeker asks for facts and opinions; this person attempts to secure clarification of the issues being discussed. The *opinion seeker* attempts to discover the values underlying the group's task. The *information giver* presents facts and opinions to the group members while the *opinion giver* presents values and opinions and attempts to spell out what the values of the group should be. The *elaborator* gives examples and tries to work out possible solutions, trying to build on what others have said. The *coordinator* spells out relationships among ideas and suggested solutions. The coordinator also coordinates the activities of the different members. The individual serving the *orienter* function summarizes what has been said and addresses himself or herself to the direction the group is taking as well as to the digressions of the group members. He or she attempts to provide the group members with a clear picture of where they are going. The *evaluator-critic* evaluates the groups decisions or proposed solutions. This person questions the logic or the practicality of the suggestions and thus provides the group with both positive and negative feedback on their various decisions and solutions. The *energizer* stimulates the group to greater activity while the *procedural-technician* takes care of the various mechanical duties such as distributing group materials and arranging the seating. Lastly, the *recorder* writes down the activities of the group, their suggestions and their decisions. The recorder serves as the memory of the group.

Group-Building and Maintenance Roles

Group-building and maintenance roles are broken down into seven specific roles. The *encourager* supplies members with positive reinforcement in terms of social approval or praise for its ideas. This person provides the group with understanding and acceptance. The *harmonizer* mediates the various differences between group members. The *compromiser* attempts to resolve conflict between his or her ideas and those of others. The compromiser will offer a compromise by either changing his or her position half way or even by giving up his or her initial position. The *gatekeeper-expediter* keeps the channels of communication open by reinforcing the efforts of others. The gatekeeper-expediter may propose to hear from a member who has not yet spoken or propose to limit the length or frequency of the contributions from the members. The *standard setter, or ego ideal,* sets or proposes standards pertaining to

Box 16
GROUPTHINK

After examining the decisions and the decision-making processes of large government organizations: the catastrophic decisions of the Bay of Pigs and Pearl Harbor; the decision processes that went into the development of the Marshall Plan; and President Kennedy's handling of the Cuban missile crisis, Irving Janis developed a theory he calls "groupthink." Groupthink, according to Janis (1971, p. 43), may be defined as "the mode of thinking that persons engage in when *concurrence seeking* becomes so dominant in a cohesive ingroup that it tends to override realistic appraisal of alternative courses of action." The term itself is meant to signal a "deterioration in mental efficiency, reality testing, and moral judgments as a result of group pressures."

There are many specific behaviors of the group members that may be singled out as characteristic of groupthink. One of the most significant behaviors is that the group limits its discussion of possible alternatives to only a small range. It generally does not consider other possibilities as alternatives. Once the group has made a decision it does not reexamine its decisions even when there are indications of possible dangers. Little time is spent in discussing the reasons why certain of the initial alternatives were in fact rejected. For example, if high cost led the group to reject a certain alternative, the group members will devote little time, if any, to the ways in which the cost may be reduced. Similarly, the group members make little effort to obtain expert information even from people within their own organization.

The group members are extremely selective in the information they consider seriously. Facts and opinions contrary to the position of the group are generally ignored while those facts and opinions that support the position of the group are welcomed. The group members generally limit themselves to the one decision or one plan. They fail to discuss alternative decisions or plans in the event that their initial decision fails or if it should encounter problems on the way to implementation.

The following symptoms should help in recognizing the existence of groupthink in the groups we observe or in which we participate.

1. Group members think the group and its members are invulnerable to dangers.
2. Members create rationalizations to avoid dealing directly with warnings or threats.
3. Group members believe their group is moral.
4. Those opposed to the group are perceived in simplistic stereotyped ways.
5. Group pressure is put on any member who expresses doubts or questions the group's arguments or proposals.
6. Group members censor their own doubts.
7. Group members believe all members are in unanimous agreement whether such agreement is stated or not.
8. Group members emerge whose function it is to guard the information that gets to other members of the group especially when such information may create diversity of opinion.

Box 17
RISKY-SHIFT PHENOMENON

Many of our everyday decisions involve some degree of risk. Given two alternatives, one usually involves more risk than the other and the amount of risk we are willing to take will play some part in our decision-making process. A most interesting phenomenon concerning risk has emerged from research on small group communication and has come to be called the *risky-shift phenomenon.* Generally, it has been found that decisions reached after discussion are riskier than decisions reached before discussion. Thus, if we have to choose between two alternatives we would be more apt to choose the riskier alternative after discussion than before. It has also been found that decisions are more risky in group-centered rather than in leader-centered groups.

Although the procedures to investigate the risky shift have varied greatly from one researcher to another, the general procedure is to present participants with a number of cases involving a decision between a safe but relatively unattractive alternative and a risky but relatively attractive alternative. For example, M. A. Wallach, N. Kogan, and D. J. Bem (1962, p. 77) used the following case: "An electrical engineer may stick with his present job at a modest but adequate salary, or may take a new job offering considerably more money but no long-term security." The subjects would then indicate their decisions individually and then discuss the case in a small group. After the discussion each subject would indicate his or her decision a second time. In terms of our example, before discussion the engineer would be advised to stick with his present job but after discussion to take the job offering the higher salary but less security.

Research has indicated that the risky-shift phenomenon seems to hold for both sexes, for all subject areas, and for both hypothetical and real situations. The inevitable question that arises is, Why does this happen?

Some possibilities are: (1) risk is highly valued in certain roles; (2) taking risks is a cultural (American?) value and people raise their status by taking risks; (3) the risky individual is the most influential member of a group and therefore succeeds in influencing other group members in the direction of greater risk taking; and (4) individual responsibility is diffused in a group whereas when alone the responsibility is the individual's own.

the functioning of the group or to their solutions. The group *observer and commentator* keeps a record of the group process and uses this in the group's evaluation of itself. Lastly, the *follower* goes along with the members of the group. He or she passively accepts the ideas of others and functions more as an audience for the other members than as an active member.

Individual Roles

Eight specific types are considered under individual roles. The *aggressor* expresses negative evaluation of the actions or feelings of the group members. The aggressor attacks the group or the problem being considered. The *blocker* provides negative feedback, is disagreeable, and opposes other members or suggestions regardless of whether he or she has reasonable grounds for doing so or not. The *recognition seeker* attempts to have attention focused on himself or herself and achieves this by boasting and talking about his or her own accomplishments rather than the task at hand. The *self-confessor* expresses his or her own feelings and personal perspectives rather than focusing on the group. The *playboy* (and *playgirl*) possesses all the negative features we think of when we talk of playboys and playgirls. This person is cynical and plays around without any regard for the group process. The *dominator* tries to run the group or the group members. This person may attempt to achieve this by pulling status, by flattering members of the group, or simply by acting the role of the boss. The *help seeker* expresses insecurity or confusion or deprecates himself or herself and thereby attempts to make the other members sympathetic toward him or her. Lastly, the *special interest pleader* disregards the specific goals of the group and pleads the case of some special group whether it is labor or management, students or faculty, miners or farmers, or of some minority group. To this person all problems are seen as opportunities to plead for a special interest.

LEADERS' ROLES IN SMALL GROUP COMMUNICATION

In the relatively formal small group situations such as politicians planning a campaign strategy, advertisers discussing a campaign, teachers considering educational methods, or among any people gathered together for a purpose, the leader has a number of specific functions that should be pointed out.

These several functions are not the exclusive property of the leader; rather they are functions that when performed are performed by a person serving a leadership role. Put differently, it is more important that these functions be served than who serves them. In situations where a specific leader is appointed or exists by virtue of some position or prior agreement, these functions are generally expected to be performed by him or her. It is important to note that leadership functions are performed best when they are performed unobtrusively—when they are performed in a nonobvious, natural manner. Leaders serve six major functions.

1. Activate the Group Interaction

In many situations the group needs no encouragement to interact. Certainly this is true of most groups with definite goals and an urgency about their mission. On the other hand, there are many groups which for one reason or another need some proding, some stimulation to interact. Perhaps the group is newly formed and the members feel a bit uneasy with each other. Here the leader serves an important function by stimulating the members to interact. It is also important to note that this function needs to be served when the individuals of a group are acting as individuals rather than as a group. This is often the case in classroom situations when some members of a class know each other from other classes or perhaps when they graduated from the same high school. These students may stick together and function as subgroups rather than as equal members of the large groups. In this case the leader must do something to make the members recognize that they are part of a group rather than of a subgroup or pair.

2. Maintain Effective Interaction Throughout

Even after the group is stimulated to group interaction it is necessary for the leader to see that the members maintain effective interaction throughout the discussion and throughout the membership. Discussions have a way of dragging after the preliminaries are over and before the meat of the problem is gotten to. When this happens it is necessary for the leader to again prod the group to effective interaction. Also, interaction is seldom shared by all members equally, but this in itself does not create problems. Problems are created, however, when this disproportionate participation is extreme or when members feel an uneasiness about entering the group interaction.

3. Keep Members on the Track

The leader should recognize that most individuals are relatively egocentric and have interests and concerns that are unique to them. Because of this, each individual will tend to wander off the track a bit. It is the leader's task to keep all members on the track—perhaps by asking relevant questions, by interjecting internal summaries as the group goes along, or perhaps by providing suitable transitions so that the relationship of an issue just discussed to one about to be considered is made clear.

4. Ensure Member Satisfaction

The leader should recognize that all members have different psychological needs and wants and many people enter groups because of these needs and wants. Even though a group may, for example, deal with political issues, the various members may have come together for reasons that are more psychological than political or intellectual. If a group such as this is to be effective, it must not only meet the surface purposes of the group (in this case political) but also the underlying or psychological purposes that motivated many of the members to come together in the first place.

One sure way to ignore these needs is for the leader to insist that the group members do nothing that is not directly related to the surface purposes of the group. Digressions, assuming that they are not extremely frequent or overly long, are significant parts of the small group communication process and should be recognized as such.

5. Encourage Ongoing Evaluation and Improvement

All groups will encounter obstacles as they attempt to solve a problem, reach a decision, or generate ideas. No group is totally effective. All groups have room for improvement. This, of course, is an obvious statement. What is not so obvious is that it is the responsibility of the group members (encouraged by the leader) to seek out these obstacles and to attempt to improve the process of group interaction. This is an extremely important but an extremely difficult task for any individual or group to undertake. No one wants to confront their shortcomings or be told that they are not functioning as effectively as they might. And yet, if the group is to improve it must focus some attention on itself, and along wtih attempting to solve some external problem must attempt to solve its own internal problems as well.

6. Prepare the Group Members for the Discussion

Groups form gradually and need to be eased into any discussion that is meaningful. It is the function of the leader to prepare the group members for the discussion and this involves both preparing the members for the small group interaction as well as for the discussion of a specific issue or problem.

Diverse members should not be expected to just sit down and discuss a

---

Box 18
NINE CENTRAL PERSONS

There are many approaches to examining and describing leaders and leadership. One of the most interesting is the description based on the concept of a central person—the person around whom the group processes take place. Donald W. Calhoun distinguishes nine such central persons.

The *machine* person is supported by "the machine"—whether political, corporate, or educational—and exchanges patronage for support.
The *ideologist* questions the status quo with new ideas that are his or her specialty.
The *organizer* moves in to structure things after change has been initiated.
The *creative innovator* possesses the qualities of the organizer but keeps an eye toward change.
The *father figure* demonstrates both the knowledge and the concern of the real father.
The *courageous sibling* challenges parental authority; this is the child who defies the existing powers.
The *romantic object* is physically attractive, projecting obvious sexuality to those who gather around.
The *savior*, like the courageous sibling, questions authority but the savior fights for everyone.
The *saint* gives of himself or herself, denying the world of material gain.

Source: Adapted from Donald W. Calhoun, *Persons-in-Groups. A Humanistic Social Psychology* (New York: Harper & Row, 1976), pp. 137–145.

problem without becoming familiar with each other at least superficially. Similarly, if the members are to discuss a specific problem it is necessary that a proper briefing be introduced. Perhaps materials need to be distributed to group members before the actual discussion or perhaps members need to be instructed to read certain materials or view a particular film or television show. Whatever the prediscussion preparations, it should be organized and coordinated by the leader.

These are just a few functions generally considered to be the responsibility of the leader. Obviously there are additional tasks of the leader that are unique to each individual situation. These tasks will become apparent as the group interacts and as the members develop greater skill in the process of small group interaction. The few functions presented here should provide some initial guidance in conducting and leading an effective small group discussion.

LEADERSHIP STYLES

The six functions of the leader may be served in various different ways or under different leadership styles. Generally three types of leadership are distinguished: laissez-faire, democratic, and authoritarian (Figure 24.1). Each type actually designates a class of leadership within which there is considerable variation. The laissez-faire and the democratic leaders are at times difficult to distinguish as are the democratic and the autocratic. And yet, there is enough difference among the styles—at least in their pure forms—to warrant our considering them as different approaches to leadership. In the real world these three styles inevitably appear in varied forms.

Laissez-Faire

The laissez-faire leader allows the group to develop and progress on its own and even allows it to make its own mistakes. This leader gives up or denies any real leadership authority and so this type may well be called a nonleadership style rather than a leadership style. The laissez-faire "leader" does an-

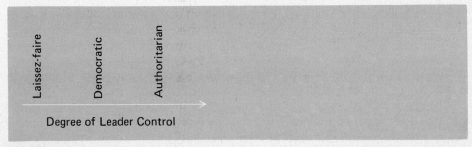

Figure 24.1
A Continuum of Leadership Styles

swer questions or provides relevant information but he or she does this only when specifically asked. This leader gives little if any reinforcement to the group members; at the same time this leader does not punish either and so is nonthreatening. This leader takes no initiative in directing or suggesting alternative courses of action.

Democratic Leader

The democratic leader provides direction but allows the group to develop and progress the way the members wish. The group members are encouraged to determine group goals and group procedures. The democratic leader stimulates self-direction and self-actualization of the group members. Unlike the laissez-faire leader the democratic leader does give the members reinforcement and does contribute suggestions for direction and alternative courses of action. Always, however, this leader allows the group to make its own decisions.

Authoritarian Leader

The authoritarian leader is the opposite of the laissez-faire leader. This leader determines the group policies or makes decisions without consulting or securing agreement from the group members. This leader is impersonal and communication goes to the leader and from the leader but rarely from member to member. This leader attempts to minimize intragroup communication. In this way the leader's role becomes even more important.

The authoritarian leader assumes the greatest responsibility for the progress of the group and wants no interference from group members. This person is concerned with getting the group to accept his or her decisions. It should be noted that this leader often satisfies the group's psychological needs; he or she rewards and punishes the group much like a parent does. And like a parent the leader concentrates responsibility on himself or herself.

A number of important studies have been conducted to examine the relative effectiveness of these various leadership styles. In one study (Ralph White and Ronald Lippett) groups of boys were led by the three different styles. It was found that in the lassez-faire group, the discussion was member-centered but the boys were inefficient. In the democratic group, cohesiveness was greatest as was member satisfaction. The work completed was less than that produced by the authoritarian group but it was judged to be of higher quality. In the authoritarian group the boys were most productive and efficient. However, the morale and satisfaction were lower than in the democratic group. Marvin Shaw found that a gorup led by an authoritarian leader made fewer errors, took less time, and communicated with fewer messages in solving mathematical problems than the democratic group.

Cecil Gibb (1969, p. 259), in summarizing the results of a series of studies on democratic as opposed to authoritarian leadership, notes that the authoritarian (compared to the democratic) group produced "(1) a greater quantity of work, but (2) less work motivation and (3) less originality in work; (4) a greater amount of aggressiveness expressed both toward the leader and other group members; (5) more suppressed discontent; (6) more dependent and submissive behavior; (7) less friendliness in the group; and (8) less 'group mindedness.' "

Each of these leadership styles has its place and we should not consider one style superior to the others. Each is appropriate for a different purpose. In a social group at a friends house any leadership other than laissez-faire would be difficult to tolerate. But as Cecil Gibb notes, when speed and efficiency are paramount, authoritarian leadership seems the most appropriate. When all members are about equal in their knowledge of the topic or when the members are very concerned with their individual rights then the democratic leader seems the most appropriate.

SOURCES

On members' roles see Kenneth D. Benne and Paul Sheats, "Functional Roles of Group Members," *Journal of Social Issues* 4 (1948):41–49. On leadership roles see any of the references noted in Unit 23. On styles of leadership see the seminal study by Ralph White and Ronald Lippitt, *Autocracy and Democracy* (New York: Harper & Row, 1960). Also see Marvin E. Shaw, "A Comparison of Two Types of Leadership in Various Communication Nets," *Journal of Abnormal and Social Psychology* 50 (1955):127–134, and J. F. Sargent and G. R. Miller, "Some Differences in Certain Communication Behaviors of Autocratic and Democratic Leaders," *Journal of Communication* 21 (1971):233–252. Perhaps the single best source on leadership is Cecil A. Gibb's "Leadership," in G. Lindsey and E. Aronson, eds., *The Handbook of Social Psychology,* 2d ed., vol. 4 (Reading, Mass.: Addison-Wesley, 1969), pp. 205–282.

For groupthink see the works of Irving Janis. A useful overview is provided in his "Groupthink," *Psychology Today* 5 (November 1971): 43–46, 74–76. A more detailed account is presented in Janis' "Groupthink among Policy Makers," in *Sanctions for Evil,* N. Sanford and C. Comstock, eds. (San Francisco: Jossey-Bass, 1971). Janis's *Victims of Groupthink: A Psychological Study of Foreign Policy Decisions and Fiascoes* (Boston: Houghton Mifflin, 1972) presents the most thorough discussion.

For the risky shift phenomenon see Marvin Shaw, *Group Dynamics: The Psychology of Small Group Behavior* (New York: McGraw-Hill, 1971), for a general overview, and Roger Brown, *Social Psychology* (New York: Free Press, 1965) for some interesting insights into this phenomenon. The study cited by M. A. Wallach, N. Kogan, and D. J. Bem was titled "Group Influence on Individual Risk Taking," *Journal of Abnormal and Social Psychology* 65 (1962):75–86. D. Cartwright, "Determinants of Scientific Progress: The Case of Research on the Risky Shift," *American Psychologist* 28(1973):222–231, provides an excellent review and analysis of the area.

EXPERIENTIAL VEHICLE

24.2 ANALYZING LEADERSHIP STYLES

Divide the class into six groups of equal size. Two groups should be assigned a laissez-faire leader, two groups an authoritarian leader, and two groups a democratic leader. All groups should be given the same three problems presented below. The groups should discuss the problems in the order given and should complete the first problem before going on to the next one.

Each group should discuss the problem and attempt to reach a decision regarding the solution. When any group has arrived at a unanimous solution they should raise their hands and the instructor will tell them only if their answer is correct or incorrect. If the answer is correct then the time it took to arrive at that answer should be recorded and the group should go on to the next problem. Be sure to note starting time so that total time for completion may be accurately recorded. If the answer is incorrect the group should be so informed and they should continue discussing the problem until they reach the correct solution. The times for completion should be recorded on the Time Chart. In addition, general discussion should center on the questions following the Time Chart.

Problem 1

A man bought a horse for $70 and sold it for $80. He then bought the horse back for $90 but soon sold it again for $100. How much money did the man make or lose or did he break even in his horse trading?

Problem 2

Construct Figure B from Figure A by moving not more than three circles.

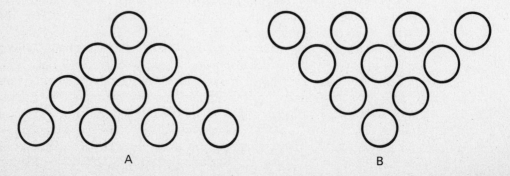

A   B

Problem 3

Draw four straight lines without removing pencil from page and without crossing over (i.e., retracing) lines to connect all nine dots.

. . .
. . .
. . .

TIME CHART   *GREAT DIRECTION*   *MIDDLE GROUND EQUAL*

	Laissez-faire leader		Authoritarian leader		Democratic leader	
	Group 1	Group 2	Group 1	Group 2	Group 1	Group 2
Problem 1						
Problem 2						
Problem 3						

Questions for Discussion

1. Did the leaders perform according to those characteristics noted in the text? How might their performances have been improved? Be as specific as possible.
2. Describe any differences in time among the three types of leadership. Among which types of leadership were the differences greatest? Would these same differences manifest themselves in real-life small group communication situations? Explain.
3. What are the implications of the differences in the time it took the groups to solve the problems? How do you account for these differences?
4. Would these same time differences manifest themselves if the problems did not have a definite answer, for example, if they had been ethical issues requiring group agreement? Explain.
5. How did the members of the different groups enjoy the task? That is, was there a difference in the degree of satisfaction with the task among the members of the different groups? How do you account for the differences?
6. How did the leaders of the different groups enjoy the task? Were there differences in the degree of satisfaction with the task among the leaders of the different groups? If so, how do you account for the differences?

UNIT 25
Small Group Analysis and Evaluation

Interaction Process Analysis
Interaction Diagrams
Rating Scales
Productivity and Satisfaction Indexes

LEARNING GOALS

After completing this unit, you should be able to:

1. explain the function(s) of interaction process analysis
2. identify the four main categories for messages in interaction process analysis
3. utilize interaction process analysis to analyze the group's messages
4. identify the purposes of interaction diagrams
5. identify at least two ways that messages can be recorded using interaction diagrams
6. utilize interaction diagrams to analyze groups process
7. construct an original rating scale to evaluate some aspect of group process
8. utilize a rating scale to evaluate a group's performance
9. construct an original satisfaction scale to evaluate the satisfaction of the group members
10. utilize a productivity index to evaluate the group's end product

As already illustrated, small group communication is an extremely complex process. And one of the best ways to further our insight into this process is to stand back a bit and attempt to analyze and evaluate it. In this unit we present four general approaches to the analysis of small group interaction: interaction process analysis, interaction diagrams, rating scales, and productivity and satisfaction indexes. Each of these methods of analysis provides us with a slightly different perspective on the small group communication act.

INTERACTION PROCESS ANALYSIS

Perhaps the most widely used system of analysis is that proposed by Robert Bales known as interaction process analysis, or IPA. *Interaction process analysis* is a form of content analysis, a method that classifies messages into four general categories: (1) social-emotional positive, (2) social-emotional negative, (3) attempted answers, and (4) questions.

Each of these four areas contains three subdivisions giving us a total of twelve categories. It is assumed that all the messages occurring in small groups may be classified into one of these twelve categories:

Social-Emotional Positive

    to show solidarity
    to show tension release
    to show agreement

Social-Emotional Negative

> to show disagreement
> to show tension
> to show antagonism

Attempted Answers

> to give suggestions
> to give opinions
> to give information

Questions

> to ask for suggestions
> to ask for opinions
> to ask for information

Note that the categories under social-emotional positive are the natural opposites of those under social-emotional negative, and those under attempted answers are the natural opposites of those under questions. With even brief experience in using this system, one can categorize the various messages with relative ease.

Generally, charts are constructed to record the type and frequency of messages communicated in the small group. A typical chart would look something like that presented in Figure 25.1.

From this chart, which represents the messages communicated in a relatively short period of time, we can already see that certain members are taking on various roles. Grace seems negative; she is high on antagonism, tension, and disagreement. Linda seems particularly positive with numerous messages showing solidarity and asking for suggestions and opinions. Helen, on the other hand, seems particularly tense but does nothing to relieve the tension or to display positive feelings. We can make more significant observations after observing a longer period of interaction.

INTERACTION DIAGRAMS

Interaction diagrams are particularly useful for recording the number of messages addressed to one person from another. They enable us to quantify who speaks to whom. There are various different ways to draw these interaction diagrams. Perhaps the most popular method is to represent each member by a circle and draw arrows from the source to the receiver, as in Figure 25.2. The arrows drawn to "group" indicate that the comments were addressed to all members of the group.

Alternatively we might begin with a model of the group with arrows connecting each possible dyad and simply mark off each comment on the appropriate line, as illustrated in Figure 25.3.

	Judy	Helen	Linda	Grace	Rhoda	Diane
Shows solidarity	/		卌 /			/
Shows tension release						
Shows agreement	///		//			//
Shows antagonism				卌 //		
Shows tension		卌		///		
Shows disagreement	///			卌		
Gives suggestions				//	///	
Gives opinions		//				
Gives information	///			/		
Asks for suggestions			////			卌
Asks for opinions			///			
Asks for information	卌					

Figure 25.1
Interaction Process Analysis Form

In each of these cases we have a record of who spoke to whom and how often. As can be appreciated, the diagrams can become pretty messy if there is much communication or if there are many members. Therefore an interaction diagram of the form presented in Figure 25.4 seems more workable. With slash marks we can easily record the various messages. Viewing the names on the left as the sources and those at the top as receivers, we can easily separate, for example, those messages from Joe to Helen (second column, top row) from those from Helen to Joe (first column, second row). Also included is a slot for those messages addressed to the group as a whole.

This model seems the most practical of the three since it allows for a clear recording of the messages regardless of how many members there are or how many messages are communicated.

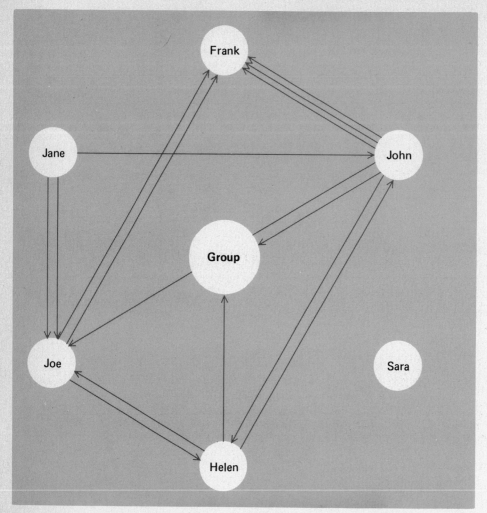

Figure 25.2
Interaction Diagram—I

RATING SCALES

Ratings scales are by far the easiest of all the methods of evaluation. Rating scales may be completed by the small group members themselves or by outside observers.

The scales may focus on any of the numerous variables present in small group communication. For example, we might construct a scale to focus on a communication pattern, an interpersonal relationship, adherence to some set of rules or principles, and any of the numerous aspects of small group process.

One sample of such a scale follows.

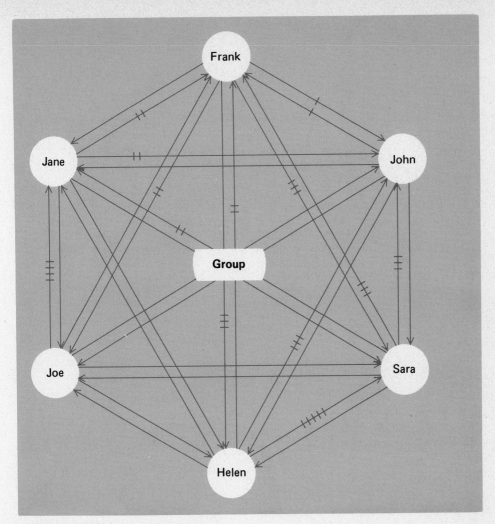

Figure 25.3
Interaction Diagram—II

This discussion was:

interesting	____ : ____ : ____ : ____ : ____ : ____	uninteresting
clear	____ : ____ : ____ : ____ : ____ : ____	unclear
purposeful	____ : ____ : ____ : ____ : ____ : ____	nonpurposeful
optimistic	____ : ____ : ____ : ____ : ____ : ____	pessimistic
shared equally by all members	____ : ____ : ____ : ____ : ____ : ____	monopolized by one or a few members

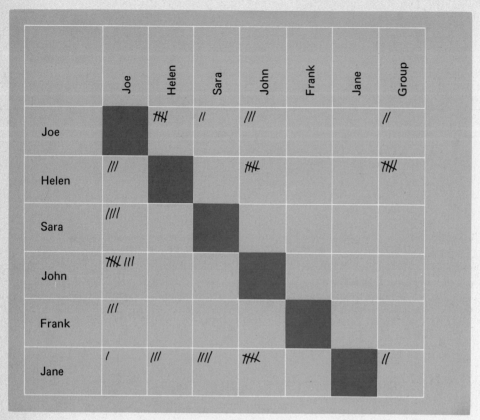

Figure 25.4
Communication Matrix for Recording Interactions

PRODUCTIVITY AND SATISFACTION INDEXES

Productivity and satisfaction indexes may be used to evaluate (1) the quantity and/or quality of the end product of the small group, (2) the time it took the group to reach the solution or end product, and (3) the satisfaction the group members feel as a result of the group process and/or the end product.

It should be recognized that quality, and even some aspects of quantity, are extremely difficult to measure. Further, by focusing on the end product we are deemphasizing the processes that went on among the members to achieve that particular end. Satisfaction presents even further difficulties especially when we attempt to account for the reasons why members feel satisfied or dissatisfied. A simple satisfaction index follows and is identical to the one we used in the "Small Group Communication Patterns" experiential vehicle (23.4).

I found this discussion:

interesting	___ :	___ :	___ :	___ :	___ :	___ :	___ boring
enjoyable	___ :	___ :	___ :	___ :	___ :	___ :	___ unenjoyable
dynamic	___ :	___ :	___ :	___ :	___ :	___ :	___ static
useful	___ :	___ :	___ :	___ :	___ :	___ :	___ useless
good	___ :	___ :	___ :	___ :	___ :	___ :	___ bad

EXPERIENTIAL VEHICLES

25.1 ANALYZING SMALL GROUP INTERACTION

The purpose of this experience is to enable you to become more familiar with the methods for analyzing small group interaction.

Six class members should be selected to discuss one of the following topics for approximately ten minutes.

1. What alternatives are there to the current grading system?
2. What are the major characteristics of an effective teacher?
3. What makes a person educated?
4. What does *love* mean?
5. How might our educational system be improved?

All other members should select a method of analysis and record the group interaction on the Interaction Diagram, the Communication Matrix, or the Rating Scale. After approximately ten minutes the discussion should be stopped and the six group discussion members should then complete the Satisfaction Index.

Interaction Diagram

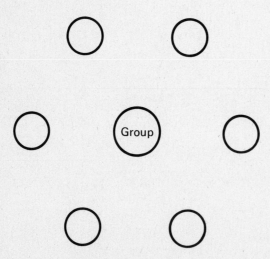

COMMUNICATION MATRIX FOR RECORDING INTERACTIONS

Fill in the appropriate names in all columns and rows.

Names							Group

RATING SCALE

This discussion was:

interesting	____ : ____ : ____ : ____ : ____ : ____ : ____	uninteresting
unclear	____ : ____ : ____ : ____ : ____ : ____ : ____	clear
purposeful	____ : ____ : ____ : ____ : ____ : ____ : ____	nonpurposeful
pessimistic	____ : ____ : ____ : ____ : ____ : ____ : ____	optimistic
shared equally by all members	____ : ____ : ____ : ____ : ____ : ____ : ____	monopolized by one or a few members
efficient	____ : ____ : ____ : ____ : ____ : ____ : ____	inefficient

SATISFACTION INDEX

(To be completed by members of the group discussion.)

In this discussion, I felt:

satisfied	____ : ____ : ____ : ____ : ____ : ____ : ____	dissatisfied
pleased	____ : ____ : ____ : ____ : ____ : ____ : ____	displeased
bored	____ : ____ : ____ : ____ : ____ : ____ : ____	excited
happy	____ : ____ : ____ : ____ : ____ : ____ : ____	sad

After each member has completed at least one analysis form, respond to all questions in connection with the method of analysis you used.

1. What are some of the advantages in using the method of analysis you selected?
2. What are some of the difficulties or disadvantages in using your method of analysis?
3. Does this method help you to describe what happened in the group? Explain.
4. Does this method help you to evaluate the quality of the discussion?
5. What other aspects or dimensions of the group process should be included in the analysis forms? Put differently, what do these analysis methods omit?
6. How reliable are the methods used? Test this by comparing how similar-dissimilar the analyses are when performed by different people.
7. How valid are the methods used? Do they enable you to analyze what they claim to help analyze?

25.2 POSITIVE WORDS*

This exercise is performed by the entire class. One person is "it" and takes a seat in the front of the room or in the center of the circle. (It is possible, though not desirable, for the person to stay where he or she normally sits.) Going around in a circle or from left to right, each person says something positive about the person who is "it."

Note: For this exercise only volunteers should be chosen. Students may be encouraged but should not be forced to participate. Although this exercise is perhaps more appropriate to the content of the earlier units, it is best done when the students know each other fairly well. For this reason, it is put here.

Persons must tell the truth, that is, they are not allowed to say anything about the person that they do not believe. At the same time, however, all statements must be positive. Only positive words are allowed during this exercise. Persons may, however, "pass" and say nothing. No one may ask why something was said or why something was not said. The positive words may refer to the person's looks, behavior, intelligence, clothes, mannerisms, and so on. One may also say, "I don't know you very well but you seem friendly" or "You seem honest" or whatever. These statements, too, must be believed to be true.

After everyone has said something, another person becomes "it."

After all volunteers have been "it" respond to the following questions individually:

1. Describe your feelings when thinking about becoming "it."
2. How did you feel while people were saying positive words?
3. What comments were the most significant to you?
4. Would you be willing to be "it" again?

* This exercise was suggested by Diane Shore.

5. How do you feel now that the exercise is over? Did it make you feel better? Why do you suppose it had the effect it did?
6. What implications may be drawn from this exercise for application to everyday living?
7. Will this exercise change your behavior in any way?

After you have completed all these questions, share with the entire class whatever comments you would like to.

UNIT 26
Preliminaries to Public Communication

26.1 Some "Principles" of Public Communication

The Nature of Public Communication
Public Communication
Subjects of Public Communications
Methods of Presentation

LEARNING GOALS

After completing this unit, you should be able to:

1. define public communication
2. define four major purposes of public communication
3. explain how specific speech purposes are defined in terms of behavioral objectives
4. identify at least three qualities which should govern the selection of subjects of public communications
5. identify and define the four methods of presentation in public speaking

EXPERIENTIAL VEHICLE

26.1 SOME PRINCIPLES OF PUBLIC COMMUNICATION

Before beginning this section on public communication, respond to the following statements by writing *T* if the statement is generally or usually true and *F* if the statement is generally or usually false.

_____ 1. The most important principle of public speaking is delivery (voice and body actions).

_____ 2. The most effective speeches are written out in their entirety.

_____ 3. A good essay is automatically a good speech and vice versa.

_____ 4. A course in public speaking should enable you to speak with some facility on almost any subject.

_____ 5. Nervousness always hinders one's speaking effectiveness.

_____ 6. A good public speaker uses logic instead of emotion in order to persuade.

_____ 7. The styles of an effective speech and an effective written composition are basically the same.

_____ 8. The effective speaker is born rather than made.

_____ 9. The systematic study of public speaking is a relatively recent development.

_____ 10. The ethical speaker is always an effective speaker.

_____ 11. The speaker should strive to make his or her audience realize that his or her voice and body actions are especially good.

_____ 12. The accomplished speaker has learned, and the beginning speaker should learn, the various gestures and vocal patterns used to express the various emotions.

_____ 13. The speaker should prepare his or her speech so that he or she knows exactly what words will be used.

_____ 14. Effectiveness should be the sole criterion that guides the speaker.

_____ 15. A good public speaker should strive to persuade the audience by means of the speech and not by means of his or her own character and personality.

_____ 16. The truly great speaker relies solely on verbal communication.

_____ 17. A speech should be composed in the order it will be delivered—introduction, development, and conclusion.

_____ 18. The speaker should always strive to speak in grammatically correct sentences.

_____ 19. Like great literature a great speech will be effective with all people at all times.

_____ 20. If a speech is effective when delivered it is effective when read.

_____ 21. Unlike literature the effect of a speech must be immediate, otherwise it is not effective.

_____ 22. The great speeches throughout history have been spontaneous efforts.

_____ 23. A great speech is an effective speech.

_____ 24. If a speech is not listened to it is ineffective.

_____ 25. A speaker with extreme stage fright should memorize his or her speech.

Small groups or the class as a whole may then discuss their responses to the statements.

THE NATURE OF PUBLIC COMMUNICATION

Public communication or public speaking exists when a speaker delivers a relatively prepared, relatively continuous address in a specific setting to a relatively large audience that provides the speaker with relatively little feedback.

First, we should include a note on the word *relatively*. No form of communication can be defined in absolute terms; all forms seem to exist on a continuum. Dyadic communication seems to lead into small group communication which seems to lead to public speaking which leads to mass communication and so on. The word *relatively* is inserted repeatedly to eliminate the inevitable but fruitless questions about how large an audience must be for there to be public speaking, how prepared a speech must be for it to be a public speech, and so on.

More importantly, we need to consider the essential characteristics of public speaking as noted in the preceding explanation. The notion of a relatively prepared speech is included to emphasize the ideas that a public speech does not occur because people happen to be in public when they open their mouths but only results from preparation prior to actual utterance. A person can easily speak in public without any preparation but he or she is not delivering a public speech. A speech, by definition, is a prepared composition and hence a *public speech* is a prepared composition delivered to a public audience.

A public speech is a *relatively continuous address*. A speech is not broken as in a dialogue or small group communication with one person speaking and then another. In a public speech the speaker speaks and the audience, hopefully, listens. It should also be noted that the audience members provide the speaker with *relatively little feedback.* The trained speaker will be able to read subtle feedback cues that the members of the audience give off; the novice speaker will let these go unnoticed. Relatively speaking, however, there is little feedback. The speaker has some opportunity to adjust his or her message on the basis of audience reaction but not as much as would a member of a dyad or small group.

The receiver of the message is a *relatively large audience.* It is larger than a small group but smaller than in a mass communication situation. Generally, the audience is in close proximity with one another as distinguished from the audience of a mass communication which is widely scattered. The audience may be homogeneous or heterogeneous. Generally, they are more heterogeneous than a mass communication audience but less homogeneous than small group members.

Public speaking also occurs in a *specific setting.* Unlike mass communication where the audience members are in numerous different settings, the public speaking audience is in a specific, definable context. And in any evaluation

---

Box 19
"NOBEL PRIZE ACCEPTANCE SPEECH"

William Faulkner

William Faulkner (1897–1962), one of the leading American writers of the twentieth century, was awarded the Nobel Prize for literature in 1949 and the Pulitzer Prize in 1955. Although Faulkner wrote poems, short stories, movie scripts, and a play he is best known for his novels, for example, *The Sound and the Fury* (1929) and *The Reivers* (1962). Faulkner delivered the following speech on December 10, 1950, in Stockholm, Sweden, reportedly in his first dress suit and before television cameras for the first time.

The speech is instructive for its clarity of style and purpose, and the universality of its theme.

I feel that this award was not made to me as a man, but to my work—a life's work in the agony and sweat of the human spirit, not for glory and least of all for profit, but to create out of the materials of the human spirit something which did not exist before. So this award is only mine in trust. It will not be difficult to find a dedication for the money part of it commensurate with the purpose and significance of its origin. But I would like to do the same with the acclaim too, by using this moment as a pinnacle from which I might be listened to by the young men and women already dedicated to the same anguish and travail, among whom is already that one who will someday stand here where I am standing.

Our tragedy today is a general and universal physical fear so long sustained by now that we can even bear it. There are no longer problems of the spirit. There is only the question: when will I be blown up? Because of this, the young man or woman writing today has forgotten the problems of the human heart in conflict with

of a public speech it is necessary to take that specific setting into account. Students in a large lecture class, for example, are in a clearly different setting from members attending a political rally who in turn are different from members of a rock concert audience.

PUBLIC COMMUNICATION PURPOSES

A public speech may have any number of different purposes. Literally there are thousands of specific purposes for making a public speech. However, there are three general purposes that are useful to define: to inform, to entertain, and to persuade.

General Purposes

Speeches delivered *to inform* the audience are many and varied and range from the lectures in college classrooms to a newscaster's presentation of some relevant facts to a friend explaining how the internal combustion engine works. It is particularly important to note that a speech to inform must do just

itself which alone can make good writing because only that is worth writing about, worth the agony and the sweat.

He must learn them again. He must teach himself that the basest of all things is to be afraid; and, teaching himself that, forget it forever, leaving no room in his workshop for anything but the old verities and truths of the heart, the old universal truths lacking which any story is ephemeral and doomed—love and honor and pity and pride and compassion and sacrifice. Until he does so, he labors under a curse. He writes not of love but of lust, of defeats in which nobody loses anything of value, of victories without hope, and, worst of all, without pity or compassion. His griefs grieve on no universal bones, leaving no scars. He writes not of the heart but of the glands.

Until he relearns these things, he will write as though he stood among and watched the end of man. I decline to accept the end of man. It is easy enough to say that man is immortal simply because he will endure; that when the last ding-dong of doom has clanged and faded from the last worthless rock hanging tideless in the last red and dying evening, that even then there will still be one more sound: that of his puny inexhaustible voice, still talking. I refuse to accept this. I believe that man will not merely endure: he will prevail. He is immortal, not because he alone among creatures has an inexhaustible voice, but because he has a soul, a spirit capable of compassion and sacrifice and endurance. The poet's, the writer's, duty is to write about these things. It is his privilege to help man endure by lifting his heart, by reminding him of the courage and honor and hope and pride and compassion and pity and sacrifice which have been the glory of his past. The poet's voice need not merely be the record of man; it can be one of the props, the pillars, to help him endure and prevail.

that and it must contain information not previously known to the audience or information that is presented in a new or different way. The college teacher who presents information the audience already knows is not giving an informative speech.

Speeches *to entertain* may range from the comic monologues of television personalities like Johnny Carson, or Bill Cosby, or Joan Rivers to the speeches given at dinners or testimonials. In all of these cases the purpose is to entertain or amuse the audience. Information is secondary and may be new or old, accurate or inaccurate. It may deal with serious themes in a humorous way or with trivial themes—with fictional or real events, and so on. With speeches to entertain there are many less restrictions on what may and what may not be communicated.

Speeches *to persuade* are concerned with reinforcing or changing attitudes, beliefs, or behaviors. Here we are concerned with making the audience think something or do something. The speech to persuade may seek to have us believe that one candidate is better than the other or to get us to contribute to this candidate's campaign fund or to vote for him or her in the next election.

Some theorists make a distinction between speeches designed to reinforce or change attitudes and beliefs on the one hand and speeches designed to alter behavior on the other. The former are designated speeches to convince and the latter, speeches to persuade.

It should be noted that no speech is solely one of information, entertainment, or persuasion. Rather, elements of all three probably appear in most real life speeches. The college lecture on the history of California, for example, will probably contain new information, will contain some entertaining elements, and will probably lead the audience to think differently (change an attitude) about California. When we talk about general purposes we are really referring to the major purpose and not the sole purpose of a given speech.

Specific Purposes

Just as each speech has a general purpose, each speech also has one or more specific purposes. And, of course, there are various degrees of specificity one might wish to distinguish. For our purposes it is best to distinguish the major issues of any given speech as the specific purposes.

In informative speeches the specific purposes refer to the information the speaker will present to the audience. For example, one specific purpose might be to inform the audience of the five major stages in language development in children, of the major land purchases of the United States, or of recent experiments in memory.

With speeches to entertain the specific purposes are generally not as clear cut as they are in informative speeches. A specific purpose in a speech to entertain might be to entertain the audience with anecdotes from the lives of several comedians or with stories of talking animals.

With speeches to persuade we state in the specific purpose what we hope to persuade the audience to think or do. For example, one specific purpose might be to persuade the audience that Senator Smile should be reelected; that New York City should become our 51st state; or that the Academy Awards should be abolished. Note that in speeches to persuade it is not necessary that the audience be able to act on the basis of their belief or attitude. For example, we might well wish to convince high school students that Senator Smile should be reelected even though they cannot vote themselves. In other types of speeches to persuade we define the specific behavior we wish the audience to engage in. For example, we might attempt to persuade the audience to buy savings bonds, to read a news magazine, or to buy a Pontiac rather than a Dodge.

Specific Purposes in Terms of Behavioral Objectives

The previous discussion on speech purposes has been, for the most part, based on traditional and contemporary speech communication theory. The theories are useful ones and have certainly stood the test of time. Presented here, however, is another approach to the specific purposes of a speech. Use whichever theory or approach seems the more useful or the easier. The new approach is simply to state the specific purpose of your speech in terms of behavioral objectives—in terms of what you want the audience to be able to do as a result of having heard your speech. Each unit of this text is prefaced in a similar way with behavioral objectives that state what you should be able to do after reading the unit.

In the speech to inform state the information that the audience will learn from the speech and how the audience will be able to demonstrate this learning in behavioral terms. For example, a specific purpose might be phrased as: The audience will be able to state the five stages of language development in the child; the audience will be able to list the five major land purchases of the United States in the nineteenth century; or, the audience will be able to summarize the essential methods and findings of three recent experiments in the psychology of memory. Note that in stating the purposes in this way we are stating not only what we want the audience to learn but also how we want them to demonstrate it. These same purposes might have been put in other forms, that is, we might have said that the audience would be able to *recognize* the five major stages in the language development of the child or *define* the five major stages once they know the names of the stages. Put differently, include in the statement of purpose the type of learning that is to be demonstrated. This may be designated by using such terms as *recognize, identify, summarize, list, state,* and so on.

In the speech to entertain the statement of the specific behavior is a bit more difficult than with the speech to inform. Yet, we might state that the audience will laugh and verbally and nonverbally express enjoyment in hearing anecdotes about the lives of several comedians; or the audience will watch the next episode of "Maude"; or the audience will smile and provide other specific expressions of positive reinforcement to the speaker.

In the speech to persuade we may rely on oral or written expressions of agreement or change. We could state, for example, that the audience will state their preference that Senator Smile be reelected, that they will argue in favor of New York City becoming the 51st state, and so on. Or we could use written methods and say, for example, that the audience will change their opinion in favor of Senator Smile on a shift of opinion ballot or that in a mock election they would vote for Senator Smile. We might also focus on behavior and state the behavior we wish the audience to exhibit; for example, we might say that the audience will buy savings bonds, read a news magazine, or buy the Pontiac.

In using behavioral objectives to state speech purposes we force ourselves to state specifically what we wish the audience to be able to do after hearing our speech. This statement then provides an important reference point against which all other parts of the speech may be checked. For example, for every bit of supporting material we would use we would ask ourselves if this helped the audience to attain the behavioral objectives noted in the purpose. If it does not advance the behavioral objective in some way then it should not be used.

SUBJECTS OF PUBLIC COMMUNICATIONS

As should be clear from listening to public speeches, whether on television, at local organizations, or at school, the topics seem to know no boundaries. Every possible topic is appropriate for a public speech. It is impossible to conceive of a topic that would not be appropriate to at least some specific audience, and herein lies the major criterion for evaluating a topic for a public speech—appropriateness to some specific audience. Exactly what constitutes appropriateness will not always be easy to determine but it should be a major consideration of each speaker. Generally, intuition and some good common sense will guide the would-be public speaker away from the inappropriate to the appropriate. Nevertheless, some specific suggestions are advanced.

First, the topic should be considered worthwhile to the audience. The audience members should be able to view the speech and the topic as a worthwhile investment of their time and energy. Whether the purpose is to entertain, to persuade, or to inform, the audience members should feel that their time was well spent. Put differently, the audience members should consider themselves better off for having heard the speech; they should have gained something as a result of hearing it.

Second, the topic of a public speech should be interesting or, more importantly, must be made interesting by the speaker. We may assume that all subjects are potentially interesting but we should not assume that all subjects are already interesting or are inherently interesting to any audience. In fact,

Box 20
THE GETTYSBURG ADDRESS

Abraham Lincoln

Abraham Lincoln (1809–1865) delivered his famed Gettysburg Address in 1863. At the dedication of the National Cemetery at Gettysburg, Edward Everett, an influential Unitarian Pastor and popular orator, was invited to deliver the dedication address which he did. Lincoln also attended and as President was asked to say "a few appropriate remarks." The few remarks was the Gettysburg Address—perhaps the most popular speech in all of American history. Some newspapers ridiculed the speech, some praised it, but only few recognized its greatness at the time.

It is included here because it is a model of stylistic excellence and one of the best examples of "appropriateness."

Fourscore and seven years ago our fathers brought forth on this continent a new nation, conceived in liberty and dedicated to the proposition that all men are created equal. Now we are engaged in a great civil war, testing whether that nation, or any nation so conceived and so dedicated, can long endure. We are met on a great battlefield of that war. We have come to dedicate a portion of that field as a final resting place for those who here gave their lives that that nation might live. It is altogether fitting and proper that we should do this. But, in a larger sense, we cannot dedicate—we cannot consecrate—we cannot hallow—this ground. The brave men, living and dead, who struggled here have consecrated it far above our poor power to add or to detract. The world will little note nor long remember what we say here, but it can never forget what they did here. It is for us, the living, rather to be dedicated here to the unfinished work which they who fought here have thus far so nobly advanced. It is rather for us to be here dedicated to the great task remaining before us—that from these honored dead we take increased devotion to that cause for which they gave the last full measure of devotion; that we here highly resolve that these dead shall not have died in vain; that this nation, under God, shall have a new birth of freedom; and that government of the people, by the people, for the people, shall not perish from the earth.

the speaker will probably be better off if he or she assumes that it is the speaker's total obligation to make the subject interesting. At times this is easy and at times it will tax the most imaginative of speakers. It takes little effort to make a speech on increasing teacher's salaries interesting to teachers but much effort to interest the same audience in a speech on Latin vowels or the history of football.

Third, and perhaps most important, is that the topic of a public speech must be limited in scope and purpose. Probably the major problem with beginning speeches is that they attempt to cover everything in five minutes: the history of Egypt, why our tax structure should be changed, the sociology of film, and the like, are clearly too broad and attempt to cover too much. The inevitable result is that nothing much gets covered—everything is touched but only on the surface. No depth of insight is achieved with a broad topic and all that the speaker succeeds in doing is telling the audience what it already knew. Invariably the audience feels cheated, that it has gained nothing as a result of listening to this speech.

Perhaps the best way to narrow and limit the topic is to begin with a general topic and divide it into its component parts. Then, take one of these parts and divide it into its component parts. Continue with this general process until the topic seems manageable as one that can reasonably be covered in some depth in the allotted time. For example, take the topic of television programs as the first general topic area. This might then be divided into such subtopics as comedy, children's programs, educational programs, news, movies, soap operas, quiz programs, and sports. We might then take one of these topics, say comedy, and divide it into subtopics. Perhaps we might consider it on a time basis and divide comedy into its significant time periods as presented on television: pre-1950, 1950–1960, 1960–1970, and 1970 to the present. Let us say we are most interested in the current period, 1970 to the present. Divide this into further subtopics such as "major programs"—"Mary Tyler Moore," "Sanford and Son," "All in the Family," "Maude," and so on. We might then take some portion of this subtopic and begin to construct a speech around a specific topic. Some such topics might be "Women in Television Comedy," "Race Relations in Situation Comedy," "Comedy Spinoffs," and so on. The important point, regardless of whether you would have subdivided the topics in this way or not, is that the resultant topic is at least beginning to look manageable, whereas "television programs" without some specificity would take a lifetime to cover adequately.

METHODS OF PRESENTATION

Once the speech is prepared, it is ready to be delivered to an audience. How it is delivered, however, will often count as much in terms of the effectiveness of the speech as will the organization, style, or research that went into the speech writing. Generally four methods of presentation are distinguished: impromptu, extemporaneous, memorized, manuscript.

The *impromptu speech* is one given without direct preparation. Obviously no commitment is given to the organization that will be used or to the specific terminology or style that will be employed. Instead, we here talk "off the cuff." Although there may be a place for this type of public speech, it is generally a method of presentation that leaves a great deal to be desired. Many college lectures, unfortunately, are of the impromptu type.

The *extemporaneous speech* is thoroughly prepared, organized in detail, and certain aspects of style are predetermined. The major headings in the speech are memorized as is the order and type of supporting materials. But there is no memorization of the exact wording.

The *memorized speech* is committed to memory verbatim. The most important feature here is that there is total commitment to memory of the exact words that will be spoken. Nothing is left to chance.

The *manuscript speech* is one read from a script. The speech is written out word for word and read by the speaker.

It is apparent that there are significant differences among these four types of speeches. What is more important to notice, however, is that these modes of presentation are useful for different purposes. When the president gives a speech, he is forced to read it from manuscript lest there be things said that were not intended, or that were ambiguous, or that might later prove embarrassing. And so, manuscript reading is essential here. A comedian giving a monologue cannot read his or her speech even though so much depends on the exact wording, so the comedian must memorize his or her speech. For the college teacher, the extemporaneous method is the preferred mode of presentation since it allows for a certain flexibility but provides enough structure to prevent wandering off the topic.

SOURCES

There are probably more books on public speaking than on any other aspect of communication. The following four books seem to provide a sampling of different points of view: Martin P. Andersen, E. Ray Nichols, and Herbert W. Booth, *The Speaker and His Audience* (New York: Harper & Row, 1974); Donald K. Darnell and Wayne Brockriede, *Persons Communicating* (Englewood Cliffs, N.J.: Prentice-Hall, 1976); Robert C. Jeffrey and Owen Peterson, *Speech: A Text with Adapted Readings,* 2d ed. (New York: Harper & Row, 1975); and, James C. McCroskey, *An Introduction to Rhetorical Communication,* 2d ed. (Englewood Cliffs, N.J.: Prentice-Hall, 1972). The Andersen, Nichols, and Booth text is a traditional performance-oriented text, giving detailed and specific advice on all phases of speech preparation. The Darnell and Brockriede text attempts to begin formulating a theoretical foundation for communication and actually goes considerably beyond public speaking. The Jeffrey and Peterson book is another traditional performance-oriented text but contains numerous readings on various different aspects of public speaking. McCroskey's book is probably the best of the numerous public-speaking texts; it's main contribution is that it synthesizes the experimental research and bases its conclusions and principles on hard evidence.

UNIT 27
The Speech in Public Communication

Structure in Public Communication
Supporting Materials
Stylistic Considerations

LEARNING GOALS

After completing this unit, you should be able to:

1. identify and define at least five patterns of organization for a public speech
2. identify the three functions of an introduction
3. identify the three functions of a conclusion
4. define the following types of supporting materials: *example, illustration, statistics, opinion, quotation, testimony, comparison,* and *contrast*
5. identify several types of multimedia that might be incorporated into a public speech
6. identify at least six principles of style

In this unit, we consider the speech in public speaking. First, we will cover organizational patterns—the ways in which the main points of a speech can be arranged and the nature and functions of the introduction and conclusion. Second, we will cover the various types of supporting materials. Third, we will consider style—the prescriptions and proscriptions of wording the speech. These three major topics should provide a firm foundation for constructing a public speech.

STRUCTURE IN PUBLIC COMMUNICATION

Organizational Patterns

All speeches are difficult to understand. The audience hears a speech but once and must instantly make sense of this complex mass of verbiage. Often an audience will simply tune out the speaker if the difficulty of understanding becomes too great. Because of this the speaker must aid the listeners in any way possible. Perhaps the best way to aid comprehension is to organize what is to be said in a clear and unambiguous manner.

Each speech demands a somewhat unique treatment and no set of rules or principles may be applied without consideration of the uniqueness of this specific speech. Consequently, some general organizational schemes are presented here with the warning that they must be adopted to the needs of the specific speech, speaker, and audience.

Problem-Solution/Solution-Problem Pattern

One popular pattern of organization is to present the main ideas in terms of problem and solution. Under this system the speech is divided into two basic parts: one part deals with the problem and one part with the solution. Generally the problem is presented first and the solution second but under certain conditions the solution may be more appropriately presented first and the problem second.

Let us say we are attempting to persuade an audience that teachers should be given higher salaries and increased benefits. Here a problem-solution pattern might be appropriate. We might for example discuss in the first part of the speech some of the problems confronting contemporary education such as the fact that industry lures away the most highly qualified graduates of the leading universities, that many excellent teachers leave the field after two or three years, and that teaching is currently a low status occupation in the minds of many undergraduates. In the second part of the speech we might consider the possible solutions, namely that salaries for teachers must be made competitive with salaries offered by private industry, and that the benefits teachers receive must be made at least as attractive as those offered by industry.

The speech might look something like this in outline form.

I. There are three major problems confronting contemporary education.
   A. Industry lures away the most qualified graduates.
   B. Numerous excellent teachers leave the field after two or three years.
   C. Teaching is currently a low status occupation.
II. There are two major solutions to these problems.
   A. Salaries for teachers must be increased.
   B. Benefits for teachers must be made more attractive.

Temporal Pattern

Organizing the major issues on the basis of some temporal relationship is another popular organizational pattern. Generally, when we use this pattern we organize the speech into two or three major parts, beginning with the past and working up to the present or the future, or beginning with the present or the future and working back to the past. There are, of course, various ways in which a temporal pattern may be actualized. We might, for example, divide up the major events of our topic and consider each as it occurs or occurred in time. A speech on the development of speech and language in the child might be organized in a temporal pattern and would be divided something like this:

I. Babbling Stage
II. Lallation Stage
III. Echolalic Stage
IV. Communication Stage

Here each of the events is considered in temporal sequence beginning with the earliest stage and working up to the final stage—in this case the stage of true communication.

A temporal pattern might also be appropriate in considering the major developments in the history of communication. We might construct a speech outline that looks something like this:

I. Gutenberg invents movable type.
II. Bell transmits the first telephone message.
III. Edison invents the phonograph.
IV. Marconi sends and receives wireless messages.

Most historical topics lend themselves to organization by temporal patterning. The events leading up to the Civil War, the steps toward a college education, the history of writing, and the like will all yield to temporal patterning.

Spatial Pattern

Similar to temporal patterning is patterning that organizes the main points of a speech on the basis of space. Instead of organizing events or main points according to a temporal pattern (time), we organize them on the basis of spatial relationships. Physical objects generally fit well into organization by spatial patterning. For example, we might give a speech on landmarks in New York City and we might go from south to north, considering first some of the essentials of Manhattan. The base outline for such a speech might look something like this:

I. Greenwich Village
II. Murray Hill
III. Times Square
IV. Midtown

Similarly the structure of a hospital, school, skyscraper, or perhaps even of a dinosaur would be appropriately described with a spatial pattern of organization.

Cause-Effect/Effect-Cause Pattern

Similar to the problem-solution pattern of organization is the cause-effect or effect-cause pattern. Here we divide the speech into two major sections, causes and effects. For example, a speech on the reasons for highway accidents or birth defects might yield to a cause-effect pattern, where we first consider, say, the causes of highway accidents or birth defects and then some of the effects—the number of deaths, the number of accidents, and so on.

Structure-Function Pattern

At times we may wish to consider the structure and the function of, say, a particular organization or perhaps of a particular living organism. Here the obvious pattern would be a division into structure and function, with either one being considered first, again depending on the specifics of the topic, the purpose, and the audience. We might wish to explain the complex nature of a college and might consider the various structures—the major persons (president, deans, department chairpersons, faculty, students) and the various functions of each.

As might be appreciated from this example, the structure-function pattern may be approached in various ways. One way is to divide the speech into two major parts: structure and function. The various structures might also be structured with their various functions considered in turn. Thus, for example, the president would be considered first and his or her various functions considered. The second point would focus on the deans and their various functions. The major alternatives would look something like this:

Alternative One

I. There are five major persons or groups of persons (structures) in a university
   A. President
   B. Deans
   C. Department chairpersons
   D. Faculty
   E. Students
II. Each performs different functions.
   A. President's functions
   B. Deans' functions
   C. Department chairpersons' functions
   D. Faculty functions
   E. Students' functions

Alternative Two

I. The President
   A. Structure
   B. Functions
II. Deans
   A. Structure
   B. Functions
III. Department Chairpersons
   A. Structure
   B. Functions

IV. Faculty
    A. Structure
    B. Functions
V. Students
    A. Structure
    B. Functions

Topical Pattern

Perhaps the most popular pattern of organization is the topical pattern, a pattern that organizes the speech into the major topics without attempting to organize them in terms of time or space or into any of the other patterns already considered. This pattern should not be regarded as a catch-all for topics that do not seem to fit into any of the other patterns, but rather should be regarded as one appropriate to the particular topic being considered. For example, the topical pattern is an obvious one for organizing a speech on the powers of the government. Here the divisions are obvious:

I. The legislative branch is controlled by Congress
II. The executive branch is controlled by the president
III. The judicial branch is controlled by the courts

A speech on important cities in the world could be organized into a topical pattern as well as speeches on problems facing the college graduate, great works of literature, the world's major religions, and the like. Each of these topics would have several subtopics or divisions of approximately equal importance; consequently a topical pattern seems most appropriate.

Introductions and Conclusions

Introductions

The introduction to a speech, like the first day of a class or the first date, is especially important because it sets the tone for what is to follow. It hopefully puts the audience into a receptive frame of mind and builds up a positive attitude toward the speech and the speaker.

The introduction to a speech, although obviously delivered first, should be constructed last—only after the entire speech including the conclusion have been written. In this way you will be in a position to see the entire speech before you and will be better able to determine those elements that should go into introducing this now completed speech. If the speech were not completed first, you would be constructing an introduction to a speech you were not very sure of. This same advice also pertains to written compositions; the introductions should always be constructed last.

Although there are many specific purposes an introduction may serve, three general ones are singled out here.

First, the introduction should gain the attention of the audience. In many situations this is not a particularly important problem but in others it is. In a college classroom if a number of students are giving speeches, it is particularly important that the attention of the audience be secured and maintained in the introduction. Similarly the college teacher needs to secure attention at the beginning of his or her lectures lest the class continue to think thoughts and trade stories of the weekend.

Second, the introduction should establish a speaker-audience relationship that is conducive to the achievement of the speech purpose. This relationship is aided if the audience likes the speaker, if they respect the speaker, and if they think the speaker a knowledgeable individual. It is no easy task to instill these attitudes in the audience in the introduction, as can be appreciated. Unit 6 on credibility elaborates on this important area.

Third, the introduction should orient the audience in some way to what is to follow in the speech. The main points of the speech may be noted here or perhaps a statement of the general conclusion that will be argued or perhaps the way in which the material will be presented.

Conclusions

The conclusion is often the most important part of the entire speech since it is the part that the audience will in many instances remember most clearly. It is the conclusion that will in many cases determine what image of the speaker is left in the minds of the audience members. Particular attention must, therefore, be devoted to this brief but crucial part of the public speech.

Like the introduction, the conclusion may have many specific purposes. Yet, three general ones may be singled out. First, and perhaps the most obvious function, is to summarize the essentials of the speech. This function is particularly important in an informative speech and less so in persuasive speeches or speeches designed to entertain. In informative speeches, however, it is essential that the speaker wrap up in a convenient summary some of the issues he or she has presented. Eventually, the details that the speaker has spoken will be forgotten; the conclusion and especially the summary will probably be remembered longer.

A second function—most appropriate in persuasive speeches—is that of motivation. In the conclusion the speaker has the opportunity to give the audience one final push in the direction he or she wishes them to take. Whether it is to buy bonds, vote a particular way, or change an attitude in one way or another, the conclusion can be used for a final motivation, a final appeal, a final argument. Generally, this final motivation should not introduce material that is completely new to the speech since the aim here is to motivate the audience and not to reintroduce the main discussion. The conclusion is too late to introduce new material.

The third function of a conclusion is to provide some kind of closure. Often the summary will accomplish this but in many instances it will not be sufficient. The speech should come to a crisp and definite end and the audience should not be hanging on wondering whether the speaker has finished or whether he or she will continue after a short pause. Some kind of wrap up, some kind of final statement is helpful in providing this feeling of closure. It is probably best not to say "thank you" or "It was a pleasure addressing you" or some such trite phrase; these are best left implied.

SUPPORTING MATERIALS

In constructing a speech, we must flesh out the essential points or issues on which to focus. We cannot simply state our propositions and let it go at that. We must make these propositions live in the minds of the audience. We must elaborate on them and make them understandable or believable. We do this by utilizing what are called supporting materials.

Of the numerous types of supporting materials that may be identified, we here consider five general classes: (1) examples and illustrations; (2) statistics; (3) opinions, quotations, and testimony; (4) comparisons and contrasts, and (5) multimedia.

Examples and Illustrations

Perhaps the most common way to support a proposition or clarify an issue is to use an example or an illustration. Examples may be real or hypothetical and may consist basically of one specific instance. If I were to explain the nature of soap operas to someone who had never heard or seen one, I might offer "Mary Hartman, Mary Hartman" as an example and explain it. Or in a discussion of violent films, I might make reference to *Taxi Driver*. These examples help to make specific a discussion that might otherwise remain too abstract for easy comprehension. We cannot conceptualize soap operas or violent films without thinking of specific examples. When the speaker provides us with an example or two he or she is helping us focus our thinking more concretely. In some cases, it is more helpful to construct a hypothetical example to make your point more clearly. We might, in a discussion of the effects of violent films create a specific instance of a young person who, after seeing a violent film, recreates the crime witnessed on the screen. Depending upon our purpose we might draw this example in brief or make it rather extended. If the latter, it is called an illustration. While the example merely specifies or identifies, the illustration draws a detailed picture.

Statistics

Statistics are organized sets of figures and may range from the very elementary type of statistics that we learned in elementary school to the most sophisticated type. Most useful in public speeches are measures of central tendency and measures of dispersion.

Measures of central tendency tell us essentially what the average of something is. We must distinguish here the mean, median, and the mode. The *mean* is the arithmetic average of a set of numbers (for example, the mean income for families living in this community is $12,000). The *median* is the middle score, the score that separates the total list of scores into two equal parts. Half of the scores are higher than the median and half are lower. For example, if we found that the median income of teachers at this college was $15,000, it would mean that half the teachers make more than $15,000 and half make less. The *mode* is the most common score—the score that occurs most frequently in a given set of scores. For example, if we said that the mode score for the last examination was 93, it would mean that more students got a score of 93 than any other score.

Measures of dispersion tell us how widely the scores differ from some hypothetical average. The range and percentiles are the most useful for the public speaker. The *range* is the difference between the highest score and the lowest score. Teachers will frequently report the range of scores on a test. A range of 45, for example, would mean that the lowest score was 45 points lower than the highest score on the test. A high range would mean that the class members differed widely in their performance on the test; whereas, a low range would indicate that their scores were more similar. Actually, this is not entirely true. It is conceivable that on a test, one student would score very high, say 98, and one student score very low, say 42, and most of the students score very close to 75. In this case the high range (56) would be misleading if taken as an indication of the variability of the performance of the students in the class.

Percentiles refer to the percentage of scores below a particular point. For example, if you scored 700 on the College Entrance Examination Board test you were in approximately the 97 percentile, meaning that 97 percent of the people taking that test scored lower than 700. The 50 percentile score (also called the median) would mean that 50 percent of the scores were below this particular score. Often it is useful to talk of quartiles. The lower quartile is the 25 percentile and means that 25 percent of the scores were below this point. The upper quartile is the 75 percentile and means that 75 percent of the scores were below this point.

When teachers curve examinations to determine final grades, it is sometimes more important to know your percentile rank than your actual score. If the teacher assigns grades so that about the upper 15 percent get *A* and the lower 15 percent get *F,* 20 percent get *B,* 20 percent get *D,* and 30 percent get *C*—a fairly typical curve—your percentile rank will tell you what percentage of the class you fall into whereas your actual score will not. For example, you may have a score of 67 which would normally be a *D* or *D+* but if this score of 67 is in the 95 percentile, your final grade will be *A* or *A+.*

These measures of central tendency and dispersion are the simplest available, and yet they are the ones that should prove most useful to most audiences. Even though the speaker may know how to compute the variance or standard deviation, if the audience does not know what these statistics mean, it is useless to include them without a lengthy explanation.

Opinions, Quotations, and Testimony

Opinions, quotations, and testimony are forms of supporting materials that are similar in many respects and may be considered together. An *opinion* is a personal evaluation of an event, person, or thing. We may say that "it is my opinion that . . ." or that "Dr. Jones, professor of political sciences, has argued that. . . ." Obviously, the more credible the source the more impact the opinion will have. Thus, in choosing opinions to include in your speech they should be chosen with this standard in mind. There is little sense citing the political science professor if the topic is chemistry, for example.

An opinion in the form of a verbatim statement is a *quotation.* Quotations should be used sparingly. Many a beginning speaker will sprinkle the speech too liberally with quotations, some of which are relevant but others, although not relevant, are included because they seem to have a nice ring to them. Quotations are useful if used in small doses and if they relate directly to the issue at hand. Nothing seems more artificial than a quotation that the audience knows the speaker threw in just because it was clever or because it was by some well-known person.

Lastly, there is *testimony*—statements by an actual witness about an event or happening. This generally is the lawyer's principal type of supporting material, the type that seems the most persuasive in a court of law. Testimony, whether used to support a proposition in a public speech or the arguments of a prosecuting or defending attorney, is useful only to the extent that the witness is reliable in the minds of the audience or jury. To the extent that the witness is perceived to have some ulterior motive or not to be well equipped to witness the happening fairly and objectively, the testimony will be disbelieved.

Opinions, quotations, and testimony, in addition to supporting a particular issue, also add a human personalized touch to the speech. Listeners want to hear, in addition to facts and statistics, what human beings say and think.

Comparisons and Contrasts

In developing a comparison we consider the similarities among objects, people, or events. Usually, but not always, a *comparison* juxtaposes something that is known with something that is unknown or is being introduced for the first time. Comparisons may be of two general types: literal and figurative. A literal comparison involves two like things: two people, two mountains, two colleges, two courses, two students, and so on. A figurative comparison compares two things that are unlike each other or that are from different classes and yet are alike in one essential respect. A figurative comparison might compare, for example, a freshman student with a lion cub, or a college with a family, or a book with a friend, and so on. Here we have two things that are different and yet we compare them because we are emphasizing one particular characteristic that they have in common. The lion cub and the freshman student are both young but will grow strong very shortly; the college and the family both watch out for the young; and the book and the friend both dispense useful advice.

When comparisons are used to prove a particular point the process is generally referred to as reasoning by analogy. We might for example develop a comparison which involves reasoning that since violent movies did not influence violent actions in viewers that violent television programs would not influence violent actions either. Or we might reason that since Burt Reynolds' last film was a good one that the next one will be a good one, too. Or, to use an example we probably use implicitly everyday, we might reason that since this particular person gave us good advice yesterday that he or she will give us good advice today.

Contrast, on the other hand, seeks to consider the essential dissimilarities and differences among the objects, events, or people being considered. This type of supporting material is especially useful if we wish to emphasize the uniqueness of a particular system as compared with all other systems. We might wish to contrast democracy with communism or socialism, or we might wish to contrast Catholicism today with Catholicism 50 years ago, or perhaps contrast pornography as viewed today with the way in which it was viewed in Victorian days.

Multimedia

The public speaker today is competing with varied other forms of communication—television, radio, films, and the like. It is essential therefore that the speaker use all the means possible to make his or her speech interesting and attention getting. Perhaps the best example of this is seen in the classroom, especially in the large classrooms of from 100 to 1000 students. And although this situation is often not very pleasing to students, it is one that is sure to prevail and even increase in frequency. The teacher who simply lectures without any assistance from media is going to have a hard time securing and maintaining the interest and attention of the students. Further, without any assistance from media the teacher is limiting himself or herself to only one channel of communication. Although not a panacea, the incorporation of multimedia into the classroom "lecture" or the public speech will normally help a great deal.

Music is perhaps the most obvious type of media to add and yet it is extremely difficult to incorporate it effectively into the speech or lecture. Pieces that are too long will bore the audience or will allow them to drift away from the main topic of the speech or lecture. Pieces that are too short will not enable the audience to feel what the speaker wishes them to feel. Similarly, the speaker must be careful to use music that will not stir up emotions and feelings in the audience that are contrary to the purposes of the speech. A well-intentioned lecturer who wants to appear youthful and plays songs that are out of date will surely give the audience reason to wonder about his or her all-around honesty.

Slides are perhaps the most useful and the easiest to control of the media products. A simple system with one projector in front of the screen will allow the speaker to control the slides. More complex systems with three or four projectors can also be controlled by the speaker by remote control but require a great deal of advanced planning. But the speaker should consider using slides if the facilities are available since they serve the dual function of maintaining attention and communicating information. Word slides are easy to prepare and enable the speaker to highlight the essential points or issues as he or she is talking. Picture slides enable the speaker to say visually what he or she is saying verbally. Thus, in lectures dealing wtih the contributions of various people, pictures of the persons themselves enable the students to see a bit more than would be possible if one just talked about the ideas of the people. To talk about animal communication, for example, without showing pictures of the animals would seem a bit half done. Again, the speaker must be careful not to use too many slides since they can detract from what the speaker is saying.

More sophisticated than slides is the use of films but films must be handled very carefully lest they disrupt the audience into forgetting what the purpose of the communication was. But brief excerpts from various films to illustrate select points will go a long way toward making the speech something more than just another speech.

On a less complex level there are simple visual aids such as charts and diagrams that the speaker brings with him or her to the speech. Complex diagrams or tables are often made a lot more understandable when presented by the speaker on a chart as a visual aid rather than when simply talked about.

These five general types of supporting materials are clearly not the only ones available to the speaker. A few of the other more common and useful types are mentioned here briefly.

Definitions are always useful but especially when the concepts are somewhat unfamiliar to the audience or when a somewhat different twist is to be communicated.

Repetition, repeating something in exactly the same words, and *restatement,* repeating something in somewhat different words, are useful when dealing with complex ideas or when you wish the audience to remember a specific concept or idea.

Asking the audience a provocative *question* is an excellent way of supporting a particular point if you can be reasonably certain that the audience will answer your question the way you want them to.

Using *description,* the re-creation of a particular scene, or *narration,* the verbal creation of some event, will help the audience to see what the speaker sees and feel what the speaker feels.

STYLISTIC CONSIDERATIONS

In constructing a speech for a public audience, style is of prime importance. The way in which ideas are phrased will surely influence the way in which they are received as well as the way the audience regards the speaker himself or herself. Here are several prescriptions and proscriptions that should result in a more effective speech style.

Box 21
SECOND INAUGURAL ADDRESS

Abraham Lincoln

Abraham Lincoln (1809–1865) delivered his second inaugural address in Washington on March 4, 1865, at a time when a northern victory in the Civil War was virtually assured. (Lee surrendered to Grant at Appomattox Courthouse on April 9, 1865.)

Like the Gettysburg Address, the Second Inaugural Address will prove a model of style and of careful audience adaptation.

Fellow-countrymen: At this second appearing to take the oath of the presidential office, there is less occasion for an extended address than there was at first. Then a statement, somewhat in detail, of a course to be pursued seemed very fitting and proper. Now, at the expiration of four years, during which public declarations have been constantly called forth on every point and phase of the great contest which still absorbs the attention and engrosses the energies of the nation, little that is new could be presented.

The progress of our arms, upon which all else chiefly depends, is as well known to the public as to myself, and it is, I trust, reasonably satisfactory and encouraging to all. With high hope for the future, no prediction in regard to it is ventured.

On the occasion corresponding to this four years ago, all thoughts were anxiously directed to an impending civil war. All dreaded it, all sought to avoid it. While the inaugural address was being delivered from this place, devoted altogether to saving the Union without war, insurgent agents were in the city seeking to destroy it with war—seeking to dissolve the Union and divide the effects by negotiation. Both parties deprecated war, but one of them would make war rather than let the nation survive, and the other would accept war rather than let it perish, and the war came. One-eighth of the whole population were colored slaves, not distributed generally over the Union, but localized in the Southern part of it. These slaves constituted a peculiar and powerful interest. All knew that this interest was somehow

1. Use Simple Terms and Sentence Patterns

Recall that a speech in normal circumstances is only heard once and because of this it is not possible for members of the audience to look up an unfamiliar word or unwind complicated sentence patterns in order to get at the meaning the speaker wishes to convey. On the other hand, overly simple language can turn off the audience and lead them to think that the speaker has nothing of value to communicate. Even more important is that the speaker should never "talk down" to the audience; condescension impedes communication. Simple language and grammatical constructions will result in immediate comprehension but will not insult the audience. Generally, simple, active, declarative sentences are preferred to the more complex, passive sentences because the forms are easier to understand and grasp with just one exposure.

---

the cause of the war. To strengthen, perpetuate, and extend this interest was the object for which the insurgents would rend the Union by war, while the government claimed no right to do more than to restrict the territorial enlargements of it.

Neither party expected for the war the magnitude or the duration which it has already attained. Neither anticipated that the cause of the conflict might cease when, or even before the conflict itself should cease. Each looked for an easier triumph, and a result less fundamental and astounding. Both read the same Bible and pray to the same God, and each invokes His aid against the other. It may seem strange that any men should dare to ask a just God's assistance in wringing their bread from the sweat of other men's faces, but let us judge not that we be not judged. The prayer of both could not be answered. That of neither has been answered fully. The Almighty has His own purposes. Woe unto the world because of offences, for it must needs be that offences come, but woe to that many by whom the offence cometh. If we shall suppose that American slavery is one of these offences which, in the providence of God, must needs come, but which having continued through His appointed time, He now wills to remove, and that He gives to both North and South this terrible war as the woe due to those by whom the offence came, shall we discern there any departure from those divine attributes which the believers in a living God always ascribe to Him? Fondly do we hope, fervently do we pray, that this mighty scourge of war may speedily pass away. Yet if God wills that it continue until all the wealth piled by the bondsman's two hundred and fifty years of unrequited toil shall be sunk, and until every drop of blood drawn with the lash shall be paid by another drawn with the sword, as was said three thousand years ago, so still it must be said, that the judgments of the Lord are true and righteous altogether.

With malice toward none, with charity for all, with firmness in the right as God gives us to see the right, let us finish the work we are in, to bind up the nation's wounds, to care for him who shall have borne the battle, and for his widow and his orphans, to do all which may achieve and cherish a just and a lasting peace among ourselves and with all nations.

2. Mix the Levels of Abstraction

Most people seem to prefer a mixture of the abstract and the concrete, the specific and the general. By mixing these levels of abstraction we communicate in a much clearer, a more interesting, and a more meaningful fashion. By mixing the levels of abstraction the speaker can more actively involve the audience in his or her speech. If a speech concentrates solely on low-level abstractions, that is, on concrete terms and sentences, the audience will probably become bored. Similarly, if the speaker only talks in terms of high-order abstractions, using highly abstract and all-inclusive terms, the audience will again become bored.

3. Avoid Sexist Terms and References

I should preface this discussion by noting that other writers and researchers in communication would not necessarily agree with the following advice on sexism in language. Yet, it seems only logical to me. The sexist aspect of language has only recently become the center of a great deal of interest. Basically, the masculine pronoun or professions designated by masculine names should not be used generically. Nor should the term *man* be used to refer to human beings. Many, of course, will disagree with this and yet with a bit of reflection we can easily see why these constructions should be avoided. Why should a hypothetical doctor, dentist, or lawyer be referred to with masculine pronouns and references? Similarly why should the hypothetical individual be called *he*? Because this is traditional or even convenient are not satisfactory answers although these seem the only arguments ever used.

It is probably best to use *he and she* or *person* instead of just *he* or *man*. Similarly, terms such as *chairman* should be replaced by *chairperson.*

In a similar vein terms that were at one time used to refer to a woman in a specific position (normally originating from a masculine term) should be avoided; for example, *poetess, Negress, Jewess, heroine,* and the like. On the other hand, terms in wide usage that appropriately designate a female, such as *actress* and *waitress* should be maintained.

4. Use Transitional Phrases

Listening attentively to a public speech is difficult work and consequently the speaker should assist the audience in any way he or she can. One of the most effective ways is to use frequent transitional phrases that provide a kind of bridge between one set of ideas and another or between one piece of evidence and another. Phrases such as "Now that we have seen how _____, let us consider how _____," will help to keep the audience on the right track. Even terms such as *first, second, and also, although,* and *however* help the audience to better follow the thought patterns of the speaker.

Box 22
SEXIST PRONOUNS

A number of proposals have been advanced to eliminate the common gender masculine pronoun. Here are three examples.

Example 1

she, he	tey
her(s), his	ter
her, him	tem
mankind	genkind
manhood	genhood

The professor lectured to ter class on the history of genkind and genhood. Tey talked of ter childhood which had a great influence on tem.

Example 2

she, he	co
her(s), his	cos
her, him	co
herself, himself	coself

The professor lectured to cos class coself. Co talked of cos childhood which had a great influence on co.

Example 3

she, he	ve
her(s), his	vis
her, him	ver

The professor lectured to vis class. Ve talked of vis childhood which had a great influence on ver.

Sources: The first example comes from Casey Miller and Kate Swift, "One Small Step for Genkind," *New York Times Magazine,* April 16, 1972, and reprinted in Joseph DeVito, ed., *Langauge: Concepts and Processes* (Englewood Cliffs, N.J.: Prentice-Hall, 1973). The second and third examples come from Mary Orovan and Vardo One, respectively, and are cited in Donald D. Hook, "Sexism in English Pronouns and Forms of Address," *General Linguistics,* 14 (1974), 86–96.

5. Use Marker Terms, Phrases, and Sentences

Much like transitions, markers will help audience comprehension. The speaker should make frequent use of marker terms that will provide signposts to the audience. Numbers and letters are perhaps the most obvious examples, but phrases such as "The second argument is . . . ." or "The last example I want to provide . . . ." help to focus the audience's thinking on the kind of outline the speaker is using.

6. Use Repetition, Restatement, and Internal Summaries

Much like transitions and marker phrases help to keep the audience on the same track with the speaker, repetition (repeating something in exactly the same way), restatement (rephrasing an idea or statement), and internal summaries (summaries or reviews of subsections of the speech) all help the listeners to better follow the speaker.

Speakers often hesitate to include such stylistic elements because they feel it makes the speech seem simple and elementary. But the speaker feels this way because he or she is so familiar with the speech that to him or her it is elementary. The listeners however, who will hear the speech but once, will surely appreciate these aids to comprehension.

7. Use Appropriate Language

The use of appropriate language is perhaps one of the most important aspects of style but one of the most difficult on which to offer specific advice. Most would agree that language should be appropriate but what appropriateness

". . . to have and to hold in counterproductive as well as productive time frames, so long as you are bilaterally capable of maintaining a viable life-style. . . ." (Cartoon by Donald Reilly.)

consists of cannot easily be agreed upon. Perhaps one guide is that the language should never make an audience uncomfortable; it should never be insulting or offensive in any way. If it is, the audience will surely respond negatively to the speech as well as to the speaker.

8. Create Images for the Listeners

Creating visual images is a most difficult suggestion on which to offer specific advice, and yet it is often this element of imagery that distinguishes the mediocre from the superior performance. Whenever possbie try to present the audience with sensory images, colors, tastes, textures, odors, and the like. These images will greatly assist the listeners in feeling along with the speaker—to see, hear, taste, touch, and smell as the speaker does.

9. Use Personalized Language

Although public speaking is a relatively formal kind of performance, it seems to help if some personalization can be introduced. This is perhaps most clearly seen in the college lecture situation where the teachers who seem to really reach their students are the ones who personalize their courses and lectures, who introduce some of themselves into the discussions. The same is true in public speaking even if you will only face this audience once.

The best guide to what is personalized language is to focus on the language of everyday conversation and note its characteristics. This is invariably personalized language. It makes frequent use of personal pronouns, of *I, you, he, she;* it makes use of contractions, simple sentences, and short phrases; it makes use of repetition and restatement. It avoids long, complex, and passive sentences. It avoids the use of the pronoun *one* or phrases such as "the speaker," "the former/the latter" (which are difficult to retrace); and in general those expressions that are more popular and more expected in the language of written prose rather than in the language of everyday communication. This is not to say that the language of a public speech should be common or trite. Quite the contrary! The language of the speech should be as polished as the language of the written essay but it should be conversational in tone and direct in reference.

SOURCES

Structure and supporting materials are covered thoroughly in Jim D. Hughey and Arlee W. Johnson, *Speech Communication: Foundations and Challenges* (New York: Macmillan, 1975). Organization is clearly handled in Judy L. Haynes, *Organizing a Speech: A Programmed Guide* (Englewood Cliffs, N.J.:

Prentice-Hall, 1973). James C. McCroskey, *An Introduction to Rhetorical Communication,* 2d ed. (Englewood Cliffs, N.J.: Prentice-Hall, 1972) covers both organization and style clearly and with emphasis on experimental support for his conclusions. Style is most thoroughly covered in Jane Blankenship, *A Sense of Style: An Introduction to Style for the Public Speaker* (Belmont, Cal.: Dickenson, 1968).

For the stylistic suggestions I relied heavily on the findings of experimental research as much as was possible, particularly the following: Joseph DeVito, "Some Psycholinguistic Aspects of Active and Passive Sentences," *Quarterly Journal of Speech* 55 (December 1969): 401–406; "Comprehension Factors in Oral and Written Discourse of Skilled Communicators," *Speech Monographs* 32 (June 1965); 124–128; and, "Relative Ease in Comprehending Yes/No Questions," in *Rhetoric and Communication,* Jane Blankenship and Herman G. Stelzner, eds. (Urbana, Ill.: University of Illinois Press, 1976), pp. 143–154.

EXPERIENTIAL VEHICLES

27.1 SPEECH ANALYSIS

This experience is designed to enable you to explore in greater depth some of the properties of a speech, namely the organizational development, the supporting materials, and the style.

Carefully read the following speech, "I HAVE A DREAM," by Martin Luther King, Jr. and respond to the questions presented below.

1. What organizational pattern is used? It is effective?
2. What method(s) is used for introducing the speech?
3. What method(s) is used for concluding the speech?
4. Are the introduction and conclusion appropriate? How is "appropriateness" determined?
5. Identify at least four different types of supporting materials used in this speech.
6. Is the speech stylistically effective? Specifically:

    a. Is the simple rather than the complex term or sentence used? Explain.
    b. Are the levels of abstraction varied? Identify specific instances of high and low levels of abstraction.
    c. Are there any sexist terms or references? Identify specific instances.
    d. Identify any transitional phrases used? Are they helpful?
    e. Are marker terms, phrases, and sentences used?
    f. Is repetition, restatement, or internal summaries used?
    g. Is the language used appropriate to the speech, subject, audience, and occasion? Explain.
    h. Is the language vivid? Does it help create images as you read it?
    i. Is the language personalized? Identify specific instances of such personalization.

I HAVE A DREAM
Martin Luther King, Jr.*

I am happy to join with you today in what will go down in history as the greatest demonstration for freedom in the history of our nation.

Source: Copyright © 1963 by Martin Luther King, Jr. Reprinted by permission of Joan Daves.
* Martin Luther King, Jr. (1929–1968), Baptist minister and civil rights leader, won the Nobel Prize in 1964 for his nonviolent struggle for racial equality. The following speech was delivered on August 28th, 1963 at the Lincoln Memorial in Washington, D.C., to some 200,000 blacks and whites holding a demonstration. Some ten civil rights leaders—after meeting with President Kennedy—addressed the crowd. It seemed generally agreed that King's speech was the highlight of the demonstration.

Five score years ago, a great American, in whose symbolic shadow we stand today, signed the Emancipation Proclamation. This momentous decree came as a great beacon light of hope to millions of Negro slaves, who had been seared in the flames of withering injustice. It came as a joyous daybreak to end the long night of their captivity.

But one hundred years later, the Negro is still not free. One hundred years later, the life of the Negro is still sadly crippled by the manacles of segregation and the chains of discrimination. One hundred years later, the Negro lives on a lonely island of poverty in the midst of a vast ocean of material prosperity. One hundred years later, the Negro is still languished in the corners of American society and finds himself an exile in his own land. So we have come here today to dramatize a shameful condition.

In a sense we've come to our nation's Capitol to cash a check. When the architects of our republic wrote the magnificent words of the Constitution and the Declaration of Independence, they were signing a promissory note to which every American was to fall heir. This note was a promise that all men—yes, black men as well as white men—would be guaranteed the unalienable rights of life, liberty, and the pursuit of happiness.

It is obvious today that America has defaulted on this promissory note insofar as her citizens of color are concerned. Instead of honoring this sacred obligation, America has given the Negro people a bad check; a check which has come back marked "insufficient funds." But we refuse to believe that the bank of justice is bankrupt. We refuse to believe that there are insufficient funds in the great vaults of opportunity of this nation. So we've come to cash this check —a check that will give us upon demand the riches of freedom and the security of justice. We have also come to this hallowed spot to remind America of the fierce urgency of *now*. This is no time to engage in the luxury of cooling off or to take the tranquilizing drug of gradualism. *Now is the time* to make real the promises of Democracy. *Now is the time* to rise from the dark and desolate valley of segregation to the sunlight of racial justice. *Now is the time* to lift our nation from the quicksands of racial injustice to the solid rock of brotherhood. *Now is the time* to make justice a reality for all of God's children.

It would be fatal for the nation to overlook the urgency of the moment. This sweltering summer of the Negro's legitimate discontent will not pass until there is an invigorating autumn of freedom and equality. Nineteen sixty-three is not an end, but a beginning. Those who hope that the Negro needed to blow off steam and will now be content will have a rude awakening if the nation returns to business as usual. There will be neither rest nor tranquility in America until the Negro is granted his citizenship rights. The whirlwinds of revolt will continue to shake the foundations of our nation until the bright day of justice emerges.

But that is something that I must say to my people who stand on the warm threshold which leads into the palace of justice. In the process of gaining our rightful place we must not be guilty of wrongful deeds. Let us not seek to satisfy our thirst for freedom by drinking from the cup of bitterness and hatred.

We must forever conduct our struggle on the high plane of dignity and discipline. We must not allow our creative protest to degenerate into physical violence. Again and again we must rise to the majestic heights of meeting physical force with soul force. The marvelous new militancy which has engulfed the

Negro community must not lead us to a distrust of all white people, for many of our white brothers, as evidenced by their presence here today, have come to realize that their destiny is tied up with our destiny. And they have come to realize that their freedom is inextricably bound to our freedom. We cannot walk alone.

And as we walk we must make the pledge that we shall always march ahead. We cannot turn back. There are those who ask the devotees of civil rights, "When will you be satisfied?" We can never be satisfied as long as the Negro is the victim of the unspeakable horrors of police brutality. We can never be satisfied as long as our bodies, heavy with the fatigue of travel, cannot gain lodging in the motels of the highways and the hotels of the cities. We cannot be satisfied as long as the Negro's basic mobility is from a smaller ghetto to a larger one. We can never be satisfied as long as our children are stripped of their selfhood and robbed of their dignity by signs stating "For Whites Only." We cannot be satisfied as long as a Negro in Mississippi cannot vote and a Negro in New York believes he has nothing for which to vote. No, no, we are not satisfied, and we will not be satisfied until justice rolls down like waters and righteousness like a mighty stream.

I am not unmindful that some of you have come here out of great trials and tribulations. Some of you have come fresh from narrow jail cells. Some of you have come from areas where your quest for freedom left you battered by the storms of persecution and staggered by the winds of police brutality. You have been the veterans of creative suffering. Continue to work with the faith that unearned suffering is redemptive.

Go back to Mississippi, go back to Alabama, go back to South Carolina, go back to Georgia, go back to Louisiana, go back to the slums and ghettos of our northern cities knowing that somehow this situation can and will be changed. Let us not wallow in the valley of despair.

I say to you today, my friends, so even though we face the difficulties of today and tomorrow, I still have a dream. It is a dream deeply rooted in the American dream.

I have a dream that one day this nation will rise up and live out the true meaning of its creed: "We hold these truths to be self-evident; that all men are created equal."

I have a dream that one day on the red hills of Georgia the sons of former slaves and the sons of former slaveowners will be able to sit down together at the table of brotherhood; I have a dream—

That one day even the state of Mississippi, a state sweltering with the heat of injustice, sweltering with the heat of oppression, will be transformed into an oasis of freedom and justice; I have a dream—

That my four little children will one day live in a nation where they will not be judged by the color of their skin but by the content of their character; I have a dream today.

I have a dream that one day down in Alabama, with its vicious racists, with its governor having his lips dripping with the words of interposition and nullification, one day right there in Alabama little black boys and black girls will be able to join hands with little white boys and white girls as sisters and brothers; I have a dream today.

I have a dream that one day every valley shall be exalted, every hill and mountain shall be made low, and rough places will be made plane and crooked places will be made straight, and the glory of the Lord shall be revealed, and all flesh shall see it together.

This is our hope. This is the faith that I go back to the South with. With this faith we will be able to hew out of the mountain of despair a stone of hope. With this faith we will be able to transform the jangling discords of our nation into a beautiful symphony of brotherhood. With this faith we will be able to work together, to pray together, to struggle together, to go to jail together, to stand up for freedom together, knowing that we will be free one day.

This will be the day. . . . This will be the day when all of God's children will be able to sing with new meaning "My country 'tis of thee, sweet land of liberty, of thee I sing. Land where my fathers died, land of the pilgrim's pride, from every mountainside, let freedom ring," and if America is to be a great nation—this must become true.

So let freedom ring—from the prodigious hilltops of New Hampshire, let freedom ring; from the mighty mountains of New York, let freedom ring—from the heightening Alleghenies of Pennsylvania!

Let Freedom ring from the snowcapped Rockies of Colorado!

Let freedom ring from the curvaceous slopes of California!

But not only that; let freedom ring from Stone Mountain of Georgia!

Let freedom ring from Lookout Mountain of Tennessee!

Let freedom ring from every hill and mole hill of Mississippi. From every mountainside, let freedom ring, and when this happens. . . .

When we allow freedom to ring, when we let it ring from every village and every hamlet, from every state and every city, we will be able to speed up that day when all of God's children, black men and white men, Jews and Gentiles, Protestants and Catholics, will be able to join hands and sing in the words of the old Negro spiritual, "Free at last! free at last! thank God almighty, we are free at last!"

27.2 INTRODUCTIONS AND CONCLUSIONS

Perhaps the best way to understand the functions served by the introductions and the conclusions of public speeches and the methods by which these functions may be achieved is to examine a number of different introductions and conclusions.

Here we include five introductions and five conclusions from a variety of public speeches—speeches addressed to varied audiences, by very different speakers, at very different times, and with many different purposes. Note the functions each introduction and conclusion serves and the methods used by each speaker.

Introductions

1. Let us ask ourselves, what is education? Above all things, what is our ideal of a thoroughly liberal education?—of that education which, if we could begin life again,

we would give ourselves—of that education which, if we could mould the fates to our own will, we would give our children. Well, I know not what may be your conceptions upon this matter, but I will tell you mine, and I hope I shall find that our views are not very discrepant.

—Thomas Henry Huxley, "A Liberal Education"

2. Mr. President: No man thinks more highly than I do of the patriotism, as well as abilities, of the very worthy gentlemen who have just addressed the house. But different men often see the same subject in different lights; and therefore, I hope it will not be thought disrespectful to those gentlemen, if, entertaining as I do opinions of a character very opposite to theirs, I shall speak forth my sentiments freely and without reserve. This is no time for ceremony. The question before the house is one of awful moment to this country. For my own part, I consider it as nothing less than a question of freedom or slavery; and in proportion to the magnitude of the subject ought to be the freedom of the debate. It is only in this way that we can hope to arrive at truth, and fulfil the great responsibility which we hold to God and our country. Should I keep back my opinions at such a time, through fear of giving offense, I should consider myself as guilty of treason towards my country, and of an act of disloyalty toward the Majesty of Heaven, which I revere above all earthly kings.

—Patrick Henry, "Liberty or Death"

3. There was a South of slavery and secession—that South is dead. There is a South of union and freedom—that South, thank God, is living, breathing, growing every hour. These words, delivered from the immortal lips of Benjamin H. Hill, at Tammany Hall in 1866, true then, and truer now, I shall make my text tonight.

—Henry W. Grady, "The New South"

4. Mr. President: When the mariner has been tossed for many days in thick weather, and on an unknown sea, he naturally avails himself of the first pause in the storm, the earliest glance of the sun, to take his latitude, and ascertain how far the elements have driven him from his true course. Let us imitate this prudence, and, before we float farther on the waves of this debate, refer to the point from which we departed, that we may at least be able to conjecture where we now are. I ask for the reading of the resolution before the Senate.

—Daniel Webster, "Second Speech on Foote's Resolution—Reply to Hayne"

5. I doubt if any young woman on this University ever approached a tough assignment with more trepidation than this not-so-young woman is experiencing over this assignment. For a commencement address *is* a tough assignment for the most experienced of speakers. But when the speaker is not experienced, when she is not even a speaker, you can, if you'll put yourselves in her quaking shoes, imagine her state of mind. I find myself experiencing the familiar panic of that recurrent nightmare peculiar to actors in which a ghoulish bevy of directors and fellow players are bustling one onto a strange stage shouting "Hurry! Hurry! You're late!" And one has no idea of what one's part is, or for that matter what the play is. And one arrives before the audience completely speechless and, often as not, completely naked. Things are not quite that crucial for I do seem able to speak and I do appear to be clad.

—Cornelia Otis Skinner, "To Maximize One's Life"

Conclusions

1. If we can stand up to him all Europe may be freed and the life of the world may move forward into broad sunlit uplands; but if we fail, the whole world, including the United States and all that we have known and cared for, will sink into the abyss of a new dark age made more sinister and perhaps more prolonged by the lights of a perverted science.

Let us therefore brace ourselves to our duty and so bear ourselves that if the British Commonwealth and Empire last for a thousand years, men will still say "This was their finest hour."
—Winston Churchill, "Their Finest Hour"

2. I am endeavoring to show to my countrymen that violent noncooperation only multiplies evil and that as evil can only be sustained by violence, withdrawal of support of evil requires complete abstention from violence. Nonviolence implies voluntary submission to the penalty for noncooperation with evil. I am here, therefore, to invite and submit cheerfully to the highest penalty that can be inflicted upon me for what in law is a deliberate crime and what appears to me to be the highest duty of a citizen. The only course open to you, the judge, is either to resign your post, and thus dissociate yourself from evil if you feel that the law you are called upon to administer is an evil and that in reality I am innocent, or to inflict on me the severest penalty if you believe that the system and the law you are assigning to administer are good for the people of this country and that my activity is therefore injurious to the public weal.
—Mohandas Gandhi, "Nonviolence"

3. I can conceive of nothing worse than a man-governed world except a woman-governed world—but I can see the combination of the two going forward and making civilization more worthy of the name of civilization based on Christianity, not force. A civilization based on justice and mercy. I feel men have a greater sense of justice and we of mercy. They must borrow our mercy and we must use their justice. We are new brooms; let us see that we sweep the right rooms.
—Lady Astor, "Women and Politics"

4. I am against our participation in this war not only because I hate war, but because I hate fascism and all totalitarianism, and love democracy. I speak not only for myself, but for my Party in summoning my fellow countrymen to demand that our country be kept out of war, not as an end in itself, but as a condition to the fulfillment of all our hopes and dreams for a better life for ourselves and our children, yes, and all the children of this great land. The extraordinary shifts and changes in European alliances should but confirm our resolution to stay out of Europe's war, and, ourselves at peace, to seek as occasion permits, the peace of the world.
—Norman Thomas, "America and the War"

5. Let me make myself perfectly clear. I do not want any Catholic in the United States of America to vote for me on the 6th of November because I am a Catholic. If any Catholic in this country believes that the welfare, the well-being, the prosperity, the growth and the expansion of the United States is best conserved and best promoted by the election of Hoover, I want him to vote for Hoover and not for me.

But, on the other hand, I have the right to say that any citizen of this country that believes I can promote its welfare, that I am capable of steering the ship of state safely through the next four years and then votes against me because of my religion, he is not a real, pure, genuine American.
—Alfred E. Smith, "Religion and Politics"

UNIT 28

The Speaker and Receiver in Public Communication

Audience Analysis
Delivery

LEARNING GOALS

After completing this unit, you should be able to:

1. identify and explain why at least six audience variables should be taken into consideration by the speaker preparing a public speech
2. identify the two characteristics that should apply to both the voice and the bodily actions of the public speaker
3. define *volume*, *rate*, *pitch*, and *clarity* as characteristics of effective vocal presentation
4. explain the recommendations made in this unit for the effective use of eye contact, facial expression, gesture, and movement

419

AUDIENCE ANALYSIS

A public speech exists only to be delivered to an audience in order to secure a specific response. Whether that response is laughter, increased knowledge, a change in belief, or specific action, the speaker must keep the nature of the audience and the specific response he or she wishes constantly in mind. Preliminary to ensuring that the audience responds as the listener wishes is an understanding of who they are. With such understanding we will be better able to predict the kinds of stimuli (i.e., messages) to which the audience will respond and the ways in which they will respond. If we can predict how an audience will respond to selected messages, we can effectively move them to respond as we wish.

Audience Variables

Some of the major characteristics that a speaker should consider in his or her attempt to understand the audience are considered here. We must recognize that at times we may be unable to secure any information about our intended audience. At times, we are simply asked to speak to a group of "concerned citizens" or to a group of "students." Clearly this is not of much help. But, in most instances we can, with some effort, learn significant details about the composition of our audience.

Sex

The sex of the audience is perhaps the most readily apparent characteristic and at one time it would have been relatively easy to take the sex factor into consideration in composing the speech. Today, however, the sex of members of the audience is a most difficult variable with which to deal.

At one time, it was possible to talk about women and men as if all women thought or believed alike and as if all men thought or believed alike. Then differences between the sexes could easily be pointed out and adjustments in the speech made. Actually, this was never true but today it is even more false than it was yesterday. Men as a group and women as a group are extremely heterogeneous. We can no longer speak of "men" or of "women" without recognizing that there is great individual variation within each class. Some women are liberated and others are considered unliberated; some men are liberated and others are considered unliberated.

We should be especially careful that we do not employ the familiar but offensive sexual stereotypes: the woman as housekeeper, the man as provider and protector; the woman as sexually naive and restricted, the man as sexually experienced and free; the woman as a nonprofessional—the secretary, salesperson, or waitress, and the man as professional—the doctor, the lawyer, the scientist.

Age

Age is a peculiar variable especially as it is viewed by students of college age. From my experience in introducing strangers to students and asking them to estimate the age of the stranger, I find that students are notoriously poor judges and will miss estimating correctly by 15 or 20 years. Students view their parents who are in their late thirties or forties as old and high school students who are perhaps two or three years their junior as very young.

Perhaps the most commonly noted characteristic of age difference is the difference in liberal versus conservative attitudes. We tend to think that the young are more liberal than the old and that college students particularly are among the most liberal of all. But I think this is changing. College students seem to be becoming more and more conservative in their attitudes toward capital punishment, foreign involvement, welfare, and various other political, social, and economic issues.

Generally, the young want their rewards immediately; the older seem more capable of delaying rewards. Children, at the extreme, want their rewards without a moment's delay. The amount of delay that people can tolerate seems in part a function of age or, perhaps more correctly, maturity. College students generally want relatively immediate rewards. To freshmen, a college degree seems extremely far off; to a middle-aged person four years seems relatively short.

Box 23
"WOMEN'S RIGHT TO VOTE"

Susan B. Anthony

At a time when women's rights are so in the news it is instructive to go back in history for one of the early women's liberationists. Susan B. Anthony (1820–1906) pioneered for women's right to vote and was president of the National Woman Suffrage Association. Her efforts helped greatly in the passage of the Nineteenth Amendment, granting women the right to vote.

In this speech, given in 1873, she defends her "illegal" voting. The speech is an excellent example for studying audience analysis and adaptation. It may also prove interesting to compare Anthony's speech with those given by contemporary liberationists.

Friends and fellow citizens:—I stand before you tonight under indictment for the alleged crime of having voted at the last presidential election, without having a lawful right to vote. It shall be my work this evening to prove to you that in thus voting, I not only committed no crime, but, instead, simply exercised my *citizen's rights,* guaranteed to me and all United States citizens by the National Constitution, beyond the power of any State to deny.

The preamble of the Federal Constitution says:

"We, the people of the United States, in order to form a more perfect union, establish justice, insure *domestic* tranquillity, provide for the common defense, promote the general welfare, and secure the blessings of liberty to ourselves and our posterity, do ordain and establish this Constitution for the United States of America."

It was we, the people; not we, the white male citizens; nor yet we, the male citizens; but we, the whole people, who formed the Union. And we formed it, not to

Freedom is something that is valued very highly by the young, probably because they have not experienced it in all its forms yet. College students want the opportunity to doubt existing values, to question and to evaluate events, people, and objects with their own standards. They want freedom—to do as they wish, to think as they wish, and to live as they wish. They resent parental interference and yet they recognize that they would interfere in probably similar ways with their own children.

They resent the prejudices of their parents and yet seem also to recognize that they have prejudices of their own. Almost without exception, however, they have fewer prejudices than their parents and the students seem more ready to change in light of new information. They seem to have fewer beliefs that they are unwilling to question.

Educational Background

Those of us who have received the benefits of a college education and beyond often forget that the rest of the world has not been through college and has not received its benefits. We sometimes forget that the references to philoso-

give the blessings of liberty, but to secure them; not to the half of ourselves and the half of our posterity, but to the whole people—women as well as men. And it is a downright mockery to talk to women of their enjoyment of the blessings of liberty while they are denied the use of the only means of securing them provided by this democratic-republican government—the ballot.

For any State to make sex a qualification that must ever result in the disfranchisement of one entire half of the people is to pass a bill of attainder, or an *ex post facto* law, and is therefore a violation of the supreme law of the land. By it the blessings of liberty are for ever withheld from women and their female posterity. To them this government has no just powers derived from the consent of the governed. To them this government is not a democracy. It is not a republic. It is an odious aristocracy; a hateful oligarchy of sex; the most hateful aristocracy ever established on the face of the globe; an oligarchy of wealth, where the rich govern the poor. An oligarchy of learning, where the educated govern the ignorant, or even an oligarchy of race, where the Saxon rules the African, might be endured; but this oligarchy of sex, which makes father, brothers, husband, sons, the oligarchs over the mother and sisters, the wife and daughters of every household—which ordains all men sovereigns, all women subjects, carries dissension, discord and rebellion into every home of the nation.

Webster, Worcester and Bouvier all define a citizen to be a person in the United States, entitled to vote and hold office.

The only question left to be settled now is: Are women persons? And I hardly believe any of our opponents will have the hardihood to say they are not. Being persons, then, women are citizens; and no State has a right to make any law, or to enforce any old law, that shall abridge their privileges or immunities. Hence, every discrimination against women in the constitutions and laws of the several States is today null and void, precisely as in every one against Negroes.

phers or to even broad areas like sociology, physics, and anthropology may be unknown to an audience that has not been to college. At the same time we must recognize that college degrees do not divide the world into the "haves" and the "have nots." There are many with degrees who are functional idiots and many without degrees who are functional geniuses.

I mention these "obvious" points here because very often we behave as if we did not know them. Perhaps the classic example I witness all too frequently is the teacher who attempts to address beginning students in a particular subject as if they were graduate students, or the teacher who goes to the other extreme and speaks to the students as if every word needs defining and every concept repeated three different ways. Admittedly, it is difficult to adjust our language and our ideas to the educational level of the audience yet we must attempt it.

Economic Status

That we all differ in terms of the amount of money we have is obvious. What is not so obvious is that this economic difference influences a great many factors. Most importantly, for our purposes, it influences the values, attitudes, and beliefs of people and consequently the audience's economic status should influence the way in which a speech is constructed.

The speaker who talks to people from the lower economic classes in terms of upper-class values or to upper economic classes in terms of lower-class values will surely lead the listeners to doubt the speaker's sincerity or at best his or her understanding of them. For example, the speaker who wants to increase welfare payments will surely have to use different reasoning and support for an upper class and a lower class audience. Similarly, the speaker who wishes to raise real estate taxes will find the poor, who own nothing, to be generally in favor of it while the rich, who own homes and apartment houses, to be against it. These of course are obvious examples and yet even the illustrations we use will affect how an audience will respond.

Religion and Politics

In many instances the religious and political views of the audience members will not make much of a difference. But when they do make a difference, they really make a difference. Issues such as abortion, censorship, socialized medicine, welfare, immigration, and similar topics would all be greatly influenced by the audience's religious and political beliefs.

We should recognize that in considering politics and religion we must consider not only what political and religious affiliations the audience members have but also the degree to which they are "loyal" members or the degree to which they follow the "party line." This is the most difficult aspect to analyze. While it is relatively easy to discover the most common religion of the audience, it is extremely difficult to discover how they allow that religion to influence their lives, their thoughts, and their behaviors. There are Catholics and Orthodox Jews who are in favor of abortion and there are liberals who argue for rigid censorship and so on. Labels that may legitimately be placed on people will inevitably be inadequate to cover all of their behaviors.

Racial and Ethnic Background

At one time it was considered "poor form" to state openly that one even noticed the racial or ethnic make-up of an audience. If, for example, a person was Indian we were implicitly taught that that fact should not only be of little consequence in our dealings with this person but that we were not even to notice the fact that the person was Indian. And so it went for all racial and ethnic groups. Of course we did notice the racial or ethnic group to which the person belonged; we just were not supposed to acknowledge it.

Today, however, racial and ethnic groups are fighting to retain their identity. On college campuses clubs are formed to preserve the ethnic heritage of the students and to educate others to the contributions of the various groups.

Similarly, ethnic groups have banded together to fight for political reforms or concessions. In all of these cases we see a pride in one's heritage. Diversity is now regarded as good and sameness as bad. This is somewhat oversimplified but probably more right than wrong.

The speaker who faces audiences of varied ethnic and racial backgrounds must learn something, about their cultures. The speaker must understand their values, opinions, attitudes, and beliefs.

The speaker must often be prepared to be distrusted at least somewhat if he or she is of a different racial and ethnic background than the majority of the audience members. Furthermore, the speaker must be careful not to attempt to present any false evidence for purposes of identifying with the audience. The "some of my best friends are . . ." technique is trite and more importantly dishonest.

Occupation

The occupation of audience members, like religion and politics, sometimes plays little role but when it does operate, its role is extremely important. Approximately one-quarter of our lives is spent on our jobs. In many instances the amount of time spent is greater. Teachers, doctors, lawyers, and store owners, for example, often spend a great deal more than one-quarter of their time at their jobs. Consequently, when it comes to issues that relate to one's occupation (even indirectly), we need to take this into consideration. Much like the situation with the different races, people in different occupations have difficulty communicating with one another. For example, one of the problems I have witnessed is between laborers and, say, teachers. Laborers have difficulty understanding how teachers can get tired from sitting at a desk or from lecturing to a class. Teachers have no such difficulty. On the other hand, teachers feel that they must always be on their job. It does not end when they come home for dinner. At night and on weekends they must grade papers, prepare lectures, make up examinations, work on committees, keep up with the new developments in the field, and of course write articles and books. And so many teachers look with envy upon laborers who are finished with their job when they come home at night. On Saturday and Sunday the laborer does not have to worry about preparing for Monday but the teacher does. The teacher, on the other hand, has difficulty understanding how physically exhausting bricklaying or paperhanging or trucking can be. Similarly, those who are not going to college have difficulty recognizing that the college student's life can be a difficult one. Sitting in class, listening to lectures, and taking notes may seem easy to someone who has never done it.

This is just one example but it should illustrate that it is not easy to empathize with those who work at very different occupations. Perhaps we can at least recognize that everyone can easily perceive the difficulties with their own job but have difficulty perceiving the difficulties with the jobs of others.

We should also recognize, in a status conscious society such as ours, that people will inevitably see their job as deserving of higher status than will others. Any teacher who assumes that everyone recognizes the higher status of teaching as compared with say firefighting or nursing, for example, is in for a most rude awakening upon encountering a fireman or a nurse.

Attitudes

We must also take into consideration the audience's attitude toward the topic or subject of the speech, the purpose of the speech, the occasion, and the speaker.

The most common problem with an audience's attitude toward the topic or subject of a speech is that they are generally not interested enough in it to maintain attention. When they are uninterested in the subject they will probably have no definite feelings about the purpose of the speech. And so this disinterest, while presenting some problems, at least provides the speaker with an audience that is not violently opposed to the purpose of the speech.

Given this disinterest, however, the speaker's first task is to make the subject interesting, to relate it to the needs of the audience. He or she must show the audience why this topic is crucial, why they should listen.

Generally the speaker is best advised to begin where the audience is. If the audience is in favor of his or her position then he or she may start by stating it and proceed from there. If the audience is against the purpose of the speech then the speaker must recognize this and proceed to eliminate or lessen their attitudes in some way. The same speech on abortion given to a "right to life" group and an adamantly pro-abortion group would be ludicrous.

Most speakers assume, although wrongly, that if an audience is present for a speech that they wish to be there and hence have positive attitudes toward the occasion. These speakers should walk into a college classroom in which the teacher takes attendance and counts it heavily into the grade. The class will be crowded but to say that the audience is positive toward the occasion would be stretching things. The speaker must recognize that listening to speeches is not exactly perceived as the most interesting pasttime by most people. And although the speaker should not overemphasize this, he or she should recognize that it is best to devote some attention to getting the audience to see the occasion as a more positive one than when they walked in. Showing the audience why this topic is important to them, involving them in some way in the proceedings, putting them into a relaxed mood, and similar methods are at the speakers disposal for altering initially negative attitudes.

Lastly, and perhaps the most difficult aspect to analyze objectively, is the attitude of the audience toward the speaker as a person. At times, of course, the audience gathers to hear a particular person because of what that person has accomplished. Perhaps the speaker is a famous politician, scientist, or writer. The audience gathers to hear or see that particular person and often the topic of the speech is of secondary importance. But in most cases the attitudes of the members of the audience are neutral or relatively so and these must be made more positive if the speaker is to have any effect on the audience's thinking. The audience has a right to know why this speaker is speaking on this particular topic. That is, they want to know the speaker's qualifications. Most audiences do not want to hear a man talk about childbirth or a person who has never had children talk about the difficulty in raising children. Similarly we do not want to hear a rich person talk about how to live on a budget or a poor person talk about how to make it big in the stock market. Of course these are extremes which are easily recognized, but most speakers are in the same situation—the audience must recognize the speaker's authority to address his or her subject.

Thus we need to let the audience know that we are qualified to speak on the topic. We need to state our qualifications subtly and with grace and, at the same time, we must not make the audience feel that we are engaging in self indulgent bragging.

Analysis and Adaptation During the Speech

All that has been said has been directed at the preparation stages of the speech. That is, the variables we considered are ones that the speaker should consider as he or she prepares the speech for delivery before an audience. But there is also analysis and adaptation which must be done during the speech, and this is more difficult.

The speaker should constantly be on the lookout for feedback that might help in understanding how the audience members are reacting to the speech. If there are howls of laughter and wild applause at appropriate places, the speaker can be pretty sure of success. Similarly if half the audience walks out and the other half stays to boo and curse the speaker, he or she can be pretty certain of failure. But what of the speakers who fall between these extremes?

Most beginning speakers should attempt to look for some of the more obvious signals. In a classroom if the students are talking among themselves or if they are sitting with bored looks on their faces or reading the newspapers, some adjustment must be made. I have witnessed teachers lecture to a class in which not one student was paying attention and yet the poor teacher just continued on as if everything was fine. This teacher of course should be fired. But this teacher and thousands of similar ones continue to bore a potentially stimulating audience.

One of the most difficult things to do as a speaker is to see negative reactions as clearly as we see positive reactions. Few of us have difficulty seeing favorable responses but we need to train ourselves to see the unfavorable responses so that we can adjust what we are saying and turn that unfavorable reaction into a favorable one.

Box 24
"ALL FOR LOVE"

Edward VIII

Edward VIII (1894–1972), perhaps more widely known as the Duke of Windsor, was King of Great Britain from January 20 to December 10, 1936. On December 11, 1936, Edward VIII delivered the following farewell address, abdicating the throne so that he might marry the twice-divorced Wallis Simpson—a marriage that the British hierarchy could not accept.

The speech is a model of effective audience adaptation and style.

At long last I am able to say a few words of my own. I have never wanted to withhold anything, but until now it has not been constitutionally possible for me to speak.

A few hours ago I discharged my last duty as King and Emperor, and now that I have been succeeded by my brother, the Duke of York, my first words must be to declare my allegiance to him. This I do with all my heart.

You all know the reasons which have impelled me to renounce the throne. But I want you to understand that in making up my mind I did not forget the country or the empire, which, as Prince of Wales and lately as King, I have for twenty-five years tried to serve.

But you must believe me when I tell you that I have found it impossible to carry the heavy burden of responsibility and to discharge my duties as King as I would wish to do without the help and support of the woman I love.

And I want you to know that the decision I have made has been mine and mine alone. This was a thing I had to judge entirely for myself. The other person

Again, we must remember that being overly concerned with audience response can make us too nervous to communicate effectively. And so we need a judicious rather than obsessive surveillance of audience feedback.

DELIVERY

Perhaps the topic of most concern to the beginning public speaker is that of delivery. The speaker seldom worries about organization or even the language of the speech. Instead he or she concentrates on delivery, generally worrying a great deal more than is necessary. Although each speaker must develop a manner of presentation that is suitable to his or her own personality, some general suggestions are offered here. Again we must recognize that these suggestions must be modified in light of the specific audience, specific purpose, and specific topic.

Perhaps the most important characteristic of effective delivery—of the voice as well as of the body—is *naturalness.* The speaker should appear natural to the audience. Studied gestures, planned movements, and overly precise ar-

most nearly concerned has tried up to the last to persaude me to take a different course.

I have made this, the most serious decision of my life, only upon the single thought of what would, in the end, be best for all.

This decision has been made less difficult to me by the sure knowledge that my brother, with his long training in the public affairs of this country and with his fine qualities, will be able to take my place forthwith without interruption or injury to the life and progress of the empire. And he has one matchless blessing, enjoyed by so many of you, and not bestowed on me—a happy home with his wife and children.

During these hard days I have been comforted by her Majesty my mother and by my family. The ministers of the crown, and in particular, Mr. Baldwin, the Prime Minister, have always treated me with full consideration. There has never been any constitutional difference between me and them, and between me and Parliament. Bred in the constitutional tradition by my father, I should never have allowed any such issue to arise.

Ever since I was Prince of Wales, and later on when I occupied the throne, I have been treated with the greatest kindness by all classes of the people wherever I have lived or journeyed throughout the empire. For that I am very grateful.

I now quit altogether public affairs and I lay down my burden. It may be some time before I return to my native land, but I shall always follow the fortunes of the British race and empire with profound interest, and if at any time in the future I can be found of service to his Majesty in a private station, I shall not fail.

And now, we all have a new King. I wish him and you, his people, happiness and prosperity with all my heart. God bless you all! God save the King!

ticulation, for example, only call attention to the speaker and listeners find themselves concentrating on the delivery instead of on the speech. This concept of naturalness does not mean that the speaker should slouch, chew gum, and speak in his or her local slang; that too would call attention to the delivery instead of to the concepts being discussed. The speaker should appear natural for the particular occasion and the topic; attention should not be drawn to the manner of delivery.

A second general characteristic of delivery is *variety.* Both speech and bodily movement should be varied. Nothing puts an audience to sleep faster than a monotonous voice and a body that does absolutely nothing. Vary both the voice—rate, volume, pitch—and the body with some movements of the face as well as of the arms and legs. Again, the movements should never call attention to themselves. Rather, they should appear natural and spontaneous, generated by the moment and not studied in front of a mirror at home.

Naturalness and variety are two general characteristics that apply to both the voice and the bodily actions of the public speaker. More specific suggestions for increasing the effectiveness of the voice and bodily actions follow.

Voice

Although many characteristics of the voice may be considered (and certainly many characteristics are significant), only a few can be considered here. We limit our consideration here to those characteristics which the individual can improve (volume, rate, pausing, pitch, and clarity) rather than those characteristics that must be dealt with by a trained speech therapist.

Volume

Volume is a particularly difficult concept to discuss since we do not hear ourselves the way others do. Generally, speakers have no idea if they are speaking at a proper volume or not. In a small classroom, volume seldom presents too many problems, but in a large auditorium volume must be carefully studied.

We need to be aware that the speaker can err in either direction. Generally, we err in the direction of speaking overly soft. Perhaps this is due to fear, perhaps to a reticence to take control of the situation; but whatever the reason it should be clear that no speaker will be effective if he or she cannot be heard. The speaker should also recognize that by speaking too loudly he or she makes the audience uncomfortable. Within this relatively normal range that is easy to hear and yet not too piercing, the speaker should vary the volume, speaking certain key words or phrases at a somewhat higher volume and perhaps lowering the voice when the occasion seems to require it. If the speaker has a clear understanding of the topic, the places where the volume should be increased or decreased will suggest themselves.

Rate

Rate refers to the speed with which we speak and also to the pauses we use. A normal speech rate is between 120 and 180 words per minute and the normal rate within this range is quite varied. The speaker must be careful to avoid either extreme. Speaking at too slow a rate will surely bore the audience, their minds will wander, and it will be almost impossible to get their attention back to the speech. Similarly, speaking at too fast a rate will confuse the audience and they will be unable to follow the ideas presented by the speaker. The rate should be fast enough to keep the interest of the audience but slow enough so that they can follow the speaker's ideas. The rate should be varied so that monotony does not set in. Certain examples may be spoken more rapidly than perhaps an important conclusion. Again, if the speaker understands what he or she is saying, the rates should suggest themselves.

Pauses are extremely important to the speaker and should be utilized to guide the audience in following the speaker's line of reasoning. The speaker should realize that he or she has gone over the speech a number of times but that the audience is hearing it only once. Consequently, the audience needs time to "digest" significant points and to make important connections.

Pitch

Pitch refers to the highness or lowness of the voice. In the sentence "Are you going to marry that beast?" we can change the meaning of the sentence by varying the pitch of the various words. Compare, for example, the following versions:

Are YOU going to marry that beast?
Are you going TO MARRY that beast?
Are you going to marry THAT BEAST?

Each of these, as can easily be appreciated, means something quite different.

In everyday conversation we vary our pitch without any conscious awareness. Generally the meaning we wish to convey guides us in raising or lowering our pitch. If public speaking, as many have put it, is enlarged conversation, then we may at times have to exaggerate some of the changes in pitch so that our meaning is extra clear to the audience.

We have to be very careful, however, that our pitch changes do not seem phony. We must also be very careful that our pitch changes do not result in a sing-song effect—up and down, up and down. This is perhaps the one thing worse than a totally monotonous pitch.

Clarity

Clarity really pertains to articulation and pronunciation rather than to the voice. Clarity of articulation is the production of individual sounds that are free from distortions produced by excessive noise. By clarity of pronunciation we mean the production of words and phrases in the ways considered acceptable for your region.

Do not attempt to imitate the Oxford professor or the street bum; speak in public as you do in private. Generally, be careful to avoid any attempts at overly precise speech. This appears artificial and is insulting to an audience. It in effect says that the speaker is attempting to put something over on them. At the same time the speaker should avoid slovenly speech. The speech of the public speaker should be dignified without being artificial, conversational without being sloppy.

When the speaker is in doubt about the pronunciation of a particular word he or she should make sure to consult a dictionary. Even one word incorrectly pronounced may make the audience think the speaker knows nothing of the topic and may well lead the audience to tune the speaker out.

Box 25
"THE MURDER OF GANDHI"

Jawaharlal Nehru

Jawaharlal Nehru (1889–1964) became the first prime minister of independent India in 1947. Nehru delivered the following speech on the occasion of the death of Mohandas Gandhi, one of India's most beloved leaders, at the hands of a Hindu nationalist.

This speech is included here because it is one of the best examples of a eulogy— a speech in praise of some individual. Although the speech is about one person, there is still a timelessness and a universality to it.

Friends and comrades, the light has gone out of our lives and there is darkness everywhere. I do not know what to tell you and how to say it. Our beloved leader, Bapu as we called him, the father of the nation, is no more. Perhaps I am wrong to say that. Nevertheless, we will not see him again as we have seen him for these many years. We will not run to him for advice and seek solace from him, and that is a terrible blow, not to me only, but to millions and millions in this country, and it is a little difficult to soften the blow by any other advice that I or anyone else can give you.

The light has gone out, I said, and yet I was wrong. For the light that shone in this country was no ordinary light. The light that has illumined this country for these many years will illumine this country for many more years, and a thousand years later that light will still be seen in this country and the world will see it and will give solace to innumerable hearts. For that light represented the living truth . . . the eternal truths, reminding us of the right path, drawing us from error, taking this ancient country to freedom.

All this has happened when there was so much more for him to do. We could never think that he was unnecessary or that he had done his task. But now, particularly, when we are faced with so many difficulties, his not being with us is a blow most terrible to bear.

Bodily Action

The public speaker should give considerable attention to bodily action and yet not let it become the most important element in the total public speaking process.

Eye Contact

Perhaps the most important aspect of body language is that of eye contact. Most researchers in nonverbal communication have found that more information is communicated by the eyes than by any other part of the body—even the voice. Intuitively we are apt to rely on the eyes to give us information about another individual; we say we trust the eyes or that the eyes tell the truth while the mouth lies. When a person professes a deep interest in us and yet glances

A madman has put an end to his life, for I can only call him mad who did it, and yet there has been enough of poison spread in this country during the past years and months, and this poison has had effect on people's minds. We must face this poison, we must root out this poison, and we must face all the perils that encompass us and face them not madly or badly but rather in the way that our beloved teacher taught us to face them. The first thing to remember now is that no one of us dare misbehave because we are angry. We have to behave like strong and determined people, determined to face all the perils that surround us, determined to carry out the mandate that our great teacher and our great leader has given us, remembering always that if, as I believe, his spirit looks upon us and sees us, nothing would displease his soul so much as to see that we have indulged in any small behavior or any violence.

So we must not do that. But that does not mean that we should be weak, but rather that we should in strength and in unity face all the troubles that are in front of us. We must hold together, and all our petty troubles and difficulties and conflicts must be ended in the face of this great disaster. A great disaster is a symbol to us to remember all the big things of life and forget the small things, of which we have thought too much.

It was proposed by some friends that Mahatmaji's body should be embalmed for a few days to enable millions of people to pay their last homage to him. But it was his wish, repeatedly expressed, that no such thing should happen, that this should not be done, that he was entirely opposed to any embalming of his body.

Tomorrow should be a day of fasting and prayer for all of us. Those who live elsewhere out of Delhi and in other parts of India will no doubt also take such part as they can in this last homage. For them also let this be a day of fasting and prayer. And at the appointed time for cremation, that is, 4:00 P.M. tomorrow afternoon, people should go to the river or to the sea and offer prayers there. And while we pray, the greatest prayer that we can offer is to take a pledge to dedicate ourselves to the truth and to the cause for which this great countryman of ours lived and for which he has died.

around the room or at the floor, we intuitively begin to doubt the sincerity of what is being said.

Years ago I remember being told that when speaking to a large audience one should focus on something on the back wall, like the clock or the door, and not to worry about looking at the audience. That bit of advice ranks among the dumbest of all things ever said about public speaking. If public speaking is to be effective the speaker must address the audience and that includes looking the audience in the eyes. The audience needs to feel that the speaker is maintaining contact with them and this is best achieved by direct eye contact. Similarly, the speaker needs to have some way of gaining information as to how the speech is going and he or she can best get this from reading the expressions in the eyes of the audience. Put differently, direct eye contact enables the speaker to communicate his or her message to the audience more effectively and at the same time allows the speaker an opportunity to read the messages from the audience more effectively.

Facial Expression

Second in importance to eye contact is facial expression (not easily separated from eye contact). With the face we again feel intuitively that we can rely on what it tells us. A smile, a frown, a smirk, or a grin can all communicate a great deal of information. If the information the speaker communicates with his or her face differs from that communicated by the speaker's verbal messages, the audience will believe the facial messages. Consequently, the speaker must take special care that the messages communicated by the face supplement and complement rather than contradict the messages coming from his or her mouth.

Gestures

At one time in history the major portion of public speaking instruction was given over to instructing the would-be speaker in the use of the hands and arms. The various meanings of each gesture were carefully calculated and the speaker needed to study each meaning and each gesture. When he or she wished to express anger, the speaker could clench the fist and bring it down rapidly into the open palm of the other hand. With this type of knowledge it was thought the speaker would always have a ready arsenal of gestures to supplement what was being said. Although the general idea of this type of training seemed reasonable enough, there were two major problems associated with it. The first was that there are many ways to express the various emotions and that what is appropriate to one person may not be appropriate to another person. Not everyone expresses anger by a clenched fist. Furthermore, as can easily be appreciated, if everyone used the same gestures the whole believability of the gestures would be lost. And this is related to the second major problem with this type of training and that is that effective nonverbal communication for the public speaker seems to be that which occurs in a spontaneous manner rather than that which is studied and rehearsed in detail. This, of course, is contrary to what the actor would tell us; his or her gestures are carefully planned. But actors' training enables them to make the gestures appear spontaneous and hence effective.

The public speaker should rehearse his or her speech using gestures but should not plan the gestures to the point that he or she knows when each gesture will appear. Rather, a rehearsal with gestures should be such that the speaker will feel comfortable using gestures in front of the audience. Put differently, we should be careful not to use gestures that appear studied and artificial but, at the same time, we should practice our speech enough so that we do not feel inhibited in using gestures.

Movement

The public speaker should move about a bit but not to the point that he or she becomes difficult to follow. We feel more relaxed when we see a speaker who is relaxed and one of the best ways to signal relaxation and a feeling of comfort is to move about. However, the problem of stationary microphones and television cameras makes it more and more difficult for the public speaker to move about. If the speaker is equipped with a hand or neck microphone it is easier to walk around, yet the cord always seems to get caught under many speakers' feet.

Movement should again be consonant with the purpose of the speech and with the specifics of the message being communicated. A step forward, for example, may be a convenient way to signal the beginning of a major point and a step back may help to signal the audience to pause for a moment to reflect on what has been said. A walk to the left or to the right helps to keep the entire audience in the purview of the speaker so that no one feels slighted. Again, however, too much or to little movement will hinder the speaker in achieving a naturalness of delivery.

In incorporating any of these delivery suggestions into public speaking behavior, the speaker should keep clearly in mind the two characteristics of effective delivery—naturalness and variety.

SOURCES

On audiences see, for example, Kenneth E. Andersen, *Persuasion: Theory and Practice* (Boston: Allyn & Bacon, 1971) and Paul D. Holtzman, *The Psychology of Speakers' Audiences* (Glenview, Ill.: Scott, Foresman, 1970). On audience analysis see Theodore Clevenger, *Audience Analysis* (Indianapolis: Bobbs-Merrill, 1966) and James W. Gibson and Michael S. Hanna, *Audience Analysis: A Programmed Approach to Receiver Behavior* (Englewood Cliffs, N.J.: Prentice-Hall, 1976).

Discussions on voice can be found in Joseph A. DeVito, Jill Giattino, and T. D. Schon, *Articulation and Voice: Effective Communication* (Indianapolis: Bobbs-Merrill, 1975).

EXPERIENTIAL VEHICLES

28.1 AUDIENCE ANALYSIS (CLASS)

Since most of your introductory speeches will be delivered in this class, it is perhaps best to start with an analysis of the class as your audience.

Take a good look at the class members and complete the following Audience Analysis Form. In most instances you will have no reliable evidence so just make the best predictions you can.

After the form has been filled out, each of the variables should be discussed with the class as a whole so that accurate and inaccurate predictions may be discovered and so that each member will have an accurate analysis of the audience. It may be helpful to pass around a form with each of the variables listed so that each member can fill in his or her personal information which can be conveniently tabulated.

AUDIENCE ANALYSIS FORM

1. *Sex*
   Identify the percentage or number of males and females; also note the common marital status.

2. *Age*
   Approximately how many members are in each of these major age groups:

   _____ 17–20, _____ 21–25, _____ 26–30, _____ 31–35, _____ 36+

3. *Educational Background*
   Since in most college classes the educational backgrounds are very similar, note here if a significant number attended private, religious, or public schools or other colleges or whether some members attended college some years ago. Also note if members have had other educational experiences such as music, art, or drama instruction, trade instruction, and so forth.

4. *Economic Status*
   Note here the various income categories of the class members:

   _____ Below $10,000, _____ $10,000–$20,000, _____ $20,000–$30,000, _____ $30,000–$40,000, _____ $40,000+

5. *Religion and Politics*
   Identify the major religious and political preferences of the class members as well as how strongly they identify with these religious and political groups.

6. *Racial and Ethnic Background*
   Identify the major racial and ethnic groups to which class members belong. As in the case of religion and politics, try to assess how strongly they identify with their racial and ethnic backgrounds.

7. *Occupation/Occupational Goals*
   Note the major present occupations of the class members, either parttime or full time, as well as the professional goals of the members.

8. *Attitudes*
   Try to predict what the attitudes of this audience would be to the following speeches. On what specific factors do you base your predictions?

   a. speech in favor of antiabortion legislation
   b. speech against school busing to achieve racial balance
   c. speech in favor of strong censorship laws
   d. speech in favor of increasingly high college admissions requirements for new entering students
   e. speech against the current welfare system
   f. speech in favor of socialized medicine

   What kinds of speech adaptations would you make in light of this audience analysis? Be as specific as possible.

28.2 ANALYZING A MASS AUDIENCE

The purpose of this experience is to familiarize you with some of the essential steps in analyzing a mass audience on the basis of relatively little evidence and in adapting various speeches to this audience.

The class should be broken up into small groups of five or six members. Each group will be given a different magazine and its task is to analyze the audience (i.e., the readers or subscribers) of that particular magazine in terms of the variables noted on the following analysis form and discussed in this unit. The only information the groups will have about their audience is that they are avid readers of the given magazine. Pay particular attention to the type of articles published in the magazine, the advertisements, the photographs or illustrations, the editorial statement, the price of the magazine, and so on.

Appropriate magazines for analysis are: *Gentlemen's Quarterly, Movie Life, Ms., Playboy, Playgirl, Scientific American, Field and Stream, Family Circle, Good Housekeeping, Reader's Digest, Book Digest, National Geographic.*

Magazines differing widely from each other are most appropriate for this experience.

To complete the analysis, try to assess the attitude of the audience to the speeches identified in the *Attitudes* category and indicate the kinds of adaptations you would make in light of the findings of your audience analysis.

Each group should then share their insights with the rest of the class.

AUDIENCE ANALYSIS FORM

Record here your analysis of the readers of the specific magazines assigned in terms of percentages.

1. *Sex*

   _____ males, _____ females

2. *Age*

   _____ below 18, _____ 19–25, _____ 26–35, _____ 36+

3. *Educational Background*
   (Note the highest level reached.)

   _____ elementary school, _____ high school, _____ college, _____ graduate school

4. *Economic Status*
   (Note status of audience members or of their families when they live with their family.)

   _____ below $10,000, _____ $11,000–$20,000, _____ $21,000–$30,000, _____ $31,000–$40,000, _____ $41,000+

5. *Religion and Politics*

   _____ Protestant, _____ Catholic, _____ Jew, _____ Atheist, _____ other

   _____ democrat, _____ republican, _____ socialist, _____ liberal, _____ conservative, _____ communist, _____ other

6. *Racial and Ethnic Background*
   (Identify the major racial and ethnic backgrounds.)

7. *Occupations/Occupational Goals*
   (Identify the major occupations or occupational goals of the audience members.)

8. *Attitudes*
   Try to predict what the attitudes of this audience would be to the same speeches noted in exercise 28.1, that is:

a. abortion
b. school busing
c. censorship
d. increasingly high college admissions requirements
e. current welfare system
f. socialized medicine

28.3 THE PUBLIC SPEECH

The following speech topics should provide sufficient suggestions for the preparation and delivery of a public speech. These topics are intended as suggestions, not limitations, on what would serve as a suitable topic for a public speech. In utilizing this exercise the instructor may wish to make all or some of the following guidelines more specific:

1. the time limit for presenting the speech
2. the criteria governing the specific subject of the speech
3. the nature and extent of the research needed for the speech
4. the type and form of the speech outline
5. the ways in which the speech is to be structured
6. the method of delivery to be used
7. the types of supporting materials to be used
8. the general purpose—whether informative, entertaining, or persuasive
9. the specific purpose in terms of behavioral objectives
10. the specific audience to be addressed, whether this class or some hypothetical audience the class members are to role play

Suggested Speaking Topics

1. a speech explaining one or more of the technical terms used in communication (see glossary for beginning ideas)
2. a speech on any subject of economic, philosophical, political, or socio-psychological importance
3. a speech in which you attempt to answer the question, "Who Am I?"
4. a speech on some current event of local, national, or international importance
5. a speech on the life of some historical figure
6. a speech to motivate the audience to behave in a certain way
7. a speech in which you take issue with some current situation, belief, or mode of behavior
8. a speech to reinforce some existing attitude or belief of the audience
9. a speech to reduce audience apathy toward some aspect of their environment
10. a speech to enhance the credibility of yourself or of some other individual
11. a speech in which you analyze the effectiveness-ineffectiveness of a spe-

cific communication, for example, a public speech, a book or newspaper article, a television program, a film, and so on.

12. a speech to answer any one of the following questions:

   a. what is effective communication or an effective communicator?
   b. what are some barriers to effective communication?
   c. what is the importance of self-disclosure?
   d. what ethical principles should govern advertising, big business, classroom activities, government, religious groups, therapist-patient relationships, the medical profession, or the legal profession?
   e. what role does credibility play in politics, in education, or in advertising?

UNIT 29
The Nature of Mass Communication

A Definition of Mass Communication
Forms of Mass Communication
The Audiences of Mass Communication

29.1 Models of Mass Communication

LEARNING GOALS

After completing this unit, you should be able to:

1. define mass communication
2. explain the one-way process view of mass communication
3. explain the two-way selection process
4. explain the relationship between technology and the need for media
5. explain the nature of the audiences to which the media appeal
6. explain the social nature of the mass media
7. identify and explain the major forms of mass communication and the major functions each serves

A DEFINITION OF MASS COMMUNICATION

As the term implies mass communication is a form of communication, a special kind of communication. At a very general level two characteristics of this form of communication may be considered definitional. First, mass communication is communication addressed to the masses, to an extremely large audience. This does not mean that the audience includes all people or everyone who reads or everyone who watches television; rather, it means an audience that is large and generally rather poorly defined. Second, mass communication is communication mediated by audio and/or visual transmitters. Mass communication is perhaps most easily and most logically defined by its forms: television, radio, newspapers, magazines, films, books, and tapes. Mass communication is indeed all around us. It is, in fact, the principal means by which we obtain information and form attitudes.

Charles Wright, in his *Mass Communication,* notes in a somewhat more extensive definitional approach, that mass communication depends on three variables: the nature of the audience, the nature of the communication experience, and the nature of the communicator. First, the mass communication audience is a relatively large one. Second, the audience is a heterogeneous one composed of people from varied social groups and with varied and different characteristics. Third, the audience is an anonymous one; the audience members and the communicator are generally not personally known to one another.

The mass communication experience is a public one; everyone has access to it. Unlike a talk at a bar or a classroom lecture, mass communications may be received by anyone. The communication is also rapid; the messages are sent to an audience as soon as they are received by the communicators. This characteristic of speed has a number of qualifications, however. A novel may take years to write and a television series years to put together. And yet once they are completed there is little time lost in the transmission of the message. This rapid nature of mass communication refers most specifically to the broadcasting of news items and events. We can see fires, robberies, political rallies, and speeches while they are in progress and this, to use Marshall McLuhan's term, has turned us into a "global village" where world events are common knowledge. Third, the communication experience is transient; the message is meant to be consumed once and it is gone. It is much like human speech in its transient, evanescent character. This characteristic also has qualifications. Video and cassette tapes and libraries have preserved many of our mass communications and have enabled us to see television shows and read messages again and again. But the general nature of mass communication, nevertheless, seems to be transient.

The nature of the communicator is that of a complex organization that goes to great expense to construct and transmit the communication messages. Television programs are put together by enormous teams of people. Even this book, although written by one person, was put together by an entire staff of people. An editor signed up the book; a designer was needed to select the typefaces and design the pages. Photographers were needed to take the pictures. Typesetters and printers were needed to compose and print the actual pages. Proofreaders and editors were needed to see that typographical and grammatical errors did not remain. A production editor coordinated the various efforts of the entire staff. People were needed to design the advertisements and salepersons were needed to sell it. Book stores had to stock it and teachers had to order it for you to have it now. A book such as you are now reading might cost the publishers $30,000 to produce. Although this seems like a great deal recall that it took millions to produce *Cleopatra* or *Bluebird* and how many even remember these films? Although mass communications cost a great deal to produce they cost the receiver or consumer very little, at least in direct cost. The price of a book is perhaps the most expensive media product because the price of a book must meet the entire cost of production. It costs us nothing to watch a television program or to listen to a radio show because the consumer pays for the shows indirectly by purchasing the advertisers' products. The advertiser assumes the direct cost of the communications through the purchase of "air time" for commercials.

Rivers, Peterson, and Jensen, in their *The Mass Media and Modern Society* offer five general characteristics of the process nature of mass communication; these should help to further clarify the nature of mass communication.

1. Mass communication is essentially one way, going from source or sources to receivers. In interpersonal communication, on the other hand, com-

munication goes from source to receiver and then from receiver back to source and continues to alternate between the parties involved. But in mass communication the messages flow from the media to the receivers but not back again except in the form of letters to the editor, audience ratings, box office receipts, and the like. It is true, as Nicholas Johnson says, that we can talk back to our television sets but we can only do so indirectly and with considerable delay. This special kind of message (feedback) is discussed at length in Unit 30.

2. There is a two-way selection process involved. The first part of this selection process refers to the media selecting that portion of the total population that it will attempt to make its audience. For example, the media might attempt to gain unmarried women in their twenties and thirties as their principal audience and so will direct their messages to this particular group of people. The second part of this selection process refers to the selection, from all the media available, of that particular subsection of media to which that individual will attend. Some will read *Photoplay,* others will read *Ms.,* others will read *Time,* still others will read *Playboy,* and so on.

3. As technology advances the need for different media decreases. Consider, for example, what it would take to transmit a hand-written note to a large audience across the country. Thousands of people would have to be involved or someone would have to march across country and deliver the note to each person in turn. But with advanced technology the situation changes dramatically. One television station can reach millions at the same time, a photograph can be reproduced in the offices of every major newspaper in the country in a matter of minutes, one newspaper can be distributed throughout the country within one day's time. Put differently, relatively few media are needed to reach audiences of millions.

4. Because of the vast number of persons receiving mass messages, it is impossible for the media to adapt to each person, even generally. It is necessary for the message to be directed to some "mythical modal point at which the largest number of people cluster," as Rivers, Peterson, and Jensen put it. In this way the media attempt to secure the largest number of possible receivers as their audience.

5. Mass media are social institutions that are influenced by the social environment in which they function. Conversely, the media in turn influence the social environment. There is, in other words, a transactional relationship between the media and the society; each influences the other. Thus, for example, the media influence the economic conditions of the society but they are also influenced by the economic conditions as well. And the same transactional relationship holds for the political and educational dimensions as well.

FORMS OF MASS COMMUNICATION

Of the numerous forms of mass communication, seven are singled out for consideration: television, radio, newspapers, magazines, films, books, and records-tapes-cassettes.

Television

Without a doubt television is the most pervasive and the most popular of all the mass media in this country and throughout a large part of the world. Although there are many nations in which television is not as popular or as widespread as in the United States, the televisionless world is shrinking rapidly and will soon be gone completely.

It is reported that the average television set is on between 5 and 6 hours per day. This is a total of 1825 to 2190 hours per year or between 76 and 91 complete days per year. Each week this comes to 35 to 42 hours, which is approximately the amount of time people work or sleep. It is, in short, a significant and vital part of the American way of life. Although we might argue over whether it would be for the better or for the worse, it would have to be agreed that American life without television would be drastically different.

Although there are only 721 television stations in the United States (compared with 4357 AM stations and 2448 FM stations), Nielsen estimates that of the 70 million homes in the United States in 1976, 100 percent are television homes, 74 percent are color television homes, and 43 percent have two or more sets.

Television is a particularly good example of what Marshall McLuhan calls a "cool" medium. A "cool" medium is one that requires the audience to supply a great deal of information; a fuzzy television picture requires that the viewer fill in the missing information and this requires active participation by the audience. A "hot" medium, on the other hand, requires little audience participation; an example would be a cinemascope movie. The distinction McLuhan draws is actually a perceptional one. The television screen presents its pictures by transmitting an enormous number of small dots of light. The central nervous

---

Box 26
THE TEN TV SHOWS MOST POPULAR WITH TEENAGERS

"Starsky and Hutch"
"Laverne and Shirley"
"The ABC Sunday Night Movie"*
"Happy Days"
"Welcome Back, Kotter"
"What's Happening!!"
"Charlie's Angels"
"The Six Million Dollar Man"
"M*A*S*H"
"Barney Miller"

Source: These shows were rated as the most watched by teen-agers by the A. C. Nielsen Company and were based on one two week period (from January 9 to January 22, 1977) and were reported in TV Guide, April 23, 1977.
* The movies were: *The Reincarnation of Peter Proud* and *Little Ladies of the Night.*

system has to organize these into meaningful wholes, hence television requires active participation.

McLuhan does not leave the issue of hot and cool here, however. Rather, he extends its implications to account for, for example, the tendency of the television generation to get involved actively in social issues. People raised on hot media did not feel the need to become so involved. Academically, the television generation finds lectures, however logically presented, boring; they want to become actively involved in the educational process and resent functioning solely as receptacles into which teachers pour their knowledge.

Obviously not everyone agrees with McLuhan. But his theories certainly are interesting and provocative. And, as Tom Wolfe said, "What if he is right?"

Radio

Before the advent of television radio was the dominant mass communication system. Much like families who now gather to watch the hit television shows, families used to gather to listen to the hit radio shows—"Jack Benny," "Charlie McCarthy," "The Shadow," "The Lone Ranger"—shows we remember from trivia quizzes and from stories told by those in their forties, fifties, and sixties.

Television has surely usurped the dominant role of radio and because of this radio has had to redirect its focus. Instead of appealing to the large audience that television has permanently won over, radio has concentrated on the smaller audiences and attempts to cater to these more specialized interests, for example, opera and symphony music lovers, news enthusiasts, country and western or rock and roll fans, and so on. At the same time, radio remains dominant in those situations in which sufficient visual attention cannot be given to the media and it serves as a kind of background noise while resting on the beach, working in the office, or driving to school. Here television cannot compete and so radio seems to be relatively secure—at least it seemed that way before the coming of tape decks and cassette players. These may eventually take over those functions radio now serves. They seem to have done this with a significant portion of the young already.

Newspapers

Although newspapers are clearly a form of mass communication, they are less "mass" than, say, radio or television. Today, everyone watches television, even the highly educated who at one time resisted, and similarly everyone listens to the radio at least at some time. But not everyone reads newspapers. Newspapers are read by the more educated and by the older.

Newspapers serve two general functions. First, and perhaps most obvious, is that they are sources of information. The older and the more educated readers use newspapers for this function. The young and the less educated generally use newspapers for their secondary function—entertainment, whether it is the arts, sports, or pornographic revelations.

TEN NEWSPAPERS WITH HIGHEST CIRCULATION

New York News	1,902,717
Wall Street Journal	1,465,633
Los Angeles Times	1,004,718
New York Times	841,476
Chicago Tribune	747,715
Spokane Chronicle	641,841
Detroit News	627,461
Detroit Free Press	622,339
Chicago Sun Times	560,124
Philadelphia Bulletin	555,381

Source: Audit Bureau of Circulations' *FAS-FAX Report*, 1976, and *The World Almanac and Book of Facts*, 1977, p. 428.

Newspapers may also be classified in terms of the size of the audience they reach. First, there are general newspapers such as the *New York Times* or the *Washington Post.* These papers are addressed to the largest segment of the population. Second, there are the local newspapers such as neighborhood weeklies or small city dailies. Third, there are the specialized papers which might better be called magazines, such as the *Village Voice, Variety, Billboard, Women's Wear Daily,* and the like. These papers are addressed to a specialized audience and although they rely on their news value it is news in the very specialized sense of trade information or gossip. The same seems true of the *Wall Street Journal* which has a very large but very specialized audience.

Magazines

Much that applies to newspapers also applies to magazines. Magazines are both general and specialized. The general magazines would include *Readers Digest, TV Guide,* and *Family Circle.* The specialized magazines would include all of those that appeal to a specific and relatively small audience. For example, *Science* appeals to that relatively small group of persons concerned with sophisticated scientific developments. *Scientific American* appeals to a similar audience but one that is somewhat less specialized, almost to the general but educated reader interested in science. *Gentlemen's Quarterly* appeals to fashion-conscious men much like *Vogue* appeals to fashion-conscious women.

Films

Films represent a paradox. On the one hand, television severely cuts into the profits of the movie industry, leading to the closing of numerous theatres

Box 28
TEN MAGAZINES WITH HIGHEST CIRCULATION

TV Guide	19,168,096
Reader's Digest	18,142,923
National Geographic	9,039,374
Family Circle	8,364,442
Woman's Day	8,167,108
Better Homes and Gardens	8,126,644
Ladies' Home Journal	7,067,039
McCall's	6,801,287
Playboy	5,701,007
Good Housekeeping	5,250,597

Source: Audit Bureau of Circulations' *FAS-FAX Report,* 1976, and *The World Almanac and Book of Facts,* 1977, p. 429.

throughout the country and to a drop in the percentage of entertainment income spent on the movies. On the other hand, films are today better than ever. Contrary to what so many people would say, namely that they will never make films as good as they did years ago, it seems to me that the best films are being made now. The twenties, thirties, forties, and fifties have nothing to offer to compare with *Midnight Cowboy, In Cold Blood, The Godfather, Zorba the Greek, Dr. Strangelove, West Side Story, Gypsy, The Hustler, A Clockwork Orange, The French Connection, Seven Beauties, They Shoot Horses Don't They?, 2001: A Space Odyssey, Bonnie and Clyde, Taxi Driver, Rocky,* and numerous others. True there is *Casablanca, Lost Weekend, Gentleman's Agreement, Gone With the Wind,* and *The Grapes of Wrath* so perhaps it is impossible to argue for or against such a proposition. What should be obvious is that some of the most creative writing, the most expert photography, and the most ingenious music is being directed into contemporary film.

Today, films are youth oriented and constitute one of the most convenient places for the social activities of today's teenagers. They are relatively inexpensive and easily accessible to the young. At the same time they afford the young a judicious mixture of the company of peers and yet an opportunity to maintain sufficient privacy.

Because of the widespread popularity of television, films are attempting to do what television cannot do and perhaps the most obvious direction is in the making and showing of pornographic films. Throughout the major cities of the United States and even in the smaller, more conservative communities, the pornographic film has become extremely popular and as the films gain even a pseudorespectability they will be shown in theatres that normally cater to *The Sound of Music* set. Eventually of course they will be seen on television on regular channels while they are now restricted to cable TV.

Box 29
TEN LARGEST GROSSING FILMS*

Jaws	$102,650,000
The Godfather	85,747,184
The Sound of Music	83,891,000
Gone with the Wind	70,179,000
The Sting	68,450,000
The Exorcist	66,300,000
Love Story	50,000,000
The Graduate	49,978,000
Airport	45,300,000
Doctor Zhivago	44,390,000

Source: The People's Almanac by David Wallechinsky and Irving Wallace (New York: Doubelday, 1975), p. 830; figure for *Jaws*, reported in the popular press.

* Because these films are periodically re-released, the figures change radically from month to month. By some calculations the following movies would also be included: *American Graffiti, Butch Cassidy and the Sundance Kid, Mary Poppins, The Poseidon Adventure, The Ten Commandments, Towering Inferno,* and *One Flew Over the Cuckoo's Nest.* Recent films which may well make the ten largest grossing films list next year might include *Rocky, King Kong, Network,* and *Star Wars.*

Books

Of all the mass media, books are perhaps the most elitist. They are read by the intelligencia of the mass communication audience and this is true even when we add the popular pornographic pocket books to this list. Generally, people who read books earn higher incomes, have attained a higher level of education, and live in the city rather than in rural areas.

Television is currently having some impact on book sales and book reading and in the years to come will probably have a great deal more influence. For example, some time ago Irwin Shaw's *Rich Man, Poor Man* was shown on television over a period of weeks. It proved an excellent and popular way of getting books to the general public. Its success led to the best sellers series and to the dramatization of Alex Haley's *Roots. Book Digest*'s current popularity seems to be due to its ability to appeal to a large group of people who want to read books but who are unwilling to invest the time required and so here they have convenient summaries of the best sellers.

Records-Tapes-Cassettes

Although not generally discussed much in works on mass communication, records, tapes, and cassettes are becoming more and more important in entertainment and in education. Stereo records account for at least as much and probably more of the spending of college students than do books.

Many publishers of books are now becoming interested in the use of cassette tapes to supplement and even replace the traditional methods of presenting information.

THE AUDIENCES OF MASS COMMUNICATION

The title to this section is the Audiences of Mass Communication because there is really no single audience, only many different and diverse mass communication audiences. Obviously, the audience must be regarded as the single most important element in any conception of mass communication. Marshall McLuhan sees the audience as the center of numerous attacks by the different media, rather like the diagram in Figure 29.1. McLuhan refers to this as a media implosion where the media are directed toward the audience and bombard the audience with all sorts of sensory stimulation rather than a media explosion where the direction is outward and where the audience would influence the media.

In any given situation we may reasonably ask why an audience chooses to select a particular medium. Wilbur Schramm in his *Men, Messages, and Media* proposes a formula:

$$\frac{\text{promise of reward}}{\text{effort required}} = \text{probability of selection}$$

Under the promise of reward Schramm includes both immediate and delayed rewards. The rewards would focus basically on the satisfaction of the

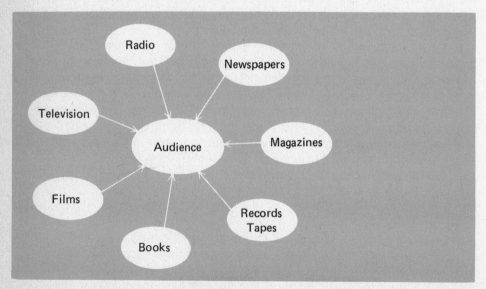

Figure 29.1
The Mass Media

needs of the audience. That is, we attend to a particular mass communication because it satisfies some need. The specific nature of these needs are covered from a somewhat different perspective in our discussion of the functions of mass communication. The effort required for attending to mass communications may be looked at in terms of the availability of the media and the ease with which we may use the media. We must also consider such factors as the expense involved and the time investment it would take to satisfy these needs. For example, there is less effort required—less expense, less time lost, extreme ease in using the media—in watching television than in going to a movie and there is less effort in going to a movie than there is in going to a play. When we divide the *effort required* into the *promise of reward* we obtain the *probability of selection* of a particular mass communication medium.

John Merrill defines three basic subgroups of audiences. The *illiterates* comprise the largest group, perhaps some 60 percent of the mass communication audience. Some of these are functionally illiterate while others are merely attitudinally illiterate, that is, even though they are able to read they choose not to. These people rely on the picture media (television, films, etc.) rather than on the print media (newspapers, books, etc.). They are passive rather than active members of society. They are oriented to fulfilling their own needs rather than to concentrate on ideas. Economically they constitute the poorer classes and advertisers are not too thrilled that these people constitute such a large segment of the audience.

The *pragmatists* constitute about 30 percent of the total mass audience. Unlike the illiterates the pragmatists are active rather than passive members; they are doers rather than watchers. They expose themselves to numerous different media; they watch television and go to the movies but they also read newspapers, magazines, and books. They are ambitious and status conscious; they seek information so that they can advance in business or in the eyes of their peers. These people are more concerned with material attainments than with ideas and so they are the major audience the advertiser seeks.

The *intellectuals* constitute the remaining 10 percent of the entire audience. The term *intellectual* should not be taken to mean intelligent although many of this group would normally be labeled intelligent. These people are concerned with issues, ideas, aesthetics, and philosophy rather than with material things and again, as with the illiterates, the advertisers have little to work with here. Intellectuals do not care much for mass communications because they cater to the lower levels of society. This group seeks mental rather than physical or material stimulation.

We might also, along with John Merrill, distinguish between the general public audience and the specific or specialized audience. The *general public audience* includes just about everyone and the *specialized audience* includes individuals who have something in common and who, because of this commonality, select the same media to read, listen to, or watch. The medium of television, for example, appeals to the general public since there is something on television for everyone but it is the specialized audiences that are appealed to by "Wild Kingdom," "The Galloping Gourmet," and "Fat Albert." Both audiences are heterogeneous but the general audience is obviously more so.

SOURCES

For overviews of the mass communication process I would recommend a number of general works. Perhaps the best introduction to the area is Wilbur Schramm's *Men, Messages, and Media: A Look at Human Communication* (New York: Harper & Row, 1973). Another excellent overview is Melvin L. De-Fleur's *Theories of Mass Communication,* 3d ed. (New York: David McKay, 1975). Two books of readings that are particularly useful are Wilbur Schramm, ed., *Mass Communications: A Book of Readings,* 2d ed. (Urbana, Ill.: University of Illinois Press, 1960), and Wilbur Schramm and D. F. Roberts, eds., *The Process and Effects of Mass Communication,* rev. ed. (Urbana, Ill.: University of Illinois Press, 1971). For information on the audiences of mass communication, see Schramm's *Men, Messages, and Media,* cited above; and John C. Merrill and Ralph L. Lowenstein, *Media, Messages, and Men: New Perspectives in Communication* (New York: David McKay, 1971); and William L. Rivers, Theodore Peterson, and Jay W. Jensen, *The Mass Media and Modern Society,* 2d ed. (San Francisco: Rinehart Press, 1971). An excellent anthology devoted to television is Horace Newcomb, ed., *Television: The Critical View* (New York: Oxford University Press, 1976).

EXPERIENTIAL VEHICLE

29.1 MODELS OF MASS COMMUNICATION

The purpose of this exercise is to further sensitize you to the essential elements and processes involved in the mass communication act. The class should be divided into groups of five or six members. Each group should then select one of the mass communication situations listed below and should construct a diagrammatic model of the elements and processes involved. That is, each group should retrace (in the form of a model) the essential elements and processes that were prerequisites or prior steps to one of the behaviors listed below. In other words, identify those things that had to be done before one could watch a film or TV commercial, read a magazine article, listen to the car radio, and so on.

Be sure to include, as a minimum, *source, encoder, gatekeeper, channel, noise, decoder, receiver, feedback, message, context,* and *effect.* Note that in mass communication situations there will be several sources, messages, effects, and so on.

1. watching a motion picture
2. watching a TV commercial
3. reading a magazine article on off-shore oil
4. listening to the top 40 on a car radio
5. reading the morning newspaper's account of yesterday's bank robbery
6. listening to a new record album

UNIT 30
The Functions of Mass Communication

Entertain
Reinforce
Change or Persuade
Educate
Socialize
Confer Status
Activate
Focus Attention
Narcotize
Create Ties of Union
Ethicize

LEARNING GOALS

After completing this unit, you should be able to:

1. identify and explain at least eight functions of mass communication
2. provide at least one example of how the media performs each of the functions identified
3. explain the distinction between functional and dysfunctional effects of the media
4. define the narcotizing and the ethicizing functions of the media

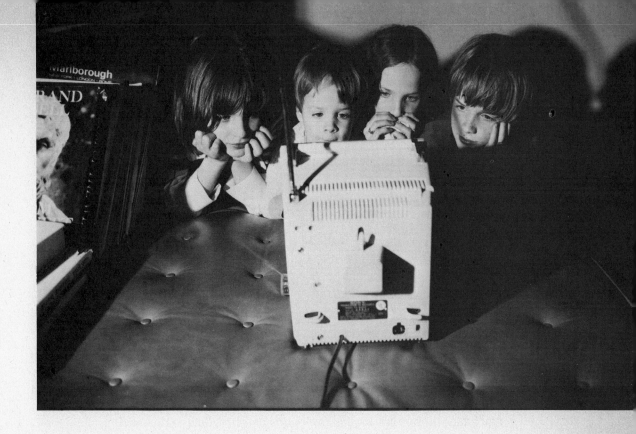

The popularity and pervasive influence of the mass media can only be maintained by its serving significant functions. Eleven of the most important functions are to entertain, to reinforce, to change or persuade, to educate, to socialize, to confer status, to activate, to focus attention, to narcotize, to create ties of union, and to ethicize.

I purposely offer such an extensive list of functions—rather than follow the standard practice of discussing three or four functions—in order to more effectively sensitize you to the numerous ways in which the mass media impinge on our everyday lives. These 11 functions are neither all equal in importance nor does each mass communication event necessarily serve all these functions. Rather, all 11 functions are significant to an understanding of mass communication and each mass media event possesses the potential for serving any or all of these functions.

As will become obvious throughout the discussion, these functions often overlap and interact with each other. It is doubtful, for example, that a communication could change an individual's attitudes or behaviors without also educating or focusing attention.

These functions of the media are also the reasons why people attend to the media. John Merrill, for example, considers three motivational factors that lead people to the media: loneliness, curiosity, and self-aggrandizement. These three factors and numerous others that might be cited are covered under the various functions. For example, the media's creation of a tie of union satisfies loneliness; the educational function deals with curiosity, and the reinforcement and educational functions focus on the self-aggrandizement motive. Bradley S. Greenberg, on the other hand, lists seven reasons for watching television that, it seems, would also pertain to other forms of mass communication: to pass time, for enjoyment, for companionship, for arousal, to learn, for relaxation, and as a source of refuge. These reasons or motivational factors are also covered under the various functions as will become clear as we consider these 11 functions.

ENTERTAIN

If you were to ask the typical television or film viewer why he or she watched television or went to the movies, they would probably say something about being entertained, assuming they were not on guard and prepared to give the more socially acceptable response of learning or gaining information. Similarly, if you asked typical people why mass media existed they would say something about the media being designed to entertain. And it is true that the media design their programs to entertain. In reality of course they are attempting to entertain in order to secure the attention of as large a group as possible so that they may in turn sell this attention to advertisers. This seems to be the major reason why mass communications exist. They exist so that they may sell viewers to advertisers. In societies where the state supports the media, the process is different. In our society, however, if the media did not entertain they would no longer have viewers and would quickly be out of business. At least this is true for the most part. Certainly, many books are published that are not primarily for entertainment—dictionaries, reference books, textbooks, and the like are not designed primarily to entertain. Yet take a close look at your current textbooks. Notice all the features designed to entertain—the colors used, the fancy typefaces, the pictures. All of these features and more are designed to secure the attention of an audience so that a publisher may in turn sell that attention to instructors or to a school system.

REINFORCE

It is difficult in any situation to convert someone from one attitudinal extreme to another, and the media, with all the resources and power at their disposal, are no exception. For the most part the media rarely achieve conversion but they do function to reinforce or make stronger our beliefs, attitudes, values, and opinions. Democrats will expose themselves to democratic persuasion and will emerge reinforced from the experience. Similarly, religious persons will expose themselves to messages in line with their beliefs and will emerge reinforced or stronger in their convictions.

The problem the media face in achieving something beyond reinforcement, of course, is that we are the ones who choose the messages to which we will attend and we generally do not choose to expose ourselves to messages that may contradict our existing belief structure.

This reinforcement view applies to situations in which persons are relatively polarized in their beliefs, values, and opinions. The media will achieve some conversions with those who are in the middle on any individual dimension. Thus, those who are torn between the Republicans and the Democrats may well find themselves converted to one side or the other on the basis of the media's messages.

Even those communications we think are changing attitudes are often only reinforcing existing ones. For example, it had long been assumed that "All in the Family" was changing attitudes toward prejudice and stereotyping. The entire program was assumed by many to be a satire on prejudice. Archie, in particular, was assumed to be close to an idiot who was constantly being put down by his daughter and son-in-law. But the studies that have been done on this show and similar shows indicate that this is not the case. For example, Neil Vidmar and Milton Rokeach in their study, "Archie Bunker's Bigotry," found that the show reinforces rather than reduces racial and ethnic prejudice. "The data," notes Vidmar and Rokeach, "seem to support those who have argued that the program is not uniformly seen as satire and those who have argued that it exploits or appeals to bigotry."

Another aspect of this function is that we actively search out the reinforcement that the media provide. Thus, persons who continue to smoke although they may have nagging doubts and feelings that they should quit, may well seek out cigarette advertisements in the newspapers and magazines. These advertisements will reinforce their behavior. The advertisements will tell these people in effect that their behavior is just fine; cigarettes are low in tar and nicotine and in the process they are getting all this pleasure. Who could resist?

CHANGE OR PERSUADE

While the media do not function primarily to change our behavior or to persuade us, they do perform this function at times and in certain situations. As already noted in the discussion of reinforcement, changes or conversions seldom occur with extremists but they do occur with the middle-of-the-roaders.

Minor behavior changes, however, are frequent. The changes in our toilet-paper-buying behavior may well be greatly or even totally influenced by the media; but except to toilet paper manufacturers, few people care about which toilet paper is used. Similarly, we may chose stuffing instead of potatoes, Revlon instead of Hazel Bishop, or L'Oreal instead of Toni, but in the total scheme

Box 30
THE ADVERTISING CODE OF AMERICAN BUSINESS

1. *Truth* . . . Advertising shall tell the truth, and shall reveal significant facts, the concealment of which would mislead the public.

2. *Responsibility* . . . Advertising agencies and advertisers shall be willing to provide substantiation of claims made.

3. *Taste and Decency* . . . Advertising shall be free of statements, illustrations or implications which are offensive to good taste or public decency.

4. *Disparagement* . . . Advertising shall offer merchandise or service on its merits, and refrain from attacking competitors unfairly or disparaging their products, services or methods of doing business.

5. *Bait Advertising* . . . Advertising shall offer only merchandise or services which are readily available for purchase at the advertised price.

6. *Guarantees and Warranties* . . . Advertising of guarantees and warranties shall be explicit. Advertising of any guarantee or warranty shall clearly and conspicuously disclose its nature and extent, the manner in which the guarantor or warrantor will perform and the identity of the guarantor or warrantor.

7. *Price Claims* . . . Advertising shall avoid price or savings claims which are false or misleading, or which do not offer provable bargains or savings.

8. *Unprovable Claims* . . . Advertising shall avoid the use of exaggerated or unprovable claims.

9. *Testimonials* . . . Advertising containing testimonials shall be limited to those of competent witnesses who are reflecting a real and honest choice.

Source: Developed and initially distributed by: the Advertising Federation of America; the Advertising Association of the West; the Association of Better Business Bureau, Inc. Reproduced by permission of the American Advertising Federation.

of things these decisions matter little. Political preferences, religious attitudes, social commitments, and the like, however, are not so easily changed as a decision to switch from Scotts to Teri or from Kool to Salem.

EDUCATE

When we think of education we generally think of a formal school situation, with a teacher in front of the classroom and the students taking notes, hoping to get down on paper what will eventually appear on an examination. But, with a little reflection it should be clear that most of the information we have has been attained not from the schoolroom but from the media. We have learned music, politics, film, art, sociology, psychology, economics, and a host of other subjects from the media and not from high school or college classrooms. We learn about other places and other times much more effectively from seeing a good movie than from reading a history textbook. A brief section in an American history book can hardly picture the Civil War as effectively as does *Gone With the Wind.* Nor can we learn to understand the plight of the Indians from reading about what some university professor thinks might have happened. How much more valuable it is to see relevant films.

One of the nice things about learning from the media is that it is less "painful" than learning in schools (at least in too many cases).

SOCIALIZE

One of the main functions of any media system is to socialize its viewers. The media provide viewers with the values, the opinions, the rules that society judges to be proper and just. They do this in stories, in discussions, in articles, in comics, in advertisements and commercials. In all of these situations, the values of the society are expressed but in an almost unspoken manner. We are taught how to dress for different occasions, the proper way to eat, what a proper meal should consist of, how to hold a discussion or conversation, how to respond to people of different national and racial groups, how to behave in strange places, and so on.

CONFER STATUS

If you were to list the 100 most important people in the world they would undoubtedly be people who have been given a great deal of mass media exposure. Without such exposure, the people would not in fact be important, at least not in the popular mind. Paul Lazarsfeld and Robert Merton, in their famous "Mass Communication, Popular Taste, and Organized Social Action" put it this way: "If you really matter, you will be at the focus of mass attention and, if you are at the focus of mass attention, then surely you must really matter." Conversely, of course, if you do not get mass attention then you do not matter and if you do not matter then you do not get mass attention.

Consider the guests on a show like "The Tonight Show" (Johnny Carson). They actually get paid very little, at least in comparison with what they would normally get for performing. Yet, they get mass exposure that is perhaps more financially rewarding than getting their normally high salaries. In effect, they are made national personalities from this type of exposure. For example, what does Orson Bean do? What does Phyllis Newman do? What does Carol Wayne do? True, Bean tells stories, Newman sings, and Wayne tells jokes, but their major claim to fame seems to be that they are personalities created by and for the media.

ACTIVATE

From the advertisers point of view, the most important function is to activate— to move to action. Put simply, they function to get the viewer to buy the bread,

Box 31
TEN LARGEST U.S. ADVERTISERS

Proctor and Gamble Co.	$360 million
General Motors Corp.	225 million
Sears, Roebuck and Co.	225 million
General Foods Corp.	203 million
Bristol-Myers Co.	170 million
Warner-Lambert Co.	169 million
American Home Products	138 million
Mobil Oil Corp.	135.9 million
R. J. Reynolds Industries Inc.	113.6 million
U.S. Government	113.4 million

Source: Based on figures for the year 1975 reported in *Advertising Age,* September 13, 1976.

to use Gillette, to chose Brut and not Canoe, and in general to make all the decisions we think so trivial but that advertisers and manufacturers consider important.

The advertiser's objective is to get us to buy their product and not someone else's, as well as to buy their product instead of nothing. Room deodorizers, for example, should be a substitute for cleanliness though it is never put in these terms.

If we did not buy what advertisers want us to buy they would no longer pay for the time or space to advertise and we would no longer have the variety of media we now have.

FOCUS ATTENTION

Wilbur Schramm in *Men, Messages, and Media* expresses this function well: "A reasonable hypothesis is that the most powerful effect of the mass media on public knowledge—comparable even to the effect of the realism with which it can present distant events and places—is the ability of the media to focus public attention on certain problems, persons, or issues at a given time. This may be an effect controlled in part by people who are able to use the media skillfully, but it is clearly important. It feeds the conversation that goes on interpersonally. It stimulates other viewing, listening, or reading. It encourages reporters to dig deeper and commentators to interpret a problem in great depth."

Notice the things we think are important. They are in fact the very things on which the media concentrates. The obvious question is whether they are important and the media, therefore, concentrates on them or whether the media concentrates on them and they, therefore, become important. What does seem clear is that the media surely do lead us to focus attention on what they focus attention.

NARCOTIZE

One of the most interesting and the most overlooked functions of the media is the narcotizing function. This refers to the media's function of providing the receiver with information that is in turn confused, by the receiver, with doing something about something. As Lazersfeld and Merton explain it: "The individual reads accounts of issues and problems and may even discuss alternative lines of action. But this rather intellectualized, rather remote connection with organized social action is not activated. The interested and informed citizen can congratulate himself on his lofty state of interest and information and neglect to see that he has abstained from decision and action. In short, he takes his secondary contact with the world of political reality—his reading and listening and thinking—as a vicarious performance. He comes to mistake *knowing* about problems of the day with *doing* something about them."

Lazarfeld and Merton term this *dysfunctional* rather than functional "on the assumption that it is not in the interest of modern complex society to have large masses of the population politically apathetic and inert." And with five or six hours of television viewing each day, there is little wonder that knowledge of problems and issues is confused with or is a substitute for action.

CREATE TIES OF UNION

One of the functions of mass communication that few persons ever think of is the ability of the media to make us feel like a member of a group. Consider the lone television viewer, sitting in his or her apartment watching television while eating a TV dinner. The television programs make this lone soul feel a part of some larger group. Whether the individual is watching members of his or her own racial group, or those who think or worship as he or she does, the viewer is made to feel a part of this larger, and by virtue of the media coverage, this important group of persons.

ETHICIZE

By making public certain deviations from the norms, the media arouse people to change the situation. It provides viewers with a collective ethic or ethical system. For example, without the media coverage of Watergate it seems unlikely that there would have been such a public outcry over the events that led Richard Nixon to eventually resign.

"In mass society," note Lazarsfeld and Merton, writing some 15 years before Watergate, "this function of public exposure is institutionalized in the mass media of communication. Press, radio, and television expose fairly well known deviations to public view, and as a rule, this exposure forces some degree of public action against what has been privately tolerated. The mass media may, for example, introduce severe strains on polite ethnic discrimination by calling public attention to these practices that are at odds with the norm of nondiscrimination. At times, the media may organize exposure activities into a 'crusade'."

In evaluating and analyzing these general functions of the media we should keep in mind at least three related issues. First, each time we turn on the television, read a newspaper, or listen to a radio, we do so for a *unique* reason. Each and every mass communication event serves a unique function, a function at least a little bit different from every previous function. Second, every mass communication event serves a different function for each individual viewer-reader-listener. The same television program may serve to entertain one person, to educate another, and to narcotize still another. Third, we should recognize that the functions served by any mass communication event for any individual will be different from one time to the next. Where a particular record once served to entertain it may now function to socialize or to create ties of union.

SOURCES

On the functions of mass communication see Charles R. Wright, *Mass Communication: A Sociological Perspective,* 2d ed (New York: Random House, 1975); Paul F. Lazarsfeld and Robert K. Merton, "Mass Communication, Popular Taste, and Organized Social Action," in Lyman Bryson, ed., *The Communication of Ideas* (New York: Harper & Row, 1951), pp. 95–118 and reprinted in Wilbur Schramm and D. F. Roberts, eds., *The Process and Effects of Mass Communication,* rev. ed. (Urbana, Ill.: University of Illinois Press, 1971), pp. 554–578; and Wilbur Schramm, *Men, Messages, and Media: A Look at Human Communication* (New York: Harper & Row, 1973). I relied on all three of these excellent works. For a somewhat different perspective see Frank E. X. Dance and Carl E. Larson, *The Functions of Human Communication: A Theoretical Approach* (New York: Holt, Rinehart and Winston, 1976). For the study on "All in the Family" cited in the text and a review of previous studies in this area see Neil Vidmar and Milton Rokeach, "Archie Bunker's Bigotry: A Study in Selective Perception and Exposure," *Journal of Communication* 24 (Winter, 1974), 36–47. The sources for the reasons why people attend to the media are John C. Merrill and Ralph L. Lowenstein, *Media, Messages, and Men: New Perspectives in Communication* (New York: David McKay, 1971) and Bradley S. Greenberg, "Mass Communication and Social Behavior," in Gerhard J. Hanneman and William J. McEwen, eds., *Communication and Behavior* (Boston: Addison-Wesley, 1975), pp. 268–284.

EXPERIENTIAL VEHICLE

30.1 ANALYZING THE FUNCTIONS OF MASS COMMUNICATION

Select one of the television shows listed below and identify the specific ways in which this program has fulfilled at least five of the functions of mass communication discussed in this unit and listed here.

Functions of Mass Communication

1. entertain
2. reinforce
3. change
4. educate
5. socialize
6. confer status
7. activate
8. focus attention
9. narcotize
10. create ties of union
11. ethicize

Television Shows

1. "All in the Family"
2. "Sonny and Cher"
3. "Today"
4. "Mary Hartman, Mary Hartman"
5. "Hollywood Squares"
6. "Dinah"
7. "The Tonight Show"
8. "Wild Kingdom"
9. "Kojak"
10. "Sanford and Son"
11. baseball
12. news

After completing these functions, consider at least the following:

1. Which functions are easy to distinguish? Difficult to distinguish? Explain.
2. Which functions do you feel a program *must* serve if it is to become or remain popular? Why?
3. Is there a hierarchy or prerequisite structure among the functions of mass communication? That is, is it necessary that certain functions be fulfilled before other functions can be fulfilled? Explain.
4. Which of these functions are we consciously aware of? Which are we generally not consciously aware of? Is there general agreement on which are which? Explain.

The functions noted for the various shows and the individual responses to the questions posed may be discussed in small groups of five or six or may be considered by the entire class in a general discussion.

UNIT 31

The Flow of Mass Communication

From Media to Audience
From Audience to Media: Feedback

31.1 Mass and Mini Communications

LEARNING GOALS

After completing this unit, you should be able to:

1. explain the two-step flow of communication hypothesis
2. explain the concept of diffusion of information
3. define *gatekeeping*
4. provide examples of the gatekeeping process
5. identify at least four characteristics of mass media feedback

FROM MEDIA TO AUDIENCE

The Two-Step Flow of Mass Communication

Perhaps the issue in mass communication creating the most interest in the popular mind is the way in which mass communication has an effect on people's thoughts and behaviors. One obvious explanation of this is that people read the newspapers or watch television or listen to the radio and are persuaded by what they read, see, and/or hear and, as a result, change their thoughts and behaviors. But this explanation is overly simplified and perhaps not as accurate as we would want.

A somewhat more sophisticated proposal was presented by Paul Lazarsfeld, Bernard Berelson, and Helen Gaudet in their *The People's Choice*. In this study of the voters in the 1940 presidential election these Columbia University researchers found that people were influenced more by other people and less by the mass media (then primarily newspapers and radio). Those who did the influencing were termed opinion leaders. Mass communications, the researchers proposed, do not affect the people directly. Instead of this one-step process, they proposed a two-step process where messages from the mass communications influence opinion leaders and these opinion leaders then influence the general population in more interpersonal situations.

Elihu Katz in his 1957 "The Two-Step Flow of Communication: An Up-To-

Date Report on an Hypothesis,'' concluded that ''most opinion leaders are primarily affected not by the communication media but by still other people.''

At times these opinion leaders come from the same social or occupational class as the people they influence but at other times they come from social classes above those they influence. Rarely if ever do opinion leaders come from classes lower in status than the people they influence. Generally when people have a significant need for new information, they will be influenced by opinion leaders who know more than they know and who are of a higher class or status. But when people have no important need for the information, they will get the information from people of the same social class.

In the early stages of adopting new information the mass media seem especially important, but at later stages interpersonal contact seems more important.

As Wilbur Schramm has noted the two-step flow concept, although useful and revealing, is perhaps a bit too simple. For one thing it is not always true; much of our information comes right from the media, whether television or newspapers or magazines. As the media become more and more a part of our everyday life, the media grow as our initial source for information on a variety of issues.

Second, the concept of an opinion leader must be looked at in terms of degree and not in either-or terms. Some opinion leaders are more opinion leaders than others. Some are leaders of leaders whereas others are leaders only of followers. Some leaders therefore get their information from the media while others get their information from other leaders.

Third, and perhaps most important, is that the flow of communication seems more reasonably characterized as a reciprocal process rather than a step process. That is, there seems more of a back and forth process from the media to people to the media to people and so on. We may hear about something on television, then talk to a friend about it, then hear about it again on the evening news and then read about it in the morning newspaper and then talk about it with friends at work. This especially seems true today where media are so much a part of our lives. It also seems logical in terms of the findings that people who expose themselves to one media will often expose themselves to other media as well. Inevitably the same issues and news items will be covered in the different media and we must further assume that interpersonal interaction occurs in between.

The Diffusion of Information

Closely related to the two-step flow of communication is the concept of the diffusion and adoption of innovations. *Diffusion* refers to the new information, the innovation, or the new process as it passes through the society at large or through the relevant social system. *Adoption* refers to individuals' positive reactions to the innovation and its incorporation into their habitual behavior patterns. In the process of adoption McEwen (in Hanneman and McEwen) identifies three general stages:

1. *Information acquisition*—the information relevant to the innovation is secured and understood, for example, a teacher learns about a new approach to teach mass communication.
2. *Information evaluation*—the information relevant to the innovation is evaluated as good or bad or anywhere in between these extremes, for example, the teacher recognizes that the new method is more effective than the old.
3. *Adoption or rejection*—the innovation is either adopted or rejected by the individual, that is, the teacher begins to teach mass communication by this new method.

Obviously all people do not choose to adopt or reject the innovation at the same time. Nan Lin, for example distinguishes five types of adopters.

1. *The Innovators.* These are the first to adopt the innovation and constitute less than 3 percent of the total population.
2. *Early Adopters.* These people adopt the innovation next and make up about 14 percent of the total population.
3. *Early Majority.* These adopt the innovation next and constitute about 34 percent.
4. *Late Majority.* This group also constitutes about 34 percent of the total population and are next to the last in adopting the innovation.
5. *Laggards.* Lastly, there are those who either adopt the innovation last or who never adopt it at all. These constitute about 16 percent of the total population.

It has been found that early as opposed to late adopters—the innovators as compared with the laggards—are generally younger, of a higher socioeconomic status, have more specialized occupations, are more empathetic, are less dogmatic, are most oriented toward change, make more use of available information, are closer to the actual agents of change, have a more cosmopolitan orientation, and are generally opinion leaders.

Gatekeeping and Gatekeepers

In the passage of a message from the source of mass media to the actual individual viewer or listener there intervenes what is referred to as a gatekeeper.

The term *gatekeeping* was originally used by Kurt Lewin in his *Human Relations* (1947) to refer to (1) the process by which a message passes through various gates as well as (2) to the people or groups that allowed the message to pass (gatekeepers). Gatekeepers may be individual persons or a group of persons through which a message passes in going from sender to receiver. A gatekeeper's main function is to filter the messages that an individual receives.

Teachers are perfect examples of gatekeepers. Teachers read the various books in an area of study, read various journal articles, listen to convention papers and talk among themselves about developments in the field, and conduct their own research in the field. From all this information teachers pass some of it on to the students and, at the same time, prevent other information from getting through to the students. In the passage of the information from researchers to students, the teacher in effect filters what he or she knows about an area of study. A cameraperson is another clear example of a gatekeeper. From all that he or she can possibly photograph, certain areas are selected for photographing and then are shown to the viewers. Editors of magazines and publishing houses are gatekeepers; they allow certain information to get through and do not allow other information to get through.

The gatekeeper, then, limits the messages that we receive. The teacher, for example, limits the information the students receive. Without the teacher, however, the students would learn a great deal less. The teacher expands the informational awareness of the students through his or her distillation of the material, organization of the information, and analysis of the findings and results of study. That is, without gatekeepers we would not get half the information we now receive.

In terms of the model of communication developed by Harold Lasswell (Who Says What in What Channel to Whom with What Effect) we might say that the gatekeepers function as decision makers determining who is to communicate information, what is communicated, in what channel it is communicated, to whom it is communicated, and with what effect it is communicated. The gatekeeper may add to the original message, subtract from the message, or alter the message that is received in terms of content, form, emphasis, intent, and so on.

We might diagram the gatekeeping process as in Figure 31.1. Note that the messages (M_1, M_2, M_3) received by the gatekeeper come from various different

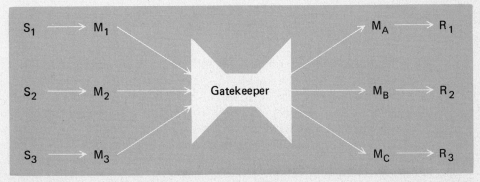

Figure 31.1
The Gatekeeping Process

sources (S_1, S_2, S_3), so one of the functions the gatekeeper serves is to select the messages to be communicated from the ones which will not be allowed to pass. The gatekeeper then transmits numerous messages (M_A, M_B, M_C) to different receivers (R_1, R_2, R_3) and, it should be noted, may transmit certain messages to some receivers and other messages to other receivers. Teachers, for example, do not pass on the same messages to different classes: advanced courses get very different messages from elementary courses. Perhaps the most important aspect to note about this process is that the messages received by the gatekeeper (M_1, M_2, M_3) are not the same as the messages the gatekeeper sends (M_A, M_B, M_C); the extent to which they differ is the measure of the gatekeeper's changes.

FROM AUDIENCE TO MEDIA: FEEDBACK

Letters to the editor of a newspaper or magazine, sales of a novel or textbook, Nielsen ratings for "Maude" or "Mary Hartman, Mary Hartman," sales for Charmin toilet tissue and Lipton Tea, book reviews appearing in professional journals or in the daily newspapers, receipts for *Jaws* and *Behind the Green Door,* subscriptions to *Cosmopolitan* and *Penthouse,* and numerous other responses to the mass media are mass communication feedback. As already noted, feedback is information that is fed back to the source from the receiver which in turn tells the source something about how his or her messages are being received. In interpersonal communication, this feedback is immediate and can result in an almost instantaneous adjustment of the message by the source. In mass communication, the feedback is of quite a different nature.

Ray Hiebert, Donald Unqurait, and Thomas Bohn in their *Mass Media* distinguish six characteristics of feedback in mass communication. These six characteristics will enable us to distinguish feedback in mass communication from feedback in interpersonal, small group, or public speaking situations and at the same time will help to define the nature of mass communication in more specific detail.

Representative

Because the audiences of mass communication are so large and so scattered throughout a huge area, it is impossible to secure feedback from all viewers or listeners. Instead a sample is selected which ideally is representative of the entire audience. This sample, it should be noted, is extremely small in comparison with the total number in the real audience. In order to record this feedback television sets are equipped with electronic devices that record the programs watched, as with the Nielsen ratings; telephone calls are made to secure reactions; or perhaps a studio audience is given a questionnaire to fill out. In all of these cases, the individuals from whom feedback is sought are ideally supposed to represent the entire audience. Before this textbook was published, it was reviewed by a number of different communication teachers.

These reviewers, it was assumed, were representative of the entire audience of communication teachers and what the reviewers had to say was assumed to be representative of what this larger audience would say had they been asked. Similarly the students who read and commented on earlier versions of this book were considered representative of the college student audience throughout the country.

Indirect

In interpersonal communication, the feedback from a receiver goes directly to the source, at least usually. In some interpersonal communication situations, the receiver may talk with a third party about a conversation he or she had with the source and the source may then hear about this person's reactions from still another person. The feedback here would be indirect. In most interpersonal situations, however, the feedback is direct. As a source you can read the feedback from the receiver—you can see the puzzled looks or the smiles, you can hear the words of agreement, the questions, or the disagreements—without the intervention of a third party. With mass communication, however, the situation is different. Consider your responses to an editorial in the *New York Times.* You may send a letter to the paper but the editor will probably only read your letter if it gets published in the paper through some third party. Or the editor may be given summary statistics; for example, of the 250 letters received on Tuesday's editorial on domestic affairs, 200 expressed disagreement, 30 expressed agreement, and 20 asked for further clarification. Similarly our responses to ''Mary Hartman, Mary Hartman'' do not go directly to Louise Lasser or Norman Lear (the producer), instead they are filtered through some third party, a program director, an agent, or some such paid intermediary.

Delayed

Perhaps the characteristic of mass communication feedback most often considered as defining is its delayed nature. Mass communication feedback is almost always delayed, perhaps by days, perhaps by weeks, perhaps by months or even years. Surveys, censuses, and the like take enormous amounts of time to complete so the results are never immediate. Sales records for a new product or a new advertising campaign may take months to compile. Generally, the more detailed the analysis or feedback, the more delayed it will be.

Because of this delayed nature, mass communication feedback results not in immediate changes in the messages of the media, as in interpersonal communication, but rather in long-range changes or alterations.

Cumulative

Feedback in mass communication may be cumulative or noncumulative. An example of noncumulative feedback might be a reaction of an audience to a particular segment of a comedy series, say "The Mary Tyler Moore Show." This is helpful to the program directors and to everyone concerned with the show, yet it is not as important as cumulative feedback which would entail responses from a large number of persons over a long period of time, say an entire season. Thus, the responses to the Jefferson family while they were on "All in the Family" that were relevant to the producers was the cumulative feedback. In other words, one would need to be sure that the Jefferson family were well received over a long period of time before the time and money to create a new series was invested. Both "Rhoda" and "Phyllis" proved themselves popular characters on "The Mary Tyler Moore Show" for quite some time before they were launched into their own series. Similarly, before launching a new detective series, the audiences' cumulative feedback toward detective series would be secured. Generally, cumulative feedback results in influencing long-range decisions whereas noncumulative feedback will result in influencing short-range decisions.

Institutionalized

Because of the difficulty in securing accurate and reliable feedback from the mass media audience, it is necessary to engage sophisticated research organizations in the task. A. C. Nielsen's organization for obtaining feedback on the number of viewers watching various television programs is perhaps the most well known example. The various public opinion polls such as Gallup, Harris, and Roper are also conducted by relatively complex organizations and are representative of the institutionalized nature of feedback-obtaining organizations.

Quantitative

Mass communication feedback involves so much data from so many different people that it must be put into quantitative form if it is to be useful in redirecting the messages of the source. If Oldsmobile wishes to advertise its new cars in various publications it must know the type of audience that reads the particular magazine under consideration. It needs to know, for example, the economic status of the readers, their location (whether urban or rural), and so on. If you wish to advertise in *Playboy* you might want to know that of its male readers between the ages of 18 and 34, 4,760,000 are college educated, 5,296,000 are married, and 3,696,000 come from households earning $15,000 or over. If you wished to run a four-color advertisement on the back cover of *Playboy* in their national edition, for one issue (based on 1973 rates), it would cost you $53,685. Data such as these would be impossible to handle were it not in quantitative form. Book reviews, on the other hand, would be an example of a qualitative type of feedback. If a publisher wished to buy the paperback rights to a book, it might first want these reviews put in quantitative form, specifically, it might wish to know how many reviews were favorable, and how many were unfavorable.

SOURCES

For the discussion of gatekeeping and feedback I relied heavily on the work of Ray Eldon Hiebert, Donald F. Ungurait, and Thomas W. Bohn, *Mass Media: An Introduction to Modern Communication* (New York: David McKay, 1974). For the two-step hypothesis see Paul F. Lazarsfeld, Bernard Berelson, and Helen Gaudet, *The People's Choice* (New York: Duell, Sloan and Pearce, 1944) and Elihu Katz, "The Two-Step Flow of Communication: An Up-to-Date Report on an Hypothesis," *Public Opinion Quarterly* 21 (Spring 1957):61–78. For the diffusion of information discussion see E. M. Rogers and F. F. Shoemaker, *Communication of Innovations: A Cross-Cultural Approach* (New York: Free Press, 1971). Nan Lin in *The Study of Human Communication* (Indianapolis: Bobbs-Merrill, 1973) also provides an excellent summary of this area.

EXPERIENTIAL VEHICLE

31.1 MASS AND MINI COMMUNICATIONS

The objectives of this exercise are:

1. to become acquainted with some of the diverse media of mass and mini communication
2. to become aware of some of the differences and similarities between these two media
3. to become familiar with some audience variables
4. to obtain some practice in audience analysis
5. to provide some experience in discovering communication principles
6. to become acquainted with some of the effects of mass and mini communications

Instructions

1. Select an example of a print medium of mass communication, for example, a newspaper or magazine addressed to a large audience.
2. Select an example of a print medium of mini communication, for example, a newspaper or magazine addressed to a relatively small audience.
3. Analyze the audience of each of these publications. Consider, for example, the following factors: age, sex, educational level, status, occupation, political persuasion, religion, income, marital status, ethnic background, special interests. In this analysis point out both the similarities and the differences between the audiences of these two media.

   Clues for this analysis may be found throughout the publication, for example, in the editorial policy, in the advertisements, in the articles and authors, in the special features, in the pictures, in the letters to the editor, and so forth.

   This audience analysis may take any number of different forms. For example, you may construct a profile of the typical reader of each publication. This would take the form of a listing of the characteristics common to most of the readers. Or you may construct your analysis on predicted percentages, for example, 75 percent of the readers are male, 90 percent are unmarried, 15 percent are college professors, and so forth. Support your inferences with specific references to the publications analyzed. For example, if you say that the typical reader is male, give your reasons for making this inference. What is contained in the publication that leads you to this conclusion?

4. On the basis of your analyses state *one* principle of communication that you feel these communicators (publishers, editors, or advertisers) are following. What is your reasoning/evidence for this conclusion?
5. On the basis of your review of these publications state what you feel are some of the effects of these media on the readers. Do these publications also have effects on nonreaders? Explain.

Notes

1. Bring these publications to class so that everyone can examine them.
2. Be prepared to discuss your findings with the class.

UNIT 32
Culture, Subculture, and Communication

Culture and Communication
Subculture and Communication

32.1 Values in American Culture
32.2 Six Sublanguages

LEARNING GOALS

After completing this unit, you should be able to:

1. define *culture* and define a *culture*
2. define *intercultural communication* and give examples
3. define *sublanguage, subculture, codifiability, cant, jargon, argot,* and *slang*
4. explain the functions of sublanguages
5. explain the relationship between the frequency of synonyms for a concept and the importance of that concept to a culture or subculture
6. identify how sociological variables influence the form of address used

CULTURE AND COMMUNICATION

Alfred L. Kroeber and Clyde Kluckhohn, in their *Culture—A Critical Review of Concepts and Definitions,* identify 164 different definitions of culture. Apparently, anthropologists are no better at defining culture than psychologists are at defining personality or communicologists are at defining communication. But regardless of the difficulty of definition, the terms must be tackled if we are to begin understanding intercultural communication.

Borrowing a distinction utilized in linguistics between Language (with a capital *L*) and a language (small *l*), Culture and a culture will be distinguished. *Culture* (with a capital *C*) may be defined as a knowledge of the appropriate and inappropriate thought and behavior patterns of a group. *A culture* may be defined as a learned set of thoughts and behaviors common to a number of people that defines them as members of the same group and as nonmembers of other groups.

These two definitions distinguish between the *knowledge* of thought and behavior patterns (i.e., Culture) and the actual *performance* of these thoughts and behaviors (i.e., a culture). Put differently, all people throughout the world may be said to have essentially the same Culture; namely, we all have knowledge concerning appropriate and inappropriate patterns of thoughts and behaviors. But we differ in terms of what those patterns of thoughts and behaviors are. That is, we differ not in terms of Culture but in terms of a specific culture to which we belong.

Box 32
SOME CULTURAL WORDS OF WISDOM

All cultures phrase their teachings in brief, easy-to-remember sayings. One of the characteristics of such sayings is that they are made to appear true and appropriate for all times and for all situations. The absurdity becomes apparent when opposites are juxtaposed.

Two is company; three is a crowd   The more the merrier

When it rains, it pours   Every cloud has a silver lining

A chain is only as strong as its weakest link   In unity there is strength

Better late than never   The early bird catches the worm

Jack of all trades, master of none   If you want a thing well done, do it yourself

Out of sight, out of mind   Absence makes the heart grow fonder

A bird in the hand is worth two in the bush   Nothing ventured, nothing gained

Rome wasn't built in a day   Make hay while the sun shines

He who hesitates is lost   Look before you leap

All work and no play makes Jack a dull boy   Keep your nose to the grindstone

Too many cooks spoil the broth   Many hands make light work

One swallow does not a summer make   Where there's smoke, there's fire

---

The essential characteristics of both definitions may now be considered together. First, both Culture and a culture refer to learned or acquired knowledge, thoughts, and behaviors. For example, patterns of behavior that we follow and which we recognize as somehow natural to our society were learned when we were infants. Persons born in other cultures would have learned totally different sets of behaviors. The behavior patterns learned were learned from the society in which we grew up and not on the basis of our biological parents. A child of German parents raised among the Chinese will learn the culture of the Chinese and not of the Germans. With most lower animals, on the other hand, the animal acquires the behavior patterns of its biological parents and not the behavior of those with which it grows up. The Italian honey bee raised by Austrian honey bees will acquire the communication patterns of its biological Italian parents and not of its adopted Austrian parents.

Culture and a culture both deal with thoughts and behaviors. The term *thoughts* is used broadly to refer to attitudes, beliefs, opinions, and values. Thus, the attitudes we have toward authority, religion, and education; the beliefs we have in a supreme being, magic, and an after life; the opinions we have concerning politics, education, and marriage; and the values we place on industry, competition, and cooperation constitute our cultural system. Similarly, the behaviors we engage in when we speak with someone, when we sneeze, and when we eat or go to the bathroom are likewise part of our cultural system. We have acquired these thought and behavior patterns from those around us who in turn learned them from those around them and we in turn will teach them to the next generation.

Culture is a group property. While personality belongs to the individual, culture belongs to the group. For a culture to exist the thought and behavior patterns must be shared by a relatively large number of persons.

Culture deals with the knowledge of appropriateness, that is, what is thought to be proper and improper within a given social group. Generally, no culture is assumed to be evaluatively better than any other culture and so what is and what is not appropriate pertains only to a specific group. All cultures are assumed by most researchers to be equal on a good-bad scale. Certain cultures may be more competitive than others, may value education more highly than others, may place more emphasis on the family unit than do others, and so on. But it is assumed that what one culture does is not any better or any worse than what any other culture does. It would be ethnocentric at best, the argument goes, to evaluate a culture with the standards or system of values derived from another culture. That is, we cannot fairly use the standard of one culture to evaluate another culture.

On the other hand, we might wish to object to this rather democratic view of things and argue that there are certain universals that should be highly valued by all people and all cultures. Those cultures that do not place a high value on these universals, the argument goes, are not equal to those that do. For example, a culture that believes in killing and that war against outsiders is a positive good might not be considered the equal of a culture that believes in helping the sick and in loving their neighbors. Of course here we are using the standards of our culture to evaluate another culture but perhaps this is justified in some instances.

Lastly, attention should be drawn to the characteristic of a culture that defines certain people as members of a particular group and as nonmembers of other groups. Our specific culture defines us as members of, say, the American culture but at the same time it defines us as nonmembers of the Chinese, Arabic, or African cultures. Our values, beliefs, opinions, attitudes, and behaviors define us as members of a particular culture and at the same time set us apart from members of all other cultures.

Given this general notion of culture, what then is intercultural communication? *Intercultural communication* is communication between or among members of different cultures. More specifically, it is communication between persons who share different patterns of thoughts (attitudes, beliefs, values, opinions, and the like) and behaviors. In concrete terms it is communication between men and women, between young and old, between easterners and westerners, between black and white, between rich and poor, between the educated and the uneducated. In short, intercultural communication exists when communication occurs between members of different groups when such groups are culturally determined.

Box 33
PUCKER UP, AMERICA—THE KISS IS CHIC

Angela Taylor

"Jenny kissed me"—Leigh Hunt was so excited, he wrote a poem about it. Well, I don't think it's anything to brag about. These days, Jenny kisses me and so do Bob and Carol and Ted and Alice. And so do a lot of strangers. As when a woman I know slightly introduces her husband. Before I get a chance to say "How do you do?" the gent leans over and kisses me.

Of course, they're not real kisses. They're planted lightly on the cheek or not planted at all—just a gesture of faintly touching cheeks and kissing into the air behind one's ear. Everybody is kissing everybody else: At parties, on the street, in restaurants. Any day now, I'll find myself being kissed by the headwaiter and the doorman.

This kissing business has been going on for some time now. Europeans have always done it, then Americans who consider themselves well-traveled picked it up. It's a status thing, like having a suntan in the middle of winter. It proves you hobnob in sophisticated circles.

And now it has become epidemic over here. Beautiful People are automatic kissers, so are Seventh Avenue types. Southerners kiss more readily than New Englanders. It probably has something to do with everybody being kin to the whole town, down South. Theatrical people are enthusiastic kissers, they hop from table to table at Sardi's calling one another "darling" and smooching madly. They kiss like crazy on television, especially talk shows.

The situation is getting out of hand, and it's time somebody laid out ground rules: Who kisses whom and whom do you kiss back? How do you know if it's going to be a simple, one-cheek kiss or do you offer the other cheek for a double kiss à la Français?

The etiquette mavens are no help. Emily Post's book goes into the kissing of the bride and the Cardinal's ring. And having your hand kissed by a man. The last rarely happens to me, and then only if the man is French or Italian. And even then, he doesn't actually kiss my limp hand, but makes a soundless smack four inches above my wrist. I always feel let down. If he's gone as far as to raise my hopes, I think he should complete the gesture.

Amy Vanderbilt's tome explains about men kissing each other in Latin countries and the two-cheek kiss exchanged by men when one of them is being presented

SUBCULTURE AND COMMUNICATION

Language is a social institution designed, modified, and extended (some purists might even say disorted) to meet the ever-changing needs of the culture or subculture. As such, language differs greatly from one culture to another and, equally important though perhaps less obvious, from one subculture to another.

Subcultures are cultures within a larger culture and may be formed on the

with a medal. But it doesn't tell how to behave when a six-foot near-stranger suddenly lunges at me. My hairdresser kisses me. But then there's my doctor. He never even offers to shake hands in the office. But I ran into him in a restaurant the other day and he planted a smack on my cheek.

In the early days of the kissing fad, only women I knew well would touch cheeks with me, both of us careful not to smear each other with lipstick. That was a nice gesture, particularly if I hadn't seen my friend since yesterday. Then their husbands' tried it, the shy ones looking pained and only doing it because it was expected of them. Unless a man is a bit of a lecher, it must be awfully boring to have to kiss each woman in the room, whether she's his type or not.

Just as I got used to the one-cheek kiss, the two-cheek affair got popular. It puts you in a delicate situation. You never know when you offer a cheek, if one kiss is going to settle things once and for all. You back off after the first one and then realize your opponent is flexing for another, and there you are, banging heads. It's embarrassing. If the double kisser is a woman, she feels you don't like her. If it's a man, he thinks that you've interpreted a gesture as a pass and that you're probably frigid.

At a large party the other night, I air-kissed at least a dozen men and women whom I knew reasonably well, although our acquaintance had been mainly on the business side. Then a woman I had talked to briefly only once crossed my path. Before I could say "Hi," she put her hands on my shoulders and kissed me. Oh, well, I thought, it's going to be that kind of evening and so was prepared when another woman (whom I knew better) bent her head toward me and I dutifully offered mine. She hadn't meant to kiss me at all, but was leaning toward somebody over my shoulder. By that time, I was off-balance and lurched into her. I suppose she thought I was drunk.

Since Emily Post has told about kissing the Pope's ring in case I find myself at a private audience in the Vatican, I think it would be helpful if an expert would show me how to handle the stranger who's puckering up and ready to attack.

Then there's the problem in reverse. For instance, Robert Redford and I were introduced at a cocktail party a couple of years ago. He dimpled and my heart fluttered. Wouldn't you think that being a Hollywood extrovert, he might have offered me a small peck? I had everything to do to get him to shake hands.

Source: The New York Times, March 7, 1976, p. 48. Reprinted by permission of The New York Times.

basis of religion, geographical area, occupation, sexual orientation, race, nationality, living conditions, interests, needs, and so on. Catholics, protestants, and Jews; New Yorkers, Californians, and mountain folk; teachers, plumbers, and musicians; homosexuals and lesbians; blacks, Chinese, and American Indians; Germans, Italians, and Mexicans; prisoners, suburbanites, and "ghettoites"; bibliophiles, drug addicts, and bird watchers; diabetics, the blind, and ex-convicts may all be viewed as subcultures depending, of course, on the context on which we focus. In New York, for example, New Yorkers would obviously not constitute a subculture but throughout the rest of the world they would. In the United States as a whole protestants would not constitute a subculture (though Catholics and Jews would). In New York City, on the other hand, Protestants would constitute a subculture. Blacks and Chinese would be subcultures only outside of Africa and China. As these examples illustrate, the majority generally constitutes the culture and the various minorities generally constitute the subcultures. Yet this is not always the case. Women, although the majority in our culture, may be viewed as a subculture primarily because the society as a whole is male oriented. Whether a group should be regarded as a subculture or a culture, then, would depend upon the context being considered and the orientation of the society of which these groups are a part.

Each individual belongs to several subcultures. At the very least they belong to a national, a religious, and an occupational subculture. The importance of the subcultural affiliation will vary greatly from one individual to another, from one context to another, from one time or circumstance to another. For example, to some people in some contexts an individual's religious affiliation may be inconsequential and his or her membership in this subculture hardly thought of. When, on the other hand, the individual wishes to marry into a particular family this once inconsequential membership may take on vast significance.

Because of the common interests, needs, or conditions of individuals constituting a subculture, sublanguages come into being. Like language in general, sublanguages exist to enable members of the group to communicate with each other. And, again like language in general, there are various regional variations, changes over time, and so on. There are, however, other functions that sublanguages serve and these functions constitute their reason for existence. If they did not serve these several functions they would soon disappear. It should not be assumed, of course, that all sublanguages must serve all the functions noted.

Functions of Sublanguages

One of the most obvious facts about language and its relation to culture is that concepts that are important to a given culture are given a large number of terms. For example, in our culture money is extremely important; consequently, we have numerous terms denoting this concept: *finances, funds, capital, assets, cash, pocket money, spending money, pin money, change, bread, loot, swag,* and various others. Transportation and communication are other concepts for which numerous terms exist in our language. Without knowing anything about a given culture we could probably make some pretty good guesses as to the important concepts in that culture by simply examining one of its dictionaries or thesauruses. With sublanguages, the same principle holds. Concepts that are of special importance to a particular subculture are given a large number of terms. Thus one function of sublanguages is to provide the subculture with convenient synonyms for those concepts which are of great importance and hence are spoken about frequently. To prisoners, for example, a prison guard—clearly a significant concept and one spoken about a great deal—may be denoted by *screw, roach, hack, slave driver, shield, holligan,* and various other terms. Heroin, in the drug subculture, may be called *H, Harry, smack, Carga, joy powder, skag, stuff,* or just plain *shit.*

A related function of sublanguages is to provide the subculture with convenient distinctions that are important to the subculture but generally not to the culture at large—and thus distinctions that the general language does not make. For example, the general culture has no need for making distinctions among various drugs—all may be conveniently labeled *drugs.* But to members of the drug subculture it is essential to make distinctions which to outsiders may seem unimportant or even trivial. The general culture, for example, does not distinguish between "getting stoned" and "on a high." Yet to the members of the drug subculture these are two different states that need to be distinguished. Put differently, sublanguages serve to increase the *codifiability* of the general language. Codifiability refers to the ease with which certain concepts may be expressed in a language. Short terms are of high codifiability; long expressions are of low codifiability. All languages and sublanguages seem to move in the direction of increasing codifiability. As a concept becomes important in a culture or subculture the term denoting it is shortened or some other simpler expression is adopted to denote it; thus *television* becomes *TV, motion pictures* becomes *movies,* and *lysergic acid diethylamide* becomes *LSD* or simply *acid.* The expression "turn on" is the drug subculture's highly codifiable term for the general culture's low codifiable expression "to take a drug or participate in some experience which alters one's awareness." Similarly, it is much easier to say "lid" than "an ounce of marijuana" and "dex" than "dextroamphetamine capsules."

Sublanguages also serve as means of identification. By using a particular sublanguage, speakers identify themselves to hearers as members of that subculture—assuming, of course, that hearers know the language being used. Individuals belonging to various nationality-based subcultures will frequently drop a foreign word or phrase in the conversation to identify themselves to their hearers. Similarly, homosexuals and ex-convicts will at times identify themselves by using the cant of their subculture. When the subcultural membership is one that is normally hidden, as is the case of homosexuals and ex-convicts, the clues to self-identification are subtle. Generally, they are only given after the individuals themselves receive some kind of positive feedback which leads them to suspect that the hearer also belongs to the subculture in question or that the hearer is at least sympathetic. In a similar vein, the use of sublanguages also functions to express to others one's felt identification with that subculture. For example, blacks may address each other as brother and sister when meeting for the first time. The use of these terms by blacks as well as the frequent use of foreign expressions by members of various national groups communicates to others that the speaker feels a strong identification with the group.

Sublanguages also enable members of the subculture to communicate with one another while in the presence of nonmembers without having their conversation completely understood. Under certain situations, of course, the sublanguage may mark the individual as a member of a particular subculture and so he or she would refrain from using the sublanguage. This is often the case among criminals when in a noncriminal environment. At other times, however, the use of a sublanguage does not lead to an individual's identification as a subculture member, and the sublanguage serves the useful purpose of excluding nonmembers from the class of decoders.

A less obvious function of sublanguages, though a particularly important one, is that they serve to provide the group with a kind of identity and a sense of fraternity. Because ex-convicts all over the country know the same sublanguage they are, in a sense, bound together. Obviously, the more the subculture has a need to band together the greater the importance of a specialized language.

Kinds of Sublanguages

Sublanguage has been used here as a general term to denote a variation from the general language that is used by a particular group or subculture existing within the broader, more general culture. But there are different kinds of sublanguages and these should now be distinguished.

Cant is the conversational language of a specific subculture which is generally understood only by members of that subculture. *Jargon* is the technical language of a particular subculture; it is the "shop talk" of the group. *Argot* is the cant and the jargon of a particular subculture, generally an "underworld" or criminal subculture such as forgers, bank robbers, thieves, and the like. *Slang* is a more general term denoting the language used by special groups (for example, different social or age groups) which is not considered proper by the general society. Slang may be viewed as consisting of those terms from the argot, cant, and jargon of the various subcultures which are known by the general population.

With the passage of time and an increased frequency of usage, slang terms enter the general language as socially acceptable expressions. When this happens new terms are needed and are therefore coined by the subcultures. The old terms are then dropped from the sublanguage since they now serve none of the functions for which they were originally developed.

This is just one of the ways by which new words enter the language and by which sublanguages are kept distinct from the general language.

SOURCES

For varied definitions of culture see Alfred L. Kroeber and Clyde Kluckhohn, *Culture—A Critical Review of Concepts and Definitions* (New York: Random

House, n.d.), originally published in Papers of the Peabody Museum, 47, no. 1a, 1952. Extended discussions of culture and cultures are provided in most recent anthropology texts. See, for example, John Friedl, *Cultural Anthropology* (New York: Harper & Row, 1976).

For sublanguages see H. L. Mencken's *The American Language* (New York: Knopf, 1971). Mencken's chapter on "American Slang" is surely a classic work and, it should be added, a most interesting one at that. Much interesting research relevant to sublanguages is reported in the various works on sociolinguistics, for example, Joshua A. Fishman's *The Sociology of Language* (Rowley, Mass.: Newbury House, 1972) and Dell Hymes' *Foundations in Sociolinguistics: An Ethnographic Approach* (Philadelphia: University of Pennsylvania Press, 1974). One of the most insightful essays is that by Paul Goodman, "Sublanguages," in *Speaking and Language: Defence of Poetry* (New York: Random House, 1971). The theory and research on forms of address are thoroughly covered in Roger Brown, *Social Psychology* (New York: Free Press, 1965).

For an introduction to intercultural communication, see for example, John C. Condon and Fathi Yousef, *An Introduction to Intercultural Communication* (Indianapolis: Bobbs-Merrill, 1975) and K. S. Sitaram and Roy T. Cogdell, *Foundations of Intercultural Communication* (Columbus: Charles E. Merrill, 1976). Interracial communication is surveyed in Andrea L. Rich, *Interracial Communication* (New York: Harper & Row, 1974) and in Jon A. Blubaugh and Dorthy L. Pennington, *Crossing Difference . . . Interracial Communication* (Columbus: Charles E. Merrill, 1976).

EXPERIENTIAL VEHICLES

32.1 VALUES IN AMERICAN CULTURE

The purposes of this experiential vehicle are to enable you to explore in greater depth the values of American culture and also to see how these values are reflected in the mass media.

Carefully examine one of the ten most popular mass circulation magazines: *TV Guide, Reader's Digest, National Geographic, Family Circle, Woman's Day, Better Homes and Gardens, McCall's, Ladies' Home Journal, Playboy, Good Housekeeping.*

What values of American culture can be seen in these periodicals? Look for these values in the magazine's editorial policy, its advertisements, its feature articles and pictures, and in the letters to the editor. List five values that the magazine assumes are held by its readers and the evidence (articles, advertisements, etc.) you have for each value.

32.2 SIX SUBLANGUAGES

Presented below are a few brief lexicons of some sublanguages. Note how these terms serve the functions discussed in this unit and how many of them are in the process of passing into the general language.

Assuming that you might like to test your knowledge of the various sublanguages, these lexicons are presented as matching quizzes. Write the number of the sublanguage term (left column) next to the letter of the corresponding general language term (right column).

CRIMINAL TALK

1. maker, designer, scratcher, connection	a. bank burglar
2. paper, scrip, stiff	b. false key
3. jug stiff, cert	c. rackets involving violence
4. beat, sting, come-off	d. forger
5. buttons, shamus, fuzz	e. wallet
6. mark, hoosier, chump, yap	f. a parcel with a trap side for hiding stolen merchandise
7. poke, leather, hide	g. burglar alarm
8. cold poke, dead skin	h. an iron safe
9. gun, cannon, whiz	i. forged check
10. boosters	j. pickpocket
11. booster box	k. dynamite
12. bug	l. forged bank check
13. dinah, noise	m. shoplifters
14. double	n. watchman
15. gopher	o. policeman
16. hack	p. negotiable securities
17. soup, pete	q. pickpocket victim
18. jug heavy	r. nitroglycerine
19. stiffs	s. empty wallet
20. heavy rackets	t. picking a pocket

PRISONER TALK

1. fish	a. prison waiter
2. kite	b. prison chaplin
3. drum	c. prison barber
4. to slam off	d. a new prisoner
5. to gut	e. to escape from jail
6. sleeping time	f. prison guard
7. college	g. prison doctor
8. greenhouse	h. roast beef
9. Cupid's itch	i. meat
10. big noise	j. letter smuggled out of jail
11. screw, roach, hack, slave driver, shield	k. venereal disease
12. frocker, goody, psalmer	l. prison
13. croacker, cutemup, pill punk, salts, iodine	m. soup
14. scraper, butcher	n. sausage
15. leather, young horse	o. cell
16. water	p. to die
17. chalk	q. milk
18. beagle, dog, balloon	r. prison morgue
19. pig	s. a short sentence
20. soup jockey	t. warden

GAY TALK

1. auntie	a. burlesque of one's own homosexuality
2. bring out	b. to introduce someone to homosexuality
3. bull dyke	c. one who wears the clothes of the opposite sex
4. butch	d. to let others know that one is homosexual
5. camp	e. one who engages in homosexual activity but does not consider himself homosexual
6. chicken	f. homosexual
7. closet queen	g. to enter the gay life
8. come out	h. masculine homosexual woman
9. cruise	i. old homosexual, generally effeminate
10. drag queen	j. effeminate male homosexual
11. fag hag	k. to be undecided between heterosexuality and homosexuality
12. to be on the fence	l. masculine appearing homosexual, male or female
13. to drop one's pins	m. to search for a sexual partner
14. leather bars	n. a young boy
15. mother	o. one who introduces another to the gay life
16. gay	p. a promiscuous homosexual
17. number	q. homosexual bars whose customers are motorcycle riders who wear leather clothes and jeans
18. queen	r. a casual sexual partner
19. trade	s. a male homosexual who does not actively participate in the gay social life
20. whore	t. a heterosexual who prefers to socialize with gays

MOUNTAIN TALK

1. a-fixin'		a.	hard rain
2. doin's		b.	bag
3. fetch		c.	look at
4. put out		d.	getting ready to do something
5. aim		e.	get rid of
6. smart		f.	hurt
7. book read		g.	clean up
8. lollygag		h.	function or event
9. crick		i.	loaf or loiter
10. biggety		j.	nervous
11. plumb		k.	bring
12. shed of		l.	stiffness
13. poke		m.	a great distance
14. red		n.	angry
15. skittish		o.	geographical area
16. gander		p.	intend, plan
17. parts		q.	exactly, on the dot
18. smack-dab		r.	completely
19. fur piece		s.	educated
20. gully-washer		t.	snobbish, stuck up

DRUG TALK

1. smack, H, Harry, Carga, joy powder, skag, stuff, shit	a.	get high
2. head	b.	ineffective dosage of drugs
3. joint, stick	c.	a regular user of LSD
4. flip	d.	LSD experience
5. acid	e.	lysergic acid diethylamide
6. poppers, snappers	f.	user of psychedelic drugs
7. straight	g.	narcotics agent
8. stoned	h.	bad LSD experience
9. trip	i.	marijuana
10. narc, narco	j.	depressants
11. spaced out	k.	one who watches over an individual on an acid trip
12. zero	l.	marijuana cigarette
13. guide	m.	high on marijuana
14. acidhead	n.	high on LSD
15. Bernice, C, candy, coke, dust, flake, snow	o.	cocaine
16. lift off	p.	stimulants
17. freakout	q.	someone who does not take drugs
18. boo, tea, grass, bush, hay, hemp, jive, pot, weed, Mary Jane	r.	amyl nitrate
19. ups, uppers	s.	become psychotic
20. downs, downers	t.	heroin

CB LANGUAGE

1. green stamps	a. unmarked police car
2. good buddy	b. other CB owners/operators
3. seat covers	c. state police
4. X-ray machine	d. overnight stop
5. plain wrapper	e. radar unit ahead
6. ranch	f. diner
7. bear cave	g. FCC (Federal Communications
8. cut some *Z*'s	Commission)
9. clean	h. fog
10. ground clouds	i. money
11. boy scouts	j. toll ahead
12. handle	k. low overhead
13. bean store	l. get some sleep
14. green stamp road	m. traffic tickets
15. keep your nose between the	n. passengers
ditches and smokey out of your	o. drive safely; watch for speed
britches	traps
16. mama bear	p. no police in sight
17. big daddy	q. CBer's name for CB transmission
18. invitations	r. police station
19. haircut palace	s. police radar
20. brush your teeth and	t. police woman
comb your hair	

UNIT 33
Language Relativity and Universal Languages

Language Relativity
Universal Languages

33.1 Word Coinage

LEARNING GOALS

After completing this unit, you should be able to:

1. define *language relativity*
2. provide at least two examples of some semantic aspects of language relativity
3. provide at least two examples of some structural aspects of language relativity
4. define *universal language*
5. identify at least three examples of proposed universal languages
6. explain at least two of the arguments in favor of the establishment of a universal language
7. explain at least three of the arguments against the establishment of a universal language

LANGUAGE RELATIVITY

In George Orwell's *1984,* a futuristic novel set in Oceania in the year 1984, the average citizen is a rather helpless creature, forbidden to love, forbidden to even think thoughts contrary to the party. Everywhere the telescreen is watching you and everywhere there are posters with a picture of Big Brother with the caption "Big Brother Is Watching You." There were three slogans of the party and together these give us a first glimpse of the role of language in *1984:*

WAR IS PEACE
FREEDOM IS SLAVERY
IGNORANCE IS STRENGTH

The aspect of the novel particularly relevant to intercultural communication is that which deals with Newspeak—a newly developed language that is expected to replace English by the year 2050. Already in *1984* people are speaking this new language, newspapers are using the language, and books are being written and rewritten in Newspeak. The aim of Newspeak and the very reason for its creation was to control thought. By eliminating the words for concepts and ideas that were contrary to the party line, the assumption was that the thoughts themselves could be eliminated.

This general idea that language influences thought and ultimately behavior got its strongest expression from linguistic anthropologists. In the late 1920s and throughout the 1930s the view that the characteristics of language influence our cognitive processes was formulated. And since the languages of the world differ greatly in regard to their semantic and structural characteristics, it seemed logical to argue that people speaking widely different languages would also differ in the way in which they viewed and thought about the world. This view of language generated a great deal of interest among linguists, anthropologists, psychologists, sociologists, and communicologists. The theory itself is referred to by different labels: linguistic relativity, Whorfian hypothesis, Sapir-Whorf hypothesis. The latter two titles come from the people who are most closely associated with the formulation of the hypothesis, namely Benjamin Lee Whorf and Edward Sapir.

In 1929 Edward Sapir wrote in his famous *Language:*

> The "real world" is to a large extent unconsciously built up on the language habits of the group. The worlds in which different societies live are distinct worlds, not merely the same world with different labels attached. We see and hear and otherwise experience very largely as we do because the language habits of our community predispose certain choices of interpretation.

Whorf, who gave the linguistic relativity hypothesis its strongest statement, noted:

> The background linguistic system (in other words, the grammar) of each language is not merely a reproducing instrument for voicing ideas but rather is itself the shaper of ideas, the program and guide for the individual's mental activity, for his analysis of impressions, for his synthesis of his mental stock in trade. . . . We dissect nature along lines laid down by our native languages. The categories and types that we isolate from the world of phenomena we do not find there because they stare every observer in the face; on the contrary, the world is presented in a kaleidoscopic flux of impressions which has to be organized by our minds—and this means largely by the linguistic systems in our minds.

In examining this hypothesis we will first look at some of the semantic aspects, and second at some of the structural aspects of language relativity.

Some Semantic Aspects of Language Relativity

A great deal of anecdotal evidence has been assembled on the relationship between the semantics of a language and the way in which the speakers of that language see the world or behave. Perhaps the most famous examples are those that refer to the fact that in Eskimo there are many words for snow whereas in English there is only one. In Arabic there are many words for different types of horses whereas in English there are just a few. The Trobrian Islanders have numerous terms for yams at the various stages of their development whereas speakers of English have but one term. Conversely, in English we have three words for what the Hopi Indian denotes with one word. In English we distinguish plane, fly (the insect), and pilot, but in Hopi all three of these nouns are denoted by *Masa'ytaka*. The Hopi distinguishes *pahe* (running water as in the ocean or from a waterfall or fountain) from *keyi* (still water in a glass or bowl) whereas we make no such distinction in English.

One of the most interesting examples is the way in which the Eskimo language classifies the different kinds of seals. In Eskimo there is one category of nouns which denotes a young spotted seal, a female harbor seal, and a swimming male ribbon seal. The giant bearded seal although belonging to the same mammalian classification as the former seals is not in the same language category. The reason is that the division in the Eskimo language is not based on the anatomy of the seal but rather on the hunting practices of the people. The three seals of the same linguistic category can all be hunted and killed by a single hunter; they therefore form one group. But the giant bearded seal can only be killed by a group of hunters and so is put into a different language category.

In an attempt to explore the extent to which words influence what we see and how we behave, a study conducted some years ago by John Carroll may be used as an illustration. Carroll's study focused on speakers of Hopi and English. Groups of three pictures each were shown to speakers of Hopi and to speakers of English; all the subjects were to do was to group the two pictures that seemed to go best together. It was hypothesized that the Hopi and the English speakers would group the pictures differently because of differences in their respective languages. For example, of the three pictures in Figure 33.1, the English speakers grouped A and C or B and C together but the Hopi grouped A and B together. The reason offered is that in Hopi there is a word *leluwi* which means "to apply or spread over a surface" and this encompasses pictures A and B whereas in English the word *painting* covers both B and C and *decorating* covers both A and C.

Of the three pictures in Figure 33.2 the Hopi grouped A and B together because the actions exemplified here are covered by the related terms *wehekna* (spilling a liquid) and *wa:hokna* (spilling a nonliquid). The word *dropping*, however (picture C), is denoted by a totally unrelated term, *po:sna*. English speakers grouped B and C most often because these were both covered by the term *accidental*.

Evidence such as this, and there are numerous other examples that could be

Figure 33.1
Grouping Experiment I (Carroll)

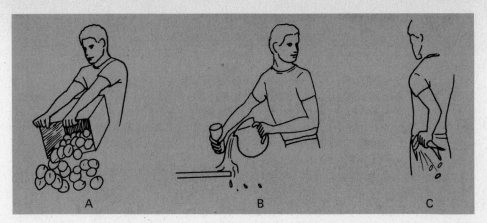

Figure 33.2
Grouping Experiment II (Carroll)

given, has been used to argue that the vocabulary of a language determines in part the world we see and the world to which we respond. It does seem reasonable to conclude that by looking at the vocabulary of a language we can tell something about what is important to the speakers of the language. If there are many words for snow in Eskimo and for yams among the Trobrian Islanders then it seems logical to argue that snow and yams are important to these particular cultures. Similarly, the vocabulary of a language may well focus our attention on certain aspects of reality rather than on others. And so the distinction between spilling and dropping in Hopi and between accidental and nonaccidental dropping in English may well direct our attention to specific facets of the world.

What seems equally clear, however, is that these differences may be learned relatively easily. That is, if we cared enough about yams we would soon learn the various distinctions and would in all likelihood notice whatever the Trobrian Islanders notice.

Some Structural Aspects of Language Relativity

The more convincing (if the not the more interesting) examples of linguistic relativity center on the grammar rather than the vocabulary of the different languages.

For example, in English we make distinctions on the basis of tense; we distinguish present from past and future. This is the extent of our distinctions in terms of verbs. But in Hopi distinctions are made in terms of the validity of a statement. Some of these differences are illustrated in Figure 33.3. Notice that a statement of fact from immediate observation is distinguished from a statement of fact from memory and that both are distinguished from a statement of

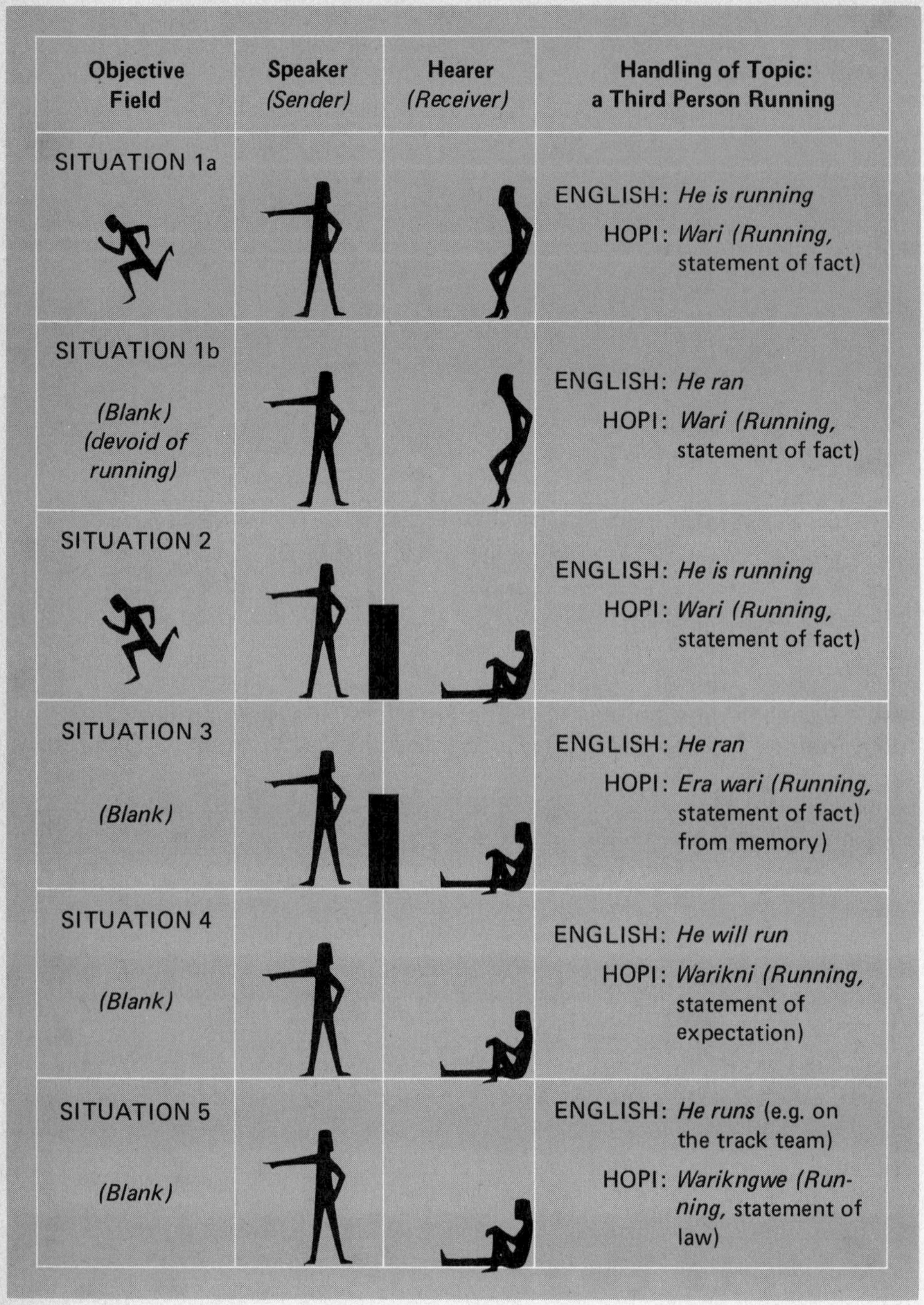

Objective Field	Speaker (Sender)	Hearer (Receiver)	Handling of Topic: a Third Person Running
SITUATION 1a			ENGLISH: *He is running* HOPI: *Wari (Running, statement of fact)*
SITUATION 1b *(Blank) (devoid of running)*			ENGLISH: *He ran* HOPI: *Wari (Running, statement of fact)*
SITUATION 2			ENGLISH: *He is running* HOPI: *Wari (Running, statement of fact)*
SITUATION 3 *(Blank)*			ENGLISH: *He ran* HOPI: *Era wari (Running, statement of fact) from memory)*
SITUATION 4 *(Blank)*			ENGLISH: *He will run* HOPI: *Warikni (Running, statement of expectation)*
SITUATION 5 *(Blank)*			ENGLISH: *He runs* (e.g. on the track team) HOPI: *Warikngwe (Running, statement of law)*

Figure 33.3
Some Differences Between the Hopi and English Languages

expectation and a statement of a general law. Whorf argued that the absence of tenses as we know them in Hopi was consistent with their timeless and ahistorical view of the world; past, present, and future all belong to a continuous span of time where sharp divisions are unnecessary. Hopi therefore distinguish the duration of events and their certainty rather than the specific time at which they occurred. Notice in English how differently we treat time. We can *waste* time or *save* it; we can *buy* time and *sell* time. We keep records, diaries, accounts, and histories. We develop elaborate schedules to keep us on time and it is imperative not only that the show go on but that it go on on time. The Hopi do not measure time in the same way. For the Hopi it is more important to be concerned with the proper sequence of events rather than the time in which the events took place. An English-speaker building a house would attempt to get the house built as soon as possible but the Hopi would not rush and may well take years to build the house without any apparent frustration about losing time. What is most important to the Hopi is that the sequence of events occurs in the right order.

It has also been proposed that English is an inductive language where the noun is preceded by the various adjectives. French and many of the Romance languages, on the other hand, are deductive—the noun comes first and is followed by the various adjectives. This difference has been related by Edmund Glenn to the differences in the English and French way of looking at the world. The English legal system is largely inductive where a series of precedents culminate in a general law. The French legal system on the other hand is largely deductive where a general rule comes first and is used to deduce the various specific applications. Similarly, Glenn notes the French have more concern for broad philosophical issues whereas the English and Americans have more concern for details.

One of the most interesting examples of a different world view has been supplied by Peter Farb. Japanese women who married Americans were interviewed at different times—at times in English and at times in Japanese. During these interviews a few of the same questions were asked in both languages. The women were, for example, asked to complete different sentences. The responses they gave varied depending on the language in which they were interviewed. For example, when asked to complete the sentence, "When my wishes conflict with my family's . . ." they answered in English "I do what I want" but they answered in Japanese "It is a time of great unhappiness." The sentence, "I will probably become . . ." was answered in English with "a teacher" but in Japanese with "a housewife." The sentence "Real friends should . . ." was completed in English with "be very frank" but in Japanese it was answered with "help each other."

In a study very similar in design to that reported by John Carroll, Joseph Casagrande compared the grouping responses of Navaho and English children. In Navaho it is necessary to include some reference in the stem of the verb to the form of the object being considered. For example, if asked to hand me an object in Navaho I must distinguish the form of the object and would say *Sanleh* if it were a long flexible object like a piece of string, *santiih* if it were a long rigid object, and *sanilcoos* if it were a flat, flexible object such as a piece of paper. Because of this grammatical feature it was hypothesized that Navaho children would group objects on the basis of form whereas English children—as has been shown repeatedly—would group objects on the basis of color. The children were presented with two objects and were asked to select the object that best went with a third object. For example, the children were presented with a yellow rope and a blue stick and were asked to select the one that best went with a blue rope. Navaho children grouped the two ropes together but English children grouped the two blue objects together.

Differences such as these do not seem particularly great and seem to be such that they could easily be changed if there were such a need. That is, from the purely linguistic point of view the similarities among languages seem to far outweigh the differences. And in terms of perception and behavior it seems that there are even greater similarities. The differences in language and, concomitantly, in perception and behavior seem largely differences in terms of ease of reference rather than in terms of the ability or inability to express certain ideas or thoughts. So while we may conclude that differences among languages do not make for insurmountable problems, they do present us with a sufficient number of examples to sensitize us to some of the possible problems that may arise. And perhaps this increased sensitivity will help us to eventually avoid misunderstandings brought about by language differences.

We might extend this idea of linguistic relativity and note that even within any one language there are sublanguages and these sublanguages have different vocabularies much as do different languages. Thus, the teacher who utilizes the professional jargon of his or her field should recognize that that sublanguage is not a part of the vocabulary of his or her sudents. The vocabulary of the students may not be the vocabulary of their parents and so on. It should be further recognized that these differences are not inevitable obstacles to communication. Rather they are differences in languages which can be reconciled; the vocabularies can be taught to others and perhaps this is one step necessary to closing the gaps between people.

UNIVERSAL LANGUAGES

With one language spoken and understood by everyone, human beings could do just about anything, or so the story of the Tower of Babel tells us. And conversely, with many diverse mutually unintelligible languages, difficulties would confront our every cooperative effort.

The desire for a universal language appears an ancient one; we have, it seems, a desire to join our fellows in some common bond—to have a demonstrable similarity. Voltaire once remarked that ''the difference of languages is one of the greatest misfortunes of being.'' And perhaps it is.

Box 34
THE TOWER OF BABEL, GENESIS 11:1–9

The whole earth used the same language and the same speech. While men were migrating eastward, they discovered a valley in the land of Sennaar and settled there. They said to one another, "Come let us make bricks and bake them." They used bricks for stone and bitumen for mortar. Then they said, "Let us build ourselves a city and a tower with its top in the heavens; let us make a name for ourselves lest we be scattered all over the earth." The Lord came down to see the city and the tower which men had built. And the Lord said, "Truly they are one people and they all have the same language. This is the beginning of what they will do. Hereafter they will not be restrained from anything which they determine to do. Let us go down, and there confuse their language so that they will not understand one another's speech." So the Lord scattered them from that place all over the earth; and they stopped building the city. For this reason it was called Babel, because there the Lord confused the speech of all the earth. From there the Lord scattered them all over the earth.

For anyone who has had to stay up nights learning the vocabulary and the very conjugations of a foreign language or for anyone who has tried to order a meal in a foreign country, the idea of a universal language seems a most appealing one. The waste in time and energy in learning other languages and in translating important works would be eliminated. By speaking the same language we would better understand people in other parts of the world; where now we are divided by language differences we would be united by language similarities. Mario Pei reports that a Gallup poll conducted in the United States in 1950 found that 76 percent voted yes when asked about the desirability of a world language, and when repeated in 1961, 84 percent voted yes. But the arguments are not so one-sided as may have appeared.

A universal language, as the phrase implies, is a language that is understood and used by all people; it is universal among people and may be a natural language that comes to be used universally or an artificial language created and designed as a universal language.

Some Universal Languages

Since the first proposal for an international language by the French philosopher Descartes in the seventeenth century, approximately 1000 systems have been proposed for a universal language. Some of the more popular candidates include Latin, Volapuk, Esperanto, Interlingua, and Basic English.

Latin, it was argued, would be an excellent choice for a universal language since it once served the function of a universal language at least among the intelligencia of Western Europe. Lawyers, teachers, priests, doctors, and in

Box 35
SOME EXAMPLES OF UNIVERSAL LANGUAGES

Volapuk (The Lord's Prayer)

"O Fat obas, kel binol in süls, paisaludomöz nem ola! Kömomöd monargän ola! Jenomöz vil olik, as in sül i su tal! Bodi obsik vädeliki givolös obes adelo! E pardolos obes debis obsik, äs id obs aipardobs debeles obas. E no obis nindukoläs in tentadi; sed aidalivolös obis de bad. Jenosöd!

Basic English (New Testament)

And all those who were of the faith were one in heart and soul: and not one of them said that any of the things which he had was his property only; but they had all things in common. . . . And no one among them was in need; for everyone who had land or houses, exchanging them for money, took the price of them, and put it at the feet of the Apostles for distribtuion to everyone as he had need.

King James Bible (Acts 4:32)

And the multitude of them that believed were of one heart and one soul: neither said any of them that ought of the things which he possessed was his own; but they had all things common. . . . Neither was there any among them that lacked: for as many as were possessors of lands or houses sold them, and brought the prices of the things that were sold, and laid them down at the apostles' feet: and distribution was made unto every man according as he had need.

general all the educated or professional classes used Latin for writing and "thinking" as well as for general communication. But with the rise of the middle and lower classes, with the increase in their participation in intellectual endeavors, and with the rise in nationalistic spirit, Latin declined in importance and French, Italian, Spanish, and the like took its place. There arose what Mario Pei calls "linguistic nationalism."

Volapuk (from the words *vol* meaning "world" and *puk* meaning "speak" or "language") was invented by a Bavarian priest, Johann Martin Schleyer, in 1879. In Volapuk words were pronounced exactly as they were written; there were no exceptions. The accents always appeared on the last syllable. All together 283 societies were formed for the propagation of Volapuk. Books and journals were published in Volapuk and over 1000 teachers were trained to teach this new language which (as you can guess) did not catch on. One of the difficulties with it was that it was a totally new language that did not make use of any existing languages for its roots. Consequently, it had to be learned from scratch.

On the heels of Volapuk came *Esperanto,* invented by a Polish doctor, Ludwik Zamenhof. Esperanto was built on English, German, French, Italian, and

Interlingua

Professor H. Oberth, un del pioneros in le campo del rochetteria scientific in Germania e plus recentemente un associato de Dr. W. von Baun in su recercas de roccheteria al arsenal Redstone in Alabama, ha elaborate un vehiculo adoptate al exploration del luna. Un tal vehiculo debe esser capace a superar le difficultates extraordinari del terreno e del ambiente del luna que es characterisate per le absentia de omne atmosphere, per un gravitate reducite, per extrememente acute alterationes de temperatura, c per un superficie plus pulverose que ullo cognoscite in terra.

English

Professor H. Oberth, one of the pioneers in the field of scientific rocketry in Germany and more recently an associate of Dr. W. von Braun in his research on rocketry at the Redstone Arsenal in Alabama, has elaborated plans for a vehicle adapted for lunar exploration. Such a vehicle must be capable of overcoming the extraordinary difficulties of the terrain and surroundings of the moon, characterized by the absence of any atmosphere, by reduced gravity, by extremely sharp changes of temperature, and by a more dusty surface than any known on earth.

Esperanto

La astronomo, per speciala teleskopo fotografas la sunon, la lunon, kaj la planedojn.

Modernaj delikataj instrumentoj permesas la detalan ekzamenon de la strukturo de la atomo.

La teorio de Einstein, la nova principo de relativeco, presentas komplikan problemon.

English

The astronomer, by means of a special telescope, photographs the sun, the moon, and the planets.

Modern delicate instruments permit the detailed examination of the structure of the atom.

The Einstein theory, the new principle of relativity, presents a complex problem.

Spanish and attempted to simplify every conceivable aspect of language. The entire grammar, for example, consisted of just 16 rules that could be learned in a matter of hours. Esperanto is still with us, although its aim of becoming a universal language has faded. There are still societies that hold conferences in and on Esperanto and "The Voice of America" used to broadcast programs in Esperanto as well as in various other languages. It is estimated that some 1 million people make some use of Esperanto today.

Interlingua was another candidate and was built out of existing words of other languages. That is, rather than create new words, Interlingua's words are simply lifted from an existing language such as French, Italian, Russian, or English. Interlingua was invented by an American, Alexander Gode, who attempted to build a language that could be understood with little specific training. Since the language made use of the common terms from other languages, a knowledge of one or more of these other languages would generally be sufficient to understand at least basic writings in Interlingua.

Basic English, developed by I. A. Richards and C. K. Ogden, was not originally intended as a universal language. It consists of approximately 850 basic English words which, it is claimed, can be manipulated to say just about anything except the technical or scientific. As can be appreciated though, it would be a bit cumbersome to express ideas with long phrases when we now have a single word. For example, instead of saying "screwdriver" we might have to say "the tool for putting in the screw."

As these examples illustrate most attempts to develop a universal language have relied on conventional alphabets and grammatical principles, although in much simplified form. But there have been other systems which have deviated widely from what we normally think of as conventional languages. *Solresol,* for example, utilized a musical scale and *Translingua* used a numerical system where each word was denoted by some combination of numbers.

Some Problems with a Universal Language

Although the idea of a universal language seems a most practical and functional one, there are numerous problems that beset the acceptance of such a language.

All languages change through time and there seems no reason to suppose that a universal language—whether artificial or natural—would not change also. With such changes will come dialects and eventually mutually unintelligible languages will spring up from the universal language. That is, the situation which arose when Latin led to the Romance languages and eventually to mutually unintelligible languages will repeat itself.

A second problem, but only a problem in relation to the language catching on, is that there are usually too few speakers to make any impact. Esperanto, which is by far the most popular of the universal languages, numbers less than 150,000 among its fluent speakers and it is difficult to imagine the numbers growing without any concerted effort on the part of governments or universities. Yet, with the push from governments a universal language could, for example, be taught in all the schools and within 20 or 30 years the majority of the population would have changed languages or, rather, would have acquired a working knowledge of the universal language.

Almost invariably these universal languages have been designed by and for the Western world. In addition, they have made most use of Western languages. And yet of the four major languages in the world only English (with 345 million speakers) is a Western language. The other major languages are Chinese (with 773 million speakers), Hindustani (with 256 million speakers), and Russian (with 220 million speakers). Naturally this situation has led to resistance among the speakers of non-Western languages.

In the creation of any worldwide system there seems to be implied that the system chosen is somehow superior to the others. Since language is so closely related to culture and to nationalism the further implication is that the new

---

Box 36
MAJOR LANGUAGES OF THE WORLD

Language	Number of Speakers
Chinese	773 million
English	345 million
Hindustani	256 million
Russian	220 million
Spanish	202 million
German	120 million
Arabic	117 million
Bengali	116 million
Portuguese	116 million
Japanese	108 million
Indonesian	90 million
French	85 million
Italian	60 million
Telugu	52 million
Punjabi	52 million
Tamil	50 million
Korean	50 million

---

system has a cultural or national superiority. But no language is superior to any other language; all languages are capable of expressing whatever needs expressing in the particular culture. (It should be added, however, that not all researchers would agree with this view. Some anthropologists and linguists would argue that some languages are superior to others by virtue of their ability, for example, to incorporate new words into the existing vocabulary and by virtue of their larger vocabularies.) Similarly, it would be difficult to argue that one culture is superior to another without invoking the values and the standards of a particular society to make the comparison. Languages such as Esperanto and Interlingua which have relied so heavily on western European languages are viewed in some quarters as racist attempts at worst and ethnocentric mistakes at best.

Still another obstacle is the sense of nationalism that prevents any country from adopting the language of another. The fierce linguistic battles in Canada over English and French and in India over Hindi, Urdu, and English and throughout numerous other parts of the world attest to the strong relationship that exists in the popular mind between language and culture, between pride in one's language and pride in one's culture and homeland.

One last and perhaps obvious problem should also be noted, How is the language to be chosen? Some would argue that a universal language should be an invented one so that no country has any advantage over any other and so that logical improvements may be made in the language. Rene Descartes, the French philosopher, scientist, and mathematician argued that "an artificial language is possible and it is possible to establish the science upon which it depends. With its aid the peasant will find it easier to reason about the essence of things than do philosophers today." The possibilities are surely tempting.

Others argue that there exist numerous languages that could serve this purpose and that a language should be chosen by the majority vote of the people of the world. If that is the case then Mandarin Chinese would probably become the universal language of the world since it has more speakers than any other language. If divisions are further made on the basis of the alphabet, then the Latin alphabet would be chosen since most speakers of the world use this alphabet.

Although the arguments against a universal language seem convincing and the problems which beset its adoption great, the idea of a universal language that would enable us to communicate with any person in the entire world is too exciting a prospect to let die because of arguments and problems. "The need is acute," says Mario Pei. "In the years to come," Pei continues, "that need will become more acute as international travel and international communications and relations of all kinds take on even broader scope. Eventually, the need will force itself upon the consciousness of even the most unresponsive of government bureaucrats." It seems likely, then, that we will continue to test prospects for a universal language for a long time to come.

SOURCES

An excellent general introduction to this area is provided in *Language* by David S. Thomson and the editors of Time-Life Books (New York: Time-Life Books, 1975).

On language relativity see the classic works of Edward Sapir and Benjamin Lee Whorf, namely Edward Sapir, *Language: An Introduction to the Study of Speech* (New York: Harcourt Brace Jovanovich, 1921); Sapir's collected writings edited by David G. Mandelbaum, *Edward Sapir: Culture, Language and Personality* (Los Angeles: University of California Press, 1962); and John Carroll, ed., *Language, Thought, and Reality: Selected Writings of Benjamin Lee Whorf* (New York: Wiley, 1956). An overview is provided in Joseph DeVito, *The Psychology of Speech and Language: An Introduction to Psycholinguistics* (New York: Random House, 1970). For a more popular and recent account see Peter Farb, *Word Play: What Happens When People Talk* (New York: Knopf, 1974).

For universal language see Robert A. Hall, Jr., *Linguistics and Your Language* (New York: Doubleday, 1960) and Jacob Ornstein and William W. Gage,

The ABC's of Language and Linguistics (New York: Rand-McNally, 1964) and Mario Pei, *Language for Everybody* (New York: Pocket Books, 1956) and "Prospects for a Global Language," *Saturday Review* (May 2, 1950). A more recent popular essay appears in David Wallechinsky and Irving Wallace's *The People's Almanac* (New York: Doubleday, 1975).

EXPERIENTIAL VEHICLE

33.1 WORD COINAGE

Although language and culture are closely related and although the language closely reflects the culture, there often seem to be concepts important to a culture or a subculture for which the language does not provide a convenient one word label.

Sometimes slang or "substandard" forms fill this void, for example, *youse* or *you all* for "you" (plural) or *screw* for "prison guard." Sometimes words are created because of some social issue, for example, *Ms.* for a form of address for women regardless of marital status or *ecdysiast* for "stripper."

In order to gain greater insight into the relationship between language and culture/subculture and in order to become more familiar with the dimensions and functions of words, perform the following exercise in groups of five or six.

1. Create a new word for some concept that is important to the culture or to a particular subculture and for which a single word label is not available.
2. Define this word as would a dictionary and identify its part(s) of speech.
3. List its various inflectional forms and definitions.
4. Provide two or three examples of how the world would be used (sentences in which the word is used).
5. Justify the coinage of this new word considering, for example, why this word is needed, what void it fills, what it clarifies, what its importance is, what its effects might be should it be used widely, and so forth.

UNIT 34
Some Intercultural Communication Conflicts

Males and Females
Gays and Straights
Blacks and Whites
Teachers and Students

LEARNING GOALS

After completing this unit, you should be able to:

1. identify at least two sources of communication problems between males and females
2. identify at least two sources of communication problems between gays and straights
3. identify at least two sources of communication problems between the races
4. identify at least two sources of communication problems between teachers and students
5. explain the role of the media in maintaining the differences between the sexes, gays and straights, the races, and teachers and students

507

In any culture that is reasonably large, various smaller groups will inevitably come into conflict with one another. No culture is totally homogeneous and the heterogeneity that exists often gives rise to conflicts and assorted communication problems—interpersonal, public, or mass. Here we consider only a few of these possible conflicts: namely those between males and females, homosexuals and heterosexuals (gays and straights), whites and blacks, and teacher and student. In the brief discussions to follow we will attempt to focus on some of the causes for the failure of these groups to communicate as effectively as they might. At this point, however, we are more concerned with asking questions than with providing answers. Specifically, examine more closely your own communication behaviors and attitudes as they operate in these intercultural communication situations. To this end, there are a series of five questions included after each of these brief discussions; they are designed to focus this self-examination on specific issues. The same five questions are used for each of the four conflict situations so that comparisons and contrasts among the potential conflicts might be more easily appreciated. The discussions will focus on (1) values and how they influence communication,

(2) the role of the media in such conflicts, (3) increasing personal awareness of "the other" groups, (4) the principles for increasing communication effectiveness, and (5) responses to selected verbal stimuli.

Particularly relevant to these discussions is our consideration of the general nature of conflict and conflict resolution covered in Unit 20. In reading about the conflicts presented here we should attempt to focus on at least the following issues raised in our previous consideration of conflict: (1) the problems as well as the benefits to be derived from conflict and especially from attempts at conflict resolution, (2) the influences that conflict has on communication and communication has on conflict, and (3) both the pseudomethods and the steps involved in conflict resolution.

MALES AND FEMALES

The conflict between men and women is one of the most talked about today, and there are many attempts today to legislate a fairer shake for women.

Despite the numerical superiority of women, our culture is largely male-dominated and male-oriented. Men control the major businesses, politics, education, and even make the more important decisions in the home. Men get paid more for the same job, are more quickly hired, and are promoted faster than women. And although there have been attempts to change this situation, it is extremely difficult to alter that which has been with us for so long.

But perhaps more important than male control of business or politics are the cultural roles that are defined for men and for women. The role of a woman, as defined in everything from elementary school readers to television advertisements, is that of a domestic, a person whose major task is to have children, raise them properly, and make a comfortable home for her husband and family. These roles are particularly apparent in the old movies where Loretta Young gives up her political aspirations for those of Robert Preston, where Nora Charles is an assistant to Nick Charles in their pursuit of justice, and where James Bond does the important jobs while the women are for decoration and for the pleasure of Agent 007.

It is true that the situation is changing somewhat. Mary Tyler Moore is independent but still very "little girlish," cries a great deal, gets upset at the least little thing, and invariably runs to Lou Grant (her boss) to solve her problems. "Rhoda" and "Phyllis," spawned from "The Mary Tyler Moore Show," and "Maude" are somewhat more independent and more in control of their situations. Even here, however, Rhoda, for all her independence is grossly insecure and only receives comfort from Joe—a character who is not particularly appealing, or from other males. Phyllis is constantly building her life around finding a man and seems to be able to do nothing right—an image that women have had to contend with for years. Maude is the exception; she is the dominant one in the family and has been since the show's inception. And yet, con-

Box 37
WOMEN IN ADVERTISING

The following excerpt is taken from the report "Advertising and Women: A Report on Advertising Portraying or Directed to Women" prepared by a Consultive Panel of The National Advertising Review Board.

What the Panel Recommends

The Panel offers no hard and fast rules for dealing with advertising appealing to or portraying women. The scene is changing too rapidly. Accordingly, we have not attempted to compile a list of current ads that the Panel thinks merit praise or criticism.

Recognizing that principles are more enduring than specific cases, the Panel has distilled its many months of study into a checklist of questions for advertisers and agency personnel to consider when creating or approving an advertisement. We realize that there will probably be differences of opinion about some of the items on this checklist, but we believe that whatever discussion may be stimulated by the controversial ones will be helpful in clarifying the issues.

CHECKLIST: DESTRUCTIVE PORTRAYALS

- Am I implying in my promotional campaign that creative, athletic, and mind-enriching toys and games are not for girls as much as for boys? Does my ad, for example, imply that dolls are for girls and chemistry sets are for boys, and that neither could ever become interested in the other category?
- Are sexual stereotypes perpetuated in my ad? That is, does it portray women as weak, silly, and overemotional? Or does it picture both sexes as intelligent, physically able, and attractive?
- Are the women portrayed in my ad stupid? For example, am I reinforcing the "dumb blonde" cliché? Does my ad portray women who are unable to balance their checkbooks? Women who are unable to manage a household without the help of outside experts, particularly male ones?
- Does my ad use belittling language? For example, "gal Friday" or "lady professor?" Or "her kitchen" but "his car?" Or "women's chatter" but "men's discussions?"
- Does my ad make use of contemptuous phrases? Such as "the weaker sex," "the little woman," "the ball and chain," or "the war department."
- Do my ads consistently show women waiting on men? Even in occupational situations, for example, are women nurses or secretaries serving coffee, etc., to male bosses or colleagues? And never vice versa?
- Is there a gratuitous message in my ads that a woman's most important role in life is a supportive one, to cater to and coddle man and children? Is it a "big deal" when the reverse is shown, that is, very unusual and special—something for which the woman must show gratitude?
- Do my ads portray women as more neurotic than men? For example, as ecstatically happy over household cleanliness or deeply depressed because of their failure to achieve near perfection in household tasks?

(A note is needed here, perhaps. It is not the Panel's intention to suggest that women never be portrayed in the traditional role of homemaker and mother. We suggest instead that the role of homemaker be depicted not in a grotesque or stereotyped manner, but be treated with the same degree of respect accorded to other important occupations.)

· Do my ads feature women who appear to be basically unpleasant? For example, women nagging their husbands or children? Women being condescending to other women? Women being envious or arousing envy? Women playing the "one-upmanship" game (with a sly wink at the camera)?
· Do my ads portray women in situations that tend to confirm the view that women are the property of men or are less important than men?
· Is there double entendre in my ads? Particularly about sex or women's bodies?

CHECKLIST: NEGATIVE APPEALS

· Do my ads try to arouse or play upon stereotyped insecurities? Are women shown as fearful of not being attractive to men or to other women, fearful of not being able to keep their husbands or lovers, fearful of an in-law's disapproval, or, for example, of not being able to cope with a husband's boss coming for dinner?
· Does my copy promise unrealistic psychological rewards for using the product? For example, that a perfume can lead to instant romance.
· Does my ad blatantly or subtly suggest that the product possesses supernatural powers? If believed literally, is the advertiser unfairly taking advantage of ignorance? Even if understood as hyperbole, does it insult the intelligence of women?

CHECKLIST: CONSTRUCTIVE PORTRAYALS

· Are the attitudes and behavior of the women in my ads suitable models for my own daughter to copy? Will I be happy if my own female children grow up to act and react the way the women in my ads act and react?
· Do my ads reflect the fact that girls may aspire to careers in business and the professions? Do they show, for example, female doctors and female executives? Some women with both male and female assistants?
· Do my ads portray women and men (and children) sharing in the chores of family living? For example, grocery shopping, doing laundry, cooking (not just outdoor barbecuing), washing dishes, cleaning house, taking care of children, mowing the lawn, and other house and yard work?
· Do the women in my ads make decisions (or help make them) about the purchase of high-priced items and major family investments? Do they take an informed interest, for example, in insurance and financial matters?
· Do my ads portray women actually driving cars and showing an intelligent interest in mechanical features, not just in the color and upholstery?
· Are two-income families portrayed in my ads? For example, husband and wife leaving home or returning from work together?
· Are the women in my ads doing creative or exciting things? Older women, too? In social and occupational environments? For example, making a speech, in a laboratory, or approving an ad?

CHECKLIST: POSITIVE APPEALS

• Is the product presented as a means for a woman to enhance her own self-esteem, to be a beautiful human being, to realize her full potential?
• Does my advertisement promise women realistic rewards for using the product? Does it assume intelligence on the part of women?

HUMOR

The Panel is not so sobersided as to suggest that humor has no place in woman-related advertising. At the same time, the Panel feels called on to point out that sometimes meanness is expressed in the guise of humor. In its study of current advertising, the Panel came across some examples of attempted woman-related humor which could not have been funny to those who were the butt of the jokes. It is healthy for people to laugh at themselves, but usually this is a luxury only the secure can afford. Effective humor often has a cutting edge, and it requires extraordinary care to insure that the cut is not made at the expense of women's self-esteem.

In the present context, for example, the Panel suggests extreme caution in making fun of efforts to improve the status of women and the opportunities available to them.

Source: From *Advertising and Women: A Report on Advertising Portraying or Directed to Women* by a Consultive Panel of The National Advertising Review Board, 1975. Reprinted by permission of the National Advertising Review Board.

sider how Maude is portrayed. She is seen as a manic-depressive and a woman who has been unsuccessful in four different marriages. Although Maude is her own woman, she is not a very effective woman.

These observations are supported by the numerous studies currently being conducted on the role of women in the media. Helen Franzwa, for example, concluded that "the images of women portrayed in the media and in school are limited to the role of housewife and mother." And in a study on women's roles in advertising Courtney and Whipple found that "the typical female product representative is a young housewife, pictured in the home, using the advertised product in the kitchen or bathroom. The world for women in the ads is a domestic one, where women are housewives who worry about cleanliness and food preparation and serve their husbands and children." On the other hand, "men are portrayed as the voices of authority. They are ten times more likely to be used as the voice over and twice as often seen as the product representative during the evening programming hours. . . . Men are shown in a wide range of occupations and roles in both their out-of-home working and leisure lives. . . . Men are portrayed as the dominant sex in the promotion of most products and services which are significant to the family and where the decision-making process is at all extensive.''

Males and females in our society have clearly defined permissible and non-permissible communication behaviors. And although this, too, is changing, it seems to be changing at an extremely slow rate. For example, college women in my classes tell me that they cannot call a man up for a date, they cannot approach a man in a single's bar but must wait until he approaches them, and must not, under any circumstances, appear overly interested or overly anxious with a date. Although women may verbalize an agreement with the general idea that they should be able to do these things, they also seem to be in agreement that the actual practice of doing these things is quite different.

All this is not to say that there are no real differences between men and women beyond the rather obvious anatomical differences. Corinne Hutt in her *Males and Females* offers an excellent summary of some of the essential differences:

> The male is physically stronger but less resilient, he is more ambitious and competitive, he has greater spatial, numerical and mechanical ability, he is more likely to construe the world in terms of objects, ideas and theories. The female at the outset possesses those sensory capacities which facilitate interpersonal communion; physically and psychologically she matures more rapidly, her verbal skills are precocious and proficient, she is more nurturant, affiliative, more consistent, and is likely to construe the world in personal, moral and aesthetic terms.

According to Hutt, some of these differences have biological bases and are adaptive for the various roles that males and females play in society. For example, Hutt notes that ''for more effective communication and socialization a greater emphasis and reliance on linguistic skills and moral propensities has proved valuable.'' The fact that a mother will reinforce the babbling of a daughter more than of a son ''probably helps to emphasize even further the vocal and verbal proclivities of the female.''

It should be clear that other researchers would argue that the differences that do exist between males and females—again, aside from the physical differences—are caused by differential social and cultural factors and not by biological factors.

At the present time it seems impossible to determine the relative influence of biological versus social factors. What does seem clear, however, is that there are many instances in which males and females are discriminated against because of their sexual differences rather than because of any differences in ability, behavior, or attitude. Too often individuals are not permitted to engage in certain behaviors or entertain certain thoughts or hold certain beliefs and attitudes because of their sexual identity and not because of their competence. Cases abound in which communication barriers are erected between males and females because of each other's sex.

Box 38
DE-SEXING THE ENGLISH LANGUAGE

Casey Miller and Kate Swift

On the television screen, a teacher of first-grades who has just won a national award is describing her way of teaching. "You take each child where you find him," she says. "You watch to see what he's interested in, and then you build on his interests."

A five-year-old looking at the program asks her mother, "Do only boys go to that school?"

"No," her mother begins, "she's talking about girls too, but—"

But what? The teacher being interviewed on television is speaking correct English. What can the mother tell her daughter about why a child, in any generalization, is always *he* rather than *she?* How does a five-year-old comprehend the generic personal pronoun?

The effect on personality development of this one small part of speech was recognized by thoughtful people long before the present assault on the English language by the forces of Women's Liberation. Fifteen years ago, Lynn T. White, then president of Mills College wrote: "The grammar of English dictates that when a referent is either of indeterminate sex or both sexes, it shall be considered masculine. The penetration of this habit of language into the minds of little girls as they grow up to be women is more profound than most people, including most women, have recognized: for it implies that personality is really a male attribute, and that women are a human subspecies. . . . It would be a miracle if a girl-baby, learning to use the symbols of our tongue, could escape some wound to her self-respect: whereas a boy-baby's ego is bolstered by the pattern of our language."

Now that our langauge has begun to respond to the justice of Women's Liberation, a lot of people apparently are trying to kick the habit of using *he* when they mean anyone, male or female. In fact, there is mounting evidence that a major renovation of the language is in progress with respect to this pronoun. It is especially noticeable in the speeches of politicians up for election: "And as for every citizen who pays taxes, I say that he or she deserves an accounting!" A variation of the tandem form is also cropping up in print, like the copy on a coupon that offers the bearer a 20 per cent saving on "the cost of his/her meal." A writer in the New York newspaper, *The Village Voice,* adopts the same form to comment "that every artist of major stature is actually a school in him/herself."

Adding the feminine pronoun to the masculine whenever the generic form is called for may be politically smart and morally right, but the result is often awkward.

Some of the devices used to get around the problem are even less acceptable, at least to grammarians. It is one thing for a student to announce in assembly that "Anybody can join the Glee Club as long as they can carry a tune," but when this patchwork solution begins to appear in print, the language is in trouble. In blatant defiance of every teacher of freshman English, a full-page advertisement in *The New York Times* for its college and school subscription service begins with this headline: "If someone you know is attending one of these colleges, here's something they should know that can save them money." Although the grammatical inconsistency of the *Times*'s claim offends the ear—especially since "they" in the headline can refer only to "colleges"—the alternatives would present insurmountable problems for the writer. For example, the sentence might read, "If someone you know . . . etc., here's something he or she should know that can save him/her money." Or, in order to keep the plural subject in the second clause, the writer might have begun, "If several people you know are attending one or more of these colleges . . ." But by that time will the reader still care?

In the long run, the problem of the generic personal pronoun is a problem of the status of women. But it is more immediately a matter of common sense and clear communication. Absurd examples of the burdens now placed upon masculine pronouns pop up everywhere. "The next time you meet a handicapped person, don't make up your mind about him in advance," admonishes a radio public service announcement. A medical school bulletin, apparently caught by surprise, reports that a certain scholarship given annually "to a student of unquestioned ability and character who has completed his first year" was awarded to one Barbara Kinder.

Since there is no way in English to solve problems like these with felicity and grace, it is becoming obvious that what we need is a new singular personal pronoun that is truly generic: a common-gender pronoun. Several have been proposed, but so far none appears to have the transparently logical relationship to existing pronouns that is necessary if a new word is to gain wide acceptance. Perhaps a clue to the solution is to be found in people's persistent use of *they* as a singular pronoun.

In the plural forms, both genders are included in one word: *they* can refer to males or females or a mixed group. So why not derive the needed singular common-gender pronouns from the plural? *They, their,* and *them* suggest *tey, ter,* and *tem.* With its inflected forms pronounced to rhyme with the existing plural forms, the new word would join the family of third person pronouns as shown in the box below.

Someone will probably object to the idea of a common-gender pronoun in the mistaken belief that it is a neuter form and therefore underrates sexual differences. The opposite is true. Once *tey* or a similar word is adopted, *he* can become exclusively masculine, just as *she* is now exclusively feminine. The new pronoun will thus accentuate the significant and valuable differences between females and males—those of reproductive function and form—while affirming the essential unity and equality of the two sexes within the species.

Language constantly evolves in response to need. It is groping today for ways to accommodate the new recognition of women as full-fledged members of the human race. If the new pronoun helps anyone toward that end, tey should be free to adopt it.

If anyone objects, it is certainly ter right—but in that case let tem come up with a better solution.

| | Singular | | Plural |
	Distinct Gender	Common Gender	Common Gender
Nominative	*he* and *she*	*tey*	*they*
Possessive	*his* and *her* (or *hers*)	*ter* (or *ters*)	*their* (or *theirs*)
Objective	*him* and *her*	*tem*	*them*

Source: Reprinted by permission of the authors.

In large part such barriers are due to the roles and the rules we expect and teach males and females to follow. For example, males are not supposed to disclose a great deal of personal information about themselves whereas women are encouraged to do so. Males are permitted to talk freely about sex with males and to a lesser degree with females; women are not supposed to talk openly about sex with anyone but especially not with males. Women are supposed to be more tactful in their speech and more indirect; men are encouraged to be direct, even blunt. Women are allowed to express greater emotionality than are males. Women are allowed to touch each other while communicating; men are discouraged from touching each other. Women are permitted to be excited by various crises; males are only permitted to be excited by major crises and even then in relatively controlled ways. Women are allowed to be concerned about their appearance and are even permitted to exhibit a degree of conceit; males are supposed to appear in the rough and to shun any conceit over physical appearance. Males are supposed to be thick-skinned and not easily hurt; women are supposed to be soft and easily hurt. Males are supposed to be aggressive and authoritative; women are supposed to be submissive. Such a list might be continued for several pages. But the point here is that the communications of males and females are different in great part because of our expectations and our differential training. For example, we reward aggressiveness in men and punish it in women; we reward emotionality in women and punish it in men. To the extent that restrictions are placed on communicating our true feelings (if women must hide "toughness" and males must hide "softness," for example), communication between males and females will be unproductive, dishonest, and unsatisfying.

Before leaving this topic, two points should be made explicit. First, the points presented here about males and females obviously do not apply to all males and females. Rather, the intention was to characterize some of the stereotypes under which both sexes in at least some parts of our culture operate. Certainly patterns of behaviors, expectations of males and females, and various other variables that influence male and female communication are constantly changing and so what was true yesterday is not necessarily true today and (hopefully, at least) what is true today will not be true tomorrow.

Second, it should be clear that the discrimination expressed, the restrictions imposed, and the barriers erected are not only the work of male against female or of female against male but of male against male and of female against female.

Examine Your Attitudes and Behaviors

1. How do the values of males and females differ? How do these differing values influence communication between males and females?
2. What might the media do to improve communication between males and

females? That is, what changes might be instituted that would facilitate more meaningful interaction between the sexes?

3. How might you increase your own awareness, understanding, and empathy for males (if female) or for females (if male)? How might this increased sensitivity make your own interpersonal communications more effective?

4. As a communicologist what principle(s) might you offer for making communication between males and females more effective?

5. If word association tests were given to males and females how might they each respond to the following terms: *male, female, marriage, rape, abortion, housework, children, pregnant, financial success, happiness, divorce, tears, love*? What do the differences in responses mean for communication between males and females?

GAYS AND STRAIGHTS

Unlike the situation with males and females or with blacks and whites, we cannot tell who is gay (homosexual) and who is straight (heterosexual) from looking at them. Contrary to the popular myth no one—not straights and not gays—can tell from looking at someone whether the person is straight or gay. This seems at once an advantage and a disadvantage. It is an advantage to gays in that it enables them to appear straight and thus secure jobs and move in any social group they wish without anyone knowing their sexual preference. But this has worked as a disadvantage also. It has enabled the straight majority to force gays into a closet and to hide their "gayness." We cannot ask that a black appear white or that a white appear black but we do ask that a gay appear straight.

Because of the diversity of the discriminatory laws gays must be gay in secret. It would be difficult at best for a college professor, a family doctor, a community lawyer, a local politician, or a carpenter to openly admit that he or she is gay. Clearly they would have to be prepared to lose a great deal. But, it is claimed by many gays, that they would gain a great deal also; they would gain in self-respect and they would finally come to terms with their own gayness—an essential part of their personality.

Because of discrimination and the resulting inability of many gays to live openly gay lives, they are usually portrayed as extremely unhappy individuals. One character in *Boys in the Band* echoes this popular image, saying "Show me a happy homosexual and I'll show you a gay corpse." Some people argue that the unhappiness is caused by the inner conflicts over one's sexual preference while others would argue that the unhappiness is caused by the society making life difficult for the gay. Interestingly enough, however, a recent *Psychology Today* survey on happiness found on the basis of over 52,000 responses that "happiness is not a matter of sexual preference." "Homosexuals in this sample," concluded the researchers, "are neither more nor less happy than heterosexuals.'' Perhaps gays are unhappy only in the minds of straights.

The discriminatory laws and even more importantly the public hostility toward gays have forced many to marry, have children, and to, on the surface, lead lives that are straight. It has been estimated that one out of every six males is gay and that only slightly fewer women are gay. If this figure is at all accurate then a large number of our relatives, our friends, our fellow students, our teachers, and our neighbors are gay.

Because of the need to hide their gayness, gays have developed a sublanguage that is generally unknown to the straight world or at least to the large majority of the straight world. Some of the more popular terms are illustrated in Experiential Vehicle (32.2) on sublanguages. This sublanguage, like all sublanguages, enables the group members to communicate among themselves without others being aware of what is going on and at the same time provides the group members with a group identity, a feeling of belonging to some larger whole.

Like women, gays have had to deal with a negative and often inaccurate image, an image etched firmly in the popular mind. Here the gay male is portrayed as effeminate, bumbling, with a high voice, perhaps even a lisp. He is a hairdresser or perhaps an interior designer, drinks martinis (never beer and never ever beer out of the can), smokes with the pinkie extended, and wears fluffy sweaters and lots of jewelry. This image is perhaps overdrawn but it is noted here in this way to draw attention to some of the stereotypes attributed to people. The gay woman, on the other hand, is seen in the opposite way. She is extremely masculine with a low voice, perhaps even a Brooklyn accent. She is engaged in some traditionally masculine occupation such as cab driving or physical education teacher. Unlike her male counterpart she will drink beer and preferably out of the can and will hold her cigarette like a man (whatever that means).

Perhaps these pictures are exaggerated. Few of us would have such clearcut and extreme mental pictures, and yet we would all recognize these images without any difficulty. They are drawn for us in films, in novels, and on television; they are joked about by comedians and regardless of the details of the specific image drawn it is clear that we all have relatively clear images of what a gay man or gay woman looks and acts like.

In terms of communication between gays and straights it should first be realized that gays may be truck drivers, police officers, firemen, teachers, politicians, doctors, sanitation workers, bus drivers, and in fact may be in every profession or occupation imaginable. Further, they may be rich or poor, educated or uneducated, tall or short, witty or dull, creative or uncreative, and so on.

Second, it should be realized that gays and straights will approach many topics from an entirely different perspective; marriage, children, divorce, sex, dating, and the like, topics that are significant to most college students, will be treated very differently by gays and straights. Likewise, it should be clear that the degree of either group to empathize with the other group is limited. Generally, gays will understand straights better than the other way around simply because straight society is more accessible to inspection. The same is true with blacks and whites. Blacks will understand whites better than whites will understand blacks simply because the white culture has been portrayed more often and in more different types of situations than has the black culture.

Of all the intercultural conflicts, the media seem most reluctant to deal with that involving gay and straight. The more elitist media—books and intellectual magazines, for example—have dealt with homosexuality on at least a semiregular basis. But the more popular media, particularly movies and television, have done very little to alter the image of the gay male and female or to present anything that would facilitate communication and understanding between gay and straight. In such movies as *Reflections in a Golden Eye, Midnight Cowboy, Boys in the Band, The Killing of Sister George, Fortune and Men's Eyes,* and *The Children's Hour,* for example, homosexuals are portrayed as mentally unbalanced and it is made clear that it is the homosexuality that causes the imbalance. There have been some notable exceptions—*Sunday, Bloody Sunday* and *The Man Who Fell to Earth*—but these have been few.

The television image is not much better. On the now defunked "Nancy Walker Show" her secretary is a gay male, or as he put it, he was "g-a-y." For the most part he was to be laughed at rather than laughed with and was probably more harmful than helpful to mutual understanding. In *That Certain Summer* we find probably the first sympathetic portrayal of homosexual males played by Hal Holbrook and Martin Sheen. Yet, on closer inspection, we note that the only physical contact allowed these two was holding hands and their discussions of homosexuality indicated that it was a negative rather than a positive or neutral experience.

In the more recent *Alexander: The Other Side of Dawn* we again note that physical contact between two homosexuals was never shown although that between female and male prostitute was shown in relatively graphic detail. Perhaps the most anti-homosexual aspect of this television film was its implication that the Alexander's problems were all going to be solved now that he was back with his girlfriend Dawn and removed from gay society.

Recently on "Alice," Linda Lavin finds a man she thinks is ideal—handsome, considerate, and unattached. The only obstacle was that he was gay. The situation developed, however, toward the more significant and sophisticated issue of whether Alice should allow her son to go fishing with this man, played by Denny Miller (interestingly enough a former "Tarzan"). Echoing the fears of so many people who have had no experience with gays, she worries that her son might be molested. She does admit that she would not have similar fears if a daughter were alone with a straight male. The situation is resolved when she allows her son to go fishing and he returns "unharmed."

That same week on "Phyllis" Cloris Leachman encountered a somewhat similar situation and became attached to a male she later discovered was gay.

The situation revolved around his telling his parents about his life-style, a confession Phyllis supported in an uncharacteristically level-headed way.

We seem to have few comparable depictions of female homosexuality. The recent "Glitter Palace" was a notable exception to the media's neglect of lesbianism. News and talk shows have been a bit more progressive and are now giving some time to discussions of male and female homosexuality— interviews with lesbian mothers and gay athletes are becoming more and more frequent and seem to be having some good effect. At least some of the mystique has been dispelled. Perhaps most important is that people are beginning to realize that bringing homosexuality "out of the closet" does not create any catastrophes—no great numbers of people have had heart attacks, gays have not taken over politics or sports, and marriage and heterosexual dating are still popular.

Examine Your Attitudes and Behaviors

1. How do the values of gays and straights differ? How do these differing values influence communication between gays and straights?
2. What might the media do to improve communication between gays and straights? That is, what changes might be instituted that would facilitate more meaningful interaction between gays and straights?
3. How might you increase your own awareness, understanding, and empathy for gays (if straight) or for straights (if gay)? How might this increased sensitivity make your own interpersonal communications more effective?
4. As a communicologist what principle(s) might you offer for making communication between gays and straights more effective?
5. If word association tests were given to gays and straights, how might they each respond to the following terms: *gay, straight, marriage, children, divorce, sex, love, gay liberation, oppression, bisexuality, lesbian, disco dancing?* What do the differences in responses mean for communication between gays and straights?

BLACKS AND WHITES

Perhaps the most thoroughly discussed of all the conflicts among people are the racial conflicts. In our society the conflicts between blacks and whites are perhaps the most significant. Controversy over busing to achieve school balance among the races, the quotas demanded by racial groups to achieve a balance in various occupations, and the changes argued for in local laws discriminating against the nonwhite minority are common enough in our daily newspapers.

On a more interpersonal level there are problems because of different world views, different expectations, and different interactions permitted and not permitted by family, friends, or the general population.

(*Beetle Bailey* by Mort Walker. Copyright © King Features Syndicate, Inc. 1976.)

Each of us views the world differently, yet those of the same race have a great deal in common. Many common values are shared by members of the same racial or ethnic group including history, religion, ethical principles, politics, and the like. Consequently, there is a greater similarity in the world view of members of the same racial group than in members of different racial groups. Time is the classic example. White culture demands promptness; to be late for a class or an appointment is a serious offense. Black culture asks only for a general promptness. Black students who are frequently late to class generally do not think there has been any serious infraction of the rules; white students do. And when the teachers are white—as most teachers are—this small difference can create serious problems. Even the values that the groups place on literature, history, and economics will vary drastically. Put differently, the shared field of experience is much more limited when we are communicating within the same race.

Similarly, we all have different expectations of ourselves as well as of others. That is, we have various prejudices and stereotypes which, in effect, tell us what to expect of the members of other races. Thus we may expect the black male to be a super athlete or very strong. We can expect the Italian to have a good voice and to be popular sexually. We expect the German to be intellectual and organized. We expect the Spaniard to be religious and loyal to family. And these are only the positive expectations. For these groups as well as for any other group we also have negative expectations and these cause even greater problems.

Jon Blubaugh and Dorthy Pennington, in their *Crossing Difference . . . Interracial Communication,* identify a number of assumptions one group makes about the other group that impede effective interpersonal communication. These assumptions lead us to expect certain behaviors and attitudes and to not expect others. Some of the assumptions that whites make about blacks that are potentially damaging in interpersonal communication include: blacks try to use whites, blacks are all alike in their behaviors and attitudes, blacks are oversensitive and are embarrassed by open recognition of color, and—

Box 39
NAMES

Harry Edwards

What's in a name? For blacks, slavery. Edwards tells why his daughter's name is
Tazamisha Imara.

Names have always been of great importance to people. Mohammed admonished his followers to "Name your children with good names"; Proverbs 22:1 advises that "A good name is rather to be chosen than great riches." Then there's the statement "Things, animals and slaves are named by their owners and masters; if a people are to be free they must name themselves." That was said to me a few years back by the Honorable Jamel Abdul Almen (formerly H. Rap Brown).

Today increasing numbers of blacks have divested themselves of their slavery-generated property labels by changing their names. The reason for these changes has nothing to do with attempting to become more acceptable to the American mainstream, or to impede identification or to sound professionally "flashy." Rather, the reason is the attempt to develop a more honest self-image and to initiate a more realistic perspective on relations between black and white America. Some blacks have changed their names as part of adopting a religious philosophy. Thus we have had to accustom ourselves to looking at Muhammed Ali without seeing Cassius Clay; to watching Kareem Abdul-Jabbar play basketball without remarking that Lew Alcindor was a great college player. Other blacks, especially young blacks, have adopted names native to black African tribes and nations. Whether as a result of religious conversion or cultural identification, however, discarding Anglo-American names and taking on African or Muslim names—even if the name is only an "X"—constitute a step toward a new self-awareness and social and political perspective.

After all, the names borne by most black people are obvious insignia of a lack of common identity and unique sense of peoplehood. During slavery, blacks were deprived of their African names and ultimately all knowledge of them. Often a black slave would be given the last name of his slave master. After emancipation, many ex-slaves, not knowing any other names, chose Anglo-American names. Many voluntarily took the last names of their former slave masters and of certain white slavers who they had been taught to regard as heroes. To this day, therefore, black people in America bear such names as George Washington Jackson and Thomas Jefferson Jones, these names having passed down through the generations from parents to children with dignity and pride. But you can't make chicken pie out of chicken shit. While these names are appropriate for whites and their descendants, the fact remains that black people have been for generations naming their progeny in a style derived from the very people who enslaved their ancestors and reduced them to chattel, and who oppress and discriminate against them today.

The children of any people hold in sacred trust the heritage of that people. They are the buds from which new life springs; they insure a people's immortality. In recognition of these facts, my wife and I are not going to pass on to our children a name that labels them as property and that glorifies the oppressors of both our ancestors and us. We have chosen Swahili names instead. We chose

Imara as the family name because it means "strength"—black people must be strong in spirit, in mind and in dedication if we are to survive America. We decided to name our first girl child Tazamisha, which means "attractive," because the beauty of any people is most readily apparent in its women. And we chose as her middle name Heshima, which means "dignity," because the dignity of any people is no greater than that exhibited by its women. All of our children will have the last name of Imara and African first names.

By the time Tazamisha is in school she will have heard us explain hundreds of times the significance of her name. Some people may laugh at her name or ridicule her about it. But we will teach her to be patient with and considerate of other people's attitudes toward her name and the fact that it is different from that of her parents. If they are willing to listen, she can explain it to them. Afterward, she can ask them to explain the significance of their own names. What, for instance, is the meaning of "Margie Sue Hickenson," "Bubba Joe Johnson," "Cornbread Smith," "Jefferson Davis Williams," "Bolivar Q. Shagnesty" and the like? And after they have answered this question, they and Tazamisha can all sit down and have a good laugh together. Tazamisha may marry a Jones or a Smith, but she doesn't have to take his name. Yet, it is not *just* the name but the initiation of a political and cultural education that will go on through the years.

But why give our daughter an African name and not change our own? Because our goal is to educate our daughter politically and culturally and at the same time to minimize the risk of launching her on a pseudocultural trip. My wife and I will eventually change our names. And we will make a big family occasion of it. But this will only be *after* we have raised our children. If one or both of us should die before that time, we have chosen our African names and we will be buried under them. For the present, however, the political condition of black people in America and our love and concern for our children demand that we retain the names we have. They will grow up hearing us explain time and time again the significance of this unconventional situation. This will provide a means of constantly reinforcing their understanding of themselves, their knowledge of the relationship they share with other black people and the nature of their condition in American society. This is the first step in the development of a more realistic perspective that will allow them to see the steamroller of racism before it has rolled over them.

Beginning with their names, we will dispense with all the little "white lies" that blacks have become accustomed to telling themselves and each other, because every lie, every delusion, weakens our ability to deal intelligently with reality as it affects us. In an increasingly bureaucratic society, the simple fact that our name is different from our children's will provide invaluable opportunities for their political and cultural education. And the lessons will not be whispered in some closet or alleyway but spoken boldly with pride and conviction. When friends ask us what our daughter's name is, we will explain; when we enroll her in school, we will explain; whenever the question arises, we will explain—patiently, thoroughly, and not so much for the benefit of the listener as for our daughter, Tazamisha Heshima Imara. And she will be there—listening, learning, understanding.

Source: Reprinted by permission of the author.

perhaps most damaging—white society is superior to black society. The assumptions blacks make about whites are equally damaging and would include: whites are all alike, are all deceptive and do not try to understand black society, whites try to use blacks, and, the most extreme, all whites are racists.

Assumptions such as these are not confined to blacks and whites but are repeated, in perhaps slightly different form, by each racial or national group about other racial or national groups. To the extent that these stereotypes persist, meaningful interpersonal communication between the races will be impossible. The communication that does occur is likely to be superficial and, at least in part, dishonest. We might illustrate—as have Blubaugh and Pennington—that each of these stereotypes is logically false. But most of us probably know that already. Assumptions such as these, it seems, must be challenged and proven false through our own actual experiences. An intellectual awareness of the illogic of such assumptions provides a necessary first step but this must be followed by more visceral experiences and ultimately an emotional awareness of and rejection of such stereotypes.

Along with our expectations of the different racial groups we also have ideas as to what interactions are permissible and what interactions are not permissible with members of the different racial groups. For example, it may be permissible for a white male to go bowling or to a ball game with black males but it may not be permissible for that same white male to go on a date with a black female. Or, the more liberal will allow that dating may take place but it may not progress beyond that and certainly marriage would be ruled out in many cases. Similarly, we may find it permissible to work with members of different racial groups but we may find it totally nonpermissible for them to live in our neighborhood or in the same apartment house as we do. Or we might find it permissible for them to attend the same school as we do but not the same church or the same social club. And it should be noted, the strictures against such interactions come from both blacks and whites.

All three of these areas (world view, expectations, and permissible and nonpermissible interactions) will stand as obstacles to meaningful interracial communication.

The media presents further problems in any attempt to achieve meaningful interracial communication. Most often blacks and Chicanos and Indians and in fact most persons who are not of the white Anglo-Saxon protestant majority are portrayed as members of a racial group rather than simply as people who incidently happen to be members of a particular racial group. For example, "Sanford and Son" plays on the fact that they are black rather than white and we laugh at Fred's prejudices against whites and Chicanos but we never are allowed to forget that he is black. Similarly with "Good Times" and "The Jeffersons," their blackness is written into the script as a major plot. Notice, however, that on "The Mary Tyler Moore Show," Mary Richards made very little of her being a protestant or for that matter of being white. This is true, with most of the programs—to be white is incidental but to be nonwhite is essential to the plot. This state of affairs is particularly unfortunate since it prevents the viewing of the nonwhite minorities as people first and as members of the various racial groups second. Not all persons feel this way. Many members of minority groups feel that, for example, the blackness of a character should be emphasized. But it would seem that while this might have been true in the beginning, it does not have to be true now. Gregg Morris was black on "Mission Impossible" and no one doubted that but he was first a person and second an engineer and the color of his skin happened to be black. The same was true, though to a lesser extent, of Bill Cosby.

We seem to have come full circle over the past several decades. At one point in history no one was supposed to notice the race of any other person. When a boxing match was telecast years ago when everyone had a black-and-white set, it always amazed me that the announcers would attempt to distinguish the fighters not by saying the black or the white but by noting that one fighter had a purple stripe on his trunks whereas the other fighter had a blue stripe. We were in effect afraid to notice color, or for that matter religion or nationality. Some years ago with the rise of black consciousness we were asked to take notice of the race, religion, and nationality of the people. And we were asked not to forget it. People became justifiably proud of being whatever they were and so we were asked to take notice of specific characteristics. But we may now have passed that stage and perhaps what we should now notice is that this one person has done X, Y, and Z and that this other person has done A, B, and C and not that one person's parents were born in Algeria and another person's parents were born in Syria or in Russia or in Greece.

Examine Your Attitudes and Behaviors

1. How do the values of blacks and whites differ? How do these differing values influence communication between blacks and whites?
2. What might the media do to improve communication between blacks and whites? That is, what changes could be instituted that would facilitate more meaningful interaction between the races?
3. How might you increase your own awareness, understanding, and empathy for blacks (if white) or for whites (if black)? How might this increased sensitivity make your own interpersonal communications more effective?
4. As a communicologist what principle(s) might you offer for making communication between blacks and whites more effective?
5. If word association tests were given to blacks and whites, how might they each respond to the following terms: *black, white, liberation, South Africa, black power, interracial dating, prejudice, Ku Klux Klan, Civil War, racism, soul, stereotype*? What do the differences in responses mean for communication between blacks and whites?

TEACHERS AND STUDENTS

Perhaps the most immediately significant conflict for most college students is the conflict between teachers and students. This is not to say that they are not working for the same goal or that there is open conflict between the two. Quite the contrary. The conflict with these two groups centers on immediate goals and aims and the methods used to achieve those goals. Perhaps the conflict is manifested in a symbolic way by the asymmetrical forms of address used in most colleges and universities throughout the country. Specifically, most college teachers will call their students by their first names but will receive from the students a title plus last name. This brings to the fore the different status

---

Box 40
FORMS OF ADDRESS

Roger Brown and his associates, in their investigation of the pronouns of address in European languages (Brown and Gilman, 1960) and of the forms of address in English (Brown and Ford, 1961), provide excellent examples of the relationship between speech and source-receiver relationships. In many European languages there are two pronouns of address where English has only one, *you.* One pronoun would be used by a subordinate to a superior; for example, in French the servant speaking to his master would say *vous,* in Spanish *Usted,* in Italian *Lei,* and in German *Sie.* The other pronoun would be used by the superior addressing his subordinate; in French, Spanish, and Italian he would say *tu,* in German *du.* Following Brown, V may be used to symbolize the pronoun of address used by a subordinate to a superior (upward communication) and T to symbolize the form used by a superior to a subordinate (downward communication) on the basis of the Latin *vos* and *tu* from which many of the modern forms derive. When equals are communicating both use the same pronoun, that is, there is reciprocal usage. If they have much in common or are very friendly T is used; if they have little in common or are strangers both use V. During the Middle Ages, however, status determined which form would be used. Reciprocal V was used by the nobility while reciprocal T was used by the lower classes.

There are two basic dimensions of social relationships: power versus equality (that is, status) and solidarity versus nonsolidarity (that is, friendship or intimacy). Power relationships are established on the basis of a number of different criteria. Age, wealth, social position, and occupation are probably the most obvious determinants. Those who are older, richer, of higher social status, or in higher occupations use T in addressing those who are younger, poorer, lower in social status, or in lower occupations. These latter persons in turn use V in addressing members of the former groups. Similarly, solidarity relationships are established in a number of ways. When, for example, persons work at the same job, have the same parents, attend the same school, or play on the same team, their relationship is one of solidarity and they would use T in addressing each other. In the situations described there is no conflict; there is no doubt as to the correct pronoun to use. There are

levels between teacher and student. And of course even if reciprocal forms of address were used the status difference would not be eliminated, nor would it necessarily be a good thing if this status difference were eliminated.

Underlying much of the differences between teachers and students is a different value system, particularly those values pertaining to education itself. Most college teachers were good students when they were in school and so they have difficulty empathizing with the point of view of the less diligent, less academically-oriented students. Similarly they place a different value on education. Whereas many of today's students are in college so that they can obtain better jobs when they get out, teachers are seldom concerned with the vocational aspects of education.

---

situations, however, in which there is doubt as to the correct pronoun of address. These conflicts appear in situations in which both power and solidarity and non-solidarity exist. For example, in the case of a younger brother addressing his older brother both power and solidarity are present and each dictates a different form. The power relationship requires that the younger brother use V but the solidarity relationship requires T. The conflict does not exist for the older brother since both power and solidarity dictate T. In the other situation the conflict centers on the form to be used by the more powerful member. For example, in the army the soldier says V to his officer since both power and nonsolidarity demand this form. However, what does the officer say to his subordinate? His superiority dictates T but his nonsolidarity relationship dictates V.

According to Brown and Gilman, these conflicts were resolved, at least up to the middle of the nineteenth century, on the basis of power. Thus in the above examples the younger brother would have given V in addressing his older brother and the officer would have given T in addressing the soldier. More recently, however, solidarity has become the more significant, as judged from questionnaire results obtained from native speakers of various European languages. Today the younger brother says T and the officer V—the forms dictated by their solidarity and nonsolidarity relationships. This is not to say that power is no longer influential. In fact, as Brown and Gilman point out, power determines who may initially introduce reciprocal T. The suggestion to use reciprocal T or its first use cannot come from the less powerful; it can only come from the more powerful.

Use of the pronouns of power and solidarity has an interesting parallel in English. Similar social relationships are reflected in the use of the first name (FN) or a title plus the last name (TLN). Even more so than in the case of pronouns, the form of address used in English is not predictable from a knowledge of the addressor or addressee, however detailed that knowledge may be. The forms used can only be predicted from knowledge of the relationship existing between the two parties involved in the communication act.

Source: From *The Psychology of Speech and Language: An Introduction to Psycholinguistics,* by Joseph A. DeVito, Copyright © 1970 by Random House, Inc. Reprinted by permission of the publisher.

Another difficulty is created because of the difference in age. All the difficulties in communicating across generations exist to some degree between teachers and students. Teachers were students and know that many of the problems that students are now going through will iron themselves out in short order. But they forget that the student does not have the advantage of this time perspective. Students see their problems as significant and demanding immediate solution; teachers see them as temporary difficulties that will shortly be forgotten.

Perhaps the one area where the most conflict occurs is over grades. Students hate them and teachers hate them, at least the vast majority of teachers and students seem to feel this way. But they are required and so teachers attempt to give out grades as fairly as possible—at least generally. Few teachers want to give F's and D's but if the A's and B's are to be meaningful indices of level of achievement, then the lower grades have to be meaningful as well. Students forget that teachers do not have a magical formula for giving grades and often struggle over the difference between a C+ and a B−. And teachers forget that to a student a grade means a great deal; it may mean the approval or lack of it from family and peers. It may place the student one step closer to graduate school or law school. No one wants to be critically evaluated, especially negatively, and students are no exception.

In many instances the issue of grades also prevents meaningful interaction between teacher and student. Often a teacher will develop a particular fondness for a student and may wish to pursue this and yet is restrained from doing so because of the necessity of evaluating this student at a later time. Similarly many students may wish to become more friendly with a particular teacher but may hesitate because it may seem that he or she has ulterior motives.

Sexual attraction is another one of those inevitable but difficult to handle issues. Teachers will often be attracted to students and students to teachers. For the most part this should raise no problems, and yet it does. First it creates problems in the minds of those with whom the teacher and the student have to live. Colleagues are always leery of the teacher who is dating a student and similarly fellow students are a bit suspicious of the student dating a teacher. This is to say nothing of their respective families. But another problem is created in that a student will often be attracted to a teacher because of what he or she sees the teacher doing in the classroom; the student may not see that outside the classroom the teacher is actually quite ordinary and may, in fact, be relatively ineffectual. Similarly, the teacher sees the student as youthful and eager and bright but also fails to see the student in his or her own environment, which may be much less flattering. Often the attraction is for the teacher or the student rather than for the individual himself or herself. This seems to be the reason why so many of these relationships are short-lived. While the teacher may stand out as a mature, worldly individual in the classroom, he or she becomes quite ordinary in other circumstances and quickly loses the magical charm in the mind of the student. And the same seems true in reverse. None of this is to say that there is anything basically or morally wrong with such behavior, it is only one of the many problems confronting meaningful student-teacher communication.

Examine Your Attitudes and Behavior

1. How do the values of teachers and students differ? How do these differing values influence communication between teachers and students?
2. What might the media do to improve communication between teachers and students? That is, what changes could be instituted that would facilitate more meaningful interaction between teachers and students?
3. How might you increase your own awareness, understanding, and empathy for teachers (if a student) or for students (if a teacher)? How might this increased sensitivity make your own interpersonal communications more effective?
4. As a communicologist what principle(s) might you offer for making communication between teachers and students more effective?
5. If word association tests were given to teachers and students how might they each respond to the following terms: *teacher, student, grades, education, tenure, plagerism, professor, student rights, examinations, graduate school, teacher evaluation*? What do the differences in responses mean for communication between teacher and student?

SOURCES

Much is currently being written on sexism. Particularly relevant works from the point of view of communication include Robin Lakoff's *Language and Women's Place* (New York: Harper & Row, 1975); Cheris Kramer, "Women's Speech: Separate but Unequal," *Quarterly Journal of Speech* 60 (February 1974):14–24; Casey Miller and Kate Swift, "One Small Step for Genkind," in Joseph DeVito, ed., *Language: Concepts and Processes* (Englewood Cliffs, N.J.: Prentice-Hall, 1973); and, *Words and Women: New Language in New Times* (New York: Doubleday, 1976). An excellent overview is provided by Bobby R. Patton and Bonnie Ritter Patton, *Living Together . . . Female/Male Communication* (Columbus, Ohio: Charles E. Merrill, 1976).

The studies cited on the role of women in the media are: Helen H. Franzwa, "Working Women in Fact and Fiction," *Journal of Communication* 24 (Spring 1974):104–109, and Alice E. Courtney and Thomas W. Whipple, "Women in TV Commercials," *Journal of Communication* 24 (Spring 1974):110–118. The Spring 1974 issue of the *Journal of Communication* carried an entire series of articles on women in the media.

On the gay-straight issue there is again much that is currently being written. See, for example, James W. Chesebro and Caroline D. Hamsher, *Orientations to Public Communication* (Palo Alto, Cal.: Science Research Associates, 1976). An excellent collection, useful for raising the consciousness of both gays and straights, is *Out of the Closets: Voices of Gay Liberation* (New York: Douglas, 1972). The results of the happiness survey may be found in Philip Shaver and Jonathan Friedman, "Your Pursuit of Happiness," *Psychology Today* 10 (August 1976):26–32, 75.

On racism see Andrea Rich, *Interracial Communication* (New York: Harper & Row, 1974); Arthur Smith, *Transracial Communication* (Englewood Cliffs, N.J.: Prentice-Hall, 1973); and, Jon A. Blubaugh and Dorthy L. Pennington, *Crossing Difference . . . Interracial Communication* (Columbus, Ohio: Charles E. Merrill, 1976). On both racism and sexism see N. J. Demerath and Gerald Marwell, *Sociology: Perspectives and Applications* (New York: Harper & Row, 1976).

On teachers and students see Neil Postman and Charles Weingartner, *Teaching as a Subversive Activity* (New York: Delacourte, 1969), and Gustav W. Friedrich, Kathleen M. Galvin, and Cassandra L. Book, *Growing Together . . . Classroom Communication* (Columbus, Ohio: Charles E. Merrill, 1976). Another useful source is David Rubin's *The Rights of Teachers* (New York: Avon, 1972). Many of the principles discussed by Sven Wahlroos, *Family Communication: A Guide to Emotional Health* (New York: New American Library, 1976) are applicable to teacher-student communication.

An overview of conflict between the races, sexes, and generations is provided by William D. Brooks and Philip Emmert, *Interpersonal Communication* (Dubuque, Iowa: Wm. C. Brown, 1976).

EXPERIENTIAL VEHICLES

34.1 MALE AND FEMALE

This exercise is designed to increase awareness of those matters which may prevent meaningful interpersonal communication between the sexes. It is also designed to encourage meaningful dialogue among class members.

The women and the men are separated; one group goes into another classroom and one group stays in the original room. The task of each group is to write on the board all the things that they dislike having the other sex think, believe, do, and/or say about them. The women should write on the board all the things that men think, believe, say, or do in reference to women which they dislike and which prevents meaningful interpersonal communication from taking place. The men do likewise.

After this is completed, the groups change rooms. The men go into the room in which the women have written their dislikes and the women go into the room in which the men have written their dislikes. The men discuss what the women have written and the women discuss what the men have written. After satisfactory discussion has taken place the groups should get together in the original room. Discussion might center on the following:

1. Were there any surprises?
2. Were there any disagreements? That is, did the men (or women) write anything that the women (or men) argued they do not believe, think, do, or say?
3. How do you suppose the ideas about the other sex got started?
4. Is there any reliable evidence in support of the beliefs of the men about the women or the women about the men?
5. What is the basis for the things that are disliked? Put differently, why was each statement written on the blackboard?
6. What kind of education or training program (if any) do you feel is needed to eliminate these problems?
7. Specifically in what ways do these beliefs, thoughts, actions, and statements prevent meaningful interpersonal communication?
8. How do you feel now that these matters have been discussed?

34.2 VALUES AND COMMUNICATION

The class is divided into groups of approximately five or six members each. Each group is charged with the same basic task, but each discharges its task from a different perspective. The general task is to select those objects that best reflect American values.

By "values" we mean those objects or ideas that people regard as positive or negative, beautiful or ugly, clean or dirty, pleasant or unpleasant, valuable or worthless, moral or immoral, just or unjust, true or false, and so forth, and those objects or ideas that influence the judgments and decisions people make.

The only limitations or restrictions are that 1) five objects be selected—no more and no less; size, weight, and cost are of no consequence and should not influence your decisions, and that 2) the objects be in existence at the present time in the same form they will be in when chosen; that is, you may not construct objects specifically for selection nor combine several objects and count them as one.

Each group is to select objects representing American values as seen from the point of view of one of the following groups:

1. the previous generation
2. the current generation
3. the next generation
4. males
5. females
6. the poor
7. the rich
8. the middle class
9. homosexuals
10. heterosexuals
11. college students
12. professors
13. blacks
14. whites
15. American Indians

Each group then reports to the entire class the selections made and the specific values each selection represents. Discussion may then focus on any number of communication related issues such as:

1. the accuracy with which each group represented the values of the group it was assigned
2. the difficulty of communication across generations, sex, economic class, race, and so forth
3. the degrees of stereotyping evidenced by the objects and values selected
4. the degree to which the members' own values influenced their selections of values for the group assigned
5. the role of values in influencing communication generally and of divergent values in hindering communication

6. the ways in which communication might be facilitated when basic values differ

34.3 FORMS OF ADDRESS

For each of the following persons indicate the form of address you would use in speaking to them *and* the form of address you would expect them to use in speaking to you.

Use the following shorthand:

TLN — title plus last name
FN — first name
TFN — title plus first name
T   — title

	You to Them	*Them to You*
1. Your college professor	_____	_____
2. A fellow student	_____	_____
3. A younger child	_____	_____
4. Your doctor/dentist	_____	_____
5. Your employer	_____	_____
6. Your employee	_____	_____
7. Your high school teacher	_____	_____
8. Your uncle/aunt	_____	_____
9. Your nephew/niece	_____	_____
10. Your grandfather/grandmother	_____	_____
11. Your state senator	_____	_____
12. The college president	_____	_____
13. Your minister/priest/rabbi	_____	_____
14. Your parents' friend	_____	_____
15. Burt Reynolds/Sophia Loren	_____	_____
16. A street bum	_____	_____
17. A millionaire	_____	_____

On what bases were your decisions made, that is, what sociological variables influenced your decisions?

34.4 HEROES

At the end of this exercise are listed the names of 100 noted personalities currently in the news. Some of these persons you will recognize and will probably know a great deal about. Others, however, may seem totally unfamiliar. Your task is to select the five persons you would nominate for your personal hall of fame. That is, select the five people you feel could serve as your personal heroes.

Either of two general procedures will prove useful. After each person has selected five people from the list given here, the names should be written on index cards and collected anonymously. A tabulation of the number of votes for each person should be made and the 10 persons receiving the highest number of votes should be noted. This method will provide an anonymous procedure and will probably result in a much more candid final list.

An alternative procedure is to form groups of five or six. After each person has selected his or her own choices from the list. The task of each group is to select a final list of five persons the group would nominate for its personal hall of fame. After each group has selected its "heroes" the names should be put on the board. This procedure, although the easier and more efficient to follow, does not allow for anonymity and hence will probably result in the selection of more socially acceptable heroes.

DO NOT READ ANY FURTHER UNTIL YOU HAVE WRITTEN DOWN AND TURNED IN THE FIVE NAMES.

Discussion may then center on some or all of the following questions:

1. The "Heroes" list contains 50 male and 50 female names. Are there more men or women represented in the final list(s)? If there are differences, how do you account for them? Is the original list weighed unfairly in terms of one sex rather than the other by having more prominent males than females or vice versa. If so, how might that imbalance have been corrected? Did anyone feel an obligation to select both males and females? An obligation to select from only one sex? Explain.

2. Did the male and female voter patterns differ significantly? If so, why do you think this happened?

3. On the "Heroes" list of 100 people there are fifteen blacks. How did blacks do in the final list(s)? Explain. What other blacks might have been included on the list?

4. If sexual preference (gay or straight) had been listed along with the name, or if the information had been known (as with sex and race), would the gays have been selected? Do not accept a simple yes for this question. This may be a socially acceptable response among college students but a deeper analysis might reveal different attitudes.

5. What areas of accomplishment are represented most frequently in the final list(s)? Why do you feel this is so?

6. How do you think the votes given here would differ if, say, your parents or your teachers did the voting? Explain.

7. Of the names on the "Heroes" list, which were the least well known? From what areas of accomplishment are these? How do you account for this?

8. What values do the class members hold that can be deduced from the final list of heroes? Are there any surprises?

HEROES

Bella Abzug
Muhammad Ali
Idi Amin
Neil Armstrong
Joan Baez
F. Lee Bailey
Pearl Bailey
James Baldwin
Christian Barnard
Ingmar Bergman
Julian Bond
Marlon Brando
Leonid Brezhnev
Helen Gurley Brown
Carol Burnett
Truman Capote
Jimmy Carter
Cesar Chavéz
Julia Child
Shirley Chisholm
Salvator Dali
Angela Davis
Sammy Davis, Jr.
Doris Day
Jean Dixon
Queen Elizabeth
Werner Erhard
Betty Friedan
Indira Gandhi
Niki Giovanni
Billy Graham
Ella Grasso
Edith Head
Patty Hearst

Lillian Hellman
Xaveria Hollander
Lauren Hutton
Mick Jagger
Elton John
Erica Jong
Barbara Jordan
Ted Kennedy
Billie Jean King
Coretta King
Henry Kissinger
Louise Lasser
Sophia Loren
Charles Manson
Shirley MacLaine
Paul McCartney
Mary McGrory
Rod McKuen
Marshall McLuhan
Maharishi Mahesh Yogi
Margaret Mead
Golda Meir
Liza Minnelli
Sun M. Moon
Mary Tyler Moore
Patricia Murphy
Ralph Nader
Richard Nixon
Joyce Carol Oates
Jacqueline Kennedy
   Onassis
Elizabeth Ray
Pope Paul
Norman Vincent Peale

Isabel Peron
Sylvia Porter
Ayn Rand
Harry Reems
Nelson Rockefeller
Anwar Sadat
Jonas Salk
Arnold
   Schwartzenegger
Neil Sedaka
Bobby Seale
Tom Seaver
Fulton J. Sheen
Carley Simon
O. J. Simpson
Frank Sinatra
B. F. Skinner
Kate Smith
Margaret Chase Smith
Alexander
   Solzhenitsyn
Elizabeth Taylor
Shirley Temple
Sister Teresa
Pauline Trigêre
Margaret Truman
Abigail van Buren
Gore Vidal
Barbara Walters
John Wayne
Lina Wertmuller
Roy Wilkins
Tennessee Williams
Stevie Wonder

34.5 PARTING GIFTS

This exercise is an excellent one to use at the end of the semester as a kind of final parting "gift" which one member gives to another.

In a group of five or six persons each member indicates a "gift" that he or she would wish to obtain for each of the other members of the group. (It is sometimes helpful to write down the names of each person in the group and the gift you would want these people to have next to their names.)

These gifts are symbolic gifts and are not actually given. Rather they are wished for the other person. As such the gifts may be material or spiritual, concrete or abstract, expensive or inexpensive, general or specific. In all cases, however, they must be positive gifts.

This exercise may be used in conjunction with the Positive Words exercise presented in Unit 25.

Discussion may center on the reasons for the selections made, their appropriateness-inappropriateness, what they say about the person for whom the gift is intended, what they say about the relationship between the persons, and so on.

GLOSSARY

Listed here are definitions of the technical terms of communication—the words that are peculiar or unique to this discipline. These definitions should make new or difficult terms a bit easier to understand. For the most part the words included here are used in this text. Also included, however, are terms which, although not used here, may be used in the conduct of a course in communication.

A Culture. A learned set of thoughts and behaviors common to a number of people which defines them as members of the same group and as nonmembers of other groups. See *culture.*

A Language. The infinite set of grammatical sentences generated by the grammar of any language, for example, English, French, Bantu, Chinese. See *language.*

Abstraction. The process by which we derive a general concept from a class of objects.

Accent. The stress or emphasis that is placed on a syllable when pronounced.

Action Language. Movements of the body, for example, the way one walks, runs, sits.

Allness. The assumption that all can be known or is known about a given person, issue, object, or event.

Ambiguity. The condition in which a word or phrase may be interpreted as having more than one meaning.

Argot. A kind of *sublanguage;* cant and jargon of a particular class, generally an underworld or criminal class, which is difficult and sometimes impossible for outsiders to understand.

Attention. The process of responding to a stimulus or stimuli.

Attitude. A predisposition to respond for or against an object.

Authoritarian Leader. A group leader who determines the group policies or makes decisions without consulting or securing agreement from group members.

Belief. Confidence in the existence or truth of something; conviction.

Bit of Information. That amount of information which is necessary to divide the possible alternatives in half. If, for example, you are trying to guess which number will be chosen from 1 to 8, and you are told that it will not be 1, 2, 3, or 4, then one bit of information has been communicated since it reduced the number of alternatives by half.

Blindering. A misevaluation in which a label prevents us from seeing as much of the object as we might see; a process of concentrating on the verbal level while neglecting the nonverbal levels; a form of *intensional orientation.*

Body English. Popular term referring to *tactile communication.*

Body Language. A form of nonverbal communication in which messages are communicated by gesture, posture, spatial relations, and so forth; a popular term covering all aspects of nonverbal communication.

Brainstorming. A technique for generating ideas among people.

Bypassing. A misevalaution caused when the same word is used but each of the individuals gives it different meaning.

Cant. A kind of *sublanguage;* the conversational language of a special group which is generally understood only by members of the subculture.

Channel. The vehicle or medium through which signals are sent.

Channel Capacity. The maximum amount of information that a communication system can handle at any given time.

Chemistry-Binders. A class of life, characterized by the ability to combine chemicals in order to grow and survive; plants are chemistry-binders.

Cliché. An expression that is overused and calls attention to itself; to describe a man as "tall, dark, and handsome" would be considered cliché.

Code. A set of symbols used to translate a message from one form to another.

Cohesiveness. The property of togetherness. Applied to group communication situations it refers to the mutual attractiveness among members; a measure of the extent to which individual members of a group work together as a group.

COIK. Acronym for "clear only if known," referring to messages that are unintelligible for anyone who does not already know what the messages refer to.

Communication. 1) The process or act of communicating; 2) the actual message or messages sent and received; and 3) the study of the processes involved in the sending and receiving of messages. (The term *communicology* (q.v.) is suggested for the third definition.)

Communication Gap. The inability to communicate on a meaningful level because of some difference between the parties, for example, age, sex, political orientation, religion.

Communicology. The study of communication and particularly that subsection concerned with human communication.

Competence. The knowledge of language that a speaker has in his or her head. See *performance.* One of the dimensions of *credibility.*

Complementary Relationships. A relationship between two or more persons in which one person's behavior serves as a stimulus for a different type of behavior from the other person(s). The classic complementary relationship would be the relationship between a sadist and a masochist. Other examples of complementary relationships would be those between the dominant and the submissive, the talker and the listener, the lover and the loved. See *symmetrical relationships.*

Complementary Transaction. In transactional analysis, a transaction involving messages that are sent and received by the same ego state for each of the participants. For example, if person A is in the Parent ego state and if person B is in the Child ego state, then in a complementary transaction person A will address the Child ego state of B and B will address the Parent ego state of A. Thus complementary transaction would involve lines connecting ego states that are parallel to each other, as in the example given here:

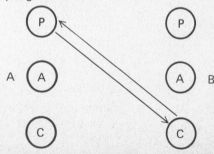

Connotation. The evaluative, potency, and activity dimensions of meaning; the associations of a word. See *denotation.*

Consonance. A psychological state of comfort created by having two elements (for example, cognitions or beliefs) one of which follows from the other. For example, consonance would exist for the following two cognitions: 1) X is healthy, 2) I engage in X.

Context of Communication. The physical, psychological, social, and temporal environment in which communication takes place.

Credibility. The degree to which a receiver perceives the speaker to be believable. See *ethos.*

Crossed Transactions. In transactional analysis, a transaction involving a message being sent to one ego state but being responded to by another ego state. For example, if person A (in the Adult state) addresses person B's Adult but person B responds in the Child state to A's Parent state. A crossed transaction then would involve lines connecting ego states that literally cross each other. A diagram of this example would look as follows:

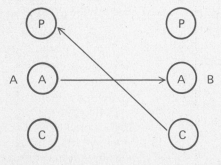

Culture. The knowledge concerning the appropriate and inappropriate patterns of thoughts and behaviors of a group.

Date. An extensional device used to emphasize the notion of constant change and symbolized by a subscript: for example, John Smith$_{1972}$ is not John Smith$_{1978}$.

Decoder. That which takes a message in one form (for example, sound waves) and translates it into another code (for example, nerve impulses) from which meaning can be formulated. In human communication, the decoder is the auditory mechanism; in electronic communication the decoder is, for example, the telephone earpiece. See *encoder.*

Decoding. The process of extracting a message from a code, for example, translating speech sounds into nerve impulses. See *encoding.*

Delayed Reactions. Reactions that are consciously delayed while the situation is analyzed; a symbol reaction.

Democratic Leader. A group leader who stimulates self-direction and self-actualization of the group members.

Denotation. Referential meaning; the objective or descriptive meaning of a word. See *connotation.*

Dialect. A specific variant of a language used by persons from a specific area or social class; dialects may differ from the ''standard'' language in phonology, semantics, and/or syntax, but they are intelligible to other speakers of the language.

Displaced Speech. Speech used to refer to that which is not present or in the immediate perceptual field.

Dissonance. A psychological state of discomfort created by having two elements (for example, cognitions or beliefs), one of which would not follow given the other. Two such elements might be, for example: ''X is harmful'' and ''I engage in X.'' These two elements represent dissonance, since given one of them the other would not follow. See *consonance.*

Dyadic Communication. Two-person communication.

Dysfunctional Effects of Mass Communication. Effects of the media that are not in the interest of society.

Elementalism. The process of dividing verbally what cannot be divided nonverbally, for example, speaking of body and mind as separate and distinct entities.

Empathy. The feeling of another person's feeling; the feeling or perceiving something as does another person.

Encoder. That which takes a message in one form (for example, nerve impulses) and puts it into another form (for example, sound waves). In human communication the encoder is the speaking mechanism; in electronic communication the encoder is, for example, the telephone mouthpiece. See *decoder.*

Encoding. The process of putting a message into a code, for example, translating nerve impulses into speech sounds. See *decoding.*

Entropy. A measure of the extent of disorganization or randomness in a system. Entropy is a measure of the degree of uncertainty that a destination has about the messages to be communicated by a source. Entropy is high if the number of possible messages is high and low if the number of possible messages is low.

E-Prime A form of the language that omits the verb "to be" in all its forms, designed to eliminate the tendency toward *projection,* that is, assuming that characteristics that one attributes to a person (for example, in "He or She is brave") are actually in that person instead of in the observer's perception.

Etc. An extensional device used to emphasize the notion of infinite complexity; since one can never know all about anything, any statement about the world or event must end with an explicit or implicit *etc.*

Ethicizing Function of Communication. The media's function of providing viewers with a collective ethic or ethical system.

Ethics. That branch of philosophy which deals with the rightness or wrongness of actions; the study of moral values.

Ethos. That aspect of persuasiveness which depends on the audience's perception of the character of the speaker; to Aristotle *ethos* or ethical proof depended upon the speaker's perceived good will, knowledge, and moral character. *Ethos* is more commonly referred to as *speaker credibility.*

Evaluation. A process whereby a value is placed on some person, object, or event.

Experiential Limitation. The limit of an individual's ability to communicate, as set by the nature and extent of his or her experiences.

Extemporaneous Speech. A speech that is thoroughly prepared, organized in detail, and in which certain aspects of style are predetermined.

Extensional Devices. Those linguistic devices proposed by Alfred Korzybski for keeping language as a more accurate means for talking about the world. The extensional devices include the *etc., date,* and *index,* the working devices; the *hyphen* and *quotes,* the safety devices.

Extensional Orientation. A point of view in which the primary consideration is given to the world of experience and only secondary consideration is given to the labels. See *intensional orientation.*

Fact-Inference Confusion. A misevaluation in which one makes an inference, regards it as a fact, and acts upon it as if it were a fact.

Factual Statement. A statement made by the observer after observation, and limited to the observed. See *inferential statement.*

Feedback. Information that is fed back to the source. Feedback may come from the source's own messages (as when we hear what we are saying) or from the receiver(s) in the form of applause, yawning, puzzled looks, questions, letters to the editor of a newspaper, increased or decreased subscriptions to a magazine, and so forth. See *negative feedback, positive feedback.*

Field of Experience. The sum total of an individual's experiences which influences his or her ability to communicate. In some views of communication, two people can only communicate to the extent that their fields of experience overlap.

Frozen Evaluation. See *static evaluation.*

Game. A simulation of some situation with rules governing the behaviors of the participants and with some payoff for winning.

Gatekeeping. The process of filtering messages from source to receiver. In this process some messages are allowed to pass through and others are changed or not allowed to pass at all.

General Semantics. The study of the relationships between language, thought, and behavior.

Grammar. The set of rules of *syntax, semantics,* and *phonology.*

Group. A collection of individuals related to each other with some common purpose and with some structure among them.

High-Order Abstraction. A very general or abstract term or statement; an inference made on the basis of another inference. See *level of abstraction.*

Honorific. Expressing high regard or respect. In some languages certain pronouns of address are honorific and are used to address those of high status. In English such expressions as Dr., Professor, and the Honorable are honorific.

Hyphen. An extensional device used to illustrate that what may be separated verbally may not be separable on the event or nonverbal level; although one may talk about body and mind as if they are separable, in reality they may better be referred to as body-mind.

Identification. In General Semantics, a misevaluation whereby two or more items are considered as identical; according to Kenneth Burke, a process of becoming similar to another individual; Burke sees identification as a necessary process for persuasion.

Idiolect. An individual's personalized variation of the language.

Impromptu Speech. A speech which is given without any direct prior preparation.

Index. An *extensional device* used to emphasize the notion of nonidentity (no two things are the same) and symbolized by a subscript, for example, $politician_1$ is not $politician_2$.

Indiscrimination. A misevaluation that is caused by categorizing people or events or objects into a particular class and responding to specific members only as they are members of the class; a misevaluation that is caused by failing to recognize that each individual is an individual and is unique; a failure to apply the *index.*

Inferential Statement. A statement that can be made by anyone, is not limited to the observed, and can be made at any time. See *factual statement*.

Information. That which reduces uncertainty. See *bit of information*.

Intensional Orientation. A point of view in which primary consideration is given to the way in which things are labeled and only secondary consideration (if any) to the world of experience. See *extensional orientation*.

Interaction Diagrams. Diagrams used to record the number of messages sent from one person to another.

Interaction Process Analysis. A content analysis method which classifies messages into four general categories: social emotional positive, social emotional negative, attempted answers, and questions.

Interpersonal Communication. Communication between or among persons, generally distinguished from mass communication and from public communication. Often used as a general term to include intrapersonal communication, dyadic communication and small group communication.

Interpersonal Conflict. A conflict between two persons; a conflict within an individual caused by his or her relationships with other people.

Intrapersonal Communication. Communication with oneself.

Jargon. A kind of *sublanguage;* the language of any special group, often a professional class, which is unintelligible to individuals not belonging to the group; the "shop talk" of the group.

Kinesics. The study of the communicative dimension of facial and bodily movements.

Laissez-Faire Leader. A group leader who allows the group to develop and progress or make mistakes on its own.

Language. The rules of *syntax, semantics,* and *phonology;* a potentially self-reflexive structured system of symbols that catalogs the objects, events, and relations in the world.

Level of Abstraction. The relative distance of a term or statement from the actual perception; a low-order abstraction would be a description of the perception, whereas a high-order abstraction would consist of inferences about inferences about descriptions of a perception.

Linguistic Determinism. A theory that holds that language determines what we do, say, and think and in fact limits what we are able to do, say, and think.

Linguistic Relativity. A theory that argues that the language we speak influences what we perceive and think. Since different languages catalog the world differently, speakers of different languages will see the world differently.

Linguistics. The study of language; the study of the system of rules by which meanings are paired with sounds.

Low-Order Abstraction. A description of what is perceived. See *level of abstraction*.

Macroscopic Approach to Communication. The focus on broad and general aspects of communication.

Manuscript Speech. A speech designed to be read from a script verbatim.

Mass Communication. Communication addressed to an extremely large audience which is mediated by audio and/or visual transmitters, and which is processed by gatekeepers before transmission.

Message. Any signal or combination of signals that serve as *stimuli* for a receiver.

Metacommunication. Communication about communication.

Metalanguage. Language used to talk about language.

Microscopic Approach to Communication.   The focus on minute and specific aspects of communication.

Model.   A physical representation of an object or process.

Multiordinality.   In General Semantics, a condition whereby a term may exist on different levels of abstraction.

Multivalued Orientation.   A point of view that emphasizes that there are many sides (rather than only one or two sides) to any issue.

Narcotizing Function of Communication.   The media's function of providing receivers with information the knowledge of which is, in turn, confused by receivers with doing something about something.

Negative Feedback.   Feedback that serves a corrective function by informing the sources that his or her message is not being received in the way intended. Negative feedback serves to redirect the source's behavior. Looks of boredom, shouts of disagreement, and letters critical of newspaper policy would be examples of negative feedback.

Negative Reinforcement.   The strengthening of a particular response by removing an aversive stimulus. See *positive reinforcement.*

Noise.   Anything that distorts the message intended by the source. Noise may be viewed as anything that interferes with the receiver's receiving the message as the source intended the message to be received. Noise is present in a communication system to the extent that the message received is not the message sent. Noise may originate in any of the components of the communication act, for example, in the source as a lisp, in the channel as static, in the receiver as a hearing loss, in written communication as blurred type. Noise is always present in any communication sys-

tem and its effects may be reduced (but never eliminated completely) by increasing the strength of the signal or the amount of redundancy, for example.

Nonallness.   An attitude or point of view in which it is recognized that one can never know all about anything and that what we know or say or hear is only a part of what there is to know, say, or hear.

Nonelementalism.   See *elementalism.*

Object Language.   Language that is used to communicate about objects, events, and relations in the world; the structure of the object language is described in a *metalanguage;* the display of physical objects, for example, flower arranging, the colors and clothes we wear.

Object Level.   The nonverbal level of sense perception which we abstract from the event level; the level on which we live our lives.

Objective Abstracting.   A form or type of abstracting in which we group individual units into a class of which they are all members as, for example, all chapters being grouped into a book.

Olfactory Communication.   Communication by smell.

Openness.   See *productivity.*

Operant.   A response emitted without a clearly identifiable prior stimulus; a bit of behavior controlled by its consequences.

Operant Conditioning.   A process whereby reinforcement is contingent upon a particular response with the effect that the response is strengthened, or a process whereby punishment is contingent upon a particular response with the effect that the response is weakened.

Paralanguage.   The vocal (but nonverbal) aspect of speech. Paralanguage consists of voice qualities (for example, pitch range, resonance, tempo), vocal characterizers (for example, laughing/crying, yelling/whispering), vocal qualifiers (for example, intensity, pitch height), and vocal segregates (for example, *uh-uh* meaning "no," or *sh* meaning "silence").

Perception. The process of becoming aware of objects and events from the senses.

Performance. The actual utterances that a speaker speaks and a hearer hears. See *competence.*

Persuasion. The process of influencing attitudes and behavior.

Phonology. That area of linguistics concerned with sound.

Pictics. The study of the pictorial code of communication.

Pitch. The highness-lowness of the vocal tone.

Polarization. A form of fallacious reasoning in which only the two extremes are considered; also referred to as "black or white" or "either-or" thinking.

Positive Feedback. *Feedback* that supports or reinforces behavior along the lines it is already proceeding in, for example, applause during a speech.

Positive Reinforcement. The strengthening of a particular response by making a reward contingent upon it. The process may be visualized in three stages: 1) a response is emitted, for example, a child says "daddy"; 2) a reward is given, for example, a smile or candy or touching; 3) the response, "daddy," is strengthened, that is, it is more likely to occur under similar circumstances. See *negative reinforcement.*

Projection. A psychological process whereby we attribute characteristics or feelings of our own to others; often used to refer to the process whereby we attribute our own faults to others.

Proxemics. The study of the communicative function of space; the "study of how man unconsciously structures microspace—the distance between men in the conduct of their daily transactions, the organization of space in his houses and buildings, and ultimately the layout of his towns."

Public Communication. Communication in which the source is one person and the receiver is an audience of many persons.

Public Speaking. Communication which occurs when a speaker delivers a relatively prepared, continuous address in a specific setting to a large audience that provides little immediate feedback.

Quotes. An *extensional device* used to emphasize that a word or phrase is being used in a special sense and should therefore be given special attention.

Rate. The speed with which we speak, generally measured in words per minute.

Receiver. Any person or thing that takes in messages. Receivers may be individuals listening to or reading a message or a group of persons hearing a speech or a scattered television audience or a machine that stores information.

Redundancy. That quality of a message which makes it totally predictable and therefore, lacking in information. A message with zero redundancy would be completely unpredictable; a message of 100 percent redundancy would be completely predictable. All human languages contain some degree of redundancy built into them, generally estimated to be about 50 percent. All human messages, therefore, have some redundancy.

Reflexiveness. That feature of language which refers to the fact that human language can be used to refer to itself, that is, we can talk about our talk, create a language for talking about language. See *self-reflexiveness*.

Reinforcement.   The strengthening of a particular response. See *positive reinforcement, negative reinforcement*.

Relational Abstracting.   A form or type of abstracting in which relationships among items are abstracted and represented in some kind of formula or equation or diagram; for example, the formula $a^2 = b^2 + c^2$ expressing the relationship among the sides of a right triangle is the result of relational abstracting.

Response.   Any bit of overt or covert behavior.

Role.   The part an individual plays in a group; an individual's function or expected behavior.

Self-Acceptance.   Being satisfied with ourselves, with our virtues and vices, abilities and limitations.

Self-Concept.   An individual's self-evaluation; an individual's self-appraisal.

Self-Disclosure.   The process of revealing something significant about ourselves to another individual or to a group, which would not normally be known by them.

Self-Reflexive Abstracting.   A form or type of abstracting in which the abstraction is of itself as when, for example, we think about our thinking, love our love, fear our fear.

Self-Reflexiveness.   The property of being able to refer back to itself; for example, language is self-reflexive in the sense that it can be used to refer to itself. See *reflexiveness*.

Semantic Differential.   A device for measuring connotative meaning consisting of seven-point, bipolar scales; generally, three dimensions of meaning are measured: evaluation, potency, and activity.

Semantic Differentiation.   The process of measuring meaning in a three-dimensional space consisting of evaluative, potency, and activity dimensions.

Semantic Reaction.   A total reaction; a reaction of the organism-as-a-whole; a reaction that is determined by what the whole situation means to an individual.

Semantic Space.   The connotative meaning of a term viewed as existing in a three-dimensional space consisting of evaluative, potency, and activity dimensions.

Semantics.   That area of language study concerned with meaning.

Semantogenic.   Caused by semantics or labels; used most widely in reference to a problem or disorder whose origin may be found in the labels. For example, stuttering has been labeled semantogenic, that is, stuttering develops because some particular behavior was labeled ''stuttering'' according to the semantogenic theory.

Sexist Language.   Language derogatory to one sex, generally women.

Sign.   Something that stands for something else and that bears a natural, nonarbitrary relationship to it, for example, dark clouds as a sign of rain. See *symbol*.

Signal Reaction.   A conditioned response to a signal; a response to some signal that is immediate rather than delayed. See *symbol reaction*.

Sign Language.   Gesture language that is highly codified, for example, a hitchhiker's gesture.

Slang.   The language used by special groups which is not considered proper by the general society; the language made up of the *argot, cant,* and *jargon* of various subcultures which is known by the general public.

Source.   Any person or thing that creates messages. A source may be an individual speaking or writing or gesturing or a group of persons formulating an advertising policy or a computer solving a problem.

Space-Binders.   A class of life that maintains itself by moving about in space and combining materials from various different places; animals.

Speech.   Messages utilizing a vocal-auditory channel.

Speech Community.   A group of persons using the same language.

Static Evaluation.   An orientation that fails to recognize that the world is characterized by constant change; an attitude that sees people and events as static rather than as constantly changing.

Stimulus.   Any external or internal change that impinges upon or arouses an organism.

Stimulus-Response Models of Communication.   Models of communication that assume that the process of communication is a linear one, which begins with a stimulus which then leads to a response.

Structural Differential.   A model of the abstraction process consisting of an event level, an object level, and first, second, third, and so forth, verbal levels.

Sublanguage.   A variation from the general language used by a particular subculture; *argot, cant,* and *jargon* are particular kinds of sublanguages.

Symbol.   Something that stands for something else but that bears no natural relationship to it, for example, purple as a symbol of mourning. Words are symbols in that they bear no natural relationship to the meaning they symbolize. See *sign.*

Symbol Reaction.   A reaction that is made with some delay. See *signal reaction.*

Symmetrical Relationship.   A relation between two or more persons in which one person's behavior serves as a stimulus for the same type of behavior in the other person(s). Examples of such relationships would include situations in which anger in one person encourages or serves as a stimulus for anger in another person or where a critical comment by one person leads the other person to respond in like manner. See *complementary relationship.*

Syntax.   That area of language study concerned with the rules for combining words into sentences.

Taboo.   Forbidden; culturally censored. Taboo language is that which is frowned upon by ''polite society.'' Themes and specific words may be considered taboo, for example, death, sex, certain forms of illness, and various words denoting sexual activities and excretory functions.

Tactile Communication.   Communication by touch; communication received by the skin.

Theory.   A general statement or principle applicable to a number of related phenomena.

Time-Binders.   A class of life that survives by passing information on from one generation to another, thus making knowledge cumulative; man.

Trust.   Faith in the behavior of another person; confidence in another person which leads us to feel that whatever we risk will not be lost.

Two-Step Flow of Communication.   An hypothesis that states that the influence of the media occurs in two steps: 1) the media influence opinion leaders, and 2) the opinion leaders influence the general population through interpersonal communication.

Two-Valued Orientation. A point of view in which events are seen or questions are evaluated in terms of two values, for example, a right and a wrong, a good and a bad. Often referred to as the fallacy of black or white or polarization.

Ulterior Transactions. In transactional analysis, an ulterior transaction is one in which more than two ego states are involved and in which there is an unspoken or hidden agenda which is generally communicated nonverbally. For example, a woman (A) applies for a job and in her Adult state addresses a question to the personnel director (B) in his Adult state, "Do I have the job?" The personnel director, leering at her chest, responds, "What can you do besides type?" This transaction is an ulterior one and would be diagrammed as follows: (the ulterior transactions are denoted by dotted lines):

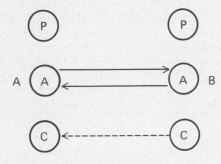

Undelayed Reaction. A reaction that is immediate; a signal response; a reaction made wtihout any conscious deliberation.

Universal Language. A language understood by all people and which all people have the ability to use.

Universal of Communication. A feature of communication which is common to all communication acts.

Universal of Language. A feature of language that is common to all known languages.

Value. Relative worth of an object; a quality that makes something desirable or undesirable; ideals or customs about which we have emotional responses, whether positive or negative.

Variable. A quantity that can increase or decrease; something that can have different values.

Volume. The relative loudness of the voice.

INDEX

Numbers in parentheses refer to box numbers.